Miracle Sales Guide

student edition

Mark Jones
James Healey

Chabot College

PRENTICE-HALL, INC., Englewood Cliffs, New Jersey

Library of Congress Cataloging in Publication Data

JONES, MARK
    Miracle sales guide.
    Includes bibliographical references.
    1. Salesmen and salesmanship. I. Healey, James
joint author.   II. Title.
HF5438.H425 1973   658.85   73-8619
ISBN 0-13-585646-9

© 1973 by PRENTICE-HALL, INC.,
Englewood Cliffs, N.J.

All rights reserved.
No part of this book may be reproduced
in any form or by any means
without permission in writing
from the publisher.

10 9 8 7 6 5 4 3 2 1

Prentice-Hall International, Inc., *London*
Prentice-Hall of Australia, Pty. Ltd., *Sydney*
Prentice-Hall of Canada, Ltd., *Toronto*
Prentice-Hall of India Private Ltd., *New Delhi*
Prentice-Hall of Japan, Inc., *Tokyo*

Printed in the United States of America

TABLE OF CONTENTS

WHAT IS SELLING

Lets come to selling terms—Selling and economics—The marketing mix—Of historical note—The marketing concept—Selling, ethics and society—Which way in selling—How to get that sales job you want

Detailed Table of Contents .... **Page 801**

THEORY BEFORE PRACTICE

The need for product knowledge—What you need to know—Where to get product facts—Understanding what motivates buying action—How to translate product features into benefits

Detailed Table of Contents .... **Page 901**

BREAKING INTO SELLING

A simple formula for valuing your time—Setting your sights for higher earnings—Five ways to increase production—Selling more to your present customers—How to move up to bigger buyers—Breaking into big selling through better time-planning—Mature salesmanship

Detailed Table of Contents .... **Page 1003**

PROSPECTING FOR VOLUME BUSINESS

Finding full-potential prospects—Qualifying specific prospects for buying potential—Finding and rating the "key" prospect in a group—Additional aids to profitable prospecting—Guides to better territory coverage

Detailed Table of Contents .... **Page 2001**

IDEAS FOR CREATIVE SELLING

You must be creative to make big money—How to train your mind to create ideas—Stepping up your creativity—Creative ideas that make bigger buyers—Ideas to keep you constantly creative—Using creative ideas on yourself

Detailed Table of Contents .... **Page 3001**

SUCCESSFUL STRATEGIES FOR PRE-APPROACH—MAKING THEM LISTEN—CALL-BACKS

Winning sales through a successful pre-approach—Making the prospect listen—Putting your finger on the prospect's reason to buy—Making call-backs pay off

Detailed Table of Contents .... **Page 4001**

MAKING A GREAT PRESENTATION

A great presentation must be prepared—Preliminary preparation for developing the presentation—The outline is the blueprint—Guides for a sure-fire demonstration—Masterful use of sales tools in a presentation—How to achieve a lean, sharp, "electric" quality—Adding power with "vivid-picture" language—Putting the presentation into words—Actual successful presentations—How to give your presentation

Detailed Table of Contents .... **Page 5002**

POWER-CLOSING TECHNIQUES

Close ealy—close often—close late—12 tested ways to get the signed order—There must be a "hooker" to close—Ideas for working out your own closing techniques

Detailed Table of Contents .... **Page 6001**

MAKING OBJECTIONS WORK FOR YOU

How to use the objection to make the sale—Strong techniques for converting objections into sales—The answer attitude that wins—Answer guide to specific objections

Detailed Table of Contents .... **Page 7001**

SELLING AT CONCERT PITCH

How to build and maintain enthusiasm—Self-management for more profitable selling—Self-management techniques to gain selling time—Self-management to make a positive impression—How to make the most of your personality

Detailed Table of Contents .... **Page 8001**

PERSONAL RECORDS, INFORMATION SOURCES AND CASE PROBLEMS

Helpful personal records to reach high-bracket goals—How to find information about people and companies—Case problems: "How would you do it?"

Detailed Table of Contents .... **Page 9001**

INDEX .... **Page 10,001**

Preface

The Prentice-Hall Miracle Sales Guide has proven itself to be of the utmost value to everyone in sales. It has helped thousands of salesmen and women reach star selling status and the income and prestige that goes with it. It has done this by stressing dynamic how-to-do-it advice with lively illustrations. In short, it has earned its place in the briefcase of the professional salesperson.

This Student Edition of the Prentice-Hall Miracle Sales Guide merges the inspirational message of the basic Guide on how-to-do-it-big with background material on selling essential for a college salesmanship course. Selling is positioned in our economic system and in the macro and micro levels of marketing. A synthesis is made of the volatile elements of the salesman's attitude and his ethics along with buying motives and consumerism. The case studies in the text and the teaching suggestions in the instructor's manual provide opportunities for application of selling principles and evaluation of accomplishment.

The contributions of Walter Horvath and other sales training greats, formerly available only to salesmen, are now available in this Student Edition to the college student. In addition to the contributors recognized on the following acknowledgment page, we wish to thank those who have made the Student Edition possible, Prentice-Hall's Jack Pritchard with Dean Olson launched the project and Cary Baker saw us through it. Guidance was also given by the following sales educators: Ross Atkinson, Richard Casey, and Ralph Wilderman of San Jose City College; James Goss of West Valley College; David Hopkins of Monterey Peninsula College; Gale Hurley of Canada College; Eugene Kresan of Foothill College and Richard Purvis of Cabrillo College.

Our thanks also go to Colette Conboy of Prentice-Hall for her guidance throughout the production, and to Faye Di Giordano for her typing.

Mark Jones
James Healey

WHAT IS SELLING 1

Let's Come to Selling Terms
Selling and Economics
The Marketing Mix
Of Historical Note
The Marketing Concept
Selling, Ethics and Society
Which Way in Selling
How to Get That Sales Job You Want

TABLE OF CONTENTS

	Starts at Paragraph [¶]
Miracle Guide to What Is Selling	801

Let's Come To Selling Terms

What Selling Means	802
The Practice of Selling	803
Can You Be a Professional	804

Selling And Economics

The Economic System	805
The Cost of Goods	806
Marketing Is a Flow	807

The Marketing Mix

Positioning Selling in Marketing	808

Of Historical Note

Older-Than-the-History Heroes	809
The Merchant Princes	810
The Economists Recognize That Trade Is Productive	811
Early American Salesmen	812
Emergence from the Production Era	813

The Marketing Concept

From Production to Marketing	814

Selling, Ethics, And Society

	Starts at Paragraph [¶]
Ethics as an Individual	816
Ethics as a Salesman	817
Relations with Buyers	818
Relations with Employers	819
How Are We Doing	820

Which Way In Selling

Classifying Sales Occupations	822
Selling to Consumers	823
Selling to Industrials and Business Firms for Their Own Use	824
Selling to Distributors for Resale	825
Levels of Pay	826
Methods of Compensation	827
Expense Allowance and Fringe Benefits	828
Basic Characteristics for Success	829

How To Go After That Sales Job You Want

Sell Yourself with a Résumé	830
What to Include in Your Résumé	831
How to Prepare a Résumé That Sells	832
Writing the Cover Letter	833
What You Should Know About the Company Before You Apply	834
Other Essentials for a Winning Cover Letter	835
Selling Yourself in the Job Interview	836

What is Selling

¶ 801 ⇒MIRACLE GUIDE TO→ What is Selling?

It is hard to think of an isolated salesman, and if there were one, he would be a desolate salesman. A salesman touches the lives of others; he brings organizations into relationship with other organizations; he fires the imagination; he sparks the economy; and the products of his efforts pervade society. He is a goer; he is a mover; he is a doer; and his unique skills combined with his restiveness produce change. So let's first explore the elements of change in selling and in the environments in which selling has operated.

This section is concerned with defining selling and positioning it in marketing, in history, in society, and with placing the individual in a selling career. The remainder of the Miracle Sales Guide shows you, as a salesman, how to be successful in becoming a professional salesman and making big money.

Let's come to selling terms

¶ 802 What selling means

The closest we can come to a synonym for *selling* is *persuasion*. In selling someone, you move him to a belief, a position, a point of view or a course of action. In many cases this may not immediately put money in your pocket. The term may be used in other than the commercial sense. A marriage proposal may require selling or persuasion; a legislator must sell his constituents on himself, and his peers on his bills; a minister sells the principles of his faith; and a citizen sells his neighbors on participating in community service. How often have we heard the statement "I'm sold on that"?

Even in a commercial sense the ultimate selling of a product or service is the culmination of a series of persuasions. Persuading someone to grant you an appointment may first be necessary. Then the prospect must be persuaded to recognize a series of benefits available to him and persuaded to your point of view as he voices doubts and objections, before he is actually sold. The American Marketing Association has defined selling in a commercial sense as: "the personal or impersonal process of assisting and/or persuading a prospective customer to buy a commodity or a service or to act favorably upon an idea that has commercial significance to the seller." [1]

¶ 803 The practice of selling

It would follow then, that *salesmanship* is the practice of selling. This practice may be good or bad depending upon the skill of the salesman. What is so often overlooked is that selling skill is built on a recognition that, whether it be in the form of product, service, or idea, what is really sold is *satisfaction*. This is where modern salesmanship and persuasion may part company. If the prospect is persuaded to buy that which will not benefit him, then there will be no long run benefit to the seller. Salesmanship is buyer oriented, and the result must be mutual and continuous satisfaction to the buyer, to the salesman, and to his company. A most appropriate definition of salesmanship is "selling goods that won't come back to people who will."

Another definition of salesmanship often used, due to the memorable way in which the basic concept is presented, is the "seven-peas-in-a-pod" definition: "personally persuading people to purchase products pleasurably for profit." This distinguishes personal selling from advertising or sales promotion. It emphasizes *persuasion*. The words *pleasurably for profit* must be interpreted as the essential, continuing satisfaction to buyer and seller.

¶ 804 Can you be a professional?

Now what is meant by the term *professional salesman?* A profession differs from a vocation or occupation in that it requires:

1. Organized programs for intellectual preparation.
2. A measurement of proficiency before certification as a professional.
3. Adherence to an accepted code of ethics.
4. Continuous learning and development.
5. A continuing attitude of service to others.

There is little doubt about law, medicine, and religion, but most would agree that seldom would salesmanship qualify as a profession. However, it is moving in that direction and may fully qualify now in such cases as the Certified Life Underwriter and the Chartered Property and Casualty Underwriter in the insurance field.

Although salesmanship may not technically qualify as a profession, there is a wide difference between a salesman and a professional salesman. This difference is one of:

- *Honesty.* Without basic honesty and personal integrity, a person cannot be a true professional in any field. This is the base from which talent must operate.
- *Attitude.* The key to a professional attitude is empathy—the ability to put yourself in the other fellow's place and appreciate his feelings. Coupled with this empathy must be the desire to help others.
- *Knowledge.* The professional must seek knowledge about his prospects and customers. He must have extensive, precise information about his products. Through the knowledge of selling principles and techniques he fits those products to those customers in such a way that will insure continuing satisfaction.
- *Performance.* The professional is one who can so skillfully perform the selling function that he gains customer loyalty, public recognition and respect, a high income and a world of personal satisfaction.

Yes, there are professional salesmen. Over 6,000,000 of our citizens call themselves salesmen, but a very small percentage qualify as true professionals. A briefcase in hand, a counter to lean on, a desk to sit behind, an extensive wardrobe, a glib tongue, or an impressive expense account do not make a professional salesman. Success and professionalism in selling starts with *honesty* and is the result of desire, tenacity, training, practice and persistense until the *attitude, knowledge* and *performance* is achieved which marks one as the true professional.

Selling and economics

¶ 805 The economic system

The purpose of our economic system is to satisfy human wants. It must do more than just produce useful items — that is only the start of the job. Useful items are of no use until they are made available to people at the time when they can be used beneficially. When this happens then there is satisfaction of human wants.

Economists use the term *utility* in the explanation of this want satisfaction process. *Utility is the capacity for things to satisfy human wants.* There are four types of utilities

selling and economics

which must be created before the economic system can achieve its purpose:

- *Form utility* is created when the products of nature are changed into a form which has a potential usefulness. This is the function of production or manufacturing.
- *Place utility* is created when goods are made available where they can be used. The transportation function is the important factor here.
- *Time utility* is created when goods are made available when they are wanted. The storage of goods is a function which is particularly important when there is either a fluctuating supply of or demand for goods.
- *Possession utility* is created when the goods are placed in the possession of those who can use them. This is the traditional province of advertising, sales promotion, and personal selling. These activities make people aware of certain needs, persuade them to satisfy these needs, and facilitate the transfer of ownership.

⟫REMEMBER→ Marketing activities are productive. They create place, time, and possession utilities which enhance the capacity of goods to satisfy human wants.

The foregoing may be considered to be a very theoretical way of looking at our economy. If you should ask any businessman down on Main Street why he is in business, the answer would probably be "to make money." It is doubtful that he would answer "to satisfy human wants." Yet, there is a definite, continuing relationship between these concepts. The object of the economic system, of business, of marketing, of salesmanship, is to satisfy human wants. The incentive for businessmen to assume the tremendous risks of endeavoring to satisfy human wants is *profit*. If businessmen are successful in satisfying human wants the reward is *profit*.

Our economic system functions because of profits. Profits are dependent upon sales. Goods will not be produced nor moved to the consumers unless, through sales, those involved in these activities can acquire purchasing power to meet expenses and to buy other goods.

⟫REMEMBER→ Without sales, our economic system would not function.

¶ 806 The cost of goods

The economic system can be viewed in the following manner.

- *Production.* Form utility by manufacturing; 50% of money spent for goods.
- *Marketing.* Place and time utility by warehousing and storage; 25% of money spent for goods. Possession utility by advertising, sales promotion and personal selling; 25% of money spent for goods.
- *Consumption.* Satisfaction of wants as a result of utilities; payment for values permitting continued creation of utilities.

Most people feel that the costs of production are necessary and valid. The costs attributable to marketing, however, are often suspect and believed to be not only excessive but wasteful in our economy. Actually marketing costs have remained stationary or declined slightly relative to production costs since World War II. Labor-saving devices, new technologies, and new methods are not reserved to production but are constantly being applied to marketing.

⟫REMEMBER→ Marketing, as well as manufacturing, adds value to goods. The values added are not so obvious but are just as essential to the satisfaction of human wants. It is well-known that the price which one pays is equal to the values which he expects to receive.

¶ 807 Marketing is a flow

The American Marketing Association has defined marketing as "the performance of business activities that direct the flow of goods and services from producer to consumer or user." In working with the Association's definition we should start with the root word *market*.

The word *market* may be used in many ways, but in explaining the marketing process it is considered to be comprised of three elements:
- People
- Purchasing power
- Inclination to buy

It is obvious that people alone do not constitute a market. Sales are not possible until there is purchasing power, be it cash or credit.

Even if there are people with money, they may not need or may not desire certain types of goods.

When the Association refers to consumer or user it is distinguishing between two types of markets — the market for consumer goods and the market for industrial goods. The customers for many businesses are other businesses, not the ultimate consumer. However, these intermediate businesses exist only for the satisfaction of the wants of the ultimate consumer. Thus the sale of industrial goods such as installations, accessory equipment, raw materials, parts, and operating supplies to the industrial market is dependent upon how those in that market interpret the sales possibilities for their products in the various consumer markets.

⟫⟫REMEMBER→ Marketing begins with the consumer and ends with the consumer. The heart of the Association's definition is "the flow of goods or services." However, marketing consists of many flows.

▶ *Flow of information from the market to to the producer.* The needs of a market cannot be fulfilled unless the nature of the needs is known. Millions of dollars are spent each year on market research. Information is sought on each of the three elements of the market. One of the primary functions of a sales force should be to provide a flow of information from the field. It is also marketing people who must interpret this information in the determination of what goods or services should be produced.

▶ *Flow of information from the producer to the market.* Once a product or service has been developed, it is then necessary that the benefits of this offering flow to the market. Again, it is advertising, sales promotion, and personal selling which must deliver these persuasive messages.

▶ *Flow of goods or services to the market.* Once the third element of a market — inclination to buy — has been successfully stimulated, then goods and services begin to flow.

▶ *Flow of revenues from the market through the marketing channels to the producer.* This permits all in the productive and distributive process to earn compensation for their contribution and to permit the continuation of their operations.

▶ *Flow of costs into satisfaction.* As utilities are created, costs are incurred. These costs accumulate as products flow through the marketing channels. However, they flow into satisfaction of human wants, which, in turn, generates a continuation of the marketing flows. If there is no satisfaction, then the flows related to a particular product or service end.

⟫⟫REMEMBER→ The salesman plays a key role in all of the marketing flows — "selling goods that won't come back to people who will."

The marketing mix

¶ 808 Positioning selling in marketing

A synonym for business might well be *decision making*. The final decision as to whether to go or not to go in any step of marketing is the culmination of four areas of decision making, called the *marketing mix*:

- Product
- Price
- Channel of distribution
- Promotion

The decisions about what to produce, how it should be designed, how it should perform, how it should be packaged, and what services should surround it are all part of product policy. These decisions can only be made after analysis of the market elements. No longer does production produce a product and tell the sales department to sell it. We are in the marketing era, and marketing people have a powerful voice in making product decisions since they know the market.

Price considerations may often cancel tentative decisions to produce an item. The price must enable the product to move through the marketing channel and be equivalent to the value placed on it by the ultimate consumer or user. In some cases the price may be too low, so that the buyer doubts the value of the product.

A *channel of distribution* or *trade channel* is the course taken by a product in its journey from producer to consumer or to a user. If the form of the product is changed, the channel ends. If the product is an industrial good that becomes part of a subsequent product, a new channel begins for the new product. A channel includes those middlemen or marketing institutions that render services in the buying and selling of the product as it flows to consumer or user. Some of these middlemen are termed merchant middlemen since they take title to (buy) the product and then resell it. Wholesalers and retailers are the typical merchant middlemen. Some middlemen are termed agent middlemen since they only negotiate or facilitate the buying and selling process without taking title to the product. Brokers, manufacturers' agents, selling agents, and commission houses are typical middlemen.

⇛OBSERVATION→ A salesman is not a middleman, but he may operate at any part of a trade channel. He may sell for a manufacturer, a merchant middleman, or an agent middleman. He may sell in industrial goods channels or in consumer goods channels.

Promotion as a part of the marketing mix is actually a mix in itself. The *promotional mix* of a company includes advertising, sales promotion, and personal selling. Seldom can a company eliminate any one of these forms of promotion. Advertising is essential to make the personal selling effort more productive, but outside of a mail order operation it cannot do the whole job. Personal selling is the primary way in which marketing programs are implemented. Sales promotion coordinates advertising and personal selling and enhances customer relations.

Of historical note

¶ 809   Older-than-the-history heroes

Miriam Beard has traced the development of business from earliest times. "Three thousand years before Christ, the Mesopotamian merchant had a considerable accumulation of technique and experience behind him; he was seasoned in affairs, wary in drawing up contracts, and stout in litigation. By 2500 B.C., he was forming trading-companies for penetration into distant realms; he was trafficking in many kinds of wares, wool, spices, soda, silver, ointments and 'fair-skinned slaves,' bringing them by caravan or sailing-ship to the cities of Ur, Uruk, Uma and other ancient centers of commerce, which are now being uncovered from the desert sands by the spades of excavators. How far back this development goes, no one can say, but some idea of its antiquity may be obtained by remembering that Ur is as much older than Rome as Rome is older than New York." [1]

Commerce and trade fed the needs of the war-oriented societies until 146 B.C. when warrior-Rome levelled the two great trading cities, Corinth and Carthage. Came the decline of the Roman Empire, and the town economy of the ancient world gave way to a village economy of the early middle ages. Business during the fourth to twelfth centuries was termed petty capitalism and marketing was most limited. There were the shopkeepers who sold what they produced as weavers, shoemakers, blacksmiths, or other craftsmen. There were also storekeepers who manufactured nothing and were dependent upon travelling merchants for their merchandise.

The travelling merchants were the antecedents of today's salesmen. They were a hearty, courageous lot who were forced to travel in groups for protection, as law and order was not an outstanding characteristic of the times. Most of the town magistrates forced them to sell to consumers before selling to the stores. They were then the first door-to-door salesmen as well as wholesalers.

The business historians Gras and Larson have noted another contribution of early merchants. "The travelling merchants, all unwittingly, developed a body of law and a set of procedures that have had considerable importance in legal development. We refer to the 'law merchant,' a mercantile law of the Middle Ages which in modern times in England was absorbed in the common law. In this mercantile law there were no lawyers. A court was improvised at a market place or at a fair — the so-called 'dusty-footed court' — made up of the principal parties to the dispute and others near at hand who know the facts or were familiar with the type of transaction at issue." [2]

During this period the Church was the source of economic thought and trade was considered dangerous to the soul; it was far safer to engage in agriculture or the handicrafts. The chief economic doctrines which the Fathers held and urged upon their followers were concerned with commerce. St. Jerome went so far as to maintain that what was one man's gain was another's loss. This is a far cry from our current belief that as the result of professional selling there is benefit to the buyer, to the salesmen, and to his company.

"It was St. Augustine, author of the *City of God*, who fixed in the minds of the people the idea of a just price (as distinct from a market price). He said that a man should pay a just price for a book even though the seller did not himself know or demand its real value." [3]

As the towns slowly grew up, businessmen began to play a dominant role in society. In the twelfth and thirteenth centuries they forced the Church to make exceptions in favor of a freer market. "In his *Theological Summary* he [Thomas Aquinas] asks a number of questions which indicate that the businessmen of the newly developing towns were taking their problems to the Church. Is it lawful to sell a commodity for more than it is worth? Is sale unlawful because of a fault in the thing sold? Is the seller bound to divulge a fault in the thing he is selling? Is it lawful to sell an article for more than was paid for it? Generally speaking, Aquinas made exceptions to the old doctrines of just price, which while quite casuistic at times nevertheless lent themselves to the needs of the period." [4]

¶ 810 **The merchant princes**

In the fourteenth and fifteenth centuries when town economics was established and trading centers emerged, petty capitalism was supplanted by mercantile capitalism, which was the beginning of big business in medieval Western Europe. This period also saw the last of Church domination of economic thought. A type of mercantile economics developed which sanctioned trade as a means of accomplishing national strength and self-sufficiency.

The more successful petty capitalists developed into sedentary merchants, commonly called merchant princes. These powerful men operated out of such trade centers as Florence, Venice, Marseilles, Augsburg, Bremen, Antwerp, Amsterdam, and London. Their operations embraced the beginning of most of our current marketing functions and institutions. They were:

• *Importers*: buying ships for their own use and becoming common carriers (transporting goods of others at established rates).

• *Exporters*: insuring cargoes and ships of other merchants; acting as commission agents for other merchants; performing banking and exchange transactions for themselves and others; buying warehouses and becoming common warehousemen (storing goods of others at established rates).

• *Wholesalers*: influencing or controlling guilds (trade associations) to obtain goods manufactured for their requirements.

• *Retailers*: operating stores to handle broken lots and odds and ends.

¶ 811 **The economists recognize that trade is productive**

In 1776, the independence of business was furthered by Adam Smith, the first of the classical or liberal economists. In his book *The Wealth of Nations* he made the following major points:

• The wealth of a nation is its total annual output of production.

• The purpose of production is consumption.

• Trade is as productive as agriculture or industry.

• Reinvestment of profits is essential for continuous economic progress.

• The government should not direct or regulate business, a principle called *laissez-faire* (let to do).

• Self-interest leads to competition, which, in turn, leads to public gain.

This was the business and economic environ- which automatically directs production and allocates goods to consumers.

¶ 812 **Early American salesmen**

This was the business and economic environment at the time of the development of our country and of the industrial revolution. The first salesmen in our country were termed Yankee peddlers and had their origin in Bos-

of historical note

ton in the late seventeenth century. At that time the colonies were not allowed to manufacture anything but had to trade their raw materials for the manufactured wares of England. Certain enterprising colonists would trade with individual sailors for buttons, pins, laces, and smallwares. They would then sell their wares to the housewives in the area.

The more successful peddlers became wholesalers and were the first to employ salesmen. These salesmen, or Yankee peddlers, followed the migration to the West carrying their wares by horseback or wagon and contributed greatly to the transportation and communication system which grew up between these new markets and the eastern seaboard. Often they would settle in one of the newly established villages and become the proprietors of the earliest retail institution — the general store.

The larger wholesale houses lacked credit information on the small and distant retailers. Particularly after the panic of 1837 they hired credit investigators to collect past due accounts and to gather business information. In the course of their duties they spread goodwill for their employers and would sell from sample — being the forerunners of the sales representative.

As retailers began to *go to market* to the wholesaling and manufacturing centers of Boston and New York, they encountered two other types of salesmen. The *greeter* would meet the retailers at the train and would invite them to the offices of his employers. The *drummer* was more aggressive. He would board the train in advance and offer entertainment to the retailers upon their arrival in the city. In this way the greeter's efforts could be countered. After the entertainment at hotel or restaurant, the the entourage would proceed to the display rooms of the merchants. The term drummer came to be applied to any travelling saleman, particularly in the West.

Dolan graphically describes the early sellers of services as well as goods. "A tinker, at that time, was a man who peddled services instead of goods. He was particularly skilled in repairing pewter and went from house to house looking for cracked or bent pewterware. He was probably the first of the service peddlers, men who were to become almost as numerous as those who sold goods." [1]

"The Yankee peddler has long been a picturesque and colorful figure; for too long we have thought of him as an idler and a vagrant, who moved from one remote settlement to another because he lacked brains or the enterprise to set up a stable business. In reality he was often a shrewd, ambitious, tough character whose dogged courage and keen imagination played a vital role in our social and economic development. It is hardly an exaggeration to say that our entire Middle West and South would have remained regions of thinly settled backwoodsmen far into the nineteenth century if the lowly peddler had not carried the materials of civilization to the people who lived there." [2]

⟩⟩⟩REMEMBER→ History is written to glorify the politician and the warrior. Yet the merchant has always been in the background wielding invisible power and bringing change. The salesman has shown courage, self-reliance, self-discipline, an insight into human motivations, and extreme adaptability to the continuing challenges which he has had to face.

¶ 813 **Emergence from the production era**

The Industrial Revolution ushered in a business system in the early 1800's which might be called industrial capitalism. New technologies were permitting the production of goods in quantities and varieties never before dreamed of. The result was the development of giant manufacturing companies. It brought businesses specializing as importers, exporters, wholesalers and retailers. It also brought about the retail specialty stores in contrast to the general store. The emphasis was on production, but the need for salesmen increased tremendously. "Figures taken from census data show that the use of travelling salesmen of the drummer type increased rapidly, when travel by railroad made regular trips possible. With about 1,000 operating in 1860, the number had increased to 7,262 by 1870, 28,158 by 1880, 58,691 by 1890, and 92,919 by 1900." [1]

The great capital requirements of mass production required men skilled in finance. The financiers, through the corporate type of business organization, became most powerful in the control and direction of business enterprises, so that from 1870 to 1930 our business system might be termed financial capitalism. The excesses of both the industrialists and financiers resulted in greater control and regulation by the government. The Sherman Anti-Trust Act of 1890, the Federal Trade Commission Act of 1914, the Securities and Exchange Act of 1934, the National Labor Relations Act of 1935, and the Wheeler Lea Act of 1938 were outstanding laws affecting government and business relations. They were quite in contrast with the doctrine of *laissez-faire*. Rather than "let to do," it became more a case of government making business conform to certain regulations. Thus, since 1930 our business economy or system might be called national capitalism in that the government has inserted itself into business operations. The purpose has been concern over maintaining economic growth, the prevention of monopolies, an equitable distribution of the national income, the health and safety of workers, and the assurance of value received by the consumer, in accordance with expectations, for the price paid.

During the 1900's the selling function became of increasing importance. In 1969 there were 6,621,670 sales workers in the United States, constituting 8.5% of all persons employed. This does not include managers, officials, or proprietors, so it is an understatement of the increasing orientation toward marketing and sales.[2]

The marketing concept

¶ 814 From production to marketing

Prior to 1930 business was primarily production oriented. The concern was efficiency in mass production and then a forcing of the products through the distributive network. Just as government has been concerned about the end results of business activities, business itself has undergone some self-analysis. As the capacity to produce became greater than the capacity to market, business goals and marketing's role in business operations were reappraised. The result has been the development of the *marketing concept*.

Still and Cundiff succinctly explain the *marketing concept* in their book *Essentials of Marketing*. "This marketing concept is a philosophy applied to the operation of a firm in which customer and consumer needs are recognized as of the utmost importance. These needs are regarded, under this concept, as the prime factors which should govern the separate planning of each function of the business, as well as the over-all plan aimed at achieving predetermined profit objectives. In other words, the marketing concept of management is based on both the philosophy that the firm is in business to serve its customers and on the determination that this is to be done profitably.

"Under the marketing concept, marketing is the catalyst that brings together the technological complex of business and the consumer and industrial markets, which have been built on the desires of individual ultimate consumers and industrial users to find better ways to satisfy their wants. This philosophy of marketing is based on two fundamentals. First, marketing has a dual job. It must direct the attention of the business to the customer's needs and desires, and it must persuade the prospective customer through all the available techniques of selling and advertising. This last phase of the job of marketing — that of persuading the customers — has long been recognized as the primary responsibility of marketing, but many businessmen have only recently begun to realize that the assessment of customers' needs is a necessary preliminary step. Of course, some retailers and sales executives have long believed that 'the customer is king.' Marketing people must point out to business the consumer needs, both conscious and unconscious, that affect the products or services to be offered. With recognition of the first phase, the emphasis in the persuasion phase has shifted from selling the product to selling the *function* that the product will perform. The second fundamental underlying philosophy of marketing is emphasis on the profit concept rather than the volume concept. Additional sales volume at any price is no longer the aim. Instead, the aim is *profitable* volume."[1]

It is the salesman who is closest to the consumer or the industrial user. Thus the salesman plays a key role in implementing the marketing concept. But it is the selling function which must pervade the company's entire organization. That is why many companies today, regardless of product produced, accurately claim *we are a marketing company*.

Consumerism (concern for the protection of the consumer) emerged in the late sixties, and Ralph Nader became its primary champion. He asserts that he believes in our free enterprise system and in our marketing system, but that both business and government have failed to serve and protect the consumer. If business fully embraces the marketing concept, there will be less cause for restrictive legislation and less criticism from consumer groups.

¶ 815 Selling, ethics, and society—a happy threesome

The salesman has come a long way. It took time before his efforts were recognized as wholesome by the Church, beneficial by government, productive by economists, and worthwhile by society. A successful selling career must begin with the salesman's belief that what he is doing is significant. Then all of the study, time, and practice to master the skills of selling must be based on an acceptable code of *ethics*.

¶ 816 Ethics as an individual

Ethics is the study of human actions with respect to their being right or wrong. The word comes from the Greek word *ethos* meaning custom or a habitual mode of conduct. The purpose of the study is to determine what makes certain actions right or wrong and what gives them a moral quality. It endeavors to establish a systematic general doctrine on moral life.

All religions have been concerned with morality and the moral judgment of the individual and of the public. The ancient Assyrians and Egyptians had religious codes of moral conduct. Judaism and its Ten Commandments, Christianity and its Golden Rule, Islam and its Koran have all been concerned with private and public morality in the conduct of everyday life. Even the humanists and existentialists find that in their individualistic efforts to determine the truth of man's existence there usually comes a recognition of a social bond among human beings.

Certain aspects of human conduct are considered unethical or immoral by nearly all approaches to ethics. Hatred, dishonesty, deceit, slander, and theft are universally held as undesirable qualities while love, truthfulness, mercy, forgiveness, and loyalty are not only closely connected with religious values, but are held in esteem by all moral philosophies.

A man is known by his actions, and his actions reflect his beliefs, which are the substance of his character. Trust comes from experience, and as one encounters repeated evidence of the accepted moral qualities of an individual, he places his trust and confidence in him. One act which is contradictory to this ethical pattern of moral conduct erodes or may completely destroy this positive evaluation of character. A person without character will find it difficult to succeed in any vocation. There are few ways of earning a livelihood which do not require the trust and confidence of others. The lack of a personal code of ethics on which society is in general agreement, or a violation of this personal code, is self-defeating.

➤➤REMEMBER→ Ethics or moral character is bedrock to success in any field. Before the *salesman* comes the *man*. Before qualification as a professional must come concern for moral precepts.

¶ 817 Ethics as a salesman

In interviewing an applicant for a sales position, the company is first concerned with "What manner of man is this?" His personal code of ethics must be compatible with those values which the company deems important. After employment, the salesman not only represents his company's products; he represents the company to the prospect. Countless sales have not been made, and accounts have been lost because an exposed flaw in the character of the salesman has destroyed the customer's confidence in the company's ability to perform.

It would be nice if there were a ready reference ethical guide covering all situations requiring application of moral principles. However, the matter becomes quite complex as it becomes apparent that *certain areas* of ethics are flexible. Approved behavior may change from decade to decade, and practices condoned in certain areas of business may be condemned in other areas. The salesman has three sources to guide him in making decisions in the field of ethics.

- His personal code of ethics, which is unchanging and embraces basic moral qualities in general acceptance by society.
- The laws, which restrain anti-social and immoral behavior.
- The policies of the company to which he must conform, if he is a loyal employee (in itself an example of required ethical behavior).

If the salesman finds that his personal code of ethics is inconsistent with any legal requirements, then he must alter his code. However, if there is a basic conflict between his personal code of ethics and his company's code of ethics as represented by company policies or practices, then there is an impasse. The only way to resolve this conflict is for the salesman to resign and seek employment with a company whose business ethics are compatible with his personal code. Fortunately, the great majority of American businesses are operated in a manner which does not cause such a conflict.

In professional selling, the buyer, the salesman, and the salesman's employer should all benefit. A test of the ethical status of an act should be viewed from the standpoint of each of these parties. In the short run or the long run will the buyer be harmed? In the short run or the long run will my company be harmed? In the short run or the long run, regardless of the gain to me, will the remembrance of this act make me feel uncomfortable? The difficult task is to answer *yes* to the last question when the apparent material gain looms large.

¶ 818 **Relations with buyers**

▶ **IDEA IN ACTION** George Brown, an industrial salesman, recognized that a buyer's secretary was definitely a VIP who could aid or seriously hamper his relations with her boss. He became most successful in selling secretaries on the benefits which would accrue to their bosses if they would schedule prompt interviews for him, handle his promotional material with tender care, and expedite his orders.

A substantial contract was to be awarded by the Gaubert Manufacturing Company on the basis of bids. Specifications were made available to all suppliers encouraging them to submit bids. George felt that because of his excellent rapport with Bernice Connolly, an executive secretary with Gaubert, it would be possible to obtain information on the bids of his two closest competitors. This would permit him to come in a bit lower. He tested this idea on the basis of benefit to the buyer, to his employer, and to himself.

The buyer would receive a lower price, thereby gaining. His company would offer a lower price only if it would be profitable; therefore his company could not lose. The commission he would receive would pay a substantial portion of the orthodontic work needed by his daughter.

George realized that this was idle daydreaming. His personal code of ethics would not permit him to take such action. It was deceit. It placed Bernice's code of ethics in jeopardy. It put the competitors at a disadvantage. It was not fair play. Also from a most practical point of view, if it were ever discovered how George came in with a lowest bid, what would he do? What would Bernice do?

▶ **IDEA IN ACTION** Cliff Romer knew cars. He was also a likeable person with a ready smile and a keen sense of humor. He knew the fundamentals of how to discern what a customer really wanted and then to move him to action. That is why Chapin Motors was so pleased with the performance of this new salesman.

In making a presentation to Alice and Gordon Newby, Cliff learned that they had a sixteen-year-old son. In order to personalize their relationship and to enhance the dialogue, Cliff mentioned his seventeen-year-old son. Actually, Cliff didn't have a seventeen-year-old son, but did have a ten-year-old daughter and an eight-year-old son.

Cliff convinced his prospects that a certain model met all of their needs and closed the sale. His prospects, now customers, exuded pride of ownership and thanked him for making the buying problem a real pleasure.

What difference does it make whether or not Cliff actually had a seventeen-year-old son? He fitted a product to a prospect — everybody was happy. This might be considered to be in the area of flexible ethics, but it takes a bit of rationalization to term this complete truthfulness.

Cliff felt most uncomfortable when the Newbys called a week later telling him of a prospect and suggesting their sons get to know each other. He had succeeded in the short run as a salesman, but failed as a man, so in the long run his continued success as a salesman will be more difficult.

the marketing concept

He has set in motion a tendency to vary from the truth if he feels there is no real harm done. He has also set in motion the need for a computer-like memory system, permitting instant recall of the timing and conditions of variances from the truth. Regardless of right or wrong, the additional burden does not permit the intense concentration on the selling situation which is required of the professional salesman.

▶ **IDEA IN ACTION** Ken Strong had sold aluminum siding for various types of industrial buildings. He felt that he was close to a sizable order with the Kingston Company. The purchasing agent called him in, closed the door, and said that the order was his if he could grant a few professional courtesies. The first was that the Kingston Company be granted a lower price for like grade and quantity than their competitor. The second was that the front frame portion of the purchasing agent's home be replaced with residential type aluminum siding. The third was that the purchasing agent and his wife would dearly love to have an evening in not too nearby New York.

Ken explained that the price concession would very likely be in violation of the Robinson-Patman Act. He said that company policy would not permit the construction on the purchasing agent's residence. He also stated that the New York trip was quite beyond his entertainment territory and expense account. However, he said that he would be delighted to have his wife join them for dinner. He then summarized the key benefits of his company's product and service and the advantages they could afford the Kingston Company as a key resource.

The purchasing agent acknowledged the long-run benefits and placed the order without further mention then or in the future of "professional courtesies."

¶ 819 **Relations with employers**

▶ **IDEA IN ACTION** Roy Stern, manufacturer's representative, traveled throughout the Southwest. His expense account permitted ten dollars a day for room and ten dollars a day for meals. Receipts were required for room, but not for meals. During each of his monthly swings through his territory he would spend three or four days in Phoenix with his brother. Both he and his brother looked forward to these visits and the continuing card games which ensued.

Roy had a rubber stamp made reading "Phoenix Pony Express Inn" with a similarly fictitious address. He then stamped a number of invoices, marked them paid, and would submit a simulated ten-dollar receipt for each night he spent at his brother's apartment. He reasoned that the company expected him to stay in a hotel, so they were not incurring any addition to planned expenses.

Roy's sales manager was rather dismayed when he tried to make reservations at the nonexistent inn on a trip to Phoenix. Roy was rather uncomfortable in making his explanations. Perhaps a clear, mutual understanding of the intent and letter of the company policy would have completely avoided an ethical dilemma.

▶ **IDEA IN ACTION** Mark Andrew's contract with the Grisson Company prohibited him from representing any other company or selling any merchandise other than that distributed by his employer. The contract was a lengthy document and although aware of the major points covered, Mark considered it just one of the formalities which accompany the employment process. Besides, several of his colleagues affirmed that companies operated under a forgiveness clause and did not hold salesmen to the letter of the contract.

As Mark became well known in his territory he began to consider going into business for himself as a manufacturer's agent, representing several manufacturers. As a preliminary test of the idea he obtained a line of merchandise not in competition with the Grisson line, but appropriate for the customers on whom he was calling. After a couple of months he gave up the idea of becoming an independent businessman but continued to sell the second line.

When Mark's sales manager learned that Mark was representing a second line, he demanded that he drop it immediately. Mark explained that it in no way detracted from his work on the Grisson line. In fact, the acceptance of the second line often enabled him to place the Grisson line, thus increasing his Grisson volume.

The sales manager was not moved by Mark's arguments and charged him with disloyalty and less than ethical conduct. Mark was incensed by what he considered narrow-mindedness and quit. Mark's personal code of ethics was rather elastic on the matter of loyalty and was not consistent with his employer's code. Rather than alter his code, he quit. In order to prevent a reoccurrence of such a situation in the future, Mark must investigate the ethical implications of a company's

¶ 819

policies and consider whether or not they are compatible with his personal code.

¶ 820 How are we doing?

"In a survey made by *Sales Review*, 500 purchasing agents were asked to 'think specifically of the salesman who calls on you that you think is the highest type of professional, and why you give him that rating.' Of the descriptive adjectives noted in the replies, the first three were *dependable*, *sincere* and *honest*."[1]

"Until all buying decisions are made by impersonal, automated calculators, just so long will *sincerity* be an indispensible item in the kit of the successful salesman. The value of product knowledge, logical approach, emotional appeal, good manners, quick thinking, and such are not to be denied. But they form the superstructure of persuasion. If they do not rest on a solid platform of integrity the whole edifice is wobbly."[2]

A professional salesman has perfected his selling skills. He has solidified his personal code of ethics. He strives to truly serve his customers. He is loyal to his company. He is fair in matters relating to his competition. He knows that what he is doing is essential for the economy and that it has social significance. The result is a world of personal satisfaction from his work.

¶ 821 Which way in selling?

As we have seen, selling is involved in the satisfaction of all human needs and takes place throughout marketing channels as goods flow to ultimate consumers or users. All types of goods, services, and ideas are sold in a wide variety of quantities by a multiple of marketing institutions using varied selling methods. In view of this selling labyrinth, it would be only natural for one to ask "which way to a selling career?"

¶ 822 Classifying sales occupations

Sales occupations can be classified in many ways. There is the selling of tangibles (products) and of intangibles (services); there is inside selling and outside selling; there is selling to ultimate consumer or to middlemen; there is selling to industrial users; there is one-time selling or continuity selling. The following classification is certainly not all inclusive, but it does serve to differentiate the best known sales occupations.

I. *Selling to Consumers*
   A. Direct
      1. Direct salesman (Fuller Brush, Avon)
      2. Specialty direct salesman (World Book Encyclopedia, Cutco Cutlery)
      3. Route salesman (Carnation Milk, Jewel Tea Company)
      4. Real estate salesman (works for licensed realtor)
      5. Service salesman (Rose Exterminator Company, Atlas Furnace Service)
      6. Insurance salesman (New York Life, Allstate)
   B. Indirect
      1. Retail store salesman (Macy's, Sears)
      2. Securities salesman (E. F. Hutton, Dean Witter)

II. *Selling to Industrial and Business Firms for Their Own Use*
   1. Manufacturer's representative (Fisher Switches, General Electric)
   2. Industrial wholesale salesman (Graybar Electric, Tournquist Machinery Sales)
   3. Sales engineer (Aluminum Company of America, Kaiser Steel)
   4. Manufacturer's agent (works as an independent businessman)
   5. Advertising salesman (The Pacific Telephone and Telegraph Co., The Los Angeles Times)
   6. Freight service salesman (Santa Fe, Shippers Express)

III. *Selling to Distributors for Resale*
   1. Manufacturer's representative (Gladding McBean; Cluett, Peabody and Company)
   2. Wholesale salesman (Skaggs Stone, McKesson-Robbins)
   3. Manufacturer's agent (works as independent businessman)
   4. Driver salesman (Hamm's Beer, Pepsi-Cola)

real estate salesman

5. Rack salesman (Hane's Hosiery, Rawson Drug & Sundry Co.)
6. Medical detail salesman (Parke-Davis, The Upjohn Co.)

¶ 823 **Selling to consumers**

Direct salesman

The shortest marketing channel is directly from manufacturer to consumer. In such a case, the manufacturer performs all of the marketing functions, including selling, which is done by its own sales force. There is considerable one-time selling on a door-to-door basis in which the salesman never sees a customer a second time. Some companies, however, such as Fuller Brush and Avon engage in continuity selling with assignment of salesmen to specific territories for continuous service to their customers.

Direct selling organizations hire both men and women, a great many of whom work on a part-time basis. Seldom are there rigid age or educational requirements and compensation is nearly always on a commission basis ranging from 25 to 40 per cent of sales. Even though one may not remain in direct selling as a career, it is excellent training for any type of promotional work. In this type of *cold canvassing* there is great emphasis on the approach to customers and quick adaption to the selling situation. It is a trying test of the salesman's persistence and emotional stability.

Specialty direct salesman

A specialty item is one which is infrequently purchased, is durable in nature, and fairly high priced. This means that there is caution and deliberation before the buying decision is made. The specialty direct salesman, although doing some cold canvassing, makes greater use of leads and does more diligent prospecting for customers. In-the-home selling by appointment, group demonstrations, and party-plans are typical of the methods used.

This may be the most practical manner in which to market radically new products or products which require demonstration. Vacuum cleaners, sewing machines, rug cleaners, cooking ware, encyclopedias, and Bibles are typical products sold in this way. Compensation is usually straight commission, with the higher unit price permitting high earnings. It taxes a salesman's initiative in maintaining a prospect list, and it requires a higher rate of successful closes than in the case of the typical direct salesman. There are few age or educational requirements, but appearance and a forceful personality are usually important factors in employment.

Route salesman

A route salesman is to the consumer what a driver salesman is to a retailer. The milk man is the typical route salesman. He strives for continuity-selling, continually prospecting for steady customers and emphasizing services to retain them. He endeavors to increase his sales through suggestion selling of related perishables such as butter, eggs, ice cream, or orange juice.

The ice man is no longer needed, and the fresh produce home-route selling is practically extinct. However, for nearly 70 years the Jewel Tea Company has operated a home-route selling service, although the company is now diversified into many different methods of retailing. Its route salesmen handle specialty food items and selected non-food durable and non-durable items, many of which are purchased on the installment plan. Although the Jewel Tea Company emphasizes profit sharing, most route salesmen work on a commission basis with a drawing account. Maturity and responsible behavior are important employment factors, as companies are interested in long-term employment of their route salesmen.

Real estate salesman

The real estate salesman works for a licensed realtor and must meet certain state requirements to sell real estate. The hours may be long and varied, as considerable time is required for a single transaction. There is in-the-office selling, on-the-site selling, and in-the-home selling with both husband and wife participating in the decision making. Many a closing takes place in the evening or on weekends.

A salesman must have a practical knowledge of business as well as specialized knowledge of real estate. Because of the importance of the decision to the buyer, the salesman must gain his full confidence and respect. It requires a great deal of selling skill and consequently the rewards are high. More and more women are entering this field and enjoying successful careers.

Service salesman

A service salesman sells a service which is intangible. He is usually a craftsman or a member of a skilled trade. Coupled with this mechanical ability is the ability to persuade people of his company's competence in performing a certain operation. He usually receives the top hourly pay of the particular craft involved and usually some type of bonus dependent upon the volume of business for which he is responsible.

Insurance salesman

Much has been done in the insurance industry to develop the professional salesman. Those who qualify for the certificates of Chartered Life Underwriter or Chartered Property and Casualty Underwriter must complete rigorous courses of study. Only a few insurance salesmen have such certificates, but all must be most knowledgeable in business matters. A minimum of two years college is almost essential with a bachelor's degree being the most common preparation for those successful in this field.

There is big money in selling insurance with incomes of $30,000 to $50,000 a year not uncommon for the true professional. After an initial training period on a salary basis, commissions and fees on policies sold and in force are the common methods of compensation.

Retail store salesman

Retailing embraces a wide variety of selling. Unfortunately a great deal of it is clerking or simply ringing up the sale. Part-time and short hours employees are used extensively due to the extended hours of operation and seasonal nature of retailing. As a result the majority of retail salespeople are paid an hourly wage.

However, there are also professional retail salesmen, working on some variation of a commission basis, who earn high incomes. In big ticket departments such as furniture and specialty departments such as women's shoes, salesmen often earn $15,000 to $25,000 a year. These high income people put to practice the principles contained in the *Miracle Sales Guide*. They don't wait for something to happen—they make something happen—and the result is sales and clientele of personal customers. Advanced degrees are seldom required, but effective sales training *is* a must for success.

For those interested in a merchandising management career, sales training is absolutely essential. Every supervisory or management training program in large retail organizations requires actual selling experience, usually in both soft line and hard line types of merchandise. Although a four-year degree was formerly a requirement for most executive training programs, more and more retailers are recruiting community college graduates for their training programs.

Securities salesman

A salesman of stocks and bonds works for a stock broker, whose operations are very closely regulated by the Securities and Exchange Commission, the stock exchange with which he is affiliated, and the laws of the state in which he is operating. As a consequence, employment standards are quite high in regard to qualities of character as well as educational requirements. A four-year degree is required by most brokerage houses, who then train their new employees in finance and brokerage operations.

There are high incomes in this field. In addition to the commission on sales, the investment knowledge gained permits many to increase their incomes greatly through effective use of their accumulated capital.

¶ 824　**Selling to industrial and business firms for their own use**

Manufacturers' representatives

A manufacturer's representative works directly for a manufacturer. The nature of his work depends upon the product and trade channel of the manufacturer. Some representatives sell industrial products to industrial or business firms who use these products in their operations. Other representatives sell consumer products to distributors for resale to other distributors or consumers. In either case he is the company, in the eyes of his prospects.

In contrast to selling to consumers, manufacturers' representatives usually have extensive territories and must do a great deal of travelling. They must be experienced salesmen, capable of making management decisions in the field and must be particularly adept in self-management. The manufacturer's representative selling industrial goods of high value is often backed up by sales engineers in the home office. Extended periods of negotiation may take place before an account is opened or a sale is made. Feasibility studies and tests are often required, which necessitates the support of a technical staff.

Because of the responsibility involved, there are opportunities for high earnings. Such earnings can only be maintained, however, by a continuous high level of performance. This is also the pathway to management positions in the company's marketing division.

Industrial wholesale salesman

Wholesale firms selling industrial goods were once called mill supply houses. Today the terms industrial supply houses or industrial wholesalers are more commonly used. They usually handle a wide variety of minor industrial equipment or supplies from many manufacturers for a particular type of industry — machinery, electronics, automotive, construction, etc.

A salesman for such a firm has a restricted territory and makes regular calls on his customers. Manufacturers' representatives assist him in becoming knowledgeable about the features and benefits of the many items which he sells. He becomes well informed about his customer's needs and becomes expert in satisfying these needs from the hundreds of items available to him. It is a more secure, steady type of selling, for which there is good pay but seldom the high incomes found in other types of selling.

Sales engineers

A sales engineer must have a technical background, if not a specific engineering degree. He may work in the same manner as a manufacturer's representative for industrial goods which are particularly intricate. He might also be a staff man providing the particular engineering know-how for specific selling situations encountered by the company's representatives. However, he is not only an engineer, he must be a *salesman*.

Manufacturer's agent

A manufacturer's agent takes the place of a salesman for a manufacturer. He is an independent businessman who represents several different, but non-competing, manufacturers in a specific territory. He differs from a wholesaler in that he does not own (take title to) the goods he sells, operating strictly on a commission basis. Most manufacturers' agents have offices, employ secretarial help, and even salesmen. Some sell industrial goods while others sell merchandise to distributors for resale. It is a case of making a business of selling, and usually this business pays very well. Many salesmen progress from various selling classifications to this independent businessman status.

Advertising salesman

Advertising space and time must be sold by printed publications and broadcasting stations. Newspapers usually employ salesmen to sell display advertising space to local businesses. Such salesmen must be able to assist small businessmen in advertising. It would be difficult to obtain national advertising in this way and most publications and broadcasters use the services of media representatives. These "reps" typically sell space or time for a number of newspapers or stations to advertisers and advertising agencies. Salesmen for media representatives must be knowledgeable about the various market characteristics and coverages of the media they represent.

Telephone companies use salesmen for the yellow pages. Specialty advertising companies sell useful products carrying advertising messages to those selling either products or services. Advertising, a selling tool, is a service which must itself be sold by personal selling.

Freight service salesman

Transportation, another marketing function, is a service which must be sold to all who are involved in the movement of goods through the marketing channels. Salesmen for freight lines must be most familiar with tariff rules, regulations, and the procedure for obtaining rates and charges for transcontinental motor, rail or air transport. The seller of industrial goods works mainly with purchasing agents while the seller of freight service works mainly with industrial traffic managers.

¶ 825 **Selling to distributors for resale**

In ¶ 824 industrial selling by manufacturers' representatives, wholesale salesmen, and manufacturers' agents was described. These same selling titles are used in the sale of consumer goods to distributors for resale. The salesman in this case is working with wholesale or retail buyers rather than purchasing agents. He must have knowledge of the characteristics of consumer markets. In many cases he must help buyers interpret trends in fad or fashion. With the massive introduction of new consumer products he must continually study the competitive offerings and evaluate the strength of his product line. He must understand inventory control and assist his customers in achieving the highest stock turnover.

The duties of a manufacturer's representative vary considerably depending on the company's product line and its channel of distribution. The company may sell directly to retailers without using wholesalers. In such cases the salesman would not only sell to retail buyers, but would hold meetings with the retail salesmen and teach them how to sell his product line to the consumer. If the manufacturer sells to wholesalers, then the representative may work closely with the wholesaler's salesmen. He may assist them in opening new retail accounts, acting as trainer, public relations man, and trouble-shooter.

Many wholesale salesmen perform a routine kind of selling termed *detailing*. It is a matter of checking the inventory of his product line in grocery or drug stores. He often stocks the shelves, and does dsplay work, as well as advising the retailer what and how much he should order.

Driver salesman

The driver salesman works for a truck *wholesaler* or *jobber* (also known as wagon jobber). He combines selling, delivery, and collection in one operation. He carries nationally advertised, fast-moving goods such as beer or soda water and perishables such as dairy products, candies, or baked goods. This is strictly service selling and does not involve a high degree of selling skill, the emphasis being on physical fitness, aggressiveness, dependability, and a friendly personality.

Rack salesman

Quite similar to the driver salesman is the rack salesman. He works for a *rack wholesaler* or *jobber,* a type of middleman who has come on to the distribution scene since World War II. He sells non-food items such as drugs, housewares, or notions to food stores. The store provides the space, and the rack salesman must keep the rack or fixture stocked with clean and well-displayed merchandise. The goods are placed in the store on a consignment basis with the store paying only for the goods which it sells.

Hanes Hosiery has been most successful in using this method of distribution for their L'Eggs brand of women's hosiery. Their program is also unique in that they use rack saleswomen rather than men.

Medical detail salesman

The medical detail salesman is unique in that he introduces his ethical drug products to doctors and sells them to drug stores for resale. Consequently, he must have a great deal of product knowledge so that he can talk intelligently with members of the medical profession. He must not only know the properties of the products but what research has been done on

medical detail salesman

TREND IN EARNINGS — EXPERIENCED SALESMEN

	1956	1958	1964	1968	1971
All Salesmen					
Average Highest Paid	$11,500	$12,900	$13,200	$14,750	$21,967
Average Lowest Paid	6,000	6,600	7,600	8,500	11,992
Average All Salesmen	8,700	9,700	10,000	11,186	14,596
Salaried Salesmen					
Average Highest Paid	$ 9,500	$11,300	$11,200	$13,000	$17,593
Average Lowest Paid	6,200	7,100	7,400	8,500	11,875
Average All Salesmen (On Salary)	7,900	9,200	9,700	10,900	13,100
Commission Salesmen					
Average Highest Paid	$15,500	$17,100	$16,500	$20,250	$29,500
Average Lowest Paid	5,500	5,600	7,500	9,000	12,050
Average All Salesmen (On Commission)	10,500	11,400	10,400	13,250	16,040
Salary/Commission Salesmen					
Average Highest Paid	$11,900	$12,500	$13,000	$15,000	$21,910
Average Lowest Paid	6,000	6,500	7,000	7,500	12,000
Average All Salesmen (On Salary/Commission)	9,000	9,500	9,900	10,578	14,790

them and validation of the results of their use. He provides doctors with samples and literature and asks that they prescribe the products or recommend them to their patients.

He must also have merchandising knowledge when he calls on drug stores. He will not only sell new products to druggists, but will also detail or obtain reorders on his products already carried by the druggists.

⇒ OBSERVATION → There are sales opportunities for men and women of all backgrounds and all educational levels. Certain types of selling require more of an individual before employment and more after employment. The more demanding the type of selling, the more financially rewarding it is. More than in any other field the rewards are directly related to one's honesty, attitude, knowledge, and performance.

¶ 826 Levels of pay

Frank S. Endicott, Director of Placement at Northwestern University, makes an annual survey of policy and practice in the employment of college and university graduates in business and industry. In 1971 the responding companies' average starting monthly salary in the field of sales and marketing was $742.[1] The average monthly earnings in 1970 of college men employed in the sales field five years previously was $1,080 and those employed ten years previously was $1,310.[2]

The 1971 Dartnell Corporation Survey, *Compensation of Salesmen*, covering 29,651 salesmen in 580 companies disclosed definite trends in earnings and methods of compensation. The following table shows the trend in earnings for experienced salesmen from 1956 through 1971.

Experienced salesmen were considered to be those who were:
- Capable of operating effectively on their own with minimum direction or supervision.
- Able to handle their territorial responsibilities efficiently.
- Well-acquainted with key decision makers within accounts they contact.
- Graduates of one or more training programs designed to increase their sales professionalism.
- Proficient in planning procedures so that calls were conducted with maximum efficiency.
- Consistently able to achieve quotas or other objectives established by management.

In the span of three years, 1968-1971, the following percent increases occurred for average experienced salesmen.
- Salaried salesmen 20 %
- Commission salesmen 21 %
- Salary/Commission salesmen 39.8%
- All salesmen 30 %

Even inexperienced salesmen had a 46.7% increase in earnings, from $7,028 in 1968 to $10,314 in 1971. These summary figures are all averages. Sales still offers the opportunity to strike it rich, in some cases up to $100,000 a year.

>>>>OBSERVATION→ There is big money in sales. The Miracle Sales Guide is intended for those who want to break into the big money and not be levelled at the median figures.

¶ 827 **Methods of compensation**

Companies must give close attention to the method used in compensating their salesmen, for their entire marketing program is usually implemented by personal selling. The method may range from straight salary to straight commission. Many variations and combinations of these two methods are used in accordance with the role that personal selling plays in the company's marketing mix and the type of selling which is required.

Theoretically, the greater the portion of straight salary, the greater control the company can have over the salesmen's activities. On a straight salary basis, it is reasoned, salesmen should not be disturbed about a particular territory assignment nor resent any non-selling duties. However, there is also concern about motivating salesmen to intensify their selling efforts. It would seem that straight commission would be the best for this purpose since the greater the production, the greater are the rewards. However, the great majority of companies use a combination plan by which part of the salesman's compensation is fixed and another part paid in proportion to sales made.

A good compensation plan should have the following characteristics:

1. *Adequacy.* It should enable the salesmen to maintain a decent standard of living.
2. *Feasibility.* It must permit a company to keep wage costs under control.
3. *Fairness.* It must be proportional to responsibility and productivity and must be considered fair by employees.
4. *Simplicity.* It must be readily understood by employees and easily administered by the company.
5. *Security.* It should provide a sense of security through regular payments and a base amount of relatively uniform earnings.
6. *Consistency with Marketing Concept.* It must encourage service to customers and discourage any acts detrimental to the interests of customers.

The 1971 Dartnell survey of compensation of salesmen indicated the trend in methods of compensating salesmen.

COMPARISON OF COMPENSATION PLANS FOR THE PAST 17 YEARS [1]

	1955	1959	1964	1968	1971*
Salary Plans	36%	40%	37%	27%	29%
Straight Salary	14	18	15	16.3	13
Salary and Bonus	22	22	22	10.7	16
Commission Plans	26%	23%	25%	28%	19%
Straight Commission	16	14	13	14.4	9
Commission with Draw	10	9	12	13.6	10
Combination Plans	38%	37%	38%	45%	52%
Salary, Bonus, Commission	8	10	6	10.0	13
Salary and Commission	30	27	32	34.9	28
Salary and Commission over Quota	—	—	—	—	11

*These figures reflect the predominating method of compensation.

The study shows a strong trend toward combination plans. More than half of all respondents, 52%, reported it as their first choice. The commission plans have fallen into great disfavor, dropping to 19%. This has been the most significant change in compensation methods since 1955. Even salary plans increased 2% from 1968 to 1971.

The great cost of training salesmen may be a factor in this shift away from the commission plans. The highest employment turnover rates are usually related to commission plans and the lowest to salary plans. However, turnover can be affected by many factors—hiring policies, training, supervision practices, promotion policies, personality conflicts, etc.

There are some salesmen who will work only on a commission basis — they know that they can sell. They also want all that is coming to them for their ability and feel that some of their rewards are being siphoned off under any other type of compensation plan. However, studies have shown that commission men have a higher earnings-to-volume ratio than do their counterparts. The fact that salesmen on salary average higher sales volume than men on commission is not due to the method of compensation. When sales volumes tend to be high, companies are more likely to use salary as their primary means of compensation.

¶ 828 Expense allowances and fringe benefits

Closely related to the basic compensation method are expense reimbursement practices and fringe benefits. Just as companies look at "the total package," so must salesmen evaluate the plan under which they can work most effectively. Regardless of non-financial motivation factors which a company might offer, salesmen's job satisfaction is closely related to their satisfaction with the method by which they are financially compensated.

The great amount of social legislation and the great advances made by labor unions in the 1930's led to an increasing importance of fringe benefits. Wholesalers and retailers were slower to develop extensive fringe benefit plans than manufacturing companies. Throughout industry and business, salesmen usually followed production and clerical workers in being accorded fringe benefits. Just as the commission plan was formerly emphasized, so were salesmen considered to be indepedent and expected to provide for themselves because they had the opportunity to earn high incomes.

¶ 829 Basic charactristics of success

We have surveyed the wide gamut of selling activities. We have seen the great variation in what is expected of salesmen and how they are compensated. We have also seen that routine work results in routine pay, but that the highest incomes are possible in sales.

The *Miracle Sales Guide* is directed to those who select the most challenging and remunerative careers in selling. Years ago the only question was "can he sell?" Now, often coupled with this, is the question "can he manage?" Business has become more complex. The salesman often finds himself selling to committees, confronted with studies and research assignments by prospects, and directed and supported by computer read-outs from his sales and marketing directors. There is a greater emphasis on managing himself, his time, his territory, his accounts, and his profitability to his employer.

Are there any basic characteristics for success in this increasingly challenging field? The basics are:

- *Honesty and Personal Integrity.* This was emphasized in ¶ 804 and ¶ 817. It is emphasized again at this point.
- *Complete Adherence to the Marketing Concept.* The recognition that the reason for the company's being is to serve the customer at a profit.
- *Empathy.* The ability to put oneself in another's place and sense what he is feeling.
- *Ego Drive.* ". . . which makes him want and need to make a sale in a personal or ego way, not merely for the money to be gained. His feeling must be that he has to make the sale; the customer is there to help him fulfill his personal need. In effect, to the top salesman, the sale — the conquest — provides a powerful means of enhancing his ego. His self-picture improves dramatically by virtue of conquest, and diminishes with failure." [1]

After seven years of field research, David Mayer and Herbert M. Greenberg concluded in their *Harvard Business Review* article that empathy and ego drive were essential to success as a salesman. "The salesman's empathy, coupled with his intense ego drive, enables him to home in on the target effectively and make the sale. He has the drive, the need to make the sale, and his empathy gives him the connecting tool with which to do it." [2]

When these qualities are superimposed on honesty and personal integrity and when there is a commitment to the marketing concept, the greatest potential for success has been found. The *Miracle Sales Guide* provides the training, methods, and techniques which will enable one with these qualities to achieve his potential.

How to go after that sales job you want

¶ 830 Sell yourself with a résumé

The man or woman who sends his prospective employer a neatly prepared résumé achieves the first critical step in selling himself. He makes a favorable impression. A résumé is an attractively presented set of facts that gives the employer a thumbnail sketch of you. Many ads for sales jobs ask the applicant to send a résumé. Even if this isn't the case with the job you are seeking, make one anyway. It may be just the thing that will give you the nod over the other candidates.

¶ 831 What to include in your résumé

A complete résumé usually includes information on your educational background, work history, hobbies and extracurricular or community activities, special skills, personal statistics (including marital and military status), and references. Since the intention of the résumé is to put your best foot forward, you can structure it to stress your strong points and minimize your weak points. Obviously, no amount of structuring or editing can cover up for a lack of requirements. If the job calls for previous experience and you don't have any, it won't be the fault of an inadequate résumé, only an inadequate background. On the other hand, assuming the job calls for a college graduate with sales experience and you have a degree but not too much experience, you can devote more space in your résumé to your education. Instead of merely listing your alma mater, you could list specific courses taken, your grade point average (if it is a good one) and any academic honors won. This way you give more space to your strengths and less to your weaknesses.

⟫CAUTION→ Don't lie or stretch the truth in your résumé. If you never actually received your degree, don't say you did. Companies usually dismiss salesmen who bend the truth. They certainly won't hire a prospect who does.

¶ 832 How to prepare a résumé that sells

It is pretty good advice to limit your résumé to one page. This may mean you will have to leave out something, but more likely you can put in everything that is really significant if you take the right approach.

⟫OBSERVATION→ A smart salesman knows that his prospect doesn't want to hear everything there is to say about his product. This is true even if he had all day to listen. A salesman can sell by stressing the outstanding features. Follow this advice when you sell yourself in your résumé.

Since the work history part of the résumé usually requires the most space on the page, there is a long and short way to list it. If you are short on experience, you will prefer the long way (see Figure 1). If you have trouble squeezing in all of your work experience, the short way is your best approach (see Figure 2).

⟫IMPORTANT→ Be sure that whatever style you choose for your résumé, you follow it consistently all the way through. The example below is inconsistent.

6-64 to 7-66
   Employer: Ace Hardware Company
   Duties: Helped customers buy, stocked shelves
   Salary: $2.25 per hour
   Supervisor: Mr. Ray Kramer

9-66 to 9-67
   Worked for BCS Building Supply. My job was to unload incoming shipments and stock them in the designated locations. My pay was $3.00 per hour. My supervisor was Mr. Jesse Costa.

The format used for the Ace Hardware job should have been used again for the BCS job and for any jobs which might have been listed.

¶ 833 Writing the cover letter

Basically there are three things you want to accomplish in your cover letter.

1. Tell who you are and why you want the job.
2. Tell what you have to offer — this assumes the question "what can he do for us?".
3. Close by asking for an interview.

The only way to write a convincing letter of application is not to write it until after you have researched the company. Common sense? Maybe. But thousands of job seekers don't bother to find out about the firm before they apply. Don't rely on their newspaper ad. They almost never tell enough.

¶ 834 What you should know about the company before you apply

Here is a list of items you should know before you write your cover letter:

1. Name of parent company (if any).

ALAN E. VANDERGRIFF   Age: 23

406 Williams Street   Height: 6'2" Weight: 173

Fremont, California 94746   Marital Status: Single

Phone: 489-0357   Willing to relocate

Education
    Castro Valley High School, graduated June 1966. "B" average.
    Chabot College, graduated June 1971. "B" average.
      Major: Merchandising

Extracurricular
    High School: Newspaper reporter, freshman baseball, varsity track,
                  Block CV Society, president of junior class
    College: Business Club, publicity chairman of Merchandising
                  Club, intramural sports, California Marketing Club
                  state contest winner

Experience
    Direct Salesman, Cutco Cutlery Company, Hayward, California
      Job: Sales Representative and College Sales Supervisor
      Supervisor: Mr. Clinton Murray, District Manager
      Dates: September 1968 -- Present

    Retail Salesman, Mervyn's Department Store, San Lorenzo, California
      Job: Men's Wear Salesman; stock work, operate register
      Supervisor: Mr. Joseph Dillon, Department Manager
      Dates: November 1964 -- September 1966

Military Service
    Served 2 years active duty, U.S. Navy (1966-1968). Advanced from
    Seaman Recruit to Storekeeper 1/c. Oakland Supply Center, inventory
    control. USS Enterprise, electronic parts issue and control.
    3 years active duty in Reserve Supply Unit 12-4 ends September 1, 1971.

Special Interests

    Swimming, skiing, trap shooting, handball, Junior Chamber of Commerce

References

    Mr. Joseph Dillon, Men's Wear Department Manager, Mervyn's
        46721 Redondo Blvd., Hayward, California 94545. Phone 782-4850

    Mr. Clinton Murray, District Sales Manager, Cutco Cutlery Co.,
        272 West Winston Ave., Hayward, California 94545. Phone 781-5762

Figure 1

JACK G. BARRON   October 2, 1972

602 El Cerrito Ave.   OBJECTIVE:

Oakland, California 91416   SALES REPRESENTATIVE

Phone: 415 - 682 - 3235

Education

    Associate of Arts Degree, San Jose City College, June 1961
      Major: Business
    Bachelor of Science in Commerce Degree, Golden Gate College, Feb. 1970
      Major: Marketing

Experience

    KGFB Broadcasting Company, Oakland, California
      Outside Advertising Salesman. 1968 -- Present
    Oakland Tribune, Oakland, California
      Retail Advertising Salesman. 1964 - 1967
    Skaggs-Stone Company, Oakland, California
      Warehouse Trainee. 1961 - 1962
      Warehouse Supervisor. 1962 - 1964

Personal Data

    Born March 8, 1943. Height 5' 11". Weight 185 lbs. Military status: draft exempt. Married, 2 children. Own home and 1968 Mustang. Enjoy camping, archery, bowling, woodworking. Belong to Big Brothers of America, Knights of Columbus.

Experience

    Started as Warehouse Trainee in 1961 with Skaggs-Stone Company, a variety merchandise wholesaler in Oakland, California. After one year, became Assistant Warehouse Manager responsible for overall planning, directing, and controlling of receiving and marking functions, including supervision of sixteen employees.

    Joined the Oakland Tribune in 1964 as a Retail Advertising Salesman specializing in the creation of effective display advertising for retail clients. Showed overall sales increase during three year employment period.

    Joined radio station KGFB Oakland in April 1968. Have held position of Sales Manager since that time. Station advertising revenues have increased at the rate of 15% per year since 1968.

Figure 2

how to go after that sales job you want

2. Name of company president and marketing executives.
3. Principal products and product lines.
4. Compensation plan.
5. Sales territories open.
6. Fringe benefits.
7. Job requirements (education, experience, age, etc.)
8. Promotion policy (from within only?)
9. Names of some of its customers.
10. Geographical coverage of distribution.

Although you may not find out all of this information before you apply for the job, you should make an effort to learn as much as you can. If it is a large and well-known company, some sources which might prove valuable are listed in Paragraphs 9071-9086.

¶ 835 **Other essentials for a winning cover letter**

No cover letter needs to be longer than three or four short paragraphs on a single page, so keep it short. Be careful not to repeat what you have said in the résumé. The prospect doesn't need to read the same thing twice. Use simple, direct language. Try to write the way you talk, but be sure you're grammatically correct. Don't use time worn or stilted phrases like "owing to the fact that," "permit me to say," "I trust that you will read my résumé."

➤OBSERVATION — 1➤ Remember, you are appying for a sales job. Your reader's first question is: "can this man communicate clearly?"

➤OBSERVATION — 2➤ Don't be afraid to sound confident. This is the mark of a man who knows he can sell. If you sound too timid or humble, you won't make a good impression on him.

See Figures 3 and 4 as guides to writing effective cover letters.

¶ 836 **Selling yourself in the job interview**

Once you have opened the door with a well-written résumé and cover letter, you have to prove your qualifications in person. The interviews you will have with company executives will make or break you. You have sold them on an interview. Now you must sell them on offering you the job. The biggest piece of advice we can give you is *Be Yourself* and use your common sense. If there are aptitude tests to take, answer them honestly. You don't want to land this job on the basis of a false personality and then have to fight from being yourself after you are hired. Here is one expert's checklist of job interview behavior.[1]

1. Be on time.
2. Come alone.
3. Dress appropriately.
4. Keep calm.
5. Fill out forms neatly and completely.
6. Watch your posture.
7. Speak clearly.
8. Smile — be pleasant.
9. Know his company and his products.
10. Leave promptly.
11. Follow up your interview with a letter or telephone call.

406 Williams Ave.
Fremont, California 94746
June 7, 1971

Mr. C.L. London
District Sales Manager - Yellow Pages
Pacific Telephone Company
386 New Montgomery Street
San Francisco, California 90762

Dear Mr. London:

    I want to be a professional salesman. After hearing you speak at the DECA Career Conference last April, I believe the job of Yellow Pages Representative is exactly what I am looking for.

    My part-time experience in retail sales work and the courses I have taken as a Merchandising Major at Chabot College will allow me to bring some fundamental knowledge and skill to your organization. But more importantly, I would come with enthusiasm and a professional attitude toward the job.

    Will you let me know when an interview would be convenient for you?

                    Sincerely,

                    Alan E. Vandergriff

Figure 3

602 El Cerrito Ave.
Oakland, California 91416
October 2, 1972

Mr. Charles Rollings
Regional Sales Manager
Systemedia Division
American Cash Register Co.
1128 Airport Blvd.
South San Francisco, California 94405

Dear Mr. Rollings:

     The enclosed record of academic achievement and success as an outside salesman should help you decide if I am the right man for your sales organization.

     The research that I have done on your firm convinces me that our interests are highly compatible. We are both seeking a high level of sales success.

     I welcome the chance to prove that I may be exactly the kind of man you are looking for. I will telephone your office next Wednesday at 10:15 AM to arrange an appointment at your convenience.

                              Sincerely,

                              Jack G. Barron

Figure 4

¶ 899   **Footnote references**

¶ 802

(1) "Definition of Terms," American Marketing Association, Chicago 1961

¶ 809

(1) Beard, Miriam, "A History of Business from Babylon to The Monopolists," pp. 11-12. Copyright © by the University of Michigan, 1938.

(2) From "Casebook in American Business History, N.S.B." Gras and Henrietta M. Larson, p. 5. Copyright 1939 by F. S. Crofts, Inc. Reprinted by permission of Appleton-Century-Crofts, Educational Division, Meredith Corp.

(3) Ibid., p. 100.

(4) Ibid., p. 101.

¶ 812

(1) Taken from "The Yankee Peddlers of Early America" by J. R. Dolan, p. 22. © 1964 by J. R. Dolan. Used by permission of Clarkson N. Potter, Inc.

(2) Ibid., p. 10.

¶ 813

(1) Russel, F. A., Beach, F. H., and Buskirk, R. H., "Textbook of Salesmanship," 8th ed., p. 10, McGraw-Hill, New York, 1969.

(2) "Statistical Abstract of United States 1970," p. 226, U.S. Department of Commerce, 91st edition.

¶ 814

(1) Still, Richard R. and Cundiff, Edward W., "Essentials of Marketing," © 1966 pp. 120-121, Prentice-Hall, Inc., Englewood Cliffs, N.J.

¶ 820

(1) Herz, Bob, "Integrity," p. 51, "The American Salesman," Vol. 15, No. 10, October 1970.

(2) Ibid, p. 46.

¶ 826

(1) Endicott, Frank S., "Trends in the Employment of College and University Graduates in Business and Industry," p. 7, 25th Annual Report, Northwestern University, Evanston, Ill., 1971.

(2) Ibid., p. 9.

(3) "Compensation of Salesmen," A Dartnell Survey, © 1971, p. 18, the Dartnell Corporation, Chicago, Ill.

¶ 827

(1) Ibid., p. 14.

¶ 829

(1) Mayer, D. and Greenberg, H. M., "What Makes a Good Salesman," p. 120, "Harvard Business Review," Vol. 42, No. 4, July-August 1964.

(2) Ibid., p. 121.

¶ 836

(1) Chiantelli, L. W., "Success for You at Your Job Interview," pp. 1-12, Golden Gate Publishing Co., 1968, P.O. Box 3527, Long Beach, Calif., 90803.

THEORY BEFORE PRACTICE

The Need for Product Knowledge
What You Need to Know
Where to Get Product Facts
Understanding What Motivates Buying Action
How to Translate Product Features into Benefits
Case Problems: How Would You Do It?

TABLE OF CONTENTS

	Starts at Paragraph [¶]
Miracle Guide to Theory Before Practice	901

The Need for Product Knowledge

Why you Must be a Product Expert	902
What to Do When You Don't Know the Answer	903
The Importance of Product Knowledge When Selling to Experts	904
What Product Knowledge Does for You	905
Three Kinds of Product Knowledge Required	906

What You Need to Know

Physical Characteristics	907
Knowledge of Replacement Parts	908
Knowledge of How the Product Can Be Used	909
Knowledge of Performance Data	910
Case Histories	911
Knowledge of the Manufacturing Process	912
Knowledge of Service Policies	913
Knowledge of Prices, Shipping Terms, and Credit Terms	914
Knowledge of Your Company's History	915
Knowledge of the Competition	916
Other Kinds of Product Knowledge	917

Where to Get Product Facts

Company Training Programs	918
Sales Manuals and Other Company Literature	919
Libraries	920
Customers	921
Trade Journals	922
Trade and Industrial Shows	923
Other Sources of Product Knowledge	924

Understanding What Motivates Buying Action

Product Facts Are Not Enough	925
People Don't Buy Facts, They Only Buy Benefits	926
You Have To Learn What Makes People Want Things	927
People Buy for Different Reasons	928
People Do Buy for Similar Reasons	929
Basic Drives Help Explain Buying Behavior	930
The Theory of the Real And Ideal Self	931
The Influence of Psychological Attitudes on Buying Behavior	932
Emotional and Rational Buying Motives	933
A Practical List of Buying Motives	934
Using Every Buying Motive in Each Interview	935
Preapproach Helps in Selecting the Right Appeals	936
Prospect's Reactions are Important Clues	937

How to Translate Product Features into Benefits

Preparing a Product Analysis	938
What The Product Analysis Does for You	939
What to Do after Making up a Product Analysis	940

the need for product knowledge

¶ 901 Miracle Guide to theory before practice

As we discussed earlier in this book, the prospective professional salesman needs to understand the importance of selling in our economic system, the role and functions of the modern salesman, and the importance of bringing to the job a professional attitude. If the would-be salesman likes the idea of thinking of himself as a problem solver, he's well on his way to a successful career. But he needs more than a positive attitude. There are two essential ingredients still missing from the recipe for success in selling. One is an expert knowledge of his products and his competitors' products; the other is gaining as much knowledge as he can about buying behavior. These two areas of information are indispensible for long-run selling success. Want proof? Ask a career salesman what makes him succeed. His answer is sure to include knowledge of the products or services he sells and an understanding of why people buy them. The man or woman who tries to succeed in selling by a shortcut that bypasses these essentials is committing occupational suicide.

→OBSERVATION→ A professional salesman is like any other professional. He keeps on learning. He strives to gain more and more knowledge of what he sells and the people he sells to. This is what the term "professional growth" really means. Certainly we expect a doctor to be more of an expert after ten years of practice than he was the day he got out of medical school. Products, the uses of products, competition, methods, and people change. The professional salesman keeps up-to-date with these changes. That's what makes him a professional.

The need for product knowledge

¶ 902 Why you must be a product expert

This is an easy question to answer. Your own experience with salesmen tells you how any prospect reacts to a "salesman" who doesn't know the answers, who makes it up as he goes along. You expect a salesman to know his product thoroughly. Isn't that what he's there for? We expect the bookkeeper to know bookkeeping principles; we expect the mechanic to know how to make repairs; we expect the barber to know how to cut hair; we expect the physics teacher to have a full knowledge of physics. These people can't help us unless they "know their stuff." Neither can the salesman. Of course, most of us don't expect a salesman to know *everything* there is to know about his products. After all, many salesmen sell literally thousands of individual items. Even doctors, lawyers, and teachers don't have a ready answer for all the questions we ask them. But wait a minute. The scope of knowledge required of a salesman is usually much narrower than that required of doctors and lawyers. A salesman is hard pressed to excuse himself for lack of knowledge. This is especially true for the veteran salesman who has had time to study and learn. One thing is certain—the more a salesman knows about what he sells, the more customers he will win.

¶ 903 What to do when you don't know the answer

There's only one thing to do when you don't know the answer to a question your prospect asks you. Admit you don't know. Then tell him you'll find out. After you do find the answer, deliver it to him promptly. Sometimes you can use the telephone to call headquarters for the needed information without leaving your prospect's home or office. If this isn't practical, you may have to terminate the interview or complete it without getting the order. In either case, after you get the answer, you have an excellent basis for a call back interview. If you are a retail salesman, there is likely to be another salesperson in your department who can supply the answer for you.

→OBSERVATION→ There are cases when a salesman could bluff the answer and still get the sale. But in addition to being unprofessional this is a risky practice. Should the answer turn out to be in error, the order could be cancelled and future orders lost. Even when the bluff works, it can lull the salesman into a false sense of confidence in his ability to make sales without thorough product knowledge. This cheats every customer and in the long run it cheats the salesman out of substantial sales and earnings.

¶ 904 The importance of product knowledge when selling to experts

The salesman who calls on experts may be prone to reasoning that since these people are so well versed in their specialties, he need not try to be an expert too. In fact he may think it would be improper of him to tell them things they all ready know better than he. This is a dangerous point of view. Although any good salesman should be careful to avoid "professoritis" (lecturing his prospects), he still is expected to be an expert on his particular product or service. Let's use an example to put this issue in perspective. Joe Adams is a medical detail salesman calling on doctors. In describing the merits of a product used for removing excess ear wax, Joe must know the chemical composition of the product, what it does inside the ear, how it works, how it should be administered, and the results the product has achieved in medical testing. What Joe does not explain is the anatomy of the human ear. He doesn't launch into a discussion of the hammer, anvil and stirrup, the operation of the semi-circular canals, and a verbal picture of the organ of Corti. He does not because it is not necessary. The doctor knows all this. He knows far more about it than Joe does.

>>>CONCLUSION→ A salesman can't know too much about his product, but he can say too much. This is true in selling any kind of product to any kind of prospect. Salesmen know this as the danger of "over-selling."

¶ 905 What product knowledge does for you

If you have had selling experience you know that the possession of thorough knowledge concerning your product and your competitor's products gives you a big psychological advantage. There's no question about it. Just think how you feel when you speak on a subject you know a lot about. Naturally, you feel confident, sure of yourself. This shouldn't be mistaken for egotism or braggadocio. It's simply a recognition of the fact that you know what you're talking about. And because you do know whereof you speak, you transfer this confidence to your listener. Result? He believes you! In the language of interpersonal communications, the person who is recognized as knowing what he's talking about is said to have a high degree of "personal proof value." In everyday English, he is believable. In selling, the confident salesman earns his customers' respect. And once he earns his customers' respect he's close to earning his customers' business. So this is the big plus that product knowledge gives the salesman, in addition to equipping him to answer all of his prospect's questions. Product knowledge pays another dividend too. The confident salesman is bound to put in more time locating and calling on prospects. He knows he can help solve their buying problems, so he's anxious to do just that. More calls and more interviews will surely lead him to more sales and higher earnings.

¶ 906 Three kinds of product knowledge required

The product knowledge required of a salesman is of three types:
1. knowledge concerning the physical product,
2. knowledge concerning the product in use, and
3. knowledge concerning ideas, things, or people directly related or associated with the product.

This last category includes, but is not limited to, the people who use the product, the manufacturing process, the reputation of the firm, distribution channels, price, service, credit, and shipping terms. A salesman's product knowledge is not complete unless he is steeped in all three of these areas. The following paragraphs serve as a checklist of the types of knowledge salesmen need.

What you need to know

¶ 907 Physical characteristics of the product

Tangible products, those you can see and feel, have a host of physical properties that can be weighed, measured, and analyzed in a laboratory. Obviously, a salesman must know all of these characteristics. Some products of course, such as TV sets and automobiles, are more complicated than others, like pencils and paper clips. Here, for example is a list of physical characteristics for a common screwdriver:

1. made of selected tool steel
2. magnetized bit
3. case hardened
4. grooved, posi-grip hard plastic, 1½″ diameter, anti-shock handle
5. full length tine
6. 8¼″ length
7. 4″ tempered blade
8. 3½ ounces
9. hammer forged

Admittedly, every buyer will not be interested in all of these characteristics. Still the salesman will have to understand all of them. Anyone of them might turn a sale on or off. You may not care what hammer forged means but the next potential buyer may care a great deal. If the salesman can't explain it, he won't make the sale.

¶ 908   **Knowledge of replacement parts**

Sometimes it is the salesman's responsibility to know what replacement parts are available, what equipment they fit, and so on. Often this is the primary responsibility of a special department in the salesman's company. The parts department of an automobile dealership is a familiar example. In industrial selling the salesman may be the one person relied upon by the customer firm and he will be expected to "talk" knowledgeably about replacement parts. In situations like this, a salesman cannot pass the buck to anyone else. If he doesn't know, he has to find out.

¶ 909   **Knowledge of how the product can be used**

Many salesmen believe this category of knowledge to be more important than any other. Their reasoning makes sense: "If you can't show the prospect how he can use your product to solve his problem, you simply won't make a sale." The same product may be bought by customers to solve entirely different problems or to solve the same problem in a different way. The key word here is *application*. The drilling company and the construction company both use compressors, but each uses or applies them in a different way. In someone's home, you might see a paperweight used for keeping a door open or a mirror used to represent a frozen lake in a Christmas decoration. The creative salesman has the ability to adapt his "fixed" products to solve a variety of customer problems. In some cases, a slight physical modification in the product might be required before it can be used successfully by the customer. The idea of taking a bound book and putting it into loose-leaf binder form is one example of physically modifying a product so it does what the user wants it to do.

¶ 910   **Knowledge of performance data**

The prospect asks, "How's the acceleration?" The salesman answers, "Zero to 60 in 11.5 seconds." This salesman's answer indicates he knows some performance data on his product. It's hard to think of any mechanical product that hasn't been tested to determine its performance capability. When the refrigerator salesman tells his prospect that the refrigerator door was opened and closed 15,000 times in factory testing, this information may help make the sale. Consider how much better a specific factual answer like this is than one couched only in general terms such as, "Oh, this is a well built door; it won't give you any trouble." You know from your own shopping experience how much more confidence you have in a salesman (and his product) when he gives you specific performance data.

Sometimes, of course, there may be data based on testing done by outside, independent laboratories, like the United States Testing Company or Consumers Union. Their test results are likely to carry more weight than results published by the manufacturing firm. The salesman must keep up-to-date with all performance data on his products, whether compiled by his own firm, customer firms, or by outside laboratories.

¶ 911   **Case histories**

Case histories are accounts of customers'

experience with the products or services they have bought. As expected, most often quality products used in a proper manner produce benefit to the buyer. The story of a product's successful use makes a case history that has great impact on potential buyers. Salesmen are wise to collect many case histories which they can incorporate into their sales presentations. These accounts carry a lot of weight, since the real proof of a product's value lies in its actual performance in the customer's hands. If the prospect's intended use for the product is similar to the use given it by a satisfied customer, the case history carries even greater persuasive impact. The salesman must also know of any cases where the product failed to fulfill its promises. He should know what the causes were and why it won't fail to do the job for this prospective user.

¶ 912 Knowledge of the manufacturing process

Salesmen who take the opportunity to see firsthand how the products they sell are manufactured gain a distinct selling advantage. For some products, the method of manufacture may constitute the chief difference between them and competing products. You've heard the automobile companies' advertising about the hundreds of quality control check points their cars must pass through before they are ready to leave the factory. One auto maker tells us that each and every car is inspected for water leaks. Your own experience may have convinced you that furniture which is only nailed together doesn't give the years of service that doweled and glued furniture gives. Maybe you've found that shoes whose soles are sewn to the uppers last longer and feel better than shoes whose soles are only cemented on. All of these differences are not only caused by differences in materials used, but primarily by differences in the manufacturing process itself. The smart salesman learns how his goods are made and uses this information to help him make sales.

In the case of custom-manufactured goods made to customer specifications, the manufacturing process may take on greater importance. Indeed, it may become the determining factor in the mind of the prospect. In this situation, the salesman must have intimate knowledge concerning how the product will be manufactured.

¶ 913 Knowledge of service policies

Would you think of buying a television set without first finding out something about the manufacturer's guarantee? Of course not. And if you asked the salesman about the guarantee and he couldn't tell you its terms and conditions, would you buy from him? Two familiar yet often confusing terms are involved in this discussion of service policies. A *warranty* is a legal statement that a product is what the maker claims it to be. This statement usually includes a phrase like — "free of defects in workmanship and materials." The *guarantee* is a statement made by the manufacturer, in which he agrees to repair or replace the item or refund the purchase price in case of product failure occurring within a specified period of time. In addition to the manufacturer's guarantee, the retailer often extends his own store guarantee. If you are a retail salesman, you will certainly take steps to be totally familiar with it. Customers are naturally impressed with a strong guarantee, especially when the company has a reputation of living up to its after sale promises. Many customers believe that a strong guarantee means that the manufacturer has confidence in his own products and is willing to make reparation should one of them fail to perform as warranted. We need not belabor the point. A professional salesman realizes the importance of knowing his company's warranty and guarantee.

¶ 914 Knowledge of prices, shipping terms, and credit terms

It may seem unnecessary to mention these aspects of product knowledge. What salesman in his right mind would make a sales call without having full information on prices, shipping terms, and credit terms? Of course, the salesman doesn't have to commit all of this data to memory. There's nothing wrong with checking a price list in order to quote the correct price. Most of the time, the shipping and credit terms will be identical regardless of the customer or the product sold. Your firm may sell everything FOB factory (buyer pays freight charges from your factory to his address) and on credit terms of 2/10, n/30 (2% cash discount if paid in 10 days, otherwise net invoice amount due in 30 days). Sometimes a salesman needs to know the pros and cons of various methods of shipment. Should it go parcel post? REA Express? Air Freight? When this kind of knowledge is important in making sales, the salesman must have the answers.

¶ 915   **Knowledge of your company's history**

When a prospect tells the salesman that he never heard of his company, the salesman should be able to give him a capsule history of his firm. This history can help with the prospect's confidence if it is told with authority and enthusiasm. How did the firm begin? What have been its successes? What unique products or processes or policies does it have? What has been its growth rate? What major customers does it have? What has been the specific history of the product being discussed? What is its credit rating? A prospect wants to be sure that the firm he is about to deal with is reputable. A salesman who knows little or nothing about his company's history will stumble over the "never heard of you" objection and find his interview terminated without success.

¶ 916   **Knowledge of the competition**

With few exceptions, no salesman has the only game in town when it comes to his product or service. And it's a good thing too. If it weren't for competition, salesmen couldn't begin to earn the high wages that are possible in selling. Anybody can sell if he's got the only source of supply. But selling pays well because so many salesmen compete for the same customer business. Because this is true, the successful salesman is always one who knows the strengths and weaknesses of his competitors. The timeworn adage that stresses the importance of knowing what you're up against applies with full force in the field of selling. Ideally, a salesman should know as much about his competitor's products, services, manufacturing process, prices, distribution, and shipping practices as he does about his own. It stands to reason that in proving your product is the best buy, you need to show why it's a better buy than the other guy's. A salesman can expect frequent direct inquiries regarding the competition. Questions like "How does this compare in price with XYZ product?" or "What can your product do for us that the one we're using can't do?" cannot be adequately answered without knowing a great deal about these competitive items. Objections like "We see no reason to change," or "We can get the same thing cheaper from another supplier," are tough to overcome when you know little or nothing about the competitor's products involved.

Retail salesmen in competing stores which sell identical items must convince each prospect that he should make his purchase here, rather than in the competing store. To do this consistently, the retail salesman must be able to tell his customer what his store does for him that the others do not. This becomes a guessing game unless he knows what the competition can offer.

⟫⟫REMEMBER→   It's easy enough to excuse yourself from knowing the competition on the grounds that you don't work for them. But the truth is you do end up working for them every time you lose a sale by reason of not knowing what they have to offer.

¶ 917   **Other kinds of product knowledge**

Depending, of course, on the type of sales job being done and the nature of the company being represented, there are other things which the salesman should have knowledge of. Every seller has some kind of returned goods policy which sets up the conditions under which purchased goods may be returned for full or partial credit. Even a life insurance policy can be surrendered or cancelled before its expiration date.

A salesman should know all of his firm's distribution practices with respect to trade channels used, trade discounts given, promotional and advertising allowances, point of purchase display materials, brochures, and other dealer aids. In addition, the salesman should be up to date on other matters that affect his and his customer's operation. A salesman who really is the manager of his own territory should know what's going on throughout the industry. In this way he can carry out his role as intelligence agent for his customers.

It's difficult to envision a professional salesman who doesn't keep up to date with nationwide political and economic conditions. These forces always have an influence on prospects' behavior. And anything that influences that "yes or no" decision is important to the salesman. Finally, there are a number of national, state, and local laws that salesmen should understand. These laws apply in a very specific way to such important practices as product pricing, advertising, and packaging. Some of the local laws go as far as to limit the freedom of a salesman to knock on a prospect's door. Space does not allow a full discussion here of all the laws that regulate a salesman's actions. Any up-to-date marketing textbook would be a good place to start learning about them.

Where to get product facts

¶ 918 Company training programs

A well-designed, well-conducted sales training program is a boon to beginning salesmen. This formal program, which typically lasts from two to three days to three to four weeks should include every phase of product knowledge mentioned in paragraphs 907-917. Most often a formal training program means a lot of study for the rookie salesman, who attends day-long classes crammed full of product knowledge, company policies, and sales techniques. Company executives as well as outside experts often participate in the program, and a heavy use of audio-visual aids and test materials is common. In many firms, two or three different sales schools may be conducted for salesmen based on their particular selling job, years of experience, or degree of success on the job. A firm which conducts formal training programs shows its belief in the need for knowledgeable and skillful salesmen. By the same token, the prospective salesman should be suspicious of any company that does not offer full-fledged sales training. The sales convention and sales meeting usually have as one of their chief purposes the dissemination of product information. These events are normally much shorter in duration than formal training clinics, but they can be an excellent and exciting way to tell salesmen what's new. It's a rare company indeed that does not devote some time during these events to giving salesmen more knowledge about old products and/or first-time facts about new products.

¶ 919 Sales manuals and other company literature

Most firms furnish salesmen with manuals that serve as a ready reference source when questions arise. Sometimes these manuals are devoted solely to statements of company policies and product descriptions, although some of them stress selling strategy and techniques too. Enlightened companies make sure their salesmen have quick access to all three types of information, i.e., product descriptions, company policies, and advice on how to sell. Recognizing that no single sales training course or sales manual can satisfy the salesman's continuous need for product knowledge, companies often follow a practice of sending out sales bulletins or audio-taped messages to their salesmen in the field. This is a quick and inexpensive way to get new product information into the hands of a salesman who may be located far from company offices.

¶ 920 Libraries

The man who told his son that the answers he sought were "in a book somewhere" gave good advice. A salesman is wise to take this advice when he seeks to expand his product knowledge. In addition to the public or city library, there are others which might house the necessary information. Colleges, teachers, companies, churches, trade associations, and commercial and professional organizations almost always maintain a library of some kind. For example, a retail salesman who wants general information on shoes could start with an encyclopedia at his public library, then go to the card catalog under "shoes," then to the *Reader's Guide to Periodical Literature* to locate articles on the subject. He could also write to a shoe manufacturer like Brown Shoe Co. and inquire of the National Retail Merchants Association. This latter source would produce a publication appropriately titled "Retail Shoe Sales Training Manual—A Handbook for Retail Shoe Personnel." How's that for hitting the bull's-eye?

where to get product facts

>>>OBSERVATION> A salesman is paid to know what he's talking about. He may have to dig up some of the product knowledge he needs on his own. Let's just say that the salesman who's willing to dig is destined to make it big.

¶ 921 Customers

Customers are an excellent source of product knowledge. As was mentioned earlier in ¶909, knowledge of the product in use is critical for selling success. Prospects want to know about customers' experience with the product.

The salesman who follows up on customers will learn not only what customers' problems have been (if any) but also what new ways they have used the product, what added benefits they have derived, which the salesman or even his company may never have envisioned. Customers are the only people who can furnish the salesman with the case histories he needs to convince new prospects to buy.

>>>IMPORTANT> Don't wait for the customer to tell you what his experience has been. Seek out your customers to discover how they have used your product. Along with the case history they'll give you, you'll gain a bonus for your efforts. You'll discover any troubles or problems before they develop into blockbusters. Providing a quick and effective remedy may very well save you a valuable customer.

¶ 922 Trade journals

Poultry Producer and *Pacific Builder* may not be magazines you subscribe to, but if you were either a feed salesman or a salesman of construction materials, one of these trade journals would be "must" reading for you. Much product knowledge and information on what's new in your industry can be obtained by regularly reading appropriate trade journals. Some journals relate specifically to a narrow line of endeavor, such as *Department Store Economist* while others like *Chain Store Age, Merchandising Week,* and *Marketing Communication Magazine* are broader in scope. In addition to information on new products, processes, and developments, some trade journals regularly feature advice on selling techniques. Others (more properly called "professional journals") are devoted almost exclusively to selling methods and management techniques. Examples of the latter are *The American Salesman* and *Sales Management Magazine.*

¶ 923 Trade and industrial shows

A trade or industrial show is just what the name implies. It is an event (often sponsored by a trade association) which has as its primary purpose the display of merchandise of competing vendors for prospective purchasers to see in the same place, at the same time. Actually, there is little doubt that the real purpose of a trade show is to sell goods. Otherwise, why go to all the trouble? Of course, the big advantage to a prospect lies in his ability to compare the wares of many vendors more conveniently than he otherwise could. In the area of product knowledge, the chief advantage to the exhibitor salesman is the chance he gets to inspect and evaluate his competitors' products.

In the course of attending a trade show, a salesman has a chance not only to appraise the competition but also to obtain a lot of feedback from customers and potential customers.

Occasionally trade shows include some kind of professional entertainment, along with cocktail parties, contest drawings, etc. This is designed to sell the event so the house will be filled with prospects.

¶ 924 Other sources of product knowledge

Although it isn't likely that a complete list could ever be compiled to fit every salesman, there are some other sources of product knowledge that are often quite productive. Other salesmen in your company, particularly the experienced and successful ones, represent a large reservoir of information. Companies that employ the buddy system of sales training recognize that the veteran salesman has much to give the rookie assigned to him. You have probably seen a new retail salesman seek out a senior salesman to help answer customer questions for him. In retailing, the tags, labels, and other literature packaged with the merchandise is a handy source of basic knowledge for salesmen. These tags usually give data on physical composition, product uses, operating or cleaning instructions, and warranty terms.

¶ 924

➤➤CAUTION➤ The retail salesman who is content to know only what is said on product labels, cannot render any real service to shoppers. They can read labels as well as he can. To know that a garment is made of Acrilan and Orlon is not enough. Knowing the characteristics of both fibers and how they differ is essential in order to help shoppers make their decision.

Two other depositories of product knowledge are your own personal experience with the product and knowledge gained by attending school. Most cities offer adult education courses, many of which are concerned with precisely the kind of product knowledge a salesman needs. Add to this the extensive offerings of free public community colleges and you've got a long list of classes to choose from —everything from aeronautics to insurance to textiles to upholstering. There's no good reason why the salesman can't keep learning more each year like the doctor, lawyer, teacher and every other person who calls himself a "professional."

Understanding what motivates buying action

¶ 925 Product facts are not enough

We realize that a salesman who lacks product knowledge will lose many sales. Likewise, the salesman who depends too heavily on product knowledge for success is doomed to disappointment. Why? If product knowledge were all that was needed to make sales, buyers could solve many of their problems without the help of salesmen by merely reading descriptive literature and making their decisions accordingly.

Let's use the two signs below to dramatize why product facts may not be potent enough to make sales all by themselves.

```
QUALITY SCREWDRIVER
   • Hammer Forged
   • Tool Steel
   • Tempered Blade
   • Frozen Tine
   • Shockproof
   • Case Hardened
   • Posi-grip handle
        Only 99¢
```
SIGN A

```
QUALITY SCREWDRIVER
     Hammer Forged
     Tool Steel
     Tempered Blade
     Frozen Tine
     Shockproof
     Case Hardened
     Posi-grip handle
       Only $3.98
```
SIGN B

Let's assume that Sign A is attached above a display of screwdrivers in a self-service store. Do the facts listed on the sign help sell these screwdrivers? No doubt they do, even though many buyers don't really understand a lot of the product features. But at ninety-nine cents, who needs to understand? As long as the screwdriver looks and feels OK, it's probably a good buy at that price.

Now, let's assume that instead of Sign A, Sign B accompanies our screwdriver display. Will sales be as great? Probably not. At $3.98 the prospective purchaser will have difficulty seeing that much value in the product, even though it may be a bargain at that price. In other words, the facts alone aren't enough to influence buying action, especially if a cheaper alternative is available. And it almost always is. What this analysis is leading up to is one of the primary truths in selling.

PEOPLE DON'T BUY PRODUCT FEATURES, THEY ONLY BUY THE BENEFITS THOSE FEATURES GIVE THEM.

¶ 926 People don't buy features, they only buy benefits

Is that $3.98 screwdriver we've been talking about worth the money? Can we convince people that it is? We can if we can show them that the benefits they'll receive equal or outweigh the price we're asking them to pay. When a product fails to sell, the fault may be in its being overpriced. The fault may also lie in its benefits being under-explained. Nobody will buy our $3.98 screwdriver until a salesman shows him that the benefits it gives him are worth $3.98. The salesman's key job is to translate product features into benefits that answer the big question in every buyer's mind:

at motivates buying action

me?" Examine your own
... You don't hand over
... you are convinced that you're
... what you're paying for in
...hermore, that this purchase
... the best way to spend that
... the alternatives open to you.
... a salesman can sell, he must
... what his product or service will
...ospect. He must translate product
... benefits. Features and benefits
...h other. Trying to sell without both
... like trying to build a table without
...mply won't work.

You have to learn what makes people want things

...en we talk about translating product
...res into benefits, we're talking about the
...fic advantages the purchaser gains from
owning and using it. The big question is: "Why do people buy?" The answer: To solve some problem. Fine. Now we have to ask: "What benefits are they looking for when they buy?"

Certainly the salesman who knows the answer to this question increases his ability to sell. As we've already emphasized, people won't buy unless they believe the product will give them the benefits they are seeking. How do you find out what these benefits are? You begin by putting yourself in the prospect's shoes. Earlier in this book, we defined this ability to see things from the prospect's point of view as the quality of empathy.

Going back to our screwdriver example, the salesman must ask himself "What would I want a screwdriver to do for me?" and the follow-up question, "What will *this* screwdriver do for the person who buys it?" Notice how product features and benefits support each other. Like the song says, "You can't have one without the other." There's no escaping the truth that a salesman can't begin to talk benefits unless he first has expert knowledge of his product.

¶ 928 People buy for different reasons

Maybe you've seen the cocktail napkin entitled, "Eight Reasons Why A Woman Buys Something." The list goes like this:

1. Her husband says she can't.
2. It will make her look thin.
3. It comes from Paris.
4. It's different
5. The neighbors can't afford it.
6. Nobody else has one.
7. Everybody else has one, and
8. Just because!

In fairness, were we to change "her husband" to "his wife" in No. 1, this list would apply equally well to male buying behavior. Later on in ¶ 934 we'll list some of the primary buying motives that lead people to buy the goods and services they purchase. But first, let's make one of the few statements in the area of human behavior that we think is irrefutable: People buy for different reasons. We really mean three things by this statement:

1. The same person may buy the same item for different reasons at different times.
   Example: Buying a wallet for yourself and another as a gift for your father.
2. The same person buys different items for entirely different reasons.
   Example: The purchase of a ballpoint pen followed by the purchase of a skillet.
3. Different persons may buy the same item for different reasons.
   Example: You buy the encyclopedia for use as a reference; I buy it to use as a living room showpiece.

About this time, it seems that a salesman has to be a behavioral scientist in order to succeed. You're right. He does. At least, the more he understands what leads people to buy, the better he can lead them to buy *his* product or service. Through reading, attending classes and seminars, and through personal experience with customers, the salesman can increase his understanding of buying motives. His study will validate what was said here—people buy for different reasons. The top-flight salesman knows how to tailor his message to fit each individual prospect. This is precisely what makes him so successful.

¶ 929 People buy for similar reasons

Despite the fact that people buy for different reasons, the evidence that many people buy for the same reasons is overwhelming. Each year, hundreds of thousands of people buy GE

¶ 929

television sets, Juicy Fruit gum, PaperMate pens, Schlitz beer, Campbell's pork and beans, and a host of other things. If we were to survey these buyers, we would very likely find that the vast majority mention good taste as their chief reason for buying Juicy Fruit gum, Schiltz beer, or Campbell's pork and beans. Other reasons would be involved too. Maybe the next four reasons would be (2) priced right, (3) recipes on the label, (4) don't like the other brands, and (5) only brands offering discount coupons. In other words, lots of these buyers might come up with identical lists of reasons for buying the product in question.

For years marketing men have spent large amounts of money and energy defining their markets. The people who make up a firm's product market share many characteristics in common. These might include: occupation, socio-economic status, age, family status, area of residence, ethnic background, ownership of home, boat, two or more cars, etc. A marketing success is a situation wherein a product which has been specifically designed for a certain group of people is bought in sufficient quantities by those people. Every marketing success is evidence of the fact that many people buy a product for substantially similar reasons. What does this mean to the salesman? It means he can count on there being a lot of people who are looking for the same benefits, the same set of satisfactions which *his* product can give them. His job is to show them how his product can deliver the benefits at a price they can afford to pay.

¶ 930 **Basic drives help explain buying behavior**

Psychologists tell us that man has several basic drives, or basic needs, as they are often called. Some of these drives (needs) are more dominant in some people than in others. Understanding what these drives are helps us explain why we tend to behave the way we do. The salesman who is conscious of his prospect's basic needs gains the kind of insight that assists him in choosing the right appeals and selling points during the sales interview.

A list of man's basic drives is given here. Although it may differ somewhat from other lists you have seen, this one is representative of most:

1. Need for approval
2. Need for recognition
3. Need for new experiences
4. Need for belonging
5. Need to maintain a fairly even temperature
6. Need to satisfy thirst and hunger
7. Need for sexual fulfillment
8. Need to act maturely
9. Need to maintain one's unity

Most of these needs are self-explanatory, but No. 9 may need some clarification. This one has to do with man's desire to be free of conflict or threats from without; to unify on one course of action at a time, without interruption. You know how unsettling it is to be interrupted by someone when you're trying to carry on a telephone conversation. You may reach the point at which you have to cover the phone and say firmly, "I'll talk to you later, after I'm through." In other words, it's next to impossible to unify on two courses of action (talking to two people simultaneously) at the same time. When you do, neither activity turns out as well as it should.

How can understanding man's basic drives help the salesman? He should develop the habit of asking himself, "What basic needs might my prospect be attempting to satisfy through the purchase of a product like mine?" For some people and products, the answer to this question may seem obvious. Surely the desire to maintain an even temperature has something to do with the purchase of air conditioning units. Likewise, the purchase of a first-time vacation trip to Hawaii seems to be related to man's need for new experiences. The fellow who seeks to maintain an even temperature by buying an air conditioner may voluntarily go out to find one. He recognizes his need. Even though he knows in general what he wants, he must still decide What make? What model? What price? What store? What terms? and so on. In general, we can safely conclude that when a particular product or service is seen to satisfy one of man's basic drives (or at least diminish its intensity) it stands a good chance of being bought. And the salesman who shows how the product will fill that need stands a good chance of making the sale. Whether he does or not depends (as always) on how effectively he can prove that his particular product will provide the greatest amount of continuing satisfaction.

¶ 931 The theory of the real and ideal self

This theory has its basis in the individual's own perception of himself and the way he thinks he is perceived by others. The way he honestly sees himself (with every defect and weakness) is called his *real self*. The kind of person he would like to be is his *ideal self*. On the other hand, the way the individual thinks he appears to others is called his *other real self* while the way he would like others to think of him is called his *other ideal self*.

For example in sizing himself up, a man may think of himself as clumsy. This is one dimension of his real self. He thinks, "I'm a clumsy guy." But he has dreams like the one in which he sees himself as a superstar basketball player, scoring thirty-eight points to lead his team to victory in the National Championships. He would like very much to be a star basketball player, even just a fair player. This is one dimension of his ideal self — about as far from "clumsiness" as he could get. And how does he think others see him? He may believe that most people see him as a fairly graceful or athletic person. Do they? Maybe and maybe not. Often, an individual can be far off-target in his perception of how others view him. And, when it comes to skills, many of his acquaintances may never have seen him perform. Perhaps they have no clear perception of him in terms of his gracefulness or lack of it. Sometimes, a dimension of an individual's ideal self will show up in identical form in his other ideal self. In other words, he wants others to see him as a graceful person just as much as he wants to see himself that way.

Contrarily, a man may promote a different version of his other self depending on where he is or who he is with. For example, he may be seen as a happy-go-lucky, fun-lover by his card playing cronies, while at the office his staff sees him as a tough, non-smiling taskmaster. Or a man may want others to see him as a loving and devoted husband and father (other ideal self), while his own ideal self incorporates the image of a jet setting playboy. Statements like, "he's got to protect his image" and "he's playing the role" are commonly heard. They refer, of course, to the efforts a person makes to have others see him in a certain way. The phrases we've quoted seem to imply a certain disapproval of people who go out of their way to influence our perception of them. We might say they are sending out false stimuli.

Although it's been overworked, the expression "doing his own thing" has been interpreted to mean that an individual's real self is in harmony with his other self. He's not trying to be or act like something he's not. Suffice it to say that we all have a concept of ourselves which probably falls far short of the kind of person we would like to be. The clothes we wear, the food we eat, the movies we see, the way we talk, laugh, and walk all communicate something about us. Consequently, the things we buy are likely to be those things that help reinforce the positive aspects of our real selves, while helping us advance closer to our ideal selves and other ideal selves.

The message here for salesmen can be summarized this way: The more you show your prospect how your product moves him closer to his ideal or other ideal self, the more readily he will buy it. The key problem is finding out what the prospect's real and ideal selves are. Once a salesman gets a good idea of who his prospect thinks he is, who he wants to be, and how he wants to be thought of, he can do a better job of helping him solve his buying problem.

¶ 932 The influence of four major attitudes in the buying process

Dr. Ernest Dichter, prominent psychologist and management consultant, says that, "the salesman's task [is] to relate his product or service to the prospect's self-image, a fluctuating image resulting from interaction of mental age, family status, professional standing and psychological income."[1]

These four major attitudes exert a profound influence on the buying decisions an individual makes. Dr. Dichter stresses the point that it is not so much how old a person is, or how large his family is, or what his actual job is, or his actual income that leads him to make certain purchases, but rather how he feels about these things. In other words, how old he feels, his attitude toward his family status, his job, and his income are what really determines what he will buy. This helps explain why the low-paid clerk buys expensive toys for his children, goes years without buying a new suit, and owns a leather bound set of *Harvard Classics*. It may also explain why a middle-aged man drives a sports car and wears mod clothes.

As Dr. Dichter says, "Every consumer is an intricate balance of several roles in life and several attitudes toward those roles."[2] The salesman's job is to help the prospect persuade himself to make the recommended purchase. He does this by stressing those benefits which are in harmony with his prospect's four major attitudes. For example, a prospect considering the purchase of a dishwasher may have these conflicts to resolve:

Psychological Age: In general he disdains having a lot of devices like this in his home. He thinks this is what makes people "soft." He's healthy. Why make a big deal out of doing dishes? He doesn't have an automatic ice crusher or electric knife. He still brushes his teeth manually. In short, he thinks dishwashers are for the old and infirm. Neither he nor anyone in his family needs this kind of help.

Psychological Income: He knows that he can afford it, but feels it would be wiser to put this money away for uncertainties or maybe add it to his children's college fund. On the other hand, the patio needs a lot of fixing up. Still, this investment would add to the value of his house. He could probably get it back when he sells. He's always believed in being thrifty, not buying things you could easily get along without. It's that sort of spending that makes rich men poor.

Family Status: He thinks he is a good father. He believes his children need to have definite responsibilities in the household. He thinks a dishwasher might tend to make life a little too easy on the kids. He doesn't want them to think of a dishwasher as a necessity. On the other hand, a dishwasher would liberate the family for an extra half-hour together after dinner. This would be nice, too. Families need to spend more time playing together.

Professional Status: As an independent insurance broker, he feels that he is important to his clients and those people he talks business to. At the same time, even though he is aware of a certain lack of public respect for salesmen, he is proud to be an entrepreneur taking the ultimate risks of private business ownership. He's an individualist with well developed opinions of his own and prides himself on not being influenced by what others think. Many times he has counseled people to buy more insurance instead of some new household appliance (like a dishwasher). On the other hand, he got into this career partly because of the material rewards it offered. A man in his position is expected to have a nice house. Wouldn't this include a dishwasher? This mini-drama gives you an idea of the conflicting attitudes that lead a man to, and then away from, a prospective purchase. If the salesman in our dishwasher example discovers these attitudes, he will try hard to let the prospect focus on things like the extra time the family can spend together, the added attractiveness of a dishwasher when he goes to sell his house, and so on. By the same token, the salesman would be unwise to stress the labor-saving advantages of a dishwasher and most unwise in using the "everybody's doing it" appeal. Again the salesman's job is to estimate his prospect's attitude toward his age, job, family status and, income and then show how his product harmonizes with one or more of these attitudes.

¶ 933 **Emotional and rational buying motives**

Traditionally, buying motives have been divided into two major categories: *emotional* and *rational*. Rational motives are usually defined as including any considerations that have to do with long-term cost and benefit of a proposed expenditure. Consequently, people are said to be buying rationally when they take the time to measure all the costs against all probable gains. In the case of an automobile, rational considerations would be things like gas mileage, resale value, average expected operating cost per mile, etc. In contrast, most authorities say that emotional buying motives are those which lead a person to buy without much regard for the long-term net gain or cost. Buying something to satisfy one's vanity or buying to win the approval of friends are examples of emotional buying motives. If the

understanding what motivates buying action

desire to make a hit with the ladies is what really leads us to buy a certain car, this would be classified as an emotional buying motive. The terms, "rational" and "emotional" often cause confusion when applied to buying behavior. Is a man who deliberates for three months before buying a Cadillac which he doesn't need and can't really afford buying emotionally or rationally? The answer is he's buying primarily for emotional reasons even though he's thought about it (been in conflict over it) for a long time. He hasn't tried to figure out in a careful, scientific way what the long-run pros and cons are. Now if we ask, "Is he *behaving* rationally?" we can answer, "He's not behaving irrationally." And maybe we answer in self-defense. After all, don't all of us make some purchases for primarily emotional reasons? People are not computers. They don't function at 100% efficiency. We all have psychological needs too. The point is, there is nothing wrong with buying for emotional reasons. We all do it. To prove this, try an experiment. For two or three months, write down everything you buy costing more than two dollars. At the end of 60 days, try to defend or explain each of these purchases to a friend of yours. You'll have trouble convincing him of the logic behind all of your purchases. That's because you have bought a lot of these things for emotional reasons.

There's a big lesson for salesmen in all of this. People will refrain from buying until they can justify their purchases. To do this, they need rational reasons for buying. A salesman can make a sale if he can add enough rational reasons for buying to the prospect's emotional reasons. The fellow who wants that expensive car won't let himself buy it until he can sanction (or rationalize) his decision. He needs the kind of reasons he can tell his friends.

⟩⟩⟩CONCLUSION⟶ Since people are naturally lead to buy certain things for emotional reasons, the wise salesman makes heavy use of rational appeals that demonstrate how the long-run benefits of ownership outweigh the costs. This strategy is actually easier than trying to win the sale using emotional appeals. The latter are difficult to identify, hard to agree on (how many people will freely admit they are buying for the "wrong" reasons?), and embarrassing to discuss (what piano salesman would actually tell his prospect that learning to play will make him the center of attention at parties?). A salesman can openly and calmly talk about the rational reasons for buying his product. Economy, labor-saving features, durability, cost-in-use and profit margins are not embarrassing topics. You can build a winning sales presentation with them. Without providing these rational reasons for buying, you're operating in a world that even psychiatrists don't fully understand.

¶ 934 **A practical list of buying motives**

There are probably as many buying motives as there are people. But because people do have so much in common, and often buy the same product or service for the same basic reasons, a list of basic buying motives like the list below, can be very useful to salesmen.

1. Love
2. Fear
3. Convenience
4. Financial gain
5. Curiosity
6. Variety
7. Prestige or social approval
8. Need
9. Pleasure (physical or esthetic)
10. Self improvement

Suppose you're selling electric can openers to consumers, which of these basic buying motives might lead someone to buy an electric can opener? Let's say we think an electric can opener can satisfy the buying motives of convenience, fear, and social approval. In this case, convenience has to do with the saving of time and effort in opening cans; fear refers to the prospect's fear of cutting himself, a fear which the electric can opener can allay; and social approval has to do with the feeling of pride the buyer may get from owning a modern appliance like this. As always, to make the sale, the salesman will have to show that HIS can opener satisfies these buying motives better or more completely than anybody else's.

¶ 935 **Pre-approach helps you select the right appeals**

A thorough pre-approach can give the salesman much information concerning his prospect. Based on this information, the salesman can make some pretty good guesses as to what might motivate this prospect to buy. This way, the salesman can plan or tailor his presentation so it highlights the benefits that seem likely to be of greatest importance to that particular prospect. The pre-approach is like using a map to learn something about territory you've never traveled through before. Or like getting a long-range weather forecast before choosing the clothes you take on a trip.

▶ **IDEA IN ACTION** Jim Pfaff sells life insurance. Before he calls on a prospect he tries to find out this important information: (1) Prospect's age, occupation, approximate income level (2) Number and ages of his children (3) Does his wife work outside the home? (4) Amount of life insurance in force (5) Any relatives or friends who sell insurance? (6) Retirement plans or investments. Pfaff makes up his "game plan" according to the information he collects. Certainly the buying motives and their relative importance in the mind of each prospect will differ depending on his situation in life. Of course Jim continues to learn more about his prospect during the interview, and he may call some "audibles" (change his game plan) when new facts are uncovered.

¶ 936 Prospects' reactions are important clues

The alert salesman gains much insight into his prospect's buying motives by paying close attention to everything he says and does during the interview. Sometimes non-verbal reactions communicate more than spoken comments. The smile, the grimace, the raised eyebrows, the set of the mouth, even the prospect's posture all reveal his feelings toward the salesman and his merchandise. If a salesman misses any of this critical feedback, he may waste a lot of time appealing to a buying motive that has little or no significance for this prospect.

Even when the prospect is asked outright what he wants the product to do for him, even when he's asked to tell you his buying motives, he may not be willing or able to do so. That's why the salesman must learn to read his prospect's reactions. The more skilled he becomes at doing this, the greater will be his satisfaction and success in selling.

¶ 937 Try out every buying motive in each sale

No matter how thorough your pre-approach, or how well you can read your prospect's reactions, you may not pick up the key buying motive that could clinch the sale. For this reason, salesmen are well-advised to work in appeals to every possible buying motive during each presentation. As was stressed earlier in ¶933, emphasis should be given to rational rather than emotional reasons for buying. Sometimes a salesman may think he's exhausted every buying motive (rational and emotional) and still the prospect remains unconvinced. In a situation like this, the problem may not be one of motivation at all. It may be that the salesman simply hasn't dramatized the advantages well enough. For example, the lady who wants to save time preparing food is quite susceptible to the basic buying motive of convenience, but this does not guarantee that she'll buy *your* blender. You, as a salesman, have got to show how and why *your* blender can save her the most time and effort. In other words, a salesman can appeal to the proper buying motives and still fail to make the sale. With poor salesmen, it happens all the time.

How to translate product features into benefits

As consumers and as salesmen we know that all too often product facts or features aren't enough to stimulate buying action. When we have a buying problem to solve, we can't always solve it by ourselves. We depend on the expert salesman to interpret product features for us, translating them into benefits. When we know exactly what the product will do for us, we can decide whether or not it solves our problem and act accordingly. The following paragraphs explain how to prepare a product analysis sheet, an indispensible procedure for the salesman who must communicate what his product can do for the buyer.

¶ 938 Preparing a product analysis sheet

One look at the product analysis sheet reconfirms the basic truth that product features

continue this procedure for all features

and benefits support each other. Here's how this product analysis sheet was developed.

1. Write in the headings at the top of the page.
2. Write in the full name of the product in the center of the top.
3. List every product fact or feature that you can think of, no matter how insignificant it may seem.
4. Starting with feature No. 1, write out as descriptively as possible what it means to or does for the user. Then in column 3, list the buying motive this benefit appeals to, and in column 4, the visual aid you will use or the demonstration you will put on to dramatize each benefit.
5. After writing each benefit, check yourself by going back and reading out loud: "Because of (*feature*) you get (*benefit*)." If after reading it out loud you think it really tells the prospect what's in it for him, congratulate yourself on a job well done.
6. In addition to describing each benefit, it's a good idea to begin developing the habit of "taking the prospect's pulse." So, after *each* benefit, write down a question designed to find out what your prospect thinks of the benefit you've just described. This procedure lets you know where you stand and whether or not you're building value (creating desire) in the prospect's mind.
7. Continue this procedure until all of the features have been translated into benefits. Don't try to do the whole job on one page. This forces you into abbreviating your benefits, but abbreviated benefits may not create enough desire to justify the price. So, a thorough job here will lead to more sales on the firing line.

¶ 939 **What the product analysis does for you**

The product analysis does for the salesman what the builder's blueprint, the tailor's pattern, and the motorist's road map does for each of them. It forces you to decide where you're going before you get there. It forces you to think in terms of customer benefits.

PRODUCT ANALYSIS SHEET

Samson Screwdriver Model S-12

(Because of) FEATURE	(You get) BENEFIT "What will it do for me?"	BUYING MOTIVE	DEMO/VISUAL
1. Hammer Forged	A bit that won't slip easily from the screw slot. "That can be a nuisance, can't it?"	CONVENIENCE	Turn screw in preset wood block.
2. Tempered Blade	A bit that won't twist or chip under heavy pressure (after demo) "Rugged, isn't it?"	GAIN (money saved not having to replace the screwdriver)	Have him apply pressure to blade held in vice. Show condition of blade and bit before and after.
3. Frozen Tine	A screwdriver that's built stronger than a welded car body. The handle will not separate from the blade. (after demo) "Do you think if you hooked your car on to this handle, you could pull it off the tine?"	GAIN	Have him pull handle while blade is held in vice.

Continue this procedure for all features

This is critical, because nobody ever buys until he knows what benefits he will get. The product analysis sheet also helps make you a product expert. By knowing, intimately, each and every product feature, you are able to answer any reasonable question to the prospect's satisfaction. Your knowledge and your confidence will help lead your prospect into a buying decision. One of the biggest advantages a product analysis gives you is in helping you decide exactly how you will demonstrate or show product benefits. There is simply no substitute for a vivid demonstration that lets your

¶ 939

prospect see how he will be better off. Getting your product into action goes a long way toward getting your prospect into the act of buying. For more guidance on how to show and demonstrate product benefits, see the material on word power and demonstrations in section 5000.

¶ 940 **What to do after making up the product analysis sheet**

The next step after filling out your product analysis sheet may vary, depending on your type of selling job. Some salesmen begin practicing or rehearsing in order to test their planned demonstrations and decide on the best order of features and benefits. Others like to match up certain key benefits for specific prospects, or write out a complete talk, striving to choose those words and phrases that communicate most clearly and dramatically. Of course, salesmen representing an extensive product line can't be expected to complete a formalized product analysis on every item they sell, but the more they do it, the greater will be their sales volume. Sooner or later your product analysis will be put to the test in the field. Here, your customers let you know how good a job you've done. They will throw out some of the benefits, add new ones you hadn't thought of, and in general reshape your product analysis for you. When this happens, you should revise your analysis sheet to incorporate all these changes. Then you'll have one that is proven. Finally, share it with your fellow salesmen.

¶ 999 **Footnote references**

¶ 932

(1) Dichter, Ernest, "How to Tailor Your Selling to the Individual Prospect," p. 36, "The American Salesman," January, 1959.

(2) Ibid.

BREAKING INTO BIG SELLING

A Simple Formula for Valuing Your Time
Setting Your Sights for Higher Earnings
Five Ways to Increase Production
Selling More to Your Present Customers
How to Move Up to Bigger Buyers
Breaking Into Big Selling through Better Time-Planning
Mature Salesmanship

TABLE OF CONTENTS

	Starts at Paragraph [¶]
Miracle Guide to Breaking Into Big Selling	1001

A SIMPLE FORMULA FOR VALUING YOUR TIME

	Starts at ¶
Objective—every customer a profitable one	1002
How to figure your time value	1003
How simple arithmetic can bring you more dollars	1004
How much must prospect be worth for you to make a call?	1005
Look hard before leaping into a change of jobs	1006
The "whopper sale" won't deceive you	1007
You're in modern selling when you select your customers	1008

SETTING YOUR SIGHTS FOR HIGHER EARNINGS

	Starts at ¶
Energize your personal goals and make every day a sales-success day	1011
Use the law of averages to raise your sales volume and dollar income	1012
Achieve your goals through dynamic planning	1013
Look at selling as a continuous process	1014
How top sales execs choose salesmen for promotions	1015

FIVE WAYS TO INCREASE PRODUCTION

	Starts at ¶
The five sources for increased sales	1021
Give your knowledge and get orders	1022

SELLING MORE TO YOUR PRESENT CUSTOMERS

	Starts at ¶
Dedicate yourself to the customer	1031
3 Ways to make your customer listen by playing the name game	1032
Creative selling is the key to boosting sales to present customers	1033
Sell across the board	1034
Concentrate on selling higher-priced units	1035
Strike at the prospect's biggest need and the sale is yours	1036
Carry in an idea—carry out an order	1037
Showing customer how to use product helps to upgrade him	1038
Show the loss entailed in excessive splitting of business	1039
Assume responsibility, based on confidence and knowledge	1040
"User calls" help you sell more to present customers	1041
Information picked up on user calls leads to more sales	1042
How to walk out of a buyer's office without tripping over the welcome mat	1043
A special service turns a small account into a big one	1044
Successful repeat sales may depend on your knowing top executives	1045
"Easy-to-sell" items can open the way to bigger orders	1046
Work with the credit manager to get the "edge"	1047
Use credit to build sales	1048

HOW TO MOVE UP TO BIGGER BUYS

	Starts at Paragraph [¶]
You can move up to bigger buyers	1051
A simple plan for selling to bigger buyers	1052
Know how your customers are faring	1053
A well-built plan of sale gets a big buyer to order	1054

BREAKING INTO BIG SELLING THROUGH BETTER TIME-PLANNING

	Starts at Paragraph [¶]
How you use time means everything	1061
Two ways to plan your calls to save time	1062
How to find the best time to call on customers in a new territory	1063
How you can double the working day and get to your goal faster	1064
How to avoid "peak and valley" selling	1065
How to lengthen the seasonal selling period	1066
Put these power-packed techniques to work for you	1067
Plan the next day's work; the second step in your day's wind-up	1068

MATURE SALESMANSHIP

	Starts at Paragraph [¶]
New developments affect your selling	1071
The "natural born salesman" is a myth	1072
Don't over-sell yourself	1073
A "prima donna" doesn't fit into today's selling	1074
Buying and selling have become more businesslike	1075
Everyone values time today	1076
Old-time persistence is not for you	1077
Backdoor selling—Yes or no?	1078
The other side of the coin	1079
Competition is a stimulant	1080
Modern times require modern methods	1081
A salesman must keep pace	1082
Be a team player—and become more valuable to your company	1083
Dickering or "horse trading" is frowned upon	1084
How changes in management have improved salesmen's opportunities	1085
"Selling" includes many non-selling duties	1086
A modern attitude is needed for required paper work	1087
Stay aware of the need for change	1088

Breaking into Big Selling

It's just as easy to sell big people as little people—and more profitable

¶ 1001 ⟫MIRACLE GUIDE to→ Breaking Into Big Selling

Any salesman who wants to make big money—who wants to earn $25,000, $50,000 or more a year—has everything in his favor today. He faces the greatest opportunity for high-volume selling this country has ever seen.

People have never had so much money to spend nor been so anxious to spend it. Industry is expanding at an unheard-of pace. The demand for goods, for services, is rising spectacularly.

Yet only one salesman in 50 is hitting this fantastic jackpot—only one in 50 really knows how to capitalize on it.

The Guide gives you the sure-fire selling techniques that will permit any man ambitious for high bracket earnings to write his own ticket.

The seven keys to making the first upward leap are right here in this section:

▶ Place the right value on your working time and work with an awareness of that value [¶ 1003].

▶ Set your sights for higher earnings. Then make your full contribution to the 6 essentials for success in reaching your goal [¶ 1011].

▶ Increase your total volume of sales by tapping the 5 sources for producing more business [¶ 1021].

▶ Sell more to your present customers by dedicating yourself to them. Use tested ideas for making dedication mean bigger income [¶ 1031].

▶ Move up to bigger buyers. It takes no more ability to sell a big buyer than a small one [¶ 1051].

▶ Break into big selling with a time-value approach to planning your work schedule [¶ 1061].

▶ Be a "modern" salesman [¶ 1071].

Use the Guide in some way every day and you will pick up ideas, hints, techniques, and inspiration that will bring you to each of your higher earnings goals.

A simple formula for valuing your time

¶ 1002 **Objective—every customer a profitable one**

You can earn big money in selling only by putting the right value on your time and never forgetting how valuable it is. If you want to take home a bigger paycheck you must be sharply aware of the dollar and cents value of each hour of your working day. About the only time you can safely forget that "time is money" is when you are getting the well-earned relaxation and rest that tune you up for the next day's successful selling.

Place your own value on your working time. Fix it in relation to what you want to earn. Then earn it by working with prospects and customers whose orders can yield you earnings commensurate with your time value.

➤➤REMEMBER➤ Time is capital to you. You must invest it for maximum return—the return that you yourself figure it is worth.

¶ 1003   **How to figure your time value**

All you need to know to calculate the money value of your time are these two facts: (1) how much you want to earn a year, and (2) there are 1952 working hours in a year of 244 working days. Divide your earnings goal by 1952 hours and you have it.

Here are the figures for some attainable goals.

Earnings Goal Per Year	Value of an Hour
$10,000	$ 5.10
$20,000	$10.25
$25,000	$12.80
$30,000	$15.35
$40,000	$20.50
$50,000	$25.60

¶ 1004   **How simple arithmetic can bring you more dollars**

Now that you know how much each hour of your time is worth you can see the importance of using your time most judiciously. You will agree that the most profitable hours are those you spend in a selling interview, telling the story of your product.

Most salesmen have just 976 hours in each year during which they face their prospects with the expectation of closing the sale. Notice how the 1952 working hours have dwindled in number and how each of the 976 hours has mounted in value:

Earnings Goal Per Year	Value of an Hour Spent in Actual Selling
$10,000	$10.25
$20,000	$20.50
$25,000	$25.65
$30,000	$30.75
$40,000	$41.00
$50,000	$51.25

Obviously, those "story-telling" hours are not going to yield their money's worth to you unless the calls you make produce a commensurate volume of business.

➤➤WHAT TO DO➤ The conclusion is clear—you must eliminate as far as possible those calls that do not pay, as measured by dollar value of orders obtained. Regardless of whether you are selling a product that requires you to call back periodically on each customer, or that involves no repeat sales, time is measured against the sales results.

¶ 1005   **How much must prospect be worth for you to make a call?**

Put yourself in the place of the salesman who asked himself that question and then took action on what he discovered.

▶ IDEA IN ACTION Gordon Miller calls on hospitals to fill their needs for supplies and equipment. He averages 25 calls per week and since he visits each account every 4 weeks, his selling list totals exactly 100 names.

Gordon's total net sales per year run about $150,000. His commissions average 8% or $12,000. Of this sum, $4,000 goes into traveling expenses; the balance of $8,000 is his net annual income.

Gordon is alerted to the fact that if he wants to make $10,000 or more net earnings he has to get more value out of each of his working hours. So he analyzes his previous year's sales and discovers that ⅓ of his customers give him only 10% of his total business, while the top ⅔ of his accounts produce 90% of his overall net sales. These are the figures he comes up with:

33 accounts yielded net sales of $15,000 or an average of $455 of net sales per account ($15,000 divided by 33).

67 accounts yielded net sales of $135,000 or an average of $2,015 of net sales per account ($135,000 divided by 67).

He realizes that it took just as much time, effort, attention, and expense to get the average of $455 net sales from each of the 33 accounts as it took to get the average $2,015 net sales from each of his 67 accounts. In fact, as he thinks about the 33 accounts, he realizes that some of them take a lot more time and effort than the other better accounts.

"Well," says he, "I must get more of those big buyers; I must stop making calls on the little fellows."

So Gordon Miller decided that on his next trip he would eliminate calling on those accounts that

a simple formula for valuing your time

fell into the category of taking ⅓ of his time while contributing only 10% of his sales. He used this free time to call on other hospitals in his territory that he had not formerly had time to see, and began to develop still more higher quality prospects. A few of these new prospects bought on his first visit; others began buying on the second or third.

Twelve months after making his analysis, Gordon found that by virtually dropping the ⅓ of his accounts that had given him only $15,000 in volume, and using the same time and effort in soliciting new accounts, he had added $35,000 of business, for a net gain of $20,000.

Since Gordon's travel expenses remained unchanged, the $1,600 in additional commissions he was now earning marked an increase of 20%, which boosted his income from $8,000 to $9,600 —and this was only the beginning.

➢➢➢WHAT TO DO➢ 1. Analyze your own selling record of the past year.

2. Identify the accounts that are cheapening the value of your time.

3. Decide whether any of those accounts are worth keeping because they are growing businesses that will shortly be in the category on which you are aiming to concentrate.

4. Drop the remaining unprofitable accounts.

5. Go after prospects with a potential unit-size order that will pay you what your time is worth.

6. Consider a job change if all else fails— but remember:

¶ 1006 **Look hard—before leaping into a change of jobs**

Salesmen who change jobs without thinking things through, often wind up worse than they were before. If you're considering a change, look at things logically and unemotionally before making a decision.

➢➢➢WHAT TO DO➢ Evaluate your job in writing. On two separate sheets of paper, list the factors you like about your job on one sheet. On the other, list the things you don't like about your present job. Then with great care—

(1) Go over your "dislike" list very carefully to make sure that the problems you have listed will not be present in a new job.

Example: You may feel your sales manager is a task-master—most sales managers are.

Thus, a change of jobs will only change sales managers; it will not change the nature of the problem.

(2) Evaluate your list of "likes." Ask yourself these and similar questions to determine whether you really stand to gain by going to another job.

"Will I be able to match the benefits of my present job if I take another position?" "Can I afford to throw away the amount of experience, the seniority, and the prestige I have with my present customers?" "Does the new sales territory give me a better profit opportunity than my present territory?"

Benefit: By putting your gripes and praises of your present job in writing, you will also be able to clearly define your problem. You just might discover that some of your complaints are not really as important as you believed. This can give you an entire new outlook toward your present selling position.

And it will also give you an honest chance to rediscover all the important plusses that made you take your present job in the first place.

➢➢➢IMPORTANT➢ Make sure you carefully take your employment history into consideration. A salesman who changes jobs frequently often runs out of new opportunities.

¶ 1007 **The "whopper sale" won't deceive you**

By keeping your time value always in mind, you can make the occasional "whopper sale" without loss of value time and other business. Here is what frequently happens—but it can't happen to you if you are invariably and intelligently time conscious:

▶ **IDEA IN ACTION** Bill Taylor sells a nationally advertised cosmetic line to retailers in the metropolitan Chicago area. His orders normally run between $50 and $400, depending on the size of the individual store. He writes four orders a day, on the average.

One day, Bill calls on a chain organization having about twenty retail outlets in the territory. The buyer says, "We are considering running a big promotion on cosmetics in a few weeks, right at the height of the season. If we do, we'll probably want to include your line. Stop back to see me in about a week, Bill, and I may have a larger order for you."

¶ 1007

Bill is elated. He quickly does some estimating and decides that if the plan goes through, the order would be at least $2,000—or perhaps even more!

"Let's see," he says to himself, "I'm to check back next Thursday. I had planned to be working out around Evanston that day, but I'll put that off till Friday. That big order is worth going after, all right, and I'll plan to work Thursday right here in Chicago."

Next, Bill realizes that on Friday he had planned to work in Forest Park—had a couple of appointments there, as a matter of fact.

"Well, I can't put Evanston off too long—so I'll just phone my customers in Forest Park and explain why I can't see them till the following Monday."

When Bill calls back to get his big order on Thursday, he is told, "We're going to have a final meeting on this early on Monday morning. Can you call back, say at 11 on Monday? Everything will be settled by then."

Bill replies, "Well, I'll arrange to be there, Mr. Crain—11 o'clock on Monday!"

When Bill eventually lands his order, it totals $1,100. The final plans have been trimmed down a bit, he is told.

Actually, Bill lost out on much more than $1,100 worth of other business because the pending big order from the chain had caused him to change many of his normal calls over a 10-day period. He was pleased to write an order more than twice as large as his usual "top" orders, but he was puzzled when he saw his final sales figures for the month—they were below his normal average monthly total!

⟶ WHAT TO DO ⟶ 1. Get the "plum" order *without* disrupting your working schedule. Use the telephone. (What Bill should have said when his appointment with the chain buyer was put off is this: "I'm sorry, but I've simply *got* to be in Forest Park on Monday. I've postponed my appointments there once already, and I can't do it again. Suppose I telephone you from there?") The buyer will respect you for keeping your appointments with other customers. You will be displaying the attitude that all buyers respect.

2. Show him you are not walking away from this extraordinary order by thinking of some way in which he can push your product during the promotion. Write him about your idea, or give it to him on the phone when you call him. Get that creative idea by reviewing the successful promotion efforts of some of your other customers: a striking display that they used; perhaps a one-color harmony, three tones of one color, that made an appealing background for the cosmetics; how one of your customers tied up its cosmetic promotion with a community event.

In this way you will guard against paying too high a price for the "plum" order, in terms of time lost, disrupted plans, and any other departure from sound work habits.

⟶ REMEMBER ⟶ Normal work habits frequently produce more total business than would be had from dropping them to try for a "plum" order.

⟶ IMPORTANT ⟶ When you raise the level of your customers' potential value you will become less dependent upon the "whopper sale" to bring up your earnings. The "whopper sales" will still come your way.

¶ 1008 **You're in modern selling when you select your customers**

You are in the vanguard of scientific selling when you search for and discover the unprofitable segments of your customer list. You are doing what the most progressive companies are doing to convert losses into profits. They are analyzing their marketing costs to see how many and what kinds of customers to sell; what territories to cover; which products to sell and at what price. Not many companies have learned and applied all the analysis techniques. But you are as much in the lead as the pace-setters of American business when you apply the formula given to you here for improving your own profit picture by weeding out the small buyers and moving up to bigger people. See ¶ 1085.

Setting your sights for higher earnings

¶ 1011 **'Energize' your personal goals and make every day a sales-success day**

"Step up your personal goals—and you'll give yourself—and your sales—a dramatic push up the ladder to success. You shouldn't settle for being just an *average* sales producer when—with a little extra effort—you can become a *great* producer." That's the advice offered by a Sales-VP for one of the country's top manufacturing outfits. *How to do it? Here's—*

setting your sights for higher earnings

⮞⮞ONE WAY⮕ "Set yourself an income that has definite, periodic increases. Then give raises toward that income by setting—for yourself—higher monthly or annual goals. And work hard to fulfill them." Here's an—

Example: John Abbott, who sells business machines in San Francisco, went from $10,500 to $17,000 in just one year. That's a 62½% jump!

Says Abbott, "As soon as I set a higher income goal, I began thinking of myself as a bigger earner. And *thinking* like a winner is half the battle. It makes you want to *act* like one.

Result: "I found myself becoming more confident every day. Now I walk into a prospect's office with the attitude that I am going to sell him. I usually do, too."

⮞⮞IMPORTANT⮕ The mere fact of setting goals alone won't do the trick. It's only a start (though a big one). The important thing is to "energize" your goals—put some action into your thinking—and above all, hard work.

The following steps will help you get started:

(1) Believe in your ability to reach your goals. Just as right thinking will strengthen your enthusiasm, so will belief in your power to reach the earning goals you have set down. Belief helps to generate enthusiasm—without it, you'll get nowhere.

(2) Look at a winner. Take an objective look at a man that you *know* is a top sales producer. Notice that wherever he goes, he carries with him an air of self-confidence. Nothing about him hints defeat. Reason. He expects to win, and because he *believes* he'll win, his attitude is inspiring. Now—take a—

(3) Look at yourself. How do you shape up? Do you *look* like a top producer? Would others say you have that 'air of self-confidence'? Well if you don't—you can.

⮞⮞IMPORTANT⮕ Before you start your drive to your goal of becoming a top producer, make sure you're willing to go all the way. If you answer "no" to any of the following questions, you may *prefer* being just 'average.'

1. Am I willing to sacrifice some pleasures and comforts if need be, to achieve my goal?
2. Is my attitude right, so that I enjoy my work?
3. Am I completely "sold" on my products?
4. Am I constantly learning to make my efforts more effective?
5. Do I bend over backwards to give my customers the service they require?
6. Do I really understand my customers, associates and friends?

Show Them Your Drive. Now that you're charged up, it's easy to convey this winning spirit to your customers. One good way to show—and prove—your enthusiasm is to:

Let them know how important they are. A Brooklyn, N.Y. salesman for a printing company uses this—

⮞⮞IDEA IN ACTION⮕ "I make written notes of my customers' likes, dislikes, interests and hobbies. I also note whether they like a little conversation before business; or whether they want me to get on with my presentation immediately."

Result: The salesman knows just how to handle each buyer.

¶ 1012 **Use the law of averages to raise your sales volume and dollar income**

The law of averages, applied to selling, works this way: the more you do the more you achieve. Thus, the more well-chosen calls you make, the more interviews you obtain; the larger the number of planned interviews, the greater the number of presentations; the larger the number of presentations, the more opportunities to close sales; the higher the number of closings, the larger your volume of sales and income.

⮞⮞REMEMBER⮕ You can perform *more* selling jobs with *no* additional time expenditure by planning your work and economizing your time. See ¶ 1061 et seq.

Put the answers to these questions to work and increase your sales volume and dollar income.

• How can I raise the number of calls I make each week?
• How can I raise the number of interviews I obtain per call made?
• How can I raise the number of presentations I give per interview obtained?
• How can I raise the number of closes I secure per presentation given?
• How can I raise the number of new prospects I see each week?
• How can I raise the number of repeat sales I succeeded in making each quarter?
• How can I raise the dollar value of my selling time?

- How can I lower the travel time I spend between calls?

¶ 1013 **Achieve your goals through dynamic planning**

Long-range goals are won only through successful planning of the many separate steps that lead to accomplishment. Learn to plan and execute small steps and you will take giant strides toward your goal of success in selling.

⟶**WHAT TO DO**⟶ Choose one or more long-range goals. Make a three column chart with these headings: Time Period, Proposed Increase, Actual Increase. Divide your Time Period and Proposed Increase into equal, corresponding subdivisions.

EXAMPLE: Your present number of repeat sales is 120 per year. Your goal is to double your repeat sales in one year. Break down the coming year into quarters and assign a goal of 60 repeat sales to each quarter period.

Time Period	Proposed increase of repeat sales	Actual increase of repeat sales (cumulative)
1st quarter (March 28)	60	
2nd quarter (June 30)	120	
3rd quarter (Sept. 30)	180	
4th quarter (Dec. 31)	240	

Now determine the simplest and most direct methods of attaining your ultimate goal of increasing repeat-sales. You might try these techniques that have worked for the big producers:
- Use follow-up letters.
- Schedule periodic check-up calls.
- Leave your card with an invitation to call if your customer needs information or service.
- Send customers literature describing your new products.
- Look for opportunities to remind your customer that you have his interests in mind.

Watch your deadlines as though your job depended on your meeting them.

At the end of each quarter fill in the number of repeat sales you have made.

Check your progress from time to time by comparing your actual progress with the planned progress shown on your chart. If you find yourself falling behind, re-examine the methods you are using for possible improvement, or check with this Guide for other ideas and methods that will be effective.

⟶**IMPORTANT**⟶ Increasing repeat sales is only one of many long-range goals. Every salesman who is aiming for top-flight achievement must increase his number of new customers. To do this he must increase the number of prospects, the number of calls, the number of presentations; and the number of interviews that result in closings.

¶ 1014 **Look at selling as a continuous process**

Each step in the selling process is related to each of the others. The final outcome of an interview is determined not by closing ability or any other single factor, but by use of the proper techniques at each and every point in *planning* as well as in *execution* of the attempt to sell.

▶ **IDEA IN ACTION** Ted Hughes sells automobiles. His appearance and manner of handling prospects are good; he makes a strong presentation and is an excellent closer. Yet Hughes turns in only an average volume of business.

This is so because his technique is under par in regard to (1) meeting objections, and (2) handling necessary selling details, such as arranging financing, explaining the trade-in allowance offer, and so forth.

By correcting these two weaknesses, Ted could immediately increase his sales volume by at least 25%. Until he does this, he will continue to be a mediocre salesman. For no salesman can really succeed until he learns the principle that *each* step in the sale affects the final outcome.

⟶**WHAT TO DO**⟶ You can easily see whether you are acting on the modern principle that each step in the selling process is related to each of the other steps. There's an analysis at ¶ 1067 which lists the various steps in selling. Rate yourself frankly on each step as shown in the analysis. If your honest rating shows that you are stronger in some of the steps than in others, you know that you must correct the weakness if you are to reach the earnings goal you set for yourself. How to begin to correct them? Well, that's what this Guide is for.

¶ 1015 **How top sales execs choose salesmen for promotions**

Another way to move up the economic ladder is via the promotion route. Which leads us to this question:

Why is one salesman promoted and another bypassed? Your editors asked leading sales figures that question. Performance was a

five ways to increase production

requisite mentioned by everyone, but there are many other factors involved. Here are some answers:

Illinois sales VP: "We look for the 'idea' man. Does he send in new selling ideas? Does he suggest new uses for our product? Does he keep his eye open for trends? A good score here moves him to the top."

Pittsburgh distributor: "We go along with the idea that the enthusiastic salesman will make the best sales manager. How do we judge enthusiasm? There are many ways. The man who is always fighting for his customers. The man who plans his schedules so that he's always set to make a backup call. The man who takes care of his paperwork—and on time. If a man shows these traits, we feel we have a winner."

Long Island manufacturer: "How a man reacts on his feet is important with us. He's under pressure as a sales manager. At a sales meeting, I call on a salesman and tell him to sell me. Naturally, I'll throw objections at him he's never heard of. If he handles them well, he'll be given top consideration."

California cosmetics manufacturer: "As far as I'm concerned performance comes first and second. If a man isn't the best performer over a stretch of time—I feel he's not ready to advance."

Five ways to increase production

¶ 1021   **The five sources for increased sales**

Regardless of the type of selling in which you may be engaged, there are *only five ways* in which you can achieve an increase in your total volume of sales. Unless you manage to tap one of these five sources, whatever effort you make or whatever plan of work you may set up is doomed to failure.

Source 1. Calling on a greater number of high-potential prospects or customers. For example, make 9 calls per day instead of 8.

⟫HOW TO DO IT→ Plan your work better and devote more of your time to actual selling. See ¶ 1061 et seq.; 8042 et seq.

Source 2. Closing a greater percentage of prospects and customers you call on. For example, close 3 prospects out of 8 instead of 2 out of 8.

⟫HOW TO DO IT→ Develop your closing power. See ¶ 6001 et seq.

Source 3. Selling larger quantities per order. For example, sell 10 gross instead of 5; or a $20,000 life insurance policy instead of one for $10,000.

⟫HOW TO DO IT→ Plan each interview and prepare for it in advance [¶ 4002 et seq.]; use a planned presentation instead of a hit-or-miss sales talk; perfect your sales presentation. See ¶ 5001 et seq.

Source 4. Selling a wider range of products. For example, sell the *full* line, rather than only the "easy-to-sell" items; sell related items rather than individual products.

⟫HOW TO DO IT→ Acquire a thorough knowledge of your product and make the most effective use of it. See ¶ 5011 et seq.

Source 5. Selling higher-priced units. For example, sell quality items instead of price items; sell the "economy size", or the large-screen television set instead of smaller and lower-priced units. See ¶ 1031 et seq.

▶ **IDEA IN ACTION** Howard Burke's sales manager questions Burke as to why he has made such a poor selling record in the year he has been with the company.

"If I had a larger territory," answers Burke, "I would do a lot better. There simply isn't enough business in the State of Maine. Give me Vermont and New Hampshire, too, and I'll double my business."

The sales manager agrees to this proposal, on a 3-month test basis.

Burke's sales do not show an increase, however, but actually decline. The reason is that in covering the larger territory, Burke's travel time is increased, with the result that he makes fewer calls than before.

This experience causes Burke to review his selling habits. In his self-analysis, he discovers a better method of closing.

"Mr. Fullbright," Burke reports to his sales manager, "I'm so busy closing sales that I find I can't cover three states after all. There are more prospects in Maine than I had realized, so I'll have to drop the two other states."

It is never consistent with true salesmanship to accept an order which represents goods or services that the buyer cannot use, does not need, or for any other reason known to the salesman ought not to buy.

¶ 1021

The second step (the closing of a greater percentage of prospects) *did* bring an increase, since it successfully "tapped" one of the sources from which it is possible to obtain additional sales volume.

There are, of course, instances when working a larger territory results in the salesman's making more calls, or in selling more "quantity users," or in some other way tapping one of the sources from which more business can be obtained. But unless a plan accomplishes this in one way or another, it will not succeed as a means to greater sales.

⋙WHAT TO DO NOW→ Examine your selling habits, your selling plan, and your selling activities in terms of the five sources of increased sales. Not every salesman can *use* each of these five sources, but every salesman can make certain that all of his thinking and effort are along lines that lead directly to one or more of these five sources.

¶ 1022 **Give your knowledge and get orders**

You must give your customer the information about your product that will make him want to buy before you can expect to get his order.

Find out if you have enough of the right information by asking yourself the following questions.

• Do I know why my customer is buying my product?

• Do I know what my customer expects from my product?

• Do I know how my customer is planning to use my product?

• Do I know other ways he can use my product?

• Do I know when my customer expects delivery?

• Have I informed my customer of my product's limitations as well as its advantages?

• If a call-back is necessary, have I left my customer with an impression of my product strong enough to overcome a competitor's sales talk?

⋙REMEMBER→ Knowledge of your product and your job increases your customer's confidence and raises your own enthusiasm. A man who knows his product thoroughly never has to misrepresent the thing he has to sell.

Selling more to your present customers

¶ 1031 **Dedicate yourself to the customer**

An important factor in gaining the buoyant, hopeful frame of mind basic to success in selling more to your present customers is dedication to them—honestly putting their interests first . . . doing your best for them . . . looking at things from their point of view . . . and selling from their point of view.

This can revolutionize your selling career, bring an explosion of success. And here's why:

• Everyone carries on continuously within himself a kind of moral bookkeeping. Salesmen are the same in this repect as everyone else.

• When you dedicate yourself to your clients' best interests, you build up within yourself a "moral credit balance"—it puts you in an expectant, hopeful frame of mind (so necessary to selling success)—you feel you have something good coming to you.

• It puts an end to the inner feelings of guilt that keep so many salesmen ineffectual—the salesmen who do things only for their own advantage and then try to kid themselves and the customer that it is being done for his sake.

• When you honestly dedicate yourself to your customers' best interests, it puts the enormous power of right on your side, and immediately fills your mind with the expectation of good to come. This continuous feeling of moral credit balance can turn a man into a giant. It gives you an assurance that nothing else can. If any man lacks self confidence, let him try it.

Stop thinking of yourself—think of the people you sell—and you won't have to think of yourself at all. You'll become an enormous selling success.

Walter Horvath, who wrote the basic material in this volume, was a leading exponent of dedication to the customer and became an enormous selling success.

At 25 he retired with a comfortable fortune—and later established his own sales consulting firm and through his writings became one of the best known sales personalities in the country.

▶ *The big change through dedication.* One of the big changes you will notice at once when you dedicate yourself to your customers' welfare is the freeing of your own creative imagination (which always takes place under the emotional stimulus of dedication to the right side of a moral issue).

Ideas for helping your people will come thick and fast—your imagination will catch fire—you'll see hundreds of opportunities to serve them which were never apparent before.

Here are a few practical suggestions to further your work in this exciting direction.

1. Learn all about your customers' problems—talk with them—let them talk. If you turn a sympathetic ear you'll get to know what a man really has on his mind—and then you can give him, not only kindly, but intelligent help.

2. When you make a call, make it with the idea of helping the man. Go in, not just to sell something, but with an idea that will be of some use to him.

EXAMPLE: You may have found through talking to your man that he's worried about a large supply of slow-moving stock. You'll find ideas to help him when you really want to help him—and instead of just making a call, you'll come through with a promotional suggestion he can use to solve his problem. It might be a consumer contest you suggest; or a sampling table, if it's a food item; a trade-in special if it's a household product; an offer of a premium; and so on.

3. Keep an idea book—with a page for each customer. In this, keep notes on what you've found out about his problems—and his special aims and interests. And on this same page put down ideas for helping him—as they come to you.

EXAMPLE: You may see a piece in the newspaper that your man could capitalize on. Mail it to him.

4. As you move about your territory, keep an eye open for good things you can pass along (something that one customer is doing that would be helpful to another). Of course, you would not use this where they are in competition with each other.

5. One salesman spends Saturday in the office—checking on the new goods that have come in for sale. First thing Monday morning he makes long distance phone calls to his people—with attractive offers—and does as much business in one day as most salesmen do in a week.

6. A very successful insurance salesman takes such a genuine interest in the personal problems of others—and is so good at helping them—that one of his customers whom he had helped asked him to have a talk with his nephew who was bogged down in an unhappy situation. He helped the young man and his client was so grateful he recommended him far and wide.

⟫OBSERVATION⟶ Most of the things you do to help your customers will be on business matters (as they should be)—but you can, with good judgment, do things of a more personal nature for them. One customer was always talking about a trip he was going to make in his boat down the inland waterway to Florida. The salesman happened to come across a magazine article on the inland waterway—and sent his prospect the magazine. He was thrilled by it.

▶ *Working into dedication.* Dedication to your customers may seem unusual at first. But it's not. You'll be following the soundest of all selling principles—to think habitually of how you can best serve the interests of your customers.

This may involve hard work until it becomes your habitual method of operation, as it did with Horvath. But if you try it you will find that it pays off with a vengeance.

Remember that this approach not only changes what takes place within you (how it dramatically releases your own powers)—but equally important a veritable explosion takes place in other people's attitude toward you.

Here are actual instances of three salesmen who made immediate sacrifices to better serve their customers (and what happened to them).

1

A real estate man had a lady come to him who wanted to buy a $50,000 home he had listed (it was an old colonial place and she was taken with its charm).

But the salesman knew she would be in for trouble if she bought it. It would cost thousands of dollars to put it into shape—and it was far too large for her purposes. The

¶ 1031

water supply was inadequate and would call for a big investment. It was a house for a rich man from the neighboring city—someone who had plenty of money to reclaim its charm. He told the lady not to buy it—and why. The story got around. The lady told everybody about how decent the salesman had been. It was such a good story—and told so often—that the salesman immediately became known as a person who looks out for his clients. People placed their faith in him—and his business thrived.

2

A salesman wholesaled dresses to retail stores. He had a small retailer who sold "better" dresses. This retailer told the salesman that he wanted to take on a line of $5 dresses and wanted to give him a big order for a full line of cheaper stuff.

The salesman (who knew the dress business) advised against it. He told the man that he could not hope to compete in $5 dresses with the big-volume stores, that they could sell them for about what he would have to pay for them. The salesman lost the order, of course, but the man was impressed with how much the salesman knew about the business and how he wouldn't take an order for something that was not good for his customer.

3

An executive wanted to buy $10,000 of life insurance and called up an agent and told him that his friend had recommended him and he wanted to place the order right there on the phone.

The insurance salesman thanked him—but told him he would rather not take the order until he had looked over the client's situation and found out what he really wanted it for—and if it would answer his purposes.

The prospect was surprised and said, "I thought you fellows were so anxious to sell insurance that you'd welcome a $10,000 policy."

The insurance man called on the prospect at his office and asked him what he wanted the insurance for—and found that the executive wanted it to protect his wife and three children.

The salesman found that they would need at least $6,000 a year to keep going without the husband's income and that the man would need $35,000 additional insurance to give him the protection he was after.

The executive took out $35,000 worth of insurance instead of $10,000.

⟫⟫REMEMBER⟶ The point of these three stories is that they show the value of looking at things from the prospect's point of view. It gets people eating out of your hand. It makes them go out of their way for you. They'll do you a good turn whenever they can. And it will end in your selling more to your present customers.

¶ 1032   **3 ways to make your customer listen by playing the name game**

Top producers are fully aware of the value of remembering their customer's name. It breaks down the impersonal barriers that often has "no sale" written on them. You too can be a name dropper and pick up extra profits. Here's—

⟫⟫WHAT TO DO⟶ *(1)* Use the customer's name often without overdoing it, of course. This point is particularly valid in the beginning of the interview when repeating his name will plant it firmly in your mind for the rest of your presentation. Preface questions with his name, and use it to end statements: "Well Mr. Jones, what do you think of my product now?"

(2) Every time you use the name of your prospective buyer, take a good look at him. Learn to associate his name with his face. By looking directly at your prospect you will appear more sincere and close contact can be reached more readily. Also, if you can recall his name upon meeting the customer in a casual situation, you stand to be regarded in high esteem when you call on him again.

(3) Make sure of the spelling and pronunciation of his name—this is absolutely vital. The more difficult his name, the more important it is that you are writing and saying it correctly. Check with his receptionist or secretary to make sure you are right on both counts. You are better off not addressing him at all, than mispronouncing his name.

¶ 1033   **The attitude that sells more to present customers**

Here is the successful salesman's attitude about selling more to his present customers: A customer who already finds it profitable to give you a substantial amount of business will listen with recep-

selling more to your present customers

tive ears to facts that show how he can profitably use *still* more.

The only time a customer is likely to feel that your suggestion is out of order is if you simply ask for the additional business as a sort of favor, without bothering to show how he, too, can profit from the added business placed with you.

⟫IMPORTANT→ You must change your attitude if you are making these mistakes:

- Mistake No. 1. You feel that you already are getting a substantial volume of business from a given account and it is nice to "leave well enough alone."
- Mistake No. 2. You say, "Well, the Jones account knows us so well that if they were interested in having more of our product they would say so."
- Mistake No. 3. You assume that the customer has a real reason for passing up part of your offerings, without first having discussed with him why he should buy. *The burden of stating reasons why a customer should buy rests on you, and not on the buyer.*
- Mistake No. 4. When a customer decides to buy a particular item, you don't have the courage to suggest a full-sized order. The only risk you run in suggesting a higher limit is that the customer will not follow your suggestion. But most of the time he will, if the item is profitable to him.

⟫IMPORTANT→ Be sure to find out how your customer uses your product, especially if it is raw material you are selling. Then you stand the best chance of selling him the quantity he really needs.

⟫IMPORTANT→ Selling more to your present customers doesn't mean that your objective should necessarily be to become the customer's sole supplier, unless (1) the customer has a small business, or (2) your product or service is not a raw material. Companies selling raw materials generally do not want *all* of a big company's business. Nor do they want to be the 100% supplier for too many small accounts.

¶ 1034 **Creative selling is the key to boosting sales to present customers**

Creative selling is necessary, if you are to sell more to your present customers; and creative selling means driving your imagination.

At ¶ 3051 et seq. are a number of ideas that great salesmen have used to make bigger buyers. Here are the means used—the creative ideas themselves are given in detail at the paragraphs mentioned.

- Upgraded a customer [¶ 3052].
- Found a hidden application for a product [¶ 3054].
- Found a new use for raw materials [¶ 3055].
- Broadened out a small customer's buying [¶ 3056].
- Opened up a whole new field of prospects among which were some big buyers [¶ 3057].
- Got the product resold and reordered by a dealer-customer [¶ 3059].

These ideas, and others under "Ideas for Creative Selling" [¶ 3001 et seq.], demonstrate that creative thinking helps in each step of the selling process. They show that your own drive can yield creative ideas regardless of what you are selling.

¶ 1035 **Concentrate on selling higher-priced units**

The higher-priced units are the more profitable units, and they take no more of your selling time and energy than the lower-priced, less profitable ones. You should therefore concentrate on those items that yield the maximum profit to you. This means, of course, that you must also select prospects who are likely buyers of big items.

▶ **IDEA IN ACTION** Bob Strand has spent six years on the road representing a manufacturer of men's clothing. His sales and his income have increased only 15% in the past three years, whereas another salesman who started out the same time as Bob has more than doubled his sales in the same three years.

Bob has almost concluded that he would be better off in some job other than selling. But he gets a new idea when he examines his selling habits and selling activities in terms of the five sources of increased sales mentioned at ¶ 1021.

Bob then realizes that he has fallen down badly because he has been selling chiefly the low-priced items in his line. On his next trip around his territory he concentrates on correcting this one point.

The result is that Bob's sales increased 40% almost immediately, and by the end of a year he had more than doubled his sales.

¶ 1035

>>>COMMENT→ Here is a concrete example of how much can be accomplished by a salesman who makes a sincere and intelligent effort to apply the principle that there are only five ways to increase sales: (1) more calls; (2) better closing; (3) selling larger quantities; (4) selling wider variety; (5) selling higher-priced units. In the instance cited, the result had a fundamental effect on a man's career. Such examples are not uncommon.

>>>REMEMBER→ The caliber of the sale counts. A high-priced product usually offers better-than-average opportunities for earning big commissions. But selling such a product takes hard work, imagination, and skill. Men who make a success of industrial selling, for example, which usually involves a high-priced product, get their turndowns like every salesman does. But they snap back quickly from their disappointments because they know that there's real profit in the next sale.

¶ 1036 **Strike at the prospect's biggest need and the sale is yours**

Little sales are often made into big ones if you strike at the prospect's most important need. This way to bigger sales works especially well in situations where the prospect starts by setting a limit on the size of his purchase.

▶ **IDEA IN ACTION** Charles Hampton, Seattle real estate broker, sold a $200,000 building to a client who wanted income property at a top cost of $50,000. He did it by selling security—which was the client's need.

"Our client," says Mr. Hampton, "was 69 years old; his wife 68. He was looking for a small apartment building, fairly new—with four or five units—one apartment for his home, and the others to supplement his inadequate income of $90 a month."

Salesman gets an idea. The client had never been covered by social security. That important fact gave Mr. Hampton the key to selling his client a $200,000 building which was the sole asset of the corporation that owned it. The client would buy the corporation and then act as building manager at a salary of $400 a month, enough to entitle him (and his wife) to social security benefits when he reached 72. This would give him the security of a steady present income, plus an element of future security that he lacked.

Prospect likes idea but hesitates. The deal looked good and after consultation with his attorney, the prospect was almost ready to close. But he was still worried about the $25,000 down payment he had to make.

Security benefits still stressed. The real estate firm solved this difficulty. It agreed to buy the property from the client after he had made himself eligible for social security benefits—provided he wanted to sell. The purchase price in this case would be $25,000 (giving the client his investment back), with $10,000 down and the balance in payments of $100 or more per month.

Sale is made. The client received what he wanted—security. Mr. Hampton earned a nice commission. The deal was made possible because the salesman met the prospect's biggest need—security.

>>>COMMENT→ Here was a creative idea thought up by associating the prospect's need with a knowledge of the social security law.

¶ 1037 **Carry in an idea—carry out an order**

Every time you call on a prospect, carry in an idea for his benefit. It will improve your chances of walking out with the order.

Brad Thomas, a New York salesman, adopted this plan, and it worked. He began getting orders from prospects who before, had given him only excuses. As a result, his sales record climbed!

Reason: Business thrives on ideas. Businessmen welcome ideas, and whenever a salesman comes along who carries sound ideas that his prospect can use, he gets the prospect's ear, he gets his confidence, and he gets his *business*.

What kind of ideas can you use? "I use just the common garden variety of ideas—nothing special," says Thomas. "One time, I carried in an idea to a dealer for a combination sale, combining our goods with a related item. Another time, it was an idea for a window display. But always, it's an idea which is in my prospect's interest."

>>>WHAT TO DO→ Follow this three-point formula to make *yourself* an idea-producing salesman:

1. *Spend a few minutes a day thinking about how you could improve your business for your prospects.* You don't have to come up with original ideas every time; sometimes the best ideas are the "oldtimers" which you revise and adapt. Keep looking all the time.

2. *When you get an idea you think will work, live with it for a few days before you spring it on your customer.* There's hardly anything prospects resent more than entertaining half-baked, impractical ideas. Work yours out thoroughly before you spring them.

selling more to your present customers

3. Present your idea briefly and clearly and be prepared to defend it against attack if need be. If you know an idea forwards and backwards, you can defend it no matter how bitterly it is assailed.

¶ 1038 Showing customer how to use product helps to upgrade him

"Stepping up" a customer to a higher-priced product is often a by-product of seeing that the customer is getting full value from what he bought. In discovering that a customer is not using the product properly, you might discover that his needs have changed and that a higher-priced product will serve him better.

¶ 1039 Show the loss entailed in excessive splitting of business

Savings on transportation costs through quantity buying is often a convincing reason for getting a customer to increase his order. This is especially true if the customer wants to divide his business among a larger number of suppliers than is necessary for safety. Here's one salesman's response to the customer who says, "We prefer to divide our business."

"That is a very charitable way of looking at it. Still, you wouldn't open your purse and give your money away, just to be sporting, would you? For instance, instead of buying in carload lots at carload bulk discounts, you are donating 7% to charity when you split up the same business between say four suppliers, and pay the case price. On your requirements for next month that would mean a loss of $163.14."

¶ 1040 Assume responsibility, based on confidence and knowledge

The big buyer is self-confident and invariably looks for self-confidence in salesmen who approach him. He wants to do business with a salesman who knows thoroughly what he is selling, who considers the prospect's requirements as paramount, and who is not afraid to assume responsibility.

▶ **IDEA IN ACTION** Morton Howitzer had his mind set to do business with a big contractor. He got the architect's specifications for a contemplated project and upon examination found some items specified that were comparable to those handled by his firm.

After requesting a copy of the plan so that he could estimate the quantity required, he introduced himself to the contractor and explained that while his company's products were not specified he had taken the privilege of estimating the quantities of materials that the contractor could use.

The contractor requested the figures and the salesman told him the quantities that would be shipped if the order were accepted.

"No," said the contractor. "You have estimated too much. You are like all of the salesmen that come around. They try to oversell on the job."

Morton gathered that the contractor was looking for someone to take responsibility for the quantities involved so that he would not be caught with materials on hand that he could not return. He therefore said emphatically, "No! My quantities are correct." He then mentioned the dimensions of the building and computed the number of square feet in the area.

"If this order is based on my computation, I will accept full responsibility for the amount ordered," said Morton.

The contractor signed the order, saying, "I have turned down the other salesmen because they had no confidence in their own figures and would not accept responsibility for quantities."

¶ 1041 "User calls" help you sell more to present customers

Many good salesmen make the mistake of not developing to the fullest the possibilities of increasing the business they do with their present customers. They fail to make the necessary "user calls" that are essential to stepping up a customer's purchases.

If yours is the kind of product that can be stepped up, you have much to gain by making "user" calls a regular part of your selling activities.

>>>**IMPORTANT**→ A follow-up call after an industrial sale is the responsibility of the salesman who got the order. It's the first "user call." During the call, he must make certain that the customer got what he was sold; that price, shipping data, method of shipment, terms, and the like, were carried out as promised. If he fails to do this, he stands a chance of losing his customer.

▶ *Some gains from user calls.* Among the many advantages of following up a user of your product are these:

• You see your product in use and can check up to make sure that it is giving satisfaction. Many a customer has been lost because the product that was sold was not used properly. A simple bit of instruction, a slight adjustment, or a little extra technical assistance might have saved these customers.

• You gain the goodwill of the customer and the employees who are concerned with your product.

• You build the basis for repeat business without going through all of the steps of selling.

• You clear the atmosphere if the customer is harboring any resentment about unsatisfactory previous purchases (from you or a previous salesman), poor service, or other complaints that he may or may not have registered with your company. By nipping the hostility in the bud, you save the account. If you do more than the customer might expect—like getting him a credit, refund, replacement, or other adjustment—you build up his goodwill and lay the groundwork for increased sales.

• You avert customer dissatisfaction before it arises.

• You pick up information that starts you thinking of the customer's needs for more of what you have to sell.

➤➤SUGGESTION➤ Plan your user calls to occur at regular intervals. Some of your customers might deserve weekly calls, others bi-weekly calls, or monthly or quarterly calls. When you can't meet your schedule, write a letter to your customer, or telephone him, to show that you are thinking of his interests.

If you sell an industrial product, regular service calls must be made to protect your customer's investment in you and your product and to assure repeat business from him. Timing the calls depends upon the amount of service demanded and the number of customers to be covered.

➤➤CAUTION➤ Do not confuse service calls with sales calls. The purpose of a service call is to render service. Although repeat sales will often result from service calls, you should let your customer bring up the subject of buying at these times.

¶ 1042 **Information picked up on user calls leads to more sales**

Every call on a customer should be thought of as the beginning of the next sale. With this thought in mind, you are bound to keep alert to new selling opportunities.

▶ **IDEA IN ACTION** Salesman Frost made a user call on a hospital and found that a new director had been appointed. He was the man who would have to be "sold" in the future. Frost used the call to get acquainted and incidentally pointed out that he had observed the increase in the hospital's activities. The interview ended in the sale of additional hospital equipment.

▶ **IDEA IN ACTION** While making a user call, the purchasing agent told salesman Denberg that the company was building a new plant in New Jersey. He asked the purchasing agent who was in charge of the project. The lead opened the way to additional sales.

▶ **IDEA IN ACTION** The first clue to a customer's need for more of salesman Atkin's product was discovered on a user call. Operators said they were overloaded with work. However, this was not sufficient evidence of the need for additional equipment. On the next user call he learned that the increase in business was requiring overtime. Later he was told that an independent contractor was being used to relieve the operators. Now he had sufficient information to justify making an "approach" call to the right man, and he was able to make the sale.

¶ 1043 **How to walk out of a buyer's office without tripping over the welcome mat**

Make sure the welcome mat is always out for you when you leave a buyer's office. This holds true whether you've just landed your first order, a big order, a small one, or whether the buyer turned you down, stalled, or promised a big order soon.

Reason: In order to sell this buyer again or for the first time, you must get back into his office. It's as basic as that.

Here are some typical situations showing how top producers say "good-bye" while in the next breath say, "I'll see you soon."

(1) First order. Any salesman is happy to open a new account, but he also knows that repeat business means profits. Here's how you could make certain that you'll get a chance to sell your new customer again:

"Mr. Jones, I have enjoyed talking with you and I appreciate this order. Maybe it's out of line, but I want to tell you how I see this order.

"You will be getting acquainted with my product in use, and I have found through experience with it that it can do a fine job of talking for itself. But, it's up to me to back up

selling more to your present customers

the product by giving you the kind of service you have every right to expect.

"If I can do that, I believe that I can look forward to many years of mutually pleasant and profitable business association with you."

(2) The promise. Here your big job is to make that promise come true. Here's one way of handling the "promiser:"

"Thanks a lot, Mr. Jones. With some people promises mean very little, but I know you mean it about this. (At this stage it's a good idea to apply a little pressure. Read what the salesman now does).

"About when would you like me to come back and finalize this—or will you just be mailing the order in? Fine. I'll tell Miss ———— to be watching for it so your order will get fast handling. Thanks again."

(3) The stall. It's up to the salesman to make sure the prospect keeps you in mind. You might try this tactic:

"Thanks a lot, Mr. Smith, for listening to my presentation. Naturally, you want to check the market to get the best deal available. You'll be getting information from several sources. Undoubtedly, some questions will pop into your mind as you look further into this.

"I certainly want to work with you to get everything squared away. I'll be in to see you on Monday, the 25th, so we can go over the ground more thoroughly." (Here again, a little pressure was used which the salesman announced when he would be back.)

(4) The turndown. You can either walk out annoyed and kiss the buyer good-bye, or you can handle the turndown like this:

"Mr. Jones, I want to say that you have treated me with courtesy and consideration. Although I didn't get this order, it was a pleasing and rewarding contact.

"I'll tell you frankly that I am looking forward to the time when I can merit your business because, whenever possible, a man likes to do business with a person he can respect."

¶ 1044 A special service turns a small account into a big one

Maybe you are getting a small share of a customer's total buying requirements because of the location of your firm. A customer often favors nearer suppliers because he assumes that nearness is essential for service. The nearby suppliers, taking for granted that proximity gives them a hold on the account, may become lax in rendering service. By giving your customer better service than your competitors you can become the favored supplier.

▶ **IDEA IN ACTION** Four competitive suppliers were selling cartons to a large manufacturer. Three of them were near the manufacturer and the fourth, whom Charles Boland represented, was some distance away.

The manufacturer was angling for a ¼ million dollar contract. If he could reduce the cost of the packaging, he was sure he could win that contract. So the manufacturer asked the nearby carton suppliers to help him solve the problem. After waiting a reasonable time without getting the service he wanted, the manufacturer presented the problem to Charles Boland.

Charles had been on the lookout for just such an opportunity to serve the manufacturer. If he could beat the competitors in finding a solution, he knew he'd get more of the manufacturer's carton business.

Charles and his carton designer worked around the clock to redesign the manufacturer's carton. By cutting out part of the inner packing, they came up with a carton that served perfectly and cost less. Charles was in the manufacturer's plant bright and early the next morning with a sample of the redesigned carton.

The manufacturer got his ¼ million dollar contract and Charles got the carton order. This was only the beginning of a steady increase in the volume of business he brought in from this manufacturer.

¶ 1045 Successful repeat sales may depend on your knowing top executives

Business with your customer may be going along nicely enough until, one day, you drop in and the executive with whom you have been dealing is no longer there. A stranger is at his desk. This new man may not feel too friendly toward your firm. He may have ideas of his own as to whom to buy from and it may look like a long, long pull to get the account back on your side.

To prepare against such an emergency, it may be wise to get to know your customer's top officials at the time you open the account.

▶ **IDEA IN ACTION** Don Stark, who sells advertising remembrance products, follows the practice of becoming acquainted with the top personnel of his customers, when he opens a new account. He says to the sales manager—the executive who usually makes the buying decision for his product:

"Bill, you know my firm builds a fine mantailored line of greetings for the exclusive use of business firms and executives. I know your president and many of the officers of your company use a greeting of some kind at the holiday season and it is important to keep those friendly contacts. We sell our distinctive line of greetings exclusively to businessmen as a personal service and it occurred to me that some of your officers would like to take advantage of making selections from our line. If you will introduce me, I will be only too glad to show them our line. It would be a pleasure for me to do so."

¶ 1046 **"Easy-to-sell" items can open the way to bigger orders**

If there are "easy-to-sell" items in your product list, you might apply the slogan of Brown & Bigelow, creators of remembrance advertising products: "Reach for the greetings (the easy-to-sell product) instead of your hat." The slogan is a reminder that you can't make big money by sticking to the easy-to-sell items, but you can use them to make each interview count. Also, you can use them to open the way for a later sale of the more expensive item that you could not sell before you turned to the easy-to-sell one.

¶ 1047 **Work with the credit manager to get the "edge"**

Today when it's especially important to increase sales, a salesman must strive to get every edge he possibly can.

One way to get the "edge" is to set up an exchange of information between himself and his company's credit manager. A salesman should keep this in mind:

A good credit executive is more than a finance specialist—he's also a contributing member of a sales team. While his chief concern is making sound credit decisions, it also involves—

(1) Evaluating sales territories;
(2) Using credit to boost sales; and
(3) Promoting customer relations.

Cooperation in these areas is essential, for the maximum effectiveness of both credit and sales.

⇒**WHAT TO DO→** Review credit agency reports with the credit exec. This will help you keep abreast of changes in your territory. It could also provide valuable insight on individual customers and prospects.

For example, if there's only favorable information on a particular prospect, you can go ahead and make your contact, just as you've planned. But if possible credit problems turn up, you may feel that your time would be better spent on some other prospect.

Naturally, no salesman will want to plunge into a sales campaign, and line up orders—only to find them turned down by his credit department. So this "groundwork" helps you avoid wasted time and effort. Besides, the company gets this—

⇒**ADDED BENEFITS→** The usual agency report is far less expensive than the usual sales call. This makes the agency report —instead of just an expense—an actual tool for savings.

And there's another reason to keep track of accounts this way. Suppose a credit executive finds that a customer's sales have been steadily increasing. He and the salesman for the account should then review the ledger card —and the salesman's own sales figures.

Why? To find out if their company has participated in the customer's growth. Information on a customer's increased sales (and presumed increased purchases) might well trigger an early sales call—long before the salesman's normal routine would require it.

Today, many firms are increasing their earnings simply by concentrating on the production of salable goods—and by finding new uses they can be put to. Here, the astute credit man's knowledge of a particular sales territory —and of industrial developments in it—can be especially valuable.

For example, if his own company supplies steel sheets used in the manufacture of lawn mowers, it will be interested in knowing about lawn mower manufacturers who also make snowblowers. A changed sales approach based on this kind of information could well result in some customer categories being changed from *"seasonal"* to *"year round."*

¶ 1048 **Use credit to build sales**

A credit manager can be a big help to the salesman when it comes to checking out credit ratings. A credit exec can tell when the ratings should be *strictly followed,* when they should be *adjusted*—or even *disregarded.*

The following example illustrates how cooperation between the salesman and the credit exec enabled a salesman to boost sales:

how to move up to bigger buyers

➤➤➤IDEA IN ACTION→ A firm had developed a $20,000 line of credit with a supplier —less than that offered by competitors, but all that the buying pattern seemed to warrant. Then the credit manager, reviewing trade reports and other information on file, noted the customer's steady growth—in sales, financial position, and number of employees. So he decided that the line of credit could be increased to $40,000—and notified sales of his decisions.

Result: The salesman was able to make a new and stronger presentation to the customer —strong enough to nail down some added sales, and eliminate some of the competition.

Credit and customer relations. The salesman and the credit exec can work together in another area—customer relations. For example, a good credit man realizes that it's a simple matter to write to the top executive of a good account, thanking him for his firm's prompt payment record, and looking forward to further dealings with him. Few suppliers bother with this knid of "unnecessary" gesture —but it's one that can create tremendous good will.

➤➤➤WHAT TO DO→ Make sure these letters get written. A simple reminder to the credit man should do the trick *(For related article, see ¶ 2066.)*

How to move up to bigger buyers

¶ 1051 You can move up to bigger buyers

You must move up to bigger buyers if your objective is to be a high-income salesman. You must feel that no company is too big, and no single individual is too important, for you to sell to. You can feel that way because *it takes no more ability to sell a big buyer than a small one.* It may take more perseverance, more creative thinking, more planning of particular sales. It does not take a greater knowledge of selling techniques than you need for everyday successful selling.

Follow three simple rules, and you will be able to face any big buyer, big executive, or person of prominence with as much ease as you would your own brother.

1. *Don't be afraid!* Some salesmen are relegated to the status of small producers because they don't have the courage to talk to big people. There's no place where courage pays off as magnificently as it does in approaching a high-caliber prospect. Before you tackle him, however, you must have complete knowledge of your product, faith in it and in your company, and skill in applying the selling strategies explained in this Guide. Once you have these bases for complete assurance, you are ready to . . .

2. *Get calling on big people.* Jump right in and begin to call on important prospects. After a few successful interviews your fear will be completely dissipated. But first,

3. *Be fully prepared for each interview.* Have a profitable idea to offer your "big prospect." The Big Idea is bound to interest him because it means profit or benefits for him particularly. The Big Idea stems out of your product knowledge and what you learn about your prospect before you go in for the interview.

¶ 1052 A simple plan for selling to bigger buyers

Doing business with bigger buyers is largely a matter of intelligent prospecting and comparing potentials of prospects in different categories.

In almost all lines of business, the market comprises several groups of prospects. In each of these groups there may be little, medium-sized, and big-potential prospects. Thus, in planning a work schedule, you must cope with two problems: (1) which groups in the market are most lucrative; (2) who are the big-potential prospects in the lucrative groups. You must tackle both prongs of the problem for the most profitable investment of your time.

▶ IDEA IN ACTION The territory assigned to Frank Elbert, who sells business systems and forms, contains more potential business than one man can cover. Frank must analyze the business in his territory and determine which markets offer the best opportunity for commissions.

In Frank's business there are these categories of buyers: wholesale, manufacturing, retail, financial, and professional men. He studies the potential existing in each and finds that a good time allotment plan is 50% industrial, 35% wholesale and retail, and 15% miscellaneous.

In each of these categories Frank analyzes the potential business which may be secured from an account and then invests his time commensurate with the volume of buying he can expect. He knows, for example, that any good retailer or wholesaler should use from $300 to $1,000 of his products per year. In the portion of his time that he spends with wholesalers and retailers, he concentrates on prospects with at least that potential. He doesn't waste time with prospects who can't buy more than $100 or $200 worth a year.

Frank is always alert to changes in business conditions in the various industries that he serves. He knows that some are hit harder than others at different seasons or are more sensitive than others to changes in the business cycle. When business falls off among certain customers and prospects, his sales to them will fall off. So he adjusts his efforts to spend less time among the temporarily depressed businesses and uses that time in selling to businesses that are enjoying good times.

⟩⟩⟩WARNING→ Being selective in reaching for big buyers does not mean concentrating all your efforts on only a few large accounts. It's exceedingly dangerous to make that mistake. The loss of one account can mean the loss of a substantial share of business and earnings in the territory. A territory composed of a distribution of accounts, both large and medium but profitable, is a stable territory and is affected little by the loss of a few accounts.

¶ 1053 **Know how your customers are faring**

Business is a dynamic venture. Some little fellows become big because they are in a growing industry and have a vigorous, progressive management. Big customers get bigger for the same reasons, or something happens and they begin to go downhill.

Eternal vigilance is the price of success in keeping your customer list properly balanced with a good proportion of big buyers. You must know how your customers are faring.

⟩⟩⟩WHAT TO DO→ 1. Keep your eyes and ears open when you call on customers and cover your territory.

2. Watch your sales records of customer buying. If a big buyer's orders keep declining over a period of time, look for the reason. Has the man at the helm become incapacitated? Has there been a change of management? Is the business suffering from inroads made by competition? Should you go after the business of the competitor who is causing your customer's business to slough off?

3. When a worthwhile account begins to deteriorate, and you no longer get value commensurate with the time you devote to it, consider adjusting your time

4. When a medium-sized buyer's record reflects vigorous growth of the customer, make the most of the added potential.

¶ 1054 **A well-built plan of sale gets a big buyer to order**

A well-built plan of sale, centered around a big creative idea from which a customer will profit, is a sure-fire way of making sales to big buyers. Planning such a sale means thinking through the entire proposal, and doing preliminary work, often leg work and research. But once this groundwork is laid, the salesman has no trouble getting the prospect's attention, arousing his interest, creating desire, convincing the prospect, and closing the sale.

▶ **IDEA IN ACTION** A part of the philosophy of Jonathan Simms, star salesman of remembrance advertising products, is to work out carefully an advertising program that will give the customer the fullest benefits from the idea used. His big sale of calendars to a large progressive bank was built around the idea of getting the bank's calendar into the home of every Boy Scout and Cub Scout. The actual distribution of the calendars would be handled by the Scouts and Scout officials, thus completely solving the distribution problem for the bank.

To accomplish this sale, Simms planned and took several steps before he approached the bank officials. When he was fully prepared, he presented the program to the bank and made the sale.

The plan that made the sale is sketched below. Simms—

• Made several personal calls on Boy Scout executives in the area of the bank.

• Learned from the Boy Scout executives the districts into which the area was divided and which districts did not have Boy Scout calendar coverage.

• Discovered that there were 5 districts or councils where the Boy Scout calendars could be placed.

• Obtained a large map of the city and outlying areas and pasted stars on this map, each one representing a meeting place for Scouts.

• Got the total number of Scouts and Cub Scouts in these councils, which gave him an accurate number of calendars needed.

• Called on the bank officials and presented the idea of putting the name of the bank into the home of every Boy Scout and Cub Scout in the area for the year. The name of the bank would be connected with the Boy Scout movement. With the hang-up calendar the bank would build identity and prestige.

• When he sat down with the bank officials to decide where their area of greatest influence would be and how many calendars would be required to get complete Scout coverage, Simms laid out his specially prepared map and membership figures before his prospects.

The planning and presentation not only made the sale of 7,000 calendars for home coverage but opened up ideas for expanding the coverage to include the schools and churches where the troops and dens meet.

Breaking into big selling through better time-planning

¶ 1061 **How you use your time means everything**

No salesman—no matter how skilled—can attain a high degree of success in his work unless he has learned, and put into effect, the practices that make for the sound utilization of time.

These practices are discussed in the following paragraphs. They show how to time each call to mesh, as far as possible, with the individual prospect's or buyer's own preference and work habits. They explain how to time call-backs so that a "hot" prospect is not called back on too late and a repeat call is not made too soon on a "lukewarm" prospect.

Also in this section are guides for eliminating "peak and valley" selling, as well as ideas for accomplishing immediate and long-term goals through the best use of time.

In addition to the planning techniques covered here, there are others in this Guide for gaining selling time through proper self-management. These are discussed at ¶ 8042 et seq.

¶ 1062 **Two ways to plan your calls to save time**

Calls can be planned in two ways depending on whether you are in "fixed route" selling or in "no route" selling. Your category will determine whether you plan your calls by using *route sheets* or *follow-up records*.

▶ *Plan for "fixed route" salesmen.* The salesman who calls back on each of his customers once each week usually makes his calls in a fixed sequence, calling on each buyer on the same day at approximately the same hour. The same pattern prevails for salesmen who call once a month or at any other stated interval.

Planning your work in such circumstances is a relatively simple task, consisting of making a *route sheet* [¶ 9056] which will permit you to see as many customers in the least amount of travel time as possible. Be sure to include the following provisions, however:

• Provide time to call on new prospects who have started in business or moved into your territory.

• Find new customers to replace those who have moved out or stopped buying for some other reason.

• Adjust for buyers' vacations or other similar interferences with the normal call pattern.

• Pay proper attention to "special matters" such as a rush order or some other unusual request or situation that you must act on yourself. For instance, inform customers of an important price change, new products, or any other developments. Use these news items to increase sales, as shown at ¶ 1047.

▶ *Plan for "no route" salesmen.* If you do not work on a fixed route involving calls at brief intervals, the *follow-up record* will keep you best informed at the least expense of time and trouble. This system involves nothing more than filling out a 3" x 5" index card for each prospect. Here is a typical card.

June 12, 19—
Woods Mfg. Co.
Mr. Grumback, Office Mgr.

Not interested now, but may need a #264 calculator in about 60 days. Best time to call is before noon. Could use a #600 but won't spend that much.

              Follow-up Aug. 20

Now for the key to this system. File your card under "August 20." The next step occurs on or about that date. You call on this customer, without making another card, and simply add the following:

    Aug. 20—Grumback on vacation
           F/U Aug. 28

On that date the following notations are added:

Aug. 28—saw Grumback. He will try to get a purchase order put through. Telephone him 2 p.m., Aug. 29

The final note in this case might be:

¶1062

Aug. 29—Ordered one #264.
F/U About Jan. 1 to see
if he needs other items—
they are expanding.

Note the advantages of this follow-up record system:

• Eliminates all need to rely on your memory.

• Does away with all need to *rewrite* data once recorded.

• Provides a healthy stream of call-backs on customers you have qualified as meriting a further call.

• Provides a constant, fool-proof source of definite appointments.

• Makes you decide and record immediately after each call the data you will find useful on your call-back, and the specific time when each call-back should be made.

File each card so that it will again "come up" on the date you select as the appropriate one.

⟫OBSERVATION→ You will find more suggested forms for planning calls at ¶ 9053 et seq.

¶ 1063 How to find the best time to call on customers in a new territory

The salesman in a new territory has no way of foretelling whether his prospect will be "too busy" the first time he calls.

A method to help you overcome this situation immediately and prevent its recurrence in future calls is given in the "idea in action."

IDEA IN ACTION Bob Gray represents a distributor of radio and television receivers. He calls on retail dealers.

Bob is transferred from Ohio to Massachusetts. His customer records for the new territory give him names, addresses, and the past buying record of each account.

On the day he starts out on his new assignment, Bob makes his first call at 9:20 a.m. He has selected an important account—a dealer with five branch stores.

"Mr. Cantrell is busy right now," says the receptionist to Bob. "He'll be tied up for another hour or so."

Most salesmen would say, "Well, I'll make another stop and then call back." But not Bob—he has a better method.

"Can you tell me," he asks the receptionist, "what is usually the best time of day to call on Mr. Cantrell?"

"Right after lunch," comes the reply. "Mr. Cantrell is rarely free mornings, but he tries to save afternoons for salesmen and other callers."

Bob thanks the receptionist, and immediately makes a note on his customer record: "Call only after lunch."

At about 1:45 Bob returns. He gets not only an interview but a good sized order.

"Mr. Cantrell," says Bob, as he is about to leave, "I mentioned a promotion we're going to launch in about three weeks. As soon as I get the material to show you, I'd like to stop by. Would you prefer to have me telephone you for an appointment, or shall I just drop in?"

"Well, Mr. Gray," says the customer, "you needn't phone in advance. Just make it in the afternoon—any day except Friday."

Bob now has two more clues to help in his timing. He adds to his notation, "Needn't phone—but don't call on Fridays."

By the time Bob has made his first swing around his territory, he has "timing" notes on practically every account.

Because he has taken the trouble to find out about his customers' habits and preferences, Bob has accomplished these two important things: (1) To a very great extent, he avoids calling at the *wrong* time; (2) enough of his customers prefer to see salesmen either early in the morning or late in the day, so that Bob can always plan to "sell" from at least 9 a.m. to 5:30 p.m.

¶ 1064 How you can double the working day and get to your goal faster

A good planner works up a call schedule for a long enough period in advance to assure high-goal earnings over the period. He then follows up with a day-to-day plan, making each day count for two, that enables him to keep pace with his long-term plan.

IDEA IN ACTION Bill Graham sells a printed business Service on a subscription basis. He earns at least $25,000 a year because he's one of the best planners in the sales organization.

During Christmas week Bill blocked out the next 60 working days. Into each block he inserted, according to his itinerary, his four best prospects for the day. He then added 4 renewal prospects who could use an additional Service (this he determined by servicing the account). He therefore had 8 prospects each and every day for 60 days. His goal was to close 2 orders a day, or 3, and why not with such planning?

Further, Bill subscribes to the order-a-day

breaking into big selling through better time-planning

philosophy. But he makes each of the 60 working days count for 2 days. This he does by dividing each block into two parts. Thus he creates *120 theoretical working days*. He then attempts to make one sale for each theoretical working day, and gets his minimum of 2 orders a day.

"This plan," says Bill, "is not difficult to do with the prospects aligned according to plan. I live with my philosophy over the three-month period (the current month and the two months planned ahead). If I blank one day I know the sales of big-priced units will make up the dollar volume I want."

¶ 1065 **How to avoid "peak and valley" selling**

A period of low or perhaps literally no productivity could undermine all but the strongest salesman. When the valleys are hit, morale tends to sag. The salesman begins to wonder whether he has "lost his touch." He begins to question whether his line and his territory are to blame. Indeed, the combination of financial hardship during the "slumps" and low morale may cause a man to quit his job—and in some cases to drop selling as a career. Such slumps usually follow a period of high productivity.

The first idea in action shows how the slump happens; the second shows how it's avoided.

▶ **IDEA IN ACTION** Mike Milford sells space in a well known trade magazine. Since there are no important seasonal factors involved, his selling pace should be a reasonably steady one. Actually, however, Mike's record is one of "feast or famine."

The explanation for this is really rather simple. When Mike finds, as he periodically does, that he has "warmed up" a number of prospects whom he expects to close shortly, he concentrates his full attention on them, thus neglecting to do the prospecting and spade-work needed to locate prospects whom he might close at a later date.

In due course Mike gets a "Yes" or "No" from each of his fully warmed-up prospects. The orders he gets makes a rather impressive total, and he writes off the failure with the remark, "You can't sell them all."

At this particular point Mike is in the position of having had a fine month's business, with correspondingly high income. Hence he isn't at all concerned when, for the next couple of weeks, he fails to close a sale.

When two weeks stretch into four, however, Mike begins to get jittery. True, he has warmed up a few new prospects during this four-week period, but they aren't ready to be closed yet. Since Mike begins to feel himself under some pressure at this point, he tries to "rush" them into buying. When he finds that won't work, his morale begins to drop.

"Five weeks with only two quarter-page sales," says Mike to himself, "and I've got to sell two pages a week to make a living!" Wryly he recalls the extra bill he ran up some six weeks ago, when all those big contracts broke, one right after another!

Much as he dislikes doing it, Mike asks his sales manager for an advance. "Got some nice things lined up that will break any day, Mr. Davids," says Mike. "I've just had some tough breaks the last five weeks, that's all. You know, Mr. Davids, that for about a month I was going great-guns. Then, wham! It ended just like that!"

Mr. Davids knows all about it, of course. He also knows that all this could have been avoided had Mike Milford only *paced* his warming-up efforts more evenly.

▶ **IDEA IN ACTION** Neal Sloan also sells space in a trade magazine. Several years ago, during a slump, he decided that if he couldn't somehow avoid "feast and famine" selling he'd change his job.

His solution was simple. "I need two pages a week as a minimum. Well, that means I ought to have four 'hot' prospects lined up all the time.

"And in order to do that, I'm going to make it an ironclad rule to spend every Tuesday and every Friday doing *nothing but* making 'warm up' calls on *cold* prospects. That will leave three days each week—plenty of time to nurse along those who are about ready to buy. And if this plan works out the way I think it will, I'll always have at least a little backlog of 'hot' prospects—instead of a record-breaking month sandwiched in between two *heart-breaking* months."

Neal's plan worked well, except when once or twice he violated his self-established rule about reserving two days *each* week for locating and warming up prospects, most of whom he couldn't close until some weeks later.

⇒**WHAT TO DO**→ Every salesman who does not have a fixed route should consider with care how he can best apply the above rule in his own work. Some men find that it pays them to devote every morning to prospecting and "warming up," thus limiting the closing efforts to the afternoon hours. Others reverse the order. Still others find a different application most suitable. The point is, of course, that you can eliminate "peak and valley" selling in almost every instance if you will so arrange your work that there is a relatively *constant* stream—rather than an intermittent one—of prospects moving up the ladder from "cold" to "hot."

¶ 1066 **How to lengthen the seasonal selling period**

If yours is a seasonal business in which the major proportion of your sales is made in a concentrated period, you gain volume by lengthening the season. The method used by one creative salesman, described below, is adaptable to most lines.

▶ **IDEA IN ACTION** Following a seasonal pattern in his trade, Al Denton sold hard from April 10 to June 15, booking orders for merchandise to be delivered to retailers late in August. In those ten weeks he had to book practically all of his year's business.

Al began to look at his limited selling period as a problem. He thought, how can I stretch the normal 10-week season into 12 weeks? If I call on the average retailer as early as April 1, he will tell me it's too early. If I call as late as June 25, he'll tell me he's all bought up.

Having stated the problem, Al then moved on to find a solution. His creative thinking led to a successful plan:

• He selected the names of five retailers who gave him the biggest orders and called on them a week ahead of the traditional date. He had no trouble in getting them to place orders because the line meant a lot to them.

• He called on other accounts ahead of the season and convinced them, by showing them the five big orders he had, that there was nothing to be gained by waiting.

• If the strategy didn't work, he would say, "Mr. Lane, I guess that since you prefer to buy considerably later in the season, I won't be too late if I call back on you, say, about June 15 or June 20?"

⟫REMEMBER⟶ This salesman recognized that his customers have buying habits. Some were, or could be made, "early" buyers; others were by inclination "late" buyers. With these facts at his command, it was easy to plan his way around obstacles.

¶ 1067 **Put these power-packed techniques to work for you**

Make every day a winner—both at home and while selling—by adopting and following three easy but effective work-and-living techniques. The results could amaze you. Instead of "coasting" you'll think you're on a roller-coaster as your life takes on added dynamism.

Beef up self confidence with self-promises

Every salesman knows he has to rely on others. This includes the customer who says "he'll buy" to the man in shipping who says "the order will go out by the 15th."

And the same holds true for the salesman's relationship to himself. If you know you can rely on yourself to do the things that must be done, you can be sure they will be done.

⟫WHAT TO DO⟶ (1) Make a special promise—to yourself. (2) Write this promise down. (3) Carry out the promise for 10 days.

No promise too trivial: What you promise doesn't matter—it's the fact that you carry out this self-pledge that builds results. With every promise kept, you become more and more certain that you can count on yourself. You'll be building up a rock-like source of inner strength. Here's—

A case in point: An experienced salesman had no trouble with his steady customers—and when he got a lead, he usually nailed down the sale, too. But he lost his zest for making cold calls. He found himself disliking the idea of walking in cold. So he made this—

⟫WRITTEN PROMISE⟶ "For the next two weeks, I will make at least one cold call a day. I will fight the urge to see only my 'sure' customers." He kept his promise, and he also—

Built up moral muscle: "Every time I made a cold call, I could feel a definite inner strengthening. There was something physical about it."

Prime the pump of new ideas

Here's a result-getting, yet easy way, a salesman can come up with more good ideas in a week than most people produce in a year. It's based on the mind's unlimited potential for creating new ideas.

⟫WHAT TO DO⟶ Take 10 minutes a day to jot down lists of ideas on subjects that interest you: How to increase your income, possible new uses for your company's products, new selling techniques, etc.

⟫REMEMBER⟶ Don't get discouraged if results aren't immediate. At this stage, you're just getting the ball rolling. Your mind is now getting started on the process of showing you significant new relationships you haven't seen before.

Case in point: One salesman felt he wasn't getting all the sales he could from his territory.

He jotted down three ideas to improve his sales situation. (1) Make the first sales call 15 minutes earlier than usual: (2) List reasons why some companies turned him down; and (3) Read company ads with an eye to getting fresh ideas.

⇒PROFIT-BOOSTING RESULT→ He went from "turned down" to "turned on." He realized that his "no sales" were because he didn't have anything new to say. He was giving the same old tired presentation. Once he perked up his presentation, sales started to come.

Bring your buried talents out in the open

A salesman may be able to turn up an ability within himself that he hardly even knew existed. You only have to do a little spade-work on possible—

"Talent show-throughs": Every person can do something at which he's a "natural," but we too often tend to overlook the clues that reveal these abilities to us.

Case in point: A salesman used to make up advertising headlines as a hobby. He didn't think any more of it until some friends in advertising happened to see a few of the ads. His friends discovered how good they were. He now supplies different advertising outfits with lists of headline ideas—at a considerable profit to himself.

¶ 1068 **Plan the next day's work; the second step in your day's wind-up**

After you have reviewed and analyzed your selling performance for the day you are ready for your second wind-up activity—preparing for your next day's work.

⇒SUGGESTION→ You should not consider your workday finished until you have outlined a detailed work schedule for the next day. With a planned order of work your selling will become more efficient and effective and you will have made it possible to earn the full dollar value of your selling time.

To arrange your calls into an orderly, economical, and effective plan is not enough. You must also provide an alternative plan in the event that someone you expected to spend time with goes out of town, is at a meeting, becomes ill, or cannot see you for some other reason.

EXAMPLE: On a certain Monday you plan to make 10 calls, but find that one appointment scheduled from 10 to 11 o'clock cannot be kept by your prospect. However, you have provided yourself with half a dozen carefully selected call-cards for the vicinity. Had you not taken the precaution of these substitute calls you would have had to "kill" the hour or spend it making random calls. Instead, you are able to use your time fruitfully.

▶ *How to plan against uncontrollable forces.*

• Determine which customers you will call on. Remember to double-check for appointments and to refer to your "follow-up" file [¶ 1062]. (The number of customers you plan to see will depend largely on your estimate of how much time each interview will take as well as estimated total travel time.)

• Prepare several substitute calls for *each* customer to be called on. Be sure to choose alternatives located close to the customer you originally plan to see.

• Estimate how much time to allot to each. Know just where you will be each quarter hour of the day, and stick to this schedule.

• Decide upon an order of call which will take the least travel time. This means either arranging your calls into a continuous line which eliminates backtracking, or arranging them into groups determined by their proximity to one another.

▶ *How to plan a successful day's work.*

• Review the past records of the customers you are going to call on. This will help guide you in deciding what items you should suggest they buy, and in what quantities, colors, and so forth. See ¶ 9053.

• Refer to notes on your customer record card to see if there are any special matters you should take up with these accounts.

• Mentally "make each call" by rehearsing what you will do and say when you get there.

You should also plan to:

• Spend more of your time with profitable customers.

• Terminate your interviews when they can no longer be profitable. Customers will rob you of selling time by merely "chewing the fat." Learn to get away from these time-wasters as quickly, but politely, as you can.

• Set a daily goal for yourself. Goals provide you with an important stimulus for your day's work.

⇒REMEMBER→ A well-planned day always lines up the minimum number of cold-canvass calls necessary to maintain a steady pace of earnings. It lines up more than the minimum if you are striving to reach a higher goal.

Mature salesmanship

¶ 1071 New developments affect your selling

We are living in a dynamic world in which monumental changes that affect selling occur while you are not looking. You cannot be blamed for missing the new developments in all of the fields of human activity; you just don't have the time—and maybe not the interest—to keep up with the discoveries of the scientists and behavioral psychologists. But if you miss the impact of the developments as they touch your own behavior as a seller of goods or services, you can and will be blamed. You will feel the blame in lost orders.

⟫SUGGESTIONS→ 1. Check your present selling methods and beliefs against the modern yardsticks, explained in ¶ 1071-1088. This self-analysis will bring you up to date.

2. Have a healthy respect for your sales manager's constructive suggestions for better selling of your particular product or service. The modern sales manager alerts his sales force to improved selling techniques as they are developed. He watches for changes that influence buyers' attitudes. He finds out what is happening by reading the current publications in the sales field, by attending conferences of sales executives in all industries and exchanging ideas with them, by studying the total market picture, and by analyzing the reports of all the salesmen in the firm.

¶ 1072 The "natural born salesman" is a myth

When anyone says today that a man is a "natural born salesman" he is perpetuating a myth. The designation implies that the ability to sell is primarily a native one; that the person is a spell-binder. Actually, any normal person, *interested in selling,* can learn, and having learned, can practice selling successfully.

The spell-binder who cannot answer technical questions is quite likely to lose the order to a competing salesman who may have a less glib tongue but can demonstrate the worth and application of his product.

▶ **IDEA IN** Alfred Whiting is a "salesman of
ACTION the old school." He relies heavily on personality, hospitality, and the like to get the prospect to sign his name on the dotted line

Alfred complains that business isn't as good as it used to be. The truth is that the people he calls on buy 50% more of his type of product today than they did 20 years ago—but they buy most of it from *other* salesmen.

For Alfred continues to sell by being congenial, while his competitors devote the interview to showing charts, tables, analyses, reports and other data that buyers require for decision-making today.

Although he does not realize it, the world of buying and selling has left Alfred—and his like—behind.

¶ 1073 Don't over-sell yourself

Popularity and friendship are genuine assets in salesmanship. But the day is gone, if it ever really existed, when the salesman who got to the top was the one who did the best job of selling himself.

▶ **IDEA IN** Bill Albee covers New England,
ACTION calling on hardware wholesalers with a specialty line.

Although Bill has become friendly with many important buyers in the three years that he has called on them, he has not succeeded in opening as many new accounts as he had expected.

Several of Bill's competitors who have concentrated on *selling* rather than on building purely personal relationships are getting the very orders that Bill feels he has earned by three years of "cementing friendships."

If Bill really understood that the yardstick is, "How much does my action contribute to the successful completion of this particular sale," he would gear his thinking and activities *more* in terms of actual orders than in terms of friendly chats.

¶ 1074 A "prima donna" doesn't fit into today's selling

The modern salesman believes in and practices complete cooperation with his employer. He not only accepts supervision, but requests instruction and guidance. He participates in his company's sales meetings, and does all he can to make such an event succeed. He joins wholeheartedly in planned "drives," and pulls his weight in such contests as may be periodically proposed.

Today, each person must be a member of "the team" or make room for someone else who will join willingly and sincerely in the common effort.

mature salesmanship

¶ 1075 Buying and selling have become more businesslike

Buyers today favor the salesman from whom they can buy most profitably.

⇛REMEMBER→ The day of the salesman who went around handing out expensive cigars, slapping people on the back, entertaining lavishly, and telling a new crop of stories on each visit is definitely gone. It went out with the change in business organization from the small individually owned enterprise to the corporate setup. That's a long time ago, but some salesmen still act as though buyers prefer to buy from the "hail fellow, well met" rather than from the man who presents the most beneficial deal.

Of course, buyers are still human, and still susceptible to attention and flattery, to friendly gestures and to personal charm. But buyers are required by today's competitive conditions as well as by a change in ethical standards to treat the *social* as subordinate to the *business* components of their transactions. The sales interview is no longer a time of persuasion by spell-binding. It has become instead a time of persuasion by education. Facts have replaced jokes and irrelevant stories; information is now preferred to cigars.

¶ 1076 Everyone values time today

The pace of business and of living is faster today than in former years. Every salesman knows that, but not every salesman acts as though he knows it. It calls for conciseness in the sales presentation, for example. If you have not trimmed your sales presentation to take the minimum time necessary to interest and persuade your prospect, you haven't kept up with the changing pace of business.

¶ 1077 Old time persistence is not for you

The modern salesman recognizes that each call and each working hour must pay for itself or be recognized as a red figure operation that cuts proportionately into overall efficiency. The old-timer regarded persistence at any cost as a selling virtue.

Here are two letters that show the difference in the evaluation of persistence between a sales manager of, say, 20 years ago, and the executive leader of salesmen today:

Antiquated Viewpoint

Dear Sam:

My hearty congratulations on the fine job you have done in opening the Lamson account! We have been trying to sell these people for 20 years, I guess, and as you may know, some years ago I personally visited them to try to get them started.

I know that you have called on them every three months for almost 10 years. Now your persistence has been splendidly rewarded. Even though your opening order is for only 10 gross, you have finally cracked the ice and I know that you will get a lot of business from them.

Hats off to you! I only wish we had more salesmen who had the guts to keep on calling after being turned down cold for 10 years. If we had, we'd also have a lot more fine accounts like Lamson's on the books.

With congratulations and best wishes,

Willard Green

Live-wire Modern Viewpoint

Dear Sam:

In reviewing your reports I notice that there are about 20 accounts that you have been calling on for two years or more without getting any business.

As you know, Sam, each call you make represents an investment on your part and on the company's. Four calls a year on each of 20 prospects runs up into the impressive total of 80 calls. Since our men average about 4 calls a day, these 80 calls are costing you approximately 20 working days per year.

There are about 20 working days in the average month, so that this group of prospects is getting one-twelfth of your time and attention with absolutely no return. As a matter of fact, when you figure time out for vacations, holidays, sales meetings, and so forth, the percentage of your time really exceeds one-twelfth.

What correctives do you suggest for this situation? Unless you feel that you should try some other approach with these accounts, do you have any specific reason to believe that you can sell them within the near future? If not, I suggest that you drop them from your call list so that you can spend this valuable field time elsewhere, where you will get an adequate return.

Please let me hear from you on this within the next week or so.

With best wishes,

Willard Green

¶ 1078 Backdoor selling—Yes or No?

Nothing irritates a purchasing agent more than a salesman who by-passes him and sells directly to some other company official. Yet salesmen frequently point out that the only way they can make their sale is by just such "backdoor selling."

Here is what two executives who sit on opposite sides of the "backdoor selling" fence have to say about this problem:

▶ *Backdoor selling—No.* David B. White, Vice President of purchasing for a large manufacturing firm, says:

"When both buyer and seller carry out their respective responsibilities, it is almost never necessary for the saleman to by-pass the purchasing department to promote a sale.

Buying techniques change. "Many salesmen are not aware of the tremendous changes in buying that have taken place over the past 5 to 10 years. We just aren't buying the way we used to. Today's purchasing agent is doing his best to upgrade his knowledge of the products he buys; he's striving to improve his buying techniques, he attends schools and seminars, holds professional meetings at which he can exchange ideas with other PA's, searches his trade journals for new ideas, and visits suppliers' plants to study their products and meet their people.

⇛IMPORTANT→ "Furthermore, today most companies want their technical people in on the buying decision. Many have product teams, production and marketing people who jointly evaluate purchases. Where the purchasing man does not control the final decision—and there are many areas where he does not—he can and often does steer the salesman to the people who make the decisions.

"To purchase materials and services effectively, most companies have evolved a buying program based on four considerations:
• Is the seller recognized as a good company to do business with?
• Is it financially sound?
• Can it meet the job requirements and specifications (quantity, size, weight, speed, efficiency, delivery, etc.)?
• Is the price right, considering all factors, including the cost of possession?

"Obviously, the salesman who cares only how he stands in relation to price doesn't render us a service.

"The purchasing agent is hired to buy the right materials from the right company at the right time in the right quantity at the right price. He must justify every decision he makes in spending his company's money.

"The salesman who helps the PA buy wisely in this way, when profits are harder to come by, won't have to waste his selling time going around to the back door.

Is any backdoor selling "legitimate"? White admits that there are times that a salesman might have to use the back door. He says:

"Now it is true that there are some purchasing people who are incapable of judging the merits of a product. But a smart salesman knows how to handle them adroitly. If he feels he must by-pass a purchasing agent, he will do it tactfully and only after he has made every effort to sell through customary channels. I would call this legitimate backdoor selling.

"The purchasing profession is not proud of purchasers who arbitrarily set up roadblocks against salesmen, as I'm sure the selling profession is not proud of salesmen who arbitrarily by-pass purchasing agents who do their jobs well.

Key angle: We object to the salesman who by-passes the purchasing agent when he *hasn't* done a good job of selling him in the first place."

¶ 1079   **The other side of the coin**

▶ *Backdoor selling—Yes.* Don Roth, Sales Manager for a chemical products firm, points out:

"If backdoor selling means cultivating someone in addition to the purchasing agent, then I say that this is necessary most of the time. And if it means seeing someone other than the purchasing agent, I have to say that this is frequently necessary, too.

"Many purchasing agents are justified in their complaints of backdoor salesmanship. Some salesmen are poorly trained or inadequately supervised. But, there would be very little backdoor selling if:
• Purchasing agents always made it possible for salesmen to have their products fairly evaluated by whoever plays a part in the buying decision.
• Purchasing agents understood many problems in their own companies.
• Everyone in the PA's company didn't want to get into the act.

"Unfortunately, these conditions *do* exist.

"A recent report states that in both large and small companies purchasing agents themselves say that final acceptance of a product or service is not generally determined by them.

The problem: "I have found that in most companies top management participates in buying decisions even down to the very normal expenditures, and that production management has an important influence on purchases in from 30 to 70 percent of industrial companies.

"In companies using materials or services of a technical nature, the engineering department or laboratory usually makes the final evaluation and the recommendation to buy.

"In talking with many salesmen, I have learned that more than 50 percent of them believe that one out of five purchasing agents must be by-passed because of the PA's partiality for favored suppliers.

▶ *Salesman's strategy #1:* "To get business, these purchasing agents must be outflanked. A demand for the product must be created behind them. Nevertheless, when you get an order through the back door, it is still good practice to let the purchasing agent know you appreciate his cooperation.

▶ *Salesman's strategy #2:* "Where the salesman is faced with a purchasing agent who cannot evaluate the product properly because he does not have the necessary technical knowledge, the salesman's obvious move is to suggest that they both present the product to the man who will make the evaluation. If the purchasing agent does not give his permission, the salesman may *have to find* a back door to the laboratory or engineering department!

"But much more common is the purchasing agent who has no real buying authority but would rather die than admit it. Such a situation clearly calls for backdoor selling.

General rule: "I think the 'backdoor' rule for a salesman must be: Where possible, approach other buying influences in a company with the cooperation of the purchasing agent —or at least with his approval. But where this is not possible, use the back door. Many times, it is the only way in!"

¶ 1080   **Competition is a stimulant**

Competition is the motivating force of the private enterprise system; it is a stimulant of both business and men. You feel the impact and pressure of it in selling today just as men before you have felt it. But it is neither as ruthless nor as uncivilized as it was a few decades ago. In fact, competitors in most industries cooperate through their trade associations to promote the interest of everyone engaged in the industry.

⟫⟫SUGGESTION→ When you meet a competitor's salesman in a hotel, be aloof without being unfriendly. You might talk to him about developments that affect the entire industry, but when it comes to direct competition, be as smug as you can be. That attitude will reflect your conviction that your product is as good as, or better than, the product of the competitor.

Salesmen with absolute confidence in the superiority of their product have been known to make sales by actually boosting a competitive product. This procedure is not generally recommended, but the following story bears out the truth that confidence in the product can support dangerous selling at times.

▶ **IDEA IN ACTION** When a prospect dropped into a car showroom, he told the salesman that he had made up his mind to buy another make of car but just wanted to compare the two.

"I understand," said the salesman, "but let me tell you about our car anyway." After he had cited all features of the car the prospect was only half convinced and expressed a desire to examine the other car once more before he made up his mind.

"If you'll step into my car," said the salesman, "I'll take you over to the other dealer. His car is a good one and deserves your study. If, after comparing it point for point with our car, you decide that ours is better, we shall be very happy to serve you."

He drove the prospect to the rival showroom and left him there. Later the prospect came back and bought. He explained his action: "Your willingness to let me see the other car; your admission that it was a good car; your offer to take me to a competitor's place of business, astonished me. But I know that you could not do that unless you had absolute confidence in your car. You evidently had no fear of competition. Your own belief made me believe. I want your car."

When you succeed in winning the customer who has favored your competitor, your enthusiasm will, of course, be high. You cannot afford to let it drop proportionately when you lose out to a competitor. When that happens your job is to find out why it happened and to do whatever is necessary to prevent its happening again. See ¶ 7032. Analyzing the results of your work each day is particularly helpful in rebuilding your enthusiasm.

Your problem is not so much how to act toward a competive salesman, but how to answer the customer who does not care to make a change, or the prospect who says that the other company puts out a better line. For meeting these situations, you have direct guidance under the tab, "Making Objections Work *For* You," ¶ 7001 et seq.

¶ 1081 Modern times require modern methods

Buying has become more professional. Today, buyers are subject to greater management control than ever before; more than ever they must "buy right." They look to the salesman to aid them in this task. To execute his proper function, the salesman must be equipped with facts, statistics, data, and knowledge of various sorts that would surprise his predecessor of only a few decades ago.

The demands on the salesman have been accelerated as the products themselves have become more technical. In many industries, the salesman's responsibility as an educator has increased several fold.

In our technological society, the salesman must always have sufficient technical knowledge to give the prospect the information he wants and needs about construction, use, economy, and features of the product offered. The way the information is given, how it is worked into the presentation, how it is used to answer objections, must be as modern as the product itself.

▶ **IDEA IN ACTION** Ted Smiley sells typewriters. On his first call one morning the office manager says, "I understand the ABC typewriter is *faster* than yours."

Ted replies, "Oh, I don't think so. We sell a lot of our machines and nobody has ever raised that objection."

Of course, Ted's competitor selling the ABC machine gets the sale. Ted's general statement, merely expressing an opinion, has *not* impressed his prospect.

Ted's second call works out differently. His second prospect says, "We are interested in cutting down *noise* in our office. Makes for better work and happier employees."

Ted is equipped to *meet* this situation. He happens to have in his briefcase an authoritative comparison—noise-wise—of his product as against leading competitive products. Ted makes this sale easily; he has *earned* it; he was modernly equipped.

¶ 1082 A salesman must keep pace

Today's salesman, whether novice or old-timer, must have a capacity for learning and must want to study. The times demand that he be eager to learn. Selling today relies fully as much on educating the prospect as it does on persuading him. But before he can educate his prospect, the salesman must educate himself.

⟫SUGGESTION→ The day of the salesman who "knows it all," the "natural born" salesman who needs no study of his craft, is definitely gone. Salesmanship, too, has become a profession. It has become more of a science than an art. It is, furthermore, a science that is still being refined. A salesman must, for example . . .

Pick up vital data that can help you outsell your competitors. How? Drop in at trade shows where they're exhibiting. Here's what a St. Louis salesman says:

"A trade show offers you the opportunity to keep abreast of latest developments. It gives you an idea of what the other fellows are spotlighting."

▶ **IDEA IN ACTION** He asks questions at the booth. "By showing enough interest, I can get a salesman to practically deliver his entire presentation. This lets me know what his company is featuring."

He then works his own presentation around the facts he has picked up. "I try to take advantage of the competition's weak points. I discuss ways we can overcome their advantages with our sales vice president and technical department."

¶ 1083 Be a team player—and become more valuable to your company

Show your sales manager and your company president that besides being a top-notch salesman, you're also a team player—always looking for ways to help your company build profits. Here are just a few of the things you can do:

1. *Spell out for the boys in the home office how you sold a particularly tough prospect.* If you changed your presentation, or stressed a "new" angle—make a note of it in your next memo.

2. *Keep the company informed on what the competition is doing.* If you find out they're stepping up their sales calls to your customer,

mature salesmanship

send the word back. If they've increased their sales force, make mention of that.

3. *Record any comments your customers or prospects make about your company or your products.* Get testimonials that can be used for advertising and promotional purposes.

⟫IMPORTANT→ Be sure to include the knocks, too. Your office must have this information also—or they'll wind up with a distorted view.

4. *Be willing to help out a new man.* Volunteering isn't a dirty word. Let your company know that you're willing to pass on any tricks you've picked up over the years. See ¶ 1086 for other non-selling duties.

¶ 1084 **Dickering or "horse trading" is frowned upon**

In the modern world of business, special price concessions to selected buyers tend to be frowned upon as a matter of general policy. Whereas in former times dickering was the rule rather than the exception, today it is engaged in but rarely. Most sellers pride themselves on practicing a one-price policy. Furthermore, there are legal restrictions covering many types of selling transactions that forbid or restrict more favorable treatment of one customer as against others.

Nevertheless, there are close-out and various other concession situations that can be taken advantage of to bring about an immediate decision to buy.

⟫REMEMBER→ A distinction is made between offering a concession that amounts to "horse trading" and offering an inducement to close. The inducement is available to *anyone* who takes advantage of it while the offer is in effect; the concession is not available to everyone.

¶ 1085 **How changes in management have improved salesmen's opportunities**

Leading businesses today are spending more time on measuring the profitability of every product sold than was ever before spent on figures. Systems are introduced under the guidance of controllers through which the costs of distribution, which means all of the expenses that have to do with selling, are analyzed and allocated to various products, customers, and the like. For example, a dry goods wholesaler may keep statistical records of the number of orders invoiced, the number of items billed, the products sold, size of the orders, number of delivery stops made for each department, and of other operations.

The statistical controls enable the company to see exactly how productive each salesman is from the standpoint of profits to the company. The studies may result in certain lines or products being dropped as unprofitable, certain items being taken out of the line that is sold by a general salesman and given to a specialty salesman, and other changes.

You may go from an employer who hasn't yet applied distribution cost analysis to one who is quite advanced in its distribution cost methods. When this happens, this is what you can expect: The company that pays attention to controlling distribution costs usually has its salesmen very much in mind. If, as a result of managerial control, a salesman's territory is changed, or he is required to eliminate certain types of customers or products, his compensation will be adjusted to enable him to continue to earn what he has been earning and to make steady progress toward higher goals.

However, don't expect the company or its controller to give you a detailed explanation of the accounting by which it arrives at its decisions to make changes.

⟫IMPORTANT→ Companies that once tried to explain their accounting practices to their salesmen have abandoned the practice. They found that the salesmen merely got involved in figures that they did not understand and wasted time in useless discussions among themselves about the system.

¶ 1086 **"Selling" includes many non-selling duties**

A big bite in a salesman's time has been made by the increase in the number of non-selling duties that has been added to the concept of selling. A salesman's duties today take in some or all of the following tasks in addition to the work of getting interviews and making sales.

1. Giving your company your opinion about its existing products and competitors' product lines, with criticisms and suggestions for changes.

¶ 1086

2. Helping your company to develop new products by offering ideas and giving advice on proposed new products.

3. Supplying information about (1) the territory, (2) the local market, (3) competition, (4) prospects' needs, (5) customers' credit positions.

⇒REMEMBER→ Salesmen are sometimes asked to conduct "survey interviews" to gather important facts about their present customers. The salesman must come up with answers to such questions as: Are they buying as much as they should? Could they be sold additional lines? What is the competition? How can the competition be displaced? What is the customer's attitude toward the company?

4. Getting dealers to push the company's merchandise, to display the product, to use the window display material, and to advertise and feature the product.

5. Training distributors' salesmen to raise their selling ability.

6. Instructing the jobbers' and dealers' salesmen in how to demonstrate the product.

7. Handling complaints and adjustments, and collecting delinquent accounts.

8. Handling correspondence with customers.

9. Attending sales meetings, conferences, and training sessions.

10. Keeping records and filing reports.

11. Keeping samples, kit, literature, and related items neat, fresh, and up to date.

⇒REMEMBER→ Fortunately, few, if any, organizations require their salesmen to do all of the jobs mentioned above. Employers know that a man can increase his activity, and therefore the company's sales volume, only if time is used effectively. To make up for the demands on the salesman's time, the progressive company steps up its training program in order to speed up the development of topnotch producers. It also improves the equipment it furnishes its men to aid them in making the best presentation. If you happen to be selling for such a company, recognize the value of their sales training efforts. Use your equipment as you are instructed to use it.

¶ 1087 **A modern attitude is needed for required paper work**

Practically all sales work requires the keeping of certain records and most sales posts carry the requirement of filing daily or other reports with the home office.

Some men are not in the least detail-minded and seek almost any escape from chores not directly connected with "signing up the customer." Others make the mistake of spending valuable hours not in the field, but in the office "taking care of a lot of paper work that's got to be done."

⇒REMEMBER→ We have already pointed out how important it is to be constantly aware of the value you place upon your time and how detrimental to earnings is the waste of precious hours that should be devoted to selling.

The detail-minded man should resolutely set a reasonable limit to the proportion of the selling day which he will devote to paper work. The salesman who is loath to fill out required reports must be reminded that the day is gone in which a salesman can say, "Oh, hang the paper work! As long as I'm out there pitching hard and writing up the orders, everything will be okay!" Such a man is out of step with the realities of modern salesmanship.

⇒SUGGESTION→ Do your paper work during non-selling hours. See the suggestions for planning your work at ¶ 8042 et seq.

¶ 1088 **Stay aware of the need for change**

You have been given a picture of the changes that have taken place over the years in business, in its attitude toward salesmen, and in salesmen's attitude toward their work.

Its message to you is that you must be modern in your outlook and in your methods. You cannot afford to continue to use antiquated methods. At some place in your selling experience you will be brought up short if you continue year in and year out to tell the same sales story, to use the same approaches, and the same presentation.

Stay aware of the continuing need for change. Life itself is a continuing process in which imperceptible changes are always taking place. They become discernible when we stop to examine the present and make comparisons with the past. Since selling is, in a sense, a catering to human needs, it changes gradually as our customs and behavior change. You must stop now and then to get your selling methods into focus with the times.

PROSPECTING FOR VOLUME BUSINESS

Finding Full-Potential Prospects
Qualifying Specific Prospects for Buying Potential
Finding and Rating the "Key" Prospect In a Group
Additional Aids to Profitable Prospecting
Guides to Better Territory Coverage

TABLE OF CONTENTS

	Starts at Paragraph [¶]
Miracle Guide to Finding Bigger Prospects	2001

FINDING FULL-POTENTIAL PROSPECTS

	Starts at Paragraph [¶]
Steps in finding full-potential prospects	2002

How to Find Good Leads (With Help of Others)

Who might supply you with leads to prospects	2003
Always "go beyond" your prospect list	2004
How to get your customer drop-outs to fall in	2005
An inactive customer blows his top and buys	2006
Calls by service department turn up prospects	2007
How to get prime prospects from customers	2008
How to use customer referrals as a source of high-potential prospects	2009
A technique for gaining permission to use the recommender's name	2010
Use your presentation to get fully qualified prospects	2011
How to get names of prime prospects from prospects you don't sell	2012
A technique to get valuable prospects from new clients	2013
Introductions to valuable prospects can be gained by using your calling cards	2014
Non-competitive salesmen can furnish excellent leads	2015
Junior salesmen can find highly qualified prospects for you	2016
A non-prospect can help you get started	2017
Social contacts can often supply you with prime prospects	2018

How to Find Good Leads (On Your Own)

Depending on yourself for leads	2019
Know the markets for your product	2020
13 Steps to success in turning cold calls into sales dollars	2021
Selling the non-user	2022
Selling the user	2023
Creative idea for improvement of customer's product turns up a high-potential prospect	2024
A creative idea from a news item leads to a prospect	2025
Creative idea, stimulated by chance remark, leads to a prospect	2026
Use direct mail to find leads	2027
Trade exhibitions yield full-potential prospects	2028
Disaster situations point up prospects	2029

QUALIFYING SPECIFIC PROSPECTS FOR BUYING POTENTIAL

Qualifying is determined by your product	2031	Exploring the "need" test	2034
"Potential" is the key	2032	A test of buying authority	2035
Three-point test to determine the potential of every prospect	2033	A test of a prospect's ability to purchase	2036
		A test to help you select "hot" prospects	2037

prospecting for volume business — table of contents

	Starts at Paragraph [¶]		Starts at Paragraph [¶]
Qualifying a prospect who comes to you	2038	Sizing up a prospect's needs on a cold call	2040
Sizing up prospects by category in cold canvassing	2039	How to qualify prospects you contact by telephone	2041

FINDING AND RATING THE "KEY" PROSPECT IN A GROUP

Three common situations requiring group decision	2051	How to locate your "key" prospect for an industrial product	2054
A system to rate a husband-wife prospect	2052	Contact the purchasing agent first	2055
Finding the key partner	2053		

ADDITIONAL AIDS TO PROFITABLE PROSPECTING

Prepare your own complete prospect source list	2061	Word-of-mouth creates prospects	2064
Identify the sources of your leads	2062	Increase your sales through well-kept prospect and customer records	2065
First sale in a new field opens the way to new prospects	2063	Cooperation with credit department helps you in prospecting	2066

GUIDES TO BETTER TERRITORY COVERAGE

Covering your territory effectively	2071	The clean-up plan for salesmen who sell one town at a time	2077
Basic routing plans that save time	2072	The broadside routing plan for door-to-door salesmen	2078
A routing plan that reduces total travel distance to a minimum	2073	Maps can be valuable to you	2079
A routing plan to stagger calls in order of customers' importance	2074	Use the telephone to increase territory coverage	2080
A routing plan for salesmen who call on customers regularly and frequently	2075	Watch for changes in make-up of territory	2081
A plan to route calls around key customers	2076	A territory cut can result in bigger volume	2082

Footnote references 3999

Prospecting for Volume Business

The "big league" salesman concentrates on prospects with real potential

¶ 2001 ⟫⟫MIRACLE GUIDE to→ Finding Bigger Prospects

One of the fastest ways to reach top bracket income is to call on top-level prospects. The quality of your prospects automatically sets the top limit of your income. This is so critically important that it can relegate you to mediocrity or make you an explosive financial success.

This section shows you how to find a continuous supply of better prospects on whom to call—and rapidly increase your income.

It ends forever the indiscriminate making of calls—just so calls can be made. It shows the ways you can cut prospecting time by finding *on the first try* the prospects who will develop into customers.

Here's the set-up:

▶ Finding Full-Potential Prospects. Covers all the methods of finding the blue-chip places to call.

▶ Qualifying Specific Prospects for Buying Potential. Includes tests and rating systems that eliminate "scatter-shot" prospecting and enable you to train your sights on the prospects who will buy.

▶ Additional Aids to Profitable Prospecting. Contains additional ideas to help you get the best results from the time you spend on prospecting.

▶ Guides to Better Territory Coverage. Includes ways to improve coverage of your territory through proper routing.

Here is mature salesmanship—prospecting as it is done by men who are serious about making money—men who don't want just interviews, but sales.

¶ 2001

Finding full-potential prospects

¶ 2002 Steps in finding full-potential prospects

Most salesmen must carefully select qualified prospects from many different sources. Only a few vendors, like those who sell to garages, drug stores, and similar buyers can drive through a territory and spot prospects with little difficulty.

Finding full-potential prospects involves two main steps:

1. Discovering all of the sources through which prospects might be located.
2. Qualifying specific prospects for buying potential.

We shall explain first the two categories of sources of leads: (a) the leads you get from others [¶ 2003], and (b) the leads you uncover yourself [¶ 2019].

How to Find Good Leads (With Help of Others)

¶ 2003 Who might supply you with leads to prospects

Your prospecting work is made easier if you can get assistance from any of the following:

• Your company. It might supply you with specific leads, prospect lists, and names of inactive accounts [¶ 2004-2006].
• Your present customers. They can help you keep your prospect list current and active by giving you names of possible buyers and referrals [¶ 2008-2014].
• Salesmen selling non-competing products and services [¶ 2015].
• Junior salesmen [¶ 2016].
• Non-prospects [¶ 2017].
• Social contacts [¶ 2018].

¶ 2004 Always "go beyond" your prospect list

Prospect lists provided by the sales manager are great aids, but they have their shortcomings. Often they are not up-to-date, and sometimes they don't prove out. You must go beyond your lists in prospecting for potential buyers.

 IDEA IN ACTION Ernest Dameron sells an improved type of sterilizing unit to hospitals. His company has furnished him with a list of hospitals in his territory.

Ernest finds, however, that he can make numerous extra sales by "going beyond" this list of prospects.

In the first place, the list, which was compiled and published by the State Association of Hospitals, contains data that are two years old. It therefore omits the names of institutions built or opened since the data were gathered. At each call, Ernest inquires for names of newly-opened hospitals.

Secondly, Ernest happens to learn that a large company located in his territory operates a private industrial clinic.

Ernest investigates further and finds that not only do many large industrial plants maintain such clinics, but also that some large non-manufacturing concerns likewise provide clinic service for their employees.

All told, these extra prospects enable Ernest to earn about 25% more commissions than he would earn if he confined his calls to prospects whose names appear on the list provided by his company.

¶ 2005 How to get your customer drop-outs to fall in

Direct a sales campaign to your former customers—it's strictly a "No-Lose" proposition for you. Here's how top salesmen view a campaign like this: Even if you don't make a single sale out of your immediate efforts you still come out ahead. Reason:

The information you receive from the people you contact will help you to prevent further customer fallout.

This is the experience of a Salt Lake City salesman:

IDEA IN ACTION He picked out a few customers in different markets who no longer bought from him. He sent this letter out. (You can either use or modify this letter.)

Dear Mr. Jones:

I miss you. My sales records show that you're no longer buying from us. And to tell you the truth, I'm a bit puzzled. Our prices are competitive and since our products rate high, I can't figure out what went wrong. That's why I'm writing this letter. Frankly, it would be nice to have you as a customer again.

But we need your help. Would you mind checking the following boxes and returning your reply in the enclosed post-paid envelope?

Yes No
☐ ☐ Have you changed to a production system that does not require our products? If so, can you give me a brief outline of the changes?

finding full-potential prospects

Yes No
☐ ☐ Did you find that one of our competitors sells a product better suited to your needs?
Yes No
☐ ☐ Do you feel our ads have misled you in any way? If so, how?
Yes No
☐ ☐ Did a competitor offer a better price?
Yes No
☐ ☐ Were our deliveries late?
Yes No
☐ ☐ Were our products arriving damaged?
Yes No
☐ ☐ Were our products poor in quality?
Yes No
☐ ☐ Did you find our credit terms out of line with those of our competitors?

Payoff: When the returns come in (and most people, buyers included, can't resist a chance to sound off) you'll have the information needed to (1) woo the dropouts back into the fold and (2) make sure that others won't fall by the wayside.

Another angle: You have a big plus going for you when you attempt to sell a former customer—he *was* satisfied with your company once before. If you can get at the source of his dissatisfaction, you stand a good chance of selling him again.

¶ 2006 An inactive customer blows his top and buys

In calling upon inactive accounts you will sometimes run into a customer who stopped buying because of a grievance that was never settled properly. When he stopped buying, your firm might have been too busy—or too short of inventory—to care. Now you want to bring the customer back into the fold. It may be the better part of valor to just listen to the disgruntled customer "blow his top," and sell him some time later, after the atmosphere has cleared.

¶ 2007 Calls by service department turn up prospects

Good service and follow-up of service calls have brought many full-potential prospects to salesmen whose companies sell a product as well as service contracts.

▶ **IDEA IN ACTION** Dick Meyers sells oil burners and oil burner service contracts. He spends a part of his selling day in calling up customers his company's servicemen have called on the day before, to see that everything is satisfactory. He is particularly sure to call new customers. This practice often leads to sales of new oil burners to replace worn out ones the servicemen have reported.

⟶ IMPORTANT ⟶ A customer who is given follow-up consideration will often mention good prospects. He is especially likely to recommend your service to someone who complains about poor service he might be getting from another company.

¶ 2008 How to get prime prospects from customers

How you ask your satisfied customers for names of prospects often determines the results. What you want to avoid is the answer, "I can't think of anyone right now." Make your request for prospects in terms of the qualifications that fit your product, and you'll get your customer thinking harder for you.

▶ **IDEA IN ACTION** Terry Lewis, insurance salesman, always asks his customers for names of prospects. If he should happen to get the reply, "I can't think of anyone right now," he comes to the aid of his customer's memory by saying, "That's only natural because you are probably trying to think of someone who is interested in buying life insurance. To be frank, I don't know of anyone who is ready to buy either. But the men I would like to meet are between thirty and forty-five, have children, and seem to be doing well. They have just had an addition to the family, or a promotion, or a raise. Whom do you know who fits into that picture?"

¶ 2009 How to use customer referrals as a source of high-potential prospects

Referral leads can be your best source for prospects in certain types of selling. For example, if the product or service is of such a "personalized" nature that the recommendation of a friend carries great weight, you should work this source of prospects for all it's worth.

▶ **IDEA IN ACTION** Roy Terhune sells membership in a local athletic club. He finds that cold canvassing and other methods "pay off," but his most important source of leads is referrals from present members.

"Yes," says a man Roy has just signed up, "I'd be glad to give you the names of a few of my friends who should be interested. There's Ed Larking, a young chap who's just become credit manager in our office. Then there's Fred Day—we used to 'work out' together at the 'Y'. There are a couple of good prospects for you."

Roy asks each new member to suggest the names of others he can call on under similar preferred circumstances.

Whenever Roy runs short of referral leads from new members, he calls on older members and asks whether they have anyone to suggest. He has found that referral leads are better, in his particular type of selling, than leads that he can develop in any other way.

¶ 2010   **A technique for gaining permission to use the recommender's name**

Your new prospect will be more impressed with you if you are able to state the name of the person who recommended him to you. There is a way to get this permission, even if at first it is denied.

IDEA IN ACTION Tom Allen gets permission to use the name of the person who has just recommended prospects to him, by saying, "I am not going to call on your friends and simply try to sell them policies. I have a service to offer, the same kind of work I did for you, and I think that it will be interesting and valuable to them. Don't you? But I don't want to call on anyone unless I have an introduction to him, and I like to have cards so that my prospects will know that I have done the same work for their friends. They may even want to ask you about it. However, when I present your card I will tell them that I asked you for it, simply to make their acquaintance and so they will know that I have given my service to someone they know."

This reasoning is difficult to argue with, and since it points up the customer's importance, he usually does not hesitate to grant permission.

¶ 2011   **Use your presentation to get fully qualified prospects**

Ask a prospect for others who are interested in the same information you have just given him in your presentation. This technique often will gain you other full-potential prospects.

IDEA IN ACTION Once Robert Parker has made his sale he says, "Mr. Jones, you say you like the job I have done for you and the method I have to work out your insurance problems. Now, whom do you know who would like to have the same type of information about his insurance?

¶ 2012   **How to get names of prime prospects from prospects you don't sell**

The extra time you have spent on a "no-sale" prospect whom you had reason to expect would buy need not be lost. You can tactfully ask him to recognize your efforts to serve him by recommending other prospects. Most prospects who don't buy are eager to "reward" you, *if you have done a good selling job,* and will make every effort to give you names of prospects they feel sure will buy.

¶ 2013   **A technique to get valuable prospects from new clients**

Prime prospects will be recommended to you by new clients if you are careful to relate your request to the *same reason* that caused your new customer to buy.

IDEA IN ACTION Richard Mason realizes that a new client he has just sold is primarily impressed with his service features. After the sale, Dick briefly reviews the customer's benefits and is quick to stress again the fact that he always keeps in touch with his customers and is available any time they need his services.

At this point Dick says, "And if you know anyone who isn't getting that kind of service from his present supplier, I'd certainly like to talk with him." The customer usually admits that he changed to Dick because of poor service elsewhere, and recommends others who are experiencing the same dissatisfaction.

¶ 2014   **Introductions to valuable prospects can be gained by using your calling cards**

A customer who does not want to be bothered writing introductions to friends will cooperate if you make it easier for him to help you. Just hand him several business cards when you make your request.

IDEA IN ACTION John Shiffman asks his customers for introductions to friends by handing them a number of his business cards. "Will you please write an introduction to several of your friends on the back of these cards?" he says. "Don't try to sell me or my service. Simply write the man's name and then under it write, 'Introducing John Shiffman' and sign your name. Thank you very much. I appreciate the favor and I will let you know how we get along."

finding full-potential prospects

If the customer objects to writing on the cards, John tells him that without such an introduction his customer's friends might miss a worthwhile opportunity by not granting him an interview.

¶ 2015 **Non-competitive salesmen can furnish excellent leads**

Salesmen of non-competitive products who cover the same territory as yours are prime sources for good prospects. Their specific knowledge of the facts surrounding a prospect will qualify their leads as almost a sure sale.

▶ **IDEA IN ACTION** Jim Blake, who sells duplicating machines, had luncheon with a paper salesman, who worked Jim's territory. In the usual "shop talk," the paper vendor bemoaned the cut in a paper order by one of his big customers to one-tenth its former size. He mentioned the reason for the decrease in his order: the company was now having their shipping labels done by an outside printer.

Jim immediately contacted the company and aroused their interest by showing them how to cut their printing bill through the purchase of one of his machines. He made a sale.

⟫⟫REMEMBER→ No one is better able to give you valuable information about a prospect than a salesman of non-competitive products who sells that prospect. He is usually able to tell you about the company's buying policy, the "key" men, the best approach, and even the reason why the prospect might buy your product. Though you have been cautioned at ¶ 1080 about fraternizing with your competitors' salesmen, the opposite of caution is recommended for salesmen of non competitive products, especially if such products are indirectly related to your own. It pays to be friendly with these salesmen and to reciprocate when you can.

¶ 2016 **Junior salesmen can find highly qualified prospects for you**

Here's an idea for the experienced salesman who finds he hasn't enough actual selling time because he has to spend too much time seeking out qualified leads. If you are such a salesman, the answer may be to employ a "junior" salesman to locate prospects. This plan is not feasible, however, in every type of selling. For example, if the arousing of interest can be accomplished only by a senior who "knows all the answers," this plan is not for you.

▶ *How the plan works.* You delegate to the junior salesman the job of finding worthwhile prospects for you. He then turns over to you only the names of prospects who are interested in buying your product. You do the actual selling.

The junior salesman is *your* man. You pay him a percentage of the commissions you receive on each completed sale. The payment must be large enough to assure your scout that he is being justly paid for his work and to stimulate him to do his best.

You train your assistant to know and do the things necessary to uncover high potential leads and to make appointments. You teach him the facts about your product that will arouse the prospect's interest. You suggest the types of prospects that are most interested in your product. And you tell him where such prospects can be found.

⟫⟫CAUTION→ A junior salesman should not repeat (in his words) your sales story. This will tempt the prospect to judge your product by what your assistant has told him. The scout should tell only those facts that will arouse the prospect's interest sufficiently to think it important that he grant you an interview. You should write out a "sales talk" for your junior salesman, and emphasize that he adhere to it.

▶ **IDEA IN ACTION** Tom Mullins sells a home study course. He finds that he must spend 75% of his time prospecting, leaving only 25% for actual selling.

Tom hires a young man whose time is worth considerably less than his own. This junior salesman spends all his time seeking out prospects. When he locates a prospect his job is to make a specific appointment for Tom who keeps the appointment and undertakes the more difficult task of making the presentation, overcoming objections, and then closing the sale.

¶ 2017 **A non-prospect can help you get started**

One way to get started successfully in a new area is to select a contact you know is a non-prospect, but who is familiar enough with your product to supply you with prime prospects. If you remember this rule—your prospects are as good as your source—then finding high-powered prospects will not be difficult.

▶ **IDEA IN ACTION** Bob Channing opened a branch office in a new territory to sell an advertising service that supplied advertising mats for retailers.

Bob's first call was on a leading retailer, who, he knew, would *not* be a prospect. But he used the first contact as a starting place from which he developed one of his company's most successful branches.

He explained his business to the retailer and stated that he was fully aware that this particular store could not use his service. Then he asked for the names of up-and-coming retailers in the area that could benefit from his service.

Bob got the names of a number of retailers who were doing well, but who were too small to have advertising departments of their own. Each of these recommended retailers in turn supplied Bob with additional valuable prospects.

¶ 2018   **Social contacts can often supply you with prime prospects**

Certain types of selling lend themselves to gaining prospects through social contacts. Men who sell life insurance, automobiles, fur coats, and similar products often make their social contacts an important source of prospects.

Included in social contacts are not only personal friends and acquaintances, but also neighbors, members of your church, club or lodge, former classmates, and any other group whose members buy the type of product or service that you offer.

Such contacts must be followed up with tact. This does not preclude occasionally "talking business" as an indirect reminder that you are glad to give friendly attention to the needs of these acquaintances.

How to Find Good Leads (On Your Own)

¶ 2019   **Depending on yourself for leads**

Unless you supplement the leads supplied to you by others, you will probably find yourself floundering for calls to make. Most salesmen must depend upon their own efforts to turn up worthwhile prospects. The basic methods of keeping your prospect lists filled with potential buyers are:
- Cold canvassing [¶ 2021-2023]
- Creative ideas [¶ 2024-2026]
- Direct mail [¶ 2027]
- Trade exhibitions [¶ 2028]

¶ 2020   **Know the markets for your product**

Markets, as used here, include all the classifications of buyers to whom your product can be sold. You find in these markets the greatest percentage of your prospects because (1) they have a need for your product; (2) they are available for contact.

EXAMPLE: Bill Burley represents an electric tool company that offers a new screw drill. Bill's company furnishes him with the following list of markets for the product:

Automotive	Kitchen and other
Car dealers	equipment fabricators
Body shops	Lumber yards
Industrial repair shops	Boat builders and
Service stations	repairers
Fleets	Contractors:
Implement dealers	Electrical
Industrial, Contractors,	Plumbing-heating
and others	Air conditioning
Plant maintenance	Building
(all industries)	Heavy construction
Woodworking	Utilities
manufacturers (all)	Vocational schools

With this list, Bill can approach prospects on a steady and complete coverage schedule; he does not have to wait for leads to come to him from his company or from others. He has no difficulty in knowing where to call because the markets have been clearly defined for him.

¶ 2021   **13 steps to success in turning cold calls into sales dollars**

For finding prospects and making sales, no substitute has been found to improve upon door-to-door, down-the-street canvassing.

No matter how much a company does to back up salesmen, ads and direct mail pieces may fail to bring in hoped-for leads. But when all other sources fail, the salesman who's been canvassing industriously needn't despair. He'll still have a pack of hot prospect cards to work from.

So that you'll be able to take home really big commissions, I have outlined below the 16 steps that I have seen thousands of salesmen use to turn cold calls into sales dollars.

1. *Turn your time into money.* A salesman fights a constant battle against an unseen, unyielding enemy: Time. To earn big money, he must be fast enough to make lots of calls, yet thorough enough to turn calls into sales.

⇛BEST APPROACH→ Park your car and work intensively as close to the car as possible. Go down the street door to door, office to office—miss no one.

2. *Look for clues.* From the moment you enter an office, digest every bit of information in sight. Look at every piece of paper. Wastebaskets, for example, are goldmines of information on paper needs, office machine needs, or mailing problems.

3. *Let your business card run interference.*

When canvassing, present the receptionist with your card, and simply say: "May I see the boss, please?" More often than not, the girl knows far better than you whom you want.

Had you told her your name and company, it would have meant nothing to her, and she'd be unlikely to pass it on correctly. But when she *sees* your name and company name on the card, she'll be able to convey the correct information to her boss immediately.

4. *Save his time—and yours.* Most businessmen appreciate your getting down to cases fast. You'll hold your prospect's interest better, and increase your chances for a sale. What's more, with the time saved, you'll be able to fit more calls into your day. And each extra chance to sell is money in your pocket.

5. *Catch his interest.* Time is precious. You are intruding on a prospect's thoughts and taking up his valuable time. To grab his interest immediately, hit him with a provocative statement. Promise concrete benefits and savings.

▶ **IDEA IN ACTION** A salesman of postage meters opens: "I can save 50% of your time and eliminate a great deal of bother in sending out mail."

Result: If the prospect answers you *"How?"*, he is qualified. If he says, *"I have only 6 letters a day and almost no parcel post,"* the salesman smiles, presents his card, a rate chart, and a piece of literature, and leaves fast.

¶ 2022   **Selling the non-user**

6. *Sell the non-user basic benefits.* Prospects fall into two types—those presently using equipment similar to yours, and those who are not. When you find a non-user, sell basic benefits. A non-user will continue to be just that until he's convinced that you have a benefit for him that's worth the cost.

Convince him that the advantages are worth the price—and the close is automatic. All that's left is deciding which piece of equipment is best for him.

7. *Point out the prospect's need.* A need is there, though your prospect hasn't seen it. If he had, he'd have done something, either installed or changed equipment. Point out his need and you create in him a desire to satisfy it.

8. *Demonstrate on the spot.* Demonstrations provide the best route to a quick close. Determine application, bring in the correct piece of equipment, and demonstrate like mad.

Tell the prospect: "Let me have 20 minutes, and I'll convince you how good this equipment is *for you.*"

9. *Be a problem solver:* Find out what problems you can solve for your prospect. Successfully demonstrate that you can in fact solve those problems and closing becomes easy.

¶ 2023   **Selling the user**

10. *Sell your expertise.* When dealing with a user, it is particularly important to sell expertise. In selling postage meters, for example, a salesman may not realize he is facing a user until he hears: "I've already got a postage meter and I'm satisfied with it."

Your answer: "Good. I don't have to waste time telling you about the advantages of a meter system. But, I may be able to help you save a great deal of time, money, and effort on your present set-up.

"If it would be possible for me to take a quick peek, I think I can tell you exactly what I can do for you, and what kind of money can be saved.

"On the other hand, if your equipment is in good condition and does an adequate job—I'll tell you that too, and go on my way."

11. *Look at the user's equipment.* Often, users are very uninformed about their equipment. They don't remember when they got it, what they paid, or what it costs to operate. They're not even sure what it does.

⇒ WHAT TO DO → Tell your prospect what he's paying and what limitations his equipment has. Ask to see his operation. Determine quickly the application that fits him (you only have a few minutes) and show him how your product is better. If you really can help him—you'll have an order. If not—no sale.

12. *Keep your briefcase with you.* When you go into a prospect's plant to look at equipment, take your sales material with you—you'll want to be ready to write up the order.

⇒ IMPORTANT → Stick close to the prospect, use your display material and keep your order pad out. Don't leave the prospect alone with one of his employees even for a minute. That may be all the time the clerk needs to put it: "Aw, we don't need it, boss."

13. *Make call-backs selling calls.* Don't skip a business that gave you a frosty reception

the last time. This only crosses potential prospects off your list.

Best approach: With good information on your prospect card, start a call-back with: "I've been thinking about your problem ever since I saw you. I think I can help you by. . ." Then start selling all over again. Tell the prospect how some other company in his field solved a similar problem.

⇒ IMPORTANT → Be sure your prospect card has complete information regarding the buyer's problem and application. You can't remember names, titles, or the small details of every call. Write it all down.

Be fully prepared on all call-backs. Act as if it's a first canvass call. Sell *benefits, improvements,* and *advantages.*

> Ideas for this article were suggested by Lester S. Schwarz, a salesman who has had abundant experience in door-to-door, to-the-consumer sales. Formerly with *Postalia,* Mr. Schwarz is now associated with *Interstate Business Forms,* New York, New York.

¶ 2024 **Creative idea for improvement of customer's product turns up a high-potential prospect**

An idea that shows a prospect how he can improve his product will almost automatically make him a full-potential prospect. The idea must present a valid reason for buying.

▶ **IDEA IN ACTION** Frank Stewart sells industrial chemicals. Frank asked his wife about the effectiveness of a new, easy-to-use cleaning compound. Her reply was that it works very well, but leaves a thin film that requires an extra rinse to remove.

Frank asks his company's chemist to analyze the compound. As a result of the analysis he writes a letter to the manufacturer to explain that the powdry film left by the compound can be eliminated by adding a solvent that his company manufactures. He also requests an interview.

¶ 2025 **A creative idea from a news item leads to a prospect**

A full-potential prospect is often found in an apparently unrelated news item about an individual or his business. By associating such facts with your knowledge of needs for your product, you will often find a valuable prospect.

▶ **IDEA IN ACTION** Al Holmes, salesman of insulating materials, learned from an article in a trade publication that a manufacturer in his territory was planning a 100% increase in his advertising expenditure.

Holmes thought, "My, that manufacturer has been operating at capacity for three years. This increase in advertising must mean he's counting on a lot of new business. That means he needs new facilities and buildings. What a prospect for insulating materials!"

Al contacted the manufacturer and found that his reasoning paid off. Because he associated an apparently unrelated news item with his product knowledge, he was able to contact his prospect well in advance of other salesmen, and turn him into a customer who placed an order worth several thousand dollars.

¶ 2026 **Creative idea, stimulated by chance remark, leads to prospect**

The salesman who keeps thinking about what he has to sell can often profit from remarks heard in ordinary conversations. The ability to associate chance statements with a selling idea is one mark of the top-notch creative salesman.

▶ **IDEA IN ACTION** Bill Mooney was returning from a convention of truck manufacturers when he struck up a conversation with a display salesman. This salesman happened to mention to Bill that a large machine manufacturer he knew was making plans to put displays "on the road." The plan was to tour various sections of the country displaying equipment from specially designed trucks.

Bill contacted the manufacturer and arranged an appointment with him. He convinced the purchasing agent and the company's engineers that with little modification his trucks would suit their purposes, and save them the large expense of purchasing specially designed trucks.

¶ 2027 **Use direct mail to find leads**

Standard form letters sent to potential users of your product might be a source of good leads if you use direct mail intelligently.

⇒ OBSERVATION → Form letters for this purpose are often supplied by the company. Usually, however, the salesman must compose his own letter and gather his own list of names for the mailing. The classified section of the telephone directory is a good source for getting a business list started.

Companies that sell by direct mail use the services of "list brokers" to obtain lists of prospects. Lists might be of new firms in an area, passenger car registrations, buyers of certain types of products, and the like. A quick way to find the names of list brokers in your territory is to inquire of someone who is doing a substantial mail order business—a publisher,

finding full-potential prospects

for example. Once you have the list broker's name, ask for his catalog. Then decide which of his lists might yield leads for you.

▶ *Key to intelligent use of direct mail.* The best way to use direct mail is to send out a small number of letters—10 or 15—at a time—and then to *follow them up* with phone calls a few days later. You must plan your work methodically if you use direct mail to find prospects. A part of a certain day each week, for example, should be devoted to this work. For example, in some lines it may work out well to mail on Monday and devote a couple of hours every Thursday morning to telephone follow-ups and making appointments for Friday and Monday.

⟩⟩⟩CAUTION→ Don't try to operate on the idea that if you send out hundreds of letters you can sit back and wait for the orders to flow in. It doesn't work that way.

▶ *Example of a letter to locate "hot" prospects.* The following letter was composed by a Smith-Corona agent, using a principal selling point to get the interview. More is told about this selling point at ¶ 7135.

⟩⟩⟩OBSERVATION→ Guidance for writing effective pre-approach letters is given at ¶ 4041 et seq.

Dear Mr. Brown:

IF YOU WERE AN ELEPHANT

Yes! If you were an elephant I know you would be interested in what I have to say, for I am talking about PEANUTS.

But PEANUTS turned into savings of dollars and cents is more interesting

You have probably shied away from buying that new typewriter you need because of the investment required to purchase it—but let's really look at this problem, using dollars and cents:

The cost of a New Smith-Corona Typewriter is PEANUTS compared with what you pay the operator:

Typical example:

You pay a Secretary $60.00 per week for 52 weeks	$ 3,120.00
For 5 years	$15,600.00
Now, by increasing her efficiency only 2% (and we know a new typewriter can easily do this) you will effect a savings in 5 years of	$ 312.00
A new machine at this time costs $238.50 less trade (your old machine is probably worth about $50.)	$ 188.50
Actual Savings	$ 123.50

You are actually saving $123.50 by trading now and also using modern, up-to-date equipment for the next 5 years.

Perhaps you feel satisfied with the present make typewriter you are using, so allow me a moment for solicitation:

The four leading American typewriters, of which Smith-Corona is one, have always led the world, both in sales and and in technical excellence. Certainly no one of the four would be where it is today if it were a poor machine—they're all good.

But just as none would claim to be perfect, there nevertheless are differences. Our claim is that when you add up what Smith-Corona offers, it comes to a more impressive total than any of the others. Why, if our only point of difference was just Half-Spacing, we'd still have a big plus.

We will be pleased to come in and discuss this in more detail with you. Return the enclosed card or Phone: LOwell 9-1333.

Sincerely,
James R. Sovine
Exclusive Smith-Corona Agent

¶2027

¶ 2028 Trade exhibitions yield full-potential prospects

Trade shows have become an outstanding means of attracting buyers to a company's product. Salesmen who are assigned to "cover" these trade fairs are in a prime position to contact highly-interested prospects.

These are the advantages you gain by using trade exhibitions as a source:

- You can meet prospects from areas you might otherwise have overlooked.
- You can meet more prospects than you could hope to contact in a normal work day.
- You can find prospects in types of businesses you may not have thought of as users of your product.
- You are in a position to talk with prospects on their "own level."
- You can consolidate your relationships with old customers you meet at such exhibitions.
- You can collect names of many valuable prospects at the exhibitions.

➤➤OBSERVATION➤ Exhibiting companies always supply their salesmen with material that helps to warm up new prospects. Cards are normally at hand for interested viewers to fill out for further information. They become leads to live prospects.

¶ 2029 Disaster situations point up prospects

One company's catastrophe can be another's opportunity. Alert salesmen follow up the occurrence of a fire or other disaster which creates a buying motive for products that must be replaced or for items or services that protect against future losses.

Qualifying specific prospects for buying potential

¶ 2031 Qualifying is determined by your product

Every prospect you contact, whether you get an order or not, costs you real money in time and transportation. A blank interview is good money lost. That is why you must qualify your prospects. The extent of qualification may vary. Three examples show the range that qualifying covers:

1. *The mass-market* (example: typewriter). Little qualifying is necessary. The typewriter salesman need only identify an office, business or factory; all are prospects for his product. His big job is to qualify the prospect as to his specific need after he contacts him.

2. *The selective market* (example: junior encyclopedia). Requires more qualifying to choose prospects who can be profitably contacted. This salesman cannot identify prospects immediately, or call indiscriminately. He must take at least these two steps to assure himself that every call has selling possibilities:

- Get names of families that include school children, using school registration lists or other sources.
- Choose a residential area with families that can afford his product.

This salesman can further qualify the prospect's family: Do parents belong to the PTA? What grade is their child in? What courses is he taking?

If your product calls for a careful selection of prospects, you must spend time qualifying them before your first call, to make the investment of your time profitable.

3. *The highly selective market* (example: pension or profit-sharing plan). The salesman who is selling a pension or profit-sharing plan for a life insurance company must fully qualify each prospect. He must be sure that the company he approaches has:

- A stable continuing management, a good record of earnings (past or prospective), and a reasonable outlook for a continuation of such earnings through its ability to market its products or services.
- A potential employee retirement problem that the management is interested in solving.
- A sufficient number of permanent employees to make the establishment of the plan feasible, and not too many to make some other type of plan, such as a Group Annuity, a more practical funding vehicle.

The salesman may contact the prospect's suppliers, an informed banker, even a competitor of the prospect, as well as many commonly used sources—like directories—to find this qualifying information. In addition, he has to "qualify" himself. Is his influence at the prospect-company sufficient to guarantee purchase of the insurance from him if the firm decides to adopt an insured pension plan?

Qualifying a prospect is an important initial step in the sales process. Do it well, and you've taken a big stride toward making the sale.

qualifying specific prospects for buying potential

¶ 2032 "Potential" is the key

For the salesman who is aiming to make every selling hour yield full time-value [¶ 1003], it is important to test each prospect for his potential as a customer. This doesn't mean, of course, that every initial sale to a new prospect must reach a fixed number of dollars or you've wasted time. In many cases repeat orders or additional orders will promise enough business to make him a profitable customer to you. He's profitable to you if your commissions will eventually average full payment for your time.

The tests that follow are useful in most lines. You can establish other tests from your selling experience that suit your particular product or service.

¶ 2033 Three-point test to determine the potential of every prospect

The key words to remember in this test are —*need, authority, capital.*

▶ *Does this prospect have a need for my product?* No matter how convincing your sales talk, your time is wasted if you give it to a prospect who has no need for your product.

▶ *Does this prospect have the authority to buy?* You may successfully "sell" a prospect who needs your product, but if he lacks the authority to buy then your talk is wasted. (However, if your job requires group selling, one "sold" member will often influence the rest. See ¶ 2051 et seq.).

▶ *Does this prospect have the necessary capital?* Although a prospect has a definite need for your product and is authorized to purchase it, he cannot actually buy unless he can meet the credit requirements of your company. Often, special credit arrangements will make a purchase possible.

¶ 2034 Exploring the "need" test

Your product must be able to help a prospect in at least one of these three ways before you can turn him into a customer.

1. Your product must save him money.
2. Your product must make money for him.
3. Your product must help him to do a better job.

You have found a full-potential prospect if you can satisfy your prospect's need for *one* of the above benefits.

¶ 2035 A test of buying authority

Human vanity often stands in the way of a salesman's attempt to find the men with buying authority. If the person you contact first tries to give you the impression that he is the "big-shot" you should see, your job is to get as quickly but tactfully as possible to the man really empowered to buy. Remember, you lose valuable time talking to the wrong man. Here are some short-cuts to test the man you meet first.

▶ *Can he buy?* After introductions and preliminary information, *but before you begin your presentation,* ask the man you are talking with if he is able to make the decision to buy. "If you are interested, Mr. Johnson, will you be able to buy? Or do you suggest I see the purchasing agent first, as is the policy in most companies?" The "as is the policy" phrase will protect his pride and invite him to be cooperative.

▶ *Who else?* If he puts you off with a remark that he will "take care of it" himself, it might indicate reluctance to admit his lack of authority. But he may also know that the man you should see is busy, or he may even wish to present your message himself. Whatever the reason, avoid the "I'll call you" putoff. Pin him down to a second interview. Ask him, "How about Thursday?" or suggest a second day if he can't see you then. Then arrange a definite hour. Leave the impression that you want to see everyone whose opinion is needed to make the purchasing decision. "I'll look forward to seeing you, and anyone else you feel should hear my presentation," should do the trick.

⟫OBSERVATION→ It's important to write the time and date in his presence. It makes the commitment stronger and more definite in his mind. (Don't write on any handy piece of paper. Use a formal call-back card, or the effect will be weakened.)

▶ *See him now.* If he implies that another's authority is needed, suggest he call that person right then. If he listens to more of your story and then agrees to call the second man, you are in an excellent position to strengthen your presentation. Refer to the first man throughout: "As Mr. Johnson himself pointed out..."

▶ *Buying policy guides.* Some large companies offer booklets describing their buying policies. A booklet might give the company's purchasing aims, name the responsible buyers, and list the products or services they are interested in buying. Be sure to profit from this data when it is available.

▶ *The P.A.* In many companies the salesman is automatically directed to the purchasing agent who will send him to the department head or buyer concerned. The purchasing agent will usually sign an order based on their recommendations. But remember, whenever the P.A. is involved, you usually run into competition. If the product involves a major expense or company policy, the decision may rest with a management team. See ¶ 2051 et seq. for ways to handle group selling.

⇒CAUTION→ To assume that you are always being directed to the right man can be costly. Check to see if there are others you can more profitably contact. One salesman had been directed to a buyer whom he saw unsuccessfully for two years. Only by accident did he discover that a better man to see, and one who also had authority to buy, was the head of the maintenance department. His second contact resulted in an immediate sale.

⇒OBSERVATION→ No rule can guide you unerringly to the "right" man. The "authority" to purchase may range from a short verbal exchange in one company, to a lengthy co-signed approval in another. One company may have a formal procedure for salesmen to follow; in contacting another, the salesman may have to rely on his wits alone.

¶ 2036 A test of a prospect's ability to purchase

The key words to remember in this test are: *observation, inquiry, decision.*

▶ *Observe the prospect. (Individual)* What kind of neighborhood does he live in? What kind of car does he drive? What is his occupation? What are his family responsibilities? *(Company)* Where is the business located? What impression does the business make on you? How are local business conditions generally?

▶ *Inquire about the prospect. (Individual)* What are his personal habits and local reputation? What organizations or associations does your prospect belong to? What trade and bank references can you explore? What is his credit rating? *(Company)* What reputation does it have? What is the business experience and ability of the management? Have you looked at a financial statement that might be available in its annual report or in other sources of information (see ¶ 9072). What is the prospect's credit rating?

⇒OBSERVATION→ If you want to be sure that your prospect has the ability to pay for your product, find out his credit rating. Although most companies check credits at the home office, every salesman should be familiar with the principal source of general mercantile credit information—the Dun & Bradstreet Reference Book. The use of this credit rating book is explained at ¶ 9075. In certain industries, such as furniture, jewelry, lumber, millinery, shoes and leather, textile, retail trade, and others, special credit agencies gather and distribute credit information about persons and firms engaged in the particular line of business. Most of these special agencies also issue rating books.

▶ *Make your decision about the prospect.* The facts about the prospect that you gather through observation and inquiry will enable you to decide whether he is a prime prospect.

¶ 2037 A test to help you select "hot" prospects

The "hot" prospect is one who will buy now. The tip-off will be supplied if you ask these simple questions:

1. *Is there a reason for the prospect to buy right now?* If you can supply a strong reason to buy immediately, a prime prospect will automatically become a "hot" prospect. For example, a prospect who has just had a new baby will be a "hot" insurance prospect.

2. *Is this the time to follow up a postponed purchase?* A prospect may have put you off to wait for a new model to come out, or to enter a new budget period, or to reach his buying season. Whatever the reason, when the time arrives, this prospect is a "hot" prospect. The reason for postponement has become the reason to buy *now*.

⇒OBSERVATION→ Timing your follow-up to coincide with the prospect's readiness to buy makes a strong impression on the prospect and helps the sale along. Your reminder system must therefore be systematic and dependable. See ¶ 1062 and ¶ 9051 et seq. for suggested follow-up systems.

qualifying specific prospects for buying potential

¶ 2038 Qualifying a prospect who comes to you

In some fields of selling, the prospect comes to the salesman. The salesman knows nothing about him, so he must begin to qualify the prospect on the spot to avoid wasting valuable time.

He may determine the three qualifying "musts" (need for product, ability to pay, authority to buy) quickly; but he knows that a successful sale to a "cold" prospect usually depends on further qualifying information.

EXAMPLE: A real estate salesman will want to find out:
1. What the prospect is interested in buying.
2. Prospect's reasons for buying.
3. The extent of prospect's inclination to buy.
4. The attitude and influence of members of prospect's family towards his buying.
5. How much prospect's family has already looked around—what they have been offered and why they did not buy.
6. What prospect already owns.
7. If a residential prospect, his church, schools, transportation, recreation, shopping district requirements.
8. If a business-opportunity prospect, the extent of his experience.

This salesman tries to find out all he needs to know the first time he meets the prospect, drives him to the listed property, and shows him the premises.

If your field of selling demands extensive qualifying of prospects, remember the value of your time, and qualify as quickly—but accurately—as possible.

¶ 2039 Sizing up prospects by category in cold canvassing

The mental-picture technique is a quick method of sizing up prospects at a glance to estimate their probable worth to you. In sizing up a prospect, you place him in a category that fits your particular needs. For example, it might suit your product to classify prospects as (1) repeat-business prospects, (2) a prospect to be won away from a competitor, (3) a small-order prospect. Other categories may have to be created to identify a prospect's potential value to you.

This technique is particularly useful in cold canvassing.

➤➤➤WHAT TO DO➤ 1. Decide upon the categories into which your prospects should be classed.
2. When you are in the prospect's office or place of business, be as observant as possible and make mental notes of what you see that might place your prospect in a particular category.
3. When you leave, immediately make notes of what you have observed and enter them on your prospect record card.

▶ IDEA IN ACTION Phil Grant, a typewriter salesman, begins to cold canvass all the offices located in a large metropolitan office building. He has little idea of the kind of office that will meet his eyes when he opens a door, but he is prepared to make a quick mental picture of what he sees.

He has already appraised the appearance of the building itself. As he enters the first office he quickly notices its general condition, size, the number of people, and condition of equipment. He looks particularly for typewriters in the office and tries to determine their age and make.

Phil not only puts his eyes to use, but listens as well. He hears that all the machines are manually operated. Most of them produce excessive noise which indicates that they are old models that have been given long, hard use.

If Phil is granted an interview during this first call, he already has a fair picture of the prospect's typewriter needs. He might talk in terms of the advantages of new manual typewriters, or perhaps electric ones, or might be able to suggest models that would better suit this prospect's business.

As Phil calls on each prospect in the building he makes similar observations. In each case he establishes immediately a general approach that fits in with the prospect's needs. He can suggest to one prospect the advantages of his models over a competitor's; to another he can suggest the advantages of a typewriter over manual reproduction.

After each call Phil jots down the full name of the prospect and what he observed, as well as the results of his call. He does this promptly in order not to forget any detail and to have a record for follow-up purposes.

At the end of his canvassing of the entire building, he finds that most of his prospects fall into one of the following categories:

1. *Repeat-business prospects.* Most of these prospects have definite schedules of replacement and are prime prospects. Schools that give typewriter instruction, service organizations, legal firms, government offices, publishers, and insurance companies are examples.

2. *Prospects who buy from necessity.* This class of high-potential prospects includes new businesses, companies that are modernizing their equipment or moving to new offices, companies that are expanding or ready to replace old equipment, and others who for some reason are compelled to buy.

3. *Prospects who should replace old equipment.* These prospects are using old machines or other inadequate reproducing equipment. They must be sold hard.

⇒⇒OBSERVATION→ Notes made about these prospects will show whether, once sold, these prospects will be big buyers or small.

4. *Prospects who are casual buyers.* Sales to these typewriter users can be made at any time, but usually depend solely upon the salesman's capabilities. Examples are: prospects who own new typewriters that don't quite fit the job; those who lack the number of typewriters needed to do all their typing work.

⇒⇒OBSERVATION→ This method of classification will help you to determine the amount of time you should spend on prospects after your first call (the value of your time compared with their potential business).

¶ 2040 **Sizing up a prospect's needs on a cold call**

When you call on a person with no advance information to help you determine his need for your product, you must find out as much as you can about his needs *while making the call*. Much of this information can be gained through observation.

▶ **IDEA IN ACTION** Jack Keely sells an internal communications system. As he approaches a cold-call prospect, he stops to look at the premises from the outside. His observations help him determine the extent of the prospect's need for his product. Here are the questions he asks himself.

• Does the company occupy more than one floor?
• Is there a loading platform at the rear?
• Is there a separate building used as an annex or warehouse?
• Is there a showroom on the ground floor with offices at the rear or upstairs?

Once inside, Jack looks for more clues that tell him if his product is needed:

• Does the firm have a switchboard, or pushbuttons on its telephones?
• Are there a number of separate offices?
• Is there an office in front and workrooms or processing rooms in the rear?

• Is some sort of crude buzzer or doorbell system being used to summon persons to the telephone?
• Are employees walking about with papers in their hands?—a sure sign of need for a communications system.

The answers to these questions tell Jack his prospect's specific needs, and also give him clues to benefits to be emphasized during his demonstration.

¶ 2041 **How to qualify prospects you contact by telephone**

Full-potential prospects can be determined by telephone contact through the "probing" technique. Probing is a method of posing statements and questions to find the answer to your unasked question: "Does this prospect need my product, and has he the ability to pay for it?"

If the answer is "yes," you can often proceed to close the sale over the phone. If your product does not lend itself to a telephone close, you should arrange for an appointment.

These guides will help you.

• Increase your chances of finding full-potential prospects by calling from selective lists. (If yours is a tangible product, constantly replaced by newer models, you can further refine your prospecting by calling only those who own old models that should be replaced by the latest one.)
• Keep your talk flexible enough to adjust to the prospect's responses, still using your written telephone approach as a guide [¶ 4025].
• Try to use the prospect's responses as a lead-in to qualifying questions or to other parts of your talk.
• If your prospect balks at an attempted close, switch back to the appointment. It's usually easier to make a sale when you are with the prospect and can give him a better idea about your product.
• Your prospect will often disqualify himself with a reason that makes further talk useless.

▶ **IDEA IN ACTION** Frank Flannery sells aluminum door and window frames to home owners. Frank makes 20 telephone calls a day to prospects located in an area heavily populated with private homes. (Frank has observed the first rule of prospecting by making sure the *group* he contacts is qualified. His job now is to qualify *individuals* in the group.)

"Hello, Mr. Mansfield?" Frank begins. "This

is Frank Flannery of Aluminum Products Company. Mr. Mansfield, beginning this week we are offering home owners a special low-payment price on aluminum door and window frames."

If the prospect does not own the home he immediately tells Frank, who then ends the conversation.

No immediate response is the signal for Frank to begin his talk to gain an interview.

If an objection is raised, Frank overcomes it and proceeds to create a desire for his product. He mentions money saved on heat bills and negligible replacement costs. As he talks, Frank continues to qualify the prospect.

"Just to give you an idea of how much money you can save on heating bills, how many windows are there in your home?"

From this and further qualification, Frank determines the number of doors and windows in the prospect's home, and the construction or condition of the home. The prospect's response when he mentions the special low-payment plan gives Frank a clue to the prospect's ability to pay.

So Frank continues to guide the conversation from statements that arouse interest, to careful mention of a few important reasons to buy. He soon has a fairly accurate picture of the prospect's needs and his buying attitude and ability. To clinch an appointment, Frank capitalizes the selling point he feels weighed heaviest with the prospect.

Phrase your telephone approach with statements and questions that will best qualify prospects for your product. Pay particular attention to the opening sentence. It is valuable if it can immediately identify non-prospects or arouse interest in prospects who might qualify further.

▶OBSERVATION▶ In the illustration, the salesman does not give details of installation, choice of product, etc. He avoids making the picture complete; he doesn't want the prospect to make an immediate decision about buying. It's too easy to say "No" over the telephone. Remember, in this particular telephone prospecting, the goal is to gain appointments, not to make sales.

Some of the ideas in this section have been suggested by the following books, obtainable from Prentice-Hall, Inc., Englewood Ciffs, N. J.

Abbott P. Smith, "How to Sell Intangibles"
David Seltz, "Successful Industrial Selling"

Finding and rating the "key" prospect in a group

¶ 2051 **Three common situations requiring group decision**

In three common situations—the family, partners, and industrial buyers—the approval of more than one person may be necessary before you can make a sale. In each of these situations, knowing the right combination of prospects to see can save you from making call-backs. It might even increase your valuable selling time if you give your sales talk only when the right prospects are present.

▶ *The family situation.* The purchase of big items such as a home and a car is almost always the joint decision of the husband and wife. Often, the opinions of other members of the family will count. When the product does not concern the family as a unit, the "combination" approval is usually not needed. However, sales to "junior" members of the family must generally be approved by a senior member, although the actual selling may have been made to the younger prospect.

▶OBSERVATION▶ An attempt is often made to get the wife or the husband to make an independent decision and sign the order, even though the objection is raised that the prospect must consult his spouse. See ¶ 7130 for ways to handle this situation.

▶ *The partner situation.* It is often necessary and almost always advisable to gain the assent of all partners when a partnership is purchasing your product. However, there are times when only one partner can be successfully sold.

▶OBSERVATION▶ The legal rights of a partner to act for the partnership are explained at ¶ 2053. See also ¶ 7127 for tips on selling to one member of a business group who wants to pass the responsibility of a decision to another or others.

▶ *The industrial situation.* A large management team is usually responsible for major purchases in industrial sales. For specific information about the "right combination" to choose in this situation, see ¶ 2054.

¶ 2052 **A system to rate a husband-wife prospect**

Here is a workable system that will show you immediately which member of a husband-wife combination is the "key" prospect. It uses a "balance of power" technique that automatically establishes the prime prospect for you as the one who scores two out of the three qualifying "tests." Here is the test:

1. Who will use my product more?
   Husband ....
   Wife ....
   Both ....
2. Whose judgment counts more?
   Husband ....
   Wife ....
   Both ....
3. Who has more "say-so"?
   Husband ....
   Wife ....
   Both ....

¶ 2053 **Finding the key partner**

The best way to find the key partner in a firm is to ask the receptionist for the "buying man." In most cases the partnership is small enough for her to know which man has the buying responsibility, so her information will be accurate.

If she hesistates to tell you, simply explain that you want to get to the right man first so that you don't waste the time of the other partners. This will usually get you immediately to the man you want to see.

⟶OBSERVATION⟶ If you are fortunate enough to know another salesman who has sold to your prospect before, or if you can check back to see who from the firm signed past orders with your company, your job becomes easier. But better check your information with the secretary; there might have been a change. "Is Mr. Johnson still in charge of buying?" or a similar verifying question will do the trick.

Here are some tips and cautions that will make your partnership prospecting easier:

• The senior partner, often designated by the firm's name, is usually the "key" man in smaller partnerships. The "Brown, Carter & Laughlin Company" would indicate that Mr. Brown is the senior partner. Be sure to check; this may be a mere alphabetical arrangement.

• A firm's name may include names of past members, retained for prestige or identification reasons: "Brown, Carter & Laughlin" might prove to be a partnership of only Messrs. Carter and Laughlin.

⟶OBSERVATION⟶ Martindale-Hubbell Law Directory is the reference source used to find information about law firms in the United States and Canada. Here you will find a list of lawyers and their addresses, firm names, the types of law practice in which the firm specializes, key personnel, and other background information that may be helpful in selling to lawyers. Every law library and almost every law office has this reference volume.

• There have been instances when a salesman "sold" one partner, only to have the sale cancelled when the other partners would not sanction the sale.

• A partner may wish to pass a buying decision on to another or others in the partnership. How to handle this situation is explained in ¶ 7127.

⟶OBSERVATION⟶ In the absence of any contrary arrangement, each partner has an equal right to participate in the management of the partnership affairs. Each partner has inherent power to act as agent for the partnership and to bind it with respect to matters relating to the partnership business. This power, however, may be limited by the terms of the partnership agreement or by any other agreement between the partners, but the limitation is not binding on outsiders who have no knowledge of it.

¶ 2054 **How to locate your "key" prospect for an industrial product**

Because the industrial sales "prospect" is often a group of three or more, you may have difficulty in finding the one person whose decision to buy will count heaviest.

This "key" prospect is usually determined by your product. If it is a major piece of machinery running into thousands of dollars, the prime prospect will most likely be a vice-president in charge of operations. If it is a new kind of hand tool, the opinion of a foreman or even an actual worker may be the important one. Other prime prospects might be the plant manager, engineers, head of the maintenance department, or the purchasing agent. Your job is to determine which one will influence the purchase most.

Here are some questions to help you locate the key man.

• Who is the head of the department that will use my product?

additional aids to profitable prospecting

- Is this position just a "title", or does it carry real authority?
- Will my product be used by more than one department?
- Is this company concerned more with purchase price or with quality of performance?

If possible, try to get the prospect's organizational chart outlining the positions and functions of the individuals in the company you are trying to sell. You may find such a chart in the company's annual report.

⟫REMEMBER→ Even though you find the key man, it is always important to see the purchasing agent first.

¶ 2055 Contact the purchasing agent first

Because most large companies clear purchases through the purchasing agent, even though the actual decision to buy might be made by another member of the management team, it always pays to see him first.

If you attempt to pass over the purchasing agent and go directly to someone else, you are likely to incur his anger and make him an opponent rather than an ally. It is his job to know the sources for as many products as possible.

In many cases it will pay you to use a telephone call or a letter to contact the purchasing agent. Often he will refer you directly to the key man.

In addition to enrolling the purchasing agent "on your side", you can gain from him information about his company's policy toward purchasing your type of product. He can also tell you about his plant's needs and whether his plant is already using your product or a similar one from another source.

Additional Aids to Profitable Prospecting

¶ 2061 Prepare your own complete prospect source list

A complete source list is a constant reminder of all the places to find prospects. Without such a list you might concentrate your prospecting efforts on a few "easy" sources and neglect or overlook others that could be equally profitable to you.

¶ 2062 Identify the sources of your leads

Knowing the source of your leads can mean the difference betwen wasting time on weak prospects and spending your time profitably in contacting high-potential prospects.

Use a symbol system for identifying and evaluating your leads. It helps to keep your prospect lists in good shape. "R" might be prospects referred to you by steady customers; "C", prospects from your company prospect list, "N" from a newspaper source, "J" from your junior salesmen, and so forth.

Each source is as valuable to you as your judgment and experience indicate.

¶ 2063 First sale in a new field opens the way to new prospects

As you gain knowledge of the business of a prospect in an unfamiliar field your approach to others in the same business becomes stronger. The natural follow-up is to uncover more prospects in the same field of business.

▶ **IDEA IN ACTION** Herb Wallace sold a service to increase office efficiency. He was called in by a prospect in a field new to him, a local hospital, to analyze the admitting procedure.

During his work, Herb also surveyed the hospital's general systems for discharging, billing, etc.

He found that he could propose a more unified procedure that would eliminate duplication and cut expenditures by $15,000 annually.

Within a reasonably short time after his recommendations were put into practice, he was able to approach and sell three more hospitals on the basis of the facts he had learned during his first hospital contact.

¶ 2064 Word-of-mouth creates prospects

The prospect-conscious salesman never hesitates to mention his profession and his product to everyone he meets.

Here's the story of one salesman who lost out by simply forgetting to say that he was in the real estate business.

▶ **IDEA IN ACTION** "I'm really mad—mad at myself. Yesterday I walked into the market to do the shopping for my wife. For the first time since I had shopped there, the owner was not in.

"I asked the boy what had happened to the boss. 'Oh,' he answered, 'he's at the new store.'

"It was the first I had heard about any new store. I realized then that I had forgotten what

¶2064

I tell everybody else—'let everyone know you're a salesman.' Here I'd been going into that market at least once a week for over a year, and never bothered to let the owner know that I was in the real estate business.

"You can be sure I won't forget again."

¶ 2065 **Increase your sales through well-kept prospect and customer records**

Your chances to make a sale will increase each time you add new information to a prospect or customer record card. When checked against data that was previously recorded, the new facts will often give you the clue to a sale.

Make certain that your records give you the exact name, title and location of your prospect. Correct names are important. "Smith-Anderson Company" is incorrect if the proper name of the firm is Smith and Anderson, Incorporated.

The first name or initials of individuals should also be carefully noted. A notation to see "Mr. Smith" is useless if there are several Smiths in the company. "Mr. John J. Smith" will always enable you to contact the right man when you write, telephone, or call personally.

Titles, too, are important. When you approach a prospect with your proposition, it is essential to know if he is the assistant to the General Manager, the Assistant General Manager, or the General Manager himself.

Be just as careful to record accurate department designations, room numbers, and street addresses.

⟫SUGGESTION⟶ Look at the forms given at ¶ 9051 et seq. and select one that will best suit your purposes.

¶ 2066 **Cooperation with credit department helps you in prospecting**

What may appear as a favor to your credit department may indeed be a favor to yourself. Your credit department may ask for your cooperation in any of the following ways; notice how you profit by doing the favor:

• A credit manager urges a salesman to call on a new company that has just placed a first order. The salesman is asked to "take a look" at the firm and report his observations. When the salesman makes the call, he is almost always greeted warmly. He establishes a strong personal contact with the new account, and gains a profitable prospect for future sales, if the firm is worthy of credit.

• An account has become doubtful and the credit man asks the salesman to call on the customer to see what has happened. When the salesman calls, he can advise the customer of ways to improve his business, thereby building a future customer, should the credit department not extend credit on present orders.

• A company sends one of its salesmen a form of report in which it asks the salesman to comment and make recommendations regarding the line of credit to be extended to a particular customer. The salesman uses his opportunity to get information that helps the credit man make a correct decision. Whether the salesman reports facts and opinions that result in suspension of credit or in extension of credit, he is helping himself by re-assessing the buying potential of the customer.

⟫SUGGESTION⟶ When you get such a form from your credit department, don't just note "O.K." or "N.G." Write a few lines, or jot down a few paragraphs on the back of the form. You might even attach a lengthier comment if the situation deserves it. By cooperating fully with your credit department you win its goodwill. You'll be the first to be offered a good lead when it comes along.

A credit man who is business-promotion minded will help his salesmen whenever the opportunity arises. Here are some of the aids you get from a credit department:

• The credit department will usually supply salesmen with periodic information about the kind of purchases the customer makes and the volume. A sharp salesman can see in this information opportunities to make bigger sales.

• The credit department's credit check of a new prospect whose potential business looks good but whose credit acceptability may be doubtful is a service to the salesman. Often a word might save the salesman the trouble and disappointment of getting an order only to have it rejected.

⟫OBSERVATION⟶ One credit department head rates his inactive accounts as the "cream" of prospect sources. His reasoning is this: if a company is still in business and you aren't selling them, someone *is*. The history of a former customer's business with your company can give you the clues to why the customer stopped buying. See ¶ 2005 for ways to revitalize inactive accounts.

Guides to Better Territory Coverage

(Adapted from Merrill DeVoe, "Effective Self-Management in Selling," Englewood Cliffs, N. J.: Prentice-Hall, Inc.)

¶ 2071 Covering your territory effectively

Unless your efforts follow a carefully thought-out plan, you are likely to find that time spent covering your territory is not rewarding you with proportionate earnings.

Your goal should be to reach your contacts quickly and effectively, to produce enough repeat and new business to compensate you fully for every minute spent "out in the field."

With thoughtful planning you can almost always save time through careful routing of calls. You avoid backtracking, criss-crossing your route, making long trips to see just one customer, by-passing customers, and needless travel.

¶ 2072 Basic routing plans that save time

Basic routing plans for each of the following routing problems are given at the paragraphs indicated.

• For the salesman who must see a definite number of dispersed customers, all equally important [¶ 2073].

• For the salesman whose customers vary in importance and who must schedule more calls to the more important ones [¶ 2074].

• For the salesman who must call on all of his customers regularly and frequently [¶ 2075].

• For the salesman whose routing is determined by the location of key customers [¶ 2076].

• For the salesman who sells one town at a time [¶ 2077].

• For the salesman who sells door to door [¶ 2078].

¶ 2073 A routing plan that reduces total travel distance to a minimum

This plan works for the salesman who calls on a definite number of dispersed customers, all of whom are equally important.

⟫⟫WHAT TO DO⟶ Pinpoint your stops on a map. Try several alternative routes based on different groupings. Use a ruler to help you determine the shortest route.

Here is one way in which a salesman grouped his calls to cut his travel distance to a minimum.

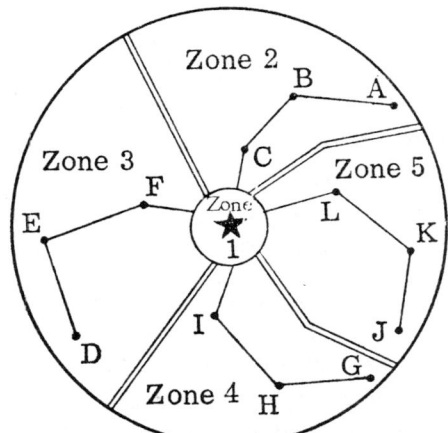

Fig 1. Grouping calls by zones.

The star in the center of the routing plan represents the salesman's base of operation. He has divided his territory into zones, and covers one zone each day.

If the salesman is unable to cover all towns in one zone on a particular day, he still works the next zone, as usual, on the following day. By not working one route two days in succession, the salesman is able to take care of individual inquiries at the smallest possible transportation cost.

For example, on the first, second, third, and fourth days of the month, the salesman may work towns in zones Nos. 2, 3, 4, and 5, respectively. On the morning of the fifth day, he might receive a call from town "B" (in zone #2) that he had been unable to cover thoroughly.

He can now take all the prospect and customer cards in town "B" of zone #2 that he had been unable to call on or follow up, take care of the inquiry, finish the calls in town "B", and work town "C" in any remaining time.

If he had interrupted his normal work schedule to spend two or three days in zone #2 and had completed his work there, he would have had to make the special trip to town "B" to take care of only this single call.

⟫⟫OBSERVATION⟶ By driving to the farthest point in each zone first and then working back, the stops not covered are those *nearest* to your headquarters.

guides to better territory coverage

¶ 2074 A routing plan to stagger calls in order of customers' importance

This type of routing allows a salesman to call on accounts with greater or less frequency according to their value to him. It is particularly valuable to the salesman who has figured the dollar value of his customers and who wishes to make more calls to more valuable customers.

⟫WHAT TO DO⟶ Divide your customers into categories that you might label "excellent," "good," "marginal." Plan to call on your best accounts every trip, the middle group every other trip, and the least important group every third or fourth trip.

EXAMPLE: John Ford sells his product to customers located in 20 cities in two states. He has divided his accounts into the above classifications. He calls on the accounts in the first group every time he is in their city, and calls on the customers in the second group during alternate trips. The third group he sees whenever possible, or when it is necessary to call on them.

This stagger plan enables John to spend more time with customers who are most profitable to him.

⟫CAUTION⟶ If the towns in your territory are very far apart it may be advisable for you to use the plan described in ¶ 2077.

¶ 2075 A routing plan for salesmen who call on customers regularly and frequently

You will save travel time by using regular-stop routing if your product (1) requires little selling, (2) appeals to an unlimited market, and (3) requires regular and frequent calls on customers. This type of routing is especially useful to men who sell food, tobacco products, a service that offers periodic check-up calls and repairs, and the like.

⟫WHAT TO DO⟶ Purchase a map that includes your territory or obtain one from your local gas service station. Pinpoint the locations of your customers. Now trace a connecting route that *most nearly* represents a straight line. Use this map to guide you on your calls until your route becomes familiar.

⟫OBSERVATION⟶ Your customers need not be located close together. Regardless of the proximity of your stops, the route must follow a continuity that is as near a straight line as possible.

¶ 2076 A plan to route calls around key customers

"Key" is defined here as those customers who demand immediate attention. A customer who must be seen right away to prevent his giving a large order to a competitor is a key customer. So is a customer who needs an immediate service call, or a prospect who is ready for closing and needs only a final interview.

Calls to key customers can be used as a routing guide by salesmen who sell in one city or in many. In either situation, the key customer becomes the one around whom all other calls are planned.

EXAMPLES: A salesman who operates in three states may have to make a sudden call to a key customer in a distant city. Before he leaves, he checks his records for other prospects or customers he might profitably contact while he is there.

A salesman whose territory is one section of a large city is called for emergency service to the other end of his territory. He checks his files for others he might see who are located near the key customer.

Key-customer routing is most advantageous to salesmen in these categories:

• Salesmen with a limited amount of accounts.
• Salesmen with a large proportion of service calls.
• Salesmen who must call on prospects in various stages of closing.
• Salesmen for whom territory coverage is less important than careful attention to accounts as they need it.

⟫CAUTION⟶ Because of its concentration on only a few customers, this routing plan does not assure you of thorough territory coverage. If you use this plan, be sure to avoid losing potential business through lack of contact and neglect.

¶ 2077 The clean-up plan for salesmen who sell one town at a time

Here is a plan that is advantageous for salesmen who call on *all* prospects and customers in a town before they go on to the next.

Because this plan allows the salesman to finish his business in any one town, its chief advantage is the economy of travel time and expense. This plan is particularly valuable for salesmen who must travel long distances.

guides to better territory coverage

A clean-up routing plan might look like this:

First Week	Third Week
Hamilton	Newberg
Margate	Plymouth
Newton	Storey
Second Week	*Fourth Week*
Waycross	Tacoma
Dorrance	Farley

Although it should be followed as closely as possible, this plan does allow a salesman to spend extra time in any town if he finds it necessary.

⇒CAUTION→ Saving travel time is not an end in itself. It may pay you to spend more time traveling if it enables you to spend more selling time with worthwhile accounts.

¶ 2078 **The broadside routing plan for door-to-door salesmen**

Broadside routing can be used in selling to homes, stores, and offices. It guarantees complete territory coverage, and is primarily valuable for one-call or first-call coverage. Figure 2 illustrates the route for thorough door-to-door coverage.

⇒CAUTION→ Call at *every* door. You will destroy the purpose of broadside routing —*intensive territory coverage*—if you skip homes or offices to call on only those that appear promising to you.

⇒OBSERVATION→ A sales manager whose product requires this type of territory coverage calls it the "hit 'em all system." He warns his men against using the "horse race system" of wandering around like a tourist, hitting a spot here and there, looking for a prospect who is a "natural." "It's a funny thing," says he, "but almost all new salesmen start using the horse race system until they learn better. They travel all over hell's half acre looking for naturals and end up with the idea that there just aren't any good prospects. Using the horse race system, they miss some of the best prospects. Using the hit 'em all system, they *can't* miss them."

¶ 2079 **Maps can be valuable to you**

Territory management can be made more effective through the proper use of maps. Maps give you a precise picture of your territory, help you see your customer locations, and aid you in planning routes that will save travel time and assure complete coverage.

Maps of towns, cities, counties, states and sections of the country may be obtained from these sources:

• The State Highway Department. Will send you state and county maps.
• City or Town Clerk. Will sell you maps of the city or town.
• Service stations. Will give you state maps, and often maps of larger cities.
• Travel bureaus
• Chambers of Commerce
• Book stores

⇒OBSERVATION→ Maps obtained from your State Highway Department often contain information valuable to you in planning your territory coverage. These maps usually pinpoint locations of radio stations, town halls, hospitals, schools, sawmills, factories, commercial buildings, and garages.

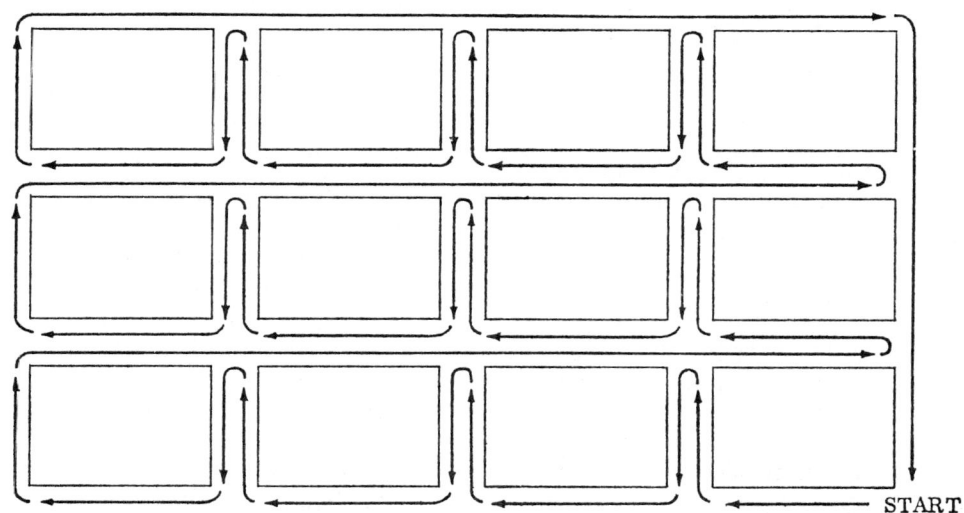

Fig. 2. Door-to-door coverage of contiguous blocks.

¶ 2080 Use the telephone to increase territory coverage

Telephone calls to supplement your personal calls on bread-and-butter customers can keep your smaller-customer relations active, improve your territory coverage, and result in extra sales.

▶ **IDEA IN ACTION** Harry Brown finds it important to spend most of his time in face-to-face contact with his best customers. Although Harry's list of customers includes many other smaller buyers, he normally sacrifices contacting them in deference to his more profitable accounts.

Harry finds a large percentage of these seldom-contacted customers becoming inactive accounts or switching to competitors. His loss in earnings, although not large, is enough to spur Harry to try supplemental telephone coverage.

On the next trip around his territory, Harry stops long enough in each town to telephone nearby smaller accounts after he has seen his bigger customers. The result is threefold: (1) contact is maintained with these accounts, assuring them that they are still thought of; (2) orders are sometimes taken over the telephone; and (3) arrangements are made for a personal call if Harry has a new line or if the customer has enjoyed an upswing in business.

¶ 2081 Watch for changes in make-up of territory

Some executives in your company—the president, sales manager, and others—are watching the growth of population of the country, if they're on the ball. They know that a big rise in population has been forecast by the U.S. Census Bureau to continue to 1980. They are watching the widespread regional shifts in the population, and the growth of metropolitan areas and their attached suburban, exurban and interurban offshoots. All of these changes affect marketing.

It is not enough for the "tops" to know how to capitalize on these changes. Each salesman must watch the developments and changes that are taking place in his own territory, and be quick to cover the newcomers in the area.

▶▶▶**OBSERVATION**▶ The shifts in industry that weaken a territory for some products strengthen it for others. For example, when farm lands are sold out for home developments, the farm implement salesman loses out, but the sales representatives who serve the shopping centers move right in. Similarly, when rezoning permits the establishment of light industry in a formerly restricted area, the salesman who is on his toes gets a line on what businesses are being "invited" in.

The more agile you are in watching developments, the better jump you get on your competitors.

▶▶▶**WHAT TO DO**▶ 1. Re-examine your routine for covering your territory. If you have not changed it in any way for the past few years, there is only one possible conclusion: your geographic area has stood still while most of the country has been doing somersaults. Make it a point on your very next trip to compare the territory with what it was when you first took it on. That will give you the clues to the sales opportunities you might have missed and will tell you whether you've been losing ground by following the old routine year in and year out.

2. Make it a point, in covering your territory, to know "what's cooking" in the community. Local newspapers, Chamber of Commerce activities, businessmen's gatherings at luncheons, are a few of the places to pick up news. And, of course, there are always your customers in the area, and the men at the gas service station, who can give you news items.

¶ 2082 A territory cut can result in bigger volume

A creative salesman does not worry about losing business volume when his territory is cut. He looks upon it as a compliment and a challenge to make bigger buyers of his present customers, and to find new profitable accounts among the prospects he previously had no time to develop.

EXAMPLE: At ¶ 3052 you will see how one salesman got more volume out of a reduced territory by upgrading his customers.

▶▶▶**OBSERVATION**▶ A sales manager usually has a good reason behind his decision to reduce a salesman's territory. In most cases he knows that there is more business in the old territory than any one man can possibly get. For example, if the company has put on a big sales promotion and advertising campaign, each salesman must work his territory more intensively to get the benefit of the promotion expenditure. He can do this better if he has less territory to cover.

IDEAS FOR CREATIVE SELLING

You Must Be Creative to Make Big Money
How to Train Your Mind to Create Ideas
Stepping up Your Creativity
Creative Ideas that Make Bigger Buyers
Ideas to Keep You Constantly Creative
Using Creative Ideas on Yourself

TABLE OF CONTENTS

	Starts at Paragraph [¶]
Miracle Guide to Creative Selling	3001

YOU MUST BE CREATIVE TO MAKE BIG MONEY

	Starts at Paragraph [¶]
Creative men are in demand	3002
You can qualify as a creative salesman	3003

HOW TO TRAIN YOUR MIND TO CREATE IDEAS

	Starts at Paragraph [¶]
Imagination has selling power	3011
Curiosity is an element of imagination	3012
Where do you fit?	3013
Train your imagination	3014
Getting ideas for creative selling	3015
Find new selling ideas to boost your earning power	3016
The formula	3017
Build up an 'idea bank'	3018
Give your ideas freely	3019

STEPPING UP YOUR CREATIVITY

	Starts at Paragraph [¶]
Adopt the attitude of a creative salesman	3031
There's always a solution to problems	3032
Discovering the bottleneck will accelerate creative thinking	3033
How a 'twist' can gain your prospect's ear	3034
Each step of the sale is a challenge to creative thinking	3035
Creative selling includes creating prospects	3036
Creative thinking wins success in the pre-approach	3037
Creative thinking helps you get by the secretary in cold canvassing	3038
Show more than savings every time you can to arouse interest	3039
How to use 'value analysis' creatively	3040
Creative ideas help to convince the prospect	3041
Offer the prospect a creative idea to overcome his objection	3042
Creative salesmen are original even in closing	3043

CREATIVE IDEAS THAT MAKE BIGGER BUYERS

	Starts at Paragraph [¶]
Creative ideas are applied in all methods of increasing sales	3051
Up-grade customers with creative thinking about benefits to them	3052
Make a big sale out of a little one with a service idea	3053
Creative salesman looks for hidden applications of product	3054

ideas for creative selling — table of contents

	Starts at Paragraph [¶]
New uses for a product challenge the creative salesman	3055
Creative salesmen look for clues to broader selling	3056
Open up a new prospect group with creative selling	3057
A creative idea wins a new important account	3058
The creative salesman follows through to get his product resold and reordered	3059

IDEAS TO KEEP YOU CONSTANTLY CREATIVE

	Starts at Paragraph [¶]
A creative idea that gets repeat orders	3071
A special service idea helps you become the main supplier	3072
Boost your sales the I. O. U. way	3073
An idea that got dealers to handle a line	3074
Offer the retailer ideas for suggestive selling	3075
Offer an idea for using existing equipment along with your product	3076
Knowledge of product and customer needs makes you creative	3077
Creativity can help avoid costly cancellations	3078
What a camera can do, if you use your imagination	3079
Reselling demands creative selling and a strong attitude against the "No"	3080
How to use the power of suggestion in creative selling	3081
Look for causes of trouble and you'll create a solution	3082
Creative salesmen use minor sales points when big ones flatten	3083
Creative salesmen help customers get full value from what they bought	3084
Creative salesmen presume every qualified prospect needs his product	3085
Creative salesmen win reciprocal favors from customers	3086
Reorganization of customer setup demands creative thinking to save account	3087

USING CREATIVE IDEAS ON YOURSELF

	Starts at Paragraph [¶]
Earn a reputation as a man who achieves	3091
Creative salesmen get that "little extra" out of every day	3092
Creative salesmen use sales tools to the greatest advantage	3093
The business picture is a stimulant to creative salesmen	3094
A "great" creative idea gives you confidence	3095

Footnote references 3999

Ideas for Creative Selling

A creative salesman always gets the lion's share of the business.

¶ 3001 ⋙ MIRACLE GUIDE to → Creative Selling

Every man who is earning big money—$30,000, $40,000, $50,000 a year—is a creative salesman. *A creative salesman creates business where none existed before.*

No one has a monopoly on creativity. There's something of that quality in *every* salesman. In fact, most salesmen are much more creative than they think they are. Don't underestimate your creative talents! They're your greatest asset.

Picking up orders is not creative selling. You get that business without any special effort. Creative selling takes imagination. You *alone* can supply this vital spark. It's the **key** to selling greatness.

To reassure yourself of using the full breadth of your creative powers, begin to train your imagination. This Guide shows you how at ¶ 3011 et seq.

Step up your creative thinking by adopting the attitudes of the top-flight creative salesmen. These attitudes are spelled out for you at ¶ 3031 et seq.

Start applying your creative thinking in each step of your work—from finding prospects to closing sales. The examples in ¶ 3035 et seq. will get you going.

To keep constantly creative, borrow ideas from others—this Guide is full of them. Get idea-minded and you will find ideas that you can adapt here, there, and everywhere—in what you read, observe, hear in conversation, or see in use.

Originate new ideas by thinking about your selling problems and arriving at a conclusion. Act on the solutions you think up.

The big hard-to-crack prospect will eventually soften if you leave an idea with him on every call. Others have won big accounts that way.

The biggest dividend to you from your creative ideas is the confidence you gain. Plan your interview around an idea you have created—big or little—and you'll feel a new power to perform.

Remember—you can't be a star salesman just by wanting to be. Will power alone won't do it; will power combined with creative selling will get you there.

¶3001

You must be creative to make big money

¶ 3002 **Creative men are in demand**

Today, more than ever before, business executives are looking for creativeness in the men they hire. That is because our times demand originality. "The man of the hour is not the man who is the strongest, craftiest, shrewdest, or most popular. He is the man of exceptional originality. He is the man who has disciplined himself to keep acquiring new knowledge and skills."

The same remark goes for salesmen. Typical of the stress upon creativeness is this statement from one company's bid for salesmen:

"Today's salesman must know not only his company's policies, products, and methods; but he must also be able to correlate them with present and future market potentials and trends. Thus, to succeed, he must be creative in his activities in order to expand markets and increase the use of better products and improved methods. Imagination, skill, knowledge, the ability to plan . . . all these are the working tools of today's creative salesman.

"The challenge is an important one . . . the opportunity is the greatest ever offered. The creative salesman who measures up to the challenge before him has unlimited avenues for advancement and for increased income. A creative sales career can be your greatest opportunity."

Any salesman can pick up orders, check stocks, answer phone or mail inquiries, and add high mileage on his car. These are necessary activities in selling, but they are *not* creative.

¶ 3003 **You can qualify as a creative salesman**

Creative salesmen earn big money because they bring their imagination and ideas into play in every step of the selling process. If you are going to make money you have to know how to create a demand for what you sell. This is the heart of selling. It takes imagination—it takes ideas—but it pays off.

If that is asking more of you than you think you can give, take stock of yourself:

• Have you ever found a prospect in cold canvassing?

• Have you ever gotten an appointment with a prospect who was hard to see?

• Have you ever created a desire for your product or services in a prospect who was not much interested when you started your interview?

If you can answer "Yes" to any of these questions, you have proved that you can be creative. Now the question is, have you been creative enough?

We are going to show you how to develop your imagination and create ideas; how to bring your imagination and ideas into play in all your selling efforts.

How to train your mind to create ideas

(*Adapted from Harry Simmons, "How to Develop Your Sales Ability," Englewood Cliffs, N. J.: Prentice-Hall, Inc.*)

¶ 3011 **Imagination has power**

Everyone has imagination. With it you dream, visualize, invent, or create.

Imagination lends a magical touch to features and talking points of a product or service. With imagination, the talking points set the fire of desire. The power of imagination makes it possible for you to help your customers visualize the profit in your company's line, the value in your merchandise, and the desirability of your cooperation.

To be helpful, imagination must be constructive. Constructive imagination has a dramatic force that sweeps away the minor arguments of competitive resistance and draws the prospect into your fold. With this quality, you are miles ahead of your competitor; without it, he may be ahead of you.

¶ 3012 **Curiosity is an element of imagination**

A salesman who is imaginative is also curious. He is eager to obtain knowledge; to find out the "why," "how," "when," "where," and "what" of everything that pertains to his job. Curiosity becomes a habit with him.

Marvin Payne, Senior Branch Manager, Remington Rand, Inc., Oklahoma City, considers curiosity an essential part of the make-up of the successful salesman. He said:

"Without it [curiosity] we cannot expect, nor even hope, to achieve any real measure of success. *We must be curious.* * * *

how to train your mind to create ideas

"Without curiosity we cannot open new avenues for the sale of our products. We remain only a parasite living upon the results obtained through the curiosity of an inquisitive predecessor."

¶ 3013   Where do you fit?

Imagination resides in the salesman who sits down quietly every evening and thinks of the things that happened during the day, trying to think up better ways to handle the situations that didn't work out well. It resides to a greater extent in the salesman who spends an hour at home each night thinking about his customers and their problems, letting his mind run riot on ways to solve their problems and build up their business so that he can sell more to them. It resides most in the salesman who tries to discover new ideas that will make his job bigger and better than it ever was before.

Wherever you fit in this picture of salesmen using their imagination, there is room for further development of your imagination—in fact, it must be developed in every salesman who has a bigger goal ahead than he has yet achieved.

¶ 3014   Train your imagination

Fortunately, the quality of imagination is one that can be acquired and developed. Regardless of what your job may be, you can acquire imagination by this simple practice:

Imagine yourself handling your job like a star salesman. Dissect your job piece by piece, and imagine all the things you would do in difficult situations. Let your imagination have boundless horizons, but try to keep your ideas practical and realistic. Write down your ideas so you don't forget them—you never can tell when they will be needed.

Don't be afraid of wild ideas—they frequently straighten themselves out when you think them through—and you can often adapt them in your job. Naturally, you don't have to use every idea that comes to you—but, as a rule, ideas go where they are welcome, which means that they develop and display themselves when and where you encourage them. Whatever it is you are doing, try to think of ways to do it better, more efficiently, more effectively, and more profitably for all concerned.

EXAMPLE: Regular practice in using imagination made a star salesman of one man known to the author. He spent half an hour a day, every evening, in silent thought. He asked himself where he could find new markets for his products; where and how he could discover new uses for them. Within a few years' time, the results of this routine became apparent, and he has been an outstandingly successful man for years. His specialty is "creative selling"—creating business where none existed before, finding customers where other salesmen do not see them.

Whenever you are forced to sit still for awhile, whether waiting, traveling, or resting, think of something constructive, something connected with your job. If you read while waiting, do it with a conscious effort to find ideas that you can apply in your work. Follow your thoughts through to a definite conclusion so that your thinking results in an idea. You will be astounded at the number and quality of helpful ideas your imaginative thinking will bring forth!

The more you use your imagination, the more imagination you will have available to use. "Use it or lose it!" is an apt warning.

⟫⟫SUGGESTION→   SCM Corporation urges its salesmen to exercise their imagination, because "imagination is not some magic quality that a few gifted men possess. It is more like a 'muscle' that all men are born with. Some men develop it by exercising it constantly to help them do the unusual, when the usual has failed. Others let it atrophy by never exercising it at all."

Salesmen are creative only so long as their mental activity remains keen and stimulated. If you hesitate or lapse, even for a short time, you may lose a week or a month in regaining your creative momentum.

¶ 3015   Getting ideas for creative selling

Getting ideas to help you create sales means driving yourself to apply your imagination to your selling job. Drive is a vital part of creative thinking. Only with drive will you get ideas from the numerous sources that are available to every salesman.

All creative salesmen get their ideas in the same way. They:

• *Borrow ideas from others.* You can apply to your own uses an idea that someone else has used to create a sale. In the section that follows you will find ideas that creative salesmen have used. Many of them can be used exactly as they are given.

▸▸▸IMPORTANT▸ When sales managers ask their salesmen to submit their best selling ideas for purposes of exchange with other salesmen, they are encouraging the men to borrow from each other.

• *Adapt ideas that others have used.* With a little applied imagination you can use other people's ideas to help you create sales. Therefore, look at each creative idea in this Guide as having some elements in them that can be used by you. You can find the way to fit them to your needs.

• *Originate ideas.* The ideas you originate to create sales are stimulated by your reading, your contacts with customers, prospects, and friends, your observations, the extra thinking you do to break special contest quotas, your concentration upon a problem. These original ideas are nothing more than a new combination of old elements. It is the fresh twist you give to an old idea that makes it original.

¶ 3016 **Find new selling ideas to boost your earning power**

You can create new sales, and boost your earning power, by finding new ideas for your presentation that will heighten your prospect's interest.

Some salesmen acquire good ideas more easily than others. They seem to 'spark' new ideas without half-trying. But most salesmen have to work hard to get enough ideas to go around.

One thing is for sure: The new ideas you need won't just come along—you have to look for them. And the harder you look, the more ideas you'll have.

▸▸▸SUGGESTION▸ Use this idea-creating, 10-step formula to help you keep plenty of good selling ideas on hand for your presentation.

¶ 3017 **The formula**

• *Spend 15 minutes a day looking for them.* Like guests, ideas come only where and when invited; invite some in daily.

• *Read more.* Non-readers start far behind the line in getting ideas. The best way is to force yourself to read for a certain period of time every day, whether you like it or not.

• *Talk as often as you can with persons who are better informed on some subjects than you are.* A good, brisk conversation with an intelligent person will make you think as you never thought before.

• *Write more letters.* Ideas grow in proportion to the need for them, and one of the best ways to have a *need* for them is by writing letters. Try writing to your prospects; say something new in each letter.

• *Learn by talking to other salesmen.* Even though you and another salesman may not live in the same selling world and sell something entirely different, mental interchange of ideas with men in your profession gives you a blood transfusion of workable ideas.

• *Travel more.* Travel is very helpful to finding new ideas. Why? Because when you see new things, you are forced out of your non-thinking rut.

• *Cultivate older people and listen to them.* Just because their hair may be white, and their hearing not up to par, don't pass older people by. Senior citizens are wise in the ways of the world, and delightful to talk to.

• *Experiment with your own ideas.* Sometimes, you'll have an idea that sounds good to you, but how can you tell if it will work until you experiment with it? Always be willing to welcome new selling ideas, and then be willing to try them out in your selling.

• *Adapt ideas from others.* Not all the good ideas you need for selling have to be startling or sensational. Some can be just ordinary ideas that work for other salesmen.

If you see an idea that another salesman is finding pat and profitable, adapt it to your prospects, and your kind of selling.

• *Consult the experts.* Don't be above asking those who are thought to be expert in your profession to contribute to your success. Whenever you have a chance to talk to such a person—do it. You will find these experts eager to share their knowledge.

¶ 3018 **Build up an "idea bank"**

The more ideas you can dig up, the more chances you have of making sales. Once you become idea-minded, you'll get ideas all the time.

To preserve the ideas that come to you at odd moments, keep a notebook handy. Jot down in it the ideas you read, or hear, or see, or think about; or the one that comes to you in an occasional "brain flash." This handy notebook is your idea bank.

Some of the ideas you come across will be in magazine articles, newspapers, or other sources that you can clip. It's a good idea to supplement your handy idea notebook with an idea file into which you place the clippings.

¶ 3019 **Give your ideas freely**

The salesman who supplies his customers and prospects with useful ideas, along with service, builds goodwill and confidence, which open the door to bigger orders. Nothing interests a prospect so keenly as a new idea, or even an old idea dressed up in new clothing.

One star salesman finally wound up with the big account he was after because he had left an idea each time he called.

Dig into your idea bank and file to find the idea that will help your customer get an extra penny per sale, or sell an extra unit per man, or make a few extra dollars per month through more efficient operations.

⟫CAUTION→ When you pick up an idea *from a customer* to put into your idea bank be sure to note where you got it. No customer wants his ideas passed on to a competitor. Also, be careful how you give your ideas. Don't give the impression that you are telling a customer how to run his business.

It can only redound to *your* advantage if you can help your customer or prospect discover or originate some new idea for his advantage. The ideas you develop yourself that will help develop *his* business, will certainly develop *your* business!

Stepping up your creativity

¶ 3031 **Adopt the attitude of a creative salesman**

To begin to step up your creativity you must adopt the attitude of a successful creative salesman. Such a salesman has these positive approaches to his work:

• He knows there's a solution to the problem and by thinking creatively he can find it [¶ 3032].

• By discovering the bottleneck he can accelerate his creative thinking [¶ 3033].

• By thinking creatively he can convert a "No" to a "Yes" [¶ 3034].

• He looks at each step of the sale as a challenge to creative thinking [¶ 3035].

¶ 3032 **There's always a solution to problems**

The creative salesman has somehow learned that in selling there exists a solution to every problem, if he can but find it. To be sure, he doesn't always find it. But his attitude is that a solution exists.

Every sales executive knows men who seem to have the habit of finding their way around sales obstacles that others find insurmountable. These men accomplish their outstanding work largely because they "stay with" a given sales problem when less creative salesmen throw up their hands in defeat. This quality is a form of persistence — not the persistence shown in "staying with" a tough *customer* but in staying with a tough *problem*. And they do this because they have learned from prior experience that tough problems, if they are to be solved at all, commonly yield only at the price of extra "brainsweat."

  IDEA IN ACTION Ralph Saunders sells automotive supplies. He is top man in his organization, but even so he is unable to sell several large chain organizations which do a large volume of business.

Other salesmen representing Ralph's company have also tried without success to "crack" these special accounts, and there is therefore reason to believe that as a practical matter his company is simply unable to sell them.

Ralph "stays with" this problem hoping to come up with a solution. He realizes that persistence in calling will not provide the answer.

Finally, Ralph has a new idea. He carefully shops several of the chain's outlets and determines exactly which competing brands they stock. He notes the resale prices of various items, and compares them with his own. After considerable work, Ralph makes a discovery. He finds that his company offers an unusually attractive value on one particular specialty unit, as compared with the lines that are established in these outlets.

Ralph telephones the buyer for one of the

chains. "Mr. Elton," he says, "I'm not calling you to ask you to consider our line. I'd like to have about five minutes with you to tell you of something I've learned about an opportunity you're missing in some of your stores."

This "curiosity" approach wins him the interview. True to his word, he does not try to present his line as such, but instead focuses the buyer's attention on the one item which he is not buying to best advantage from his present suppliers.

"Now here's my suggestion, Mr. Elton," concludes Ralph, "If you will select, say, six of your typical outlets and let me test out our #763 in them, I'm willing to let the results speak for themselves."

Mr. Elton accepts this offer.

Ralph personally instructs the salespeople in the six test stores, and persuades them to feature his #763 in their windows and to "talk it up" as a good item.

The added sales induce Mr. Elton to place this item in their entire group of stores. Shortly thereafter he says to Ralph, "You're one of the few salesmen who have ever taken the trouble to *prove* to us how we could increase our sales and profits.

"We saw no reason to change suppliers before, but we now think you've earned a break. Next time you stop in, we'll be glad to listen to your suggestions as to how we can go about introducing some of your products."

¶ 3033 Discovering the bottleneck will accelerate creative thinking

With the attitude that every selling assignment has a "bottleneck" of its own, the creative salesman looks for the bottleneck to help him step up his creative thinking on the problem. In one case the bottleneck may be in finding prospects; in another, it may be in getting the interview; in a third, the problem may be how to beat competition, and so on.

The creative salesman concentrates on finding means of overcoming the impediment that crops up often in his selling. Once he has hit upon a successful formula, he uses the same ideas and methods again and again.

▶ **IDEA IN ACTION** How to beat competition was Fred Compton's bottleneck. Here's how he beat it in one case, using methods that he found had worked in others.

The prospect, a large industrial concern with a department equipped to make time and motion studies, broke down the processing of its paper work into make-ready, set-up and running time—each operation was broken down into hundredths of a minute! Fred took these figures and translated them in terms of his company's new high-speed equipment which would result in approximately 35% more efficiency over present equipment.

In the meantime, three competitive equipment producers were contacted by the prospect; each was a threat to Fred. Here's what Fred did that beat this competition:

• He prepared an attractive proposal which was more convincing than that of at least one of the competitors because it recommended a specific piece of equipment.

• He arranged for a demonstration with the "right man".

• He gained the friendship of the department head, who kept him informed of when the competitors were to make their demonstrations.

• He arranged a luncheon with the key buyer to occur immediately after the most threatening competitor had finished his demonstration—and he brought his sales supervisor with him.

• He compared his own product with the competitor's (the one still in the running), whose equipment he knew thoroughly.

• He presented an impressive list of users and new customers who had recently purchased the same equipment.

• He brought the controller and the department head to see his company's exhibition at the Business Show.

¶ 3034 How a twist can gain your prospect's ear

BY JOSEPH FISHER,
Field Underwriter,
Washington National Life Insurance Company

Getting a prospect to listen to you can be a lot easier if you use a new twist. The edge it can give you is enough to add many sales that otherwise would never get off the ground.

Actual case: Many of my prospects, especially sole proprietors of small businesses or professional people, were reluctant to hear my story. They seemed to think they would live forever.

Fresh angle: My new approach is angled to avoid talk of life insurance. The reason is simple: A man who has built a business or a practice by himself isn't comfortable talking about "retirement" or death. That's why my new offer, a strictly business proposition, works so well.

Here's a sample opening from my presentation to a small businessman:

"Mr. Prospect, how would you like to guarantee the value of your business for the rest of your life? My company will take an option to buy your business, in the event of your death, for whatever price you name today. We will turn over to whomever you name the amount you think your business is worth. And, on top of that, we'll give the business back to your family to do with as they please."

I say these words slowly and deliberately, emphasizing the key words, so that the prospect realizes that I'm not trying to "fast talk" him. Almost everyone reacts with surprise and shock, and generally each one manages to offer at least one of these objections:

Objection #1: "I don't know what my business is worth." This is a fair objection, and indicates an open-minded and interested prospect. It's often difficult to set a price on a business or practice that would be hard to sell, and which has no clear-cut market value. But I remind my prospect of the terms of my offer.

"I told you that we'd purchase the business at whatever price you set. A fair price would be the amount that you as a 'willing seller', would or could get, from a 'willing buyer'—today."

This comment assures him that I am interested in his evaluation of the worth of his business. I give him a rundown of some important facts and figures that he could use to set a fair value on his business: annual income, value of assets, outlook for the future, the importance of his personality in bringing in business, and other factors.

But this objection is often merely a first reaction. It can be handled without too much trouble. The ones that follow aren't quite so easy.

Objection #2: "What do you get out of it?" This one makes selling a challenge. I generally begin by explaining that my company takes these options on large numbers of businesses. The charges that each one pays to retain our option more than covers the cost we have to bear. It all adds up to a guarantee for the owners and their families, and a profit for my company.

Objection #3: "What do I get out of it?" This is where you put your salesmanship to work. I give all the explanations I use to sell from the "life insurance" angle. But now, I slant them as "business income replacement" money.

This money pays the state tax, provides for the businessman's dependents, and guarantees the true value of the business against the normal need to sell which usually follows an untimely death.

My plan—the "option to buy"—assures the businessman that his heirs won't have to sell the business for a song in order to raise money quickly. Most prospects are excited to learn that they can get the full value of their business, and still retain full ownership.

Result: Since I began using this approach, I've had tremendous success — and I'm sure that it can do for you and your sales record what it did for mine.

¶ 3035 **Each step of the sale is a challenge to creative thinking**

The attitude that each step of the sale is a challenge to creative thinking makes it possible to create business where none existed before. In "cold turkey" canvassing, this attitude is the key to topflight success.

Let's take each of the steps in a sale and see how a creative idea helped to make a sale to a cold canvass prospect.

Here are the steps, so familiar in your selling; the creative ideas are given in the paragraphs indicated.

You create the prospect . . . by making him realize a need [¶ 3036].
You make the right pre-approach . . . by creative thinking [¶ 3037].
You get the interview with the prospect . . . by creatively getting by a secretary who won't let you in [¶ 3038].
You arouse his interest . . . by creatively finding the benefit that means most to the prospect [¶ 3039].
You stimulate his desire . . . by creatively building his desire for the benefits [¶ 3040].
You convince him that the benefit will work for him . . . by the creative quality of your demonstration [¶ 3041].
You overcome an unusual objection . . . by offering the prospect a new idea [¶ 3042].

¶ 3036 Creative selling includes creating prospects

A creative salesman doesn't just look for prospects, he creates them. He has to, in most fields of selling, for if he didn't create the prospect he would not sell. With each call in cold canvassing you are creating a prospect.

EXAMPLE: Most users of typewriters don't "shop" for new machines. In fact, most of them do not even want, or realize they need, new typewriters until an enterprising typewriter salesman convinces them of what a new machine can do. So a salesman, rather than just looking for prospects, actually creates them.

The same is true of many other fields where each day's plan must include several cold canvass calls.

¶ 3037 Creative thinking wins success in the pre-approach

Part of the pre-approach to a sale is to find the right man to whom to tell your sales story. It takes creative thinking to solve this problem, especially if you have been having trouble with one "right man" and are looking for an opportunity to tell your story to someone else who has authority to make the buying decision.

▶ **IDEA IN ACTION** The "right man" whom Jim Oakes had been trying to get to buy his product wouldn't budge from his established source. Jim learned one day that the "right man" had resigned from his position because of internal differences, and he saw the possibility of a more amenable prospect in his successor.

But Jim didn't know who this successor was. *Creative idea:* Although he knew that Mr. X had left, *Jim still called for him by name.* The switchboard operator volunteered the name of the person who had assumed his duties, and there Jim was, ready to greet the new incumbent by name and to congratulate him on his promotion.

¶ 3038 Creative thinking helps you get by the secretary in cold canvassing

The very first step toward the interview in cold canvassing—getting by the secretary—may call for imagination. This happens when the secretary guards her employer's time so carefully that you can't get in to see the prospect.

▶ **IDEA IN ACTION** Ordinary sales methods were of no avail to Tom Miller in trying to get an over-conscientious secretary to tell her boss that Tom wanted to see him. He had tried the technique that normally works—"selling" the secretary on announcing him and fixing a time when he could see him [see ¶ 4073]. But this guardian of the boss's time could not be won over.

Tom would not let his effort end there. He knew, from what he had observed of the prospect's place of business, and from what he knew about the prospect through pre-approach study, that he could make a sale easily if he could get in. So he pondered the situation and decided to do something bold; he would call his prospect at home after working hours.

"Mr. Smith," asked Tom, "do you have any influence with your secretary?"

"Why?" asked Mr. Smith, laughing good naturedly.

"Because," said Tom, "I have some equipment that could save you a lot of money, and I can't convince her that she ought to let me in to see you."

The prospect fixed a convenient time for an appointment for the next morning, and a week later Tom had a signed contract.

¶ 3039 Show more than savings every time you can arouse interest

Suppose your best selling point for the product you offer is the savings it enables the prospect to make. The weight of this argument may seem sufficient to you to convince any prospect that he should buy. But you can never be sure.

▶ **IDEA IN ACTION** Bill Fleming found that savings alone would not always "bring home the bacon." He was able to point out savings of more than $25,000 a year to his prospect, which to his mind justified the purchase of his product. What made the sale was Bill's switching his selling point to the space-saving benefit of his equipment. He had observed that the prospect's office was overcrowded. The space-saving advantage solved the problem and Bill made the sale.

¶ 3040 How to use value analysis creatively

You can never tell where your next selling idea will come from. But you can be assured of one thing—a good idea will seldom fall into your lap. You have to keep thinking about the needs of your customers and prospects. For example—

Applying the "what would do it cheaper?" question to your customers' and prospects'

stepping up your creativity

needs can pay off in profitable new orders. Here's how three salesmen used value analysis.

• While calling on a customer, a dictating machines salesman noticed clerks taking inventory by posting inventory data to forms. He inquired about the job and learned that the data on the forms was then transferred to punched cards.

 IDEA IN ACTION Why not have the inventory data dictated into portable machines and then transcribed directly to the cards?

Payoff: This idea cut the customer's cost of taking inventory by 30%; it also sold several portable dictating machines

• Walking through a customer's plant, a steel salesman spotted several machine parts made from competitors' steel. He examined them and discovered they were an expensive alloy. He suggested that a free-cutting stainless steel be used.

Pay off: The idea cut machining time 50% and, naturally, the salesman got a fat order.

• A salesman for a wire-bound box firm lost out when an account switched to a lower cost packaging method. However, he got it back when he used value analysis—showing that despite higher initial cost, the wire-bound box could save money. How? The company could have its distributors simply re-loop the wire-bound box around out-going shipments, and reuse it.

¶ 3041 **Creative ideas help to convince the prospect**

You might be using a demonstration to convince your prospect that the benefits you've pointed out are real. The entire demonstration takes creative thinking, as is explained later in this Guide. An extra twist, added by a creative thought, can give the demonstration greater convincing power.

Imagine having a prospect for whom you discover savings of $85,000 a year through the use of something you sell! If the saving is big, chances are the investment required by the customer is big, too. The whole proposition takes on mammoth proportions—including the salesman's commission.

You may have to convince your sales manager, when you're headed for a big deal, that the proposition merits a deviation from your usual demonstration procedure. In the case cited below, the company went to the expense of shipping the product to the customer's office, and making advance preparations so that a good demonstration, fitted to the prospect's specific needs, could be made. The trouble and expense all proved worthwhile—the big sale was made.

IDEA IN ACTION Harold Thomson had a customer who used only one of his company's products. Thomson knew there was a potential need for much more equipment, if he could but get in and make a survey.

He "sold" the survey first. One of the recommendations he made on the basis of the facts disclosed was to decentralize the operation. This meant that a unit of the product he hoped to sell would be installed in 5 different places.

The most important phase of the sale was the demonstration. 21 people from 5 different divisions had to see the demonstration. This fact, plus the size of the potential sales, justified a request that his company do everything necessary to permit an on-the-spot demonstration.

The demonstration was made in the customer's office. The on-the-spot display overcame all the objections raised by the 21 interested viewers.

⇛OBSERVATION→ This kind of deal won't happen to the $5,000-a-year man, the ordertaker, or any of the other varieties of salesmen who never reach even the $10,000-a-year class. It's for men who have confidence, courage, imagination, and a desire to tackle big buyers.

¶ 3042 **Offer the prospect a creative idea to overcome his objection**

It takes creative thinking to overcome an everyday objection in that you must make a selection of reasons on which to build your answer. But when an unusual objection arises, a new creative idea—new to the prospect—will often make the sale.

IDEA IN ACTION A Brooklyn real estate broker, Mr. Bognossian, had an attractive investment property for his client, a corporation executive. It was just what the prospect wanted and he made an acceptable offer to the owner.

A few days later the prospect called at the broker's office to say that he could not buy the property.

"Mr. Bognossian," he said, "I cannot go through with this deal. I know it's a good buy, but if anything should happen to me, my estate will need cash and too much would be tied up in that property."

The $1,500 commission looked too good to Mr. Bognossian to let it slip away. He thought quickly, using an idea that was new to the prospect.

"Mr. Investor," he said, "I agree with you as far as you go, but I'm sure I can show you how you can buy this property and still keep yourself in a cash-on-hand position."

The investor-prospect was eager to hear the solution.

"The property, after all expenses," said Mr. Bognossian, "will earn profits of about $8,000 a year. Instead of $8,000, figure the return at $7,000 and use the other $1,000 a year to buy life insurance to give you the cash your estate will need. You'll be sure, in this way, that there'll never be a distress sale of the property."

The deal was closed.

¶ 3043 Creative salesmen are original even in closing

The creative salesman thinks of ways to make his presentation dramatic, and carries the dramatic element right to the close. Asking for the order comes naturally as he brings his drama to a climax.

The following idea in action, from Charles B. Roth, "Successful Sales Presentations,"[1] illustrates the point.

IDEA IN ACTION Bill Carroll sells an intangible service — long-distance moving. He developed his presentation by devising a visual aid that made his intangible service appear as a tangible. Using a large brief case with cutaway side, he made it possible for the prospect to look into a large moving van packed with miniature furniture. Each packed piece was protected with cloth wrapping.

Bill unpacked the van in front of the prospect, showing as he did so why it was impossible for any furniture to be scratched, marred, or broken if properly packed, as his firm packed it.

As Bill unpacked the van, he reiterated the advantages of his company's careful method of preparing goods for long-distance shipping. Then he began repacking the van. This was the dramatic action that led to the close.

Having repacked the van, he would ask: "You would want your household goods handled in this safe, sure, and easy manner, wouldn't you, Mrs. Prospect?" Of course, there could be only one answer from the prospect, "Yes." He followed his prospect's "Yes" immediately by asking when the family expected to move, "so I can make all arrangements and guarantee that your household goods will be in your new home when you get there."

Creative ideas that make bigger buyers

¶ 3051 Creative ideas are applied in all methods of increasing sales

Creative ideas open doors to bigger buyers in many ways. To mention a few, creative ideas have been used to:

- up-grade customers [¶ 3052]
- find hidden applications for a product [¶ 3054]
- find new uses for raw materials [¶ 3055]
- broaden a customer's buying [¶ 3056]
- open up a whole new field of prospects among which there are some big buyers [¶ 3057]
- win important new accounts [¶ 3058]
- get the product resold and reordered [¶ 3059]

The ideas in the paragraphs noted worked for the men who originated them; they can work for you, too.

¶ 3052 Up-grade customers with creative thinking about benefits to them

You can raise the dollar volume of a customer's business by creatively thinking of how his business will benefit if he buys a better grade of the product or service you are selling. The creative ideas come to you through recalling past ideas and experiences and relating them to the problem at hand.

Go over your list of customers who already use the better grade product. Then think: how has each customer used the high-priced product? Can the man whom you are going to up-grade make a similar use of it? What is there about the business of the customer you are going to upgrade that is like the business of the customers who use the better grades?

IDEA IN ACTION The sales manager for a large envelope company noticed that Wilson Fleming had not only survived a territory cut but was actually producing more dollar volume than his old territory had yielded. It was especially noticeable because sales figures from the other territories showed no simi-

creative ideas that make bigger buyers

lar successes among the other salesmen. The sales manager called Wilson in and asked how he did it.

"Well, I did add some new customers, but most of the increased sales came from old customers," said Wilson.

"What did you do, bully them into buying more stuff than they could use?" asked the sales manager.

"No, although by concentrating on them I did get more volume. In most cases, however, I got them to buy better envelopes than they had been using—better paper, better design, better printing. Each time I'd call on an old customer I'd talk about the benefits of using higher quality, better looking envelopes. Slowly but surely it worked, and now almost half my old customers are ordering higher-priced envelopes and are happy with them."

¶ 3053 Make a big sale out of a little one with a service idea

By showing a prospect how to increase efficiency or otherwise improve his operations, you may be able to increase the size of an original order. The suggestions you are able to offer come from the knowledge you gain about his business as you prepare to make the sale of your product.

▶ IDEA IN ACTION The cashier of a bank was interested in buying a desk and called in Herb Brown, salesman for an office supply house. As the prospect talked, Herb made mental notes of the condition and arrangement of the bank furniture and operating equipment. He made no effort to close the sale at the end of the interview, but told the prospect that he would see him on the following morning.

That evening Herb prepared a scale drawing incorporating his own ideas on how the bank should be modernized. He showed how, by a new arrangement of furniture and equipment, the working efficiency would increase. The drawing interested the prospect, and that morning Herb received a $6,000 order for furniture and equipment.

¶ 3054 Creative salesman looks for hidden applications of product

When a product, like a duplicating machine, has many applications, a salesman is apt to select the most obvious one, and make a proposal that meets that particular need. The creative salesman looks for the hidden applications. A hidden application may be the one that opens the way to big orders.

▶ IDEA IN ACTION Steve Farmer had been calling for a long time on the circulation manager of a well-known firm that does a tremendous amount of direct mail advertising. The obvious application of one of his products was to save costs through use of the machine on promotional literature.

He called on the circulation manager, a top executive in this type of organization, and was brushed off. On each subsequent call on other departments he was referred back to the circulation department or the purchasing agent, and neither would see him.

One day when the circulation manager was out sick, he reached the assistant who seemed quite interested. A survey was made and a short time later a proposal was presented covering promotional literature. A saving of up to 70% was shown on one application, and a definite machine was recommended for this application.

The assistant circulation manager presented the proposal to the circulation manager and the sale died.

Farmer tried again the following year. This time, with the help of a colleague who sold another product to the same prospect, he hit upon a hidden application for a different machine and was able to get an order. Also, through this sale he got an "in" to the general manager, to whom he planned to re-issue his original proposal.

The sale was the most important of the year for Farmer for at least three reasons:
- It was the initial sale to a large non-user of long standing.
- The sale opened the door to many new applications and additional equipment for this customer.
- The application was simple though hidden by many larger and more obvious applications.

⟫⟫OBSERVATION⟶ This story also illustrates the value of "staying with" a big-buyer prospect. It demonstrates, too, the necessity for finding a way in when the "right man" for the obvious application won't buy. In large organizations, which are often the big-buyer prospects, it is easier, of course, to find another "right man" than in smaller companies.

¶ 3055 New uses for a product challenge the creative salesman

A new use for a product is best illustrated by the strides that have been made in adapting new raw materials to products conventionally made of other materials—plastic is an outstanding example of the century.

Men in the product development department of the producers of new raw materials are not the only ones thinking up new uses. Salesmen also catch the creation fever and make important creative contributions.

Your creative abilities are especially brought into play when you set out to sell a prospect the new use of your materials. You work hand in hand with the firm's engineers on such an assignment. In fact, you count more than the engineer, frequently, because without your ability to create a desire for the product in the mind of a customer, the engineer's idea would be valueless. An idea that has no value is not a creative idea.

The stimulant to selling a new use for your product is the extra sales you will make to new prospects and old customers. The very first sale of a new use opens the way to big buyers.

IDEA IN ACTION Bryan Moore's firm, a manufacturer of paper cartons, had hit on the idea of making a carton that would replace wooden containers for a hardware item. Engineers perfected a sample self-locking carton. Before the firm could undertake production, the first sale had to be made.

Bryan made the sale by being creative in every step of the selling process.

He qualified the prospect by selecting an important manufacturer of the hardware item. The name of this manufacturer, as a user, would carry weight when he approached other prospects. He "went for broke" to get in to see his man. (What he did is described in ¶ 4075.) He created a desire for the product by giving a presentation that emphasized the benefits of a carton as compared with wooden boxes. He demonstrated dramatically with his sample carton the security, lightness, and other advantages of his materials; and he closed the sale on the strength of the well-planned sales story he had created.

¶ 3056 Creative salesmen look for clues to broader selling

A customer may be purchasing all his requirements of a certain item from you. You feel that he must have need for other items in your line, or for certain services your firm offers. Your normal efforts to sell across the board have not brought results. Your customer has remained a one-item buyer.

As a creative salesman you know there is a solution to this problem of getting the customer to buy other items in your line. You keep your eyes open, your ears attentive, and your mind alert for the slightest hint of a need for other items on your product or service list. You get permission to watch the employees who use your product in performing their jobs. This kind of observation gives you the clues to the need for the "something else" you want your customer to buy.

IDEA IN ACTION A salesman for an envelope company was pleased with the envelope orders from a large mail-order company, but stayed alert for ways to make the publisher a bigger customer. Watching the operators prepare some envelopes for a special mailing, he discovered that many of the envelopes were "slugged" "Attention: Sales Manager", and that the company did this job itself.

Knowing that his plant could do the same imprinting in one-sixth the time, the salesman showed the customer how to save time, trouble and expense by letting the envelope supplier perform this service. The mail-order company was quick to see the convenience and the savings in time and money that pre-printed envelopes would mean. The salesman was happy with the bigger orders that resulted.

¶ 3057 Open up a new prospect group with creative selling

Are you in a field of selling where certain prospects will not buy because they say they get what they need through trade associations? There may be a sales appeal that will overcome this objection. In exactly this situation a creative salesman found the appeal and opened up an entire prospect group to which to sell.

IDEA IN ACTION "Don't waste your time on the textile people in your territory," was the counsel given to Dave Bell by the salesman whose territory he was taking over. "They don't want our business service because they have several trade associations that take care of these things for them."

Dave checked with his sales manager and found that the company had never done well with the textile people. The sales manager knew of no approach that would work, but thought that a way might be found.

The problem was a challenge to Dave. He in-

creative ideas that make bigger buyers

vestigated the services that the trade associations gave to their members and listed all that were similar to those offered by his service.

Then he began to make calls on the textile people. Sure enough, he was brushed off with the objection that he had been warned against.

"Well, let's see about that," was his reply. "On this sheet of paper, Mr. Prospect, I have listed all the help you get from other sources. But over here on the left I have listed those things that we do for you which you cannot get elsewhere."

"Now, do you honestly think that you don't need our service?"

That, in essence, was his presentation. Because the facts were on his side, because he had presented them in so clear a manner, he made sale after sale.

¶ 3058 **A creative idea wins a new important account**

Persistence in calling steadily on a prospect who will be a big buyer once you land him is no waste of time. But to land this prospect it takes ingenuity and creative thinking, for in the period that you have been trying to win the account you have used all the techniques in the book for breaking through the barrier of competition. The day when you can plan your interview around a creative idea you will probably make the sale.

▶ **IDEA IN ACTION** Thomas Docherty had his mind set on selling Monroe calculating machines to a firm in his territory that had the potential for becoming his biggest account. Docherty knew that this firm was the largest user of office machines in the territory. For years he had called regularly on the purchasing agent but had never been able to break through competition. To use his own language, he "could not afford to give up"; the potential volume of sales, if he overcame the bottleneck, was too promising.

Docherty has the driving power essential to creative thinking. He felt he would some day get the big creative idea that would lick his problem. He didn't know where or how.

He made a practice of keeping himself informed in every possible way about his "big" prospect's business. He always read the prospect's house organ and its annual report to stockholders. In following this routine he got the idea that finally clinched the sale.

The prospect had a wonderful profit-sharing plan for its employees. Looking through the annual report of securities owned by the profit-sharing trust, Docherty noticed that a profitable investment had been made in shares of a company affiliated with Monroe.

Immediately the idea came to him that he could use this information to advantage. Surely the purchasing agent would be interested in knowing that he and his fellow employees were indirectly owners of Monroe and would see the sense of buying machines from Monroe. The idea worked. It proved the wedge that opened the way to an order for four machines.

⟫⟫**OBSERVATION**⟶ Again we see the ramifications of creative thinking. Here it was not a product use that was thought up, or a way to broaden a customer's buying. It was just a way to come to the prospect with a fresh approach.

¶ 3059 **The creative salesman follows through to get his product resold and reordered**

A salesman who sells to others who must resell his product—either wholesalers or retailers—is deeply concerned with his *customer's* efforts to complete the sale to the ultimate consumer. He knows that reorders are almost completely dependent upon the customer's ability to sell the product to the ultimate consumer.

⟫⟫**OBSERVATION**⟶ It's human nature for the average person to shy away from things with which he is not completely familiar. If the dealer or his employees are not fully informed about your product—how to use it, what it will do, its advantages, etc.—they hesitate to push it, fearing the embarrassment of inability to answer a customer's questions. Given two competing products, the dealer's hands will reach for the one whose use and selling points he has been taught by the manufacturer!

The creative salesman is keenly aware that all of the devices his company might use to educate the dealer and the dealer's selling staff—advertising matter, sales manuals, house organs, dealers' conventions, dealers' contests, training customer salesmen—are not enough. He does all he can to contribute to the process.

▶ **IDEA IN ACTION** Charlie Aldan calls on his dealer-customer and finds that he can't get an order because the dealer is stocked-up. Being a creative salesman, he is observant. He looks around and doesn't see a single piece of material that has been furnished by his company to publicize the product and what it will do. He knows that this dealer would be selling the product if he himself, as well as people who come into the store, were reminded of the product and its benefits. Here's how he talks to this customer:

"The reason you're stocked up, Mr. Dealer, is that you aren't selling our Shino Polish fast enough. I think I know why, too. As I look around, I don't see a single one of our new lithographed displays that every one of our dealers is entitled to. As a matter of fact, I've gotten six re-orders, today alone, from stores that are using this display. It's the best silent salesman we've ever put out. Suppose I drop in tomorrow and put it up for you. Then I'll check with you again in a week or ten days—unless you need a re-stock sooner."

➤OBSERVATION➤ Tons of promotional and display materials are allowed to gather dust in storerooms and basements simply because the wholesaler or retailer, to whom they have been furnished at great expense, doesn't use them and the salesman doesn't take the opportunity to make them work for him as well as the customer. Here's an opportunity of large dimensions for the creative salesman.

Ideas to keep you constantly creative

¶ 3071 A creative idea that gets repeat orders

Repeat orders mean chunky commissions. You don't want to lose them. In some fields of selling, the idea of making a survey to convince the customer that he *cannot afford not to repeat* his order will bring in the renewal.

▶ **IDEA IN ACTION** Stanley Grant sells a line of re-membrance advertising products. When Stanley's customer told him that he didn't plan to renew his desk pad program, Stanley suggested a post card survey.

"When the post cards started flooding the customer's office," says Stanley, "the customer was astonished. He had no idea anyone would be so enthusiastic about the desk pads, and he didn't want to be spending money on them if there was nothing to be gained."

The return totaled more than 33%, and all but ten asked to be kept on the list. As a result Stanley got his renewal order.

¶ 3072 A special service idea helps you become the main supplier

You can increase your share of a customer's business by thinking up a better service for him especially. Offer him something extra: some convenience he will appreciate; some personal attention that will prove your interest in his business; some suggestion that proves your alertness to his needs. This is one way that you, as a creative salesman, can gain a customer's increasing dependence on you as a main supplier.

▶ **IDEA IN ACTION** Knowing that he had plenty of competition for the envelope business of a large mail-order concern, an ambitious salesman decided that he had to be tops in service to win the bigger orders he wanted. He spent some time mulling over the customer's requirements and came up with a big "extra" that he discussed with his manager. The manager agreed that the potential in extra orders warranted the plan.

The great idea around which he planned his next interview was this: His company would hold the customer's orders in stock and make shipments to the proper letter shops on the customer's release. This plan would save the customer the space and expense needed to stock envelopes and the trouble and cost of frequent shipments to the letter shops that handled its mailings.

With this valuable extra on his side, the salesman soon saw sizeable increases in the orders from the appreciative customer. The reward for better service was a better share of the customer's business.

¶ 3073 Boost your sales the I.O.U. way

The creative salesman realizes that if you can cash in on the favors you do a customer over the years, you stand a good chance of keeping him as a customer. Here's how you can make this idea work:

Whenever you bail a customer out of a tough spot (getting his rush order delivered on time, for example) keep a record of your good deed. You may want to claim your I.O.U.

Would you believe? Too many salesmen pass up this top selling opportunity. If the mention of the favor is tasteful, it can mean added sales for you.

➤WHAT TO DO➤ Read how two salesmen who helped get the rush order in on time picked up their I.O.U.s:

ideas to keep you constantly creative

> **IDEA IN ACTION** A Philadelphia salesman uses a letter to serve as a reminder. He lets about two weeks pass by and then he sent the following note—

I am glad that you received your order on time. You told me that it was an impossible request, but after doing business with us, through the years, you'll learn that 'Mission Impossible' is our company program. I will see you soon to write up your next order.

> **IDEA IN ACTION** A Butte, Montana, salesman doesn't try to pick up his I.O.U. until he attempts to sell the customer again. He weaves the favor into his presentation like this:

"Mr. Prospect, I'm here to do both of us a favor today. Just like last month, when we got your rush order to you on time—we could make a last minute delivery again. But why wait? Give me the order now and you'll eliminate that overtime you had to pay your men to process the material. I'll write the same order now."

¶ 3074 **An idea that got dealers to handle a line**

Uncover a few new accounts for a dealer whom you have been trying to get to handle your line and you will probably succeed in breaking through the competition that has stood in the way.

> **IDEA IN ACTION** A salesman for Magic Chef ranges was sent into a city where competition was strong and dealers were satisfied with competitive lines. His problem was to open new outlets.

The salesman concentrated on restaurant prospects. During his noon hour he would have his soup in one restaurant, his main course in a second, and his dessert and coffee in a third. In each instance he would praise the food and get into a friendly talk with the proprietor. Capitalizing on the proprietor's natural courtesy to a patron, the salesman would arrange for an appointment later on in the day. At the interview he offered to make an analysis of the restaurant's kitchen problem and in short order made a few sales which he turned over to dealers.

Within little more than a year, seven dealers were handling his line and 127 units had been sold.

¶ 3075 **Offer the retailer ideas for suggestive selling**

By helping retailers to sell related products, you win their goodwill and increase the sales of items on your product list.

> **IDEA IN ACTION** Ben Burke goes into a customer drugstore and offers to set up a sales-pulling display. If, for instance, the display advertises a hair-grooming product that Ben sells, he asks the druggist for hair brushes, combs, and other items related to a hair-grooming product.

He also asks the druggist for a few bottles of his company's hair-grooming product to use in the display. This gives the salesman a chance to check the druggist's stock. Also, by using some of the stock in the display, he can more readily find the opportunity to ask the druggist for a reorder.

¶ 3076 **Offer an idea for using existing equipment along with your product**

Many a sale is made by the creative salesman who can find a way to fit his product to a company's use without compelling the prospect to discard equipment that is still good. The savings and other benefits to be gained by the offered product loom larger if there's also a use for what the prospect already has.

> **IDEA IN ACTION** Stanley Toff considers it important, in selling office duplicating equipment, to find out what auxiliary office equipment a prospect has. He then comes up with an idea of how the prospect can combine the existing equipment with the equipment he recommends, to perfect a process that reduces costs and speeds up production.

Toff found, for example, that the combination of his particular method and a small copying machine proved very successful for one of his prospects. He had worked up a process by which both the old copying machine and the new machine would be functioning together.

¶ 3077 **Knowledge of product and customer needs makes you creative**

Knowledge of your business and a strong desire to win an order is a combination that often leads to creative thinking. This is especially true in businesses that manufacture largely to customers' specifications. You know what your firm can do, you know what your customer wants, and you think hard for a way to overcome every difficulty that might interfere with your getting the order. You sometimes come up with a solution that even the engineers have not hit upon. You find yourself much more creative than you think you are—in fact, you're quite an inventor.

IDEA IN ACTION In Bill Turner's line, every order is a special order. The customer has a packaging problem and the order that Bill finally receives is for a carton that fulfills a certain need and is reasonable in cost.

Bill's customer wanted a package for its canned juices that had an easy-opening feature. To make that package just as the customer wanted it, the sample maker at Bill's plant pointed out, would give gluing trouble.

The order was important to Bill and he got thinking about the specifications. A thought came to him of a way to get the easy-opening feature and still avoid the gluing difficulty. Bill's idea was to perforate the outer flaps. Even the sample maker considered the solution ingenious.

¶ 3078 Creativity can help avoid costly cancellations

Today, more than ever before, it is absolutely essential for you to make sure that every sale you make is a *solid* sale—not one that will come flying back in your face a few days later —marked "Cancelled."

Reason: With prices going up and up, the cost of "cancelled" sales to your company could make the last line of your company's P & L plummet.

WHAT TO DO→ Use the following sure-fire methods, passed on by other salesmen and sales executives, to make certain that your sales stick.

The anti-cancellation program: John Drew, a Dayton, Ohio salesman, uses this keep-them-sold method:

Before the order is shipped. "What I do depends on whether the order is from a new customer or an old one."

New Customer: Says Drew, "After getting the order, I call up the customer the next day and thank him again. Then I ask him if the terms, service arrangements, and guarantee are satisfactory. I also tell him to feel free to call me if he has any problems."

Old customer: "I send out a letter expressing thanks for the confidence shown in my goods. The letter then goes on to state that the customer can expect the same excellent service to continue. Again, I invite him to call if the need arises."

When the order arrives. Mike Hildebrand, a Philadelphia based salesman, has this to say:

"I keep a record of when every order is due to arrive at a customer's plant. On the arrival day, I phone the customer to (1) Remind him that we came through on time and (2) See that everything was received in workable order."

Result: "If everything's okay, the customer appreciates my concern. On the other hand, if the customer has a complaint, I'm right on the spot and can offer him a substitute delivery before he has a chance to say 'cancel'."

After the order arrives. Tony McKlain, a Los Angeles office equipment salesman, offers this advice: "The period after the product arrives is the most critical. *Example:* "I was selling one of the best units in my industry— and selling lots of them, too. Yet the rate of cancellation was extremely high. I did some checking.

"I found that most of our cancellations occurred within 10 days after the goods arrived. *What was the answer?* In most cases, it was the girls in the office—they were wary of the new machines. They couldn't understand all the knobs and buttons, and their complaints convinced their bosses to cancel."

IDEA IN ACTION McKlain now allows his customer a few days to get set up. He then stops in to make sure that everyone fully understands how to use all the buttons on the machines.

What to do when a customer cancels. No matter what precautions you take, you will get some customers who want to cancel.

WHAT TO DO→ Take action immediately. It's up to you to get the order resold. Your commission depends on it. Here's what some salesmen do to combat this ever-present problem.

New Jersey salesman: "I return to the prospect and make an all-out effort to resell. In the course of my presentation I mention the spot I'm on in the home office because of the cancellation. This man-to-man approach works very well."

Georgia salesman: "I've worked out a great deal with my own boss. He has allowed me to sweeten the pot for the customer; throw in something extra when necessary. But I still have to use this privilege with great caution. By sweetening the pot once for a customer, he may come to expect getting something extra all the time. So I only use it when the sale is all but lost."

ideas to keep you constantly creative

¶ 3079 What a camera can do, if you use your imagination

What is simpler than a camera? Everyone knows how to use one.

Creative salesmen find a use for photography that wins customer admiration of their ingenuity. But more valuable than this admiration is the time saved in making the sale. Good selling techniques come into play to hasten the customer's buying decision: he's in the act, when he is given a photograph to hold and look at; he's using his eyes—the most powerful of his senses for holding his attention; he sees proof to convince him.

Read the following examples of how salesmen made the camera work for them.

EXAMPLE 1: J. J. Hayden, San Francisco real estate dealer, has "before" and "after" pictures of renovated buildings that he sold before they were modernized. When a prospect doubts that anything attractive can be made of an old building, he quickly convinces him with the display of photographs.

EXAMPLE 2: T. C. Biddle, of Biddle Sales Inc., Mansfield, Ohio, sells kitchens. Like others in this field, he uses miniature cabinets and appliances to show a customer how the kitchen he recommends will look. But the miniatures alone didn't work well enough to suit him. Customers usually wanted to talk over the plans at home, and all he could give them was a plan drawing. That wasn't adequate.

Biddle solved his problem with a Polaroid camera. He now photographs the miniature model that he has set up for his customer, and the customer takes the picture home with her, if she can't make a decision while she is in the store. The photograph technique has made it easier for him to sell his individually-planned kitchens.

¶ 3080 Reselling demands creative selling and a strong attitude against the "No"

Some salesmen have to fortify themselves against the "No" of a prospect only long enough to make him say "Yes" once. The order that follows the "Yes" is final; the sale is made and the commission earned.

But in some fields, a prospect's "Yes" is only the beginning of a sale. A follow-through is necessary to make the sale add up to a complete transaction. In the follow-through the prospect may say "No" again. The second "No" is an even greater challenge to the salesman's stamina and creative ingenuity.

EXAMPLE: In the book publishing field, a salesman who "sells" a professor the idea of writing a college text often has to resell his man *after* the professor has consented to write the book. The reason usually is that before a contract is signed, the professor must submit his outline of the book. But often the professor gets bogged down in his normal activities and nothing happens. The salesman must see the professor again and resell him. At this stage the "No" from the professor-prospect is devastating to an ordinary salesman. The successful salesman looks upon it not as a refusal, a denial, or a negative decision, but as an attitude that can be changed. Let's see how he uses his imagination to change the negative attitude.

▶ **IDEA IN ACTION** When John Bates, approached Professor Jones in his first interview, he walked into the professor's office certain that he would have a series of noes to face before a contract would be signed. For him, the first "No" was the start, not the end of the interview. Determined not to be content with a "No," John "made the sale" and the professor agreed to submit an outline.

Weeks passed and nothing happened. The outline was not received by the publisher.

John approached Professor Jones again. The professor had many reasons for not having worked up the outline. Family obligations, illnesses, administrative details, etc., stood in the way. No, he just didn't have time to work up an outline.

John knew that if he believed this, the interview would be over. To him, this was just one of the noes of an attitude he intended to change. John expressed his keen disappointment. He let Professor Jones know that he felt let down. He asked the prospect to outline his time for the next three months to see if there really were time that could be used for writing.

In reselling his prospect, John made the professor see himself enjoying the benefits of the royalties. In 4 to 6 years his children would be of college age. He could reduce his mortgage more rapidly. If he needed a new car, the royalties would pay for it. And that long-desired European vacation could easily become a reality with the royalties. Thus, with creative selling, John recreated the professor's desire to write the book.

John did something more. He helped the professor overcome his inertia. Right then and there he got the professor started on his outline. And this time the publisher began to receive the promised material. It was good and the contract was signed.

¶ 3081 **How to use the power of suggestion in creative selling**

Originality is needed to make the power of suggestion a selling aid. How you use it depends upon what you sell and whom you sell to. What impression do you want to make, and what little thing can you do to make it? Get your mind thinking along these lines and you may hit upon an original idea for showmanship that suits your product and your customers.

▶ **IDEA IN ACTION** Hudson J. Force became known in the building industry of Akron, Ohio as a human dynamo with a flair for showmanship. In every aspect of his operation, from building homes to selling them, he displayed originality and inventiveness.

When calling on prospects, Mr. Force always carried a newspaper in his pocket. Reason? "I wear leather half boots, so when I knock on the door and am invited in, I take the boots off and set them on the paper." By showing respect for the prospect's home, he indicates that he is just as careful in the construction of his homes.

¶ 3082 **Look for causes of trouble and you'll create a solution**

Before you can get started thinking creatively and effectively about a selling problem, you must first find the reason why you are having trouble. Let's say your sales to a certain wholesaler have fallen off. You don't know why, but you are certain that the dealer's salesmen are not pushing your product. Your next move should be to discover why. When you get the facts, the right solution will often suggest itself.

▶ **IDEA IN ACTION** Sales to one of Frank Rodney's wholesaler-customers had fallen off drastically. Frank called on the wholesaler, saying, "It's almost a year since I last talked with your salesmen. When are you having them in for a meeting? I'd like a few minutes to talk to them."

"Okay," came the reply. "Next Friday at 4:30."

Frank was amazed to find that out of a group of eleven salesmen, five were "new." Here he had gone along for a whole year, confident that every salesman employed by this wholesaler knew his (Frank's) line and how and why to push it. Actually, not only had five of the men never heard the story, but most of the other six had forgotten what they had been told.

At this meeting with the salesmen, Frank told his story to the new salesmen, refreshed the memories of the older salesmen, and cleared up many a misunderstanding. In short, he "sold" his line to the men themselves.

Sales to the wholesaler picked up suddenly.

¶ 3083 **Creative salesmen use minor sales points when big ones flatten**

Special product features, quality, price, service, savings and other big sales points in your presentation will usually make the sale. But when your prospect is not responding favorably to these big selling points, your creative thinking is challenged. What can you say about your product that will make your prospect buy?

Here is where you begin to think of the secondary sales points. What were the minor points you listed when you prepared your sales presentation [¶ 5017]? One of these will come to your mind and you will create a sale with it.

▶ **IDEA IN ACTION** When Pete Strong listed the sales features of the valves he was selling to build his presentation, he included the packaging of the valves as a minor sales point. Individual boxing of each valve didn't add one iota of value to the valves themselves. Competitors weren't boxing their valves; they merely protected the outer ends.

Pete's prospect wasn't impressed with the virtues of Pete's valves as other prospects were. So he thought quickly of the "extra" selling points that he ordinarily omitted from his presentation. The individual packaging might make his valve seem sufficiently different from his competitors' to strike a responding note in the prospect. It did, and Pete made the sale.

¶ 3084 **Creative salesmen help customers get full value from what they bought**

Making certain that your customer is getting the fullest value out of what you sold him is your best protection against losing him to a competitor. Also, a customer who is not making the best use of what he bought from you is a poor prospect for repeat sales or sales of other products in your line. You can't afford to sell him and forget him. You must create the opportunities to test whether he is making the best use of your product. The simplest way is to:

• Make a service call and ask about how your product is working out.

• Pass an idea along to your customer that helps him get more value out of the product. It can be an idea you picked up from another customer who is enjoying the product fully.

¶ 3085 Creative salesman presumes every qualified prospect needs his product

A creative salesman presumes that there is a need for his product in every company that fits into a category in which he has customers. Acting on this presumption, he turns up business where "it just couldn't exist." He may even sell his product to his own competitor! Or he may sell it to a company that has *apparently* eliminated all need for his product.

EXAMPLE 1: A salesman sold his competitor a machine for preparing duplicate copies of proposals for the sale of competitive products! Reporting on this sale, he said, "Very often, in planning calls on non-users, we stumble across a name of a large concern that is closely allied with our products. We immediately begin to find reasons for not calling on them. We decide that here is a concern that surely has complete knowledge of modern business methods, so why bother. I found, to my astonishment and pleasure, that this is not true." This salesman takes nothing for granted.

EXAMPLE 2: To an uncreative man, a company that has introduced high-speed electronic methods would seem to have no need for lesser-speed equipment. But the creative salesman thinks that maybe the electronic methods don't meet all of the requirements of the company. Maybe there are some operations that can be served by some of the equipment he sells, in conjunction with high-speed electronic methods. So he is always on the lookout for that kind of business—and he makes sales.

¶ 3086 Creative salesmen with reciprocal favors from customers

Because the creative salesman finds more ways than the average salesman to help his customers, he wins reciprocal treatment from his customers. The customer reciprocates by writing a testimonial, or he expresses his willingness to tell a prospect how much he likes your product. He will also willingly furnish leads to good prospects. But even more gratifying are the unexpected ways in which a satisfied customer comes to the aid of the creative salesman, often without solicitation.

▶ **IDEA IN ACTION** One of George Blake's bank customers in Brooklyn was grateful to him for having taken the time at a "user call" to watch some operators use the machines he had sold to the bank. On this call, George had pointed out some short-cuts that had evidently been forgotten when new operators had been taken on.

One day, a Long Island bank prospect whom George had been trying to sell, visited the Brooklyn bank to review some advanced accounting operations for which the Brooklyn bank was well known. During this visit George's customer suggested to his Long Island guest that he take a look at the highly efficient operations that were being done with the machines that George had sold the bank. This was the clincher for George's sale to the Long Island prospect. He got a signed order totaling $5,300 the very next day from the Long Island bank.

¶ 3087 Reorganization of customer setup demands creative thinking to save account[1]

What shall you do when you find yourself in danger of losing an account because of a change in a customer's buying setup?

⟫COMMENT→ Such changes take place when one company sells out to another, or consolidates with another into a new corporation. It also happens when a big company "splits off" a subsidiary, or creates new subsidiaries to take over certain divisions. It happens even more frequently when a company centralizes the purchasing function and takes purchasing out of the hands of branch offices, individual plants, branch stores, and the like.

Any change in a customer's corporate structure that brings in another set of buyers or executives who make buying policy and decisions, or deprives those who have been doing the buying of their authority, or waters down their authority, may be a threat to good accounts.

▶ *Centralization that takes buying out of your territory.* You can often succeed in salvaging what might become lost accounts by taking these steps:

• Find out who'll do the buying of your product under the new setup.

• Find out what purchasing will still be done in your territory.

⟫REMEMBER→ A company that centralizes its purchasing usually prepares instructions to all centers that had purchasing authority. The memo explains the new procedure and may include a list of items that may still be bought locally. The exceptional items often cover repair and maintenance items and emergency needs. A limit is usually placed on the dollar expenditures for such items.

• Find out the motives for centralizing. Does the company want to speed up deliveries of raw materials? If so, perhaps you can keep the account by arranging for fast deliveries by air? Does it expect to get better prices through bulk buying? Perhaps you can prove to them that there are advantages in continuing to purchase from you that will offset the price advantage. You will have to contact and "sell" more than one executive, probably, to get your item into the list of exceptions.

• Continue calling on the customer, at longer intervals. You can't tell what changes might be made later that will revive local buying.

▶ *Decentralization that takes buying out of your territory.* Your account may be with a central office that is to be decentralized. Whereas you have been selling to one central office, you may find that now a number of purchasing departments are to be set up. Again you must find out how your product will be affected, the purposes of the decentralization, the personnel to be dealt with. The facts are essential before you can think about ways to salvage the account.

⋙REMEMBER→ There will be times when you will lose an account because of a change in the customer's buying set-up, either to accomplish centralization or decentralization. That doesn't mean that your company will necessarily lose the business. It's your responsibility to try to save it for your company. Get the facts you discover to your sales manager promptly. He will do the rest to save the business.

▶ *Merger of customer.* If your customer takes over another company, there are two possibilities: (1) you have an opportunity to sell more of your product, or (2) you have to watch out not to lose the account to a competitor who has been selling to the merged firm. Alertness is essential:

• Find out the purpose of the merger.

• Find out what changes are to be made in the purchasing structure.

• Get to know the new personnel who will have the buying authority.

If your customer loses its identity in the merger there's always the possibility that some of its personnel will be retained. Again, if you discover the facts, you will know how to act to save your account.

⋙REMEMBER→ You have the edge on the competitor if you have been selling to the company that will continue to do the buying after the merger, and if your competitor was selling to the company that lost its identity in the combination. That edge can become blunt in no time if you don't hasten to do a strong reselling job to keep the account. This is a time when giving your customer an idea that he can use profitably is extremely valuable. It marks you as the salesman from whom to keep buying.

Using creative ideas on yourself

¶ 3091 **Earn a reputation as a man who achieves**

Make every day a winner—both at home and while selling—by adopting and following three easy but effective work-and-living techniques. The results could amaze you. Instead of "coasting" you'll think you're on a rollercoaster as your life takes on added dynamism.

(1) Beef up self confidence with self-promises. Every salesman knows he has to rely on others. This includes the customer who says "he'll buy" to the man in shipping who says "the order will go out by the 15th."

And the same holds true for the salesman's relationship to himself. If you know you can rely on yourself to do the things that must be done, you can be sure they will be done.

⋙WHAT TO DO→ (1) Make a special promise—to yourself. (2) Write this promise down. (3) Carry out the promise for 10 days.

No promise too trivial: What you promise doesn't matter—it's the fact that you carry out this self-pledge that builds results. With every promise kept, you become more and more certain that you can count on yourself. You'll be building up a rock-like source of inner strength. Here's—

A case in point: An experienced salesman had no trouble with his steady customers—and when he got a lead, he usually nailed down the sale, too. But he lost his zest for making cold calls. He found himself disliking the idea of walking in cold. So he made this—

⋙WRITTEN PROMISE→ "For the next two weeks I will make at least one cold call a day. I will fight the urge to see only my 'sure' customers." He kept his promise, and he also—

Built up moral muscle: "Every time I made a cold call, I could feel a definite inner

using creative ideas on yourself

strengthening. There was something physical about it."

(2) Prime the pump of new ideas. Here's a result-getting, yet easy way, a salesman can come up with more good ideas in a week than most people produce in a year. It's based on the mind's unlimited potential for creating new ideas.

➤➤➤WHAT TO DO➔ Take 10 minutes a day to jot down lists of ideas on subjects that interest you: How to increase your income, possible new uses for your company's products, new selling techniques, etc.

➤➤➤REMEMBER➔ Don't get discouraged if results aren't immediate. At this stage, you're just getting the ball rolling. Your mind is now getting on the process of showing you significant new relationships yon haven't seen before.

Case in point: One salesman felt he wasn't getting all the sales he could from his territory. He jotted down three ideas to improve his sales situation. (1) Make the first sales call 15 minutes earlier than usual; (2) List reasons why some companies turned him down; and (3) Read company ads with an eye to getting fresh ideas.

➤➤➤PROFIT-BOOSTING RESULT ➔ He went from "turned down" to "turned on." He realized that his "no sales" were because he didn't have anything new to say. He was giving the same old tired presentation. Once he perked up his presentation, sales started to come.

¶ 3092 **Creative Salesmen get that 'little extra' out of every day**

Salesmen who want to keep their sales curves going up are constantly on the lookout for ways to get more selling time out of their day.

The '10-day' week. A San Antonio salesman has come up with an idea that doesn't let him "relax" anytime during the day.

▶ **IDEA IN ACTION** "Act like your workweek has 10 days in it. Here's what you can do—Multiply your time by dividing your day. I divide my day into two parts—a morning unit and an afternoon unit. Now, for the whole week, this gives me ten units, five in the morning and five in the afternoon.

"By thinking of each of these units as a separate 'working period', I go all out to make each one count. Here's why:

"I figure if I strike out in any one period, *I'm losing 10% of my weekly income.*"

Result: "I've actually increased my income by doubling my efforts through this system. Because I now have no morning or afternoon letdown, I'm psyched to work all day."

The no-business lunch break: A San Diego salesman has added four hours a week to his selling time by cutting out 90% of his business lunches. He says he 'eats less and sells more.'

"I asked myself how important the lunches were. After thinking about it for a while, I found it hard to trace more than one sale that I made in the past month, to a business lunch. And, contrary to popular opinion, most of my customers don't favor the idea of being away from their desks for two hours at a clip."

▶ **IDEA IN ACTION** The salesman has found a way to mix eating with business. He uses the business-dinner. "When I'm on the road, I sometimes invite a customer to dinner. During this time a little business is sprinkled in with good conversation. And, during the dinner, I usually set up a sales interview for the next day."

¶ 3093 **Creative salesmen use sales tools to the greatest advantage**

Here we are talking about three kinds of selling tools: (1) what the company furnishes to its salesmen to help them do a better selling job; (2) what the company furnishes to its wholesalers, dealers, and retailers to promote the sale of the product; (3) the company's advertising to get its name and products known. What use does the creative salesman make of these types of material that the average salesman does not? A few simple examples will illustrate:

EXAMPLE 1: A heater company furnishes its salesmen with a sales manual that's filled with information which helps the men to sell automatic water heaters. Each salesman uses the manual more or less. The creative salesman uses it more, thinking up his own ways of dramatizing the facts given in the manual. For instance, the company's manual cites a survey which states that in the average home the savings accomplished by automatic gas hot water amounts to $100 a year. The creative salesman dramatizes this fact. He pulls a dollar bill from his pocket and exhibits it before his prospect's eyes.

"Do you have all of these you want?" he asks his prospect.

"No," replies the prospect.

"Well, you can save lots of these a year with

¶ 3093

our automatic hot water heater. I can't tell you exactly how many, but one survey has shown that in the average home the savings amount to $100."

EXAMPLE 2: The creative salesman looks for every opportunity to tie in his own selling efforts effectively with his company's advertising and promotion campaigns. He makes sure that he is informed of these plans *well in advance,* and that he is supplied with layouts, tearsheets, proofs, or samples, as the case may be. This gives him time to study the material and to be prepared to explain what these resale aids can mean to each of his customers.

¶ 3094 **The business picture is a stimulant to creative salesmen**

The creative salesman makes a habit of reading the financial news to keep abreast of changes in the country's economy. Whatever the news is, he thinks of how it affects his market and how he can use the news to make more sales.

⟶ COMMENT⟶ Some large companies supply their salesmen with bulletins that point up important financial developments. For example, when the news shows that manufacturers are expanding their facilities, companies that sell industrial products alert their men to the new sales opportunities. When industry is contracting, they guide their salesmen to overcome the selling resistance by stressing the cost-saving benefits of their products.

Whether or not you are supplied with economic bulletins by your home office, you should always know what's happening in business generally. It will pay you to subscribe to one of the weekly financial publications, if you do not daily read a newspaper like *The Wall Street Journal* that has good business and financial coverage. Here are some weekly publications to choose from:

Business Week, published by McGraw-Hill Publishing Company, Inc., 330 West 42 Street, N. Y. 36, N. Y.

U. S. News & World Report, published by United States News Publishing Corporation, 2300 N Street N.W., Washington 7, D.C.

The country-wide economic situation is only part of the business picture. What is happening in particular industries is also important because there are always some businesses that are doing better or worse than others regardless of the general trend. See ¶ 9082 for a source of information on the state of trade in selected lines.

IDEA IN ACTION Charles Bellows read in the financial section of a New York newspaper that a large building materials corporation had inaugurated a thorough, company-wide economy drive during a recent business recession. Economy drives were the order of the day at that time. This particular economy program was going to rectify overstaffing on various corporate levels; it was going to curtail needless capital expenditures, which, Bellows learned, was interpreted as getting along *without,* wherever possible.

The gloomy news didn't faze Bellows. His thinking was: How can I find a use for our product that would contribute to this customer's economy program? Result: He received a $6,000 order for new equipment by showing a saving of $4,600 a year and a reduction of peak period overtime.

¶ 3095 **A "great" creative idea gives you confidence**

The great idea around which you plan your interview must have merit; the benefits to your customer must be crystal clear. If your idea is "great" in this respect, you have the fullest confidence that the prospect will see it and act.

Sometimes, however, for a reason that defies logic, you are turned down. But even then you feel confident that someone will see it some day and act. That is the beauty of a great creative idea. It remains good for a long time, and you "stay with" the prospect, if the potential sales to him justify continuous calling. Eventually you make the sale.

¶ 3999 **Footnote references**
¶ 2025
   (1)   Published by Prentice-Hall, Inc., Englewood Cliffs, N. J.
¶ 3002
   (1)   "The New Test for Leadership," by James T. McCay; The Prentice-Hall President's Guide, ¶ 3301.

   (2)   Moore Business Forms, Inc.
¶ 3040; 3043
   (1)   Published by Prentice-Hall, Inc., Englewood Cliffs, N. J.
¶ 3087
   (1)   "How to Adjust to New Buying," *The American Salesman,* March 1959, deals with this problem.

SUCCESSFUL STRATEGIES FOR PRE-APPROACH—MAKING THEM LISTEN—CALL-BACKS

Winning Sales Through A Successful Pre-Approach
Making the Prospect Listen
Putting Your Finger on the Prospect's Reason to Buy
Making Call-Backs Pay Off

TABLE OF CONTENTS

Starts at Paragraph [¶]

Miracle Guide to Successful Strategies for Pre-approach—Making Them Listen—Call-backs 4001

WINNING SALES THROUGH A SUCCESSFUL PRE-APPROACH

What the pre-approach entails 4002

Finding Out About a Prospect in Advance of an Interview

What to find out about a prospect 4003
Where to get information about a prospect 4004
How to get acquainted with your market 4005

Getting the Interview

Second step of the pre-approach 4011
Rules for getting the interview 4012
Why you should make appointments 4013

Making an Appointment Over the Telephone

What you gain by using the telephone 4021
The telephone has drawbacks 4022
5 ways to dial s-a-l-e-s 4023
How to use the telephone to get an interview appointment 4024
Plan what you have to say and say it 4025
Aim to capture interest immediately 4026
Say only enough to arouse interest 4027
Do not misrepresent your purpose just to get the interview 4028
Be low-pressure but persistent 4029
Use good telephone manners 4030
Relax and enjoy it! 4031

Making an Appointment By Letter

What a letter can do for you 4041
The weaknesses of a letter 4042
Keep these rules in mind 4043
Building the letter that will get an interview 4044
Capture his attention in the opening 4045
Originality is the keynote 4046
Use "you" emphasis 4047
Techniques to use in getting your prospect's attention 4048
Promise him a big benefit 4049
Tell a story to get his attention 4050
Show the prospect how you can solve one of his problems 4051
Turn your prospect's "no-decision" into a victory 4052
Get the prospect's attention through praise 4053
Openings to guard against 4054
Fan his interest into desire by showing how your benefits can fill his wants 4055
Point out that the benefits can be his 4056
Get him to agree to see you 4057

Five Special Techniques for Getting an Interview

Use the influence of a third party to get interviews 4061
How to gain an interview on your own 4062
Use a verbal direct reference 4063
Pre-approach sales material softens the prospect for the interview 4064
Make full use of company pre-approach material 4065

	Starts at Paragraph [¶]		Starts at Paragraph [¶]
Create your own pre-approach material	4066	How to handle a "brush off" by a receptionist	4072
Send an advance card announcing your intended call	4067	What to do when you are received by a "proxy" for the prospect	4073
Getting In Without An Appointment		Getting in without naming your product	4074
		Win over the secretary	4075
Sell the interview first	4071	How to avoid the reception room interview	4076

MAKING THE PROSPECT LISTEN

Every prospect is a multi-phased individual	4081	Exercise caution with the completely trusting prospect	4088
Steer the talkative prospect back to "sales"	4082	Allay the fears of the suspicious prospect	4089
Ask the silent prospect leading questions	4083	Guide the opinionated prospect to your way of thinking	4090
Pace yourself to the "fast" prospect	4084	Conform to your customer's buying habits	4091
Give the deliberate prospect your "full treatment"	4085	Get right down to the 'nitty gritty'	4092
Deal quickly with the impulsive prospect	4086	Avoid using the rebuttal instinct	4093
Be firm with the vacillating prospect	4087	Listen and your prospect will listen	4094

PUTTING YOUR FINGER ON THE PROSPECT'S REASON TO BUY

Every buyer has a buying motive	4101	Use your imagination to "think out" a prospect's strongest buying motive	4106
The ten main buying motives	4102	A different approach to the same buying motive can win the sale	4107
Three techniques to help you find a prospect's primary buying motive	4103	How to meet an "unusual" reason to buy	4108
A direct question brings out the prime buying motive	4104	How to convert buying motives into sales	4109
A trial and error method to find your prospect's major buying motive	4105	Your appeal must change with the times	4110

MAKING CALL-BACKS PAY OFF

How to set up a call-back	4121	Fellow-salesmen can give you ideas to be used in call-backs	4125
Three key queries before making a call-back	4122	Seek a higher authority after repeated calls	4126
Remind the prospect of your previous visit on a call-back	4123	Change a losing situation into a winning one	4127
A "last-ditch" attempt after several calls may make the sale	4124	Footnote references	4999

Successful Strategies for Pre-approach— Making them listen— Call-backs

Your selling power soars as you keep on using successful strategies

¶ 4001 ⟫MIRACLE GUIDE to→ Successful Strategies for Pre-approach — Making Them Listen — Call-backs

The selling strategies explained in this section bring you face to face with your prospect for a successful interview. Here are the actual selling techniques that high-bracket salesmen use to get to the right man without loss of time.

This section develops the strategies, techniques, and basic principles for winning through a successful pre-approach. It tells you what to find out about a prospect in advance of the interview [¶ 4003]; how to get the interview through appointments made in advance by telephone, letter, or other special techniques [¶ 4011 et seq.]; how to get in without an appointment when you have to [¶ 4071 et seq.].

Your presentation is, of course, the critical part of your selling activity. But before we get into that big subject, which will be treated under the next tab card, we want to be sure you know how to handle individual prospects when they display certain temperaments. Unless you do, your great presentation may lose its selling punch.

Similarly, making a great presentation is easier if you understand buying motives and the techniques for putting your finger on the prospect's reason to buy.

Another prerequisite to successful selling is a knowledge of the techniques and strategies that make call-backs pay off.

Therefore, this section includes, in addition to pre-approach guidance, the following aids to successful selling:

▶ Making the prospect listen [¶ 4081 et seq.]

▶ Putting your finger on the prospect's reason to buy [¶ 4101 et seq.]

▶ Making call-backs pay off [¶ 4121 et seq.]

You will sell your way into big money by mastering the selling strategies that are given here.

Winning sales through a successful pre-approach

¶ 4002 What the pre-approach entails

To guarantee that you get your money's worth from the time you spend with your prospect, you must prepare in advance for the interview. This pre-approach phase of selling involves two steps: (1) finding out all you can about the prospect [¶ 4003 et seq.]; (2) getting the interview [¶ 4011 et seq.].

Finding Out About a Prospect in Advance of an interview

¶ 4003 What to find out about a prospect

The better informed you are about your prospect and his needs, the better your presentation will be and the more confident *you* will be that you have something he will buy.

Here's what to learn about your prospect before you contact him:

- Exactly what the company makes or does
- Its size—approximate number of employees — net worth — extent of operations (local or national)
- What its requirements are in your line—products and volume
- Whether the company is growing
- Whether its credit is good
- Who is the right man to see (his *correct* and *full* name)
- Specific information you need for a convincing presentation. For example, a chemical salesman will want to know not only what the prospect manufactures but also which process he uses.

➤WARNING➤ You *could* get most of this information directly from the prospect by simply waiting until the interview. Don't make that mistake! The interview is for selling, not research.

➤OBSERVATION➤ There are some fields in which a salesman cannot gather the necessary information about a prospect before he sees him. For example, in highly personalized businesses like life insurance, the information has to come from the prospect himself. Similarly, in businesses that require a great deal of specialized data before a sale can be made, only part of the pre-approach information can be obtained in advance of the first interview.

There are selling situations in which a salesman is warned by his sales manager not to spend valuable time on preliminary investigation. He must find out about the prospect's needs for his product *while making the call*. See ¶ 2040 for how to do this.

A salesman who shows enough interest in a prospect to learn about him in advance gains the respect and the listening ear of that prospect. The following illustration presents two approaches made by competitive salesmen selling a stapling machine to a prospect who packages his product in cardboard cartons.

Poor approach:

"Mr. Allan, I am Jack Smith from the ABC Staple Manufacturing Company. We manufacture and distribute a full line of stapling machines. There is probably an application in your plant where we could save you considerable time in your packaging operations."

Good approach:

"Mr. Allan, my name is Fred Brown and I represent the Atlas Staple Machine Company. Let me explain briefly how you can triple your carton closing speed on overlap cartons, where I notice you are now using tape."

The second man, Fred Brown, has something definite to offer. He has taken the trouble to find out a specific application for the stapling machine.

¶ 4004 Where to get information about a prospect

In general, there are two ways to get information about a prospect—you ask someone, or you hunt it up in one of a number of sources, depending upon what you are looking for.

► *People to ask.* Any of the following people may know something about the prospect that will be useful to you.

- One of the other salesmen in your company may have called on the prospect in the past and can give you information from his experience.
- Your present customers, especially those in the same business, can be helpful.
- Other salesmen in related but noncompetitive fields are usually willing to cooperate.
- People in the neighborhood of the company in which you are interested—in a gas station or diner, for instance—often know

whether the company is hiring or laying off, is busy enough for a night shift, is contemplating new construction, and the like.

• On a referral call, the person who referred you to the prospect can usually give you pertinent information about him.

▶ *Where to look up information.* It may take a little time to look up information about companies and their executives in a printed publication, or to get information from a Chamber of Commerce, but by using such sources to prepare yourself in advance of the interview you fortify yourself with facts that make it easy to approach, please, and interest your prospect.

We have spelled out in detail for you, under the tab "Salesman's Personal Money Kit," some standard published sources for this purpose [¶ 9071]. And we show at ¶ 9083 how Chambers of Commerce help salesmen.

¶ 4005 **How to get acquainted with your market**

The more you know about the type of business in which your prospect is engaged, the easier it is to make the sale. You can visualize your product in use by the prospect, you can find new applications for it, and you can identify your product with the prospect's needs.

In addition, if you learn something of the language used in the trade, you can talk to your prospect at his own level and convince him that your product is meant for him.

▶ *Get background information from trade publications.* After you have classified your markets, as explained in ¶ 2020, find out for each market the names of the leading trade publications in the field. You can get a world of information, useful to you in selling, by looking at a few copies of the publication. Language of the trade is found in almost any issue.

➤➤SUGGESTION→ Each industry has a trade association. A list of these associations is given in *National Associations of the United States,* published by the U.S. Government Printing Office, and in *Encyclopedia of American Associations,* published by Gale Research Company, Book Tower, Detroit 26, Michigan.

The trade association can tell you the name of the leading trade publication and the publisher's address. Or you can call up any large company in the industry and find out from it the name and address of the best trade publication. If you are in a large city, you can usually look at the publication in the public library. Otherwise, send for sample copies.

Market Data and Directory [¶ 9082] also gives information about trade associations and trade publications.

▶ *Ask directly for information.* People like to talk about what they are doing. By expressing interest in your prospect's business, you will find your prospect ready to explain the workings of his business.

▶ *Use your company's guides.* If you are lucky enough to be supplied by your sales manager with special data about the markets that have need for your product, use the information to the utmost.

Getting the Interview

¶ 4011 **Second step of the pre-approach**

The second step of the pre-approach is to get the interview. Whenever possible, you should arrange to get the interview in advance. Sometimes, of course, you will be unable to do so, and your problem will then be how to walk into the prospect's office and get to see him [¶ 4071].

¶ 4012 **Rules for getting the interview**

Regardless of the method used to get the interview, you should keep in mind the following three rules:

1. It is up to you to *get* the interview. You are never *entitled* to a person's time, regardless of the benefits he would receive from your product or service.

➤➤IMPORTANT→ Many modern companies have a policy of seeing as many of the salesmen who call on them each day as possible. Their policy is explained at ¶ 1079.

2. Concentrate on seeing the right man. There is no sense in interviewing a man who can't make a decision to buy from you.

3. Sell the interview before you sell your product. A prospect who is not convinced that the interview might be worth his time will either not grant one or else be a half-hearted listener. Here is an example of a salesman who learned this lesson:

▶ **IDEA IN ACTION** Herb Ward sells a collection service. He discovered that many prospects would cut him short as soon as he revealed his company and service, even though most of them had problems with past-due accounts. Herb decided to try a new approach.

"My name is Ward," he would begin. "I stopped in to ask whether you'd be interested in what amounts to insurance against losses from past-due accounts." The usual answer was "Yes, we might. How does it work?"

Herb, having thus sold the idea of an interview, got his chance to sell his service.

¶ 4013   **Why you should make appointments**

Every salesman has had the experience of being told something like this after having made a special trip: "Sorry, but Mr. Burton is at our plant today. It's best to make an appointment to see him." The advantages of being expected by the prospect are clear:

• You save yourself hours of wasted travelling and waiting time.

• A prospect with whom you have made an appointment is at least familiar with your name and company, and, if your arrangements were made skillfully, is sold on the interview.

• Having an appointment adds prestige to your call.

⟫⟫IMPORTANT→ The techniques that we will describe are aimed chiefly at getting the initial interview. Your customers, and prospects upon whom you call more than once, will usually let you know what to do about future interviews.

⟫⟫WHAT TO DO→ Use one of the following five means of arranging for an interview:

• Make an appointment over the telephone [¶ 4021].

• Make an appointment by letter [¶ 4041].

• Send an advance card, announcing your intended call [¶ 4067].

• Have a mutual friend or acquaintance arrange the interview for you, either by phone or in a letter [¶ 4061].

• Send advance sales material and follow it up with a request for an interview [¶ 4064].

Making an Appointment Over The Telephone

¶ 4021   **What you gain by using the telephone**

The telephone can be one of your most important sales helps, *if* it is used properly. Here's what it *can* do for you:

• Quickly and inexpensively establish a time for a definite interview, without wasted travelling or waiting.

• Enable you to get an idea of the prospect's potential for buying.

• Give you a preliminary personalized contact that will ease the later selling job.

• In some cases, get you to a man whom you would not be able to see merely by stopping in at his office.

¶ 4022   **The telephone has drawbacks**

The telephone has two serious drawbacks that can kill sales before you even get started:

• It is easier for many people to say "No" over the phone than it would be if you were talking to them in person. For this reason your telephone approach must be well planned and well executed to get positive results.

• The impersonal nature of the telephone dismays some salesmen who find that they are less able to cope with objections and unexpected problems on the phone than they would be in a personal give-and-take situation. Such men are depriving themselves of a useful tool, simply because they don't make the telephone work for them.

¶ 4023   **5 Ways to dial s-a-l-e-s**

When you sell by phone, you must grab your prospect's attention with your first sentence, or you'll wind up with just a conversation—instead of a sale. Here are five quick starts that can really pay off:

(1) *Thank-you approach:* Mr. Allen, this is John Friendly of the Ace Supply House. Thanks for the order we received this morning. However, if you increase your order by $75, you'll be able to take advantage of our special price."

(2) *Service approach:* "Mrs Brown, this is Arthur Amiable, your neighborhood appliance dealer. I am calling to let you know that we accept any bank credit card. You can also use them during our coming sales week."

(3) *Inactive account approach:* "Good morning, Mr. Charles, this is Mr. Foster of Foster Meat Products. We haven't done any business with you for two months, and I thought I'd call you and find out why." (Settle any complaints at once—before you try to sell.)

(4) *Demonstration approach:* "Good morning, Mr. David, this is John Purdy of Speed Typewriter Mfg. Co. I would like to demonstrate to you and your secretaries our

winning sales through a successful pre-approach

new time-saving models. We believe they can save you valuable time."

(5) *Special sales or bargain approach:* "Good morning, Mr. Ende, this is John Alden of the Miles Widget Company, I mailed you a letter last week about our New One-Package Widget. What did you think of it?" (Follow up on his answer immediately. If he's impressed, go for a sale and if he presents an objection, counter that before you do anything else.)

¶ 4024 **How to use the telephone to get an interview appointment**

You will succeed in getting the interview you are after if you emulate top-flight salesmen who handle the telephone with great success. This is what they do:

- Plan the telephone conversation [¶ 4025].
- Capture interest immediately [¶ 4026].
- Say *only enough* to arouse interest [¶ 4027].
- Never misrepresent just to get the interview [¶ 4028].
- Persist without noticeable pressure [¶ 4029].
- Mind your telephone manners [¶ 4030].
- Relax and enjoy it [¶ 4031].

¶ 4025 **Plan what you have to say and say it**

Carefully plan what you are going to say, write it out, and then read it that way over the phone. This process eliminates awkward hesitation, or forgetting or repeating anything, and it adds assurance to your words. It *will* have spontaneity if you read the words carefully each time.

Regardless of what you are selling, develop your telephone conversation requesting an interview along these lines:

- Identify yourself by name and, usually, your company.
- Tell the prospect why he would *benefit* from seeing you.
- Ask him for an interview to explain the benefits.

¶ 4026 **Aim to capture interest immediately**

You will probably speak less than a minute in making an average appointment. That gives you little time to waste, and since your whole purpose is to make the prospect curious enough to give you an interview you should get to it at once. Unless the man is a friend, avoid pleasantries or generalities; get right down to brass tacks of *interest*.

¶ 4027 **Say only enough to arouse interest**

This will depend somewhat on what you are selling. With some products it is best to explain exactly what you want to talk about. Here is an example of this direct approach:

"Mr. Anderson, this is Mel Peters of the Paramount Automatic Machine Company calling. We felt that, because of the importance of fast, accurate machining in your business, you would be interested in spending just ten minutes to hear how you can reduce drilling costs by one-third with our newly improved multiple drill presses. May I arrange an appointment for Wednesday afternoon to tell you about it?"

Note that although the salesman was specific about the purpose of his visit, he said only enough to get the interview. He saved the facts until later.

If you have a large territory, and your problem is seeing only those people who are definitely interested, then the direct approach is the most feasible one, since it tells the prospect enough to know whether or not he wants to hear more. If you have sent out advance material and are following it up for interviews, you will use the direct approach, also, since the prospects presumably know what it is you sell from the literature you sent them.

In many businesses, however, an indirect approach is best, especially if you anticipate a negative reaction to the nature of your offering. In such cases you state the benefits that you want to give the prospect, and then ask for the time to explain just how to get those benefits. For example:

"Mr. Smith, this is Allan Temple. My firm specializes in ways to save homeowners up to $100 a year on heating bills and to make their homes more comfortable. Could I take fifteen minutes some evening to explain what it is we offer? Naturally, there is no obligation on your part; I will be obligated to explain how you can definitely save money. Would Thursday evening be all right, say about 7:30?"

Here the salesman felt that direct reference to house insulation would create a barrier in the minds of some people, so he concentrates on the benefits of insulation without revealing what he sells.

¶ 4027

In either kind of approach, avoid answering questions *if* you can do so diplomatically. Here are some phrases that show how to do this:

"That's one of several points I would like to explain in the interview."

"I will be glad to explain that when I see you."

"You would get a much better idea from seeing it than from hearing about it."

If the question cannot be avoided, or if the prospect insists on an answer, then by all means give a straightforward reply.

¶ 4028   **Do not misrepresent your purpose just to get the interview**

If you sense resistance to your service or product on the prospect's part, don't try to give him the impression that you are selling something entirely different and then hope to dazzle him in the interview. A prospect who thinks that he has been tricked into giving you his time is an angry one, and rightly so. The victim of this kind of deceitful approach will usually become aware of it and of course will then refuse to see you under any conditions.

¶ 4029   **Be low-pressure but persistent**

In keeping with the best modern selling, be strictly low-pressure when you call for an appointment. It is wise to include in your few words the assurance that you will only take a minimum of time, and that the interview will not obligate the prospect in any way.

However, you can, and should, be persistent without being high-pressure. If real success is your goal, you can't afford to let negative reactions side-track you.

Suppose you call a man and make a low-pressure approach on the subject of life insurance, and his answer is "I've already got several insurance policies." That should be your cue to try another tack, like this:

"That's exactly why you would benefit from seeing me, Mr. Brown. My customers know that my job isn't to sell them as much insurance as I can, but to see that they carry the insurance they *need*. Why not let me estimate your coverage, free of charge naturally, when I call? You might need *different* insurance, not more of it."

¶ 4030   **Use good telephone manners**

Just as appearance and other personal details are important in the actual interview, the personal impression you make over the phone is important, too.

Follow these instructions that assure success in using the telephone:

• Speak distinctly and loudly enough to be heard.

• Use a conversational tone, as you would in person.

• Think and sound cheerful and optimistic, no matter what the reaction on the other end has been.

• Keep your mouth close to the mouthpiece.

Avoid these disconcerting habits that spell failure in using the phone:

• Smoking or drinking water between phrases or sentences; in fact, smoking at all while you are on the phone.

• Putting your hand over the mouthpiece so that you can converse with someone else while the prospect is talking.

• Trying to keep the phone to your ear by hunching your shoulder; you affect both your hearing and your speaking.

• Talking against excessive background noises.

• Slamming the receiver down when you are through; the prospect may have an afterthought and still be on the line.

• Chewing gum.

Making an Appointment By Letter

¶ 4031   **Relax and enjoy it!**

If you are relaxed when you make your phone calls, your tone is more conversational, your voice more natural and lively, and your attitude one of friendliness and optimism. So follow these tips to help you relax at the telephone:

• Realize that you will not get an appointment from every call you make, no matter how good you are.

• Be well prepared. You will then be confident, and with confidence comes ease.

• Try taking a few deep breaths before you start calling. It has a calming effect and will help you speak properly.

• Remind yourself to relax.

¶ 4041   **What a letter can do for you**

A good letter can perform a very valuable service besides arranging a time for an appointment: it can *sell* the interview. If you word the letter skillfuly the prospect will not only expect you but will also welcome your visit.

¶ 4042 The weaknesses of a letter

Your letter might just happen to arrive on a day when the prospect is preoccupied and will hardly do more than glance at it. Unlike a telephone call, a letter is out of your control once you mail it. When the conditions surrounding its arrival aren't favorable, even the best letter might be overlooked.

¶ 4043 Keep these rules in mind

To write letters that will win interviews, remember these points:

- This is a selling job, and selling principles apply to the letter just as they will to the interview.
- The more accurately your letter fits in with your prospect's *wants,* the more likely he is to give you the interview. The letter is an uninvited guest, and its only chance of making itself (and you) welcome is to hit on the benefits the prospect would like to have.
- Keep the letter short and uncomplicated. You can write yourself out of an interview just as you can talk yourself out of a sale.

¶ 4044 Building the letter that will get an interview

Even in the shortest letter, you must lead the prospect through four stages:

1. Capture his attention in the opening [¶ 4045].
2. Build his interest into desire by describing the benefits you can offer and how they would fit his needs [¶ 4055].
3. Show him that he can secure these benefits [¶ 4056].
4. Get him to agree to see you for further explanation [¶ 4057].

An example of a letter that won many interviews is given at ¶ 2027.

¶ 4045 Capture his attention in the opening

Your opening must get attention immediately. People are busy, and in addition almost everybody gets sales material through the mail. They are therefore apt to glance hastily and with disinterest at mail that looks like another attempt to loosen their pocketbooks. Only a good opening can induce people to read a salesman's letter carefully enough to be convinced by it.

⇛REMEMBER→ Many purchasing agents, buyers, and other businessmen encourage salesmen to make appointments with them. Your letter is only doing half its job if such a man simply marks it "OK" and hands it to his secretary, or perhaps puts your name on his desk calendar. A good opening will make him read the letter and thus sell the interview as well as arrange it.

¶ 4046 Originality is the keynote

The letter that's *different* stands the best chance of a careful reading. You should therefore strive for originality in your letter, especially in the opening sentence. Originality does not mean that you must resort to spectacular, outlandish or tricky forms of expression; it simply means a new or unexpected slant on the subject.

There is probably no service or product that will not benefit from a fresh viewpoint in its presentation. Even a straightforward approach is made more effective if the words in it have the spark of originality. For example, how often must a toy buyer in a department store read and hear words like these:

"Our toys can raise the sales volume in your department and increase your profits."

Certainly the buyer wants to do both of these things, but his interest would be aroused more if it were put this way:

"Watch your sales climb, your customers smile, *and* your pocketbook get fatter, when you offer these popular toys."

The second sentence says basically the same thing as the first, except that it uses more vivid-picture words.

¶ 4047 Use "you" emphasis

If an uninvited letter starts off with "The Brown Service Company is the world's largest . . .", or "The new Dandy Can Opener is the best . . .", the reader's attention will immediately lag. What does he care what you are or think? He wants to know what's in it for him, and the fact that something is good doesn't necessarily mean he wants to buy it.

The Dandy people, for example, would get better response with an opening like this:

"It's a fact: you will sell more automatic can openers, and make more friends, by carrying the new Dandy Can Opener . . ."

Immediately the prospect is personally involved, because the advantage to *him* is the first thing mentioned. Keep this "you" emphasis in mind no matter which method you are using to get his attention.

¶ 4048 Techniques to use in getting your prospect's attention

There are several proven techniques that can get the attention of your man at the start of a letter:

• Promise him a big benefit [¶ 4049].
• Lead into your subject with a relevant story [¶ 4050].
• Show that you can solve a problem for him [¶ 4051].
• Take advantage of your no-decision sales talk [¶ 4052].
• Compliment him or his company [¶ 4053].

¶ 4049 Promise him a big benefit

People are attracted to a plan or product which promises, for some logical reason, great profit or income, savings of time or effort, happiness, or the like. The prospect of making or saving a sizeable sum of money is especially appealing. Consider these openers:

"Would a $10,000 boost in *net* profit next year interest you? . . ."

"Stronger, neater package sealing in half the time; that is exactly what you will get from . . ."

"Three machining operations instead of seven, *and* a better product as a result; . . ."

Any prospect having a need for one of these benefits would probably read on to see if he could use the idea.

⇒WARNING→ If you can't *deliver* the benefits *in full,* by all means avoid this approach. It will only be of use to you if the claim means exactly what it says.

¶ 4050 Tell a story to get his attention

A pertinent story that will lead the prospect into the rest of the letter is an effective opener. Here is an example:

Remember the Greek myth about Icarus, the resourceful fellow whose home-made wings fell off when the sun melted their wax fastenings? Well, your company, which is starting to take wing, will probably also meet unexpected, serious problems.

May I show you how the Benson Consultation Service has been of real help to . . .

¶ 4051 Show the prospect how you can solve one of his problems

If the first thing a man sees in a letter is a possible solution to a problem that has been bothering him, or a better way to do whatever he does, he's interested. Naturally the more specifically you touch on one of his problems, the more you deserve his interest; but sometimes the use of common problems will work. For instance, construction firms are always interested in faster, easier methods in their business. Speed means more jobs per year, less labor cost per job, and consequently a better bidding position. Here is an example of an opening capitalizing on this fact:

"Like similar companies everywhere, you can save time and money on every job by using modern high-tension nut-and-bolt techniques *where you now use rivets.* Like to know how? . . ."

¶ 4052 Turn your prospect's "no decision" into a victory

In this situation you've met with your prospect, made your presentation, and—NO DECISION. It's a draw! You've met up with one of those "I'm not sure" types.

While he's "thinking it over" prior to your next meeting, you don't have to stop trying to sell him. Rather than doing nothing but wait for his reply, seize the opportunity he's given you by his inaction.

⇒WHAT TO DO→ Write him a letter expressing your appreciation for the courtesy he's given you, and the opportunity for a second meeting. For this very special situation, here's a letter that has brought positive results on numerous occasions.

Dear Mr. Kelly:

I thoroughly enjoyed meeting you yesterday. My sincerest hope is that you found the time you took to meet with me rewarding. Between now and our next meeting I will be doing a good deal of thinking about the questions we discussed, for I have the conviction that there are a number of things I can do that may prove valuable to you. The notation has been made on my calendar that I'm to have the pleasure of seeing you again at 10:30 next Tuesday morning, and I look forward to that.

Often a first meeting may close on a rather vague note, with no firm appointment for a subsequent meeting. And that's the time to take the initiative with this letter:

Dear Mr. Allen:

Many thanks for taking time out of your busy day to see me yesterday. I thoroughly enjoyed meeting you and found it a stimulating, challenging experience.

We gave each other a number of things to think about and I look forward to exchanging ideas with you when we get together again.

I'll phone you in the next day or two to arrange an appointment that will be convenient for you.

¶ 4053 Get the prospect's attention through praise

Almost everyone is vulnerable to praise, and the prospect's vanity can be used as the target for your opening. Here is one example of opening a letter with praise:

"When a man reaches your level of responsibility he has one thing in common with successful men in any business or profession: his time is extremely valuable, and simply has to be conserved. Don't you agree that five of your valuable minutes on one day would be a good investment if you could be shown how you can save hours of time each week?"

⟫⟫WARNING⟶ False compliments must always be avoided. Also, if you feel that the prospect will not cotton to someone who flatters him, don't use the complimentary openings; choose another method.

¶ 4054 Openings to guard against

Test the opening of your letter for strength. You can't win attention and favorable action with an opening that is timorous, negative, vague, or irrelevant.

• Timorous. A timid opening will never get the prospect to do what you ask for.

(Timid opening) "May I suggest a way in which you could increase your plant's production capacity?"

(More forceful) "You can actually add 20% or more to your machine shop capacity without adding a single machine or operator."

• Negative. Anything that would create an unfavorable or unpleasant impression would be negative. Strive for a pleasant and positive reaction.

(Negative opening) "You are probably not selling your share of sportswear this season, unless . . ."

(Positive) "You are enjoying a busy and profitable season, we hope."

• Indirect or vague. An opening should not leave the reader in doubt. Be direct and specific.

(Vague opening) "Does the idea of increased profit next year appeal to you?"

(More specific) "Would a $5,000 boost in net profit next year interest you?"

¶ 4055 Fan his interest into desire by showing how your benefits can fill his wants

Your main job in a letter asking for an appointment is to make the prospect want to see you. The only reason he will agree to an interview is because he wants the benefits you speak of. It is with benefits, then, that you whet his appetite once you have gained his favorable attention. Tell him that you can save him money, make him more comfortable, protect his children, solve his production problems, eliminate paperwork headaches, add to his prestige, and so on, according to what your commodity offers. Concentrate on what your product or service can do for him, rather than what it is.

⟫⟫IMPORTANT⟶ Remember that wanting is an emotional state. The benefits that you describe should be aimed at emotional appeal; that is, at *wants* more than just needs. A vacuum cleaner salesman would appeal to the pride of the housewife in a tidy home, and to her desire to save effort, more than to the underlying necessity for cleanliness.

¶ 4056 Point out that the benefits can be his

The prospect, having given you his attention and having let you kindle his desire, will now want to know what is involved in getting these advantages. If this were a sales letter you would explain your offer in some detail, but since this letter is designed only to get an interview, you should avoid giving him too many facts. Some commodities have to be described at least partially, but even in these cases the less you say about *how* they work the better.

Instead, convey the impression that the benefits you describe can be his with a minimum of trouble and expense, and will require only a few minutes to explain. For example:

"This comfort and convenience can be yours at a pleasing pennies-per-day cost and without delay—you could be enjoying it within a few days . . ."

"This easy-to-sell line could be lifting your sales level just as it has done for others, and with just as little effort on your part . . ."

"You will be amazed at how simple it is to put this plan to work for you . . ."

The object is to make the step from *wanting* to *having* seem easy.

¶ 4057 Get him to agree to see you

Having led up to the interview as the next logical step, go ahead and ask for it. You can boost your average of "Yes" answers this way:

• Suggest a time. Unless you do, you are forcing the prospect to think up a time, which is bothersome to some people. You should not only suggest an hour and day, but should also ask him to advise you of a more suitable time if your suggestion is inconvenient for him.

⟫⟫SUGGESTION→ If for some reason the date you suggest is the only one which would be convenient for you (for instance, if you can be in Cleveland only on a certain day), state the fact in your letter. Under such conditions most people will have the courtesy to arrange to be available at that time if they want to see you, or at least they will let you know if they *don't* want to see you then.

• Point out that there is no obligation. With some people, this assurance can make the difference between giving you the interview and not doing so.

• Make it easy to respond. You can include a stamped, self-addressed return card, perhaps printed up so that the only action necessary on the part of the prospect is to "X" or check the card before he puts it in the "Out" box. Some salesmen have success by simply stating in their letter that they will telephone soon to arrange for an appointment. This, of course, involves no action on the part of the prospect.

Special Techniques for Getting an Interview

¶ 4061 Use the influence of a third party to get interviews

One of the best ways to get an interview is to have a friend or business associate of the prospect arrange it for you, or give you a recommendation.

⟫⟫IMPORTANT→ Salesmen with the highest earnings use the third party method for getting interviews. Such men aren't afraid to get others to do favors for them, and you shouldn't be either.

Usually the mutual friend will telephone and make an appointment for you. In some cases he may even introduce you personally.

⟫⟫REMEMBER→ A man who will recommend you to a friend or business acquaintance will also usually try to answer questions about that person. The questions, of course, must be obviously business ones related to the interview.

⟫⟫CAUTION→ Whatever personal information you might be told should not be revealed at the interview unless you are certain that the prospect will not resent the familiarity which personal knowledge implies.

¶ 4062 How to gain an interview on your own

If you can get a third person to pave the way for you, all well and good. But there are many times when you'll have to do it on your own.

Here are five ideas that are opening doors for salesmen around the country. These same ideas can work for you:

Be the 'no-name' salesman. An office furniture salesman uses this saleswinning card to gain his interviews:

XYZ Company, Inc.
Introduces Mr. ———————

On the card this sales ace writes, in ink, "My name is not very important to you. It means little—but my message, that's another story—and it is important to you. I can save you many dollars if you'll give me 10 minutes of your valuable time."

Result: A good response. Not many prospects can resist having a look at a no-name salesman.

Win over the secretary. The surest way to a prospect's interest is through the heart of his secretary! Here's how it works:

▶ **IDEA IN** A New York engineering company **ACTION** wanted to increase attendance at its trade exhibit. So, well in advance of the Trade Show's opening date, they sent out letters to 550 secretaries—in shorthand—which read:

Dear Secretary:

We'd like your boss to visit our suite at the Manhattan Hotel during our industry's engineering show next month. If he brings us this letter, we will send you a lovely gift. Just write your name and address at the bottom of this sheet.

Result: At the convention, almost 200 engineers walked into the suite, letter in hand. "All of them," a company representative said, "reminded us to send their secretaries the gift."

Tell him half your story. You can do your best selling only in a face-to-face interview—so don't waste your big guns on the telephone. When you call for an appointment, hold back the details, the facts and figures. Instead, give your prospect an idea of the juicy results.

▶ **IDEA IN ACTION** Mr. Anderson, this is Barry Stone of the Acme Maintenance Company. I think that I can save you thousands of dollars a year by eliminating 90% of the downtime on your trucks and heavy-duty machinery. May I arrange an appointment with you for next Wednesday to fill in the details?"

Result: You've whetted his appetite for more information. If you've chosen some valuable benefit as bait, your prospect is going to be very interested in hearing the rest of the "details."

Tell him you have an appointment. You can save the trouble of calling back to confirm your appointment by changing the last paragraph of your "Bear-Trap" letter. Instead of asking for a selling appointment, finish up *strong* by saying:

I am looking forward to discussing this in person next Thursday at 11:30. If I don't hear from you, I'll be in to see you then.

Result: Salesmen who end their "Bear-Trap" letters this way report that "it's a winner. Most men are too busy and too intrigued to write back a negative letter."

¶ 4063 **Use a verbal direct reference**

Some of your customers and friends, for one reason or another, will decline to arrange an appointment for you or even write a letter or card of recommendation, but they will not object to your using their name as a reference, if you ask for that privilege. The mention of someone's name as a direct reference, provided the person is someone whom the prospect knows and thinks highly of, is an effective interview getter.

The effect of the reference will be increased if you get the prospect to say that he knows the man who gave the reference. For example:
SALESMAN: Mr. Prospect, you know Mr. Allison at All-Color Printing, don't you? (Wait for answer.)
PROSPECT: Yes, I know Mr. Allison.

SALESMAN: Mr. Allison suggested that you could benefit in the same way that he has from my product. Let me show you how it can help you, too.

⇒CAUTION→ In direct references you must have the man's permission to say that he is recommending you. In indirect references, such as merely stating that someone uses your product, permission is not necessary.

⇒REMINDER→ Make a point of thanking those people who assist you in this way, and let them know what the results are. You will find that people who know that their favors are appreciated are usually ready to be helpful again.

¶ 4064 **Pre-approach sales material softens the prospect for the interview**

Top-bracket salesmen utilize every means for making a prospect aware of them or their product *before* they attempt to get an interview. These men reap the benefits of their company's advertising by *using* it. They also make use of pre-interview mailing material, either supplied by the company [¶ 4065], or originated by the salesman himself [¶ 4066].

¶ 4065 **Make full use of company pre-approach material**

Your company, like most business houses, probably advertises its product and has some kind of printed material that is designed to do part of the selling job. The profitable use of this material depends on the salesman; he must put it to work.

Here are suggestions for getting the full benefit from company pre-approach help:

• Know exactly what your company makes available in the way of mailings, advertising, sales literature, sales letters, and so on.

• Select the material that is best suited for your purposes. Don't send more than is necessary to arouse the prospect's interest.

• Draw upon the material you may now be using in your presentation. Some of it may be suitable for enclosure in a mailing. A small circular, for example, is easily mailed.

• Always follow up your mailings.

• When you interview prospects who have received your pre-interview material, be sure to reinforce the original effect by mentioning it, or by using it in your opening remarks.

▶ **IDEA IN ACTION** Bill Hadley's company, a large insurance firm, sends out to a list of prospects which Bill has O.K'd, a letter signed by the company president, on company stationery, and mailed from the central office. The letter mentions a new kind of policy that is available, and states that a representative will call to explain its advantages.

When Bill makes his call he begins this way: "Mr. Prospect, my name is Bill Hadley. A few days ago you received from our president, Mr. ―――――――, a letter mentioning a new kind of insurance plan now being offered by my company, the ――――― Insurance Company. I am here to explain this new plan to you. May I tell you about it?

Bill gets good results with this approach because he takes full advantage of the letter. He benefits both from the awareness that it has created and from the prestige of his president's signature.

⟫⟫SUGGESTION→ A good way to put company advertising to work is to use blow-ups or cut-outs of ads as they appeared in newspapers or magazines. Hand the ad to the prospect and ask whether he noticed it in such-and-such a magazine.

¶ 4066 **Create your own pre-approach material**

Suppose your company does not offer you much advertising or mailing assistance. You can find your own ways to soften up prospects for an interview. For example, you might write your own series of interest-getting letters, send them to the prospect at regular intervals, and follow up with a request for an appointment.

▶ **IDEA IN ACTION** Jack Blake's letters, mailed each week for three weeks, were short and simple. They stated that a certain company in the area had bought his product that week and had begun to save considerable time, effort, and money. The third letter included a request for an interview. By that time the prospect had gotten the idea that Jack's product was doing a good job for other companies and might be able to help him, too. The interview was granted.

Letters of this kind, sent directly from the salesman or from the local office, are usually more personal than central office mailings.

With imagination you can think of other types of mailings—post cards, samples, anything that will smooth the way for your approach.

Remember these two points when you prepare your own pre-approach mailing:

• Whatever you mail to a prospect should look good and be in good taste. Letters and envelopes should be neat and well typed, and the material carefully chosen.

⟫⟫CAUTION→ Humor and cleverness are effective only when used skillfully. Unless you're absolutely sure of your skill, don't try to be funny in your mailings.

• You should send out only as much material as you can properly follow up. Timing is important. You can't afford to let a prospect wait too long before you contact him personally or the effect of the mailing will be lost. Unless you normally canvass heavily by mail, warm up only a few prospects at a time.

¶ 4067 **Send an advance card announcing your intended call**

A quick, easy, and inexpensive way to arrange interviews is to mail out advance cards, informing customers or prospects that you plan to call on them at a certain time on a certain day. In many cases the salesman's company provides these cards, but if it does not, it is a simple matter to secure your own.

Advance cards are frequently no more than standard postcards, printed up somewhat as follows:

```
Our Mr. ―――――――――
will call on you on ―――――――
at about ――――― o'clock.
                 Sincerely yours,
                 Brink Mfg. Co.
```

A phrase asking the reader to advise a more suitable time is sometimes added.

Some salesmen prefer a more personalized or unusual card. It might begin:

"Hold that order! I'll be there on . . ."

One card used successfully has a real penny tipped into it, under the heading "Yep! It's real!", with the following copy underneath:

"And so are the dollars you'll make with University Frocks! At $4.75.

I'll be seeing you and showing you at
The ....
On ....
............................."

The most common use of advance cards is to notify customers of a salesman's intended

getting in without an appointment

visit. The customer will then expect him and can make plans (check stock, for example) if it is necessary. Advance cards *can*, however, be used to make appointments with prospects, too. Cards sent to prospects for this purpose should not be too informal or chummy, of course.

⫸IMPORTANT⟶ Remember that an advance card, like a letter, does not obligate the prospect in any way to see you; it cannot take the place of a definite appointment.

Getting In Without an Appointment

¶ 4071   **Sell the interview first**

No reasonable salesman is disturbed when he is denied an interview for a valid reason; for instance, if the prospect is at a meeting.

But in many cases the denial is not based on a valid reason. The buyer is chronically "too busy" to see salesmen in whose lines he does not have an active interest; or he assumes that he knows all about the proposition and that its presentation would be a waste of time; or he prejudges a proposition as not being of interest to him.

Such buyers and prospects give salesmen the "brushoff" through a secretary, or they see the salesman for a brief moment, solely to explain why it would be a mutual waste of time for the salesman to make his presentation.

Where the interview is not freely granted, the salesman's task is to "sell the interview". It is rarely possible to succeed in selling the product when the prospect is still "unsold" on the idea that he should listen to the sales story.

The sale of the interview, like the sale of the product, must be thoroughly planned and a well-developed presentation should be worked up and rehearsed. All the steps, in short, that apply to the sale of the product [¶ 5003] apply to the sale of the interview.

Special techniques must be used to "get by" the receptionist, the secretary, or the assistant who seeks to bar the interview.

But first let's see a typical instance of two salesmen at work on the same problem of getting interviews, and why one does poorly while the other succeeds.

▶ **IDEA IN ACTION**   Scotty King and Ed Bryant sell life insurance. They work out of the same office.

One morning they are told that a new medical expense policy has just been made available. Their sales manager carefully explains the features and cost of the new policy and then says, "Now, this is a real opportunity to go out and sign up a lot of people whom you couldn't sell before. Make the most of it!"

All the men proceed to their desks to work up a list of people they will call on.

At the end of the day, Scotty and Ed compare notes. "How many did you sign up, Scotty?" asks Ed.

"Two," is Scotty's glum reply. "How about you, Ed?"

"Nine," says Ed.

"Say, that's great, Ed. I wonder what you're doing that I'm not? Sit in on one of my calls in the morning, old man, and tell me where I'm missing out, will you?"

"It's a date," replies Ed.

The next morning, wth his friend at his elbow, Scotty sees his first client.

"Mr. Frisbie," he begins, "this is Mr. Bryant who works in my office. I stopped in to tell you about a brand new medical policy that has just become available. Here is what it offers you that makes it different from all other medical policies. First . . ."

"But, Mr. King, I'm not interested in any medical policy, no matter how attractive," interrupts Frisbie. "I carry hospitalization, accident, and life, as you know. That's all I need, and I've got an appointment in 5 minutes, so if you'll excuse me. . . ."

"Well, Scotty," says Ed when they get outside, "suppose you tag along with me on my first call, and see if you like the way I present the new policy. Then we can compare notes and see what the score is."

Ed led the way to the office of a Mr. Klinger, who greeted him with this remark: "I don't want to be rude, Mr. Bryant, but I don't need any more insurance—and I've got a conference coming up in a few minutes."

"Mr. Klinger," replied Ed, "I want only one minute. This is Mr. King who is with our office. I just stepped in to ask you one question, Mr. Klinger. When you bought that new car a couple of months ago, didn't you tell me you wanted protection immediately against fire, theft, and collision?"

"Sure I did! Why run risks on an investment of several thousand dollars? I didn't drive it at all until you said I was covered."

"That's exactly what I thought, Mr. Klinger," smiled Ed. "Now I want to talk to you about another risk that runs into several thousand dollars, on which you have absolutely no protection."

¶4071

Klinger looked up quickly, "What's that?"

"Liability for medical expenses for yourself and family," said Ed.

"Well," replied his prospect, "I'm not sure I'm interested, and I've got to go to a meeting in a few minutes. Can you stop back later?"

"I can, indeed. Say about 2 o'clock?"

"That's okay," answered Klinger.

As soon as they got outside, Scotty said to Ed, "Boy, am I grateful to you! Guess I'd forgotten the rule—'Never try to sell your product if the customer hasn't been sold on the interview.' Watch me go to town now!"

¶ 4072 How to handle a "brush off" by a receptionist

Receptionists are sometimes permitted, or even instructed, to "brush off" salesmen when, *in their judgment,* the executive who is being solicited would not be interested in seeing the salesman. Some receptionists develop a high degree of "brush off" skill. On the other hand, some salesmen become equally adept in "getting by" the receptionist.

Three techniques that work are described here: (1) the "outbluffing technique," (2) answering when the receptionist says, "Mr. Jones is busy," (3) answering when she says, "I know Mr. Jones wouldn't be interested."

▶ *Outbluffing the receptionist.* Your words and actions give the impression that you and your prospect know each other.

▶ **IDEA IN ACTION** Jack Winchell sells folding boxes like those used by the firm whose office he enters.

"Can I help you?" inquires the telephone operator-receptionist.

"Yes, indeed," smiles Jack, hoping that this phase of his call will run smoothly, but laying the groundwork for any eventuality. "Will you please tell Mr. Jones that Jack Winchell is calling?"

"Do you have a card?" asks the operator, following her usual pattern.

"No, I'm afraid I don't," says Jack, and then quickly adds, "Just tell Mr. Jones that I'd like to ask him a question, but if he's tied up right now, ask him whether I can see him at 2 o'clock this afternoon." And Jack promptly turns his back and examines some pictures on the wall in the reception room.

The receptionist hesitates a moment, but then decides to announce the caller. Jack has created just the impression he feels is right for the situation. His words and his manner have implied several things that he has not actually said. The receptionist is thrown off guard by his apparent assumption that he will be announced and received—either then or at 2 P.M.—without question. Jack's request that his name be sent in, without mention of his firm's name, may mean that he already knows Mr. Brown, she muses to herself. His gesture in turning makes it difficult for her to quiz him further. All in all, Jack has outwitted her.

▶ OBSERVATION ▶ This game of "bluff" can be played in various ways—instructions for playing it are difficult to spell out. The alert salesman learns by trial and error how he can best use the technique.

Some receptionists won't be outwitted. They'll persist in their attempts to "brush off" the salesman without announcing him. Regardless of the exact words such a receptionist uses, her remarks will add up to (1) "Mr. Jones is busy right now, and I can't disturb him," or (2) "I know Mr. Jones wouldn't be interested."

▶ *Answering the receptionist who says your prospect is busy.* To a receptionist who uses the "busy" excuse for keeping you from seeing your man, say, "I see. When would be a good time for me to call back—say about 11:30?"

It is usually easy to tell from the receptionist's reply whether your prospect really *is* busy at the moment or whether she is attempting to "stall." If she replies that 11:30—or any other time that she may suggest—would be better, then the chances are 100 to 1 that her first statement was sincere.

But if her reply indicates that she doesn't want you to call back, then you can apply the same technique that is suggested for answering the receptionist who decides on her own that your prospect wouldn't be interested.

▶ *Answering the receptionist who says your prospect wouldn't be interested.* A receptionist who says she "knows" that your prospect won't be interested must be prepared to take the "strong medicine" her remark invites. To break through this barrier, you must say, "You are making a very important decision that can be quite costly to your company. Are you certain you want to take the responsibility for this? Why don't you just tell Mr. Jones I'm here and let him decide whether he will see me?"

getting in without an appointment

If this line of reasoning fails to secure the announcement to the prospect himself, there is one further step you can take. Ask her, "May I have your name, please?" This question, politely voiced, usually wins the fray.

⇛OBSERVATION→ Few salesmen like to force such "strong medicine" on the receptionist, and some salesmen refuse to do so.

¶ 4073 **What to do when you are received by a "proxy" for the prospect**

What shall the salesman do when he is received by someone other than the man he has actually called to see, for example, a secretary or an assistant?

The rule is: do not try to "sell" a substitute listener on your proposition, but sell him (or her) on the advisability of *arranging for you to see the prospect himself*.

Determine whether the "proxy" listener has come forth at the specific request of the prospect or not, and make your approach fit the situation.

▶ *The prospect has sent a substitute to see you.* In this case, concentrate on a few facts that will suffice to justify an interview with the prospect.

IDEA IN ACTION Bill Williams asks to see Mr. Granger, head of a large company. The receptionist, after announcing him, tells him that Miss Davis, Mr. Granger's secretary, will be with him shortly.

"Mr. Williams," says Miss Davis, "Mr. Granger has a group meeting to attend in about 5 minutes. He's sorry that he can't see you at this time, and asked me to talk with you instead. May I ask what you wanted to discuss with him?"

Bill realizes from Miss Davis' remarks that she has actually been delegated to talk with him, and that she has been further authorized to inquire about his mission.

"Let me give you the essence of the matter, Miss Davis," began Bill.

This "opener" was designed to make it plain to her that he—the salesman—intended to tell her only that part of his story that would enable her to see that it would be advisable for Mr. Granger to hear the *whole presentation*.

"We offer a truck maintenance service, Miss Davis, that saves our customers from 8 to 20% of their delivery costs. Our service has been used for 3 years or more by these outstanding companies whose names appear on this list. That's what I want to discuss with Mr. Granger, and I wonder if you can suggest a time when we can go into the matter."

Bill has handled this situation with skill. He has told Miss Davis only a group of facts that he thinks will convince her that Mr. Granger would be interested in hearing the whole sales story. He has quoted no prices, offered no details, submitted no proof that his firm actually can save Mr. Granger's company from 8 to 20%. In other words, he has *not* given the information that would be absolutely necessary before a decision could be made on the offer itself.

By handling the matter in this way he has completely by-passed the hazard that the prospect will attempt to make a decision on the basis of a second-hand presentation of his offer.

▶ *The "proxy" was not sent out by the prospect to see you.* When you are sure that the person who receives you has not been sent by your prospect, and that he doesn't know of your presence, "sell" the proxy on announcing you to the prospect and fixing a time when you can see him.

IDEA IN ACTION Dick Holden asks to see Mr. Rutherford, vice president of a large corporation.

The receptionist announces Dick by telephone, and then says, "Mr. Holden, will you wait just a moment, please? Mr. Rutherford's secretary, Miss White, will be with you shortly."

Dick thanks the receptionist and waits. He wonders whether Miss White is coming out because Mr. Rutherford suggested it or whether she is receiving him on her own volition as a matter of established routine.

"I'm Miss White, Mr. Holden—Mr. Rutherford's secretary. Can I help you?"

Dick decides to probe for the answer to his question. "Why, yes, Miss White," he replies, "I'm sure you can. I'd like about 10 minutes with Mr. Rutherford, and if this isn't a convenient time, I wonder if you can set an appointment for sometime tomorrow morning."

"Would you mind telling me what you have in mind, Mr. Holden? This is a very busy week for Mr. Rutherford, and I hesitate to make any more appointments for him. I'll be glad to give him your message."

These remarks make it quite clear that Dick has not been announced to Rutherford himself.

Dick knows that "the other person" can't make his presentation for him. He also knows that in this instance the secretary will somehow have to be "sold" on announcing him to his prospect.

So he says, "Well, Miss White, I don't think the matter I have in mind can be handled just that way. Can we set a time for some day next week?"

In short, Dick is trying hard to avoid having the decision as to whether he will be received made by anyone other than the prospect himself.

Because he has followed the rules of sound salesmanship, Bill receives the answer he has earned.

"Can you come back about 10:30 tomorrow morning, Mr. Holden?" asks Miss White.

➤➤REMINDER→ *Never* expect another person to tell your sales story as effectively as you would yourself.

¶ 4074 **Getting in without naming your product**

In selling certain specialty products, it is important to get in to see the prospect without mentioning the name of the product. There is a reason for this tactic. In specialty selling, it is usually necessary first to prove to the prospect that a need exists (the prospect often is not aware of the need), and second, you must show the prospect that the product is designed to fit that need.

If you mention the name of your product before you have proved a need of it, you are very likely to get a quick brush-off with: "We don't need it," or "We're not interested." You want to get in and explain the need first. How you can do this, making an ally of whoever greets you first, is demonstrated below.

▶ **IDEA IN ACTION** Charles Foote sells a well-known intercommunication device. He is cold canvassing because practically everyone in business needs the product. Upon entering the outer office of one of his cold prospects, he walks up to the switchboard operator intent upon making a friend of her. She knows more than anyone else about the communication needs of the firm. She knows how often her lines get tied up by inter-office calls, how frequently long-distance calls are made, and so on. He is going to get this kind of information from her because it will help him establish the need for his product. Also, he's going to try to see the right man without letting the receptionist know what firm he represents.

"Good morning," says Charles to the receptionist, adding in an easy, informal way, "I wonder if you will help me?"

Few people can flatly reject a friendly request for help. Not one receptionist in a hundred will say "No, I can't" or "No, I won't." Almost invariably she will ask, "What about?" or "What do you want?" or "What are you selling?"

Here's where Charles does a switch. Instead of answering her question, he asks her a question.

"You must have a pretty busy switchboard at times—do you have to handle all inside calls too?" Or, "Who are the people in your company that the boss has to contact most frequently?" Or, "Does the boss talk to many people around the office through your switchboard?"

If she is willing to give Charles a few facts about their communication set-up, he'll use them when he sees the boss. Sooner or later, though, she'll get back to her question: "What do you want?" or "What are you selling?"

This time Charles' answer is: "I'd like to discuss a direct private line telephone with Mr. — uh — what's his name?"

If the receptionist gives Charles the name, he says, "That's the man I want to see—do you suppose you could get me in to see him?"

If the girl at any stage of the conversation mentions that the switchboard is overworked, or that communications are inadequate, Charles says, "I have a private direct-line telephone that will help you a lot—Whom do I have to see about it?"

So far, Charles has not revealed the product he is selling. If the girl insists on knowing, Charles says, "Oh, I'm sorry—I didn't mean to be rude. I'm asking these questions because I have a service to help your top executives—who is the head of this company?"

Charles has made *three attempts* to see the boss without naming his product. Sometimes he succeeds on the first try, sometimes on the second, often on the third. If however, the girl insists on learning exactly what company he is with and what he is selling, he tells her.

He says, "It's about a new (name of product) product especially designed *to help you* in this kind of office. (The phrase "to help you" is an effective one and Charles uses it often.)

If the boss asks what Charles wants, he tells the receptionist, "I want 5 minutes of his time to show him a private direct-line telephone I know will help him." Or, "Tell him I've made a survey of his office, and that I have something here that is designed to help him."

If the executive asks, "What firm is he with," Charles answers the question. Putting some sell into it, he says, "I'd like to show him a new (name of product) private, direct-line telephone developed especially for him."

¶ 4075 **Win over the secretary**

The surest way to a prospect's interest is through the heart of his secretary! Here's how it works:

A New York engineering company wanted to increase attendance at its trade exhibit. So, well *making the prospect listen*

in advance of the Trade Show's opening date, they sent out letters to 550 secretaries—in shorthand—which read:

Dear Secretary:

We'd like your boss to visit our suite at the Manhattan Hotel during our industry's engineering show next month. If he brings us this letter, we will send you a lovely gift. Just write your name and address at the bottom of this sheet.

Result: At the convention, almost 200 engineers walked into the suite, letter in hand. "All of them," a company representative said, "reminded us to send their secretaries the gift."

¶ 4076 **"Going for broke" to get in**

Once in a great while you feel dead sure that you will get the order if you can only get your prospect to look at your product. But you can't get in to see Mr. Right. You begin to feel that "you'll go for broke" if necessary, just to get in. You know this is a dangerous attitude, so you try again and again to get an appointment. Finally you have exhausted the ways of getting to see Mr. Right and you are again thinking of "going for broke."

You want to try something different; if it works you are in and you can proceed with the sale; if it doesn't work, you spoil your chances for approaching the prospect again. Where a great deal is to be gained if you win, you try out your "different" idea.

▶ **IDEA IN ACTION** A whole new field of non-user prospects would open up for Bryan Moore if he could get one important prospect to convert to paper cartons for packaging a hardware item that was normally packaged in wooden containers.

The product development engineers of Bryan's firm had designed a perfect self-locking carton for the purpose. But Bryan couldn't get in to see his man. Receptionists, secretaries and assistants had always said, "Mr. Right is too busy."

Bryan felt he would "go for broke" and call before 9 o'clock without an appointment, bringing with him the designer of the sample carton.

Again Bryan was given the brush-off.

"Mr. Right has an appointment at 9 o'clock," said the receptionist.

"Can I see someone else, anyone, even someone in the shipping department?" said Bryan.

An air of urgency about this unexpected call must have been sensed by the receptionist. She called Mr. Right's secretary. The young lady came flying out. Evidently, Bryan's wanting to go "under" Mr. Right's head had done the trick.

"Mr. Right will see you, but he has only 3 minutes," said the secretary.

Bryan and his designer were in. They left with the order 25 minutes later.

¶ 4077 **How to avoid the reception room interview**

It's advisable to give your presentation to a business prospect in his office. You can't ordinarily do your most effective selling in a reception room. If your prospect leaves his office to come out to hear your story, you must try to get him back into his office. Sometimes you must make several attempts.

▶ **IDEA IN ACTION** Bill Sears sells a specialty item. The major part of Bill's presentation is the demonstration. It is essential that he give the demonstration in the prospect's office.

When an executive came out to ask Bill what his business was, Bill replied, "I want to show you something—can we step back into your office for a minute?" Although this simple request works for Bill many times, this prospect persisted and again asked what Bill wanted "I've made a survey of your office layout (an honest statement in Bill's line), and I believe I have something that will help you," was Bill's second response.

As he said this, Bill picked up his demonstration kit as if he assumed that his prospect would lead the way to his office.

But again Bill's prospect balked. Bill then looked at him directly and said, "It'll take only a few minutes, and I'm sure you'll find it worthwhile."

Bill's prospect gave in to this third request and invited him into his office.

This same strategy is used effectively when Bill calls on retail stores. He says to the proprietor, "I have something here I'd like to show you—do you have an office in the back?" If he hesitates, Bill uses his best interest-getting opener: "I believe I have something here that will enable your clerks to serve your customers better." If the prospect remains reluctant, Bill goes into his third try: "It'll take only a few minutes, and I'm sure you'll find it worth your while." In most cases, one of these attempts work.

Making the prospect listen

¶ 4081 **Every prospect is a multi-phased individual**

Every salesman knows from experience that prospects and customers vary, as individuals, in their temperaments.

¶ 4081

Attempts have been made to catalog various "types" of prospects and customers and to set forth the attitude—or technique—that the salesman should adopt as he encounters each of them in his daily rounds.

None of these "systems" is completely practical, because none makes allowance for fluctuations of temperament in any one person. Although someone might be correctly described as a specific "type," that person at different times will display different temperaments.

None of us *is* a single "type," but rather a composite of several. Most seasoned salesmen have had the experience of seeing one individual display two or more different temperaments during the course of a single interview.

What, then, should you do as you encounter the shifting range of changing personality traits?

This section tells you the signals to watch for that indicate your prospect's obvious mood at any particular moment—signals that tip you off to practical ways to meet and successfully handle each one.

The following "temperament types" are treated in this section:

- talkative
- silent
- fast talker
- deliberate
- impulsive
- vacillating
- trusting
- suspicious
- opinionated

Remember, however, that any *one* individual might display any or all of these same temperaments at different times.

¶ 4082 **Steer the talkative prospect back to "sales"**

Some persons are by nature just plain talkative. The best technique is to give such a person a reasonable length of time to "talk himself out." He may finally say, "Let's see now. You wanted to tell me about your new line of spring novelties?" If, however, he doesn't "come around" in a reasonable time, you must find some means of steering the conversation back to business. Try these ways:

- Pick up a comment he has made and tie it in with the purpose of your call.

    EXAMPLE: "Your views about our economy are certainly interesting, Mr. Jones. The point you made about people spending more money at this time of year ties right in with a pre-season discount I can give you."

- At the first opening in this talk, agree with him and get into your message.

    EXAMPLE: "I certainly agree with you—we sure do need rain! Incidentally, one of the things I want to be sure to tell you about is that our new line of spring novelties . . ."

¶ 4083 **Ask the silent prospect leading questions**

The "silent man" is the most perplexing type for many a salesman. Small wonder! For he sits there, not indicating whether he is agreeing or disagreeing, or whether he is even thinking or listening.

The best remedy for this situation is to try to "draw him out" by asking questions that call for some response.

"I think that's an important advantage, don't you, Mr. Barclay?"—or—"Do any of your competitors do much volume in this line?"

The value of this technique is that usually the response, even though it is only a nod or a monosyllable, will indicate fairly clearly how the "silent man's" mind is working. His "one word" tells you how well or how poorly you are faring, as accurately as does the more talkative person's longer response.

¶ 4084 **Pace yourself to the "fast" prospect**

A fast-talking person likes *action*. He wants to be told the highlights or essence of your story, not the details; he wants to be told fast, not in a slow or deliberate way.

The rule is simple: pace your manner and delivery to match the prospect's tempo.

¶ 4085 **Give the deliberate prospect your "full treatment"**

This type of prospect wants to have every question answered to his full satisfaction, and likes to know every detail in the book.

There is no use in trying to hurry this prospect. Since you only succeed in irritating him if he feels that you are trying to rush, be prepared to give him a complete story.

¶ 4086 **Deal quickly with the impulsive prospect**

The impulsive person is apt to interrupt your sales presentation before you've had a chance to state all your points. He might say, "Okay, I'll take it," or, "No, not interested."

He is also likely to change his mind after announcing his decision. On the other hand, it is often possible to make him change his

making the prospect listen

decision by quickly stating one more fact for consideration.

It is best to deal quickly with the impulsive type and seize any opening for a favorable decision. See ¶ 6045 for a way to make "quick sales" stick.

¶ 4087 Be firm with the vacillating prospect

The vacillating prospect literally "doesn't know his own mind," and will usually accept help in arriving at a decision if assistance is properly offered.

It is often a mistake to move quickly with such a person. He responds best to guidance that is at once authoritative and deliberate. Points need to be repeated frequently, and small facts explained.

It's best not to give the prospect who vacillates a choice, but to gradually focus his attention on a single course of action. When the ground has been fully covered, and perhaps retraced, you might find it necessary to force the sale to a close. This can be accomplished again by taking a firm position.

> **EXAMPLE:** "Mr. Waycross, we've gone over the whole proposition pretty thoroughly, and I'm certain you'll be pleased if you decide on this particular contract. I know you don't want to rush into a matter of this sort, but really I don't see how you could go wrong. Here, if you'll just initial this form, I'll get started immediately to see that you get our service."

¶ 4088 Exercise caution with the completely trusting prospect

It's not often that you run across a trusting prospect, but when you do it's best to handle him with caution.

The person who has absolute faith in you will take everything you say as "gospel"; will almost always do what you recommend. Be careful to avoid misunderstandings, and be sure that you tell him the "whole truth and nothing but the truth."

If he finds, or even *believes*, that you have misled him, he will very likely tend to suspect everything you will ever tell him. But when treated squarely, such prospects usually turn into "solid" customers, and are often an excellent source of "advertising" for you and your product.

¶ 4089 Allay the fears of the suspicious prospect

The distrustful person suspects the world in general and is often convinced that every salesman he meets is trying to "pull the wool over his eyes."

Such an individual jumps at every opportunity to turn everything you say or do into "proof" of why he shouldn't trust you or buy from you.

The way to persuade this kind of prospect to buy is to "soft-pedal" yourself and your product. Make no extravagant claims, "tone down" your presentation to avoid giving him a chance to find fault with it.

If you couple this procedure with an attitude that displays courtesy and deference, he will soon get the idea that you are *not* out to "hoodwink" him, but that you are sincerely interested in serving him.

If you get the chance, you might even try some "homegrown" psychology on this individual: let him "win" some minor point of contention—give him the feeling that he's "hard to fool." These tactics can result in a sale.

¶ 4090 Guide the opinionated prospect to your way of thinking

Just as some persons don't know their own minds, so others are overconfident. Unlike the impulsive thinker (who often reverses himself in an instant), the person with strong opinions must be "guided" into changing his mind. A skillful salesman can often lead the strong-minded man to "come around." Turn to ¶ 7046 for an illustration of how a salesman successfully handles this type of prospect.

¶ 4091 Conform to your customer's buying habits

The wise salesman adjusts his approach to the buying habits of his customers, knowing that not to do so is to invite unnecessary trouble.

You don't encourage a man to listen if you start chatting with him when he prefers that you get right down to business. Nor do you create a good listening attitude in a customer who likes to chat a while, if you jump right into your sales story.

Similarly, if a customer is growing lukewarm because you are calling too often, or because you are not calling often enough, it's a signal to you to change your calling schedule.

Find out how each of your customers likes to buy, adjust your ways to his, and you'll have less trouble getting him to listen.

This is the type of information about your prospects and customers that you should know:

• Is there a special time this customer prefers to be called on?

• Does he buy small quantities frequently, or place large orders at long intervals?

• What grades, sizes, colors, models, etc., does he use?

• What are his interests, hobbies, or other data that you should remember to mention?

• Does he like salesmen to leave as soon as business is done, or to stay and chat a while?

• Does he like the salesman to drop in, or to telephone in advance for an appointment?

• Is this customer particularly impressed by what certain other customers, whom he knows and respects, decide to buy?

• Does he have any idiosyncrasies that should be remembered? (For example, has strong political opinions that should not be argued; is hard of hearing, so that he should be spoken to loudly; often cancels orders he has placed; likes to do most of the talking, and the like.)

• What competitive sources does he buy from?

Any alert salesman can add other items.

¶ 4092 **Get right down to the "nitty-gritty"**

Make sure you get right down to the "nitty-gritty" the minute you start your selling interview—and you'll see your sales average climb.

Sales-losing statistic: A large sales consultant firm in Pittsburgh claims that most salesmen talk twice as much as they should, and say half as much as they could. This firm teaches that you can't dominate the prospect by dominating the conversation. You must draw him out by letting him participate in the sales interview.

⟫WHAT TO DO→ Get right down to specifics by following these four suggestions that will help you get to the root of the prospect's problem immediately.

(1) *Start with something special.* Make each of your product's benefits seem like an exclusive feature. This can be done both verbally and visually.

EXAMPLE: If an electric heating systems salesman merely states, "Electric heat is clean," he hasn't made his point. But, if he actually can show the prospect how much dust is in the room because of the present heating system, he's well on his way to a sale.

(2) *Watch out for "positive" boredom.* Prospects tend to become bored with salesmen who ask simple questions that only demand a token "yes" or "no" response.

⟫WHAT TO DO→ Ask the prospect questions introduced by what, how, why, when and where—questions that can't be answered by a simple "yes" or "no". *Result:* This allows the prospect to open up and tell you what his needs are. Doing this also keeps the buyer involved in the interview and with the product.

(3) *Keep questions brief.* Questions a salesman asks a prospect should be short and simple to answer. Know the exact point that you are going for, and then hit that point sharply and crisply. Any question over 12 words is too long.

(4) *Take this simple test.* List as many of your product's features and the benefits of doing business with your company as possible within a half hour time period. A minimum of 15 features and 5 company benefits is passing. Then check over your list to see if you have gone right to the specifics by hitting on facts and figures, such as size, weight, number of movable parts, materials, etc.

¶ 4093 **Avoid using the rebuttal instinct**

Listening power is the key to added sales. And by far, the most difficult impediment to a salesman's listening power is the 'rebuttal instinct.' This is the tendency not to be listening at all while a customer is speaking—but rather waiting impatiently for an opportunity to interrupt.

Here's an example: You're selling a closed circuit television system to a high school. The prospect expresses concern about public reaction. He fears the public will say that your product is an expensive frill.

Rebuttal instinct: "This isn't expensive. It will save you money—as I pointed out before . . ."

Result: It's obvious that the salesman didn't take time to understand the prospect's objection.

Despite his fears that the public reaction

putting your finger on the prospect's reason to buy

will not be favorable, this prospect might still be sold. But the salesman must control his "rebuttal instinct."

Here's how a good listener might respond:

"If I understand you correctly, you are not so much concerned with whether this will actually save you money, as you are with the problem of how you'll convince the public of that fact.

"Well, you're not the first to install this type of system. As a matter of fact, the neighboring school district has just purchased one. I'll be glad to get a testimonial and full details of their plan so you can present them to the public."

Result: The good listener has led the discussion down the sales road.

➤➤➤ WHAT TO DO → Curb your 'rebuttal instinct.' Think before you answer back. Make sure you completely understand the nature of your prospect's objection. *Reason:* If you brush aside a real objection, you'll lose the sale.

¶ 4094 Listen and your prospect will listen

The prospect must get a chance to talk and ask questions, or he will have every right to resent your complete monopoly of the interview.

Be sure that your sales talk includes ample listening time. Being a listener gives you these advantages:

• You won't talk too much. You will spoil the effectiveness of your presentation if you prolong it by unnecessary chatter.

• Your prospect's questions and comments, even his objections, will tell you where you have hit the target and where you have missed, and why.

Putting your finger on the prospect's reason to buy

¶ 4101 Every buyer has a buying motive

No sale is ever made unless the buyer has a specific buying motive. This infallible rule —that behind *every* sale exists a *reason to buy* —can be a miracle key to guide you to more profitable selling.

Motives vary from prospect to prospect. One has a different motive from another for buying the identical product. The same prospect may have different motives at different times for buying the same product.

When you accurately put your finger on your prospect's primary reason to buy, you have found the "heart" of the sale. The prospect's motive—or buying desire—*wants* to be satisfied. Your sales talk can then aim to satisfy this desire to buy, and lead your prospect into *selling himself.*

¶ 4102 The ten main buying motives

Ten common buying motives account for most sales. They are:

• Desire for wealth (profit, economy, saving, etc.)
• Desire for health
• Desire for admiration from others (pride, prestige)
• Desire for gratification of some appetite
• Desire for amusement
• Desire for safety and security of self or dependents
• Desire for utility or use value
• Desire for self improvement
• Desire for saving of time, trouble, or worry
• Desire for comfort

A specific product usually appeals to only one, or a few, of the 10 reasons to buy.

Armed with the answer to the question, "Which buying motive (or motives) does *my* product satisfy?" you can formulate a successful presentation around your product's benefits that best satisfy those motives. See ¶ 5015.

¶ 4103 Three techniques to help you find a prospect's primary buying motive

As previously mentioned, one buying motive is dominant in your prospect's mind. If it should be different from the one or ones around which you have built your prepared presentation, your job is to find his particular buying motive and adjust your sales talk to meet his reason for buying.

Here are three ways that will help you find the buying motive that is strongest in your prospect's mind:

• Direct question technique [¶ 4104].
• A trial and error method [¶ 4105].
• A way that utilizes your creativity [¶ 4106].

¶ 4104 A direct question brings out the prime buying motive

Try using the direct question method to

find your prospect's motives for buying when you realize that you're on the "wrong track." When you discover the prime motive and begin to show the prospect how your product will satisfy him, he'll be in a receptive mood to listen.

▶ **IDEA IN ACTION** Frank Meltzer had done some preliminary checking before his call on a prospect whom he was trying to interest in a certain type of envelope in his line. The envelope was just the kind that Frank thought would appeal to this economy-minded prospect. Yet the prospect showed little interest in Frank's offer.

Realizing that he was making no headway and that he was appealing to the wrong buying motive, Frank stopped selling for a moment and tried a question.

"Mr. Prospect, is it possible that you've already found a low-priced envelope that suits your needs as well as the one I just showed you?"

"Well, what we actually want is a *better* envelope. You see, within the last two months we've changed the emphasis of our service and now aim at the higher-priced mailing business. Frankly, that envelope you showed me looked pretty low-grade."

Relieved, Frank brought out samples of his best material, envelopes used by other quality houses in the prospect's line, and soon had the prospect showing real interest.

A direct question enabled Frank to switch successfully from an appeal to the *economy* motive to an appeal to *prestige*. Continued appeal to his prospect's new buying motive enabled Frank to close the sale.

¶ 4105 **A trial and error method to find your prospect's major buying motive**

The alert salesman uses the "trial and error" method to determine a prospect's strongest buying motive (or motives). He uses his best judgment in the selection of sales points to present, and then observes carefully the *actual result* when he uses them in practice.

When a sales point tests out well in actual practice, the top salesman capitalizes it. He knows that a sales point that "clicks" is his most precious possession, for it indicates the buying motive uppermost in the prospect's mind. He uses it again and again—and he keeps right on using it until the sale is made.

Similarly, the successful salesman *drops* a sales point, no matter how good it seems in his own judgment, if *actual practice* proves it to be ineffective. For if a sales point tests out poorly when given a fair trial during an interview, there in no point in stressing it. Field tests are the acid test, and your prior judgment of a sales point's effectiveness should not cause you to keep plugging it if it fails to prove itself.

⟶**IMPORTANT**⟶ The trial and error technique is a continuing process. Changed conditions cause buying motivations to become more or less dominant; excellent sales points may become obsolete; your own company may launch new products that appeal to different buying motives.

¶ 4106 **Use your imagination to "think out" a prospect's strongest buying motive**

Star salesmen put their imagination to work to think out a prospect's strongest buying motive *before they meet him*. As in other phases of their selling, these "stars" perform the creative work that is always the mark of the highest type of salesmanship.

▶ **IDEA IN ACTION** Steve Shearer sells life insurance and an annuity program. During one month he sells large policies to three men whom other salesmen have tried in vain to sign up.

In the first case he emphasizes the *investment* aspect of his proposal. He does this because he knows that this particular prospect is investment minded; he had considerable holdings of securities that are worth more than he paid for them.

Steve reasons that a well-to-do man with a successful record both in business and in "the market" wouldn't be nearly so much impressed by the *protection* argument as by the investment approach *(desire for profit)*.

Steve's second big sale is made to a man in different circumstances. This prospect had recently lost his partner in an automobile accident. Steve reasoned—and rightly—that *here* was a man who would listen when he spoke of sudden death and the need for full protection for one's family *(desire for safety)*.

The third big sale was made on still different grounds. The prospect in this instance was inclined to be impressed with his own importance. "Mr. Logan," said Steve at just the right place in the interview, "there is one thing you may want to consider in connection with this matter. If you let me write up the policy as I've described it to you, you will automatically become a member of a very exclusive group. Here are the names of a few men who are already in it." Here Steve repeated the names of half a dozen of America's most successful men.

Mr. Logan's face lighted up with intense interest as Steve mentioned these names.

"Now, only a few men in America—less than 200, to be exact—have ever bought a policy in that amount. You belong in that group, Mr. Logan, and since you already understand the sound investment and security reasons for buying, I thought I should call this additional fact to your attention" (*desire for prestige*).

Steve Shearer proved his master salesmanship in each of these three cases by using his creative *imagination*. In each case the sale was made in his *own mind* before he even approached the prospect.

¶ 4107 A different approach to the same buying motive can win the sale

There are various ways to appeal to a particular buying motive. When one approach doesn't work, use another—but don't get away from the motive if it's the dominant one.

▶ **IDEA IN ACTION** Bart Merrill sells mill and factory supplies. One of his customers turns him down one day on a rather large order, saying, "There's another company that has just quoted us a little better price on the same item, and, of course, we've got to buy where we get the most for our money."

Bart realizes, of course, that the buying motive in this instance is *economy*—a form of the *desire for wealth*. He realizes that on price alone he cannot win this order. But, having been up against similar situations before, Bart has a ready answer.

"Mr. Jones," he replies, "I know you've got to buy where your dollar will get you the most, and that's exactly why I think you should place the order with us."

"How do you figure *that*? Your price is a little higher than the other quotation."

"I know it is," continues Bart, "but let's look at it this way. Not too long ago there was a shortage on certain items that you regularly use. You may remember that you were rather anxious about it and asked me whether we could fill your needs."

"Yes," answers Jones, "I recall that situation."

"Well," continues Bart, "I told you then not to worry—that we would take care of you. I explained that we're a big, reliable, old organization, one that buys right and sells right. We don't try to buy at cut prices, nor do we sell at cut prices.

"The result is that when an emergency develops, we are likely to get preferred consideration from *our* sources, and this enables us to take care of our customers.

"Now, Mr. Jones, if on that occasion you had been dealing with a less reliable company, you would have had to pay them or someone else a premium price for the scarce merchandise you needed so badly. On that one item alone you saved enough money, by dealing with us, to balance out the saving on *ten* orders. like the one you are going to place today."

Bart got the order. He found a different way to meet his customer's primary buying motive (*economy*) in spite of the higher *price*.

¶ 4108 How to meet an "unusual" reason to buy

You can "tie in" your sales talk with a prospect's buying motive even if it differs from the motive that *usually* spurs people to buy your product.

The wise salesman is prepared to meet these other individual reasons to buy with his reserve sales points if he cannot make the sale solely on the basis of his "set" presentation.

EXAMPLE: A real estate salesman of business properties gives a presentation that stresses business *security*. He meets one prospect who is interested in real estate as a means of avoiding taxes. The salesman then proceeds to stress the tax shelter (*economy*) aspects of real estate that he now knows interest his prospect most.

¶ 4109 How to convert buying motives into sales

Once you have found the buying motive that is uppermost in your prospect's mind, you can change his desire to buy into a decision to buy.

▶ **IDEA IN ACTION** Herb Vogel sells juvenile furniture to retailers. His house builds a quality line that naturally sells at prices a bit above average.

Herb knows his customers well. Hence, to a certain class of retailer, he emphasizes the *prestige* value of handling his products, rather than the volume or profit that will ensue.

¶ 4109

He does this for an excellent reason—the fact that in this particular class of trade there is an active desire to build prestige.

Yet on his next call Herb may emphasize *profit*. He will point out that while his products won't achieve the volume that less expensive articles enjoy, there is an unusually attractive profit, both dollar-wise and percentage-wise.

Again, Herb does this for a very sound reason. He has learned that this second type of retailer actively desires to increase his profit-building sales.

In a third category fall those retailers to whom Herb emphasizes *reliability* (desire to save trouble). These are retailers who would rather forego part of the profit they might earn in exchange for an assured absence of returns, complaints, and adjustments.

Herb gives his presentation so that a different point is emphasized for each class of customer. He is successful because he realizes the importance of this and proceeds accordingly.

¶ 4110 Your appeal must change with the times

You must always be alert to changes in business conditions that may change a prospect's buying motives.

Charles B. Roth gives the following illustration of this point in his "Successful Sales Presentation".[1]

IDEA IN ACTION For several years a salesman used a standardized approach to gain attention. He would request interviews with top executives and win them by promising to show the prospect a way to increase sales by 10%. The phrase "increase your sales by 10%" was always magic—and he had no trouble getting all the interviews he could handle.

But there came a time when the magic words lost their effectiveness. He would make his usual telephone calls, but get no interviews. Something was wrong. It was time to discover why businessmen were no longer interested in increasing their sales, and to change the appeal.

The salesman went at the problem by thinking up three new appeals. He made a dozen calls using each, and discovered that one was much stronger than the others. This one really worked. It got him the interviews that the old "increase your sales" phrase had gotten him.

Instead of saying he had something that would help his prospect increase his sales by 10%, he now told him of a plan that would cut his selling costs. This change, as minor as it seemed, got him in; because it appealed to executives who were now not so much interested in increasing sales as they were in cutting selling expenses.

Making call-backs pay off

¶ 4121 How to set up a call-back

Few professions can become as frustrating as sales. That's why it takes a "tough crust" to succeed. Every salesman runs into prospects who just won't buy. You could give a presentation that even the greatest sales master would be proud of, yet, you are refused at every turn.

The salesman who meets this situation by giving vent to his emotions is usually sorry in the long run. More than one salesman has stormed out of a prospect's office after several well-executed, but unsuccessful, closes with a sarcastic comment such as "If you don't want the best for your company, it's OK with me." This "sour grapes" finish will close you out of this prospect's life forever.

⟶WHAT TO DO⟶ Thank the prospect for listening to your proposals. Maintain the same cheerful attitude until you have left the premises. Try to dismiss his failure to buy with a "better luck next time" smile and comment. By never showing any animosity to a prospect you stand a very good chance of selling him at another time.

IDEA IN ACTION One very cheerful and well-liked salesman that we know tells this to prospects when his closes have failed to close, and he is about to leave the office. In a very friendly and sincere manner he says, "You know, Mr. Jones, it was indeed a pleasure meeting with you today. I would find this job much more profitable and rewarding, if I could meet with ten men a day who are exactly like you. I really mean that."

The prospect is usually taken back by these kind, but illogical words, and usually asks our friend what he means by that. The salesman in his best joking manner replies, "The trouble is I meet *twenty*."

If this anecdote is used right, it is usually good for a laugh and can put you in good stead with that prospect when you call again.

¶ 4122 Make several call-backs if your selling situation requires it

Just as there are selling situations that require a sale to be made on a single call (door-to-door selling, for example), so there are selling fields in which several call-backs must be made before a salesman can expect to make a sale.

If you are in a multi-call line, don't make the mistake of stopping your calls too soon. One extra call might be all that is necessary to put you in the group of salesmen who place the bulk of the orders.

EXAMPLE: A large company that sells supplies to builders informs its salesmen that 80% of its business is placed after the fifth call. Despite this known fact, 88% of the salesmen stop calling after 1, 2, or 3 calls. According to these figures, a majority of the company's salesmen waste their valuable time by making one to three unproductive calls.

≫ WARNING → Since it takes several calls to sell a prospect, you must be especially thorough in qualifying your prospects as to their potential buying ability.

In the following situations it's usually necessary to make several calls before you get an order:

▶ *Selling to a group.* Group selling makes it necessary for you to see more people; often to sell them individually before you get a crack at selling them together. Be prepared to call back a reasonable number of times until the sale is made. See ¶ 2051 et seq. for tips that can help you make every call count when you sell to a group.

▶ *Selling intangibles.* In selling intangibles (insurance, stocks and bonds, or services), call-backs are usually more frequent than in selling a hard-goods line. You sell an idea; often the idea is unfamiliar to the prospect. Your job is to "educate" him, and to give him time to "think it over".

▶ *Conforming to prospect's policy.* Some companies are hard to win quickly because they follow a policy of making a salesman prove himself before they will place a first order with him. Such companies usually expect to become long-term buyers and they want to know the kind of salesman they will be dealing with. When they are convinced of his reliability and worth—and it takes several calls to convince them—they close. Once the salesman has earned the confidence of such a prospect he has a loyal customer and a steady source of orders.

¶ 4123 **Three key queries before making a call-back**

The time to decide whether you are going to call back on a prospect is immediately after you have had an unsuccessful interview. When you make the decision, keep clearly in mind the value of your selling time and weigh carefully the worthwhileness of another call.

Your answers to the following two questions will help you to weed out the prospects on whom call-backs would be futile and let you see those who merit further expenditure of your time. The third question is necessary for taking action.

1. *Is this account worth another call-back?* To answer the question, you should weigh the answers to questions such as these: Is there something in the situation that makes it worthwhile to call back? (The fact that it takes several calls *usually* to make a sale in your particular line may be the "something" in the situation that justifies another call.) Do you feel that you are still making headway? Has your prospect just given your proposition full consideration? Did he show interest? What was his reaction when you suggested another call?

2. *If I call back, what strategy can I use that will get me somewhere?* Have you exhausted all the approaches that could possibly appeal to this prospect? Have you any ammunition left, or would another call be a mere rehash of previous calls? What creative idea can you develop to bring to this prospect before the next call?

3. *When is the best time to call back?* Your knowledge of each situation will enable you to determine whether to call back in a week, a month, or some other specific time.

¶ 4124 **A "last-ditch" attempt after several calls may make the sale**

A good salesman will make it a rule to call regularly on his big prospects. He insists upon "staying with" the prospect because the potential sales are great. But even such a man will reluctantly decide to give up when he discovers some fact that destroys his confidence, not in himself, but in the prospect. Before he gives up, however, he will make one last attempt and will "sell dangerously."

¶ 4124

The force of such desperation will often break the bottleneck.

▶ **IDEA IN ACTION** Ralph Foster, a business systems salesman, had called once a month for four years on a large organization that used forms supplied by competitors. On these calls, Ralph was always able to see the purchasing agent, but he had never succeeded in getting him to look at his product. The purchasing agent had promised him, however, that the next time the company needed to replenish certain forms, he would let Ralph know about it.

Through a friend Ralph learned that the prospect had bought a large quantity of forms from a competitor. Ralph felt that there was no longer any use in calling on the prospect; the purchasing agent had not kept his word. But, being a good salesman, Ralph decided to make his parting call a telling one. Getting the interview was no trouble, for Ralph had been a welcome caller for years. This time, when he approached the prospect, he said: "Mr. Prospect, I promise you that I'll never step in here again if you will look at our register and forms just once." The prospect looked, and Ralph left with a sizeable order.

¶ 4125 **Fellow-salesmen can give you ideas to be used in call-backs**

Contacting a fellow salesman for help in solving a selling problem that was brought out in call-back interviews is good practice. For example, a colleague who sells products of another division of your company to one of your prospects may give you the very information you need to make a sale.

▶ **IDEA IN ACTION** Glenn Faulke approached the president of a tool steel company to interest him in a new type of industrial grinding wheel. The president was satisfied with the grinding wheels he used. No order was received and further contact seemed stalemated.

Glenn contacted the salesman in his area who represented another division of the company. He learned from him that the prospect had another application for the same grinding wheel he had tried to sell. This different use for the same wheel in the finishing process of certain grades of steel appealed to the president and Glenn made the sale.

¶ 4126 **Seek a higher authority after repeated calls**

The man you contact first might balk at your repeated attempts to interest him in your proposition. By contacting someone higher-up, you may be able to make a sale. But remember to maintain good relations with the first man—he might be called in when a decision to buy is made.

▶ **IDEA IN ACTION** Bill Larson, a salesman of modern filing equipment, failed to "sell" the Manager of Office Services on his bid for a survey of the company's filing operations.

Bill then approached the Vice-President in charge of systems and was promptly assigned a company methods man to assist him in the survey. Bill immediately contacted the Manager of Office Services to inform him of this move, and to build his goodwill. The manager smoothed the way to a multiple sale when he was called in to help make the purchasing decision.

¶ 4127 **Turn a losing situation into a winning one**

You can turn the unlucky "circumstances" that lose you sales into "sales winners." Every experienced salesman has seen good accounts go down the drain for any one of a number of reasons which were out of his control. For example, a retailer retires or a manufacturer discontinues the product for which you supplied a component.

But how about these losses? A newly-appointed buyer or purchasing agent favors a salesman who is his personal friend, or a long-time relationship ends because of customer dissatisfaction with your quality, price or service. But, you can turn *these* circumstances into a—

▶ *Two-way street:* The same developments which work against you can operate in your favor. Here's why:

"Improved" circumstances can turn a loser into a winner. For example, (1) The prospect who was "not interested" in insurance may have since acquired a family; (2) the young man who "couldn't afford" a boat or a car may be earning more money; (3) the purchasing agent who was "bound hand and foot" to a college classmate selling your rival line may have changed jobs, or had a falling out.

⟫SUGGESTION→ Keep checking or calling back on your "no-sale" prospects. You can never tell when the circumstances will turn in your favor.

¶ 4999 **Footnote references**
¶ 4110
   (1) Published by Prentice-Hall, Inc., Englewood Cliffs, N. J.

MAKING A GREAT PRESENTATION

A Great Presentation Must Be Prepared
Preliminary Preparation for Developing the Presentation
The Outline is the Blueprint
Guides for a Sure-Fire Demonstration
Masterful Use of Sales Tools in a Presentation
How to Handle Price in a Presentation
How to Achieve a Lean, Sharp, "Electric" Quality
Adding Power with "Vivid-Picture" Language
Putting the Presentation into Words
How to Give Your Presentation
Actual Successful Sales Presentations

TABLE OF CONTENTS

	Starts at Paragraph [¶]		Starts at Paragraph [¶]
Miracle Guide to Making a Great Presentation	5001		

A GREAT PRESENTATION MUST BE PREPARED

What is a great presentation?	5002	A prepared presentation is a 'must'	5005
What a great presentation is made of	5003	Mastering your presentation gives you flexibility	5006
How long should a presentation be?	5004		

PRELIMINARY PREPARATION FOR DEVELOPING THE PRESENTATION

Know what you have to offer	5011	Turn facts into benefits	5015
Tips on listing your selling points	5012	Study your competition	5016
How a company-prepared list of sales features can help	5013	How to select the selling points for your presentation	5017
List both product and company features	5014	Make possession nine-tenths of the sale	5018

THE OUTLINE IS THE BLUEPRINT

Make an outline	5021	Provide for the demonstration when making your outline	5027
The basic pattern for an outline	5022	Provide in your outline for the use of sales tools	5028
Additional points to include in a complete outline	5023	Provide for covering price when making your outline	5029
Example of an outline for selling a product (written form)	5024	Provide for answering questions and objections as you go	5030
Example of an outline for a sale entailing a survey (chart form)	5025	Include trial closings	5031
Repeat the important points	5026		

GUIDES FOR A SURE-FIRE DEMONSTRATION

6-point guide to a successful demonstration	5041	The best demonstration is an in-use demonstration	5044
Watch out for these 'no-sale' gestures	5042		
Get the prospect into the act	5043		

making a great presentation—table of contents

MASTERFUL USE OF SALES TOOLS IN A PRESENTATION

	Starts at Paragraph [¶]
Tips for using samples	5051
Tips for using working models	5052
Make your camera click for you	5053
Tips for using a presentation manual	5054
Tips for using sales kits	5055
Tips for using a catalog in your presentation	5056
Tips on showing facts through charts and graphs	5057
Tips for using descriptive literature and similar aids	5058
Tips for using testimonials	5059
Question your speaking habits and answer your sales problems	5060
Written proposals can be used profitably to build interest in a first interview	5061
Written proposals call for creative thinking	5062
Photographs can be a useful sales tool	5063
Ask your customers for testimonials	5064
Introduce new evidence by using reproductions	5065
Clippings from newspapers and trade publications up-date your presentation	5066

HOW TO HANDLE PRICE IN A PRESENTATION

Value must justify price	5071
When to bring in price	5072
How to put off the impatient prospect	5073
Soften up your prospect with a touch of 'show business'	5074
Techniques for minimizing price	5075
Quote quantity prices to "up" the sale	5076
Know how to handle price objections	5077

HOW TO ACHIEVE A LEAN, SHARP, "ELECTRIC" QUALITY

Ways to make your presentation "great"	5081
Dramatize your presentation	5082
Use "you" emphasis	5083
Importance of language	5084
Use the power of story-telling	5085
Ask questions as you go along	5086
Appeal to the senses	5087
Use plenty of examples	5088

ADDING POWER WITH "VIVID-PICTURE" LANGUAGE

Language has power	5091
Use word power to increase your sales power	5092
3 steps to increase your word power	5093
Word power to explain a product	5094
How to enlarge your word power	5095
Avoid using cliches in your sales talk	5096

PUTTING THE GREAT PRESENTATION INTO WORDS

Developing the presentation from the outline	5101
First introduce yourself	5102

Get the Prospect's Attention

Get attention in the first sentence	5111
Use an emphatic benefit as your opener	5112
Tell him you can solve a problem for him	5113
Ask your prospect a thought-provoking question	5114
How to use an unusual or dramatic opening	5115
Use the "no-name" approach to win more sales	5116
Start your presentation with an exhibit	5117
Use an interesting news item as an opener	5118

Build Interest

Make him interested by stating benefits	5121

Turn the Prospect's Interest Into Desire

Desire must be created	5131
Build up the prospect's need for your product or service	5132
How to show your product as the best for the prospect's needs	5133
Point out to the prospect his personal stake in the sale	5134
Make your benefits sound personally satisfying to the prospect	5135
Add glamour to your product	5136

Make Your Presentation Convincing

A prospect isn't sold until he's convinced	5141
There is no substitute for the facts	5142

making a great presentation—table of contents 157

	Starts at Paragraph [¶]		Starts at Paragraph [¶]
Get the facts from your company	5143	Gather your forces before you make the final assault	5146
A thorough presentation is more likely to convince	5144	**Make a Firm Bid for the Order**	
Talk to the prospect on his own level if you want to convince him	5145	A good presentation leads into a good close	5151

HOW TO GIVE YOUR GREAT PRESENTATION

	Starts at Paragraph [¶]		Starts at Paragraph [¶]
Control of the presentation	5171	Hit hardest the points the prospect likes best	5175
A good personal impression gets you off on the right foot	5172	Look for vital clues when prospect knocks your competition	5176
Give a smooth-flowing talk	5173	Add $30,000-a-minute selling ideas to your presentation for free	5177
Be worthy of his order	5174		

ACTUAL SUCCESSFUL SALES PRESENTATIONS

	Starts at Paragraph [¶]		Starts at Paragraph [¶]
A two-call presentation to businessmen to sell the need for fire protection, make a survey, and then sell the equipment indicated by the survey	5181	A presentation to purchasing agents or shop men to sell a grinding wheel that requires a semi-technical explanation	5183
A presentation to businessmen, built around a demonstration of an office machine that emphasizes quality, performance, dependability, and value	5182	A presentation to farmers, built around the use of a visual aid (slides), to sell a premium fertilizer, stressing dependability of the supplier	5184

Footnote references 6999

Making a Great Presentation

When your prospect lets you tell your story, that's your big moment

¶ 5001 ⟫MIRACLE GUIDE to→ Making a Great Presentation

It's astounding but true that 20% of this country's salesmen bring in 80% of the sales that are made. In other words, each top salesman sells sixteen times as much as each average salesman does. Why? The answer lies in the way they present their goods to their prospects. They not only get interviews; they know how to use them to get orders.

There is only one way to reach the top in selling—you must know how to give a *great* presentation. You can't be an effective closer until you have become a convincing presenter.

Without losing sight of the fact that selling is a continuous process—that every single step in the selling process is related to each of the other steps—we are covering the presentation without discussing closing techniques. The latter are treated at ¶ 6001 et seq.

To give a great presentation, you must apply certain techniques at each of the following four stages.

▶ *Preliminary preparation.* This step entails gathering the facts about your product and service, and your competition, and deciding how to use the most telling ones [¶ 5011 et seq.].

▶ *Outlining the talk.* In this step you blueprint your sales story [¶ 5021 et seq.].

▶ *Putting it into words.* You work up each point of the outline, using *tested techniques* for achieving a sure-fire demonstration [¶ 5041 et seq.]; for making masterful use of all your selling tools [¶ 5051 et seq.]; and for handling price expertly [¶ 5071 et seq.]; you make your words "sell" [¶ 5081 et seq.; 5091 et seq.].

▶ *Learning how to give the sales story most effectively.* This means injecting your personality into selling. The know-how [¶ 5171 et seq.] gives you complete and confident control of every selling interview.

A great presentation must be prepared

¶ 5002 **What is a great presentation?**

Any explanation of a salable item or service to someone by a salesman could be called a sales presentation. *Your* objective, however, must be to develop a *great* presentation, one which will accomplish the following five tasks:

¶ 5002

- Hold the prospect's interest throughout.
- Clearly and adequately explain, in a convincing manner, what is being sold and the benefits to be derived from it.
- Establish definitely that the product or service being presented would satisfy one or more of the prospect's buying motives.
- Overcome or answer to the satisfaction of the prospect all questions and objections to buying that he may have.
- Make the prospect decide that he wants to buy.

⇒ IMPORTANT → In each of these objectives, the emphasis is on the *prospect's* point of view—on how *he* stands to gain by making a purchase. The prospect is the final judge of the effectiveness of your presentation, so put yourself in his shoes as you work it out.

⇒ REMEMBER → A great presentation is one that so convincingly satisfies your prospect's buying motives, and so persuasively removes all buying obstacles, that he decides to place an order. The success of a sales interview thus depends greatly on how closely your presentation anticipates the prospect's wants. This in turn depends on how thoroughly you know your product or service, how much you have been able to learn about your prospect, and how well you fit the two together.

¶ 5003 **What a great presentation is made of**

A good presentation is a smooth and convincing sales talk that leads in a logical manner from the opening sentence to the close of the sale. It cannot be disjointed or confusing; it must be a well-forged unit.

Even the smoothest sales talk has five definite parts, or steps. Each step must be accomplished before the presentation is complete. The five parts are these:

1. Get the prospect's attention (immediately after introducing yourself [¶ 5111]).

2. Arouse his interest by describing benefits [¶ 5121].

3. Stimulate his desire for these benefits [¶ 5131].

4. Convince him that the benefits described are true and that they can work for him [¶ 5141].

5. Get him to take action and sign the order [¶ 5151].

Like any steps, these are meant to be taken in order, but in many cases two steps can be combined into one. The opening, or attention-getting stage, for instance, might be accomplished through the immediate mention of significant benefits. Two steps (1 and 2) would then be covered in one.

⇒ WARNING → Although two or more steps in the presentation process can sometimes be combined, no step should ever be left out. Many otherwise skillful interviews have ended in failure because of the omission of a single step. Each step depends on the one before it, and so each step must be developed in turn.

¶ 5004 **Four times when doing nothing is your best bet**

Knowing when to do nothing can be as important to a salesman as having the facts and figures handy and presenting them in a reassuring manner.

After all, that *nothing*—properly timed—can lead straight to a sale—and that is something. The following example shows how a real-estate salesman uses the "nothing" approach. You'll see how you can adopt it to your own needs.

Here are four times when a salesman should be content to "do nothing"

1. After revealing the contract: Always let Prospect see the sales contract long before it's going to be put to use. Pull it out. Place it on the table. Make sure he knows what it is. Then do nothing. Let the contract do the work for you.

When you do start to do something, be casual about it. You could, for example, pick up the contract to check a fact. (Best time: When you can point out something in it that's an *advantage* to your Prospect.) Finally, you can start to fill it out, bit by bit.

But at the first it's usually a good idea to not do much of anything with a sales contract —for a while.

2. After making a strong point: "Doing nothing" at a time like this is the only way you can let your prospect think over what you've said. And the stronger the point made, the more important it is that it register. Anything you might say at this time could detract from your winning point.

a great presentation must be prepared

Leaving Mr. and Mrs. Prospect alone can be all that's necessary at this point.

3. After they've seen the house: This is another time to go off somewhere and leave the prospects to themselves.

You could say something like, "I'll just let you look about for yourselves. I'll be in the living room."

You're on safe ground if you've made all the strong points you can and if you think they're interested, then you'd be foolish to hang around.

4. After you know they're interested: At this point you had better do nothing, since any more salesmanship on your part could easily be interpreted as high-pressure. Your best bet: Ask for the sale.

¶ 5005 A prepared presentation is a "must"

Salesmen who are earning big money favor a carefully planned, word-for-word presentation. They depend on a memorized "script;" they do not extemporize. If they deviate at all from the memorized script, they do so to fit the needs of the moment. But they always get right back to the script and follow it exactly as they prepared it.

If you prepare your presentation as we instruct you to in this Guide, every word of it will count; it will be lean and hard—electric with power. It will be built from the prospect's point of view—it will be studded with supporting facts; and it will be so effectively dramatized that it will carry your prospect along to the end—the sale. It will be a great presentation. Why, then, should you not memorize it and use it in every interview?

▶ *Advantages of a prepared presentation.* Here's what you gain by preparing your presentation and following it practically word for word:

1. In the process of preparing you learn all about what you're selling and how it should be sold.

2. You are sure of covering the important points in every interview. If you master your presentation completely, you won't leave out or forget vital parts.

3. You make the best use of your interview minutes. A planned and orderly presentation is the most efficient kind; it moves logically and convincingly from one point to the next.

4. Your words, being carefully chosen, are the ones with maximum impact and persuasiveness.

5. You have the confidence that comes from being well prepared.

6. Prospects are impressed by salesmen who demonstrate that they have taken the trouble to prepare and organize their material.

7. An organized presentation enables you to control the interview and smoothly guide the prospect toward the close.

▶ *"Canned" presentations can be "great."* Don't let anyone discourage you from using what you have prepared as a great presentation because it is "canned." Some of the greatest presentations have been canned. Let's see what some salesmen find objectionable about a canned presentation and how their arguments break down, if the presentation is impelling.

1. A "canned" sales talks sounds dead and lacks spontaneity, they claim. Yet actors in long-run plays find meaning for lines they have said perhaps a thousand times. So do most really successful salesmen, who stick to a perfected and memorized presentation that for them has proved its effectiveness. Having found the best way to tell their story, they continue to use it in its best form and are not in the least mechanical, judging by their success. Even salesmen who would discredit the standardized presentation admit that any kind of presentation, if given often enough, tends to settle into a fixed pattern.

2. Some salesmen complain that interruptions throw them off when they are in the midst of a memorized sales talk. Actually any presentation can be disrupted by questions and interruptions unless you maintain control over the interview and your thoughts.

3. Another objection says that no two prospects are alike, and so your presentation must be flexible. Most salesmen, however, call on people for whom their product or service is suited, and whose wants and needs therefore tend to be at least roughly similar.

▶ *Exceptional situations.* For some products and services a completely memorized, standardized presentation may be impractical. For example, men selling a specialized product, designed to meet individual customer needs, like engineered pieces of equipment, must vary their selling talks from prospect to prospect. Nevertheless, such salesmen must go through the preliminary steps of studying their product, their competition, and their prospects' needs and buying motives. They must also go through the basic steps of selling, from getting attention to closing the sale. Although they do not have to write out a complete sales story, they must mentally plan what they are going to say in each interview.

⇒SUGGESTION→ Even if the use of a standardized presentation is not feasible in your case, you will gain by standardizing the elements that are common to all of your interviews. You will thus reduce the time necessary to prepare for each new interview, and you will arrive at the most effective way in which to present the points that are covered in most of your interviews.

¶ 5006 Mastering your presentation gives you flexibility

Flexibility means being able to switch your emphasis to appeal to a particular prospect's buying motives.

Flexibility also means being able to meet unexpected problems and interruptions and still control the interview.

If your presentation has been thoroughly prepared it has anticipated what would otherwise be "unforeseen" problems. Unexpected changes of direction will thus be kept to a minimum.

Preliminary preparation for developing the presentation

¶ 5011 Know what you have to offer

The first thing to do in developing your presentation is to take inventory and determine exactly what you have to sell.

⇒REMEMBER→ In "Mature Salesmanship," you saw that exhaustive knowledge of your product or service is essential to success [¶ 1082]. Without complete knowledge of your product you can't have a great presentation.

To be sure that you know your product thoroughly and to begin planning your presentation, list every possible selling point.

When this list is completed it will serve two purposes:

1. From it you will choose the best and most effective points as a basis for your presentation.

2. The remaining features will provide additional support to be used during the interview when it is necessary to convince a stubborn prospect.

⇒IMPORTANT→ The more you know about your product, the stronger your faith in its performance. The more faith, the more conviction you have in selling.

¶ 5012 Tips on listing your selling points

You may feel that you already know all you have to about what you are selling, but you must remember that it is the salesman who knows the *most* who reaches the top. Therefore, to be sure you've listed every selling point, follow these tips:

- Write down all the points you can think of from memory. Scrape your mind for every single feature that might be a selling feature, including ones that you are aware of but aren't using now in your presentation.
- Review carefully all company literature and bulletins for points that you have forgotten or have overlooked.
- If you sell a product, study it physically as if you had never seen it before. Take it apart, if possible. Try to get a look at it in action, where you can watch it and listen to it.
- Ask other salesmen in your company (choose *good* salesmen) what features they have the most success with.
- Ask your customers for their opinion. People who actually use a product can shed valuable light on its advantages and drawbacks.

¶ 5013 How a company-prepared list of sales features can help

In designing its products, your company tries to make them better than those its competitors have to offer. It also probably uses market research to discover the features that customers are likely to want in such a product. Since they are in on the development of the product from the beginning, the engineers

preliminary preparation for developing the presentation

and sales promotion people have a thorough understanding of what the product can do.

For these reasons the lists of sales features that your company prepares are your best source of information for building your great presentation.

⇒ SUGGESTION → In most cases you can and should enlarge the company list from your own knowledge of the product and its use. Also, be sure the company list has not become outdated by fast-moving conditions in the industry, by changes in the design of the product, or changes in competitors' products.

¶ 5014   **List both product and company features**

In your list be sure to include the benefits that customers get from buying your product *and* the ones they can expect from dealing with your company. People buy both.

IDEA IN ACTION Frank Stewart sells an industrial humidifying unit. As the first step in developing his sales presentation, he drew up a list of sales features that he knew his product offered. His unit isn't the *best* on the market for every point on the list, but he put down everything that he could think of that was *good*. Here is the list:

- Low initial cost
- Low installation cost
- Low maintenance cost
- Low operating cost
- Low depreciation rate
- Compact size
- Good appearance
- Quiet operation
- Low vibration
- More mobile unit than others
- Extra safety features
- Unit rates preferred insurance premiums
- A wider range of models and sizes
- Quicker delivery date than competition can meet

Knowing that he represented a good company, Frank also listed these advantages of buying from his company:

- Superior reputation
- Local service office insuring prompt, efficient, and low-cost servicing
- Company extends favorable credit terms, offers discounts for prompt payments
- Unit covered by a more complete guarantee than others

- Company has many similar units in operation in vicinity and throughout the country
- The company's salesmen are local residents of good reputation
- The salesmen are well trained and can make sound, on-the-spot recommendations

With a little work Frank was able to add more product *and* company benefits to his list, and he had a solid idea of just what he had to sell.

¶ 5015   **Turn facts into benefits**

Your presentation must satisfy the prospect's buying motives [¶ 4101 et seq.]. Buying motives are satisfied not by lists of impressive features, *but by the benefits that those features will give*. There is a clear distinction between the two. A person does not buy strength; he buys the durability that strength provides. He does not buy beauty; he buys the pleasure and pride that possession of a beautiful object will mean. He does not buy speed; he buys the time saving, or the greater production, or the excitement that speed gives him. Behind everything the prospect wants, there is the more important reason *why* he wants it.

⇒ IMPORTANT → When you run into a period of "bad business," and buyers are wary of making commitments because of uncertain economic conditions, or are buying with the utmost caution, it is especially important to stress benefits.

As you select the selling points from which to develop your presentation, visualize each point in terms of the benefits that it can bring.

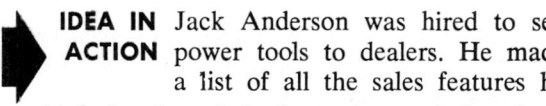

IDEA IN ACTION Jack Anderson was hired to sell power tools to dealers. He made a list of all the sales features he could find, selected the best ones, and then built a presentation around these points. His sales manager listened to the presentation and said, "But what's in it for the dealer?"

A little surprised, Jack said, "I just told you; low cost, a complete line, a popular item . . ."

"Jack," replied the sales manager, "a list like that only tells him what the product is. You've got to show him why he should buy it, what benefits he'll get. Ask yourself 'So what?' on each point you used, and then list the corresponding benefit to the dealer. You'll see a big difference."

Jack did as he was advised, and soon realized that the second list was what the dealers really

¶ 5015

wanted to hear. Here is what the two lists looked like:

Advantages	"So what?"
Popular item	Big turnover, higher sales, *better profit*
Low cost	Greater customer acceptance, less money tied up in stock
Complete line	Could service a greater percentage of customers, be a one-stop source
Manufactured locally	No delivery problems, quick service and repair
Well advertised	Big demand, customer acceptance

Jack had immediate success from the new presentation that he developed from the benefit list.

¶ 5016 **Study your competition**

After you have compiled a list of what *you* can offer, take a good look at your competition.

Knowledge of competing products enables you to evaluate your list of selling features. You want to stress benefits that are better than competitors can offer, or exclusive with your line. Studying competitors enables you to find out what those benefits are.

⟫SUGGESTION→ Although your presentation should stress the superior or exclusive features of your product or service, it must not omit other important advantages just because they are shared by competitors. Your two biggest competitors, for instance, might offer low operation costs, just as you can. You must still use this feature in your presentation, because it is an important point, even though it is not exclusive with you.

You must be aware of all local factors that make competitive conditions in your area different from elsewhere. It has a direct bearing on the sales features to be emphasized and your preparation to meet objections.

EXAMPLE: You are working for a national company, selling ferrous castings in an area where there are several local foundries. You face stiffer price and delivery competition than you would in other areas. So you select the sales features that emphasize quality and justify the price differential. You use your testimonials of satisfied customers who are some distance from your plant to prove dependable delivery.

¶ 5017 **How to select the selling points for your presentation**

You must build your talk around the *best* selling points in your list. To select the most telling sales features, *put yourself in the prospect's place*. Look carefully at every point and ask, "Is that what would satisfy my buying motives if I were the prospect? Is that something I would especially want or need in this kind of a product or service? Would that feature make my offer look any better than, or different from, other propositions the prospect will hear?" Remember that he is the judge and that he will buy only what promises to do something for *him*.

Naturally the features that help most to make your product or service stand out are its *exclusive* features. Whatever they are, major or minor, you should emphasize any feature that competitors can't offer. Even a small point carries weight when it has distinctive, only-one-in-its-field authority.

⟫OBSERVATION→ The better you know your competition, the better you can utilize the features that are yours alone.

Obviously, you can't cover every point on your list in a normal sales interview. Your presentation would take too much time. The points that are not included in your prepared presentation bolster your confidence and serve as a reserve when the going gets rough.

¶ 5018 **Make 'possession' nine-tenths of the sale**

You can get maximum results from your sales calls if you get your product into the hands of your prospect as soon as possible. Here's what one sales manager tells his men:

"Short of buying your product, the closest your prospect can come to actual possession of it is physical contact with one or more aspects of it. Encourage him therefore, to touch your product, handle it, use it. For maximum effectiveness:

(1) *"Start early*. The earlier your prospect gets the feel of things in your demonstration, the better. It's basic attention insurance.

(2) *"Make his role easy*. Don't ask your prospect to do anything too complicated. If he fails, his embarrassment may take the form of 'no sale'.

the outline is the blueprint

(3) *"Make it clear.* Tell your prospect exactly what you want him to do. If he doesn't completely understand you and consequently is not totally successful in the handling of your product, he may decide that it doesn't work, or that it's of inferior make. When you want him to hold something, show him how. Don't leave anything to chance."

The outline is the blueprint

¶ 5021   **Make an outline**

The best way to organize your material into a logical, orderly, and convincing presentation is first to make an outline. Outlining organizes your thoughts and enables you to make the best use of the facts, benefits, and sales features that you want to present to your prospect. Through an outline you can see how all of your material is going to fall into place. You thus get a clear idea of what the actual presentation will be like.

Whether the outline is simple or detailed will depend on what you sell and on your personal preference. For most men, the work that goes into a detailed outline is fully compensated by the grasp it gives them of what they must say and how they will say it. A detailed outline also simplifies the actual writing of a word-for-word presentation.

⟫⟫SUGGESTION→   Make your outline as complete as you feel it should be to help you develop the presentation. Two adaptable forms are shown in the examples: the written form [¶ 5024] and the chart form [¶ 5025].

¶ 5022   **The basic pattern for an outline**

These steps, which are the natural outline of almost any sale, provide a framework within which to develop your own presentation outline:
- *Introduce* yourself.
- Get the prospect's *attention* and keep it.
- Get the prospect *interested* in your product.
- Make the prospect *desire* your product.
- *Convince* him with proof.
- Get him to take *action* (close the sale).

By arranging the elements of your own sales story under the appropriate heading, you will see your outline fall easily into place.

⟫⟫WARNING→   Take pains to make each step connect smoothly with the next. This will be of particular importance when you put your presentation into words, following the outline.

⟫⟫IMPORTANT→   There are three exceptions to this established selling sequence:
- Steps can be combined. For example, you usually get the prospect interested by describing benefits, after you have his attention. If you can make outstanding benefit claims, you can use them to capture his attention at the start. You would then be combining the attention step and the interest step. Most sales, however, are made by leading the prospect through each step in turn.
- Conviction is not always handled as a separate stage. Some salesmen include facts, figures, testimonials and similar convincers throughout their presentation, making conviction a constant process.
- Close the sale at the earliest opportunity. Don't wait until the end of your presentation to sew up the order if the prospect is ready earlier. Trial closings should be placed at intervals in your presentation to feel out the prospect's buying readiness [¶ 6001 et seq.].

¶ 5023   **Additional points to include in a complete outline**

If you are making your outline a detailed one, you can sketch in the following elements to show where they will appear in the final presentation:
- Repetition of main points [¶ 5026].
- The demonstration, of there is one [¶ 5027].
- Visual aids and other sales tools [¶ 5028].
- Quoting the price [¶ 5029].
- Anticipating main questions and most common objections [¶ 5030].
- Trial closings [¶ 5031].

¶ 5024   **Example of an outline for selling a product (written form)**

The following is an outline of a presentation to sell a newly developed envelope designed to entice people to open it and read its contents. The new envelope for third class mailers, called the Sim-Pull and manufactured by the Tension Envelope Corporation, features a tucked-in flap at the end which comes open when the tab that protrudes is pulled, thus providing easy access to the material inside the envelope. The company has supplied the salesmen with a list of sales features, and has advised them that there will be trade ads and mailings to familiarize the public with the Sim-Pull. Some orders have already been received.

OUTLINE

Attention:
    Want a new and sure way to get your third class mailings read?
    The Sim-Pull envelope [patent pending], exclusive with us, will do it (show him).

Interest:
    Different—attracts attention
    Tab is intriguing, gets more *openings,* more *returns*
    Quick and easy to open—message put to work sooner
    Doesn't rob space from advertising or merchandising message
    Economical—only a few cents more per thousand
    Foolproof on mechanical insertion
    Company service, reputation for quality

Desire:
    Expand on benefits and personalize them

Conviction:
    Acceptance has been immediate, orders coming in (give facts, use testimonials and other evidence)

Close:
    Be the first in your industry, get maximum effect
    Briefly summarize benefits
    All this at only (quote price)
    How many will you need for your next mailing?

¶ 5025 **Example of an outline for sale entailing a survey (chart form)**

You can adapt the chart form shown in Fig. 1 in preparing your outline. The outline presented was drawn up by the Carrier Corporation for a one-call sale of a home air-conditioning system. Words are kept to a minimum, yet the outline is sufficiently detailed to provide for each step in a sale that includes selling the idea of a survey, making the survey, and closing the sale.

¶ 5026 **Repeat the important points**

As you prepare your outline, remember that the primary benefits should be brought to the prospect's attention more than once during the presentation. Repetition strengthens the effect of your statements and gives emphasis to them. A person may understand a statement when he first hears it, but he seldom absorbs its full impact unless he hears it more than once.

    ⋙CAUTION→ Try to re-phrase the points that are repeated so that you won't sound monotonous. Avoid mentioning any one feature too often.

¶ 5027 **Provide for the demonstration when making your outline**

Working up the outline for your presentation will help you decide where the demonstration belongs. If your demonstration is so complete that it will comprise most of the interview, then you will usually begin it without much delay. If you have only one or two demonstrable features, they will be shown as they become appropriate during the interview.

If the demonstration is a lengthy or involved one, fit it into the outline in steps. Then you can note along with each step the comments or benefit descriptions that will accompany it.

For more on the demonstration itself, see ¶ 5041 et seq.

¶ 5028 **Provide in your outline for the use of sales tools**

How will you use the sales tools supplied by your company to help you make your presentation? Among them may be: samples; demonstrators or working models; movies, slides, three-dimensional viewers, photographs; presentation manuals; sales kits; catalogs or catalog pages; charts and graphs; descriptive literature, blow-ups of ads, and copies of publicity stories; testimonials.

Notice that these tools all have the function of engaging the prospect's eyes: they are visual aids.

At ¶ 5051 et seq. you will find guidance for getting the best results from each of the visual aids. At ¶ 5184 you will find an example of a sales presentation built around the use of slides.

    ⋙REMEMBER→ You can develop certain sales tools on your own, to supplement or take the place of company material. See ¶5060 for do-it-yourself tools.

¶ 5029 **Provide for covering price when making your outline**

Price is an important factor in any sale. Good salesmanship demands that it be covered

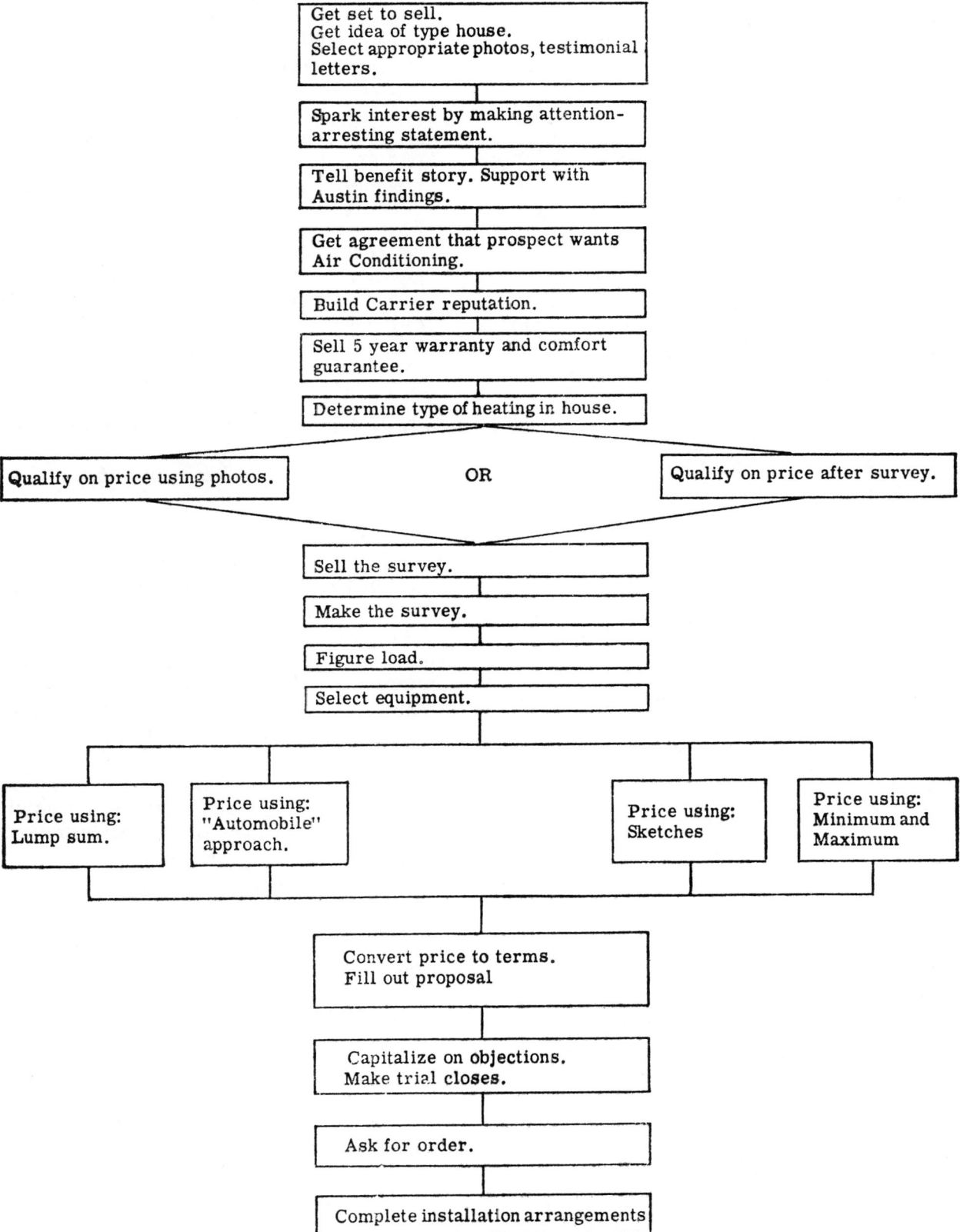

Fig. 1. Outline of Presentation in Chart Form

in your presentation, and handled with the same confident, positive attitude that marks your presentation as a whole. If you avoid covering price as a part of the presentation, you invite the prospect to believe that you are afraid to mention it because it is too high.

For a discussion of how to time the price quotation, how to quote with confidence, and how to minimize a price, see ¶ 5071 et seq.

¶ 5030 Provide for answering questions and objections as you go

A prospect's unanswered questions and objections are obstacles that block the sale. Anticipate them and build the answers into your presentation. This eliminates problems before the prospect can bring them up, and deprives him of reasons for not buying.

Here's how to go about getting the right question and objection answers worked into your outline:

- Make a list. List all the reasons you can find why a prospect—*any* prospect—might decide against placing an order. Think of every question that might be asked about what you sell.
- Opposite each objection put down the means you have to overcome it. Opposite each possible question write out the complete answer or answers. See "Making Objections Work For You," ¶ 7001 et seq.
- Select from the list the most important points and the ones you are most likely to encounter.
- As you make the outline of your presentation, work in the answers to all the important possible questions and objections you have selected. Put each answer or positive supporting fact into its appropriate section in the outline.

¶ 5031 Include trial closings

In a complete outline you can work in trial closings and give your presentation closing strength. In every interview you must make a try for the order as soon as possible, and as often after that as necessary. Trial closings fit naturally into your planned presentation after strong points and when your demonstration ends. You must also be prepared to insert trial closings during your "live performance," whenever they are feasible. See ¶ 6001 et seq.

EXAMPLE: Dictaphone Corporation supplies its salesmen with a presentation for the Time-Master, an automatic transistorized dictating machine. Built around a demonstration, the presentation is a short one that is loaded with selling power. One reason is that after each main point a trial closing is attempted. If no affirmative response is forthcoming, the salesman goes on with further demonstration and selling.

The sales presentation is reproduced at ¶ 5182. In this sales story the first trial closing comes after the salesman has sold his prospect on the *quality* of the machine; the second, after he has convinced the prospect of *performance;* the third, after he has developed the third essential, *dependability*. The final close is made on the point of *value*.

Guides for a sure-fire demonstration

¶ 5041 Six-point guide to a successful demonstration

The demonstration is that part of your presentation which makes use of the product, a part of the product, or some other tangible thing to show a benefit to be gained by buying the product. The demonstration may, at the same time, show how the product works. The prospect's needs are the keynote to the demonstration. How the product fits those needs is the meat of the demonstration.

Each demonstration must be made to fit the particular product. No demonstration can be made successfully without the most careful planning and rehearsing of the demonstration to make it accomplish its purpose.

The following pointers must be observed in planning the demonstration:

▶ *Guard against being too technical.* A demonstration should not be too technical. An involved demonstration can be as confusing as a wordy explanation. Your purpose is to show *what* the product can do for the prospect, and details on *how* this is done may be unnecessary.

▶ *Get the prospect into the act.* Try to get the prospect to take part actively in the demonstration. Automobile salesmen always include a trial spin by the prospect, because automobile salesmen know that the car will sell itself if the potential buyer drives it.

Sometimes you can get the prospect in on the

act by asking him questions that require him to observe what is happening. An example: "Can you see, Mr. Prospect, what will happen when the liquid level reaches that float?"

▶ *Ask questions.* As the demonstration proceeds, ask questions to be sure that the prospect understands, and to get him thinking about how the product fits in with his needs. As you plan your demonstration, include time for these questions between each step.

▶ *Tell what you are going to show.* Before you start the demonstration, tell your prospect what you are going to show him. In this way you build up his interest and at the same time give him clues as to what to look for.

▶ *Keep it short.* The demonstration should not be a complete one *if it will take too long.* For example, men selling a portable dictating machine limited their demonstration to eleven minutes—one for each pound the machine weighed. In that time they gave a convincing rundown of what the machine could do, but purposely left out some details of how it was done. If the prospect showed further interest, the salesman went into greater detail *after* the demonstration. Here the demonstration served its true purpose in the interview—it illustrated customer benefits.

▶ *Start the demonstration at the most advantageous time.* If your demonstration is complicated and costly, you will first want to create enough interest to warrant the demonstration. On the other hand, if your demonstration creates the interest, you should begin the demonstration as soon as possible.

¶ 5042 **Watch out for these no-sale gestures**

A gesture that is used purposely to emphasize a point or to add force to your demonstration can help make your sales. But a mannerism that diverts a prospect's attention in any manner is a fault to be corrected.

Acceptable: Many top salesmen get the order book out in the open early in their presentation. This gesture is a sales-winner. It makes it easier for the salesmen to go into their close.

Not acceptable: There are many mannerisms which salesmen use without knowing. Some of these are:
- Strumming your fingers.
- Chewing a pencil or pen.
- Toying with your eyeglasses, or objects on your prospect's desk.
- Constant crossing and uncrossing of your legs or other nervous fidgeting.
- Nodding or shaking your head unnecessarily.
- Exaggerated slapping or pounding of furniture with your hands.
- Slumping and poor posture.
- Looking bored while your prospect is discussing a point.
- Exaggerated facial expressions.
- Raising your voice unreasonably when enthusiastic or excited.

⇒WHAT TO DO→ Watch your prospect's reactions to the way you act. Check yourself while actually giving a presentation—or better yet—arrange for your sales manager to observe you under "battle conditions" to see if you commit any of these common mannerisms which can annoy, offend or distract a prospect.

EXAMPLE: A sales manager accompanied a young salesman who wasn't living up to expectations. In short time, the sales manager spotted that the salesman would shake his head in disagreement when a prospect offered an objection.

The kicker: The salesman didn't have the slightest notion that he was "annoying" his customers and buyers. Once he became aware of what he was doing, the salesman changed his ways. *Payoff:* Today he's one of the company's best producers.

¶ 5043 **Get the prospect into the act**

One of the "musts" for a successful demonstration is to get the prospect into the act. You do even better if you can also bring into the act someone who is important to the prospect. Thus, if a prospect's child is to benefit by the purchase, bring in the child; if employees are to use the product, bring one into the demonstration. If it's simplicity of operation that you want to bring out, get someone into the act whose performance will prove that the product is easy to use.

▶ **IDEA IN ACTION** The demonstration of a piece of office equipment was to be made to a superintendent of schools. The salesman prepared his demonstration in advance in terms of the customer's needs and requirements.

First, he arranged for a field demonstration at

a nearby school district where similar equipment was being used. This choice had two advantages: (1) it met the superintendent's objection to visiting the company's headquarters which would have taken him away from his office for too long a time; (2) the prospect found the machine functioning in a familiar setting.

Second, he arranged for the demonstration to be conducted by a 13-year-old student at the school. This idea also had two advantages: (1) it demonstrated the simplicity of the machine, which was of prime importance to the school district; (2) it brought the prospect as well as someone of importance to him—a student—into the act.

¶ 5044 **The best demonstration is an in-use demonstration**

You can gain two great advantages by arranging to demonstrate your product in a satisfied user's office or in his plant:

• The prospect sees the product in true operational surroundings. He can see more clearly what a similar installation or operation at his own place of business would involve. This kind of a demonstration also gives the prospect confidence in you; it shows that you have faith in your product.

• Your satisfied customer will often give you the benefit of his testimonial on the spot.

Masterful use of sales tools in a presentation

¶ 5051 **Tips for using samples**[1]

Whether you carry a complete sample of the product you sell or a part of the product, like swatches, by allowing the prospect to see the sample you whet his appetite for the product. Also, you become far more convincing about the product benefits than if you simply tell him about them.

Here are some tips on how to get the best results from displaying the samples in your presentation:

• If you have a choice of samples, select only those that are suited to your prospect's needs.

• Don't show too many.

• Use perfect samples that are clean and in good condition.

• Don't let the prospect play around with a sample if it will distract him from what you are saying.

• Attach to each sample any information such as style number, cost, color variations, and the like, to help the buyer select and identify his choice.

• Follow up promptly any buyer with whom you have left a sample.

¶ 5052 **Tips for using working models**[1]

A demonstrator or working model is a vivid way to explain the operation of your product. This device is not as often available to salesmen as a sample, but if it *is* available use it with these tips in mind:

• Tell the prospect what you are going to show him.

• Guard against being too technical.

• Get the prospect into the act.

• Ask questions as you go.

• Keep your demonstration short.

• Make it dramatic if you can.

¶ 5053 **Make your camera click for you**

Take your own photographs — and show each prospect how *your* product will meet *his* needs. There's a picture that can help you boost your sales—and it doesn't matter what you're selling.

Here are just some of the ways you can use a camera as a sales tool:

• Show previous installations.

• Illustrate successive or key stages in the development of your product.

• Show "before" and "after" situations.

• Present an illustration of what could happen without your product or service.

• Enable discussion of areas of operations that would otherwise require a walking tour of the plant.

• Indicate trouble spots or proposed installation locations, when submitting a written proposal.

As the above point illustrates, practically any salesman can put his camera to good uses. Let's look at an actual—

⟫CASE HISTORY→ Before Frank Casale, a salesman of home roofing and siding, calls on a prospect, he takes a picture of the prospect's house.

When he makes his call, he begins by handing the prospect a picture showing a beautifully reconditioned home. Quite often it's a home in the prospect's neighborhood. As soon as the prospect acknowledges the attractive appearance of the house in the photograph, Casale hands him the picture of his own home.

Here comes the sale: Once a prospect concedes that his house looks poor by comparison, Casale usually finds it easy to interest him in making improvements.

¶ 5054   **Tips for using a presentation manual**[1]

Presentation manuals come in a variety of forms, from a mere booklet to a large easel setup. They are usually intended as a step-by-step guide for the presentation. By going through the manual page by page with the prospect, you can be sure of a thorough, orderly and time-saving coverage of the important sales points. At the same time you are keeping the prospect's eyes busy, letting him see each point as you explain it.

To get the most benefit from a presentation manual, observe these tips:

• Practice using the manual so that you don't stumble through the presentation.

• Maintain control of the manual and the interview. Don't let the prospect leaf through the manual. Give him each point in turn.

• Check his understanding of one point before you proceed to the next.

• Don't read the words printed in the manual; tell him about it in different words.

• Make every effort to personalize the presentation. You don't want to appear to be parroting the prepared material.

¶ 5055   **Tips for using sales kits**

Perhaps your company is one of the many that have made up sales kits for their salesmen. These kits contain the equipment—samples, literature, visual aids, sometimes even the words—for a complete presentation. They are organized so that the sales can follow an orderly pattern. Sales kits are worked out by sales departments or sales consultants, and ensure a thorough and convincing presentation if they are utilized properly.

These tips will help you get the most from a sales kit:

• A kit is designed to do a certain job in a certain way. Don't defeat the purpose by ignoring it or using it half-heartedly.

• Practice using it. Some kits, for example, require removing and replacing samples or booklets that are kept in special pockets. You should be able to accomplish all such maneuvers without a hitch.

• Keep the kit looking attractive. Clean up samples, replace frazzled literature, and replenish give-away supplies frequently.

¶ 5056   **Tips for using a catalog in your presentation**[1]

Almost all product salesmen have catalogs or catalog pages that can serve as visual aids during the presentation. Catalogs have pictures, charts and other eye-filling items that can supplement your spoken sales talk. A catalog also indicates the range and completeness of your line. It acts as a silent salesman in your absence; the prospect can refer to it for additional information about your product.

⟫REMEMBER→ The effectiveness of catalogs in selling was proved in a survey made by the Sales Executive Club. Salesmen answering inquiries from prospects who had studied a catalog averaged 38.4 orders per 100 calls, compared with only 9.2 orders per 100 on cold calls.[2]

If your catalog is issued in loose leaf form, a page or two can make an excellent visual reference point for a presentation. These pages are easily and economically left with the prospect. You can gradually build up his supply of catalog sheets by leaving different pages on subsequent calls. Or you can capitalize on something he likes in your catalog by leaving a copy of that particular page with him.

Here are a few pointers that will help you get the maximum value from your catalog:

• Know the catalog well. If you fumble when looking for something in it, the prospect will not think of it as a quick reference source.

• Bring out the catalog only after you have acquainted him with the product so that he knows what to look for.

• Emphasize the special features of your

catalog—a better-than-average index, more engineering information, more up-to-date material. Make the catalog appear outstanding to the prospect, so that it won't be buried on a shelf or in a drawer of forgotten catalogs.

• Hand each catalog to an interested person and go over it with him.

• Keep your own copy of the catalog and those you give to customers as up to date as possible.

Avoid these mistakes in catalog usage:

• Don't base your entire presentation on the catalog. Use it instead as a supplement and a reference source for answers to questions that come up during the interview.

• Don't try to show too much of the catalog at one sitting.

• Don't give them out indiscriminately. Catalogs are often expensive items and should be placed where they will do some good.

¶ 5057 Tips on showing facts through charts and graphs

Charts and graphs of performance data, market research findings, survey results, and the like give life to statistical information. One good chart can accomplish more in a few minutes than hours of recited figures.

Even the best charts and graphs deserve the following boosts from the salesman:

• When you present a chart or graph, tell briefly what it shows or make some other explanatory comment.

• Rehearse your use of the graphic illustrations until you can smoothly handle even large ones without awkwardness, and can place them where the prospect can see them.

¶ 5058 Tips for using descriptive literature and similar aids

Most companies provide supplementary visual material such as descriptive literature, new product bulletins, blow-ups of company ads, or reprints of publicity stories. Any of these items can be handy in a variety of ways during a presentation, especially during second and subsequent interviews.

For instance, you can exhibit advertisements to dealers to show how your company helps them by creating a market for the product. You can use a colorful folder describing a new product as the basis for a presentation aimed at prospects you haven't been able to sell. You can use publicity stories as proof that, although your product may be a new one, it has already been proved in use.

Just how and where you utilize this kind of material will depend on how many other visual aids you have, and where your presentation needs visual support.

¶ 5059 Tips for using testimonials[1]

Testimonials furnished to salesmen by their sales managers take the form of letters from satisfied customers, case histories, lists of names of prominent users, photographs of the product in use, and so on.

Such testimonials are invaluable wherever proof of quality or service will help the sale. They erase doubts in the prospect's mind. They give him moral support and justify his decision to buy. This reassurance is especially important if your service or product is not well-known or is new to the prospect. If your dealings with the prospect require him to disclose personal information, testimonials help him overcome a natural reluctance to take a stranger into his confidence.

The following tips should be observed:

• Be sure that the testimonial comes from someone whose opinion the prospect will value.

• Show testimonials from users whose business and circumstances match as closely as possible those of the prospect. Local ones are best [¶ 5064].

• Give the prospect time to read the testimonial himself to get the maximum effect.

¶ 5060 Question your speaking habits and answer your sales problems

It makes sense to examine your speaking ability from time to time, since a salesman lives "by word of mouth!" Here are 13 questions which check out your Speaking Profile.

⟫WHAT TO DO→ Answer these questions about your speaking habits and then go to work on the ones that don't measure up.

	Yes	Not Sure	No
1. Do you pronounce words clearly enough to make it			

easy for the prospect to
understand?
2. Do you talk loud enough to
be heard easily?
3. Do you talk without having
objects in your mouth?
4. Do you look at the person
with whom you are talking?
5. Do you avoid doing other
things while you are talking?
6. Do you think you reflect
friendliness and warmth?
7. Do you show respect toward
the prospect even when
contradicting him?
8. Do you use positive words?
9. Do you encourage him to
ask questions?
10. Do you avoid using trade
jargon whether your prospect understands you
or not?
11. Do you avoid using large
words to impress?
12. Do you select simple and
clear words?
13. Do you avoid sarcasm?

¶ 5061 **Written proposals can be used profitably to build interest in a first interview**

A prospect will listen to a salesman who has obviously spent a lot of time preparing for that particular call. The more concrete the evidence of having prepared for the visit, the better the chances of gaining an interested listener.

One way to show your preparedness is to have in your hand a written proposal, custom-built to apply your product to the prospect's problems or needs. Such a written proposal can be used profitably in some instances, the first time you call on a prospect. It is particularly helpful in cases where a double-barreled selling job is required—first, selling the prospect on the idea of letting you gather specific facts about his situation, and second selling your product or service after the facts have been gathered.

EXAMPLE: Salesmen of the Minneapolis-Honeywell Regulator Company use an impressive written proposal to sell the *idea* of installing centralized temperature controls in the first interview.

▶ **IDEA IN ACTION** You are a Minneapolis-Honeywell salesman who has learned that a large office building in your territory plans to overhaul its heating system and add air conditioning. Using a photograph of the building as a cover, you assemble a booklet showing the advantages of centralized temperature control. In it you place several pages made up especially for the particular building, referring to it by name. You combine these custom-built pages with selected standard pages that fit the particular application. You also include a list of large buildings that have the type of control system you are recommending. And you add photographs and skeleton drawings that show probable control locations. The finished booklet is a professional looking brochure, with protective acetate covers.

You practice using the proposal until you know its contents thoroughly and can give a good presentation based on it. Then you call on the prospect with the booklet and descriptive literature on the controls it recommends. Impressed with your preparation, your prospect listens attentively to your page-by-page presentation.

¶ 5062 **Written proposals call for creative thinking**

In any line of selling that entails a fact-finding survey to establish the customer's needs, a written proposal is usually required.

EXAMPLES: An industrial salesman must often survey the customer's operations, plant, and problems before he can determine what the product he offers will do for the customer. He follows up his survey with a written proposal and then sells from his proposal. See ¶ 5181 for an example.

Similarly, a salesman who sells duplicating equipment must study the prospect's operations so far as they relate to procedures entailing duplicating processes, before he can recommend equipment that will benefit the prospect.

One who sells a transportation service must make a study of the prospect's shipping practices.

A life insurance salesman must secure such facts as applicant's birth, family data, the objectives insurance-wise, and amounts of present insurance and social security, before he can make recommendations for insurance coverage.

Since each proposal is tailor-made to fit a particular prospect's needs, the written proposal, like the problem itself, requires creative thinking both for the contents and for the appearance of the proposal.

▶ *Proposal is a tool.* The proposal is a tool for the salesman to present his recommendations and to make a sale. It gives him the opportunity to present an attractive folder that contains information exclusively for the prospect—and hence of great interest to him. It enables the salesman to sit down with his man and give the prospect a thorough idea of what the proposal will do for him.

▶ *What the proposal should include.* Bear in mind that the proposal is based on the study you have made of the prospect's problems. Since it is individualized in each instance, no pattern that fits all proposals can be presented. However, an example will suffice to show the nature of the contents. A seller of duplicating equipment covers the following items in his proposal:

- A transmittal letter showing that the report submitted is based upon a recent study of the prospect's operations and that it is designed to meet the prospect's objectives [see below for sample].
- The objectives that have been set up to meet the prospect's needs.
- The prospect's present method of performing the work.
- The recommendations made to accomplish the objectives.
- A summary of proven benefits and advantages, each being brought out as dramatically as possible.

▶ *Physical appearance of the proposal.* The report should reflect the quality of the effort that went into the survey and proposal. The following ideas will enhance its appearance:

- Include a title page which shows that the proposal has been prepared especially for the prospect. For example:

A Proposal Prepared for
NAME OF THE PROSPECT
By
NAME OF YOUR COMPANY
Presented by
YOUR NAME

- Include illustrations of the product or equipment which is recommended in the proposal, and any other related pictures, diagrams, and charts.
- Be generous in using paper. Devote a separate sheet to each subject of the report. For example, place all of the objectives on one page, spreading them out so that each is given importance.
- Allow plenty of white space in the typewritten portions. White space is obtained from the margins at the top, bottom, and sides, spacing between paragraphs and topics, and arrangement of tabular matter, such as costs of proposed operation, cost comparisons, and the like.
- Use eye appeal in setting up various portions of the report. For example, a summary of advantages can be staggered on the page; and recommendations can be placed in boxes, and so on.

▶ *The transmittal letter.* A letter of transmittal, typed on the company's best letterhead, should be attached to the report. The following example can be adapted to almost any proposal.

(Date)

The ABC Company
120 Broadway
New York, N. Y.
Gentlemen:
THIS REPORT . . .
is the result of our recent study of one phase of your business paperwork procedures.
The facts concerning your present method have been carefully gathered and analyzed—and a proposed method, designed to meet the objectives you specified, is presented in detail. For clarity in presentation, our complete report is divided into four sections:

- Objectives
  - A comparison of present and proposed procedures
  - Summary of advantages
  - Equipment recommendations

Based upon our extensive experience in business paperwork procedures, we believe the recommended method and equipment will accomplish, or exceed, the objectives of this presentation.
We would like to express our wholehearted gratitude to Mr. John Smith, Chief of your Special Services Section, for the splendid cooperation extended to us during our recent survey.
We hope you will find this report both interesting and rewarding, just as we did when preparing it for you.

Very truly yours,

¶ 5063 Photographs can be a useful sales tool

Even if you are an amateur, you can make profitable use of a camera in your selling work. Prospects are often more convinced by a snapshot than by a glossy professional job, just because it is more believable. Similarly, a picture of a *nearby* plant, office or home situation means more to the average Seattle prospect, for example, than one taken in Baltimore. A picture of places or people that your prospect knows personally has the greatest convincing power of all. For these reasons it pays to be your own camera-man.

▶ **IDEA IN ACTION** Frank Casale sells for a company that specializes in home roofing and siding repair and improvements. Before he calls on a prospect he takes a picture of the prospect's house with an inexpensive camera.

When he makes his call, he begins by handing the prospect a picture taken with the same camera, showing a beautifully reconditioned home. Quite often it's a home in the prospect's neighborhood. As soon as the prospect acknowledges the attractive appearance of the house in the photograph, Frank hands him the picture of his own home. A surprising number of prospects admit that their house looks very poor by such comparison. Frank then finds it easy to interest them in making improvements.

Other suggested ways in which you can use a camera as a sales tool are these:

- to show previous installations
- to illustrate successive or key stages in the development of your product
- to show "before" and "after" situations
- to present an illustration of what could happen without your product or service
- to enable discussion in one place, using photographs, of areas or operations that would otherwise require a walking tour of the plant
- to indicate trouble spots or proposed installation locations, when submitting a written proposal

Because the use of a camera requires imagination to make it a versatile sales tool, more is said about it in "Ideas For Creative Selling." See ¶ 3079.

¶ 5064 Ask your customers for testimonials

You can easily build up your own kit of testimonials by asking your good customers to give you a written letter expressing appreciation of your product. Or you can ask permission to quote your customer verbally.

Testimonials from your own customers can have greater convincing power than those you get from your company. Yours have a personal touch and local flavor. They carry the names of people whom your prospects, who are in the same territory, are likely to know and respect. They are also personal endorsements of your abilities and help you gain the confidence of your prospects.

You use your own testimonials in much the same way that you do your company's. You must avoid the same dangers of antagonizing or belittling your prospect [¶ 5059].

⟫⟫CAUTION⟶ If you quote your customer verbally, don't exaggerate or misquote to make the recommendation sound more convincing. Your prospect may be better informed than you realize. Furthermore, what you say may get back to your customer, perhaps through the prospect himself.

⟫⟫SUGGESTION⟶ Try to get a photograph of an installation to back up a testimonial, if your product can be seen in action.

¶ 5065 Introduce new evidence by using reproductions

A photostat or other copy of a test result, or laboratory report, is a very convincing sales tool. It is especially useful in incorporating the latest, up-to-the-minute information into your presentation. You gain the double advantage of credibility and timeliness.

Keep your eyes open for material that will lend itself to this treatment. Sometimes paragraphs or pages in company bulletins or engineering announcements can serve a purpose when reproduced.

⟫⟫OBSERVATION⟶ Reproducing material can also serve the purpose of reducing information into more compact form. Parts of testimonial letters, for instance, can be reproduced and gathered onto one page. Significant sections of documents or articles can be extracted and reproduced.

¶ 5066 Clippings from newspapers and trade publications up-date your presentation

News clippings are sales tools that you can easily add to your presentation. The useful items you can find are unlimited: product news, company expansion or merger announcements, personnel changes, performance figues, survey results, and so on.

Clippings can help in any step of your sales talk. When taken from current issues they make your presentation timely and vital. They show prospects that you keep informed on changes and improvements in your business. Result: prospects have confidence in what you say, and they regard you as a source of information.

How to handle price in a presentation

¶ 5071 Value must justify price

Your job is to convince your prospects of the true value of your product or service. People will buy the most expensive items if they are convinced that they will get their money's worth.

If you sell a quality product that is priced higher than that of competition, take every opportunity to describe the features in a way that suggests justification of the high price. Sell the difference that makes your product worth its price.

> **EXAMPLE:** Salesmen for the Dictaphone Corporation, when presenting their Time-Master Six automatic dictating machine, mention early in their presentation that the machine has "1530 precision parts." Why? Because it helps the prospect to understand how the Time-Master can do what it does, why it costs what it does, and why it's worth the money.

¶ 5072 When to bring in price

The timing of your price quotation depends on you. There is no hard-and-fast rule about when to quote price in an interview. Most salesmen feel that it is best to mention price *after* they have clearly demonstrated the value of the product or service. There are many, however, who make a point of mentioning the price several times during their presentation.

Salesmen whose products or services carry a very large price tag often prefer to make this clear early in the game, rather than shock the prospect at the end. Having stated the price and conceded that the amount seems large, these men minimize the price and promise to show that the benefits are worth every dollar of it and more, which they proceed to do. In cases where low price is a strong selling factor, salesmen frequently bring it into play early along with the other sales features.

The timing, therefore, rests with you. Plan to quote when you think the time will be right, but *plan* it.

¶ 5073 How to put off the impatient prospect

There will always be prospects who will ask the price before you're fully ready to tell them. In this situation you should postpone quoting, if you can do it without giving the impression that you are stalling. Here are sample phrases used by salesmen to avoid discussing price prematurely:

1

"I'll be happy to tell you the price in a moment. May I wait until then?"

2

"The price will depend on quantity, the style you choose, and so on. It might be better if I tell you first about one or two more features."

¶ 5074 Soften up your prospect with a touch of 'show business'

A little play acting can often soften up the most determined "price-is-all-that-counts" buyer. All the props you need for your big scene is pencil and paper. Here's how the scene develops.

You've tried a few trial closes and the prospect has stopped you with the price objection. After the second objection, it's time to get the play started. Let's say that you're selling a piece of equipment that costs $1,000 and its normal life is figured at five years.

Curtain going up: Take out your pencil and paper and start figuring out loud as follows—"Let's see, five years is 60 months . . . sixty into $1,000 . . . that comes to only $16.67 a month. There you are, Mr. Jones. That is what it costs you to enjoy the benefits of this machine . . . only $16.67 a month."

Another twist: Some salesmen like to get the prospect into the play. They hand the paper and pencil to the prospect and ask him to do the same figuring. These salesmen win support by asking the prospect like this:

"Mr. Jones, I know that I am offering you a good buy. Won't you please take this pencil and figure along with me, to see just how good a buy it is?" Now—

how to handle price in a presentation

⟫BRING DOWN THE CURTAIN→
After he figures your price per month, ask him if he doesn't think that he's getting a good buy. If he says yes, get his signature and make your exit—the play is over!

¶ 5075 Techniques for minimizing price

Several techniques can be used in quoting price to make the amount seem low:

• Use such minimizing words as "only" (It costs only $8.00); "low" (The price is a low $8.00); "mere" (It will cost you a mere $8.00), and so on. Such phrases suggest to many buyers that the price is reasonable.

• Tie the price in with a brief summary of benefits, or a statement suggesting substantial value for the money. Examples:

1

"Now the price for all this—economy, versatility, speed of operation, long life, and attractive appearance—is only $43.50."

2

"The price is $29.95, and that includes the machine, free installation, and a full year's guarantee."

• Suggest possible prices that are higher than the actual price, which will then sound low by comparison. Example: "Wouldn't you expect to pay $200 for that kind of protection, Mr. Prospect, or at least $150? Well, all it will cost you is $85."

• Break a large price down into smaller units of cost. A large lump-sum price looks less forbidding if it is broken down into cost per month, week, day or individual use.

EXAMPLE: The Simmons Company's well-known Beautyrest mattress costs more than those of many competitors. Salesmen point out that based on the mattress' long expected life, the cost is only about two cents per night. Stated this way, the difference of $20 and more between a Beautyrest and other makes of mattresses is hardly noticeable.

• Offset a large initial price by emphasizing savings. Stress savings advantages in as many ways as you can, and in dollars and cents. Express them not only as a lump-sum figure but as daily or weekly savings, or savings of so much per unit of production. Emphasize such savings as lower labor costs, reduction of overtime, elimination of errors, lower repair and maintenance costs, and the like. When you make the prospect think in terms of how much he'll save, you overcome his resistance to high price.

EXAMPLE: "Mr. Prospect, although Transite at first glance looks much more expensive than multiple duct tile, the actual material cost difference is usually no more than four cents per duct foot. That's because you save on three points:

1. There are fewer items to inventory. That means lower warehousing and inventory costs.

2. There is less handling of material from plant to job. That gives lower handling costs.

3. There is less duct breakage, and so a saving on material cost."

* * *

"Savings on installation costs of Transite will more than offset the initial price difference. The difference in labor costs between Transite and tile can reach twenty cents per duct foot, and is usually *at least five cents* per duct foot. And the installation is faster. Look at the many ways you save on even a straight line installation:

1. There is no joint material to make. The couplings are all made up and come with the sections.

2. The joint material is easier to place. Simply connect the coupling to the section.

3. Sections are lighter, easier to handle than tile.

4. Ducts are easier to position. Struggling with heavy sections for hair-line alignment is eliminated.

5. Closing of joints is easier. No tying or wrapping—just tap the section in.

6. There are fewer lengths to install, because they're longer.

7. There are fewer men required in a crew, because Transite is easy to handle.

In this way you build advantage on advantage. Each of your statements is a convincing one because it is backed by facts and illustrations, supplied by the company, that nail it down.

¶ 5076 Quote quantity prices to "up" the sale

If your prices vary with quantity, apply the technique used by a successful forms salesman. He quotes three prices: the first for the quantity mentioned by the prospect; the second for a larger quantity; the third for a still larger quantity. Quite often the prospect decides to order the middle quantity quoted to make the price saving.

¶ 5077 Know how to handle price objections

Every salesman must expect to run into price objections of one kind or another, or meet buyers who will try to bargain. To know how to handle these problems, turn to ¶ 7062 et seq. There you will find full details and examples of how successful salesmen make their prices stick.

How to achieve a lean, sharp, "electric" quality

¶ 5081 Ways to make your presentation "great"

The presentation that you develop from the outline must be more than so many descriptive words. It must have certain qualities and embody features that make a presentation great. To give your sales talk a real selling edge, sharpen it in these proven ways:

- Dramatize it [¶ 5082]
- Use "you" emphasis [¶ 5083]
- Use vivid words and good language [¶ 5084]
- Tell stories to make points clear [¶ 5085]
- Ask questions as you go along [¶ 5086]
- Appeal to the senses [¶ 5087]
- Use examples [¶ 5088]
- Use parallel situations [¶ 5089]

¶ 5082 Dramatize your presentation

The quality that will lift your presentation above the ordinary more than any other is its dramatic force. Without such force, yours is just another sales story—the kind that doesn't make a powerful impression. But if you make what you do and say dramatic, yours is the story the prospect will remember when he's comparing points of competitive products before making a decision.

Here are some ways to add dramatic flavor to your sales talk:

• Use dramatic words. Choose words that will have an impact on the prospect, words with power and color: "glide with silky-smooth power," "the rich colors, the easy-chair comfort of the interior." See ¶ 5091 et seq. for adding power with vivid-picture language.

• Use dramatic comparisons and illustrations. Note how these remarks dramatize speed, strength, and economy: "less time than it takes to light a cigarette"; the biggest football player could stand on it and not harm it"; "as economical to run as burning a light bulb".

• Use a dramatic demonstration. Servel salesmen, demonstrating the quiet operation of their gas refrigerators, would strike a match and ask the prospect to listen. The silence of that tiny flame spoke more eloquently than words for the quiet running of the Servel refrigerator. More on the advantages of dramatizing your demonstration is given at ¶ 5041 et seq.

• Be dramatic in your manner when making important points. Put emphasis on your words when you want them to have impact. Use pauses to build suspense here and there. Use your body to dramatize those statements that need force, by pointing, leaning forward, and so on. Here is where rehearsal of your presentation adds to its effectiveness; you can practice dramatic emphasis. See ¶ 5171 et seq. for more on the way to give your presentation effectively.

⟫⟫WARNING⟶ The word "dramatic" does not mean unrestrained. If you conduct your interview like a three-ring circus, the impact will be great, all right, but the message will be lost.

¶ 5083 Use "you" emphasis

Vanity is a human characteristic that must be considered in any dealings with people, and it is especially important in areas of persuasion such as selling. You must be sure that your presentation is geared to the natural vanity of the prospect, and that it satisfies his desire to be treated with respect as an individual. A benefit can even lack persuasive appeal if it is not clear that it is a benefit intended for the prospect and that you fully expect *him* to profit by it.

There are positive ways to inject the "you" emphasis into your sales talk:

• Use the words "you" and "your" frequently.

• Capitalize on opportunities to personalize the interview. Complimentary references to his responsible position, his reputation, or even a family picture that you spot on his desk, are in order.

- Indicate by common courtesy and a willingness to serve that you respect his importance as a prospective buyer, no matter what his present buying potential is.

- When he talks, listen. All interviews should include in their planning some time for the prospect to make comments.

¶ 5084 **Importance of Language**

No matter how many visual aids and demonstrations you use in a presentation, your chief communication with the prospect will be by spoken word. Correct language is the clearest and most expressive way to say anything. Ungrammatical sentences are confusing, often waste words, and make a bad impression.

⟫⟫SUGGESTION→ Here is a bonus benefit of writing up your presentation. You can take the time to polish the language. Get someone who knows good grammar to read over what you've written. That's the easiest way to check on grammatical errors. The only other way is to consult a basic grammar when you're in doubt.

The words you select for telling your sales story must obviously be chosen with care, since they have important work to do and a limited time in which to do it.

You should avoid using long or complicated words and concentrate on simple, direct ones. Long words, however descriptive or meaningful, are often hard to take in at a normal speaking pace, so their value is lost.

The words in your presentation must be vivid and expressive. They must summon up images in the prospect's mind, so that he has a clear understanding of the benefits you are describing. Your words must also carry conviction, since persuasion is your goal. For more about word power, see ¶ 5091 et seq.

⟫⟫SUGGESTION→ Most businesses have their own special words. The smart salesman gets to know some of the terms used by a prospect in his business and just how to use them.

¶ 5085 **Use the power of story-telling**

There are three reasons why successful salesmen use stories in their work:

- People enjoy hearing stories. A well-told story is interesting and entertaining as well as instructive.

- Stories put the imagination to work. Explanations and factual statements satisfy reason, but a story brings the listener's imagination into play. Imagination is the magic power that lets the prospect visualize instead of just comprehend. Most sales are not made until this visualizing is accomplished, and the prospect turns words into pictures.

- Stories can be used in any stage of the interview. They can accomplish anything from getting attention to motivating the signature on the order.

The best stories are ones illustrating the benefits that others have received from your product or service. Such stories enable the prospect to picture himself in the same circumstances and visualize the benefits as accruing to him. If your story tells about someone the prospect knows, its convincing effect is greatly increased.

⟫⟫CAUTION→ When you use a story for the purpose of illustrating how someone else benefited, make sure that it is a believable story. An anecdote that arouses doubt or disbelief works against you. There must be no doubt in the prospect's mind that what you say happened *did* happen, and that the same benefit could be his.

¶ 5086 **Ask questions as you go along**

You should ask the prospect questions as you proceed with your presentation, for these important reasons:

- First, a question serves as a form of brief summary, or re-statement after each point.

- Second, by asking a question you can be sure that he understands one point before you proceed to the next.

- Third, the answers to your questions help you judge the progress you are making toward closing the sale.

- Fourth, if the prospect can be "yes" conditioned during the presentation, his resistance to committing himself at the close is reduced.

The more often he agrees with you, the more unreasonable an arbitrary turn-down will seem at the end.

Here are examples of the kind of question that you should ask your prospect:

1

"A saving of $50 each year on cleaning bills would be nice to have, wouldn't it, Mrs. Prospect?"

2

"Wouldn't a 10% increase in production from such a small investment be a real gain, Mr. Production Manager?"

3

"Isn't the safety for your children that this gate can provide something that you want, Mr. and Mrs. Prospect?"

¶ 5087   **Appeal to the senses**

A person has five ways with which to absorb information: he can see it, hear it, touch it, taste it, or smell it. Of these, *seeing, hearing* and *touching* are the senses most important to the majority of salesmen. The more of them a salesman can engage, the stronger the impact of his message on the prospect, and the greater the chance of making a sale.

Of the three—seeing, hearing, and touching —*seeing* is by far the most effective. We understand what we see quicker than any other way, we remember it longer, and it makes a stronger impression on us. It is also true that we tend to *believe* what we see, even though we might doubt the same information if we received it through our other senses.

Make use of these factors in your presentation. Try to engage all the prospect's senses with you sales message, rather than rely on speech to do the whole job. Pay special attention to the eyes. Here are tips on what to do:

• If you sell a product, key your presentation as much as possible to a demonstration, or a sample or model, so that he can *see, touch* and *hear* about your product at the same time.

• If you sell a service, arm yourself with photographs, letters of recommendation, testimonials, copies of lab reports, printed statistics—anything he can *look* at as evidence of what he's hearing.

• Make full use of company-supplied visual aids such as films or slides, flip charts, visual portfolios, catalogs, scale models, mock-ups, cut-away sections, etc. These are designed to help put the prospect's eyes to work for you.

⇒⇒WARNING→   Two senses transmitting the same information reinforce each other and create a strong impression. But two senses trying to take in *different* information can create confusion. You must co-ordinate your demonstration and the use of visual aids with your words, so that the prospect gets one strong impression, not scattered and confusing ones. If the prospect is allowed to handle a sample or model longer than necessary, or browse at random through a catalog as you talk, his attention becomes divided. It's up to you to make his senses act as a team, by maintaining control of the presentation.

¶ 5088   **Use plenty of examples**

Examples are necessary to clarify your statements. Even if the prospect understands your point, an example gives it emphasis and can help him visualize it.

▶ **IDEA IN ACTION**   Walt Cooper sells all kind of insurance. He has found that the benefits he offers often don't really register until he gives an example of how those benefits could be needed. After he describes each feature, therefore, he states a pertinent example to show how it would work. His presentation abounds with examples phrases such as these:

"Say, for example, that a delivery man trips over a rug in the hall . . ."

"Suppose someone upstairs had a fire and the water from the hoses dripped down . . ."

"That means that if for some reason you became quite sick and were temporarily unable to make premium payments . . ."

"If, for example, you choose instead to withdraw all the money at that time to help buy a home . . ."

Each example is one in which the prospect can picture himself, and Walt, like many salesmen, says that his use of such examples is one of the biggest reasons for his success.

Adding power with "vivid-picture" language

¶ 5091   **Language has power**

Using vivid-picture language is one of the nine techniques just discussed for making your presentation lean, sharp and electric. This section will show you how to add power to your presentation by finding the right selling words

adding power with "vivid-picture" language

to *describe, explain,* or *demonstrate* your product or service.

You must take the time necessary to develop a vocabulary of selling words that make what you are selling become alive in the imagination of your prospect. You don't add power with words like "good," "fine," "nice," and other weak adjectives. Your selling vocabulary must be made up of vital, living words—picture-building words. Without them you cannot effectively transfer to your prospect the image of the sale that you make in your own mind's eyes.

¶ 5092 Use word power to increase your sales power

The words you select for telling your sales story obviously must be chosen with care, since they have important work to do and a limited time in which to do it.

The one-word close. Top salesmen know that buyers respond to the positive. The strategy is to get the prospect into the frame of mind where he agrees with you. In other words, get him in the habit of saying "Yes." Here's the way it goes:
"You like this pattern, don't you?"
"Yes," responds the buyer.
"This is a key feature, don't you think?"
"Yes," answers the prospect.
"Now you can see how our product is unique, can't you?"
"Yes," replies the prospect.

➤➤WHAT TO DO➤ Prepare a series of questions that fit your product. Once you get your prospect answering "yes", the sale is just a question or two away. *Don't you agree?*

One word that moves the hesitant prospect. No matter how smoothly you deliver your presentation, there comes a time when the prospect just won't get off the fence. He refuses to make a decision.

➤➤WHAT TO DO➤ Use the word that makes the prospect come to grips with the problem. Ask him "Why?" *Example:*

Let's say you've delivered your presentation and attempted a trial close. The prospect says he'd rather wait.

"Why do you hesitate, Mr. Bartell? Do you think our price is too high?" Or, the same question might be phrased like this *"Why* do you want to wait until the end of the month and run the risk of paying a higher price?"

Result: The question makes it easier to close. The prospect now has to put his reasons for waiting out in the open.

➤➤WHAT TO DO➤ Be prepared to ask the "why" question when your prospect is sitting on the fence. It could get him off. *Why* not give it a try?

The one-word block. We've just seen how one word can set up a sale. Now look at the word IF—that can make things difficult for you.

EXAMPLE: You've finished pour presentation, and you're ready to ask the prospect for his order.

Salesman: "If you buy right now, you'll save 10%. That seems harmless enough. You've given your prospect the big benefit and your order blank is out.

The block: The word "IF" causes the buyer to hesitate. He thought he was going to buy, and now you've suddenly given him reason to reconsider.

Right way: "When you give me your order, Mr. Jones, you get that 10% discount for buying before the 15th. Thank you." No problem here. The word "when" has created a positive line of action.

Agreeing words: This is another variation of "Yes" technique. A top salesman realizes that it's a waste of time to continue a presentation unless his prospect is agreeing with the points being made.

➤➤WHAT TO DO➤ Make sure your prospect is nodding his head in the right direction by testing him with these "agreeing" words: *"Isn't it?" "Hasn't it?" "Aren't we?" "Isn't that right?"*

These test words can help you win over your prospect in two ways:

(1) If the prospect disagrees with you, it gives you a chance to *change your course of action* before you've lost him completely; or

(2) It gets the prospect in an agreeing mood which will pay off later when you close. *Reason:* Each agreement reaction you obtain makes it easier to get the next one.

⇉**WHAT TO DO**→ Emphasize the first word so that it's implied by your inflection that agreement is expected as a matter of course. *Isn't* that what selling is all about?

¶ 5093 3 steps to increase your word power

Step 1. From your list of product features, select a strong selling feature that calls for a description of a specific attribute of your product.

Step 2. Write down all of the colorful, vivid, vital words that give the feature meaning and that help the prospect create a mental image of the feature and visualize the benefit it holds for him.

⇉**REMEMBER**→ You won't use all of the words that you gather in writing any one paragraph, but the words will be there for you to use in different parts of your presentation.

Step 3. Write a pargraph expressing what you want to convey to your prospect, choosing words from your list.

⇉**SUGGESTION**→ You must combine the words with some of the other techniques that make your presentation lean, sharp and electric. Thus, you tie in the words you choose with "you" emphasis, questions, dramatization, story-telling, specific statements, appeal to the senses, examples, and parallel situations. Make your sentences *short*. Don't let them become involved.

¶ 5094 Word power to explain a product

Product feature. The product is oil. You want to explain the main benefit to the prospect, which in this case is the lubrication of all parts of the machine to which it is applied, and to impress the prospect with the quality, duration, and vitality of the product.

Power words: "lubricate," "film," "regularity," "smooth," "density," "viscosity," "thickness," "friction," "efficiency," "slippery," "lengthens," "wearing," and "qualities."

What is said: "Mr. Prospect: Oil-e-O is not only a good oil. It is an oil that lubricates every minute part of your machine. It forms a slippery film between every moving surface and every touching part. It makes every wheel turn smoothly and easily with clock-like regularity. The low density of this oil determines its thickness and makes it just right for your particular use.

"Every molecule of this oil is geared to give the full lubricating value to your entire machine. It reduces friction and increases the efficiency of every operation. It adds many years of wear to your machine.

"Mr. Prospect, there is no oil like Oil-e-O for general lubrication, for efficiency, and for long wearing qualities. Order now."

NOTE: Earl Prevette used the above words to sell oil and led the sales force. He tells about it in "How I Sell," page 113, obtainable from Prentice-Hall, Inc., Englewood Cliffs, N. J.

¶ 5095 How to enlarge your word power

The 3-step method for adding power to your presentation through carefully chosen words should be but the beginning of your efforts to make every word you use in a presentation count. The following suggestions will help you enlarge your word power:

- List in alphabetical order the vivid words you have worked up through the 3-step method. Keep this word file active by adding to it every word or phrase you come across in your reading or conversation that has power for your selling purposes. Work these new words into your presentation from time to time.

- Be sure you understand the meaning of every word you use in your sales talk, and that you pronounce it correctly. Use a dictionary to check your usage.

- Guard against using highfalutin language. You don't magnify your word power with high-sounding phrases. It is plain, pithy, deft, impelling words that have power to carry your prospect along with you.

- Use the key words of the industries to which you sell.

¶ 5096 Avoid using cliches in your sales talk

Say the right few words at the right time and you're on your way to a sale. But say the wrong words at the same important time—and —no sale! What does this mean? Simply this. There are certain cliches many salesmen have a tendency to use that have the absolute wrong effect. Instead of winning the sale at the key moment, they destroy the sale.

What are these words? Here are some sayings that have been used repeatedly by many salesmen over the years:

- Old ways are best.
- That's not my department.

putting the presentation into words

- You are wrong about that.
- I have no time to read manuals.
- I take things as they come.
- I'll contact the home office about that—not today.
- Good things sell themselves.
- You wouldn't be interested in that.
- The public expects too much.
- There's no sentiment in business.
- It can't be done.

It is easy to fall into the habit of using sayings like these, but if you want more sales, more influence over your prospects and customers you will avoid them. *Remember this:* The trite sayings or cliches never once made a sale for a salesman. They never once added to a salesman's stature or good will.

Putting the presentation into words

¶ 5101 Developing the presentation from the outline

When your outline is completed, the next step is to write out the presentation just as you intend to give it. The problem is simply to take the information you have already decided upon, in the shape or form that your outline gives it, and put it into words. In doing this, you must include as many as possible of the techniques explained at ¶ 5081 et seq. (dramatizing, "you" emphasis, good words, and so on) to give your story selling power.

¶ 5102 First introduce yourself

Almost all initial personal interviews begin with the salesman introducing himself and stating what company he represents. Since this is the natural beginning, it should be the first thing you write in your presentation.

The importance of the first few seconds of an interview justifies a little thought about your initial introductory words. The opening is to show the prospect that you know his name and at the same time to further impress his name on your own memory. You can amplify this effect by stating the prospect's name as a question and confirming that you are in the presence of the prospect himself.

EXAMPLE:

SALESMAN: "Mr. Brady?"
PROSPECT: "That's right."
SALESMAN: "Mr. Brady, I'm Al Franklin..."

Normally, you would then explain what company you represent, although in some specialty selling this is not done if the mention of the company or product might create a negative response. See ¶ 4074.

If you want to impress your own name on prospects, repeat it right away.

EXAMPLE:

SALESMAN: "Mr. Brady, my name is Franklin—Al Franklin..."

The prospect thus hears your name twice and is likely to remember it.

Getting the prospect's attention

¶ 5111 Get attention in first sentence

As soon as you have properly introduced yourself, you must get the immediate and complete attention of the prospect. Just because you are standing there does not mean that he is paying attention to you. Your first sentence must be one that will make him an attentive listener.

The following types of opening remarks have all been used as attention-getters by successful salesmen in one field or another. Select one that will do the job for you, having in mind your product or service, your personality, and the prospects with whom you deal.

- State an emphatic benefit [¶ 5112].
- Promise to solve a problem you know he has [¶ 5113].
- Ask the prospect a thought-provoking question [¶ 5114].
- Use an unusual or dramatic opening [¶ 5115].
- Use the 'no-name' approach to win more sales [¶ 5116].
- Begin with an exhibit [¶ 5117].
- Use an item of related and interesting news [¶ 5118].

⟫COMMENT⟶ Some of these openers are similar to those you use in writing letters that get interviews [¶ 4041], where the need is the same—to get immediate attention.

Both your words and your manner should tell the prospect that something important brings you to his office. *Never* use the slighting "just happened to be in the neighborhood" opening. The remark reflects thoughtlessness of your own time and little regard for the prospect and his business, and doesn't gain attention.

¶ 5112 **Use an emphatic benefit as your opener**

The prospect wants to hear benefits that satisfy his buying motives. If you can offer a substantial benefit that will be sure to interest the prospect, use it as your opening remark.

A statement of benefit as an opening must meet these four tests:

1. The benefit should be one that the prospect wants.
2. The claim must be thoroughly substantiated in the rest of your presentation.
3. It must be a benefit that you are sure you can deliver in full.
4. It should be specific. A dollars-and-cents offer is far more effective than a sweeping generality as a means of getting attention.

Here are examples of statements indicating buyer benefits used as openers:

1

"Mr. Carlysle, what I stopped in to tell you about is a new type of truck rental service that will save you up to 15% on your present delivery costs."

2

"Mr. Worth, we have a new process that can cut operating time in your lithography department by one-third."

3

"Miss Upton, my special reason for calling today is that we are offering a special this month that enables you to have your typewriters and other office machines completely reconditioned at 25% less than the usual charge."

¶ 5113 **Tell him you can solve a problem for him**

If you are in a position to solve a prospect's specific problem, you have an ideal opening. This, too, is a statement of benefit, but a special kind because it is personal and specific. A man who is wrestling with a problem is eager to listen when someone offers to help him solve it.

EXAMPLE: "Mr. Prospect, it took me four minutes to reach your office from the street, and the return trip would double that. Multiply eight minutes by the number of your employees who go to the corner drug store for coffee every morning. Then add the time they spend waiting for it, or drinking it. The total time consumed, all non-productive, is amazing, as you probably realize. Our on-the-spot coffee service recovers that lost time and puts it back to work for you."

¶ 5114 **Ask your prospect a thought-provoking question**

A method used successfully by many salesmen is the question opening. You can frequently get a prospect's attention by asking him a question that is stimulating or thought-provoking, related to your presentation, and not confusing or obscure.

These examples show questions that have worked in getting attention:

1

"Can you afford to gamble with important mail?"

2

"Mrs. Prospect, if your family is like mine, you probably carry some sort of health insurance. It probably costs you a hundred dollars a year and doesn't do one thing toward improving your health, does it, Mrs. Prospect?"

⟶CAUTION⟶ Avoid the kind of question that implies some failing on the prospect's part. Consider the unfavorable reaction you would probably receive to these questions: "Have bad relations between management and employees got you down?" "Do you realize that your maintenance costs are probably much too high?"

¶ 5115 **Use an unusual or dramatic opening**

One of the best places to use the dramatic element in your presentation is at the beginning. Something out of the ordinary will usually succeed in getting the prospect's attention.

¶ 5116 **Use the "no-name" approach to win more sales**

Introduce yourself to more sales by using the "no-name" approach with your prospects.

Many salesmen have the idea that when they introduce themselves to a buyer for the first time, they must race in with their hand extended and say, "I'm John Jones with the Ajax Agency."

What they fail to realize, is that a prospect —especially one whom salesmen call on regu-

putting the presentation into words

larly—is not really interested in their name, or in anything they have to say. He's only interested in one thing—*himself.*

Tom Jensen, an advertising man, uses the "no-name" approach, and it has proved to be a saleswinner for him. Here's what Tom says:

"I don't even mention my name when I introduce myself to a prospect. Instead of telling *who I am,* I tell him what I'm going *to do for him.*

EXAMPLE: If I'm calling on a car dealer to talk to him about an advertising program, I begin with "Good morning, Mr. Burnes. I have an idea that will put twice as many people into your Buicks. I'm with the Ajax Advertising Agency."

"Later, when I *show* the prospect how I can serve him, he almost always says, "I'm sorry, what did you say your name was?"

Now he's interested in what I have to say. So I smile and tell him my name. Of course, I never mentioned it at all—but he didn't spot it."

➤➤WHAT TO DO➤ Practice this technique of introducing yourself until it feels natural to you. You'll be on good, solid ground because you'll be thinking in terms of the prospect's interest—how you can serve him, and what he'll get out of the sale.

Result: Your prospect will sense your interest. He'll feel that he's not in the presence of a high-pressure salesman who is going to beat him out of a lot of money, but that here is a man who wants to serve him.

¶ 5117 **Start your presentation with an exhibit**

One way to get attention is to catch the prospect's eye with an exhibit or visual attraction of some kind. Some companies provide their salesmen with scale or cut-out models, blow-ups, and the like, and in many cases these can serve to get the interview going. Salesmen who have these aids, or who sell a product that stirs curiosity by its appearance, can often get under way by simply saying something like:

"Mr. Prospect, this is the new ———, the fastest-growing home appliance on the market."

Remember that the eyes are a person's quickest and sharpest point of registration. Your prospect's eyes work for you if you have something interesting on which they can focus.

¶ 5118 **Use an interesting news item as an opener**

News of something new and big in the industry, or of something out of the ordinary that has a bearing on the interview, will help you get your prospect's attention. The closer the news affects your prospect personally, the closer he is likely to listen. The effectiveness of this method is increased if you present an actual article or newspaper clipping for the prospect to look at.

These examples illustrate how news can serve to launch the interview:

1

"Mr. Prospect, perhaps you saw the amazing results of *Fortune* magazine's recent survey of the petrochemical industry and its future. Let's look at this figure in particular, the one that concerns you most . . ."

2

"Mr. Prospect, it isn't often that a new product is exciting enough to deserve a major article in two leading trade magazines in the same month. But our new machine *is* that exciting, and here are the articles . . ."

Build Interest

¶ 5121 **Make him interested by stating benefits**

You have to change the prospect's state of attention into favorable interest. Do it by telling him what benefits he will gain from the purchase of your product or service, for it is benefits that he wants and will pay for. This is why you distilled your list of selling features until they took clear shape as benefits to the buyer [¶ 5015].

➤➤IMPORTANT➤ Choose the benefits that suit your largest class of prospects in developing your presentation.

EXAMPLE: Pitney-Bowes, Inc. makes an electrically-powered machine called the Tickometer, which counts and imprints paper forms at speeds up to 1,000 per minute. The presentation expresses the features of the product—in this case, speed, accuracy, versatility and ease of operation—in terms of *benefits* (savings and convenience), as follows:

"By comparison [with manual counting and imprinting], the Tickometer will count and imprint up to ten times faster, with improved convenience and accuracy plus big time and payroll savings."

* * *

¶ 5121

"The machine enables you to keep skilled workers at their proper jobs, and costs less per day than an average worker's pay for just one hour."

* * *

"It cuts waste on misprinted labels, lets your company meet production requirements exactly, and provides a quality control coding that is easily legible to dealers and salesmen."

* * *

"Over 100 case studies and testimonials prove . . . the savings that Tickometers have provided in payrolls, time, materials, and morale for thousands of companies."

Notice how much more meaning these statements of benefits have for the prospect than simple claims of speed or accuracy. They show what speed or accuracy means to him. Notice, too, that wherever possible the benefits are phrased so as to sound suited for the particular prospect.

Turn the prospect's interest into desire

¶ 5131 **Desire must be created**

Making the prospect *want* what you offer (creating *desire* in him) narrows the important gap between interest and a signed order. While interest is mainly a mental reaction, desire is an emotional one that incites the prospect to take action.

People *want* (1) whatever answers a strong need and (2) whatever gratifies a personal buying motive, such as comfort or amusement. You must, therefore, dwell on the need which you can answer, to make it seem like a strong one, and you must personalize your offering in every way possible.

Here are means by which to accomplish these goals:

• Build up his need, pointing it out if necessary [¶ 5132].

• Show in what way your product or service is the best answer to that need [¶ 5133].

• Point out his personal stake in the matter [¶ 5134].

• Emphasize the *satisfaction* that the benefits will bring [¶ 5135].

• Add glamour or fascination to your product [¶ 5136].

¶ 5132 **Build up the prospect's need for your product or service**

You must remind most prospects how important their need is to get them to want what you are offering. In some cases you have to point out a need or needs of which the prospect is unaware, before your story can strike a responsive chord.

No matter how obvious you feel the need for your product or service may be, therefore, restate that need to amplify the prospect's awareness of it. Then he'll begin to actively want the benefits you promise.

EXAMPLE: International Minerals and Chemical Corporation makes and sells fertilizer, something every farmer can be assumed to need. To build desire for Rainbow Plant Food, the salesman prefaces each benefit by pointing out why the farmer needs it. He does this using a visual presentation (slides).

The complete presentation is given at ¶ 5184. Notice how the farmer is first reminded of his needs and then told how Rainbow is the right answer for him. The result is to make him *want* Rainbow Plant Food.

If for some reason the average prospect does not realize that he needs your product or service, or why, then you've got to point out the need to make him want what you're selling.

EXAMPLE: The Pitney-Bowes Tickometer is designed to cut the "concealed cost" of counting or imprinting paper items by hand. Since most prospective customers haven't analyzed this situation, the Pitney-Bowes salesman must point out its importance. Here are examples of how a presentation highlights these concealed costs:

"Here's why it's so important to you. Most firms are not aware of the concealed costs of counting and marking by hand, or by inefficient hand-fed machines. But you can imagine what that concealed cost is, in employees' wages, time lost from other work, spoiled materials, and inaccurate counting or marking . . .

"Let's look at some of these costly—but necessary—operations. Counting by hand, especially when office or plant workers are drafted to do the work, is monotonous, expensive, and leads to frequent errors. These errors mean that new counts have to be made

—more time wasted, more dull work, poor morale—and maybe more errors.

"Well, one employee using the Tickometer will count 10 times as fast as she can by hand, and without spoilage or errors! The machine enables you to keep skilled workers at their proper jobs, and costs less per day than an average worker's pay for just one hour!"

In this fashion the prospect, who in most cases isn't aware of what hand counting and imprinting is costing him, is first made to appreciate his need so that he can better appreciate the benefits of automatic counting. Once he starts thinking about these hidden costs, the Tickometer becomes important to him.

¶ 5133 **How to show your product as the best for the prospect's needs**

Create desire for your product by presenting it as the best one for your prospect's needs. Make it stand out in his mind as *the* answer and he'll want it. This is especially important when you have close competition.

To do this, make full use of *exclusive* product or service features—whatever your product or service can do that others can't. Even a minor point seems important when it is proudly presented as the only one of its kind.

Knowing all about your product and its market, and where your prospect fits into that picture, helps you to portray your product as the ideal one. You know what features to stress, what changes or new ideas in the industry you can capitalize on, what will make your offer sound most up-to-date. If you run a close race with competitors, the more you know about your competition the better you can make your product appear as the best one for the prospect.

¶ 5134 **Point out to the prospect his personal stake in the sale**

You may sell to buyers for large corporations or people who otherwise have little personal connection with the materials or services they are purchasing. If this is the case, you can give your sales talk special appeal by pointing out how the prospect *is* personally involved.

If he is a purchasing agent, for example, he probably tries to do the best job he can, regardless of the nature of his purchases or his individual feelings for the things he buys. Make him want your product by connecting it favorably with success and good judgment in his responsible position. If headaches such as returns, short shipments, and incorrect billings are usual problems, emphasize the relief from them if he buys from your company.

⟫⟩CAUTION⟶ This is *not* to suggest that a purchasing agent, or anyone else, will buy flattery or an easy deal instead of a good product. The point is to combat the impersonal remoteness of some purchasing situations by highlighting the aspects of the sale that concern the prospect as an individual. He is more likely to *want* what will benefit *him*.

The following examples illustrate how this personalizing can be done after you've been specific about the benefits.

1

"Mr. Prospect, you have a responsible job and I know you are intent on doing it well. That's why I'm sure you will be enthusiastic about this service. It takes a large burden off the shoulders of your office staff. Equally important, it assures you of putting your money where it will do the most good."

2

"Isn't that important to you, Mr. Prospect, knowing that placing your orders with us will give you the comforting assurance of full-order deliveries every time, thanks to our large stock?"

3

"Mr. Prospect, my product not only does its job better than others, as I've just shown you; it also tells the people who use it that their purchasing agent knows his stuff."

In each case the idea is to promote personal enthusiasm for your product or service by searching out ways in which the prospect will benefit as an individual.

¶ 5135 **Make your benefits sound personally satisfying to the prospect**

Elaborate on the happiness, the enjoyment, the pride, the admiration or whatever other personal satisfaction you can offer the prospect. If his work will be made easier, urge him to picture the physical comfort and pleasure that less work will mean to him. If it will help him make more money, stimulate thoughts of how that extra money will provide enjoyment or supply his wants and needs. Stir his imagination into envisioning personal satisfaction, and you will succeed in making him want to buy.

> **EXAMPLE:** Say you sell home air conditioning. One of the main benefits is comfort. To make the prospect really *want* that comfort, you build up its blessings in the prospect's imagination. You remind him of the tired discomfort of hot, muggy summer days and the misery of sweltering, sleepless nights. You describe sticky trousers with no crease left in them, frayed nerves, the prospect of another steaming night spent tossing and turning. *Then,* when you describe the cool, dry home, the better appetite, and the extra hours of sleep each night that come with air conditioning, the prospect has an active desire for it.

As you write out your presentation, try to picture each benefit as bringing personal satisfaction to the prospect, no matter what the product or service is. It's this kind of touch that makes your proposition sound more *desirable* to prospects than others they hear.

¶ 5136 Add glamour to your product

A touch of the romantic or glamorous gives your product a special appeal. If there is an intriguing angle you can weave into your story, use it to create desire.

> **EXAMPLE:** Brown & Bigelow, creator of remembrance advertising products, has an item called the Touch Rest Desk Pen. This is a modern-looking desk set in which the pen is held at an easy-to-reach angle by a ceramic magnet in the base.
>
> When a Brown & Bigelow salesman recommends this pen to a prospect as a remembrance gift to customers, here's what he does. After pointing out how attractive and how useful the pen is, he capitalizes on the fascination of the ceramic magnet. He describes how modern this material is, how it is formed by baking, how tenaciously it holds its pulling power. He shows how shaping can concentrate the magnetic field in a certain area, and how the hole in the magnet in the Touch Rest base serves this purpose. Then he plays up the novelty of a magnetic pen holder and its value as a useful conversation-piece. By building up the romantic element in this practical product, the salesman makes his prospect *want* that pen as a remembrance gift. The result? Out of 800 products that the company offers, the Touch Rest Desk Pen frequently appears on the weekly list of Top Twenty order-getters.

Make your presentation convincing

¶ 5141 A prospect isn't sold until he's convinced

Conviction is "a firm belief founded on evidence," says the dictionary. That firm belief is what a prospect must feel before he makes the decision to become a customer. Your presentation must therefore do far more than convey information; it must create conviction in the prospect's mind.

The most essential ingredient in the formula for a convincing sales presentation is evidence. Include all you can of these three kinds: (1) a demonstration; (2) visual aids, especially testimonials; (3) facts and figures.

Almost as important as the evidence is the manner in which you present it and your attitude during the interview. To carry conviction, you must:
- Have enthusiasm.
- Be confident.
- Speak forcefully.
- Be sincere and willing to serve.
- Show loyalty to your company and product.
- Make only those promises that you can keep.
- Be thorough.
- Speak on the prospect's level.

¶ 5142 There is no substitute for the facts

The most fabulous benefit story in the world wouldn't sell anything if the benefits weren't backed up with proof. Making a prospect believe in your product or service depends on how well you support statements with facts. Even a demonstration isn't fully convincing without the facts that supplement and explain it.

Include plenty of hard-hitting facts in your presentation, if you want it to be convincing. See that those facts meet these tests:

▶ *Facts must be truthful.* If your prospect detects one note of exaggeration or half-truth in the facts you present, or thinks they are misleading, you stand to lose the battle. Once his confidence in either you or your product wavers, conviction becomes impossible. Stick

putting the presentation into words

to the truth, and prospects will believe what you say.

▶ *Facts must be specific.* No one decides to invest a sum of money in a product or service because it is "a lot faster" or "more efficient than other machines on the market". First he demands to know *how much* faster or *how much* more efficient. Tell your prospect exactly what your product can do for him, and then back it up with specific facts, testimonials, and the like. Never use a generality when it is possible to talk in dollars-and-cents, hours-and-minutes, percentages, numbers, and similar specific means of description.

▶ *Facts must be easily understood.* Technical language is difficult to understand. Unless a technical approach is absolutely essential to your product or service, you should keep your facts as simple as possible. Complexity creates more confusion than conviction; once a prospect gets confused, he is likely to lose interest. Remember that the prospect may be hearing these facts for the first time, and that simplicity will help him understand them clearly.

⟶OBSERVATION⟶ Don't overlook the persuasive quality of understatement. Whereas people react unfavorably to exaggeration, they tend to believe what seems understated.

¶ 5143 Get the facts from your company

Most salesmen can turn to their company for facts and figures to back up statements that are made to convince a prospect. The company is usually in the best position to secure data from their own laboratories, sales offices, outside sources, and so on. The experienced salesman can often add facts acquired in his selling efforts.

EXAMPLE: If you sold Johns-Manville's Transite Ducts, a single-duct conduit, you would have an 18-page bulletin of facts to draw from. This booklet thoroughly analyzes the material, installation and upkeep costs of underground ducts. It compares the costs of using Transite with the cost of a multiple tile duct installation. Costs are broken down to the penny, based on cost data from actual installations, and illustrations and charts make each cost factor clear. From this material you could develop a hardhitting presentation aimed at telephone company buyers and contractors, based on the claim that Transite is the lowest cost material when all cost factors are considered. The company bulletin gives the facts to prove it. The example at ¶ 5075 demonstrates the use of the facts.

¶ 5144 A thorough presentation is more likely to convince

If your presentation tells a complete story, it is more likely to be convincing than if it is sketchy. Suspicions that you have left things out or are slighting important points put a prospect on his guard. You should be thorough, even to the extent of bringing up disadvantages of your product if their omission would suggest you are afraid of his knowing them. When a prospect sees you lay all your cards on the table he knows that you have confidence in what you are selling. This gives him confidence that your statements are valid, and therefore makes them convincing.

⟶OBSERVATION⟶ Your presentation can tell a complete story although it omits some of the selling points that you hold in reserve. You must be selective of selling points in order to keep your presentation within time limits. See ¶ 5017.

¶ 5145 Talk to the prospect on his own level if you want to convince him

Prospects prefer to do business with a salesman who can speak their own kind of language. If your speech is too formal or highfalutin for the prospect to understand easily, he will miss part of your message and resent your attitude. If, because of his education or the nature of his work, he expects a more refined or technical presentation than you give him, you will fail to earn the respect necessary for conviction. Write your presentation to suit the level of the average prospect upon whom you will call.

The following statement, for example, is used by a drug salesman to sell an injected tranquilizer to doctors.

"This product has proven its effectiveness in alleviating symptoms of anxiety, tension, psychomotor excitement and other manifestations of emotional stress. It is also a highly effective antiemetic agent for the symptomatic control of nausea and vomiting due to a wide variety of causes."

To a doctor, this is "talking his language". It would be utterly unsuitable for anyone else.

¶5145

¶ 5146 **Gather your forces before you make the final assault**

When you have won all but the final battle, the close, reinforce your advantage by summarizing. The repetition enhances the effect that your sales points had when first made.

➤➤OBSERVATION➤ Summarizing is one method of bringing the sale to a close. In this respect it is a definite closing technique [¶ 6022].

A summary can be as simple as the one in the presentation of International Minerals and Chemical Corporation. See ¶ 5184.

"So, it's all there . . . a plant food designed for your soil . . . the right ingredients to help throughout the growing season and a product kept ahead of the times by International's staff of 300 scientists and agronomists. Quality? Sure . . . we've been delivering it for 50 years. Reliable? You bet. International has the mines and the plants and the people to furnish what you need right when you need it."

Make a firm bid for the order

¶ 5151 **A good presentation leads into a good close**

Your great presentation must include as an integral part a final close, the attempt to get the order after the story is told. Because this is so important, it is treated in a separate section.

Closing the sale will hold no terrors if you know just how to go about it, and remember that the prospect expects you to do so. Study the closing techniques at ¶ 6001 et seq. and give careful thought to which one will suit your situation best. Then write a close into your presentation, working at it until you're sure it's a strong one.

The trial closings you include at intervals in your presentation are tentative, but there must be nothing tentative about your final effort to get the order. A sales interview should have as a logical conclusion a buying decision by the prospect. Don't rest until your closing words are ACTION words that move the prospect to where you want him . . . the dotted line.

How to give your great presentation

¶ 5171 **Control of the presentation**

For you, as for every salesman, each interview with a new prospect is a performance with a new and critical audience. Its success hinges not only on the material (the presentation) but also on your skill in putting your story across. Here you must excel if you hope to attain the selling pinnacle you are after.

The secret of a winning performance is a simple one: *you, not your prospect, must be in charge.* You must subtly but effectively dominate the interview, and make the prospect like it. You must exert gentle control throughout, leading always politely but firmly in the direction of a sale.

Here are five moves that will put you in charge of the interview:

• Start off on the right foot [¶ 5172].
• Give a smooth-flowing talk [¶ 5173].
• Act worthy of his confidence and his business [¶ 5174].
• Hit hardest those points he likes best [¶ 5175].
• Dominate the "give and take" [¶ 5176].

¶ 5172 **A good personal impression gets you off on the right foot**

Selling is a very personal business. In most cases it involves one man dealing directly with another, and personal likes and dislikes can affect the relationship. You must recognize that the prospect is free to let his personal feelings toward you influence his action while you, as the salesman, must control your personal feelings toward him. Even an exceptional proposition may fall on deaf ears if the prospect decides that he doesn't like you or takes exception to your dress or manner.

Your first grip on the reins, therefore, depends on the personal impression you make. Here are some of the measures you must take to win your prospect's good opinion:

► *Make the first impression a good one.* The first few seconds can make or break a sale. A prospect starts to size you up the minute you come into view, just as you are judging him. By the time you have approached, shaken hands, and said your first sentence, the average man or woman will have formed an opinion of you. With some people this first judgment will be tentative, but with others it will be lasting.

how to give your great presentation

Make that first impression work *for* you; don't begin the interview with one strike against you. Pay attention to these details:

• Do everything you can to avoid having your appearance act as a detriment to the sale. The soundness of this precept is explained and illustrated at ¶ 8061 et seq.

• Get the prospect's name straight and refer to him by name during the introduction and throughout the interview. If you mispronounce his name you will definitely annoy him—so get it straight right away.

• Have a natural and confident manner. As you approach the prospect, be in a positive and friendly frame of mind, confident that both of you will benefit from the interview.

▶ *Smile to get rapport.* A smile helps you establish rapport with the prospect and to put him and yourself at ease. Your smile, so long as it is sincere, can win goodwill.

▶ *Be courteous.* An occasional prospect won't care if you leave your hat on, but since most will, you should remove it. Ignoring courtesy invites the same lack of respect that it shows. Therefore always respect your prospect's personal tastes and feelings.

▶ *Mix diplomacy with authority.* You're expected to know your business, but an overbearing attitude will work against you. Make a point of being open-minded and objective about non-business subjects that crop up.

You can demonstrate that you honor the prospect's opinion with these techniques:

• Ask his advice. Somewhere in your presentation you can arrange to ask the prospect what he thinks of a point you have made, or of a certain condition in your industry. His answer may give you important clues to his buying motives.

• Agree with or show respect for what he says. It's flattering to the speaker to find his remarks accepted or respected.

• Repeat his own words. Be alert for the opportunity to take advantage of something he has said as a way to further your own cause.

¶ 5173   Give a smooth-flowing talk

Your presentation is the main means of control, since it determines both the direction and the general content of the interview. It gives you the initiative and the advantage of knowing what comes next.

To gain maximum control, the presentation must be smooth-flowing, with all the jerkiness and rough spots worked out of it, both in the writing and in the telling. It must be lean and hard, yet complete.

Make sure your presentation, as written, doesn't meander, drag, or pull in several directions. Ask other people to read it or hear it and tell you whether it flows and progresses in logical sequence. If it doesn't flow smoothly, work on it until it does.

Learn the final version of your presentation by heart. Rehearse it until you can handle yourself, the words, and any visual aids without a hitch.

¶ 5174   Be worthy of his order

The prospect's buying decision will be greatly influenced by what impression you make on him as a man with whom to do business. It isn't enough that he like you personally; he wants to buy from a strong, competent, reliable salesman. Once he decides that you are the kind of salesman, you have gained another element of control over the interview.

Follow these hints to get your prospect to like your sales acumen:

▶ *Act with confidence.* Top success depends greatly on having and inspiring confidence, not only in your product or service but also in your company, your statements, and your own ability and judgment. Looking, acting and sounding confident gains your prospect's confidence; without his confidence the odds are decidedly against you.

There are some manageable factors that can help you feel and act confident.

• Be well prepared. Nothing helps your confidence like knowing what you are going to say and do during the interview.

• Speak forcefully. Convey confidence by speaking with authority and with emphasis. Avoid tentative or non-committal statements. Speak as though you firmly believe and *want* him to believe what you say.

⟫CAUTION→   Don't confuse confidence with boastfulness or arrogance. You don't want to try to bulldoze the prospect or overwhelm him. Your object must be to draw him along through your own inoffensive but strong expression of assurance.

- Don't knock your competition. Besides being in questionable taste, slamming your competition often reveals fear or lack of confidence. You gain stature with most buyers by welcoming comparison and by tending to emphasize your strong points rather than your competitors' weak ones.

- Show loyalty to your company and your product. A surprising number of salesmen are quick to make apologies when a prospect maligns one or the other. A loyal defense is the only logical response for a salesman in such a situation. If you show lack of respect for, or confidence in, the company behind you, or what it makes or does, so will your prospect.

▶ *Keep your enthusiasm high.* People prefer enthusiastic salesmen. You can never afford to merely "go through the motions" when you're trying to sell. You have to be enthusiastic. Enthusiasm puts life into your presentation; it distinguishes you as a man who is interested in his work and enjoys it. Buyers value this in a salesman, and are influenced by it. See ¶ 8000 et seq. for valuable advice on developing and maintaining enthusiasm.

▶ *Be sincere.* Stick to the facts, be sincere in presenting them and in promoting the prospect's benefit, and your presentation will acquire strength. A new prospect doesn't know you, and perhaps is ignorant of your product or your company. Your sincerity will help break down the barrier of strangeness and win his confidence.

▶ *Be alert and eager to serve.* Unless your selling situation is the single-call, no-repeat kind, your prospects usually judge from your first call what your attitude will be after the order is placed. Buyers like to deal with salesmen who will follow up on orders, offer helpful advice, and be there when they are needed.

¶ 5175 Hit hardest the points the prospect likes best

Emphasize the points to which your prospect responds best. If he seems to brighten when you mention product appearance, act as though appearance is an especially important feature. Your presentation will then jibe more closely with his strongest buying motives.

You've got to be on the lookout for reactions that will reveal what the prospect favors in your story. Asking questions at intervals, to be sure that he understands points as they are made, will help smoke out his response. Some close-mouthed prospects will give little indication of their feeling, but most will give signs of agreement or disagreement that will be your cue.

Use the following techniques to stress particular sales points and benefits within the framework of your planned presentation:

- Use your voice to add emphasis. Changing the pitch, volume or excitement in your voice will add punch to statements that your prospect seems to like.

- Use pauses and changes of tempo. If you see that a point has hit home, don't be in a hurry to move on. A pause gives a good point time to sink in. Slowing down as you cover a feature emphasizes it and gives it more time to register.

- Repeat a point to give it greater force. If a sales feature gets a good tumble from a prospect, repeat it, either verbatim or in rephrased form.

- Add fuel when you see a spark. If the prospect shows real enthusiasm for a particular benefit, make the most of it by elaboration. This kind of flexibility is often needed and is entirely compatible with a prepared presentation.

- Make the summary hit the high spots. In summarizing sales points, stress those statements or benefits that seemed to impress him most when he first heard them.

¶ 5176 Look for vital clues when your prospect knocks your competition

Suppose that midway through your presentation, the prospect begins a tirade against your competitor.

⟫WHAT TO DO→ Stop your presentation and listen attentively, *and don't interrupt.* Let him do all the talking.

Not only is he giving you points that you will be able to sell him on later, he is also giving you positive proof of the inferiority of your competition. Proof that you will be able to cite to other prospects.

Your role: When it is your turn to respond, play it low key. Agree with your prospect, but don't overdo it. A comment such as, "I didn't

how to give your great presentation

realize they were having so much trouble," is sufficient.

⇨ REMEMBER → Your main purpose is to play up your product—so don't waste too much time doing anything else. Just because your prospect is knocking a competitor's product does not necessarily mean he wants yours.

However, he is probably in the right frame of mind to buy your product. But now it's up to you to sell him on the merits of your product —he's already sold on the negative value of your competitor's.

¶ 5177 **Add $30,000-a-minute selling ideas to your presentation for free**

Sell like a winner! Use the explosive, nononsense television approach that is helping companies move their products at a record clip.

⇨ WHAT TO DO → What the points emphasized in those one minute ads — costing $30,000 and more — and all in 60 seconds. (Lots of commercials run only 30 seconds—or even less.) In the following examples we'll show you the TV way in action and how some salesmen are giving their prospects the 60-second treatment.

1. Zoom in on your target. *TV way:* The product is detergent and most have some "secret" ingredient. But the soap companies aren't spending $30,000 to discuss formula pH control. No, sir. They're telling a housewife how well the product softens her skin and how it brings romance back into her life. That does it.

Salesman: The product is the automobile and these salesmen are dropping "dependable transportation" and "cushioned ride" and zooming in on the points that score when selling the young set.

The car salesmen are highlighting axle ratios and cubic displacements, and quick starting because they've found that these are the factors that turn on the younger buyers.

⇨ WHAT TO DO → Determine what features of your product are most effective in making the sale. You can pick up this information by noting what points in your presentation draw your prospect out.

2. Use the cash-register word. *TV way:* The word here that makes cash registers ring is "new." Listen to the TV announcer and note how many times he mentions the word "new." He repeats it and repeats it. Why? The giants know that the audience will listen when something is described as "new." And when you get your audience listening you're well on the way to a sale.

Salesman: Painting contractors have grabbed onto the word "New" and are painting like never before. A painting contractor had this problem:

He was coasting along with customers who bought his services only every four or five years. Then he began talking up a *new* benefit his paint jobs could bring to his commercial customers when applied to their customer-traffic areas.

⇨ WHAT'S NEW → He's now selling a new reason for painting a customer's office. He's offering cool blue-green for the hot months and warm brown for the winter months.

Payoff: Business is booming. Many customers are now buying his service twice a year.

⇨ WHAT TO DO → Look for the "new" in your product. You should be able to find something new in design, construction, service, application, or enjoyment. When you find it, build your presentation around it.

3. Put on a show. *TV way:* Demonstrate is the key to TV commercials. You know how it works—dirt is whisked away with one wipe; or the toddler turns a couch into a bed; or the dancer who dances up a storm with a pen tied to his heel. These demonstrations win the battle for your eye. And, at the same time they don't detract from the product.

Salesman: Alert salesmen have gotten the message in a hurry. This isn't to imply that no salesman ever demonstrated before TV—but today it's done with a flair.

EXAMPLE: The product is a light weight machine that has to be assembled by the buyer. A salesman could take it apart and then put it together for the buyer. That's routine and dull. Instead, the creative salesman—

Sells with a flair: He walks into the prospect's office with the machine already *disassembled*. After a buildup, the salesman empties the machine on a desk and then proceeds to put it together.

Payoff: The prospect is watching every step.

Actual successful sales presentations

¶ 5181   A two-call presentation to businessmen to sell the need for fire protection, make a survey, and then sell the equipment indicated by the survey

Acknowledgment: William A. Bavagnoli, Salesman, Newark office of Remington Rand Division, Sperry Rand Corporation

First Interview

SALESMAN: Mr. Prospect, my name is John Collins, Remington Rand.

PROSPECT: Hello, John.

SALESMAN: May I sit down, Mr. Prospect?

PROSPECT: Please do.

Gets attention

SALESMAN: Mr. Prospect, this appointment was arranged specifically to discuss fire protection for your business records. Have you ever thought about being unemployed?

PROSPECT: No, I can't say I have. Business is so good, that thought has never entered my mind. We've been so busy we haven't had time to think about anything but business.

Creates interest; starts him thinking

SALESMAN: It's wonderful to hear that you enjoy such prosperity, but just consider this a moment. A fire tonight could put you among the unemployed tomorrow. The fact is, Mr. Prospect, that of all businesses whose records are destroyed by fire, 43% never reopen their doors. How would you like to be one of them?

Objection

PROSPECT: I wouldn't. We don't have anything to worry about, though, because our building is fireproof and the records are in these steel files. That's all the protection we'll ever need.

Agrees with objection, but

Answers objection with question

SALESMAN: Well sir, your first statement about your building is correct, it is fire resistive. What is stored in the building, however, is not. Don't you agree that it's possible for your stock downstairs to burn? Papers, paneling on the walls, floor covering? These can all burn and produce enough heat to burn your records. It only takes 350°F. to burn paper and any one of these can do it, don't you agree?

Gets his agreement before proceeding

PROSPECT: I'll go along with you on that, but how about the files?

SALESMAN: A steel file will protect your records from flame but not from heat, and heat is what burns. Records housed in steel containers will last approximately 4 minutes. In fact, Mr. Prospect, many of our cooking utensils are made from steel because of its excellent heat conducting qualities.

Demonstrates point

Allow me to demonstrate this point. If you will place your hand on top of this file, I will light a match under the top cover, and you tell me when it gets hot. (Waits until he does.) Do you agree that heat burns and not flame, and that steel conducts heat?

Gets agreement before continuing

PROSPECT: Yes, but I'm not completely convinced.

SALESMAN: Well, sir, then you wouldn't mind if I took one of these ledger cards with me, would you?

PROSPECT: Of course I would. It would take some time to get the information that's on that card.

Demonstrates: makes him smell fire

SALESMAN: *If* you can get it at all. Is it worth taking the chance? I have here a ledger card which was burned around the edges where all your important information is. What use, other than scrap paper, can

actual successful sales presentations

	you make of this? You see, fire can also burn your source documents, and then you would never be able to reconstruct your ledger cards.
False objection	PROSPECT: I can always depend upon my customers to furnish me with the information.
Shows why he needs protection. Creates more interest	SALESMAN: Then why keep these records at all? You're wasting time and money, if your customers will provide this service for you.
	No doubt your customers are fine people, and would probably come to your assistance, but there is always the chance that they won't. Business is business. This is the downfall of the 43% I mentioned. Don't let yourself and your business be a statistic.
	If for no other reason but to prove to your Insurance Company the current value of your Inventory or Accounts Receivable, you need record protection. Remember, the burden of proof is on the insured. What do you think you'll prove with a burned card like this?
He's interested	PROSPECT: That's a good point. I'll have to think about that some more. What exactly are you proposing to do?
Shows he has proper service and equipment to do job. Sells his company and himself	SALESMAN: Mr. Prospect, our company is in an excellent position to assist you in planning your record protection needs. Our high quality products are designed to house all types of business records. Our experience and know-how of over 50 years leaves us no reason to recommend anything but the best system and product, because we make all types.
	PROSPECT: That's fine, but what is it that you have to offer?
Closes for survey	SALESMAN: We would like to survey your records and present a proposal to you showing exactly what you will need to protect your records. Can we arrange an appointment for this Friday?
Pinpoints date	
	PROSPECT: Friday is a bad day. Next week would be better.
	SALESMAN: How about Monday afternoon at 2:00?
	PROSPECT: That's O.K.
Names a satisfied user	SALESMAN: Fine, we'll see you Monday afternoon. By the way, Mr. Prospect, Mr. Jones of the XYZ Company has just purchased our complete proposal for the very same equipment we discussed today. We also did a survey for him.
	How about visiting him to see what he purchased and at the same time we can show you the different products available.
	PROSPECT: Good. Do you think we can go on Wednesday?
Arranges to show product in use	SALESMAN: I'm sure it will be satisfactory. I'll call Mr. Jones for the appointment and then confirm it with you. By that time the survey and report should be completed. Let's make it for 10:30 at XYZ Company and 10:00 here. We can review the proposal before going.
	PROSPECT: Fine.

SECOND INTERVIEW

Goes over each part of proposal, making sure each point is understood clearly. Gets agreement on each point	SALESMAN: Mr. Prospect, before going over to the XYZ Company, let's go over the proposal so that all points will be clear in your mind.
	The letter of transmittal explains briefly what the proposal consists of and how we will proceed to carry out its recommendations.
Talks positively as though he already has the order	Part I gives a detailed breakdown of your records and how you are presently housing them.
Avoids negative phrases such as "I think," "I believe," "It may be"	Part II contains the proposed equipment and shows what protection you will have.

Part III is a summary of benefits you will receive when you purchase our equipment.

Part IV is a users' list which includes the XYZ Company.

Part V has the actual quotation on the equipment.

Price objection

PROSPECT: What? Those prices are out of this world.

Answers objection with a question

SALESMAN: Mr. Prospect, the total price may seem high to you. However, when you compare the price you will have to pay should your records burn, which price will be higher? That for the equipment, or your loss?

PROSPECT: My loss, of course, but that's assuming my records burn.

SALESMAN: True, but can you be sure that they won't? In fact, how can you be sure you won't have a fire tonight?

PROSPECT: Well, I guess you're right, nothing is sure.

Trial close; asks for order

SALESMAN: There is only one way to be sure, Mr. Prospect, and that is to purchase our fire protective equipment. Why don't we go ahead and order it now?

Buying signal

PROSPECT: Not so fast, I haven't even seen the equipment yet.

SALESMAN: Fine, then let's go over to XYZ Co. It's about time for our appointment.

AT XYZ COMPANY

SALESMAN: Mr. Prospect, may I introduce Mr. Jones, Controller for the XYZ Co. Mr. Jones, can you tell us the major reason why you placed your records in fire protective equipment?

MR. JONES: Yes, the salesman came in and made a complete study and showed us why it would cost more to reproduce records after a fire than to be safe and place them in fire protective equipment. We didn't take his word, mind you, we had to see for ourselves, so we made our own little study. Sure enough, everything the salesman said was true. At least I can go home at night now not worrying about whether I'll have a job to go to tomorrow.

PROSPECT: Yes, I'm beginning to see your reasoning.

SALESMAN: Mr. Jones, would you mind if I demonstrate your equipment to Mr. Prospect?

MR. JONES: No, go right ahead.

Covers product feature by feature. Answers objections before they are voiced

SALESMAN: Mr. Prospect, this piece of equipment is called a "Safe File" Deluxe. It is the unit we recommended to protect your open orders. Notice the sturdiness of this unit, how well built it is. Doesn't it look as though it will go through any fire?

PROSPECT: Yes, how is it made?

Shows inside of drawer

SALESMAN: It is made of a monolithic (one piece) construction, pre-cast and pre-dried. One piece construction means that the sides, top, bottom, back and even the drawer separators are all cast as one unit before the steel frame is placed over it. We pre-cast it to remove all possible imperfections in the insulation, such as cracks, air holes, and so on. It is pre-dried to less than ½ of 1% free moisture. The steel frame that is placed over the insulation would rust if **the free moisture were not removed**.

actual successful sales presentations

Gets him to say "Yes"

You don't have to worry about rust with our unit. Isn't that a wonderful feature?

PROSPECT: Yes.

Gets prospect in on demonstration

SALESMAN: While I have the drawer open, take a look at the gear-actuated full progressive suspension. Due to the weight of the drawer, we use gears instead of the normal type suspension. This provides maintenance-free operation and ease of drawer pull. Try the drawer. Open and close it a few times. Doesn't it operate smoothly?

PROSPECT: Yes, it does.

SALESMAN: Mr. Prospect, this "Safe File" Deluxe bears three labels of certification.
1. Underwriters' Class "C" which means
    a. Severe fire (reaching 1700°F) for at least one hour without interior temperature reaching 350°F.
    b. A sudden heating without producing explosion.
    c. Impact due to falling 30 feet in the clear after being heated for ½ hour and reheating for ½ hour in the invested position after impact without destroying the usability of papers or records stored inside.
2. The Safe Manufacturer's National Association "C" Label with same specifications.
3. Safe Cabinet Laboratory 1 hour label which is the label of our own laboratories, where research and development of these units are constantly being performed.

Gets agreement

Doesn't this give you a feeling of complete protection, knowing there are such organizations behind this product?

Buying signal

PROSPECT: Yes, I never realized there was so much entailed in marketing such a product. How about the locking device?

Gets prospect to try lock

SALESMAN: I'm glad you mentioned that, Mr. Prospect. Most people seem to take it for granted. It is a plunger type lock and can be made to control one drawer individually or all drawers simply by flicking this lever on the side of the drawer. Here, try it.
What do you think of this little added feature?

Buying signal

PROSPECT: Very interesting. I could use that for my personal drawer.

SALESMAN: Yes, sir, and this is one of the additional features, which is standard on the files we are recommending. If you should desire a combination lock, that, too, can be placed on the file.

PROSPECT: That's nice to know, but I don't think I'll need that much protection.

SALESMAN: Do you have any questions on what was covered thus far?

PROSPECT: No, everything is quite clear. About how long would it take to get this equipment?

Trial close

SALESMAN: If we place the order today we will have your equipment in two weeks. Shall we enter the order?

Answers "Procrastination" objection

PROSPECT: No, let me think it over a little while.

SALESMAN: It's wonderful to see you're cautious in making decisions, Mr. Prospect, but fire, unfortunately, is not. You can't afford to wait or think about this problem.

Summarizes, getting agreement again
Gets him to keep saying "Yes"

You agreed that our one-piece monolithic construction, pre-cast and pre-dried was an excellent feature, right? Certainly you concurred that the unit is well constructed. You also agreed on the excellence of our gear actuated suspension, didn't you?

197

198 *actual successful sales presentations*

You were quite pleased to hear of the organizations backing our equipment. Our locking device answers your problem of locking your personal drawer without affecting the operation of the other drawers, correct?

Closes

Asks for the order

Since you agree on all of these points and since surely you concur that fire protection is needed for your records, why wait? Why take the chance? Let's place this order today and minimize your waiting time. Each moment wasted can mean the life of your business.

Helps him make a decision

By the way, Mr. Prospect, shall we specify our surf green color to match the decor of your office?

PROSPECT: Yes, that's an excellent suggestion.

SALESMAN: Fine. Thank you very much, Mr. Prospect. I'll get to work on this immediately.

¶ 5182   **A presentation to business men, built around a demonstration of an office machine that emphasizes quality, performance, dependability and value**

Acknowledgment: Frank J. Barrett, Salesman, Dictaphone Corporation, East Paterson, New Jersey

Gets enthusiastic tempo immediately

Here it is—the all-new, all-transistor Time-Master Six! It's the *automatic* dictating machine. It makes writing as easy as phoning!

Top to bottom, inside out, it's new: in looks, in action, in sound, and in value. And it uses this Dictabelt record . . . which is years ahead of the field!

Good looking, isn't it?

Uses vivid-picture words to sell quality in looks, sound, and performance

That slim-line contour means lasting beauty. Those crisp, clean lines will wear well—will always be in style.

And that beauty is functional. Its easy operation, its fluid action promise comfortable, effortless communication. Because it's easier than shorthand, you'll like it and you'll use it. And when you use it, it will pay off—in time saved, in dollars and cents.

Every one of its 1530 precision parts works to one end: to make your dictation *effortless*.

Gets into demonstration smoothly

Slip a belt on . . . Touch this . . . Pick up the mike and it's on automatically . . . Press your thumb (dictate) *and think out loud* . . . Corrections? Touch . . . Signing off? Touch . . . Listen back? Touch . . . All right under your thumb! . . . Put it down . . . and it's off!

Now let's hear it. (Dictate.) *The automatic Time-Master Six uses new principles of recorder design. Here is the best recording to be built in a dictating machine . . .*

Wasn't that wonderful? Unmistakable fidelity. Not a syllable or inflection lost or distorted. The widest frequency response ever brought to a secretary's ear.

Gets affirmative response

That's QUALITY—in looks, in sound, and in Performance. Isn't that what you want?

Trial close on agreement as to quality

Shall we get you started using your own quality Time-Master?

Develops second essential—performance

Now let's look at this matter of PERFORMANCE, so important in a dictating machine: "what it does", and "how well it does it".

If this weren't important, people would buy the cheapest tools for their plant, their watches at drug stores, recording machines at discount houses, or inexpensive portable typewriters instead of standard office machines.

actual successful sales presentations

What is it supposed to do? Make your work easier—easier than with shorthand—to help you get things done.

How well does it do it? That depends. How fast does it work? How easy? How accurately? How reliably?

The Time-Master Six will perform as no dictating machine you've ever seen. Watch.

Explains ease of operation

Slip a belt on again... Touch the Talk Bar... Pick up the mike (there's no waiting, thanks to transistors) *and think out loud.* When you change your mind, just touch this "C" *and tell her what to do. There's nothing to erase, nothing to change.* Simple?

Two playbacks give confidential listening... or broadcast quality.

Finished? Touch "L"... Then touch this... Touch this... Tear off a slip... And it's on its way!

Time-saving feature

This pad of twenty-five slips... means you load it only once or twice a month!

Demonstrates again

Most of this effortless PERFORMANCE is made possible by this Dictabelt record. Let me slip on this belt and show you...

(Dictate.) *Watch the belt go round... you see the sound tracks forming as you write out loud: you know you're recording, know just where you are—quickly find any sentence you want to play back, and it can't be erased: belts are indelible.*

When you go back to listen like this... Then come back when you're through to the blank space like this... You touch the Talk Bar and go ahead. Don't dial, scan or skip around—you're back in the clear and off you go. That's effortless PERFORMANCE!

Translates facts into benefits

That "road-mapped" visibility means a lot to your secretary! She doesn't wait through blank spaces... for you to start again. No garbled dictation when you talked in the same spot twice... and she *knows* when you're through—never has to guess.

Prospect looks, listens, and feels

But here—let's look at a Dictabelt... It's *hand-size... mail-size... file-size... pocket-size...* and it will stand for abuse—and can still be transcribed!

It gives you straight-line *uniform recording, measured backspacing,* that all-important *place-finding,* and the *lowest cost:* You dictate, transcribe, and forget it!

With the Dictabelt record you see the recording!... and it can't be erased!

Explains built-in protections for performance

Here are some other built-in protections against doing it wrong.

Tiny transistors replace glass vacuum tubes, so you get instant starting... no dictation missed... no "down time" with tube failure... no turning off at night.

You can't do it wrong! In neutral? Hear this buzzer... Through listening? Hear it again... This bell... says to wind up. Then this buzzer... prevents lost dictation. You can't remove the belt this way ... or this... only like this.

Greatest safeguard, Company label

Effortless PERFORMANCE! These audible signals make you do the right thing, at the right time, all the time. It's even easier than shorthand!

Trial close after convincing prospect of performance

And here's the best safeguard of all—this Dictaphone label!... Shall I get your secretary started on learning how simple it is?

Develops third essential—dependability

Thirdly, you want DEPENDABILITY. You want the answer to two questions: "How do I know it will do what I want?" and "Can I count on it?"

actual successful sales presentations

This Dictaphone trademark... assures you of just that. Our seventy years' experience means *top service, and lasting satisfaction,* to you. Not for today, or tomorrow, but for keeps. You can *count* on Dictaphone!

Trial close after proving dependability

Shouldn't we get going on equipping you as soon as possible?

Summarizes 4 things prospect wants

FOUR THINGS ARE *MUSTS:* Quality, Performance, Dependability and VALUE.

Price—a 4-part story

It's not how little you spend, but how much you get! Cost? Cost is a four-part story:

    The *First* Cost—When you begin.

    The *Running* Cost—Here is where you consider things like efficiency of operation, no multiple handling, no erasure, "Road-Mapped" visibility, complete safeguards, less "Down Time".

    The *Net* Cost—Quality shows in the end: So figure on future trade-in or market value; and

Reduces price to cost per day

    The *Real* Cost—Of not having it!

    A Time-Master costs a quarter a day.

    Shorthand costs you seventeen dollars a day—and extra for overtime!

It's not what you *pay!* It's what you *save*—if you use it.

The Time-Master Six is priced with integrity to give you years of pleasure and lasting satisfaction.

Final closing

Shall we start now?

¶ 5183 A presentation to purchasing agents or shop men to sell a grinding wheel that requires a semi-technical explanation

Acknowledgment: Norton Company, Worcester, Massachusetts

SALESMAN: Good morning, Wes, how are you today?

CUSTOMER: Hi, Lou. I'm fine. What's new?

Gets attention by handing customer a piece of abrasive

SALESMAN: I've something interesting to show you.

CUSTOMER: What is this?

SALESMAN: That's a piece of green silicon carbide abrasive—we call it 39 CRYSTOLON. It's the abrasive used to make our wheels for roughing out carbide tools.

CUSTOMER: It really sparkles, doesn't it?

Creates interest in explaining how specimen is made

SALESMAN: Yes. I thought you would be interested in knowing a little about it. This is made by charging an electric furnace with silica sand and coke. When the electric current is turned on, the heat starts a reaction between the silica in the sand and the carbon in the coke, and the result is silicon carbide, like that piece you are looking at.

CUSTOMER: Then you crush it up and make wheels out of it?

Hands customer Knoop Hardness chart

SALESMAN: That's right. But, Wes, we're faced with quite a problem in making wheels to do a good job grinding carbide tools. Here, look at this chart. This chart shows the relative hardnesses of various materials. The Knoop hardness test is something like the Rockwell test, except it is used on very hard materials. You see, hardened tool steel

actual successful sales presentations

	comes out about 740. Here are your bonded cemented carbides that run between 1900 and 2000, and here is ALUNDUM, aluminum oxide abrasive, at 2050.
Uses chart to explain degree of hardness	Now some of the hard particles of tungsten carbide in the tool bit go to 2480. There is CRYSTOLON abrasive also at 2480, Norbide at 2800 and diamond at 8000, or higher.
Makes sure customer understands	You can see the problem now. In the case of green grit plate mounted wheels you have to grind the carbide with an abrasive that is no harder, or at best only slightly harder, than the carbide itself. It is like whittling on a piece of wood with a wooden knife. Do you see what I mean?
	CUSTOMER: Yes, but what about the Norbide?
	SALESMAN: Well, the Norbide is hard enough all right—in fact, it does a good job when used for lapping. But it doesn't have the necessary strength or toughness to be used as an abrasive in a wheel.
	This is why green grit wheels are usually very soft.
	CUSTOMER: They sure wear down fast.
Uses simple imagery to clarify	SALESMAN: If you think of a grain on one of those wheels, you can see that it wouldn't have to hit the carbide many times before becoming dull. If the wheel were made hard, to give you long wheel life, those grains would be held in the wheel too long and you would be grinding with dull grains. A wheel like this would grind very slowly and heat up the carbide and maybe crack it. Even if it didn't crack, the heat would probably damage it so that the edge wouldn't stand up in use. That would be bad, as you know. So the wheels have to be made soft to allow those grains to break out of the wheel as soon as they start to dull.
Creates interest in new product	In the past, wheel manufacturers have gone to open structure wheels—wide grain spacing—to try and get longer wheel life. But that did not seem to be the answer because the grains still became dull just as fast and the wheel still had to be just as soft to get rid of the dull grains, before they could damage the carbides.
	We've tried something new and now have a wheel that will last longer, cut faster, and still not heat up the carbide.
Explains with parallelism	CUSTOMER: What's that?
	SALESMAN: You know, if you have a hacksaw and are cutting something soft like aluminum, you use a blade with wide tooth spacing. But if you used that blade on a very hard material it wouldn't cut very well. As a matter of fact, the teeth would probably strip off the blade, so you go to a blade with a close tooth spacing—lots of teeth, each taking a small chip—and this blade cuts quite fast. Isn't that right?
Gets agreement before continuing	CUSTOMER: Yes.
Points out benefits resulting from product improvement	SALESMAN: Well, we have done the same thing with our plate mounted CRYSTOLON wheels; packed more abrasive grains into the wheel. Each time the wheel turns around there are more grains cutting the carbide. This makes the wheel cut faster. And, of course, any savings you can make in time are valuable, considering what labor and overhead costs today.
	Each grain still gets dull just as fast as before, but since there are more grains in the wheel, the wheel lasts longer. So you don't buy as many wheels to grind the same number of tools.

Shows him sample wheel

We call this dense structure wheel a #4 structure wheel. Plate mounted wheels are 14″ x 4″ with a 1½″ rim, and the marking would be 39C60-K4VK.

More benefits

This wheel not only saves you money because it lasts longer, but it also produces savings because it cuts faster. You can see for yourself.

Objection

CUSTOMER: It seems logical enough, but we're having pretty good luck with our present wheel.

Answers objection with a question

SALESMAN: Yes, but you wouldn't mind having a wheel that would last longer, would you?

CUSTOMER: No.

Closes

SALESMAN: Here, I'll write down the marking of this wheel and you can requisition one to test. Mark your requisition "test orders" and we will bill you at your normal quantity discount. Will you order one of these to try?

CUSTOMER: O.K.

¶ 5184 **A presentation to farmers, built around the use of a visual aid (slides), to sell a premium fertilizer, stressing dependability of the supplier.**

Acknowledgment: International Minerals & Chemical Corporation, Skokie, Illinois

Local emphasis

SALESMAN: Hello, Mr. Farmer, I'm Ted Moore. I'm with International Minerals & Chemical Corporation and live at ——————. Remember the postcard I sent last week? I mentioned that I'd like to talk fertilizer with you. I know your time is valuable. And, of course, there wouldn't be much point in my taking up your time if I had only an ordinary fertilizer to offer.

Reminds prospect of pre-interview mailing

But we have a premium plant food and I would like to tell you about it . . . also give you a brief sketch of our company and explain why it pays to do business with us. As I mentioned on the postcard, I'll need only a few minutes. Here's a slide viewer that helps you see what makes our plant food superior.

Slide 1—Bag of Rainbow mentions farmer's need

The first slide shows you the product . . . Rainbow Plant Food. It's a premium fertilizer . . . made for men like yourself who want to farm better . . . for farmers who want better than ordinary results.

Slide 2—Gas pump Explains need with parallelism

The point I'd like to make with the next slide is that Rainbow is the *modern* fertilizer . . . the kind of plant food that goes with up-to-date farming. Just like you need a high octane gas for a high compression engine, you also need a better fertilizer to give you yield and crop growth advantages.

Slide 3—Two piles of fertilizer

The next slide brings up a question: "How can you tell if a premium fertilizer is really more than ordinary and worth the little bit extra it costs?" Unless you spend a lot of time studying fertilizers, it's hard to know just exactly what you should be getting in a fertilizer.

Slide 4—Tailor-made for crops and soils

As the next slide suggests, the plant food you buy should contain what your soil needs. Sounds simple, doesn't it? But not when you think about it. Soils vary all over the country . . . rainfall varies . . . cropping practices vary . . . as a result some areas are more deficient in certain elements than others.

Yet a good many fertilizers are made the same for Illinois, California, Vermont, or any other state . . . just as though all soil needed

actual successful sales presentations

Slide 5—Help at the right time

exactly the same fertilizer. Of course, that's not the case with International. Rainbow and all our fertilizers are tailor-made for your soil.

The point I'd like to make with the next slide is that you need a fertilizer that helps out at exactly the right time. For example, some nitrogen sources give your crops a fast spurt early in the season, then fizzle out. Other sources may not go to work until later in the summer ... they work fine in August but don't help a bit in May.

You and I can't tell just by looking at a handful of fertilizer what kind of nitrogen it contains or when it will be available to plants. But the point is that one source usually isn't enough. You generally need more than one nitrogen source in the fertilizer you buy, to provide for your crops all through the growing season. That's another reason why Rainbow is better.

Slide 6—Dependable

You'll notice the word "dependable" on the next slide. And that's what you want ... a dependable fertilizer from a dependable company that keeps ahead of the times. Everything else you buy is being improved. Tractors are better ... combines are better ... and your fertilizer should be better. There is no good reason why you should settle for a fertilizer that hasn't been improved for twenty years. Our company recognizes that fact and therefore keeps up with new discoveries ... keeps Rainbow Plant Food up-to-date. That's the kind you need.

Builds up company reliability

Slide 7—New IMC administrative building

The next slide shows you our headquarters ... International Minerals & Chemical Corporation. It's a progressive company, with a fifty-year reputation for standing behind its fertilizer and other products.

Slide 8—Ac'cent well-known product of same company

For instance, take a look at that next slide. It's a product you see in most grocery stores and supermarkets. Your wife may have it in her kitchen right now ... a flavor-improver called Ac'cent. It's actually a by-product of agriculture ... the sugar beet industry. Homemakers and chefs have been depending upon it for years.

Slide 9—Print of recent ad

You've also probably seen our plant food ads. The one you see on the next slide recently appeared in leading farm magazines. You'll see more of our ads because International Minerals & Chemical Corporation has been a major factor in the fertilizer business for more than fifty years.

We're basic producers of fertilizer ingredients. For instance, we have our own deposits in Florida, where phosphate is mined and refined. The point I'd like to make with you is that we don't depend on just anybody's source of phosphorus. With our own deposits we're assured of a constant, uniform supply.

Slide 10—Super Scooper. Dependability of source

The next slide shows how it's mined. The large dragline you see is called the Super Scooper ... it digs a freight car full at one bite.

Slide 11—Clam Loader. More on dependability of company; freight savings

We also have our own potash deposits in Carlsbad, New Mexico. The slide you're looking at shows a hard working machine that loads fourteen tons per minute. It's just one of the machines that helps to make the mining of potash an efficient operation.

Slide 12—Noralyn facilities. Brings the prospect into the picture. Salesman states facts, and explains what those facts mean to the prospect

This fall we're also opening up new potash mines in Canada. This mine will be important to Midwestern farmers because it means a potash source closer to the farm with important freight savings.

Of course, you're wondering what is the point ... what does all this mean to you? Well, it means this ... more efficient production of fertilizer. It also means better quality because we have better control over what goes into the fertilizer we sell you and can keep an up-to-the-minute check on quality all along the way.

Slide 13—Quality control

At every step in the process of making fertilizer or processing the ingredients we run careful tests and quality checks. Our quality control program is concerned with more than the rigid specifications set by government officials. We have our own research and agricultural specialists who keep an eagle eye on Rainbow and demand the finest ingredients and the top performance from it.

Slide 14—Formulation check
Turns facts into benefits

In addition, samples of all the production in our plants are sent to the Plant Food Division's main control laboratory and checked for quality and proper ratio. This means that you can depend upon the formulation you buy and that the Rainbow Plant Food you buy will give you the results we say it will.

Slide 15—Storage facilities
Moves from product to service advantages

We also have modern storage facilities where the plant food is carefully cured under ideal conditions. This means two things to you . . . you get plant food that's in top-notch physical condition, free-flowing and easy to spread . . . and you can get quick service . . . you get the kind of plant food you want, when you want it.

Slide 16—U.S. map with Rainbow plants
Names nearest plant

The next slide shows the location of our plants . . . 24 plants in the Midwest, South and East. You'll notice there's one near here . . . over at —————. Even though we're a large nationwide fertilizer manufacturer, our service is local . . . we're close to you so that we can serve you better and faster.

Slide 17—Loading slide
Names plant again

More facts into benefits

The next slide shows the loading facilities we have at ————— . . . plenty of help so that your truck gets loaded fast if you pick up your fertilizer. Or, if you buy through a dealer, it means that the dealer can guarantee delivery because he knows he can depend on our faster service.

Slide 18—Agricultural Experimental Station

The point I would like to make with the next slide is our interest in plant food research. For instance, we have contributed about a million dollars for agricultural college and experiment station research projects. We help them carry out the soils and plant research that shows how to get better crops and bigger yields. Right now we are working with 20 agricultural colleges on 26 separate plant nutrition projects.

Inserts names of state, school and project

Here in ————— we're working with ————— on a ————— research project. Other projects which we have recently supported here in ————— are —————.

Slide 19—Green house

And in our own laboratories, IMC scientists check results and work constantly to develop even better plant foods . . . better methods of making raw materials work in the soil . . . keeping Rainbow Plant Food ahead of the times, tailor-made for your farm to give you better returns on fertilizer and farm investments.

Slide 20—Rainbow billboard
Summarizes

So, it's all there . . . a plant food designed for your soil . . . the right ingredients to help throughout the growing season and a product kept ahead of the times by International's staff of 300 scientists and agronomists. Quality? Sure . . . we've been delivering it for 50 years. Reliable? You bet. International has the mines and the plants and the people to furnish what you need right when you need it.

You may have heard the old saying: "Fertilizer doesn't cost . . . it pays." Well, that's certainly true of Rainbow Plant Food. Rainbow turns each acre into a profit maker.

Assumptive closing

Mr. Farmer, you have been very attentive to this demonstration. I feel sure that you have been visualizing the better crops you will get with Rainbow Plant Food. You will want it delivered to you by (date) in time for your next spreading.

POWER-CLOSING TECHNIQUES

Close Early — Close Often — Close Late
12 Tested Ways to Get the Signed Order
There Must Be a "Hooker" to Close
Ideas for Working Out Your Own Closing Techniques

TABLE OF CONTENTS

	Starts at Paragraph [¶]		Starts at Paragraph [¶]
Miracle Guide to Power-Closing Techniques	6001		

CLOSE EARLY—CLOSE OFTEN—CLOSE LATE

Multiple-close technique—the key to more closings	6002	Try for a close after strong points in your presentation	6006
When to try to close	6003	Try for a close after overcoming an obstacle	6007
		Try for a close when the demonstration ends	6008
How to close on every buying signal	6004	Try for a close on a buying signal	6009
The proper attitude toward "No" in trial closings	6005	Offer something special to get an immediate order	6010

12 TESTED WAYS TO GET THE SIGNED ORDER

Techniques that close sales	6011	Give the prospect a reason to buy now (last chance close)	6019
Three strong closing techniques that take for granted the prospect will buy	6012	The right kind of "story" will help close the sale (narrative close)	6020
Assume that the prospect is ready to buy (assumptive close)	6013	Use the names of other buyers to persuade your prospect to buy (testimonial close)	6021
Act as if the prospect will buy (physical action close)	6014	Summarize your strong points to convince the prospect to buy (summary close)	6022
Get the prospect to decide on a minor point (choice close)	6015	Ask your prospect why he doesn't buy ("why not" close)	6023
Convince the prospect of his immediate need	6016	How to close a "tough" prospect (the "hat trick" close)	6024
Offer the prospect something for deciding to buy now (concession close)	6017	Ask the prospect for the order ("ask for the order" close)	6025
Induce the prospect to close (inducement close)	6018	How to "move" the prospect who hesitates	6026

THERE MUST BE A "HOOKER" TO CLOSE

The "hooker," essential ingredient of every sale	6031	How to "buy" for your prospect—and close more sales	6033
The prospect frequently has a reason to buy now	6032	Sometimes it pays to ask the prospect if there is any reason to delay	6034

IDEAS FOR WORKING OUT YOUR OWN CLOSING TECHNIQUES

	Starts at Paragraph [¶]
Your own closing technique increases your selling power	6041
Demonstration with prospect's own records closes sales	6042
Fact that proves quality and justifies price leads into close	6043
Giving the prospect a "ready-made" idea clinches the sale	6044
Strengthen "easy" sales as much as you can	6045

Power-Closing Techniques

Closing is the most important thing in selling; you can't sell if you can't close

¶ 6001 ⟫MIRACLE GUIDE to→ Power-Closing Techniques

Many salesmen do a good job with every step of the selling process till they get to the close—and then they falter—and all their work is lost.

Because they don't know what to do in the all-important 5% of selling time that goes into the close, the 95% of their time that goes into the preliminary steps is utterly wasted.

You have to be a strong closer to make top-level income at selling—and it's something that's simple to master—something that will repay you with high-bracket earnings for the rest of your selling days.

This section gives you the closing techniques that $50,000 salesmen use. These techniques do the job for you. You use them—they do the rest. They free you from all anxiety about the close. They work even when men who have always dreaded facing the issue of closing the sale.

The techniques that will make you a strong closer are explained and illustrated in these four parts:

▶ Close early—close often—close late
▶ 12 tested ways to get the signed order
▶ There must be a "hooker" to close
▶ Ideas for working out your own closing techniques

The all-important "hooker" is explained in details. You see why no sale was ever lost because there are *two* hookers, but why hundreds of sales are lost every day because there is *none*.

¶ 6002 **Multiple-close technique—the key to more closings**

The multiple-close technique must be mas-

Close early—close often—close late

tered by every salesman who wants to move up fast in selling. It means that you must gain facility in making a series of trial closes in each interview. In each trial close you attempt to determine whether or not the prospect is ready at that moment to make a decision to buy.

In the multiple-close technique, a negative reply to a trial close is not regarded as final. It merely indicates that the prospect is not ready to buy at that point. A top-flight salesman makes, if necessary, from four to eight attempts to close during the course of an interview. That is the great secret of his closing power. He tries and tries again to close.

¶ 6003 When to try to close

Since the multiple-closing technique calls for several attempts to close, the safe rule to follow is close early—close often—close late. Thus, you begin as soon as possible with trial closes. Your own good judgment, based on the precise circumstances involved, must tell you when and how to make the necessary trial closes.

Trial closings come naturally and effectively at these times:

- After strong points in your presentation.
- After overcoming an obstacle presented by the prospect.
- When your demonstration ends.
- When the prospect indicates that he is ready to buy.

¶ 6004 Close on every buying signal

The ability to recognize a buying signal is one of the things that makes a salesman a real "pro." Another is knowing how to cash in on it—for bigger and better sales results.

⇒⇒HOW TO DO IT→ Close on *every* buying signal that comes your way. Don't fall into the trap of thinking that there's only one buying signal—and one time to close—in every sale. This idea has been discredited for many, many years—but it's still hanging around as a—

Persistent myth: There's one psychological moment in every sales talk when the buyer is ready for a close—that's when he flashes the signal. And whether or not the salesman closes the deal depends entirely upon his ability to spot—and cash in on— that one magic moment. **Don't you believe it!**

The facts: There may be a dozen or more of these crucial moments in each and every sales presentation. The right moment to close is whenever the buyer wants the product. And this want is created by you, the salesman, time and time again.

⇒⇒THE ONE-TWO PUNCH→ The multiple-close technique and buying signals work as an *action team*. When you spot a signal—drop your presentation and go into a close. If he isn't ready to say "yes"—on with the presentation. When you spot another signal, try to close again—and again and again.

¶ 6005 The proper attitude toward "No" in trial closings

A turndown on a trial close is by no means a sign that the sale cannot be made on the *next* try, or on the one following that. In using the multiple-closing technique, you know that you lose nothing by making an unsuccessful attempt, since you are prepared to carry on with reserve sales points that provide the basis for the next try.

▶ **IDEA IN ACTION** Jack Williams sells a home insulation service. He has told his story to his prospect, a Mr. Jensen, and quoted the cost of insulating his home. Jack decides that now is the time to make his first trial close.

"Sounds like a pretty profitable thing to do, doesn't it, Mr. Jensen?" says Jack.

Jack knows that there is only an off-chance that this first trial close will win him the order. Of course, if it *does*, he is ready to write it up immediately.

"Well," replies his prospect, "I'm not so sure. Even if it cuts down our heating bills as much as you say, it would take several years to pay for itself. No, I don't think I'd want to invest that amount of money."

Jack, a skillful closer, does not permit this reply to throw him "off base." He knew in advance that the odds were against a "Yes" at this point —so his response to his prospect's reply is to go into a further sales talk.

"There are some mighty important conveniences that you will enjoy from the very day your insulation is installed. First is the wonderful relief from that 'oven like' feeling when the sun has been blazing down on your roof all day. Second, you can say 'goodbye' to most of the bother of keeping a coal furnace going during the long winter months.

close early—close often—close late

"These two things alone make insulating pretty much worthwhile, don't you think?"

Jack knows that if Mr. Jensen replies favorably to this second trial close, the sale can be closed then and there. He also knows that the odds are against an early trial close evoking a "Yes"—that it may be the fourth or sixth rather than the first or second that will "do the trick." Jack knows, finally, that even when a trial close evokes a "No," he has lost nothing by the attempt. He is prepared to go right on with his sales talk, should Mr. Jensen turn him down on this second attempt.

"How long did you say I can have to pay for this job?" is Jensen's reply to Jack's second trial close.

This response indicates to Jack that Jensen is just about ready to buy. So he says, "Three years, Mr. Jensen—and I think you'll find that the modest monthly payments will be a small price for all the benefits you'll get from insulation. If you'll just okay this form, I'll see that the job is started without delay."

"All right," says his prospect, "it'll be a relief to get a good night's sleep when it gets real hot in another six weeks or so!"

¶ 6006 Try for a close after strong points in your presentation

At certain times in your presentation, you "add up" what you have been saying in one briefly stated strong point. After you deliver this "punch" line—or a series of them—try for a close.

▶ **IDEA IN ACTION** Roger Cavanaugh sells automobiles. He has told his prospect, Mr. Damron, the highlights of the story about the car he is trying to sell him, and decides to make his first trial close.

"You'll want the car for the weekend, won't you, Mr. Damron?"

"Well, first I've got to decide to buy it!" comes the response.

"Yes," replies Roger, "and let me tell you why *most* of our customers say they'd never have another make car." (Here Roger continues with his presentation. He climaxes what he says with a convincing fact about the car's pick-up and economy, then tries for another close.)

"What color will you want, Mr. Damron—this new blue shade, or the grey that's so popular this year?"

"Well, of course, I haven't decided yet whether I'm going to buy, but if I do, I'll let my wife decide that," says Damron.

Roger replies, "Yes, color means a lot to the ladies. Something you'll particularly appreciate, however, is our transmission." (After briefly explaining the features of the transmission in nontechnical terms, and making a strong point of the easy control, Roger goes into his third trial close.)

"Let me tell you about a friend of mine. He bought another make car—a popular make—that has an older type transmission." (Here Roger goes into a close that stresses his friend's regret.)

"So you see, Mr. Damron, why I think you're wise if you select the car with the best and most modern transmission I know of."

Noting that Damron is silent and apparently hesitating, Roger picks up his order book and says, "Suppose I fill out this form—"

"No," says Damron, "I guess I'll have to think it over. It's a good car all right—a good buy—but there's no point in rushing into a deal like this. I'll come back tomorrow, after I've slept on it."

"Okay, Mr. Damron, that's fine. But let me just go over the high-spots so you'll have a clear picture of what we offer . . ." (Here Roger summarizes the strong points in his presentation.)

"Now," he concludes, "let's see what all this adds up to—comfort, appearance, safety, economy, easy terms, a nice trade-in allowance—just about all you can ask for, isn't it?"

"Yes," replies Damron after this series of "punch" lines, "I guess you're right. How soon can I pick it up?"

¶ 6007 Try for a close after overcoming an obstacle

When you have successfully overcome an obstacle presented by your prospect, you have just gained a telling point in your favor; the "balance" of the sale is tipping toward you. You can best capitalize on this advantage with a trial close.

An objection raised by a prospect is the most common obstacle. A very close relationship exists between the ability to close and the ability to overcome objections. Indeed, the relationship between the two is so close that it is difficult to deal with either one apart from the other. This is true largely because the buyer is inclined to voice his objection (or objections) at the moment when the salesman attempts to get him to commit himself—unless, of course, he is ready to buy. A prospect or buyer who has no remaining objections can logically do nothing *except* buy. By the same token, a lost order always represents a situation in which there remained one (or more) objections which the salesman was unable to overcome.

Seen in this light, overcoming objections is, in a practical sense, synonymous with closing the sale.

▶ **IDEA IN ACTION** Dick Larsen represents a new company selling industrial dyes. He knows that the biggest barrier to a sale will be the "present supplier" objection. Dick prepares to overcome this objection, and to capitalize on it to make a sale.

When he is met with the "brush-off", "We've bought from the same source for 20 years. I see no reason to change!" Dick handed his prospect a portfolio of testimonial letters. He says deliberately, "Let me show you some companies you know and respect who *have* changed to our brand."

He uses the testimonials to overcome his prospect's objection, and to lead in to a close at the same time.

"You see," Dick tells his prospect, "these other companies that are comparable to yours have found it profitable to adopt our product." His prospect is impressed. Dick attempts a trial close.

"Would you like to order your usual quantities, or would you prefer to take advantage of the 5% discount we are offering this month on bulk sales?"

After a brief explanation of the savings possible with the discount, Dick's prospect signs up for an order larger than he normally places.

Whatever the obstacle may be, the technique is: overcome the obstacle and try for a close immediately.

¶ 6008 **Try for a close when the demonstration ends**

After a demonstration has been made, the time is usually ripe to try for the order. If the demonstration has been good, you have created a desire for ownership, and the close frequently is nothing more than a routine agreement on price, delivery instructions, and so on.

▶ **IDEA IN ACTION** Bill Smathers represent an internal communications system company. He has just made the last move of his demonstration and is stating his final strong point. "So you see, Mr. Hilton, use of our system permits you to contact key men in your organization instantly, and eliminates the time-consuming walk from their offices to yours."

Bill's *very next words* begin his close.

"I appreciate your undivided attention, Mr. Hilton. If you'll be kind enough to give me the number of stations you require on your control, and the location of the men who will be using this system, I'll quickly estimate the total time and cost of installation."

Bill has little difficulty getting an affirmative response to this natural and logical close.

¶ 6009 **Try for a close when you spot a buying signal**

Learn the selling tricks of the top producers and soon you'll be selling like them. Leading sellers say that every buyer—and they mean *every* buyer—tips off the salesman by some action, phrase, or expression—a buying signal —that seems to say—"*I'm ready to talk terms —if you are.*"

Are you ready? You'll go right on talking if you can't recognize the signal. And when you do, you may have talked yourself right out of the sale.

What does a signal look like? Some can be spotted a mile away—a favorable comment about your product, for example—others are more subtle. In general, they can be put into into these categories:

• *Physical Action.* Here's the classic example of this signal:

You're making a presentation—and the buyer stays mum. He doesn't even grunt. You start to wonder if you're talking his language. Suddenly he picks up the contract and reads a clause or two.

⟶**WHAT TO DO**⟶ Stop your presentation and swing into your close. You *were* talking his language after all! Now he's signalling that he's *interested*. He actually wants you to step in and help him say "yes."

What else to look for: The prospect is signalling when he steps back for a better look at your merchandise. Or when he lifts a corner and studies the label.

• *Spoken Sign.* "Don't you think the price is a little too high?" Is this an objection or a signal? The tuned-in salesman hears it as a signal. Why? It shows him that the buyer is actually thinking:

"I'm interested in your product. It looks like it can do the job for me. But maybe I can beat down the price a little."

That's the real story behind the question. The buyer is waiting for a good strong close—

actually fishing for one—that will justify his convictions and let him place an order.

→→→IMPORTANT→ Even if you have misread the signal—nothing is lost. Your closing action could lead to the sale anyhow. And the worst that could happen would be a delaying action on the part of the buyer. The chance for the sale hasn't been lost.

What else to look for: Get the order book out if the buyer should (1) Ask you to repeat a detail about your product, (2) Ask about a delivery date, or (3) Question you about your guarantee.

• *Facial Expressions.* Here are signals any salesman can miss if he doesn't watch his prospect carefully. A lifted eyebrow—a pursing of the lips—a quizzical look are all signs that it's time to close.

Here's why: These facial expressions can—and do—reflect the buyer's interest. They show he's interested in what is being said. Good closers know that certain expressions mean, *"I'll take it—just ask me."*

→→→HOW TO DO IT→ When the buying signal is flashed, stop talking—and start closing. Forget about the other points you wanted to make. The buyer has tipped his hand—he's heard what he wanted to and now he wants to buy.

¶ 6010 Offer something special to get an immediate order

Are you in a business that sells by direct mail as well as through salesmen like yourself? If so, you might whip up an immediate closing by using some of the techniques your company uses successfully in getting orders through the mail.

▶ **IDEA IN ACTION** A large publisher sells some of its products through direct mail and some through salesmen. To get direct mail orders, this company offers premium booklets which are valuable in themselves.

Bill Strong sells an information service for this company. He keeps track of all booklets that are bringing in mail orders.

When Bill tries for a close, he throws in a selection of booklets to get his prospect to give him the order *now*.

He glamorizes these booklets for he knows that each one was prepared by a specialist in the subject covered. He doesn't treat them lightly. After all, haven't they brought in thousands of orders by mail!

12 tested ways to get the signed order

¶ 6011 Techniques that close sales

Here are 12 tested closing techniques you can use to close sales effectively. All of them can be of value to you at one time or another as you use the multiple-close technique.

The skilled salesman masters them all, has at his fingertips just the right one for each trial close. Or he may try the *same* technique several times in a row, then swing into another type when he thinks more power is needed.

First master three or four of the closes that feel most "comfortable" to you. As you gain proficiency in them, incorporate others into your selling.

Remember, the ability to use all these closing techniques, and any others the salesman may evolve, distinguishes the top salesman from the average salesman.

¶ 6012 Three strong closing techniques that take for granted the prospect will buy

In three of these 12 closing techniques the salesman assumes that the prospect had decided in his own mind to make the purchase. The difference exists in the manner in which this assumption is expressed.

These differences in manner are illustrated in the next three paragraphs.

¶ 6013 Assume that the prospect is ready to buy (assumptive close)

You go into an assumptive close by making a statement that indicates that you *assume* the prospect is ready to buy. If the prospect "goes along" with this statement, the sale is safely closed; if he balks, you resume selling until you are ready to make another trial close.

▶ **IDEA IN ACTION** Paul Jackman, a medical detailer, works for a large pharmaceutical house. He has spent about 15 minutes explaining a new drug to his prospect. The prospect mentions that a gross lot costs ten dollars more than a type he has been ordering, but also shows a preference for the new drug.

Paul realizes that the time has come to try to close the sale. He stops his sales talk and says, "I'm sure you'll be satisfied with it. Suppose I write up an order for one gross."

Paul, a seasoned salesman, knows that his prospect may back away from this assumptive close by saying something like, "No, I haven't really decided yet." Paul also knows that if this occurs, he must go into a further sales talk until he reaches the proper place for a second trial close.

Although most prospects will respond to an assumptive close by either expressing agreement or backing off, some will simply say and do nothing to indicate their response.

▶ *How to handle the assumptive close.* The assumptive close should never *seem* like a closing maneuver but rather like the salesman's recognition of a decision already made by the prospect himself. When this effect is achieved, even if the prospect responds by backing off, he simply feels that the salesman's own confidence in the value of the purchase has led him to overestimate the prospect's own enthusiasm for it. Thus, no harm is done in any event.

Backing off simply means that the customer is definitely not ready to buy yet, and therefore needs to be exposed to an additional presentation to provide the basis for another trial close.

When a prospect meets an assumptive close with *silence,* the salesman must decide (1) whether he should take the chance of continuing to assume that the sale is closed, or (2) take the safer course of recognizing that the customer has actually not yet decided either way and is indicating by his silence that he is literally "on the fence." The first alternative is dangerously close to high pressure selling, which is normally not good selling. Furthermore, it tends to force an immediate decision, and since the silent response does indicate indecision, there is a relatively high chance of losing the sale.

Therefore, while the salesman would prefer a "Yes" response to his assumptive close, he is almost as well satisfied with silence at this point. He looks upon the silence as indicating two things: (1) indecision, and (2) enough interest on the part of the prospect to justify the expectation that a little more "selling" will very likely lead to the sale.

¶ 6014 **Act as if the prospect will buy (physical action close)**

Closely related to the assumptive technique is another closing technique known as "physical action." Here the salesman assumes the sale is closed, but he expresses this assumption not primarily in words, but in some physical action.

Here are some ways to use the physical action technique:

- Begin to write out the order.
- Hand the order form and pen to the prospect for his signature.
- Pick up the telephone and say, "I'll phone the order in now, to save time."
- Hand the item to the prospect and say, "I guess you want to take it with you."

The physical action close does not have the appearance of pressure—provided it is executed in a manner that leads the prospect to think that the salesman has merely overestimated the degree of the prospect's own enthusiasm or decision on the matter. If placed with some skill in the course of the interview where the salesman might logically seem to make such a "mistake," it is never offensive.

¶ 6015 **Get the prospect to decide on a minor point (choice close)**

This closing technique is an attempt to get a decision from the prospect on some detail of the salesman's offer, by having him make a choice. A decision on the choice is obtained in such a way as to imply or involve a decision *on the sale itself.*

1

REAL ESTATE SALESMAN: "Shall we prepare the lease as of May 1 or June 1?"

2

TYPEWRITER SALESMAN: "Now that you've heard the facts, Mr. Prospect, do you think our Carbon Ribbon or Standard model would best suit your needs?"

The minor point technique can be applied mildly or forcefully, to suit individual circumstances.

¶ 6016 **Convince the prospect of his immediate need (shock treatment close)**

You're losing the "battle" with the prospect. The sale is quickly slipping away. Now is the time to reverse the direction of his thinking; to get him to see your product or service in a new light. If you don't move immediately, you'll lose him for good. On the other hand, quick action can save the sale.

⇛HOW TO DO IT→ Use the "shock treatment" close. Convince the prospect of his immediate need for your product or service by hitting him with a bombshell.

12 tested ways to get the signed order

▶ **IDEA IN ACTION** Gary Keyes, a booking salesman for a hotel chain, was told by a prospect that he would rather hold off his decision for a while. Keyes responded with this shock statement: "Now, let's be honest for a minute. You'd be in a fix if the accommodations you need and desire weren't available—not just with us—but with anyone. Right?"

Result: Keyes opened the door to a sale with his shock statement. He got the sale.

¶ 6017 Offer the prospect something for deciding to buy now (concession close)

In some types of selling it is possible to get the prospect to decide to place his order immediately by offering him "something special" for an immediate favorable decision.

▶▶▶**OBSERVATION**▶ The concession close has its place here and there in the realm of selling. There are "close-out" and various other situations where negotiation, rather than a fixed quotation, is used to determine the price, terms, and conditions of the offer.

▶ **IDEA IN ACTION** Ralph Smith, a real estate agent, has finished showing the premises his prospect is interested in. He has attempted several trial closes during the course of his presentation; each time the prospect has argued for a lower price. His last close has almost "worked" and he sees that the prospect needs only a little "nudge" to help him make a decision.

"If you'll close right now, I'll drop the price of the house $100. Is it a deal?" asks Ralph.

"Okay, I'll take it," says his prospect, induced by this price concession.

¶ 6018 Induce the prospect to close (inducement close)

This technique involves offering something "extra" that is available to *anyone* who takes advantage of it. The offer of something "extra" tends to dissipate hesitation and delay. It helps close many a sale every day in the week.

1

SALESMAN (wholesale drugs): "We have a special introductory offer on this new product. The regular price is $4 a dozen, but we can take your order now at $3 per dozen."

2

SALESMAN (furniture manufacturer): "On any order you place with me now for fall merchandise, we will give you a 10% advertising allowance, to help you start the season with a good advertising campaign."

¶ 6019 Give the prospect a reason to buy now (last chance close)

When you can honestly state a condition that will or may arise in the near future that would make buying more favorable now than later, you are in a position to use the "last chance" close.

1

MANUFACTURER'S REPRESENTATIVE: "We are closing out this model, and have only 18 left to sell. They will no doubt all be sold within a week, and then you can buy only the new model at the regular price."

2

SALESMAN (photographic supplies to retailers): "There's a 7% increase in price on this item effective the first of next month. This is your last opportunity to stock up at present low prices."

This "last chance" close relies on an appeal to fear—fear that an offer that is available now will (or may) be lost if there is delay in acceptance. Since fear of losing something of value is a strong buying motive, this closing technique has a lot of power.

▶▶▶**CAUTION**▶ This technique can be used only when a factual situation exists or the possibility that such a situation will arise exists. On the other hand, the alert salesman can often find such an opportunity where others see none.

¶ 6020 The right kind of "story" will help close the sale (narrative close)

Each of us relies heavily on the experiences of others in practically every decision we make. We all tend to try to duplicate the success of others and to avoid their failures. This fact gives the narrative method of closing its force.

One facet of the narrative technique sets it apart from others. When the salesman uses it skillfully, he can, without referring to the prospect directly, point out how unwise he is in his hesitation.

1

SALESMAN (life insurance): "Why, only last week I took a check to the widow of a man who, before he was killed, had all but signed the application for the additional coverage he felt he needed. That check could so easily have been for $15,000 instead of $5,000—if only this chap hadn't hesitated the last time I talked with him!"

2

SALESMAN (real estate): "Another couple was looking at a similar lake-front property with the same idea of building a summer home. They too found just the spot they had been looking for, but because they hesitated a little too long, they lost out to another buyer."

3

SALESMAN (children's photographs): "There's a lady not far from here who just ordered a dozen additional prints of her child's photograph, on top of the six that we offer at this special price. She liked the photo so much that she sent one to relatives and old friends, many of whom had never seen the child."

In each of these illustrations the salesman is, by indirection but nevertheless effectively, suggesting that his *prospect* is being foolish in his indecision. To say so directly would be tactless; to make the nameless person in the narrative the "villain" accomplishes the same result tactfully.

⇛CAUTION→ This technique must be used with sufficient skill to make the narrative "ring true." If your listener feels that you are telling a "trumped up story," the net effffect is unfavorable rather than advantageous.

⇛OBSERVATION→ You don't have to "name names" when you use this technique. In fact, it is probably easier for the prospect to put himself in the place of the person in the narrative when no name is mentioned.

¶ 6021 **Use the names of other buyers to persuade your prospect to buy (testimonial close)**

The testimonial technique is based on the "follow the leader" instinct. If certain persons who are respected by the prospect—or great numbers of persons whose names he may not know—have decided it is advantageous to say "Yes" to a proposition, the prospect is inclined to "go along" too.

▶ **IDEA IN ACTION** A salesman selling misses' dresses to leading department stores might tell the buyers in his territory of how successful his line has proved in an outstanding store, or several such stores. He may or may not substantiate his recital by showing copies of orders, reorders, correspondence, or other material. The big point is that he mentions *names*. These names should, of course, have some special meaning to those to whom they are mentioned.

The testimonial technique relies sometimes on sheer weight of numbers. For example, a salesman may leaf through his order book, showing (on his carbon copies) the name of buyer after buyer of his product.

¶ 6022 **Summarize your strong points to convince the prospect to buy (summary close)**

Many salesmen get excellent results in closing by summarizing all the reasons for buying their product.

▶ **IDEA IN ACTION** "Let's look at it this way, Mr. Tepper," says stock salesman Mercer to a hesitant prospect. "This investment is abundantly sound—I'm sure you realize that. Second, it assures you a higher rate of return than most others of its class. Finally, you recognize the unusual prospect of appreciation in value—you know the reasons why you may very likely realize substantially more than the amount of your initial investment when you do sell. Then, too, it is so readily marketable that you can sell at almost a moment's notice.

"Now, Mr. Tepper, is there any reason to hesitate in view of these facts?"

The sales points gather impact as each one reinforces the others. Safety—high return—possibility of appreciation in value—liquidity—all these are brought up in the prospect's mind at the same time.

The salesman's enthusiasm must be discernible as he quickly reviews the list of reasons to buy. When both logic and enthusiasm are joined in such a close, there is every likelihood that the order will be forthcoming, if it is available at all.

¶ 6023 **Ask your prospect why he doesn't buy ("why not" close)**

When they are unable to close by other means, many successful salesmen stop further "selling" and simply ask the prospect why he won't buy. ("Mr. Prospect, you must have a reason for hesitating, and I'm sure it's a good one. Would you mind telling me what it is?" is one way to ask "why not?" The experienced salesman changes the wording to meet individual circumstances, but the query itself is as stated here.)

Few prospects fail to respond to such a question. The question implies that the salesman is at a loss to understand what is going on in the prospect's mind. The prospect knows that under these circumstances he must seem to the salesman to be a bit slow, or stubborn, or even unreasonable. To justify his position in the salesman's mind, he is very likely to explain his reasoning.

This closing question is advantageous to the salesman for these reasons:

• It puts the prospect on the "defensive" since his reasons must have substance or his ego will suffer.

• It enables the salesman to learn exactly what obstacles he must overcome if he is to win the sale. If the obstacle can be overcome, it is most likely that the sale will be closed.

• In stating his reason or reasons, the prospect is acknowledging to some extent that he would buy if the reasons could be overcome.

• When the prospect gives his reasons, the salesman wins another opportunity to state his case in terms most important to the prospect.

⟶REMEMBER⟶ Not every reply to this question is complete or accurate. A person who does not have authority to make the commitment may not give the true reason. Nor will the prospect give the real reason if it is inability to pay, or anything else that he does not wish to reveal. It follows that the sale is not always automatically won even if the *stated* reason is blasted away.

¶ 6024 **How to close a "tough" prospect (the "hat trick" close)**

This close is used by strong salesmen to handle "tough" selling assignments successfully. Use it when all other methods of closing have failed.

▶ **IDEA IN ACTION** Ray Remington's job is to sign up companies to lease their "company cars" rather than buy them outright. He tells a strong story of the advantages of leasing, but since acceptance of his offer involves a change in the prospect's policy and practice, he often finds it difficult to close. "I want to think it over" is frequently the reply when he tries to close the sale.

When Ray feels that he has "stayed with" his prospect as long as he should, he picks up his briefcase, reaches for his hat, and thanks the prospect for his time and courtesy. The prospect, seeing that the attempt to "sell him" is being terminated, relaxes.

Then Ray goes into his "hat trick" close. In what seems like an entirely casual afterthought, he asks, "Mr. Fulbright, do you mind if I ask one more question before I leave?"

Mr. Fulbright is glad to oblige. "Probably," he thinks to himself, "this chap is going to ask whether he can check back with me in a month, or something like that."

So he says, "Not at all, Mr. Remington."

Then Ray gets in his "extra lick."

"Do you know, Mr. Fulbright, that if my figures are correct—and I'm sure they are—it costs your company at least $45 per week for every week you delay taking on our service?"

Ray, of course, has chosen a point that hasn't been specifically stated before.

Making such a point at this moment, when the prospect's guard is down, gives him one more excellent opportunity of winning the sale.

Most salesmen can use this device in one form or another. All that is required is that the salesman, by his acts and words, indicate that he has "given up the fight." Then he does the unexpected by making one more strong appeal for the sale.

⟶CAUTION⟶ It's important to reserve a strong sales point to use in this close. If you use a weak point, or one that has already been mentioned in the interview, it might cause the prospect to feel even more justified in his decision not to buy.

¶ 6025 **Ask the prospect for the order ("ask for the order" close)**

Some orders are obtained by the simplest of all closes—by simply *asking* the prospect to buy.

The other closing techniques already discussed are, in reality, different ways of asking for the order. But they "ask" in terms of logic, or facts, or some other appeal, rather than literally in terms of saying, "Will you give me the order?"

Many salesmen prefer not to use this close, feeling that it is an appeal to sympathy or a request for a favor.

Some salesmen, on the other hand, have great faith in it. They feel its frankness and sincerity get them business they might not otherwise obtain.

Whether this close should be used or not

depends on the salesman's temperament, the type of product sold, and his prospect—how would he react to such a frank request?

¶ 6026 How to "move" the prospect who hesitates

A prospect who indicates that he wants to buy, but hesitates to make a decision, can be "drawn out" of his indecision if you ask questions that demand definite answers. The prospect is forced to respond—and will indicate by his answer the obstacle that is making him indecisive.

IDEA IN ACTION Bill Simmons sells an industrial machine. He proceeds to give his presentation to his prospect, makes several trial closes, but realizes that none of them "takes." The prospect is held back from an affirmative response by an unseen obstacle. Bill immediately begins to "force" it out by asking definite-response questions.

"This machine fits your purchasing budget, doesn't it?" The prospect's response indicates that this is not the objection.

"Its performance will meet your production standards, won't it?" asks Bill. This time his prospect expresses some concern about the machine's production capacity. Bill immediately reiterates pertinent facts from his presentation. He points out that his machine's precision minimizes rejects and actually gives a higher rate of acceptable pieces than competitors' models, even though the competitors quote a higher piece-per-hour figure than Bill's machine.

The prospect is satisfied. Bill then moves into a close and makes the sale.

➤**IMPORTANT**→ Make your questions specific. Often, the prospect himself may not know exactly why he hesitates. The blunt question, "What's holding you back?" might easily antagonize or embarrass the prospect, who often needs your help to find out what the answer is.

There must be a "hooker" to close

¶ 6031 The "hooker," essential ingredient of every sale

No salesman is prepared to make his next call until he has answered the question, "What reason can I give at the proper time—be it a big or a small reason—for the prospect to make a decision to buy NOW?"

"I'll think it over"—"I'll let you know"—"I want to discuss the matter"—these words cause many sales to flounder. When the salesman realizes that they really mean, "Give me one reason why I should decide now," he gains power to close more sales.

The "hooker"—the reason to buy now—is perhaps the most important word in the entire sales vocabulary. It closes every sale that is made, whether the salesman involved knows it or not. It can be supplied either by the prospect or the salesman. In some cases, the reason may hinge solely on the question, "Is there any advantage in waiting?"

How the "hooker" works is explained in the following paragraphs.

¶ 6032 The prospect frequently has a reason to buy now

Many prospects supply their own reasons for wanting to buy now; they may even make a point of telling the salesman what it is, to impress him with their need to buy now. At such times the salesman is relieved from supplying a convincing reason.

EXAMPLE 1: A retail merchant looks at the samples of a traveling salesman. The merchant realizes that the salesman is in town only for a day or two, and that if he wants to stock the line, he will have to place his order *without delay*.

EXAMPLE 2: The prospect is interested in planning a trip and securing reservations. Because his vacation begins in two weeks, he is eager to make arrangements *immediately*.

EXAMPLE 3: The prospects, a couple, have just bought a new home. They want to purchase new kitchen units *now*, before they move in.

➤**IMPORTANT**→ The fact that a sale can often be closed even though the *salesman* has offered no hooker leads many salesmen to believe that a hooker is not essential. Don't be fooled by this assumption. If you have not supplied a hooker, then the prospect has "hooked" himself. In some cases, the reason may not be divulged—but it is present nevertheless.

¶ 6033 Use the "fear of loss" technique to close sales fast

One of man's most vital desires is to avoid loss. While a man may remain relatively unmoved by the promise of gain, the thought that he can lose something he already possesses, motivates him to quick action. And this knowledge can be a tremendous "ace in the hole" to you.

To illustrate this often-overlooked fact, here's a short, telling story:

The late Chauncey Depew, raconteur and successful businessman, once put into very snappy English this desire of man.

"If someone were to come to my house," he said to a friend, "at three o'clock in the morning, wake me, and tell me that by going downstairs I could make $500, do you know what I'd do?"

"No, what would you do?"

"I'd kick him downstairs, and go back to bed. And so would you."

He paused and began again: "But if the same man were to awaken me and tell me that by getting up, dressing and going with him I could *save* $500, do you know what I'd do? I'd say, just wait 'til I get my pants on, and go out with him. Because fear of loss is one of man's strongest fears." Keep this in mind when trying to close a prospect.

¶ 6034 **Sometimes it pays to ask the prospect if there is any reason to delay**

If nothing more, you can always ask the hesitant prospect, "After all, is there really any reason to postpone a decision?"

Two responses are possible. If the prospect says, "No, I guess not," he creates an opportunity for you to swing into a close.

If the answer is, "Well, I'm hesitating because of...", the prospect will state his objection. This gives you a chance to overcome the obstacle and then try another close.

Ideas for working out your own closing techniques

¶ 6041 **Your own closing technique increases your selling power**

Most products and services have some unique aspects around which successful closes can be built. Sometimes the salesman's own special situation lends itself to an individual closing technique. In the next few paragraphs you see how some outstanding salesmen have evolved closing techniques that work for them. Possibly they will work for you. At any rate, they guide you to thinking about comparable situations in your own field that might become the basis for your own special closing technique.

⟶IMPORTANT⟶ Whether you evolve something special for yourself or not in closing methods, you cannot afford to by-pass the closing techniques that are explained in the preceding sections.

¶ 6042 **Demonstration with prospect's own records closes sale**

Closing immediately upon demonstrating to a prospect how a definite loss could be eliminated by use of the salesman's product was the technique one salesman found best for him. What made this the right time to close was the fact that he proved his point conclusively by *using the customer's own records of costs.*

▶ **IDEA IN ACTION** Stuart Long sells a guide that indexes domestic and foreign shipping and postal rates. These rates are commonly used by the shipping departments of many different types of concerns to determine the most economical method of shipment.

In attempting to sell one prospect, Stu was told, "I don't believe you have anything to offer that we can use. We have our shipping problems down pat."

Stu then asked to see some of the company's shipping receipts. Checking a number of these, he showed the prospect how $25 could have been saved if the company had employed his guide.

¶ 6043 **Fact that proves quality and justifies price leads into close**

Learning from experience that a unique fact about his product broke down price resistance by emphasizing quality, a soap salesman used the all-telling fact over and over again to lead into a close.

▶ **IDEA IN ACTION** Larry Sands, a soap chip salesman, has just made a trial close. "It sounds good," says his prospect, "but your price is too high."

Larry knows the fact that will break down this resistance to price.

"Are you buying soap or water?" he asks his prospect. He proceeds to quote facts (and show them in print) to point out that his soap contains 60% more soap, 60% less water than other soaps.

¶ 6043

The prospect is convinced that the price is justified, and places an order.

¶ 6044   **Giving the prospect a "ready-made" idea clinches the sale**

If you give the prospect an idea that makes it easier to get full value from what he buys, the sale can be closed.

▶ **IDEA IN ACTION** John Tulley sells gift items. He shows his prospect a new type of ash tray and succeeds in raising his interest in the product as a perfect "client gift." The prospect hesitates, until John gives him an idea that shows his prospect how to make a purchase of these gifts pay off.

"Here's a terrific idea," says John. "With each ash tray you send to your customers, you include this distribution letter. It will 'wrap up' your customers' gift item effectively, and save you the trouble of creating your own greeting."

John shows him a sample distribution letter—a catchy, friendly note intended to build customer goodwill.

The prospect is closed on the salesman's idea, and makes a sizable purchase.

¶ 6045   **Strengthen "easy" sales as much as you can**

The prospect who decides to buy a costly product before he has heard your full story has probably done some previous shopping. Nevertheless, there is danger of cancellation unless you take pains to "nail it down." One way to strengthen a "quick" sale is to "congratulate" your customer.

▶ **IDEA IN ACTION** Chris Summers sells a popular line of pleasure boats. He briefly tells one prospect about the many advantages of owning a particular model, then gives his first trial close. To his surprise, his prospect says, "I'll take it."

Despite the prospect's early decision, Chris begins to write up the order. However, he wants to "cement" the sale as tightly as possible, to insure against a later cancellation. So he says, "Let me congratulate you on a decision that I'm sure you'll be happy you made for many years to come. No other craft will serve your family purposes as safely and comfortably as this one, or be so inexpensive to maintain. Good sailing, and catch some big ones for me!"

The customer has been given a definite feeling of having bought something worthwhile, and leaves more "sold" than at the time he said he would buy.

⟶**IMPORTANT**⟶   Many salesmen use this technique after *every* sale. A psychological pat on the back, in the form of congratulations on a wise decision, makes any customer feel good.

¶ 6999   **Footnote references**

¶ **5018**

(1) Acknowledgment: Foreword to Charles B. Roth, "Successful Sales Presentations," by Allen N. Seares who was vice president of Remington Rand, Inc. when he wrote the foreword. Published by Prentice-Hall, Inc., Englewood Cliffs, N. J.

¶ **5051; 5052; 5053; 5054; 5056; 5059**

(1) You will find in "Working Salesmen Tell How They Get the Most from Sales Aids," *The American Salesman*, July, 1958, the results of a survey of salesmen's use of their selling aids made by the magazine. The suggestions, comments, "do's and don'ts" offered by salesmen who answered the questionnaire may help you increase your sales if your company supplies you with any of the following sales aids: visual presentations, flip charts, catalogs, testimonials, demonstrators, films, and slides.

¶ **5056**

(1) See above.
(2) "Industrial Catalogs: Salesmen in Print," by Goldalie Frank, *Management Methods*, February, 1959.

MAKING OBJECTIONS WORK FOR YOU

How to Use the Objection to Make the Sale
Strong Techniques for Converting Objections Into Sales
The Answer Attitude That Wins
Answer Guide to Specific Objections

TABLE OF CONTENTS

Starts at Paragraph [¶]

Miracle Guide to Making Objections Work For You 7001

HOW TO USE THE OBJECTION TO MAKE THE SALE

The big four rules 7002	Capitalize the objection 7007
Is the objection real or a mere excuse? 7003	Apply the capitalizing technique to all kinds of objections 7008
Why evasion is the right initial tactic 7004	Find the hidden objection 7009
How to evade an objection with "Yes, but" 7005	When does an objection mean "Yes, I'll buy?" 7010
Direct approach may be necessary to identify a stall 7006	What to do when the buying signal is flashed 7011

STRONG TECHNIQUES FOR CONVERTING OBJECTIONS INTO SALES

Lower the prospect's selling resistance with an *empathic* remark 7021	How to answer objections that have no real basis in fact 7027
Convert the objection into a question 7022	Minimize objection when facts can't be refuted 7028
Make the objection the reason for buying 7023	Delaying the answer to a sincere objection 7029
Get the prospect to answer his own objections by asking "why" 7024	Mere excuses may be a sign to summarize 7030
Think creatively to get around an objection 7025	Ask for the hidden objection when every sales effort has failed 7031
Mention an obstacle that doesn't exist in the buyer's mind 7026	Look for the hidden obstacle when you lose a sale to a competitor 7032
	Techniques for handling a trade-in sale 7033

THE ANSWER THAT WINS

No more fear of objections 7041	Consider the temperament of the prospect in answering objections 7046
Look upon objections as misconceptions 7042	Don't waste time on hopeless objections 7047
Answer objections without arguing 7043	Make a personal "Answer Book" 7048
Be tactful in meeting objections 7044	
Protect the ego of your prospect 7045	

ANSWER GUIDE TO SPECIFIC OBJECTIONS

How to use the Answer Guide 7061	"I can get a similar product for a considerably lower price"
"Your price is too high"	
Reasons on which to build a strong answer to price objections 7062	Reasons on which to build a strong answer to the "similar at lower price" objection 7071
Live examples of specific answers 7063-7070	Live examples of specific answers 7072-7073

making objections work for you—table of contents

	Starts at Paragraph [¶]
The prospect wants a lower price or extra discount	
How to deal with a bargainer	7074
Live examples of specific answers	7075-7077
"Your credit terms are too tough"	
How to meet the objection against credit terms	7078
Live example of specific answer	7079
"We have a lower bid from your competitor"	
How to meet the "lower bid" or "better deal" objection	7080
"I can't afford it"	
How to overcome the "I can't afford it" objection	7081
Live examples of specific answers	7082-7085
"My budget doesn't leave room for the expenditure"	
Reasons on which to build a strong answer to the "no room in the budget" objection	7086
Live example of specific answer	7087
"I'll think it over"	
Ways to get the procrastinator to act now	7088
Live examples of specific answers	7089-7095
"I'm too busy"	
How to meet the "too busy" objection	7096
Live examples of specific answers	7097-7098
"I'm not interested"	
How to get the prospect interested	7099
Live examples of specific answers	7100-7101
"I'm all stocked up"	
Ways to help a dealer move your line when he's stocked up	7102
Live examples of specific answers	7103-7105
"I can get a better guarantee from Blank Company"	
How to meet objection to your guarantee	7106
"I never heard of your house"	
Reasons on which to build a strong answer to "unknown company" objection	7107
Live example of specific answer	7108
"Your product is too new"	
Reasons on which to build a strong answer to "newness" objection	7109

	Starts at Paragraph [¶]
Criticism of your product	
How to overcome objection to the product itself	7110
Live examples of specific answers	7111-7115
"Your former salesman didn't leave a good impression"	
Live example of specific answer	7116
"I've heard that XYZ Co. had trouble with your product"	
How to overcome adverse rumors	7117
"A nearer supplier will give me faster delivery and service"	
Reasons to overcome "distance" objection	7118
Friendships or other personal ties stand in the way	
Reasons with which to break down the personal ties	7119
Live example of specific answer	7120
"We've been buying from Blank & Company for many years and are completely satisfied"	
Reasons on which to build an answer to the "loyalty" objection	7121
Live examples of specific answers	7122-7125
"We buy from a supplier who buys from us"	
How to meet the reciprocity difficulty	7126
"I must take it up with my partner"	
How to get the prospect to listen first by himself	7127
Live examples of specific answers	7128-7129
"I'll have to talk it over with my husband (or wife)"	
How to get immediate action when one spouse wants to talk over proposal with the other	7130
Live example of specific answer	7131
"The machine we have is still good"	
Reasons for replacement of equipment that is "still good"	7132
Live examples of specific answers	7133-7135
"I'll buy a cheap second-hand machine"	
How to convince prospect to buy a new machine instead of a second-hand one	7136
Live example of specific answer	7137
"Send me a case on consignment"	
Live example of specific answer	7138

Footnote references 7999

Making Objections Work for You

You can capitalize almost any objection that is tossed at you

¶ 7001 ⇒⇒⇒MIRACLE GUIDE to→ Making Objections Work for You

A strong sales presentation anticipates objections, nips them in the bud, and answers them before they arise. But objections will arise even though you have attempted to forestall them by your presentation. They might turn up at any moment. You must be ready to do more than answer them; you must make these very objections work for you, just as top-flight salesmen do.

Years of study have been given to the subject of answering objections by the country's leading sales consultants, sales managers, and salesmen. They have discovered what should and must be done—what not to do—to make each objection a stepping stone to successful closing of a sale.

You can profit immediately by what these experienced and successful sales people have discovered. By applying the vital techniques they use, you can make your income exceed even your most optimistic goal.

The first three sections [¶ 7002-7048] give you the basic principles to apply in answering any objection.

The Answer Guide to Specific Objections [¶ 7061 et seq.] furnishes a foundation on which to build convincing answers to a variety of objections you may encounter in selling your product or service. Adapt the language, ideas, and tone of the "live examples" to your particular needs.

Objections will work for you only if you follow your answer immediately with an attempt to close. For power-closing techniques, see ¶ 6001 et seq.

¶7001

How to use the objection to make the sale

¶ 7002 The big four rules

Objections aren't hard to handle, once you have mastered four basic rules that will take any man to the top. Those rules are:

- First deal with the objection as though it were a mere excuse, and evade it [¶ 7003-7006].
- Capitalize the objection [¶ 7007-7008].
- Find the hidden objection [¶ 7009].
- Obey the buying signal [¶ 7010-7011].

Beyond the "big four" rules you will find other powerful techniques to make objections work for you [¶ 7021 et seq.]; but the four that are explained at the paragraphs mentioned above must be made an integral part of your selling skills.

¶ 7003 Is the objection real or a mere excuse?

The proper *initial* response to *any* obstacle to selling is to *deal with it as though it were a mere excuse,* and *evade it.* You will quickly learn from applying this technique whether you are facing a true objection or one that is merely an excuse.

If the objection is real—one that looms large and substantial in the prospect's mind—you must meet it squarely. If the objection is a mere excuse, you will be able to by-pass it and get on with your selling.

➢➢➢WARNING➢ Do not use the evasion tactic when a prospect objects to giving you an interview; use it only in a *selling* interview. Always remember that you must sell the interview before you can sell your goods.

¶ 7004 Why evasion is the right initial tactic

The evasion tactic involves nothing more than avoiding a discussion of the obstacle on its *merits.* For instance, if a buyer says, "We're not ready to buy any spring merchandise yet," the salesman (who should assume that this is a mere excuse) may reply, "Well, I know it's early, but I'd like you to see our line now, so you'll be sure to remember it when you *are* ready to buy."

In handling the objection in this way, he has skillfully avoided discussing the merit of the claim that it's too early to buy. He has attempted to evade or by-pass the issue raised.

Now, if the objection is a mere excuse, it will be forgotten. For as the buyer looks at the line, if it appeals to him, he will no doubt buy in spite of his earlier statement to the contrary.

But if this statement is a *true objection,* he will not permit the salesman to dispose of it by the evasion tactic. He will say, "No, Mr. Rankin, we make it a firm rule here never to buy Spring merchandise until November 1. So we'd both be wasting our time if I were to look over your line now."

Thus we see that since nothing is lost by initially treating any obstacle as a mere excuse, the tactic of evasion is the proper one to begin with in every case. If the obstacle is in fact an excuse, the tactic will dispose of it. If it is an objection, the prospect's reply to the attempt to by-pass will bring out that it is no excuse. His objection must then be met squarely on its merit.

➢➢➢OBSERVATION 1➢ By-passing the objection until the prospect has raised it for a second time saves you from making too much, too hastily of every objection. This is a fault of many experienced salesmen, but not of top producers.

➢➢➢OBSERVATION 2➢ Evasion is useful sometimes toward the end of your presentation. For example, suppose that you are quite sure that your prospect is ready to buy and he then proffers a lame excuse, one that you can recognize is merely a substitute for a pause before he signs the order. You might ignore the excuse, change the subject to something quite apart from the sale, and hand him the order to sign.

¶ 7005 How to evade an objection with "Yes, but"

The alert salesman can easily swing the conversation from an excuse to some other point of discussion. The "Yes, but . . ." method is used perhaps more than any other. The following example explains how this is done.

▶ **IDEA IN ACTION** Norman Kendall sells textbooks to colleges. He is talking with the head of the geology department, who states, "Mr. Kendall, we like the text you publish, but the instructor's guide is rather sketchy. I'm afraid we'll have to pass it up."

Norman feels that this is a mere excuse, without real substance in the professor's mind. He replies accordingly by using the "Yes, but" evasive tactic in an effort to swing the conversation to another point.

"Yes," says Norman, "but when you consider, Professor Morgan, that our new edition is the only text that deals with such recent discoveries as . . ." (here he gives the facts) "it seems to me to have advantages that you cannot duplicate."

Here the "Yes, but" technique has been successfully used to do the job that is called for when a mere excuse is proffered. Since what is needed is to change the conversation without going into the merits of the excuse itself, the "Yes, but" tactic is a very useful tool.

"I guess you're right, Mr. Kendall," says his prospect, "but I don't think the index is as complete as it might be."

In reply to Professor Morgan's criticism of the index, Norman decides to use another tried and true evasive tactic. "I'll get back to that in just a moment," he replies. "First I'd like to show you these unique charts."

"I realize that the charts are valuable, Mr. Kendall," comes the reply, "but in my opinion no text is better than its index."

His prospect's reply shows that the matter of adequate indexing is not a mere excuse, but a true objection.

Norman realizes that the criticism of the index is a real objection, and therefore proceeds to discuss it on its merits.

¶ 7006 **Direct approach may be necessary to identify a stall**

In some situations you have to use a direct approach to discover whether the prospect is sincere in his objection or is using the objection as a stall.

EXAMPLE 1: Your prospect says that your credit terms are too tough. You want to find out whether he really means it, or is using this objection as an excuse. So you ask him to suggest acceptable terms. If he is sincere, he will frankly state the credit terms he considers equitable. If he is merely using the credit term as an excuse, he generally is caught off guard and states a proposition that cannot possibly be met.

⟫CAUTION→ Sometimes the prospect's floundering, when you try to pin him down to acceptable terms, shows that he requires "more selling." You must judge by the entire situation whether he's sincere.

EXAMPLE 2: Your prospect says that he cannot buy from you because he has a reciprocal setup with one of his customers who produces a product in competition with yours. You want to be sure that he's sincere and not merely stalling. So you say to him, "I'll be happy to try to get my company to buy from you as much as X Company does. If I succeed, will you then give me an order?" If he says "Yes," you know that he is sincere. A negative or non-committal reply probably means that reciprocity is not really the objection.[1]

¶ 7007 **Capitalize the objection**

Every salesman who is a big earner uses the technique of *capitalizing objections*. If you have not yet developed that technique, begin immediately to master it.

Here's the formula: Answer the objection in such a way that you make your case even stronger than if the objection had not been raised.

▶ **IDEA IN ACTION** Wilbur Gorman sells banquet arrangements for conventions. The hotel he represents is located in downtown Chicago. "No, Mr. Gorman," says a prospect, "we will have over 500 members attending our annual convention and it's just too much trouble for them to find parking accommodations in the downtown district."

Wilbur has the facts that enable him to refute this objection. He uses them, but he also uses the objection itself as an opportunity to get in some extra "plugs" for his own hotel, *which he would not otherwise have a chance to mention*.

"Mr. Raymond," says Wilbur, "you needn't worry a bit about parking. We have full service arrangements made so that all your guests need to do is to leave their cars with our doorman—he'll see that each one is properly parked, and available again on 10 minutes' notice."

Having thus completely refuted the objection, Wilbur proceeds to *capitalize* it. "You see, Mr. Raymond, our exceptional service is what has led many organizations of your type to return to our hotel again and again. Here's a list . . ."

The opportunity to show this impressive list of "repeaters" arose because of the objection. The net result of Wilbur's capitalizing tactic is that instead of being weaker because of the objection, his case is actually stronger than it would be if it hadn't been raised.

Wilbur, like other good salesmen who have learned how to capitalize objections, is constantly on the alert for such opportunities.

Hence, when a few minutes later Mr. Raymond says, "Well, we'll have to think about it; our convention is 10 months off, and there's no hurry," Wilbur again capitalizes as he refutes the "stall."

"Really," he says, "it would be wise for you to make your reservation just as quickly as possible. Here is our reservation chart for May—let's see—the organizations that have already made firm reservations with us for that month include . . ."

¶ 7008 **Apply the capitalizing technique to all kinds of objections**

Once you get the knack of capitalizing objections, you can learn to apply the technique to almost *any* objection. Strong salesmen constantly seize the opportunity to strengthen their selling talks while they answer objections.

A few short illustrations will show you how they do it.

1

PROSPECT: "We can't afford to go in for that sort of thing right now."
SALESMAN: "Actually, the good hard dollars you will save are the most attractive feature of our service. (He gives details and proof.) If it's money that you base your decision on, I frankly don't see how you can afford to pass us up."

2

PROSPECT: "I must discuss the matter with several of my associates."
SALESMAN: "Let me summarize the advantages of our offer, so you will have the whole thing clearly in mind for your discussion." (Thus he gets a chance to repeat the main points.)

3

PROSPECT: "We buy just as cheaply from the ABC Company."
SALESMAN: "I'm sure you do. But there must be some reason, don't you think, why we do the largest volume in our field?" (A strong plug.)

It takes only a few well-planned statements to equip yourself with this income-building technique. Develop the capitalizing remark you will use to follow up each objection you are likely to encounter. Memorize it from your "Answer Book" [¶ 7048] and try out the technique the very next time you have to answer an objection. You will see how easy it is to do. You'll find that it removes your fear of objections. You will no longer be put on the defensive by objections but will be in a strong offensive position with a new selling point.

¶ 7009 **Find the hidden objection**

If the prospect has an objection in his *mind* that he has not brought up, it acts as a barrier to the sale exactly as though it had been expressed. And since such a mental reservation must be met, if it is to be overcome, the need arises to get it out in the open. Thus it becomes a part of good salesmanship, under such circumstances, to *seek out the hidden objection*.

EXAMPLE: "Mr. Prospect, are you hesitating because you think prices may drop?"
"Well, yes! That's what's bothering me!"
"O.K., now here's why we are quite certain prices will not go down this year."
Or, "O.K., here's how we will protect you," and so forth.

You must keep pressing for the unmentioned objection until you uncover it. Only then can you meet it squarely and close the sale.

▶ **IDEA IN ACTION** Bill Coleman sells real estate. He has been talking with a prospect, Mrs. Long, about a house that seems to suit her wants. But although Bill feels he has overcome every obstacle that has been raised, he is unable to close the sale.

Bill knows that it is always an unresolved obstacle that keeps a prospect from buying, so he reasons, correctly, that in this instance there must remain a hidden objection. He realizes that this objection must be gotten out in the open.

"Mrs. Long," he probes, "are you hesitating because the house is eight years old?"
"No, that doesn't bother me," she replies.
"The price is right, isn't it?" continues Bill.
"Yes, I suppose I can't do any better for the money."
"Would you mind telling me, Mrs. Long, whether there's anything about the offer that doesn't seem just right?"
"Well, Mr. Coleman, I'm wondering what the neighbors are *really* like—good neighbors are so important!"

Bill has no problem left. He is able to tell his prospect much about the neighbors on both sides of the house she is considering, since he himself has previously handled several transactions on that block.

⟫OBSERVATION→ This sale might never have been made had Bill not probed for the hidden obstacle.

¶ 7010 **When does the objection mean "Yes, I'll buy"?**

A prospect will sometimes make a statement in the form of an objection, which is in fact a signal to buy. Such a situation is technically called a "buying signal." You must be quick to recognize this type of objection and try a close immediately. Words like "I suppose," "I wish I could," "it looks good," "if I could," "maybe I will," "I ought to," "perhaps I should," and others show you that the objection really means "Yes, I'll buy."

The prospect's tone of voice, facial expressions, and actions are also clues to a buying signal.

Notice the buying signals in the following remarks:

1

"Well, Mr. Salesman, I don't suppose I really *should* spend quite that much money."

2

"I *guess* it would be smart for me to wait till my partner gets back to town next week."

IDEA IN ACTION Harry Bryce sells motor boats. He is calling on a prospect who has listened to his presentation and has looked at photographs of various models of power craft.

The prospect is obviously tempted to make a decision in favor of one of the models, but has not expressed agreement on Harry's various trial closes.

"I'm sure you'll be very happy with this boat, Mr. Dodge," says Harry. "If you give me the order now, I can guarantee delivery within 30 days."

"I suppose I really should think it over for a bit," says Mr. Dodge.

Harry is elated. He is a seasoned salesman, who recognizes a buying signal when it is expressed. He knows that this sale is now "in the bag." For Harry notes that while his prospect's remark is in the form of an objection, it means "I'll buy."

Had Mr. Dodge really meant that he wanted to wait, he would have used slightly different words. He would have said, "I want to think it over." The difference in wording should be noted with care. What Mr. Dodge actually said was *qualified* by the words "I suppose."

Now, when a person says, "I *suppose* I should wait," he does not actually mean, "I definitely intend to wait."

The buying signal consists of more than *words*. Mr. Dodge's voice and facial expression also indicate that while he thinks he *should* wait, he'd rather *not*. Further, he has not put away the photo of the craft that tempts him; instead, he holds it in his hand and keeps looking at it with evident interest and desire.

¶ 7011 **What to do when the buying signal is flashed**

Why does the prospect use words that are almost in the form of an objection at the moment when he has just about decided to buy? The answer lies in the realm of psychology. In the example in ¶ 7010, the prospect knows that it would be wise to consider the matter. He is tempted to disregard the voice of wisdom. However, before doing so, he wants some *reassurance* that he is not doing the wrong thing.

Hence, his words really mean: "Mr. Salesman, you don't think I'm making a mistake, do you?"

⟫WHAT TO DO→ When a buying signal is flashed, you *must*

1. Instantly stop "selling," no matter if you are in the middle of a sentence; no matter if you have one or ten more points to make. No matter what you have planned to do, you must, when you are given a buying signal, *stop selling*.

2 Express, in a slow, matter-of-fact way, your reassurance that the prospect will *not* regret buying now. "I'm sure you'll never regret having settled this today," are words that you might well use. Such reassurance, spoken slowly and calmly, is all that is needed. You should follow up by writing up the order or with some other acknowledgement that the decision *has been made*.

⟫WARNING→ If you don't stop selling on a buying signal, you are pretty sure to lose the sale. The buyer isn't asking you for more reasons to buy; he merely wants reassurance.

Strong techniques for converting objections into sales

¶ 7021 **Lower the prospect's selling resistance with an *empathic* remark**

Before you try to answer an objection, put yourself in the shoes of the prospect. Doing that is called *empathy*. Say something that shows you understand how he feels, and then go on to answering the objection. Your *empathic* remark won't be an out-and-out agreement with the prospect, but it will have a softening effect on the prospect and will give you an easy lead into the solid answer to his point. A few examples will show you the type of remark that does the trick.

1

PROSPECT: "I'll talk it over with my wife."
SALESMAN: "Mr. Prospect, I'm a married man myself and I know how it is."
See ¶ 7131 for an answer to the objection.

2

PROSPECT: "I buy only from local merchants."
SALESMAN: "Certainly, madam, it is only natural to enjoy trading with your neighbors."

3

PROSPECT: "I hate to change. We've been buying from Jones & Company a long time."
SALESMAN: "Yes, we all hate to change. But we usually change if we can better ourselves, and when we know it is better to change, the sooner the better."

⫸RECOMMENDATION⟶ You may have to use this technique more than once in your sales talk. Therefore, you must gain facility in varying your empathic remark. Make a list of your own, say five such remarks, from your own vocabulary to suit the objections you encounter in selling your product or service. Memorize your list, and you will be able to draw upon it automatically for the right response.

¶ 7022 Convert the objection into a question

Think of every objection raised by a prospect as a *question* that you can answer, and not as an objection. You avoid the negative influence of the word "objection" and you build a positive attitude that inspires confidence.

Get your prospect, too, to think that he is raising a question, and not posing an objection, and you will put him in the frame of mind to listen for your answer.

▶ *Proof that objections are questions.* Let's look for the proof that every objection is really an unanswered question in the mind of the prospect. Here are some simple objections and the questions that they imply.

Your price is too high! *Question:* Will I get my money's worth for the price asked?
Your company is too small! *Question:* Will this salesman's company give me the kind of service I get from the bigger suppliers?
I can do without it. *Question:* What have I to gain by taking on this additional expenditure?

▶ *How to condition your mind to the positive attitude.* For each objection you encounter in your selling, find the question the objection implies and note in down in the "Answer Book" we recommend at ¶ 7048. Learn these answers by heart. You will thus train yourself in the technique of treating objections as questions.

▶ *How to condition your prospect to think he has a question and not an objection.* The prospect will begin to think that he has a question and not an objection by your leading him to that attitude.

⫸HOW TO DO IT⟶ 1. Agree with him that he has posed a "question."
PROSPECT: "Your company is too small for our account."
SALESMAN: "That does bring up a question. The question is, can our company give you the kind of service you get from the bigger companies. As a matter of fact, because we are smaller, our company's setup is made to order for you. Instead of being relegated to the status of a small account in a large company, your account would be one of the biggest in our shop. As such, you would be sure of all those many valuable services that you can only expect when you are sure of really personal attention." [Continues with convincing facts that convert the objection into the prospect's biggest reason for buying his product or service.]

2. Get the prospect to agree that the objection is really a question.
PROSPECT: "Your price is too high."
SALESMAN: "What you are really asking me, aren't you, is whether you are going to get your money's worth from these batteries."
PROSPECT: "Yes."

⫸OBSERVATION⟶ By saying "Yes" the prospect has invited the salesman to convince him that his batteries will outlast the ones he can get elsewhere for less money.

3. If the prospect does not agree with your question interpretation of his objection, get him to tell you what the question is. When you have done that, you have established in your prospect's mind that he has a question and not an objection.
PROSPECT: "We tried something like it a while ago; it didn't work."
SALESMAN: "You are really asking why my product will work if the other one didn't, aren't you?"

strong techniques for converting objections into sales

PROSPECT: "No, that is not the question."
SALESMAN: "Then what is the question?"

Every time you answer the question you have made of the objection, you must go right into a close.

¶ 7023 Make the objection the reason for buying

This is a technique to be used when you face the prospect's strongest objection. After you have given him an empathic response that softens his resistance, you take the very objection that he has raised and make it work for you as a reason to buy.

EXAMPLE 1: A prospect tells you he cannot afford your product. You show him that if he uses your product it will make more money for him. In other words, he cannot afford it now because he isn't using your product. Or you show him that if he uses your product it will reduce his costs of doing business and he'll have more money. His very reason for not buying becomes his reason for buying.

EXAMPLE 2: A prospect says he doesn't need your product because what he has has lasted a long time and it's still good. Show him that just because it has lasted a long time is the very reason for buying—it's toward the end of the life of some products that they begin to give maintenance trouble which adds to cost, or other kinds of trouble that impede production results.

EXAMPLE 3: PROSPECT: "We can't use your machines now. We're replacing about a third of our truck fleet."

SALESMAN: "I can't think of a better reason why you should install our machines right now. I can show you by simple arithmetic how you can write off a very sizable part of your investment in replacement, right in the next six months, from the new profits you're bound to make by stepping up your production. Here's the way I figure it—."

¶ 7024 Get the prospect to answer his own objections by asking "why"

Getting the prospect to answer his own objection is a technique employed by many powerful salesmen. Sometimes you can get the prospect to explain away his own objection by merely saying, "I wonder if you would mind telling me why." Other times you must raise the question more adroitly.

"Why" gets the prospect talking. It can't be used repeatedly with the same prospect, of course, but you can start off by asking "Why do you hesitate?" "Why do you believe it is too costly?" "Why do you want to wait until fall?" As you follow up his reply, you must vary the question until you have overcome his objection by asking—not telling.

▶ *Adroit questioning.* Here is an example of adroit questioning to overcome a prospect's objection to tying himself down to monthly payments over a period of years.

▶ **IDEA IN ACTION** Knowing that the prospect was anxious to buy an annuity to protect his family but objected to the "long haul" of future payments, the salesman said:

"Are you paying for a car?"
"Yes."
"How much time elapsed between the time you paid for your last car and the time you bought the new one you now have?"
"About the same, I guess."
"Well," said the salesman, "for most of us, buying automobiles is an endless procedure of payments. Still we never seem to get tired of them or let them bother us too much, do we?"
"I guess we don't seem to."
"That's right, and it just goes to prove that usually we'll carry out a contracted obligation, doesn't it?"
"Yes, I guess so."
"Now in this case you already have the obligation. This idea of ours is merely a contract which will carry it out. You are fortunate that you can buy security for your family on the installment plan."
"How much insurance are you proposing?" the prospect asked. "You know I recently bought a policy from another company. My application was originally for $5,000 but I cut it down to $1,000 because I was afraid I couldn't carry it."
"Does the amount make any difference as long as it is enough to do what you want done for your wife and little girl and you can put aside the deposit?"
"When you put it that way, I guess it doesn't."
The application was signed on the spot.

¶ 7025 Think creatively to get around an objection

In some lines of selling you can get around an objection with a concrete suggestion that gets the prospect thinking along entirely different lines. In other words, you let the prospect have his own way, but you show him how he can gain by following your constructive idea. The big-money salesmen in many fields are constantly getting around objections through creative thinking.

Notice at ¶ 3042 how a real estate salesman offered his prospect a new idea to overcome an objection, and thus made the sale.

¶ 7026 Mention an obstacle that doesn't exist in the buyer's mind

By getting the prospect to agree that a given point (or series of points) is, in fact, not an obstacle, the sale can often be expedited.

The purpose of raising the objection that you know is not a real objection in the buyer's mind is to get him to express the things he likes about what you are selling. Repetition of the points that are not obstacles can go far toward making the sale.

⟩⟩⟩OBSERVATION→ When you raise the objection yourself, you should be quite sure that the prospect is going to agree that he has no such objection. But even if the prospect doesn't agree, you can easily answer the objection because you have selected one that does not create a serious problem.

The following example demonstrates three keys to meeting objections successfully:

• Get the prospect to repeat what he likes about your product.

• Capitalize the objection that you yourself have purposely raised.

• Smoke out the hidden objection through raising non-existing objections.

IDEA IN ACTION Bill Graham is in the new car department of a popular automobile dealer. He has just given his sales talk to a prospective buyer, Mr. and Mrs. Smith, and has taken them for a demonstration ride. Now back in the showroom he is attempting to close the sale, but realizes that something is preventing them from making the final commitment.

Bill begins to raise "objections" by reiterating the sales points he has made, hoping to smoke out the hidden obstacle to the sale.

"Did you both feel the fast getaway power packed into that Jet-8 engine?" Mr. and Mrs. Smith agree. (Bill is strengthening his sales talk by getting them to agree.)

"And do you like the greater control and easier driving power that power-steering gives you?" Yes, they think that is fine.

"By the way, did I mention how easy it is to park in crowded city conditions with this one-finger control power-steering wheel?" (Now he is capitalizing on an objection he raised.)

Bill keeps trying. "And think of all the fun driving a brand new convertible is going to be with vacation time just around the corner." Here the couple hesitate. Bill knows they like the convertible but he sees a possible lead to their hesitation.

"How many children did you say you have, Mr. Smith?"

"Two; boy and girl," he replies.

"And Tommy's going into first grade next year," adds Mrs. Smith. (Bill has found the hidden objection.) Immediately he says, "Why, then, you want the safety-designed de luxe sedan with the new five-rib steel roof engineered for greater protection. It has safety grip handles, and door locks placed way up front out of the youngsters' reach. Let me show it to you."

The sale will be safely closed because Bill was skillful enough to raise objections he knew he could put to his own advantage.

¶ 7027 How to answer objections that have no real basis in fact

An objection that has no real basis in fact, whether it relates to the price or quality of your product, your company, or anything else, is the easiest to answer. All it requires is that you refute the objection by introducing facts and/or an explanation that removes the substance from the objection.

EXAMPLE: Wallace Bruno sells time for a television broadcasting station. His prospect turns down his offer on the ground that his rate is higher than that of a competitive broadcasting station. Wallace easily overcomes this objection by proving that, because of a larger audience, the cost *per person* in the audience is actually lower than the cost *per person* reached by his competitor.

▶ *Direct denial.* A direct denial is, of course, sometimes the only way to meet an objection that is not based on fact. For example, if a customer says that some of the parts of your machine are made of aluminum when actually they are made of stainless steel, you can be emphatic about setting him straight, without offending him.

▶ *Counterattack with facts.* When you run into a prospect who is inclined to keep raising objections about construction of your product, and other features, showing that he does not have the facts, you might let him talk himself out. Don't interrupt; don't object; don't argue; just listen. When he has finished, come back at him with a strong counterattack of *facts*, supported by *proof*.

⟶OBSERVATION⟶ A prospect who makes several assertions about your product or service that you know are contrary to fact, is giving evidence of his interest in your product. He may have gotten the misinformation from your competitor and his attitude may be that he is not going to let you put anything over on him. Recognize the need for answering and closing in the present interview before the competitor takes the sale away from you.

¶ 7028 Minimize objection when facts can't be refuted

In some cases, the most that the salesman can do, in view of the facts themselves, is to *minimize* the objection. Although this is less effective than *complete refutation*, it often serves to overcome objections. Thus, when times are uncertain, the salesman can minimize the condition by fighting fear with faith.

▶ **IDEA IN ACTION** A young man, hesitating to buy a policy, told the representative, "Times are too uncertain. Something is liable to happen and then I'll be stuck with the policy and have to let it lapse because I may not be able to pay the premium."

The agent said, "Well, *something* must be left to hope. You only have one premium to pay today, and for every future premium there is a whole year ahead in which to pay it. We must have faith that the years which require the future premiums will bring with them the necessary money. Almost every venture we make must have this element of faith in the future. Most of us marry without very much idea of how we are going to maintain a home and a family. We start on a business venture without seeing the whole road, but we have faith in the future. When we have courage the future usually justifies our faith. Shouldn't we be equally courageous in the purchase of life insurance?"

¶ 7029 Delaying the answer to a sincere objection

The key rule in answering objections is *first* to evade any obstacle raised by the prospect in an effort to find out whether the objection is real or just an excuse [¶ 7004]. You must discover quickly whether the objection is sincere, and answer immediately if it is. Otherwise your prospect might keep his mind on the objection until you answer and thus miss what you are saying. His mental fixation diverts his attention and you are the loser. He may even decide in his own mind that you can't answer him and thus begin to lose confidence in you. But sometimes delaying the answer may be the best procedure, and if handled skillfully can help to win the sale.

Here's your guide to delaying the answer to a sincere objection:

▶ *Momentary delay*. You are usually safe in delaying the answer to a sincere objection for a moment if you are in the midst of your presentation and you know you are going to answer the objection momentarily. In such cases tell your prospect that you are about to cover that point in a moment. Be sure you do cover it *in a moment*. Your purpose in delaying the answer briefly is to avoid breaking into the thought you are in the midst of developing.

▶ *Prolonged delay*. Suppose the prospect's interruption with an objection comes in the midst of your presentation and you don't expect to reach the question in a moment. You want to delay the answer because it can be covered most effectively as you logically proceed with your sales story. You feel that if you break in immediately to answer you will disturb the orderliness of your sales story and that you may lose control of the interview. In that case, frame your response along these lines:

• Agree that he has raised an interesting point.
• You intend to discuss it in connection with another feature of importance to him.
• You would like first, with his permission, to be sure that he is thoroughly familiar with the features just discussed that are vital to him.

Don't pause or wait for his permission; go right on from where you left off.

▶ *Delay in answering price objection*. Now suppose that early in the interview your prospect interrupts you with a price objection before you have given him the story of the merits of the product. Are you going to answer the price objection immediately, or put it off until you have covered the real selling points of the product or service? You know that you can prove the value of the product to him, if you can get him to listen to the sales story. Frame your response along these lines:

- Agree that price is important.
- You are certain that if the product doesn't provide the benefits it has given to hundreds of users (profit making, cost cutting, time saving, etc.) the prospect won't want it at any price.
- Let's look at what it will do for you, Mr. Prospect. Then proceed *immediately* to explain and demonstrate the value of the product to the prospect.

▶ *Delay to find the answer.* You must, of course, delay answering an objection when you don't have a ready, correct answer. Tell the prospect frankly that you don't know the answer, but that you will get it for him. Then be sure to carry through on your promise.

≫CAUTION→ Don't make the mistake of trumping up an answer if you don't know what it is. The fabrication won't fool your prospect; it will only antagonize him and lower his opinion of you.

¶ 7030 Mere excuses may be a sign to summarize

Mere excuses offered by a prospect after you have completed your presentation may mean that the prospect is interested, but that he merely has not had time to think over everything you have said. He isn't saying "No," and he isn't saying "Yes," but is stalling for time to weigh your offer and reach a decision.

This is a signal to you that your presentation must be made more clear-cut. Probably a good summary of your proposition is needed, with emphasis on the benefits the buyer will gain, a restatement of facts, and a review of the evidence. Testimonials and names of users of your product carry extra conviction at such times.

¶ 7031 Ask for the hidden objection when every sales effort has failed

After every sales effort has failed and you can think of no reason why the prospect does not buy, you might get a fighting chance to close the sale if you smoke out the key to your failure by asking the prospect directly why he has not bought.

▶ **IDEA IN ACTION** You have called on a prospect several times. Every call has strengthened your conviction that he stands to profit by your offering. You decide to use a direct question to get at the hidden objection. So you say:

"Mr. Stonewall, I have been calling on you for some time. I haven't sold you—but I think I can do you a service by selling you. You need my product. You're a difficult man to sell, because you never openly state your objections. Will you do this for me?

"If I'm going to be licked on this account, I'd like to know the reason why, because it'll teach me a valuable lesson in salesmanship. On the other hand, if you're not buying because of some objection you've failed to state plainly, will you tell it to me now and give me a sporting chance to answer it?"

¶ 7032 Look for the hidden obstacle when you lose a sale to a competitor

The technique of asking the prospect for the reason why he will not buy can be used profitably when you have lost a sale to a competitor. In finding out *why* the competitor beat you, you may discover much more than a hidden objection. Here's an example of what you might discover.

▶ **IDEA IN ACTION** Bill Daly was selling an electronically operated paper cutting machine. He had been working with a prospect whose plant could use two such machines. Bill expected to earn a sizable commission on the sale.

Everything went well with his presentation. He had the purchasing agent's full attention during two interview calls. When the prospect asked for a written proposal with full specifications, Bill felt quite sure that he would get the order on his third call back.

But on his next call he didn't get the order—because the order had been placed with a competitor! Bill was determined to find out why he lost the order. He wanted to know what his competitor did that he did not do, since he knew that the competitor did not have a superior product and could not offer any price advantage. The selling points of his product and the competitor's were the same—safety and speed. The construction differences in the two competing machines were really immaterial.

Here's what he discovered in a talk with the purchasing agent after he had lost the sale. *There was no hidden objection.* But the competitor's salesman had used **two important strate-**

gies that won him the order: (1) he had asked to meet the plant superintendent after he had told his selling story to the purchasing agent; (2) he had explained to the plant superintendent, an engineer, the technical ways in which the company had engineered the machine to acquire greater speed and safety (actually the machine was not superior in these respects).

By probing for the obstacle that lost the sale, Bill learned how to overcome the competition. He immediately improved his presentation and his strategy. In all future selling of the machines he made it a point to "sell" the plant manager as well as the purchasing agent. He gave more attention in his presentation to speed and safety. In the future, the purchasing agent would always be able to convince the factory people that the speed and safety of the machines were the best that could be had.

⫸IMPORTANT⟶ Always find out why competition got the business when you lose out to a competitor. Get the reasons out of hiding and you will be able to overcome them.

¶ 7033 **Techniques for handling a trade-in sale**

Trade-in allowances have a strong appeal to customers in some fields, such as automobiles, industrial machines, typewriters, household equipment like vacuum cleaners, refrigerators, electric stoves, and other items. If the product turned in has real trade-in value, because it can be repaired or reconditioned and sold, or sold as is, the trade-in allowance can be used to spur a sale; if it has little value, the problem is to keep the prospect's disappointment from hurting the sale.

▶ *Sell the new product first*. Even when a trade-in allowance helps close a sale, and certainly when the trade-in value in not significant, it is important to sell the new product first on its merits. Get the prospect's mind off the trade-in by assuring him that he will be allowed a fair value for the article he turns in, and proceed with your sales presentation.

⫸OBSERVATION⟶ In selling automobiles, for example, the salesman first finds out whether the prospect has a car to be traded in, gets the keys to the car, and turns the car over to the appraiser on location. Having thus gotten the old car out of the way, he goes about selling the new car with even greater emphasis on the values to be gotten from it.

▶ *How to handle the trade-in allowance*. After you have sold the customer on the merits of the replacement, use the trade-in allowance as an inducement to buy. Don't make the mistake of taking a quick look at the trade-in and offending your customer with derogatory remarks about its condition or its uselessness. Instead, try to get the prospect to tell you what he expects to receive for it. Before giving him *your* allowance figure, explain what must be done to make the article salable, if indeed it can be resold. Build up your customer's confidence in your fairness by being businesslike and dignified in your discussion of the trade-in allowance.

▶ *How to answer the objection that a better trade-in allowance can be obtained elsewhere.* Your prospect may actually have been offered a better trade-in allowance from one of your competitors, and he will quickly tell you so. You must then explain why your allowance is just as good, if not better, all things considered, than the higher offer. Your product is superior; it will have a bigger trade-in value eventually than the competing product; it will last longer; it will be more economical to maintain. In other words, you are really answering a price objection.

▶ *A way over the trade-in obstacle*. A trade-in allowance might present an obstacle in selling to an industrial user whose controller makes a careful economy study to justify a replacement. The trade-in allowance may be the decisive figure in the calculations that affect the capital recovery period (the length of time in which the investment must be recovered). When your prospect refuses to buy because the trade-in allowance is a problem in its amortization structure, and you can't give him as big an allowance as he wants, you can still win. You can do it by showing substantial savings in operating costs to be made with your equipment. The higher the savings, the shorter the recovery period. Thus, with convincing savings figures you have the ammunition for overcoming the trade-in problem.

▶ *Show economy of regular short-term trade-ins*. You may be able to convince your prospect that it is more economical for him to replace the equipment every few years than to hold on to old equipment until it has to be replaced. To do this, you must have the facts and figures that apply to your product. The key factor in some cases, that induces owners to replace old equipment with new, is the "expensive pair of hands" that uses the equipment—in other words, the high-salary cost as compared with the low-investment cost. A sample comparison used in the sale of typewriters is given at ¶ 7135. The computation given there shows the method of preparing the comparison.

The answer attitude that wins

¶ 7041 Sell 'old-hat' objections with new-profit answers

Use hard-hitting answers that reflect the buying picture of the 70's and you'll sell more buyers who attempt to stall you with old-hat objections.

Here's the picture: The profit squeeze is on. Your prospect is being pushed— and pushed hard—by his boss to make sure he's getting the best possible deal before he signs for an order.

⇒WHAT TO DO→ Handle objections— the ones you've heard time and time before— with this in mind: Today, each objection is the buyer's way of asking "Is this the best deal— and how can I justify this purchase?" Here are a few objections:

"Your price is too high". You have to use the same arguments—better quality, service and delivery—but the change is in the emphasis. Let's say you're selling a machine that costs $1,000 and has a life expectancy of 10 years.

1970's way: "Mr. Prospect, you're right when you say my machine costs more than the one the Jones Company sells. But look at it this way. Over a 10-year span, our machine will cost you $100 a year, or about $15 more a year than what you would pay our competitor. But, look at what your $15 will buy."

You then list the old standbys and conclude with "Now those benefits are worth a lot more than $15, aren't they?"

Result: If you've stacked the cards in your favor, you should get a "yes" answer and then the deal is just a signature away.

"Your company is too small." Your first impulse is to become a "name-dropper" and mention some of the top companies you're now servicing. Under normal circumstances, this is a powerful argument. But, remember the prospect is under pressure. That's why you should use the—

1970's way: "You're right, Mr. Smith, when you say we're small—but that's the big reason why you should buy from my company.

"It's a big reason if you're concerned about meeting deadlines and avoiding money-eating delays. Here's the point:

"Instead of being just another account, as you would be with one of the giants, you'll be Mr. Big with us. When you place an order, it will get VIP treatment. You won't have to alter your schedules waiting for a shipment."

Result: You've given your prospect the dollars and cents reason why he should buy from you and then you solidified your argument by showing him that he's in good company when he does business with you.

¶ 7042 Look upon objections as misconceptions

Prospects often make negative statements not because they don't want to buy or want to get rid of the salesman, but because they lack information or have some misconceptions about the product.

If you regard the prospect's negative statements as arising from his misunderstanding or misconceptions, you avoid becoming argumentative. This attitude also impels you to give the prospect proper information or more information to correct his viewpoint.

¶ 7043 Answer objections without arguing

When objections are raised, the skillful salesman differs with his prospect without being blunt or brusque. He does not argue or invite an argument, knowing that to win an argument is often the way to lose a sale. He schools himself to soothe, rather than ruffle, the other person's feelings at every point, but especially at those points where a difference of opinion must be resolved.

▶ **IDEA IN ACTION** Elmer Holsman sells a well known home encyclopedia. This is not an easy selling assignment, since an order represents a commitment of several hundred dollars. The sale is usually made to both husband and wife and each interview is likely to bring its full share of resistance.

"You have a nice set of books there," says Prospect Jones, "but our own encyclopedia is only 10 years old, and we're quite satisfied with it."

Now Elmer doesn't agree with that conclusion. Were he a less tactful salesman, he would express this disagreement along the following lines:

"Now, Mr. Jones, you seem to think that because the paper and the binding of your old set are almost as good as new that you've got a good source of information Actually your books are quite out of date, and you can prove this to yourself by looking at the headlines in this evening's newspaper and then trying to run down the information about places and events in the news in your 10-year old books!"

But Elmer knows better than to talk that way. So he frames his rebuttal more tactfully.

"Mr. Jones," says Elmer, "I know exactly how you feel. You have a very fine encyclopedia, and I can see it's in excellent condition.

"You may wonder, Mr. Jones, why many people, who have a set just like your own decide to replace it with the edition you and I have been talking about. The answer is really quite simple. These people tell me that in the majority of cases when they turn to their encyclopedia, it isn't just for casual reading but because something specific has turned up on which they want up-to-date information.

"I'm quite certain, Mr. Jones, that if someone were to offer to trade you a twenty-year old encyclopedia for your *own* set, giving you, say, $25 in addition, you'd turn it down. That extra 10 years that *your* set covers makes quite a difference.

"But let's look at it this way," continues Elmer, turning to the lady of the house. "I think you told me, Mrs. Jones, that you have a daughter 14 years old and a son who is almost 12."

"That's right."

"Well, modern education, as you of course know, emphasizes discussion and study of *current events*. I'm sure that both of your children frequently look things up in the encyclopedia. If they don't find what they need for their special purpose, not only do they find that their classmates have better reports, but they may actually lose their interest in doing research, which will become more and more important as they get further on in school."

Instead of challenging his prospect to prove whether his present material would help him understand today's headlines, the salesman painted a picture of years of benefit and advantage to the two children in the family.

¶ 7044 **Be tactful in meeting objections**

In a sales interview it is normal for the salesman to emphasize reasons why the buyer should *buy,* and for the buyer to stress reasons why he hesitates to buy or even why he should not buy.

If the sale is to be made, the salesman must succeed in either convincing or persuading the buyer that each of his objections to buying is overruled by some reason or fact. The process of answering objections presents many moments when the salesman must reply forcefully and still avoid overstepping the bounds of tact.

 IDEA IN ACTION Ralph Blount sells a moving and storage service. His calls are based on leads that have come in by telephone.

Ralph works on straight commission, and each sale he succeeds in making means an important addition to his weekly commission check.

This fact, plus the fact that his is a highly competitive business, has been responsible for Ralph's gradual adoption of an unfortunate mannerism. The double tension he works under has put him on the defensive, and his reaction is a gruff sort of aggressiveness that is displayed in tactless remarks.

"We can do the whole moving job for you for $110, lady," says Ralph.

"Isn't that a little high for such a short move?" counters his prospect.

"Well, you might get somebody else to do it for a little less, but don't blame us if some of the stuff gets broken."

The answer is tactless and does not make the sale. Ralph should be equipped to answer the objection to price with reasons like those given at ¶ 7062. If he were so prepared, he would not be put on the defensive by the combination of high stakes plus stiff competition.

¶ 7045 **Protect the ego of your prospect**

Don't argue; be tactful! If both of these commands are obeyed, there is little danger of losing ground by offending the prospect's ego. But in some situations, you must be particularly careful to protect the listener's ego; even to build it up.

Take the case, for example, of the prospect who made a bad purchase in the past and is now objecting to buying your product because it reminds him of the one he was stuck with. You find out from him what happened and you see that he made mistakes in judgment. Any reference by you to his poor judgment, or telling him how he might have avoided the mistake, will do you no good. Reminding the prospect of his shortcomings is the surest way to lose a sale, no matter how right or logical you may be.

Under such circumstances, you should win the customer's goodwill by building up his confidence and pride. One way would be to tell him an interesting story of how some well-known person experienced adversity through an error of judgment and used the lesson of this very mistake to build an extraordinarily successful business. Then go on to point out what the prospect now knows about buying such a product as yours.

¶ 7046 **Consider the temperament of the prospect in answering objections**

Every good salesman is sensitive to the temperament and mood of his prospect and takes all circumstances into account in answering his objections. Here's an example of suiting a reply to one type of temperamental prospect—the opinionated person.

A prospect who is cocksure of himself considers it almost a disgrace to reverse an opinion once he has expressed it. In answering objections raised by this type of person, you must be careful never to put him in the position of having to modify his opinion because of something *you* said. Instead, you must make it appear that he has changed his mind because of his own superior judgment. Below in a case that illustrates how a skillful salesman accomplishes this feat.

▶ **IDEA IN ACTION** Bob Reynolds, a real estate broker specializing in office space, learns that the Smith Company is seeking new quarters in a suburb of Chicago. Bob knows of space that seems entirely suitable, at 100 Main Street, and calls on Mr. Edgecomb of the Smith Company to try to arrange a lease.

After listening to Bob's proposal, Edgecomb turns it down in no uncertain terms.

"We wouldn't think of going into that section," he says. "Why, nobody in any business similar to ours is located within several blocks of that address! No sir, not a chance! Let me know if something really good turns up."

Bob could easily disprove his prospect's contention then and there. But as a smart salesman he knows that a more delicate approach is needed in such a case. So he says, "Well, you know exactly what you want, Mr. Edgecomb, and my job is to try to find it for you. It would be very helpful if you would tell me the types of companies who would occupy offices in a building that you *would* consider."

"Why," replies Edgecomb, a bit pompously, "dignified firms—first-class legal firms, or architects, or insurance companies—people of *that* sort. See what I mean?"

Bob proceeds with care at that point. "Isn't that a coincidence," he says, with a disarming smile, "that you should mention an insurance company! I know you're not interested in 100 Main Street, Mr. Edgecomb, but when you mentioned an insurance company—well, let me make sure now—I have a list of all the tenants at 100 Main—and if I'm not mistaken . . "

Bob takes the tenant list from his briefcase and reads off a name here and there. "Wilcox & Bannigan, the big law firm—Corrigan & Corrigan, the architects who get most of the big deals—oh yes, here it is, Star State Insurance Company!

"I thought they were at 100 Main. Well, I'll go over some tenant lists for other buildings, and call you when I've found something interesting."

"Does Star State have *offices* there, or only a small agency?" cagily inquired Edgecomb.

"Well, they have the entire sixth floor," replies Bob. "Here, Mr. Edgecomb, let me leave this tenant list with you—it tells who's there, what space they occupy, and so on."

When Bob telephones in a day or two to suggest another building, he is not at all surprised to hear, "You know, I happened to be in 88 Main yesterday, and I went over to 100. That building has changed a lot in the last couple of years, hasn't it? I might just take a quick look at the premises you mentioned—just to make sure."

Bob has handled an opinionated prospect in just the right way.

¶ 7047 **Don't waste time on hopeless objections**

You were advised at ¶ 4003 to make advance preparations before you meet the prospect, and get as much information about him as you can. That's usually your assurance that you are approaching a live prospect. But sometimes the prospect is really not a prospect for your product for a reason that you cannot overcome. In that case, leave the prospect immediately, in a friendly way. Don't waste time on him.

EXAMPLE: You are selling stainless steel valves that are designed for corrosive, hard-to-handle fluids. Your prospect is a chemical company. In your interview you discover that the prospect uses only dry chemicals. He has no need for valves. This is a hopeless objection—one you cannot answer.

⇒**OBSERVATION**→ Such an experience should caution you to find out the manufacturing process of the prospect in advance, if possible.

answer guide to specific objections

>>>CAUTION→ Be absolutely sure that the objection is hopeless.

¶ 7048 Make up a personal "Answer Book"

How are you going to benefit immediately and permanently by the techniques explained in this section for making objections work for you?

Do you remember your old school books with their "drill exercises" at the end of each lesson? They were put there because drill is a necessary part of instruction in any art or branch of knowledge.

We strongly recommend, therefore, that you get up your own "Answer Book" to develop facility in answering objections the way top-notch salesmen do.

>>>WHAT TO DO→ 1. Get a loose-leaf binder and list on a separate sheet each objection you are likely to meet in your particular selling job.

2. On each sheet, write the question the objection implies [¶ 7002], and how you will get the prospect to agree that he has really raised a question.

3. Write in the answer to the question, which is really the answer to the objection.

4. Then write: "I am glad you brought that up, Mr. Prospect. It gives me the opportunity to tell you some very important things that make my case stronger." Vary this remark from page to page so that you have a number of different ways of leading into the remark that will capitalize the objection [¶ 7007].

5. Write in the capitalizing statement that strengthens your story, gives you a chance to bring in testimonials, lets you summarize the reasons why the prospect should use your product, and so on.

6. *Now study your "Answer Book"* until you know it by heart.

Your Answer Book can become your most valuable tool for increasing your earnings. Add more pages as you run into unexpected resistances that need solving just as you solved the expected objections. Don't hesitate to change a page when you have found through experience a better way to overcome an objection. Keep up the drill by reviewing your Answer Book regularly.

>>>WHAT TO DO→ Prepare the blank pages of your answer book with these side headings to be sure that you cover each of the five points mentioned:

1. Objection.
2. Question implied by objection.
3. Answer to question or objection.
4. Lead-in to capitalizing.
5. Capitalizing statement.

>>>COMMENT→ The answer book is desirable even though you have smoothly worked into your presentation the objections you commonly meet and your answers to them. In your selling experience you may run into other objections that you feel should be anticipated because they come up often. When that happens, you will want to change your presentation to cover the omission. At such times your answer book is your reference source for working up the strongest handling of the objection in the step-by-step presentation of your sales story.

Answer guide to specific objections

¶ 7061 How to use the Answer Guide

To help you reach your greatest power in converting objections into sales, two special aids are given here: (1) The objections you will usually run into and how you can build the strongest answer to overcome them; (2) live examples of tested answers to the most important objections.

>>>REMEMBER→ The live examples were used by actual salesmen. Because they are only excerpts from a selling effort, they cannot always show how the salesman applied the four key rules in overcoming objections [¶ 7002]. Nor can they demonstrate all of the techniques given at ¶ 7021 et seq. However, the various techniques have been adequately illustrated in the text.

Use the aids in this section as follows: Look through the paragraph immediately following the objection and select the items that apply to your product or service. The ones you select will have to be fully developed to make the most of them for your particular product. Then read over the live examples

---

Acknowledgment is made to Michael Gore, Advertising, Merchandising, and Sales Promotion Consultant, and founder of *The American Salesman*, for many of the live answers to objections that are included in this Section.

to find ideas and language to strengthen your response. Test your answer against the principles in ¶ 7002 et seq. to be sure you have made the best use of the guidance given there.

"Your price is too high"

¶ 7062 **Reasons on which to build a strong answer to price objection**

1. The price is justified by quality of materials, superior workmanship, design, construction, durability, built-in conveniences, etc.

2. Price is relative. Your price is actually lower than your competitor's when economies of operation, quality, and service are considered.

3. Your company could produce a lower-priced product, but experience shows that this is the product that gives complete satisfaction.

4. An inexpensive product costs more in complaints, mishaps, breakdowns, etc.

5. When selling to a dealer: higher-priced products are prestige builders for the dealer; also there's more profit in it for him; national advertising of your company helps the dealer sell your product; an inexpensive product costs more in loss of customers and in customer dissatisfaction.

6. High-grade performance is what the customer is buying. It is the result of years of experience and specialized "know-how".

7. Your company produces at the lowest possible cost and sells at a fair price.

8. If a less expensive method of production were developed, your company would be the first to apply it.

See ¶ 5071 et seq. for treatment of price in the presentation.

¶ 7063 ⟫Live example→ **Capitalize the objection by showing your volume of sales**

PROSPECT: "Your price is too high."

SALESMAN: "Yes, we are the highest-priced in our field, yet we do six million dollars a year at these same prices. We couldn't do that if our values weren't mighty fine, could we?"

¶ 7064 ⟫Live example→ **Capitalize what your competitor can't — beat price with proof**

SALESMAN: "All right, Mr. Prospect, here's a list of our users right in this city who are now operating pumps which have pumped more than two million gallons of gasoline with practically no repair costs. These pumps are still in splendid condition, and they require only normal care. Now I suggest that you take this list of names and addresses and go to see these pumps. Give them a careful inspection. Then ask the other company if they can furnish you with such a list. They can't do it. Their pumps will not stand up."

¶ 7065 ⟫Live example→ **Be ready with exclusive features when prospect wants to shop for better price**

Ken Morgan sells electric motors and related supplies and equipment to large industrial plants.

"Mr. Morgan," says one of his customers, "which size transformer do you suggest we install in our new heat treating department?"

Ken reaches for the catalog issued by the ABC Transformer Company. "Here are the capacities, Mr. Young, of all the units manufactured by the ABC Company. Let's see—they're on page 6."

"Well," says Young, "model 69BB seems to fit our needs. How much does it weigh?"

Ken replies, "I'll tell you in a second. Weight and other specifications for model 69BB—yes, here they are—on page 54."

"Fine," says Young. "That gives me the picture on the ABC product. But they're a bit higher priced than some other manufacturers, aren't they? Guess I'll have to look around before deciding."

But Ken is prepared for this, too. "Mr. Young," he replies, "ABC has several exclusive features that I think you ought to consider." Here Ken produces a circular furnished by the manufacturer. It not only pictures one of their typical units, but also lists two special features that Ken has referred to. Further, there is a copy of the guarantee that backs up every one of their units, and a list of big company users.

Mr. Young examines this with some care. He is obviously impressed. Finally, he says, "Well, Mr. Morgan, I guess this is the transformer we should buy, even if it does cost a bit more."

¶ 7066 **How to get customers to accept higher costs for special orders**

You can keep your customers and new prospects ready to buy special orders even when you have to charge them more for such orders. Just make sure you have the facts on why your company must tack on a boost.

Here are three typical special order require-

answer guide to specific objections

ments and successful ways to justify the higher prices.

Tell why earlier delivery will cost more. Remind your customer that if he must have the goods sooner than usual, your company will run into any one, or all, of the following problems:

- The order won't fit into the production schedule your company has set up on the item;
- Overtime work will be needed to get the order out on a rush basis;
- Running off the item ahead of schedule will call for a special machine setup thus adding to our production costs.

Tell why a special finish will cost more. Let your prospect know you'll be glad to furnish the item finished any way he wishes, but that changing from the standard could turn up costs because your company doesn't have the right equipment to apply the finish he wants

This means that your company will have to either buy new equipment for the job or subcontract the work. Either way, you'll run into increased costs. But by assuring the prospect that neither you nor your company will make any extra profit from the additional costs could give him the added incentive to place that special order.

Tell why a smaller quantity will cost more. Explain to the customer that although he is free to buy just a small quantity of an item, his cost per unit will naturally run higher because—

- The small order does not qualify for a high discount;
- A small order requires special packaging which might add to the cost;
- Your company's overhead expenses are the same for each order—whether large or small.

⟫WHAT TO DO→ Inform the customer in advance the reasons why it's going to cost him more. When you take a special order, this fair-play approach will take the sting out of the higher price and help avoid a cancellation.

¶ 7067 ⟫Live example→ **Plead guilty to high price and sell him**

SALESMAN: "Yes, my price *is* too high—if you're thinking of the $1.98 customer. Our product, frankly, isn't manufactured for that market. For the $3.50 customer who walks into your store, this lamp is the biggest eyeful of value you could possibly offer him. In fact, wherever this number has been set up alongside the $1.98 item, it actually has sold better than when displayed without that competition. The comparison is so striking that customers don't hesitate to pay the difference. Why should you? Incidentally, the $3.50 market must be growing like wildfire, because last month alone we doubled our volume of the same month a year ago."

¶ 7068 ⟫Live example→ **Use prospect's own slogans to meet prime objection**

An advertising agency client found himself on the point of okaying a fairly big job when he wavered, venturing that the price seemed rather high.

SALESMAN: "Very well, I can cut corners here and there and probably get the work done at a lower figure. But I like to feel, as you do, (and here he casually pointed to the slogan on his firm's own calendar) that 'quality is remembered long after price is forgotten.' Two or three months from now, the important thing with you will be not whether this job could have been cheapened by forty or fifty dollars, but whether I put everything into it that would bring you the most business possible. Don't you really think so?"

⟫SUGGESTION→ Look into your customer's own advertising and sales literature and the chances are you'll find words of his own to counteract the price objection.

¶ 7069 ⟫Live example→ **Make your higher price an asset**

If your price is a selling liability, make it an asset. Let Lyle Straight tell you how standard-brand products (oil burners, in his case) get across the price objection.

"In our line of business, we are forced to meet the competition of numberless oil burner companies which have rushed into the market with a hastily made burner. They depend on price alone for their sales.

"When a buyer or prospect comes to us, one who has been considering the cheap burners, I do not try to conceal the fact that ours is higher in price. Rather, I make it a selling point, instead of trying to dodge the issue. First, I explain the heater and give a demonstration. Then I concentrate on the reputation, the financial responsibility and the standing of our house.

" 'There are a lot of oil burner companies that are making burners in one corner of their plant.

There are other companies who have organized hastily, and are turning out an inferior product to meet a price. Now, remember, when you buy a burner you are letting yourself in for a lot of expense, if you buy the wrong burner. We have the financial responsibility to guarantee the proper service.

" 'Here is a list of users who bought cheap burners and had to throw them out. They have spent their money and today they haven't the money *or* the burner either. You'll probably buy our make sooner or later. Why not get it now and save that extra expense of having to throw out a burner that won't heat your house? Remember, it is heat and comfort and economy of operation you are buying, not just some sort of machine to put in your basement and forget about.' "

¶ 7070 ⟫Live example⟶ **Prospect's own products are not the cheapest**

PROSPECT: "No, I simply won't pay any such price. Why, I can beat that by 15 per cent."

SALESMAN: "Mr. Prospect, it wasn't my impression that your products are the very cheapest in your field. Was I wrong?"

⟫OBSERVATION⟶ Nine times out of ten that does it. For 90% of the people you call on, whether manufacturers, doctors, merchants, or others, do not operate on a single "I'm the cheapest in town" appeal. And what's equally important, they really know that price is meaningless when it is considered apart from quality. All you have to do is to tell them in the fewest possible words that you know they know it!

"I can get a similar product for a considerably lower price."

¶ 7071 **Reasons on which to build a strong answer to the "similar at lower price" objection**

1. The two products may look the same but they are very different in quality and performance. Supply the facts that prove there's a difference.

2. Account for differences in the special advantages offered by your company—a guarantee, better service, easier terms, reputation for reliability, etc.

3. Use reasons given in ¶ 7062 to answer price objection generally.

¶ 7072 ⟫Live example⟶ **Lose the argument —win the sale**

PROSPECT: "Why, I can get these goods from So-and-So for 50¢ a gross less than you're quoting me."

SALESMAN: "Probably so. I wouldn't argue that point with you for a minute. Mr. So-and-So is much better qualified than I am to tell you exactly what his goods are worth. But I do know what my goods are worth and I know that at the price I've quoted they'll be a better buy than anything else you can get, no matter what the price. Of course, you can get more expensive goods than ours and you can get stuff a lot cheaper, but for your purpose ours is the best buy because . . ."

¶ 7073 ⟫Live example⟶ **Compete on merit, not price**

PROSPECT: "I can buy the same line for a good deal less from X Company."

SALESMAN: "My house knows that line; but we don't make it. No doubt, if we did, our price would be as low as theirs. On the other hand, if the X Company made our line, *maybe* their prices would have to be as high as ours. You've got to figure my product, its sales appeal to your trade, and decide if my product—and only my product—pays you the profit you've a right to make. We don't compete in price. If we did, there'd be no bottom. But we do compete on the merits of our products; and if price, which sets profits, were the all-dominating reason to guide your purchases so as to insure satisfactory sales, then the lowest-priced product would be your best-selling product. And that isn't true, is it?"

The prospect wants a lower price or extra discount

¶ 7074 **How to deal with a bargainer**

1. Tell him that you don't cut prices nor does your company. Then sell him on the merits and quality of your product.

2. Use the *fair play* argument. The prospect would not himself cut the price of the product he sells, so why does he expect you to?

3. Point out that if you reduce your price your prospect would feel that you are reducing prices for other customers, and maybe giving them an even better deal.

⟫OBSERVATION⟶ The salesman who sticks to his price and terms is bound to gain the respect of the prospect. He may not get the order the day he refuses to lower his price, but the next time he calls on the prospect there'll be no play for a cut or special treatment, and the order will be won on merit.

¶ 7075 ⟫Live example⟶ **Stand pat on price**

A produce firm was in the market for two tractors. Bill Burton submitted his price, and so did his competition. Not long after, Bill was told by the prospect that his competition had submitted a new price on the tractors. Since the new competitive price was considerably lower than the first quotation, the prospect wanted to give Bill the same opportunity to lower his bid.

Here's how Bill handled the situation: He reminded the firm that in the beginning he had been asked to offer his best price. "That's exactly what I've given you," Bill said. "Consequently, even if I could cut the price now, I wouldn't—you'd no longer have any faith in me or the Company. After all," Bill went on, "you can't expect to do business with a man if you don't trust him —and you can hardly trust him if he doesn't keep his word."

Bill concluded by reminding the prospect once again that he had submitted his best price initially and that he would stand on that price.

Apparently, his explanation struck a responsive chord, because the prospect gave Bill an order.

¶ 7076 ⟫Live example→ **Play on his vanity and hold to your price**

PROSPECT: "No sale unless I get an extra 5%."
SALESMAN: "Mr. Dealer, I haven't been selling half as long as you have been buying these goods. I know that I'd be no match for the average merchant I call on. They know the market at least as well as I do. I also know that you are a darned good judge of values yourself so that you would know in a minute if I added a single nickel to the rock-bottom price for which these goods can be sold. I figure prices down to the last penny in the first place and let it go at that."

¶ 7077 ⟫Live example→ **How to handle the discount hog**

W. L. Barnhart, late Vice-President of National Surety, used to tell how one of his men would handle the customer who always thought the price too high.

"Sometimes," said Barnhart, "the reason for the price problem is that the buyer thinks he should be able to get a special price or discount of some sort. In the early days of adding machine selling, the buyers were not so accustomed to having printed prices mean exactly what they said. Everybody wanted a special discount over the advertised price, which was then $375.00 for one particular machine.

"One salesman, encountering this objection, went around to a dozen or more of his leading customers, banks and the largest businesses in town, and got them to give him the cancelled checks they had given in purchasing their adding machines. Then he used these actual checks in demonstrating his machine, adding them up on a slip while the prospect watched over his shoulder.

"Thus, in one demonstration, the salesman showed each prospect that a dozen or more of the biggest business houses in town had bought and that they had all paid full price for their adding machines."

"Your credit terms are too tough"

¶ 7078 **How to meet the objection against credit terms**

1. Judge whether the prospect is sincere or merely using the credit terms as an excuse.
2. Defend your credit terms as standard in the trade.
3. Ask the prospect to suggest acceptable terms.

¶ 7079 ⟫Live example→ **Ask what terms are acceptable**

PROSPECT: "Your company's credit terms are too tough."
SALESMAN: "Actually, our terms are just about standard with the rest of the industry. However, if you tell me now just what terms you feel would better suit your situation, I'm sure that my company will accept any reasonable proposition."

"We have a lower bid from your competitor"

¶ 7080 **How to meet the "lower bid" or "better deal" objection**

1. Ask to see the specifications on which the competitor made his bid. You want to be sure that there has been no misunderstanding of some of the requirements, that competitor's bid is on the same quantities and quality of material as yours.
2. Ask for the details of the proposition, then point by point clarify why your deal is as good as, if not better than, the competitor's.
3. Resell on quality, performance, low cost of maintenance, service, reputation of your firm for giving customer satisfaction, and so on.
4. Use reasons given in ¶ 7062 to answer price objection generally.
5. Assure the prospect that you can give him as good a deal as the competitor because you have been doing that for years.

"I can't afford it"

¶ 7081 **How to overcome the "I can't afford it" objection**

1. Use the objection as the reason for

buying, if what you are offering has money-saving advantages.

2. Present a proposition that makes it possible for the prospect to buy, like easy terms, partial payments, trade-in, if you can legitimately do this.

≫REMEMBER→ You can't earn big commissions by selling to persons who really can't afford to buy your product. A salesman who is aiming to get into high-bracket income will by-pass the financially insecure prospect and concentrate on full-potential prospects.

¶ 7082   ≫Live example→   It's the reason for buying

PROSPECT: "I can't afford it."
SALESMAN: "Mr. Jones, I'm glad you mentioned that, because one of the big features of our equipment is the money it saves you, from the very first minute you install it."

¶ 7083   ≫Live example→   Itemization of daily expenses proves a convincing argument when prospect "can't afford it"

Quite often when a prospect says that he cannot afford to make a purchase it is because he has not analyzed his assets correctly. The following argument presented by a life insurance salesman showed the prospect how his income was being spent and the advantage of putting aside something for himself.

SALESMAN: "Mr. Prospect, when you are paying your bills every month, does it ever seem to you as if you are working for everyone but yourself? Now these figures are not absolute, but in general they are probably pretty close. Let us assume that a man has received his check for the month and that he is writing out checks to pay his bills.

- 8 days' pay is going to the grocer, butcher, milkman.
- 8 days' pay is going for rent, light, heat.
- 3 days' pay is going to doctors and dentists and professional men.
- 4 days' pay is going for clothing.
- 4 days' pay is going for cigarettes, movies, golf and luxuries.
- 3 days' pay is going for the automobile.

"If you will add these up, you will find that 30 days' income is used and if you are lucky and the month has 31 days, this extra day's income you may save for yourself.

"Now my thought is this: Instead of working for all these other people, pay the one who is making all of this possible. **Pay yourself first.** There must be a figure between $1 and $15 that you feel you should be putting away each week for yourself."

¶ 7084   ≫Live example→   Ask for a time payment proposition

PROSPECT: "I can't afford one now."
SALESMAN: "Well, what sort of a time payment proposition would you like? Your old machine deteriorates and loses trade-in value, so you might really save money by buying now on satisfactory terms."

¶ 7085   ≫Live example→   Get a delivery date

PROSPECT: "I have no money now."
SALESMAN: "That doesn't matter. Tell me exactly when you expect to be ready for it and I'll put the order through for any date you say. All you have to do now is let me have a small deposit and tell me which of these two colors you prefer."

"My budget doesn't leave room for the expenditure"

¶ 7086   Reasons on which to build a strong answer to the "no room in the budget" objection

1. The prospect is always ready to save money; delay in savings is the same as adding to costs. Show specifically how the savings are made and total them up, mathematically, to show that they come to more than the expenditure.

2. The prospect is always ready to make more profits on his sales and delay means a loss of profits. Show specifically how the profits mount through faster turnover or larger mark-ups than on other items he sells.

¶ 7087   ≫Live example→   Figure the savings

Dan White, who sells office equipment, called on a firm that was at the tail end of its budget year. Consequently they were hesitant to go into any capital expenditure. Dan's customer was using two units of a particular model which kept up with their demands for two weeks of the month. However, the other two weeks would be hectic and involve three hours a night overtime on the part of two operators. In making a survey, he found that a net saving of $80 could be realized if production could be increased to eliminate overtime costs. A demonstration of the machine he recommended, with a selling proposal, closed the deal.

Dan correctly concludes that in spite of a so-called shortage of funds a company can find the

answer guide to specific objections

money if the salesman has a sound proposition and follows the steps of a sale.

"I'll think it over"

¶ 7088 **Ways to get the procrastinator to act now**

1. Ask "why." It may bring out a hidden objection or resolve the prospect's uncertainties.

2. Show him what he can gain by an immediate decision. Make him feel the penalty of postponement. Perhaps he'll be entitled to a special discount if he buys now; or will get delivery in time to meet the initial demand that is sure to arise from a national campaign your company is launching; or prices may be slated to go up. At any rate, quicker enjoyment of the product's benefits will be gained by an immediate decision.

3. Ignore the remark and proceed with your strong selling points, dramatizing savings and other gains.

4. Indicate that your prospect now knows all he has to know about the value of the product; you are right there now to answer any specific questions.

5. When you sense that the prospect is sincere and not just looking for an "out," tell him you understand how important the decision is to him, and summarize the benefits of your product. Then make an appointment immediately for a call-back. Leave him something to remember you by. Possibly arrange to come back with someone; bringing a "specialist" to the next interview might give you the psychological edge for making the sale.

6. Ask him what you can do for him when he says he'll think it over. He might be looking for some special inducement.

7. Suggest that you'll put off seeing someone else to whom you were going to make a similar offer. The rivalry might stimulate him to decide now.

8. Leave the product with him for a trial period, if possible, or make use of your guarantee.

⟫⟫OBSERVATION 1→ When a business recession is changing to recovery, buyers in lines of business that are slow to feel the improvement will tend to put off buying until their own business has turned the corner. They need reassurance that the recovery is real. Salesmen can give this reassurance by quoting current economic data published in a recognized business service or in the press.

⟫⟫OBSERVATION 2→ The procrastinator who puts off a buying decision because he doesn't like the way things look in Washington, Europe, or somewhere else in the world, has to be shown that the future is usually unpredictable. For example, in 1928 and 1929 optimism ran high, and few people predicted a depression. In 1931 and 1932, we had just the opposite situation. And after World War II almost all the "experts" predicted a postwar decline and we actually had a boom.

¶ 7089 ⟫⟫Live example→ **Make prospect see why he can decide now**

A. F. Tripp recites a typical sequence in which a prospect begins by agreeing that the insurance policy described sounds worthwhile, but ends with "I'll think it over. Call back in a week."

SALESMAN: "Aren't there just two things to think about: (1) Do you need it and (2) Can you pay for it?"
PROSPECT: "I guess you're right."
SALESMAN: "You know just as well *now* as you will next week whether you need it or not, don't you?"
PROSPECT: "Yes."
SALESMAN: "And don't you know just as well *now* as you would a week from now whether or not you can pay for it?"

The prospect, in most cases, admits he does—and the case is closed.

¶ 7090 ⟫⟫Live example→ **The power of the "why" over the procrastinator**

Elmer Wheeler, America's dynamic master of "Sizzlemanship," declares that the hardest question for a wavering prospect to answer is the simple word *why*. The prospect will struggle to answer your "why," says Wheeler. He will find it difficult to put his objection into suitable words. His vague, distant, hidden objection is often so imaginary it *can't* be framed in words. For instance, observe this example:

PROSPECT: "I'll think it over."
SALESMAN: "Why?"
PROSPECT: "Well, I—it just seems best."

⟫⟫COMMENTS→ By using this rule of "why" you gradually bring out all the objections of the prospect. Soon all the questions seem answered—but still the prospect won't buy. *One key objection* still worries the prospect. What is it? Cost? Weight? Construction? Practicability? Can't realize the need? Feels another has better features?

Keep using the word "why"!

SALESMAN: Is that your ONLY reason for not buying?

PROSPECT: Yes, that's my only reason for not buying.

→COMMENT→ The prospect has committed himself! He is behind *one* objection! Now answer this key objection, and the sale will soon be yours. When you do answer the objection, be sure to say: "You told me that was your *only reason* for not buying—so now I imagine you are ready to have me make delivery."

¶ 7091. →Live example→ **Show what it costs to delay decision**

PROSPECT: "I'll think it over."

SALESMAN: "The last time I was here I sold Browne, across the street, one of our machines. That was three months ago. This morning he told me that it had saved him over $600 since he had it. At that rate, every month you spend in thinking it over costs you $200.

¶ 7092 →Live example→ **Ask him if he's delaying his own sales**

PROSPECT: "I'll wait and see how the election turns out."

SALESMAN: "Well, Mr. Richards, if that's your only reason for not buying now, let me ask you a question. Are your own customers waiting to see how the elections turn out before sending you any more business? No, they're not! In fact, last week's nationwide business index shows a slight increase over the week before. Are you laying off your sales force until you see how the elections turn out? Of course not! If you did, you might as well close up shop for the next six months and take a vacation till November rolls around. Besides, with steel prices going up as they are, you'll certainly have to pay a lot more for this equipment after the election. Why not save money and start realizing profits—right now?"

¶ 7093 →Live example→ **Get him to listen a little longer**

PROSPECT: "I'll let you know later."

SALESMAN: "Mr. Prospect, I am glad you want to think this over. You don't buy this kind of service very often and I can see that you are careful in making decisions. That's the kind of customers we like; they appreciate our careful workmanship. Now, if you will give me a few more minutes of your time I'll show you how you can make your work a lot easier immediately and you won't have to bother to let me know later."

→COMMENT→ With a little pleasant persuasiveness you may be able to get your prospect to listen a little longer while you bring out an advantage that will make him act immediately.

¶ 7094 →Live example→ **Get action—now —from a prospect who is "in no hurry"**

PROSPECT: "I like the idea of a Retirement Income policy, but I'm in no hurry. I have five months to go before my 'insurance age' changes."

SALESMAN: "It is very easy to put off taking the policy for five months, but then your first Retirement Check will also come five months later. If you had to wait five months longer for the income it would provide, this might cause you some discomfort. It might even make you dependent on someone else for a time—which is exactly what you want to forstall in the first place. Why not make sure of enjoying your retirement five months earlier?"

¶ 7095 →Live example→ **Leave him something to remember you by**

If you're convinced the sale won't jell right then and there, here's one way to keep the door wide open:

SALESMAN: "All right. While you're thinking it over, perhaps you'd like to see the whole picture. I've a booklet here that will help you study the proposition at your leisure. I've only got two left and I need them till the new ones come in, but I can lend it to you and drop back sometime later to pick it up. Here you are!"

"I'm too busy"

¶ 7096 →Live example→ **Test out the "too-busy-to-talk" prospect**

You can get an interview with the prospect who is "too busy to talk" by testing him out to see if he really is overloaded with work—or is just trying to stall you.

You can use any of these three tests:

Be direct with him. "We're both busy," Mr. Prospect. "If I wasn't sure my proposition would prove unusually interesting and profitable to you, I certainly wouldn't waste your time or mine. I know how to be brief. Will you let me explain now?"

answer guide to specific objections

Be less direct. "I know you're busy, but the element of time enters into this idea of mine, too. I know it'll make money for you, but you must strike while the iron is hot. Here, let me show you my plan . . ."

Appeal to his curiosity. This is another way to get to the "too busy" prospect. If he's merely stalling, he'll forget he told you he's overloaded with work if you use this approach:

"I appreciate your telling me how busy you are, and I know what it means, because I myself am busy from morning till night. However, I'd be doing you—as well as myself—an injustice, if I didn't ask you for a little time this morning. I'm not making a routine call—I have a specially prepared proposition to submit to you. It's one which will make you more sales and easier profits. Would you like to hear what I have to say?"

¶ 7097 ⟶Live example⟶ "11 minutes" does the trick

Mandus Bridston, master salesman of appliances, gives his treatment for the busy man. Says he:

"I've discovered that the best way to calm down that awfully rushed buyer is to pin him down to a few minutes. 'You've got 11 minutes, haven't you?' I might say.

"He'll mutter something about nobody ever sticking to what they say in regard to time, but will concede that he probably has that much time.

" 'Well,' I take out my watch, 'that is all the time I want: just eleven minutes. I'll lay out my watch and go to it, and please don't mind if I talk fast.'

"I do lay out my watch and I time my talk. If the dealer gets interested in my proposition, I ask his permission before I take more time. It is always granted with a grin."

¶ 7098 ⟶Live example⟶ Get order for "specially priced" items now

PROSPECT: "I can't spare the time right now."
SALESMAN: "All right, I'll come back to see you on my next trip. But I'm here today with a chance for you to take your pick from a list of specials at markdowns which can save you from twenty to forty per cent. Some of the more important items that are on my list will shoot back to catalog price within the next week or ten days. Why not just see me long enough to pick what you want from our list of specials and let me come back next time for the regular items?"

"I'm not interested"

¶ 7099 **How to get the prospect interested**

1. Find the reason for lack of interest and overcome that reason. Has he tried such a product once before? Does he have a binding contract?

2. Give an example of one of your customers who said he wasn't interested but bought because he saw the chance to profit through use of the product.

⟶REMEMBER⟶ If a prospect says he's not interested after you have told most of your sales story, and doesn't give you a concrete reason for his lack of interest, it's time to do some self-questioning about why you failed to interest him. See ¶ 1015.

¶ 7100 ⟶Live example⟶ Answering the man who has tried once

PROSPECT: "We tried something like it a while ago. It didn't work. We're not interested.
SALESMAN: "Mr. Prospect, have you ever eaten a dinner that didn't agree with you—gave you indigestion? Of course you have! Yet you didn't give up eating just because that dinner didn't click. You say you've tried my plan before but it didn't work. Isn't it possible that the plan itself is as good as you thought it was when you decided to try it last year—that the only reason it flopped was the method used to put it over? I not only know your judgment was correct, but I've got a method that's been tested over and over—and it works!"

¶ 7101 ⟶Live example⟶ Build interest by example

PROSPECT: "I'm not interested."
SALESMAN: "A couple of hours ago I called on another very busy executive, and he wasn't interested either—until I had the chance to show him how he could save $60 a month that he's been literally throwing away for years. I don't know exactly how much you may be losing on returned goods every month, but I'll bet I can show you in the next eight minutes how to save at least $500.00 a year, and maybe a whole lot more. Here's an example of what I mean—"

"I'm all stocked up"

¶ 7102 Ways to help a dealer move your line when he's stocked up

1. Get behind all of the company's efforts to secure dealer cooperation.

》》OBSERVATION→ Many companies use such dealer aids as lower prices for quantity purchases; discounts and rebates; premiums to consumers; coupons entitling consumer to a discount or extra free product; contests among consumers; samples; trade-ins.

2. Get the dealer to feature a display of your product on his counter and shelves.

3. Get dealer cooperation in window displays.

4. Influence the dealer to advertise and feature your product.

》》OBSERVATION→ Manufacturers take the initiative usually in offering assistance to the dealer. They furnish dealers with advertising mats, dealer ads to tie in with the manufacturer's own ads, direct mail circulars to be used by the dealer, ideas and layouts for dealer signs and billboards, and the like. The salesman helps carry out the manufacturer's efforts.

5. If he's stocked up, but not with your line, prove that your line moves regardless of his general stock condition, and is a sure money-maker.

6. Make him see the profit possibilities that will result from your company's forthcoming special promotion campaign, if such advertising is actually planned.

》》CAUTION→ If your prospect is really overstocked and he is not merely using the objection as an excuse, don't overload him. Arrange to come back at a definite time when he is no longer overstocked—and move on to a better prospect.

¶ 7103 》》Live example→ Get an order and display when the prospect is "stocked up"

When a merchant wearily tells you that he's "all stocked up," ask him to come outside with you to see something you want to show him in his own window. Select a position (one you picked out before you entered the store), and tell him that your money-making display, which just fits that spot, will pay him good rent for a space which isn't producing a nickel's worth of profit for him. "And you know only too well, Mr. Merchant, that your rent is really the cost of your windows."

You've got him sold the moment you plant this idea. If he rejects the spot you point to, you can ask him to select a better one. In either case, you not only get the order but the precious display space as well.

¶ 7104 》》Live example→ Remember "Old Man Turnover"

PROSPECT: "I can't make any money on your goods. The profit is too small."

SALESMAN: "Yes, Mr. Dealer, your *gross* profit is small, but you've forgotten Old Man Turnover. Consider your investment in that slow-moving line over there (you'll find some in every store). You double your money on that, Mr. Dealer, but you do it only once a year. Our gross profit is only half of that, but you turn our goods over four times a year. Thus you make a lot more on the same investment. You need a fast-moving line like ours to balance the slow turnover on the goods you've got to keep on hand."

¶ 7105 》》Live example→ Get an order for later delivery

CUSTOMER: "We've got too many gloves in stock *now*. Couldn't place an order with *anybody* today!"

SALESMAN: "If your inventory is heavy, I certainly wouldn't suggest that you add to it at this time. But here's what I *do* suggest. Place an order now for delivery in 30 days, when your inventory will be in need of some additional fresh styles."

"I can get a better guarantee from Blank Company"

¶ 7106 How to meet objection to your guarantee

1. If your guarantee is for a shorter period than your competitor's, justify the duration of your guarantee by showing that: (1) experience and factory research have proved that defects, if any, show up in the first six months; (2) the guarantee terms you offer are simple and clear-cut as compared with the complicated clauses in other guarantees that give the manufacturer numerous "outs."

2. If you don't have a written guarantee but the company stands firmly behind its product, offer a writen guarantee if company policy permits you to.

"I never heard of your house"

¶ 7107 Reasons on which to build a strong answer to "unknown company" objection

1. Although your company is not as well

known as others, it will be soon because of the caliber of the management.

2. Although your company is small, it can give your customer as good service as any well-known company, and better individual attention. See example in ¶ 7022.

3. You have become associated with the company because of your confidence in the management, the excellence of the product, and your conviction that the company is bound to grow.

4. If your company is well established, but unknown to the prospect, use your testimonials.

¶ 7108 ⟶Live example⟶ Use testimonials

SALESMAN: "Our line, Mr. Dealer, has been handled for years by such stores as Lord & Taylor's and Filene's. If our goods don't give permanent satisfaction, and if our service is not the best, do you suppose for a minute that firms like these would continue to sell our products?"

"Your product is too new"

¶ 7109 Reasons on which to build a strong answer to "newness" objection

1. Newness means progress; every product that today is commonplace, like radio and TV, was once "too new."

2. Your new product has been completely tested in use, as shown by your list of testimonials and list of users.

3. Show what your company has been doing to advertise the product.

4. Sell on superiority of quality, product benefits to the customer, advantages.

5. Popularity of well-known brands is not necessarily an indication of their superiority. Instead of putting its money into advertising, your company may have been putting it into research, development, and improvement of the product.

6. Your company has earned a reputation for customer satisfaction that can't be beaten by producers of the better known products.

Criticism of your product

¶ 7110 How to overcome objection to the product itself

1. A dynamic display of confidence in your factory's judgment will often work wonders if the design of a product is criticized, or when the prospect says that a competitor puts out a better line.

2. Use testimonials of other users, or show reorders, if a dealer-prospect says the product won't sell.

¶ 7111 ⟶Live example⟶ Make your confidence contagious when the product is criticized

PROSPECT: "Your product isn't built right."

SALESMAN: "Well, I'm not a mechanic, and I don't know all about the why's and wherefore's of that hinge, but I do know the man who makes them, and I know that if it wasn't the best thing of its sort in America for that particular place, *it just wouldn't be there,* that's all!"

¶ 7112 ⟶Live example⟶ Be specific when a competitor's product is alleged superior

PROSPECT: "The other company puts out a better line."

SALESMAN: "I believe the company I am with puts out the best line in the country. If I thought there was a better one, I would be carrying it, and with my record, I'd have no trouble in changing. Why, in seven ways at least, our products are better made and easier to sell than anything on the market. Take this camera, for example—"

¶ 7113 ⟶Live example⟶ Appeal to the customer's pride

PROSPECT: "There's no demand for your product."

SALESMAN: "Did you ever stop to think why you go to the post-office for stamps? Funny question, isn't it? But, listen! You go to the post-office for stamps because you know you can get them there! That's why, too, a lot of trade does *not* go to some stores for up-to-date merchandise, because they are accustomed to finding the same old stock there and don't expect to see the newest popular merchandise. When 86 stores out of every 100 in this city find our canned goods one of their fastest-selling lines, there must be quite a demand that *you* could capitalize right here in this store. Why not make me prove it? Give our line a 60-day trial. Suppose I send you our special deal, as long as you can make 15% extra profit at the same time you try out our line."

¶ 7114 ⟶Live example⟶ Break down the style objection

PROSPECT: "The styles are wrong. Our customers won't go for them."

SALESMAN: "Well, sir, on this trip out with this new line, I've heard those comments from three other mighty good merchants—men who are almost as good judges of merchandise as you are. And it just shows you that *nobody* can tell *what* the women will go for. Here—look at these repeat orders from Syracuse and Rochester and Buffalo. And as you know, right here in your own town you've seen things that sell like hotcakes—things that a mere man would say no sensible woman would wear to a dog fight. But the point is, Mr. Dealer, that compared with styles that your women customers will see pictured in the magazines and elsewhere, these styles are anything but extreme!"

¶ 7115 ⇛Live example→ Use facts to overcome a criticism that once prevailed

PROSPECT: "I have heard that your machines are not very good and you don't sell as much as other companies."

SALESMAN: "You are basing what you say on facts that existed many years ago. If you have not seen the modern XYZ machine in the past six years, I can understand your making that statement, but today we have a machine that is second to none. Our customer acceptance is world-wide. In the past 14 years our sales have tripled and today our company's sales of this machine are at their highest point."

Your former salesman didn't leave a good impression

¶ 7116 ⇛Live example→ Sell yourself

SALESMAN: "I'm new in this territory myself, and I suppose I'll make some mistakes. But I know I won't build this territory by not satisfying people. So the first thing I want to do is apologize for my predecessor and hope you won't hold me responsible. I certainly want to make friends for my company."

"I've heard that XYZ Co. had trouble with your product"

¶ 7117 How to overcome adverse rumors

This kind of objection comes as a surprise. You usually don't know of the trouble and can honestly say that you don't. You can assure the prospect that the company has undoubtedly taken care of the complaint, if indeed there was one. You might point out that the prospect, like every other businessman, has at some time had a misunderstanding with a customer, and he certainly wouldn't think it fair if his other customers acted on a rumor without having heard both sides of the story. To bring the prospect to a good listening mood, you might offer to find out whether there had been trouble, and what it was, and let the prospect know.

With such a disposition of the prospect's negation, you can proceed to show the benefits to be derived from the product, to emphasize quality and service, and to use your testimonials and list of well-known satisfied customers to build confidence in the company's reputation and its product.

"A nearer supplier will give me faster delivery and service"

¶ 7118 Reasons to overcome "distance" objection

1. Present facts that assure the prospect that there will be no delay in delivery or service. For example: your company uses air freight for delivery; it guarantees that a service man will call within 24 hours of notice; and so on.

2. Use testimonials of satisfied cutomers who are also some distance from your company's headquarters.

Friendships or other personal ties stand in the way

¶ 7119 Reasons with which to break down the personal ties

1. It's to the prospect's advantage to switch, because your product is superior, has certain benefits and savings.

2. It is often difficult to get as good quality of service and attention from a friend or relative as from an outsider.

3. The prospect may sometimes feel that he'd rather not give his relatives or friends information he must impart to obtain the full benefit of the product or service. He can discuss his needs more fully with an outsider.

⇛COMMENTS→ Personal ties are often deeply rooted. Yet few men's devotion to their friends goes deeper than their own selfish interests. It is good strategy to admit openly that you admire loyalty toward friends. You wouldn't be a good sport if you didn't. But don't let this admirable trait of yours keep you from emphasizing the advantages, the dollars and cents benefits that your prospect will gain by doing business with you. Remember that he continues to favor his friend, for the simple

answer guide to specific objections

reason that *no one has as yet sold him a practical reason why it is to his greater advantage to switch*. Remember also that he is in business to make a profit for his *company,* not to support his friends.

Even the closest friend doesn't expect a man to continue doing business with him when it is obviously to his disadvantage to do so. Your job, therefore, is to put your finger on one or more points of superiority, either of product or service, which enables you to offer a reason for buying from *you*.

Your best bet is to make a play for an insignificant part of the prospect's business, and then "go to town" on performance, letting nature take its course with what should be the resulting contrast between your service and the other fellow's.

¶ 7120 ≫Live example→ Breaking down the friendship objection

PROSPECT: "I have a couple of good friends in the business."

SALESMAN: "Mr. Prospect, if there were a deficit of income to your family, would these friends of yours make up the shortage out of their own pockets? Of course not! Well, if I can give you some ideas that will guarantee security for your family and yourself, is there any reason why I could not have your business?"

"We've been buying from Blank & Company for many years and are completely satisfied"

¶ 7121 Reasons on which to build an answer to the "loyalty" objection

1. Prospect's first duty is to himself to make the best buy.

2. It is important to diversify in order to assure a continuous supply at all times.

3. The prospect's business is big enough to handle more than one line; his sales will show how well your product stands up.

4. No one can afford to stand still; progress requires change.

5. Your product is newer, better, made to meet today's needs.

6. Perhaps the prospect is complacent because he doesn't know, having stayed with one source of supply, how far ahead your company has moved as a producer in the field. A test order will prove that it pays to broaden the source.

7. Prospect can gain a definite profit by buying your product.

8. Point out the benefits to be gained from your product. They may be benefits that the other supplier never thought of stressing because they are obvious.

9. If your product is for resale, and it has become well-known through the firm's advertising policy, your prospect should be carrying it or his customers will go elsewhere for it. Thus, your prospect might lose not only the profits on your product but other business in addition.

10. You don't expect him to drop his present source; it is to his own advantage to share his business.

¶ 7122 ≫Live example→ You have something attractive to show

PROSPECT: "We've been buying our equipment from the Smith Company for almost 20 years. We have confidence in them and their values, and we've learned how to use their product, so it's no use."

SALESMAN: "Mr. Prospect, you've put your finger right on the big point! We know, of course, that you buy from Smith, and that they're a fine outfit, and that you're accustomed to their product. We know that we'd simply be wasting your time as well as our own if we didn't have something awfully attractive to show you to overcome that big handicap. And if we do, I'm sure the least you want to do about it is hear our story."

¶ 7123 ≫Live example→ Edge in by showing extra profit

PROSPECT: "I don't care to make a change."

SALESMAN: "In that case I don't expect you to discontinue your present connections, just because I happen to want your business. All I'm suggesting is that you add from $100 to $200 extra profit a month to your business with hardly any extra capital investment on your part. You'll find that my line supplements, rather than competes, with the line you are carrying, and brings you extra sales that you're actually passing up. Look at these records of re-orders from a half dozen typical department stores—stores that carry from three to five other lines all the time."

¶ 7124 ≫Live example→ When it pays to be blunt with the prospect who has a contract

If you're the kind who can sense when to break rules and regulations, you will save this one for the prospect who can't be budged because he has a contract. Change the language to suit your style, but try the idea when you've exhausted your regular ammunition. Remember that few companies dare tie themselves up 100% with any supplier—that there's usually a wicket through which, say, 10% of the goods of non-contracted suppliers still can gain admittance.

SALESMAN: "You're in kind of a bad hole. Blank's have got you where they want you. They're shrewd, all right. I don't doubt they're giving you service, but how do you know that service is top-notch? Have you got anything with which to compare that service? Have you got stick, stone or club to keep Blank on their toes to serve you? No, you've shut the door to competition; you've turned them into the clover field. What's more, you've closed your eyes to competing products. You've served notice that you are not progressive enough to want to keep up on the latest improvements. If every company in America did just what you have done there would never be any more improvements in the machines we make. Research departments would be thrown out the window. Twenty years from now your company would be using the same machines it uses today." Then you make him a proposition.

"All I ask is the chance to put my machines in here to the extent of 10% of your requirements. That will cost you no more than you are paying Blank, but you'll get more for your money—not only from me and my company, but also from Blank. You will have two suppliers competing on service. You will have two kinds of products competing on the basis of quality of work and cost of operation. You will have the advantage of what I know to be my machine's superiority in certain work. You will have at your service all that I and my company's mechanical experts can show you about special applications of our product. Perhaps we will be able to help you solve some difficult problem. One thing I can promise you as a dead certainty—you will get service from us the like of which you have never seen before because we will feel that we have to make good."

¶ 7125 ⟫⟫Live example→ **We have standardized on another make**

PROSPECT: "While I like your machine, we have standardized on another make for economy."

SALESMAN: "Yes, standardizing is economical. But sometimes what was once genuine economy in time becomes false economy. Our machine is the best for the money that you can buy on the market today. It is designed for more efficiency and is easier for the operators to use than any other machine. So you really would be economizing if you standardized on our machine. We know that a complete turnover of your inventory of machines now would be impractical. But by purchasing a few of our machines and putting them side by side with your present equipment you will be convinced that there is real economy in standardizing on our machine. You can make the change-over little by little."

"We buy from a supplier who buys from us"

¶ 7126 **How to meet the reciprocity difficulty**[1]

You run into this objection especially with big-company prospects who favor their own customers in making purchases, rarely with small companies. When you encounter this objection, use the following points in trying to overcome it:

1. Find out whether the objection is real or just a stall. See ¶ 7006.

2. Sell the special benefits of your product. Your prospect may realize that he is losing a valuable benefit under his reciprocal arrangement.

3. Show him in dollars and cents how much he can save by buying your product. It gives your prospect a basis for comparing the profits he makes on his customer with what it is costing him to carry through the reciprocal arrangement.

4. Use the reasons that help to win orders from prospects who buy from friends or have other personal ties to a supplier, given at ¶ 7119.

⟫⟫OBSERVATION 1→ The purchasing agent might become your ally if he has found the reciprocal arrangement irksome. Suppose, for example, that he has had to put up with poor deliveries and poor quality that he would not tolerate but for the reciprocal plan. He might be glad to help you get to top management of his company to present your case.

⟫⟫OBSERVATION 2→ Some companies instruct their salesmen to report the facts to them and not try to cope with the reciprocity problem themselves. Management has its own ways of dealing with the problem. It is in a better position than its salesmen to weigh the seriousness of the situation and look into its legal aspects. Also, management might consider becoming a customer of the prospect. It can investigate whether it is using the pros-

answer guide to specific objections

pect's products or service directly or indirectly. Top management might even know someone in the prospect organization who can help you make the sale.

"I must take it up with my partner"

¶ 7127 How to get the prospect to listen first by himself

Point out that the partner (or associate) will want the opinion of the man you are talking to. He can form that opinion now by knowing the merits of the product. Then, arrange an appointment at which both parties will be present. Among partners, one often has a stronger influence than the other, in some matters, either because of personality or partnership arrangements. At the joint meeting, try to detect which of the individuals will influence the decision, and direct your strongest appeals to him.

¶ 7128 ⇛Live example⇢ You be the one to explain your product

PROSPECT: "I must take it up with my partner."
SALESMAN: "Right. Would you do me this favor—let *me* be the one to explain the machine to him? I probably know more about typewriters, and if I were there I could answer his questions on the spot and save time all around."

¶ 7129 ⇛Live example⇢ Why bother the board of directors?

PROSPECT: "I'll take up your proposition with our board."

⇛COMMENT⇢ The fear of assuming a new kind of expense often frightens a junior executive into passing the buck to his board of directors. With a bit of imagination, however, you can so minimize the weight of responsibility on his shoulders that he will feel the purchase is a relatively insignificant, routine matter.

SALESMAN: (selling a Depositors' Forgery Bond): "You don't call your executive committee together when you need to put on a new night watchman, do you?"
PROSPECT: "No, I don't."
SALESMAN: "And what do you pay a new watchman?"
PROSPECT: "$50 to $60 per week."
SALESMAN: "Well, I propose to act as night watchman and day watchman over the most vital factor in your business, your bank account. I'll act as watchman on every check you draw no matter where it goes or who may intercept it, and I'm going to charge you only $— a week for my services for the three-year period covered by this bond. Do you need a meeting of the executives to hire me?"

And the prospect agreed, when he saw the matter in that light, that it could doubtless be fixed up in a few minutes.

"I'll have to talk it over with my husband (or wife)"

¶ 7130 How to get immediate action when one spouse wants to talk over proposal with the other

1. Point out to the wife that she doesn't talk over every purchase with her husband—purchases like groceries and children's clothes. These expenditures amount to much more a year than she would spend on your product, which will serve her every day of the year.

2. Arrange to meet husband and wife together at a convenient time.

3. If you can't arrange to meet both people together, be sure that the one you are interviewing knows the important points that you want him or her to pass on to the other.

⇛COMMENT⇢ If the sale involves a substantial sum, you may risk having the order cancelled, or the product returned, if you induce the wife to buy without consulting her husband. The best strategy in the face of this objection, usually, is to do your best to arrange for a call when husband and wife are present. By the time the woman has recited your selling talk to her husband, it may be so diluted as to have no persuasion with the treasury watchdog. Your presence will enable you to do whatever additional selling is necessary with the husband.

¶ 7131 ⇛Live example⇢ Make him a hero to his wife

PROSPECT: "I'll talk it over with my wife."
SALESMAN: "Mr. Jenkins, I'm a married man myself, and I know how it is. As a rule, I'd do the same thing exactly. But when you buy a gift for your wife, you don't tell her about it beforehand. That's just what this oil-burner is—a gift that will save your wife many a backache, a gift that will protect her from winter colds by assuring the right temperature throughout the house all the time, a gift that many women would rather have than a new fur coat. Men seldom realize what a wonderful present an oil-burner is to a woman. Why not surprise your wife by keeping her away from the house this Thursday or Friday and arranging to let us install the burner as a gift of permanent comfort—from you to her?"

¶7131

"The machine we have is still good"

¶ 7132 Reasons for replacement of equipment that is "still good"

1. By keeping his present old machine, the prospect is losing the advantages of all improvements that have been made in the equipment—improvements that speed up production, reduce work-over costs, increase safety, etc.

2. The prospect's competitors have already replaced their machinery with the newer types.

3. The longer the prospect keeps his old equipment, the more costly it becomes. Costs of material and labor used on repairs and time lost by factory employees during breakdowns eat up the profits.

4. The older the present equipment becomes, the lower its trade-in value becomes.

5. It is wise for the prospect to maintain the value of his investment by trading it in for modern equipment before it becomes obsolete.

¶ 7133 ≫Live example→ Development of economy reason for replacement

A typewriter salesman uses the following reasons to convince a prospect that there is real economy in replacing an old machine with a new modern one.

1. Increased production. New machines will usually increase typing production in many ways.

2. Better looking work. New mechanical and operating features make the machine quieter, less fatiguing, less wasteful, and turn out better-looking work.

3. Less waste. Fewer errors are made and less work has to be retyped, for mechanical defects or worn parts do not exist in new machines.

4. More modern and business-like appearance of office.

5. The insignificant yearly cost of a typewriter, compared with the operator's salary and other expense, such as ribbons, carbon paper, stationery, etc.

6. Psychological effect upon operator. Most girls are happier with their jobs when new typewriters are furnished.

≫OBSERVATION→ Of the above, item 5 is, as a rule, the most potent reason of all for replacing old equipment. The salesman brings out this economy with "sharp pencil selling," as explained at ¶ 7135.

¶ 7134 ≫Live example→ New model is more efficient

PROSPECT: "We can get along all right with our present equipment."

SALESMAN: "I'm sure you can, Mr. Blank, and I appreciate that you know more about office management than I ever will. But couldn't you say that about almost any old automobile in fair condition? It will run, and you get places and back. The reason a new model obsoletes an old one is not that the old one is bad, but that the new one is so much more efficient and productive.

"I've read that the English as a rule are very reluctant to scrap old machinery because it will still run—whereas the Americans will scrap even a late model if they find the latest model will save them time and money. The whole point is that we have a brand new model typewriter which will do brand new things for you" (and so into a brief sales follow-up).

¶ 7135 ≫Live example→ "Sharp pencil selling" shows insignificant yearly cost of new typewriter

Facts and figures will appeal to the average business man or department head to a far greater extent than a long verbal sales story. It is a very potent means of turning the prospect's thoughts from the capital expenditure involved in buying a new typewriter to the much greater investment in the *expensive pair of hands* using the equipment. Rightly used, the phrase "expensive pair of hands" can be a key factor in inducing owners to replace old equipment with new.

≫OBSERVATION→ The above statements are applicable to many types of machinery and equipment that are traded in. The following computation can easily be adapted to prove to a prospect that regular replacement of old equipment with new is economical.

▶ *Table showing comparative costs when machines are traded in after 3, 5, 7 and 9 years.* The following table furnishes the salesman with ammunition for convincing a prospect that now is a good time to trade in his old machine. There are many ways to present the argument. An example is given below. The salesman does his figuring on a scratch pad, *right before the prospect's eyes.*

From inspection of the following table, it will be seen that a man who trades in his typewriters every 3 years has an annual cost (initial plus upkeep) of $56.17.

answer guide to specific objections

	3 Years	5 Years	7 Years	9 Years
Initial Cost	$225.00	$225.00	$225.00	$225.00
Approx. Trade-in Value	65.00	55.00	45.00	35.00
	$160.00	$170.00	$180.00	$190.00
Estimated Service Costs:				
1st Year (a)	0.00	0.00	0.00	0.00
2nd Year (b)	4.25	4.25	4.25	4.25
3rd Year (b)	4.25	4.25	4.25	4.25
4th Year (b)	—	8.50	8.50	8.50
4th Year (c)	—	30.00	30.00	30.00
5th Year (b)	—	8.50	8.50	8.50
6th Year (b)	—	—	8.50	8.50
6th Year (c)	—	—	35.00	35.00
7th Year (b)	—	—	8.50	8.50
8th Year (b)	—	—	—	8.50
8th Year (c)	—	—	—	40.00
9th Year (b)	—	—	—	8.50
Total Service, est.	$ 8.50	$ 55.50	$107.50	$164.50

(a) New machine
(b) Yearly incidental service
(c) Major servicing (cleaning, re-adjusting, new rubber, etc.)

	3 Years	5 Years	7 Years	9 Years
TOTAL COST	$ 168.50	$ 225.50	$ 287.50	$ 354.50
COST PER YEAR	56.17	45.10	41.07	39.39
PAID OUT IN SALARY @ $50.00	$7,800.00	$13,000.00	$18,200.00	$23,400.00

A man who trades in every 5 years has an annual expense of $45.10 which is $11.07 less per year (or 92 cents per month) than on the 3-year basis.

A man who trades in every 7 years has an annual expense of $41.07 which is $15.10 less per year ($1.26 per month) than on the 3-year basis, and $4.03 less per year (34 cents per month) than on the 5-year basis.

A man who trades in every 9 years has an annual expense of $39.39 which is $16.78 less per year ($1.40 per month) than on the 3-year basis, $5.71 less per year (48 cents per month) than on the 5-year basis, and $1.68 less per year (14 cents per month) than on the 7-year basis.

Total cost on 3-year basis ($168.50) is 2.16% of operator's salary, on 5-year basis—1.73%, on 7-year basis—1.58%, and on 9-year basis—1.51%.

▶ *Use of trade-in information to sell the prospect.* Now let's suppose that the salesman has made a good demonstration and good impression on the owner of a seven-year old typewriter.

SALESMAN: "Now that you've seen this beautiful new Smith-Corona, Mr. Blank—is this a good time to discuss trading in your seven-year-old?"
PROSPECT: "Oh, I don't think so. That old typewriter will last quite a while yet."
SALESMAN: "That's probably true, Mr. Blank—most good machines can be kept running, whether they're automobiles or typewriters. But actually you're paying for a new typewriter right now, without getting the benefit of it. Give me two minutes more, and I'll show you.

"First, you'll agree the big cost of a typewriter is not the machine, but the *expensive pair of hands* that run it. (He starts figuring for him on a scratch pad.) Let's say you pay the typist $50 a week. 52 weeks—that's $2600 a year. One-twelfth of that is $217 per month. A new 11" Smith-Corona costs $225—just about what you pay her in one month.

"On a 7-year old machine, say the trade-in value is $45. $45 from $225 is $180. That would be your cost for a new machine. Over the next three years, you'll pay the operator $7,800—plus stationery, ribbons and carbons. $180 is 2.3% of the salary cost. So with a brand-new machine against a 7-year old one, your operator only has to be 2.3% more efficient to pay you back the whole cost! Why, against a breakdown, high repair costs, loss of use, waste of supplies, poor-looking work, lower production—2.3% is a modest figure.

¶7135

"So we see that each day a user keeps an old machine after it has passed its prime, he's paying for a new one, in lowered efficiency and higher upkeep—but he isn't getting the new machine's value! And the old machine drops a little each year in trade-in value.

"In other words, Mr. Blank—think of a typewriter as a tool, figure what it costs to run that tool—and you can make a mighty good case for keeping that tool up-to-date. I'd certainly be glad to have you approve that reasoning."

"I'll buy a cheap second-hand machine"

¶ 7136 **How to convince prospect to buy a new machine instead of a second-hand one**

1. Show by facts and figures that a second-hand machine will cost more in the long run.
2. Minimize the saving. Compare first cost of new equipment with the salaries paid to operators.
3. Stress quality performance from new equipment that will be lost.

¶ 7137 ⟫Live example→ **Minimize the savings in purchasing used equipment**

SALESMAN: "I don't need to tell you that it will cost you more. When you buy a used machine, you buy something someone else has taken the good out of and then discarded. You'll have higher service costs, and lower trade-in value—but most of all you won't get the quality of work you want. Ever stop to figure that a typewriter is just a tool, and that its first cost is less than you pay *in one month* for the hands that run it? It's actually cheaper to buy a new machine, and get what you pay for!"

"Send me a case on consignment"

¶ 7138 ⟫Live example→ **How to educate the dealer who wants a shipment on consignment**

SALESMAN: "I wish I could—but I can't. The only way we can keep our costs down to a level that allows you a 40% profit is by operating on a sound business basis. We're in the manufacturing, not the banking business, and we've got to get our money promptly enough to be able to take advantage of purchasing opportunities. If we distributed our goods on consignment, we'd be paying interest to the bank for working capital—and in the long run you and your customers would have to absorb our higher cost of production. Now, I'll tell you what I'll do, though. I'll send you a case on our regular liberal 30-day terms. Then, if within two or three months, you still have more than half the lot unsold, I'll get the home office to exchange the stock for any other numbers in our line. I can have the goods here by Friday—."

⟫OBSERVATION→ Company policy may require you to refuse all requests for consignment. However, the policy may be worth reconsidering. A farmer who raises and sells seeds consistently refused to deliver seeds on consignment. He weakened on one occasion and left a consignment of seeds with a customer. In a short time he had re-orders; in fact, a surprisingly large amount of seed was sold by the customer. Here's the explanation given to him by the customer: "Your seeds are out on the floor where I can see them, so I sell them."

¶ 7999 **Footnote references**

¶ 7006
  (1) Acknowledgment: "How to Outsell a Reciprocal Buying Setup," by Gertrude Charloff, *The American Salesman*, March 1959, p. 7.

¶ 7096
  (1) "How I Raised Myself from Failure to Success in Selling," p. 198, published by Prentice-Hall, Inc., Englewood Cliffs, N. J.

¶ 7126
  (1) Acknowledgment: "How to Outsell a Reciprocal Buying Setup," by Gertrude Charloff, *The American Salesman*, March 1959, p. 7.

SELLING AT CONCERT PITCH

How to Build and Maintain Enthusiasm
Self-Management for More Profitable Selling

TABLE OF CONTENTS

	Starts at Paragraph [¶]
Miracle Guide to Selling at Concert Pitch	8001

HOW TO BUILD AND MAINTAIN ENTHUSIASM

	Starts at Paragraph [¶]
The power of enthusiasm	8002
Create a buying atmosphere	8003
Enthusiasm helps you put it all together	8004
Find something to admire in everyone	8005
Pleasing your customers raises your own enthusiasm	8006
Knowledge stimulates enthusiasm	8007
Make a habit of associating with successful people	8008
Keep physically fit	8009
An increased income goal will increase your enthusiasm too	8010
Believe in your ability to reach goals	8011
Planning builds enthusiasm	8012
A job behind you gives momentum	8013
Be creative and you'll be enthusiastic	8014
Whole-heartedness is a by-product of enthusiasm	8015
How to become more relaxed—control your nerves	8016
Strengthen your morale through good company relations	8017
Use a no-sale as the basis for renewed enthusiasm	8018
Create enthusiasm by changing your customer's "No" to "Yes"	8019
Change your attitude if it's glum	8020
Overcoming negative influence of the past	8021
Learn to generate your healthy, positive emotions	8022
How to keep defeatism out of your selling day	8023
Four key problems	8024
Talk yourself into self-confidence	8025
How to overcome fear of the "tough" customers	8026
A good laugh will banish tension	8027
Review, analysis, and planning restore enthusiasm	8028

SELF-MANAGEMENT FOR MORE PROFITABLE SELLING

	Starts at Paragraph [¶]
Your guide to self-management	8041

Self-Management Techniques to Gain Selling Time

Determine the time you spend in each selling activity	8042
Figure your gain from added selling time	8043
Increase the selling hours by scheduling desk work last	8044
Where to cut time wastes	8045
What to do when your customer keeps you waiting	8046
How to save time in handling collections, adjustments, and complaints	8047
How to prevent "wasted motion" from killing your prime selling hours	8048
Prepare a work schedule for profitable use of your time	8049
Make the most of rainy days	8050
Consider your prospects' work habits in deciding best time to call	8051

	Starts at Paragraph [¶]		Starts at Paragraph [¶]
Self-Management To Make A Positive Impression		Overcome your prejudices	8098
		Resolve that your prospect will find you friendly	8099
How the buyer sizes you up	8061		
Use enthusiasm as a sales aid	8062	Understanding the "unapproachable" customer helps you like him	8100
Don't offend your customers by smoking	8063		
Shake hands meaningfully	8064	Capitalize a mark of individuality in your customer	8101
Walk with assurance	8065		
Practice poise	8066	You must be a self-starting salesman	8102
Undue familiarity might damage customer relations	8067	You can strengthen your character through self-reliance	8103
Enthusiasm doesn't condone brashness	8068	Check your habits	8104
Keep your troubles to yourself	8069	Personal mannerisms can affect a sale	8105
Why good speech is essential	8070	Punctuality shows that you are in control of your job	8106
How to use your voice effectively	8071		
It's important to learn your sales talk perfectly	8072	Don't make yourself hard to buy from	8107
		Get the buyer in your corner—don't put him on the defensive	8108
How to train your memory	8073		
Role-playing prepares you for the actual sale	8074	Avoid putting the customer "on the spot"	8109
		Use the right word to avert unpleasant situations	8110
How To Make The Most Of Your Personality			
		A display of optimism can often make a sale	8111
Your personality is a composite of many factors	8091	6 ways to change stress from enemy to friend	8112
Plug up your personality leaks to step up your sales	8092	An effective last remark will often gain a second interview	8113
Sincerity will pay off	8093	Win or lose, leave them smiling	8114
Courtesy advances your customer relations	8094	Self-management can turn you into an expert closer	8115
Tact turns opposition into agreement	8095		
Use your power of charm	8096		
You can help keep at peak selling by acquiring patience	8097	Only you can follow through on self-management	8116

Footnote References 8999

Selling at Concert Pitch

The "star" manages to lick tough territory, tough prospects, tough breaks, and other obstacles

¶ 8001 ⇛MIRACLE GUIDE to→ Selling at Concert Pitch

How would you like to sell all the time at concert pitch?

When an orchestra plays at "concert pitch," the hard preliminary work has already been done; the long rehearsals are over. Now, at the concert, the individual instruments fuse together into one harmonious flood of sound. Smoothly and powerfully the orchestra carries the audience with it.

So it is with selling. When you are selling at concert pitch you are carrying your prospect with you, without seeming effort. You take him along with you, from sales point to sales point. You have charge of the interview—quietly and inoffensively, it is true, but you are in the saddle all the way. The interview concludes with the prospect buying from you. And what is even more important, both the prospect and you have a sense of personal satisfaction—he that he has made a good purchase, and you that you have made the sale.

How you achieve this confident, concert pitch frame of mind, and maintain it as your day-to-day selling technique, depends in large part upon yourself. That you can do it there is no question. And it is certain that you must do it if you are to win your way into the big money in selling.

In the following pages you will learn from the experience of others who have developed this priceless method of selling. They will tell you what the ingredients are that make up the successful formula.

See ¶¶ 8002-8028 which show you how to develop and maintain the enthusiasm which is the crux of "concert pitch" selling—and see ¶¶ 8041-8051 which show you how to manage yourself to multiply your selling power.

Then see ¶¶ 8061-8116 which give you the miracle approach that puts your product and your personality across with a bang—the second "must" for "concert pitch" high-bracket selling.

¶ 8001

How to build and maintain enthusiasm

¶ 8002 The power of enthusiasm

Many top salesmen have testified to the power of enthusiasm in their sales lives. In fact, so much has been said in recent years about enthusiasm that perhaps now we tend to disparage the salesman or sales manager who preaches "be enthusiastic." But to disparage enthusiasm is one of the costliest mistakes we can make. It plays a special role in selling. It is the key to greatness in this field.

There is a sound psychological basis for the power of enthusiasm in selling. Every salesman, even more than most people, is subject to forebodings and fears. He fears to make the first call of the day . . . he is afraid of the greeting he may get from a tough prospect . . . sometimes he is afraid to ask for the order, or for a big order. One of the chief values of enthusiasm is that it replaces fear. Fear is negative and crippling; but when the emotional force of fear is used to generate enthusiasm, our fears disappear. We become filled with positive power.

¶ 8003 Create a buying atmosphere

Let your enthusiasm "show through" during your presentation—and you'll influence buyers and win added sales. *Why?* Because an enthusiastic salesman *creates* a buying atmosphere.

EXAMPLE: To show you how enthusiasm can work to boost your sales record—let's follow a salesman from the time he enters his prospect's door until he closes.

• *Entrance:* Walk in like a winner. (The enthusiastic salesman *knows* he has the right product for his buyer). Greet your prospect with a smile and get started with, "My demonstration will show you how my product can cut your costs dramatically."

Wrong way: Walk in like the buyer is doing you a favor for letting you show him how your product will save him money. If you start off with, "I know you're a busy man—but I hope you'll give me a few minutes to demonstrate my product", you're already heading for a fall. (If he made an appointment, he *expects* you to give a presentation.)

• *Presentation:* "Know what you're saying and know what you're doing," is the motto of one top producer. When you're sure of yourself, your enthusiasm leaps out at your prospect.

"It's not enough," he says, "to know how your product is put together—you have to know how your prospect can *use it*. That's what makes the sale." Here's what this salesman does before he makes his sales calls:

> **IDEA IN ACTION** "If I'm selling the prospect for the first time, I call to confirm the date. While doing this, I also ask him a question or two that might give me a lead as to the nature of his problem or what his needs are."

This salesman doesn't stop there. He checks with his fellow salesmen to see what highlights they use to sell similar type customers.

Wrong way: Give every customer the same presentation. After all, if it was good enough for the Jones Company, why shouldn't it work with the Smith Company.

• *Give-and-take:* The key here is to make others feel important. If you do this, then you become important to them. In practically every presentation, the buyer has either some questions or an opinion he wants to get across.

The confident — enthusiastic — salesman doesn't back away when the prospect breaks into his presentation. Instead, he welcomes the exchange. He realizes that this is the prospect's way of (1) showing off his knowledge and (2) asking to be convinced that he's making the right decision.

The salesman sprinkles his answers with phrases that everyone—and buyers are no exception—likes to hear. Here are a couple of key phrases:

"That's an excellent point, Mr. Jones."

"An observation like that makes it obvious that I'm dealing with a pro."

• *Rebuttal:* After letting the buyer know that you have respect for his ability, you must gently—but firmly—show him how his observation doesn't apply to your product.

Something like this doesn't "destroy" the buyer—or put him on the defensive: "That would be the case with similar products, but my company has designed a special button which eliminates that problem."

Wrong way: Get careless with your answers —"I thought I made that point clear," or "You haven't understood what I've said"—and you might as well prepare to leave (without the sale).

how to build and maintain enthusiasm

¶ 8004 Enthusiasm helps you put it all together

• *Close:* The enthusiastic salesman has no fear of this moment. He knows he's dealing from strength. The salesman has set things up right from the start. He—

• Gained instant attention with his informative beginning.

• Held the prospect's attention with a presentation geared to his needs.

¶ 8005 Find something to admire in everyone

Deliberately looking for and finding something to admire in everyone you approach makes it easier to meet that person enthusiastically. The very liking of the person stimulates you to want to do your best, and best efforts carry their own enthusiasm.

¶ 8006 Pleasing your customers raises your own enthusiasm

You will enjoy enthusiasm and success in the degree to which you make a point of pleasing your customers.

⟶WHAT TO DO⟶ 1. Make a written note of your customer's likes and dislikes, his interests and hobbies.

2. When you are with him, say something you know he will like to hear.

3. Send your customer cards for appropriate occasions.

4. Between calls phone or write your customer.

¶ 8007 Knowledge stimulates enthusiasm

Learn more about yourself, your product and your customers and the extra knowledge will give you greater confidence and security. Your enthusiasm will increase in direct proportion to your knowledge of your job.

⟶WHAT TO DO⟶ 1. Schedule periodic classroom sessions with yourself. Do this in your non-selling time.

2. Test yourself with questions about your product, your customers, and yourself.

3. If you don't have the answers to the questions you raise, find them out as quickly as possible.

4. Use the personal check charts at ¶ 9058.

¶ 8008 Make a habit of associating with successful people

You can increase your enthusiasm and in some measure increase your success if you make a habit of associating with people who have become successful.

When you seek out the successful person, listen to what he has to say. Ask him for his opinions and advice. You will find that almost invariably he is a positive thinker and willing to help you.

It's important to keep your association with successful people a two-way street. Be willing to share your ideas, too.

¶ 8009 Keep physically fit

Keeping physically fit is one of the requisites for building and maintaining enthusiasm.

Give yourself plenty of rest, the right foods, and normal cleanliness. Your body will then perform willingly and with energy.

⟶REMEMBER⟶ You will find yourself able to make more calls, speak with a stronger, more convincing voice, and give more forceful presentations. You will also have enough "drive" at the end of each day to plan your next day's sales.

¶ 8010 An increased income goal will increase your enthusiasm too

Free yourself from the limitation that an unchanged earnings outlook places on your enthusiasm. If you think of "balancing your budget" solely in terms of your present income and do not raise your goals from time to time, the self-imposed limitation will retard your professional growth.

⟶WHAT TO DO⟶ Plan an income that has definite, periodic increases. Give yourself "raises" by setting yourself higher monthly or annual income goals. Having chosen a definite goal concentrate all your energy and thought toward its accomplishment.

It is necessary to keep increasing your goals if you are to become, say, a $30,000 a year man. As soon as you seriously set a higher goal of earnings than your present achievement, you begin thinking of yourself as a bigger earner. And thinking of yourself as a big earner makes you act like one when you are with a prospect. You become strong, confident, and able. These are qualities that influence men to buy from you.

¶ 8011 Believe in your ability to reach goals

Just as right thinking will strengthen your enthusiasm, so will a belief in your own power to reach the earnings goal you have set. Belief helps to generate enthusiasm.

Frank Bettger, a mighty powerful salesman,

¶ 8011

says in "How I Raised Myself from Failure to Success in Selling:"[1]

"Let's see how starting off with a good fifteen-minute workout of the smile muscles helped me during the day. Before entering a man's office I would pause for an instant and think of the many things I had to be thankful for, work up a great big, honest-to-goodness smile, and then enter the room with the smile just vanishing from my face. It was easy then to turn on a big, happy smile. Seldom did it fail to get the same kind of smile in return from the person I met on the inside."

¶ 8012 **Planning builds enthusiasm**

The salesman who hasn't the least notion of what the morrow holds for him has literally nothing to be excited about. Planning each day's work is therefore essential to building enthusiasm.

⇒WHAT TO DO→ Get a head start on the day's work by preparing for it the night before. You will rest easier and you'll eliminate the morning rush, confusion and upset caused by last minute preparation. See the planning forms at ¶ 9051 et seq.

¶ 8013 **A job behind you gives momentum**

Momentum accelerates enthusiasm. You can get some momentum before your first call of the day by getting one of the necessary, but not so profitable, jobs behind you before you get going at your main task—selling. Filling out a report completely and carefully is an accomplishment that gets you on the way with some momentum. Finding the information you promised to give a customer is another accomplishment to give you the feeling of going forward. Try to select a job that you can complete in the time available, or at least one on which you can make substantial progress.

¶ 8014 **Your timing is important**

There are only two important times during the day for you to make sales calls.

The first is immediately after you have *made* a sale. The second is immediately after you have *failed to make* a sale.

Why? Because there is never a time when you are in better shape to give a prospect your best than just after you have closed a sale. You then have the smell of success in your nostrils, the feel of success in your muscles. Then, if ever, you are a giant.

On the other hand, it is doubly important to make another call immediately after a failure. That's the time when you need a call to restore the confidence and enthusiasm you lost when you failed to make that sale.

¶ 8015 **Whole-heartedness is a byproduct of enthusiasm**

One test of whether enthusiasm has become part of your equipment for volume selling is whether you are doing all parts of your job, even the routine ones, wholeheartedly. Take the non-selling duties of keeping records, making reports, planning work, and studying new products. If you are doing these tasks well, promptly, and willingly, you know that your enthusiasm has developed into a habit.

¶ 8016 **How to become more relaxed— control your nerves**

In this tense, high-pressured world today, it's sometimes difficult to maintain your enthusiasm. Therefore it's important for a salesman to know how to keep control of his emotions and not let his nerves get the upper hand.

⇒WHAT TO DO→ Take the advice of several of the country's leading doctors, who offer these tips for 'outwitting' your nerves:

(1) *Be systematic.* Exert more control over yourself, your actions, your habits, and put system to work. (9 times out of 10, these experts say, nervousness is caused by a simple lack of system in living.)

⇒WHAT TO DO→ Organize your thoughts and plan a mental schedule of what you want to accomplish. And, follow it through —giving yourself ample time for what you must do.

(2) *Learn how to decide.* You become nervous, the doctors say, because you cannot decide things—so, you don't try.

⇒WHAT TO DO→ Start making decisions, today. Begin with the little everyday ones, working up to the big or major decisions. They will then be easy because you'll be in training for them.

(3) *Develop more will power.* When you make up your mind, stick to your decision. Follow through on what you say you will do.

⇒CAUTION→ Don't allow your nerves to play havoc with you *after* you've made a decision. Once you've made the decision—stop worrying about it.

(4) *Laugh more and develop your own sense of humor.* Most people who are ner-

how to build and maintain enthusiasm

vous take everything—especially themselves—much too seriously.

→ WHAT TO DO→ Learn to laugh at trifles. Learn to laugh at *yourself*. This is a very hard lesson, but the most *valuable* one.

(5) Learn to live easily. This does not necessarily mean "easy living." "But," the doctors conclude, "staying relaxed, poised and self-possessed is a must for nerve control."

→ WHAT TO DO→ Budget your time so that you have an opportunity to unwind. You can't go at a top speed all day, everyday. Give yourself some time to relax.

¶ 8017 Strengthen your morale through good company relations

If you feel that your home office "doesn't know what it's doing half the time", you have created a morale-destroying conflict between yourself and your employer. Your dissatisfaction will make it impossible for you to maintain enthusiasm and perform in your best style. Your critical attitude is bound to be detected and as your fellow employees in the home office learn that it is hard to please you, they will stop cooperating with you.

▶ **IDEA IN ACTION** Lester Smallwood has been a salesman for his company for 17 years. More as a habit than anything else, he has progressively been more and more critical of the home office. One day this conversation takes place between two clerks:

"Here's a wire from Sam Toomey asking us to rush out an order," says Frank, the shipping clerk.

"Well, I was just getting ready to fill this rush order Les Smallwood sent in," answers Tom, his helper. "We can't get them *both* out today. Which one shall we ship?"

"Well," answers Frank, "better ship Sam's. Sam doesn't mark *every* order 'rush,' but Les is so sure we don't know what we're doing that he'll squawk no matter whether we fill his order today or tomorrow."

→ WHAT TO DO→ If you find yourself continually "griping," candidly ask yourself, "Would I really be any happier with another company, or have I for some reason allowed my own morale to slip to the point where I no longer see straight on things that affect me and my job?"

Look for the things that are right about your company and your working conditions. They will help you change your attitude and restore your enthusiasm.

When you have a justified criticism, offer a constructive suggestion at the same time, but watch the tone of your communication to be sure it will not be interpreted as carping.

¶ 8018 Use a no-sale as the basis for renewed enthusiasm

Pave the way for an enthusiastic return interview with your unsold customer by making him your friend.

→ WHAT TO DO→ 1. When you fail to close a sale, act as pleased as if you had made it.

2. Ask the buyer why he failed to buy from you. You will often get a surprisingly honest and helpful answer.

3. Let your customer know you appreciate him and his business even though you don't sell him all the time.

¶ 8019 Create enthusiasm by changing your customer's "No" to "Yes"

You can create enthusiasm and increase your income at the same time if you make a habit of simply ignoring your customer's first "No". Remember that this first "No" is seldom a final decision and that if you stop at this point you will frequently lose his confidence and business.

→ WHAT TO DO→ Learn how to make objections work for you [¶ 7001 et seq.] and the technique of multiple closing [¶ 6001 et seq.] and you will learn how to turn your customer's "No's" into an enthusiastic "Yes!".

¶ 8020 Change your attitude if it's glum

If you feel fear, apprehension, or anxiety about a particular selling job, be guided by the sound psychological principle that you can change your feeling and thoughts to cheerfulness and confidence through proper direction of your thinking. It will take conscious effort, and even some pressure behind the effort, to substitute healthy emotions like courage and determination for the stress emotions, but it can be done! Begin by repeating over and over to yourself: "I am going to keep my thinking and my attitude calm; I am going to do this job successfully."

Then make your actions suit the counsel. Don't fritter away your energy and time on trivial tasks that suddenly seem important. Direct your steps toward actions that will bring you nearer to the fulfillment of your determination. Prepare your approach to the customer;

review your presentation; decide to try to close often. You will find that your thinking and feelings have changed from fear to eagerness.

¶ 8021 Overcoming negative influence of the past

It is good to learn from past failures, mistakes, or disappointments, but it is disastrous to dwell upon them in self-accusation, self-pity, or self-justification. Once you have discovered how to profit by the error, dismiss it from your mind. Mulling over it will simply cripple your energies, will-power, and chance for success.

If you find it hard to throw off the dejection, try these sound spirit builders:

1. Go to see a friend or acquaintance who emanates enthusiasm and always makes you feel good. Stay away from people who are habitual failures, who talk negatively about their past, present and future.

2. Find a hobby that will absorb your interest. The new skills and information that you acquire through such hobbies as painting, photography, collections of various kinds, gardening, do-it-yourself repairs, and the like, will make you feel alive and vital. There's nothing like the new experience of a hobby to keep you from cogitating on your troubles. Try it!

3. Go where you are part of an audience. Seeing others in action will make you less aware of yourself and your worries. At competitive games you will observe the skill, determination, and enthusiasm of the players—all pointed reminders that selling requires the exercise of these same qualities for winning.

¶ 8022 Learn to generate your healthy, positive emotions

Dr. John A. Schindler in his book "How to LIVE 365 Days a Year," states that 50% of those seeking medical aid today have emotionally induced illness.[1] In other words, unhealthy emotions cause and contribute to illness. Whether a person is well or ill, generating the healthy emotions of cheerfulness, determination and courage produces salutary effects. It can build your confidence and raise your enthusiasm. The following guides to generating healthy emotions are based upon the sage observations in Dr. Schindler's now famous book.

• Like your work. Work is therapy and liking your work will be a constant stimulus to your healthy emotions.

• Learn to like the people you work with.

• Learn to accept your adversities. By taking setbacks in your stride you can change them into stepping-stones to success.

• Meet all your problems with decision. Don't turn a problem endlessly over in your mind. Decide what's to be done—then do it.

• Make the present an emotional success. Don't live in the future, but enjoy each moment as it comes along.

¶ 8023 How to keep 'defeatism' out of your selling days

Become an even bigger producer by making sure that 'defeatism' doesn't creep into your overall sales thinking. You should be on your guard when (1) planning calls, (2) seeing customers, and (3) asking for the order.

Here are some examples of how defeatism could cost you sales and what you can do to prevent it from bogging you down:

¶ 8024 Four key problems

Problem #1: What time to start the selling day?

Defeatism: "I'll give the prospect a chance to open his mail and get set before I call." *Result:* First call: 10:15.

Right way: "I'll nail at least one man every day before he gets a chance to get nettled by his normal business problems. I might steal a jump on the competition." *Result:* First call: 8:45-9:00.

▶ **IDEA IN ACTION** Try to visit a growing account when making an early call. *Reason:* Your eagerness and enthusiasm should impress him. It's your way of saying that you and your company put in a full day.

Problem #2: What time to close up shop?

Defeatism: "There isn't much sense in calling a prospect when he's liable to be short-tempered and anxious to get home." *Result:* Last call: 4:15.

Right way: "I'll revamp my presentation to take into account that my prospect has had a long day and he could be a bit upset." *Result:* Last call: 5:15.

▶ **IDEA IN ACTION** Let the prospect know just how long you're going to take when making an end-of-the-day presentation. This will help you keep his attention and he won't be constantly watching the clock and wondering how much longer you're going to be.

Problem #3: Can the Jones Company be sold?

Defeatism: "Everyone knows that Jones is tied up with its present supplier. There is no chance of cracking that account." *Result:* No chance for new sales.

Right way: "This account is too large to let it go uncontested. There isn't a company that isn't on the lookout for a better offer." *Result:* New sales.

▶ **IDEA IN ACTION** There are many ways to break a competitor's stranglehold on a prospect. One way is to cite the many disadvantages of doing business with one supplier. Here are three ways to get the point across:

A. "The lone supplier tends to take you for granted."

B. "You'd improve your chances of getting a rush order if you had a supplier in reserve."

C. "You'd get top-flight service from us. We're out to prove ourselves."

Problem #4: Should a steady customer be asked for added business?

Defeatism: "I've been calling on the Edwards Company for years. You can't aggravate a good account by being pushy." *Result:* Stagnant sales.

Right way: "The Edwards Company is losing money by staying with its present equipment. I'll show them how, by stepping up to our higher-priced model, they'll actually cut costs in the long run."

▶ **IDEA IN ACTION** Stress the positive. Point out to your customer all the advantages he can get by stepping up. Show him examples of how your other customers—who already use the better (and higher-priced) product have benefited.

This approach gets the customer to re-evaluate whatever earlier reasons he had for refusing to buy other—perhaps more expensive—items in your line. *Result:* Added business, happier customer.

¶ 8025 Talk yourself into self-confidence

This is a technique that is especially helpful when your business or outside concerns are sapping your energy, enthusiasm, and spirit. What you need at such moments is a realization that a change of thoughts works wonders in changing your outlook.

⇛**WHAT TO DO**⇾ 1. Pick a meaningful self command to raise your spirits, like "I can, I will, I must have confidence in myself."

2. Repeat the words to yourself every now and then, or say them out loud, till they become part of your attitude.

⇛**REMEMBER**⇾ The locker room "pep talk" is built upon this idea. The principal difference, however, is that the ball team depends upon the coach to raise their enthusiasm and the players depend upon each other to "talk up" their strength. Most of the time you must depend upon yourself to be both coach and team. Fortunately, any salesman who has built or is on the way to building an annual net income in five figures has the capacity to be his own self-motivator when a change of spirit is needed.

¶ 8026 How to overcome fear of the "tough" customers

If you decide in advance that a customer is "too tough to be sold" you are depriving yourself of a selling opportunity. When you believe that even the "tough" customer is a subject for good salesmanship you will overcome defeatism and pave the way for more sales. You will take on all of the "hard to sell" people with confidence.

You will increase your chances to sell such a customer by following these simple guides:

• Win his attention. The customer who has a reputation for being "tough" is most likely a demanding buyer. He will not be satisfied with a run-of-the-mill approach. This type of buyer demands your best. However, once he is sold he will probably be sold "hard".

• Pay attention to his wishes. The hard-to-sell customer probably got his reputation through setting high standards. Remember, he is in a better position to know what he wants than you are. If you satisfy him you have a good chance to sell him.

• Establish confidence. The tough buyer may be a cautious buyer. It's up to you to establish confidence by showing that you're willing to serve him.

• Remember to close. Some salesmen are frightened off by a "hard" buyer and so never get as far as the close. If you remember to try to close, not once but many times, you will have a good chance to succeed.

¶ 8026

¶ 8027 A good laugh will banish tension

Laughter can often relieve tension between your customer and you. If witticism doesn't come to you spontaneously, you can at least think about the situations that try your patience and be prepared with an appropriate remark or story that you know gets a laugh. A little practice in the telling will give you assurance.

Although a "good story" will never take the place of a good presentation, knowing when to make a humorous remark will often carry you over a delicate situation that may arise in your interview.

EXAMPLE: The salesman was about to demonstrate the model he had just gone over point by point when his prospect said "No." Anxious to avoid antagonizing his prospect, but unwilling to stop his presentation, he overcame the situation by saying, "Do you mind if I plug it in anyway? I haven't seen the darn thing work for over two weeks." The customer laughed and the relaxed salesman went on to make the sale.

¶ 8028 Review, analysis, and planning restore enthusiasm

At the end of a day well spent in selling, your enthusiasm will decline to a relaxed level—like that of the artists who perform at concert pitch. But you have two wind-up activities that will restore it to a good tapping level for the next day—your evaluation of your own performance and your planning for the next day.

How to evaluate a day's work is discussed under the tab, "Breaking Into Big Selling," ¶ 1067; how to plan for increased production is explained at ¶ 1068.

Self-management for more profitable selling

¶ 8041 Your guide to self-management

To be a really big earner you have to know how to manage not only the selling end of your business but you have to know *how to manage yourself.*

On this "personal" side of the problem—this "subjective" side—is where many men who could be big salesmen fall down.

This section of the Guide shows how to manage yourself for greatly increased income.

• It tells how to keep yourself at concert pitch day after day—so every day becomes one of your good days—so you're energetic and clear-headed and filled with buoyant expectancy.

• It shows how to handle the personal management of time so you have more of it for the actual job of selling—the only time that means money to the salesman.

• It shows what you can do to make a better personal impression—how to put yourself across with your prospects—and thus make sales more easily.

• It shows how to make the most of your personality—how to capitalize on your unique strengths—how to correct the shortcomings that hurt you in selling.

• It shows how to prepare yourself for greater selling effectiveness—how to use your "personal" time for increasing knowledge and skills.

Self-management techniques to gain selling time

¶ 8042 Figure your gain from added selling time

Every hour added to your selling time increases your income. Selling time is the time you spend face to face with a customer. Take the value of each selling hour and see how much more you can earn by adding 1, 2, 3, 4 or more selling hours to your day.

⟫⟫WHAT TO DO→ Divide the number of hours you spend in interviews each week into your weekly income. The answer is the value of your selling hour.

EXAMPLE: A salesman spends an average of 20 hours in interviews and earns approximately $200 a week. His selling time is worth $10 an hour. For each selling hour that he adds to his average of 20 he can earn an average of $10 more a week.

This table shows you how much your income can be increased.

Value of selling hour	Earnings increase per week by adding			
	1 hr.	2 hrs.	3 hrs.	4 hrs.
$ 5	$ 5	$10	$15	$ 20
10	10	20	30	40
15	15	30	45	60
20	20	40	60	80
25	25	50	75	100

¶ 8043 Determine the time you spend in each selling activity

A record of the time you spend on each of your selling activities will enable you to manage your time for best results and to quickly attain your higher income goal. It will show you which activities are cutting unnecessarily into your potential earnings, and which activities need more of your time.

⟫WHAT TO DO→ Use a small note pad to record the exact number of minutes you spend performing each activity. Travel time, time spent waiting for customers, interview time, "break" time, and time spent in desk work are the activities you can list. You will have to refer to a watch to be accurate.

 IDEA IN ACTION Glenn Robinson kept a record of his time. This is what it showed after one week.

¶ 8044 **Increase the selling hours by scheduling desk work last**

If you have "things to take care of at the office," seriously consider the advantages of setting aside the last hour of the day rather than the first hour for this purpose.

IDEA IN ACTION George Wilkins represents a manufacturer of portable power tools.

He does not schedule an appointment for 9 o'clock in the morning but devotes an hour or so to take care of the morning mail and to clear away paper work. Since his customers know that George is at his office during this time they call him for information, quotations, special services, etc. He is conscientious and takes

	Monday	Tuesday	Wednesday	Thursday	Friday	Total
Travel	1½ hrs.	1¾ hrs.	2 hrs.	1¾ hrs.	1¼ hrs.	8¼ hrs.
Waiting for Customers	1¼ hrs.	40 min.	1¼ hrs.	45 min.	1 hr.	5 hrs.
Interviews	2 hrs.	3¼ hrs.	2¾ hrs.	3 hrs.	2½ hrs.	13½ hrs.
"Breaks" (including lunch)	1½ hrs.	2 hrs.	1¾ hrs.	1½ hrs.	1¼ hrs.	8 hrs.
Desk work	45 min.	1 hr.	50 min.	1¼ hrs.	40 min.	4½ hrs.

Glenn saw that he spent too much time traveling. He cut down on this non-profitable activity by routing his calls economically [¶ 2071]. He also cut down on time spent waiting for customers by using the pre-approach methods that assure prompt reception [¶ 4013]. Glenn noticed that he never spent less than 1¼ hours on "break" time. He decided to limit himself to one hour a day. Desk work was done at home in the evening, giving Glenn approximately 4½ additional hours each week to devote to calls.

As a result of this time-management record, Glenn became aware of the extent to which he wasted potentially profitable hours. He increased his interview time by cutting down on unprofitable jobs.

⟫SUGGESTION→ You have to work harder when economic conditions are unfavorable. In such times, devote more time to actual selling each day and you'll make up for the extra calls it takes to get the order.

the time and trouble to fulfill these requests immediately.

George finds that he is not ready to begin selling until almost lunch time, and his first appointment is often not until 1:30. When he sees that his sales are dipping dangerously he decides to make his first call at 9 in the morning and to stay out in the field until 4:30. George then finds that during this later hour he can take care of things at the office more efficiently and with fewer interruptions. His sales increase because he has more than doubled his selling time by this one simple technique.

Do your non-selling jobs after normal selling hours. In practically no instance are you justified to take time for desk work at the start of the day.

¶ 8045 **Where to cut time wastes**

You can increase your time spent in actual selling by plugging the leaks where waste occurs. Examine the following list; then manage every minute of your time to pay off in dollars earned.

- Waiting for customers. You can cut down on time spent waiting for customers by setting up definite appointments.
- Talking to customers who can't buy. You may be wasting your time if you "take a chance" by calling on a "customer" about whom you know little or nothing. Even cold canvassing requires some qualifying of customers. See ¶ 2031 et seq.
- Talking to the wrong man. Be sure that your customer is the man who is authorized to buy. See ¶ 2035.
- Talking about the wrong product. Be sure that you know which of your products will best fill your customer's needs before you give him an unnecessary run-down of your line.
- Losing time in traveling. Schedule your calls to reduce travel time. See ¶ 2071 et seq.
- Miscalculation of customers' potential. Always keep in mind the dollar value of your time and you won't be spending more time on customers than they're worth to you.
- Talking too long. Once you have finished the business of your interview you should leave.
- Too many "breaks." Limit yourself to one or two breaks a day, and be willing to sacrifice them if they interfere with your job of selling.
- Too many calls on friends or others who are not prospects.

⋙WARNING→ Let's assume that each of your selling hours is worth $5.00. Each 15 minutes wasted costs you $1.25. A dime cup of coffee that causes you to waste 15 minutes costs you at least $1.35. The greater your earnings objective, the costlier the cup of coffee. Each time you are tempted to waste selling hours, ask yourself this question—is the cause worth the cost?

For more ideas on how to plan your time for bigger selling, see ¶ 1061 et seq.

¶ 8046 **What to do when your customer keeps you waiting**

Mentally weigh the value of the sale you can make to your customer against the value of your time, if you have to wait for him. Your selling time is too precious to spend waiting for business that is too small to be profitable to you.

If you decide that it is worthwhile to wait, don't let yourself become irritated while waiting. Irritation destroys enthusiasm. Spend the time profitably: review your presentation; think creatively about your job; read something that has a bearing on your work.

Once you have decided not to wait, give a good reason for leaving and make an appointment for your return call.

¶ 8047 **How to save time in handling collections, adjustments and complaints**

Adjustments, complaints, and collections, if required of you, should be handled efficiently, but with the minimum disruption of your normal selling schedule and with the least possible waste of your selling time.

Make it a rule to get all the facts before you attempt to settle the matter in question.

You should temper the time-honored maxim, "The customer is always right," with this other modern sales rule: "Get the facts—all the facts—and then let your own good judgment, as well as your customer's, indicate the proper settlement."

You will lose valuable selling time if you start discussing the trouble upon hearing the customer's side of the story. Furthermore, you are actually in danger of losing, rather than encouraging, customer respect and good will if you immediately accept the blame when a customer states that something has gone wrong.

You will save your time and temper as well as that of your customer if you tactfully but firmly insist upon delaying the discussion until you possess all the pertinent facts that exist on both sides.

¶ 8048 **How to prevent 'wasted motion' from killing your prime selling hours**

Stop "wasted motion" from gobbling up your "prime" selling hours! Most salesmen waste some valuable selling time each day. How? By doing things in a way that doesn't produce any profits—in other words, "wasted motion." Every minute you can save from "wasted motion" means more sales for you.

⋙WHAT TO DO→ Develop a program that makes each hour of your day count. Here are two ideas you should be able to use:

self-management techniques to gain selling time

¶ 8049 Be a morning glory

The idea here is to sell when the selling is good. Hardly anyone will dispute the fact that the best selling times are the morning hours. Yet many salesmen find all kinds of reasons for staying in the office in the A.M. They argue that paperwork piles up and "just has to be handled." But if you consistently spend your mornings in the office, you'll end up with this—

⟶ SAD RESULT→ Any morning dropped from your in-the-field selling time costs you approximately one-fifth of your "prime" selling hours—and that's a lot of time, and a lot of sales!

Here's how one salesman learned the hard way: Tom Harding used to do his paperwork from 9 to 9:30 A.M. But soon his customers got wind of that fact.

"They used to start calling me right at 9:00," he told us. "One call followed another—until I didn't even get the paperwork done that I had intended to do. Two or three service calls or requests for information would chew up an hour."

"Then the morning mail would come in and by the time I read it and sorted it into piles for action, I had killed off more than two hours of my morning. I didn't seem to be able to put off the calls either. I felt I had to take care of them *right away*. Sometimes, it was noon before I could tear myself away."

Tom sees the light. "None of my customers knew, of course, what they were doing to my selling time with a 10-minute conversation. But then I realized it wasn't their problem at all, it was my own fault."

▶ **IDEA IN ACTION** "Now, I don't go near my office at all until *after* I have my day's selling work done. Then when I do go in—usually after 4:30 P.M., I take care of my mail and any minor service calls I have.

Result: "There's no question about profitability. I found I could add 10 hours a week to my prime selling time by *staying away from my office* in the morning. I still get all the paperwork accomplished, but my sales record sure shows the results of the switch."

⟶ WHAT TO DO→ Make your mornings, "money mornings." Stay away from your office and its non-paying paperwork during the early hours. Instead, schedule your paperwork for late afternoons, evenings, or perhaps even weekends.

¶ 8050 Know when to change your schedule

Every salesman must handle emergencies with reasonable promptness. But reasonable promptness does *not* have to mean dropping everything and upsetting a well-thought-out time schedule—or a carefully laid-out route sheet. The "I'll do it right away" attitude can be quite costly to your sales.

Reason: If you're going to extract all the "sales juice" that is in your territory, you must organize yourself expertly and then strictly follow your plan. Here's how Bill Ferris, paper salesman, found this out:

"I used to be the 'I'll get to it right away' type salesman. Every time an emergency came up, I'd alter my schedule to fit the customer in as my next call. This was great for my service record, but it wasn't helping out my sales record at all. I was wasting valuable time darting back and forth, and my schedule was always messed up."

▶ **IDEA IN ACTION** "Now, I plan my day so I can make as many of my scheduled calls as possible before noon. Sometimes, if I think any one company will take unduly long, I try to fit it in later in the day. This leaves my mornings jam-packed with sales opportunities and my afternoons more flexible. I'm able to take care of any unexpected calls without disturbing my sales plan. My customers generally don't mind if I see them later in the day, and I save time for selling."

⟶ WHAT TO DO→ Handle the unexpected call with finesse. First, find out what the "emergency" is. If it's minor, explain that you'll be there later in the day. If your customer has a genuine problem then it's better to alter your schedule and get there as soon as possible.

¶ 8051 Consider your prospects' work habits in deciding best time to call

Good timing is a primary factor in the success of a call. If you call at a time when the prospect is habitually not in a mood to be interrupted, he will refuse to see you or will give you only cursory attention and limited time.

⟶ CAUTION→ Don't try to solve the timing problem by making *general* rules that you won't make any calls before 9:30 in order to give the prospect time to read his mail; or after 11:30 because the prospect might have a luncheon appointment; or after 4 p.m. because the prospect may have his mind on signing letters or clearing his desk for the day. Such rules cut drastically into your valuable selling time. Also, they ignore the fact that work habits vary with different occupations.

⇒WHAT TO DO→ 1. Find out what is the best time to call on particular customers by direct inquiry. Discreet inquiry of the telephone operator, the prospect's secretary, or a member of his family, if evening selling is contemplated, will tip you off to a time when you will most likely find him in.

2. Study the work habits of your customers and prospects and base your timing on what you discover over a period of time.

Earl Prevette describes in "The Power of Creative Selling"[1] what in his findings were over half a century of successful selling. His vast experience is reflected in the following summary of what he calls "the scientific time" to call on prospects engaged in various pursuits.

- Executives and self-employed prospects: after 10 a.m.; between 2 and 5 p.m.
- Physicians, surgeons, etc.: between 9 a.m. and 12 noon; between 1 and 4 p.m.; between 7 and 9 p.m.
- Dentists: between 8:30 and 9 a.m.
- Lawyers: between 11 a.m. and 2 p.m.; between 4 and 5 p.m.
- Stock brokers, bankers, etc.: before 10 a.m.; after 3 p.m.
- Contractors, builders: before 9 a.m.; at noon; around 5 p.m.
- Professors and school teachers: *not* during school hours; between 6 and 7 p.m.
- Public accountants: any time during the day, but not from January 15 to April 15 (though some accountants finish their busy tax season between March 15 and April 15).
- Druggists and grocers: from 1 to 3 p.m.
- Insurance brokers: between 9 and 10 a.m.; at noon time; at 4:30 p.m.
- Publishers: after 3 p.m.
- Merchants, store heads: 10 a.m. to noon; from 2 to 5 p.m.
- Chemists and engineers: between 4 and 5 p.m.
- Clergymen: any time after Tuesday.
- Salaried people (under $5,000) and wage earners: between 8 and 9 p.m. at home.
- Housewives between 9:30 and 11:30 a.m.; between 1:30 and 4:30 p.m.

Self-management to make a positive impression

¶ 8061 How the buyer sizes you up

Put yourself in the place of the buyer and examine yourself for the impression you make. If you find yourself falling into an unfavorable "type"—one of those mentioned below—it's time to correct the impression you give through proper self-management.

- The superior salesman. If you approach a buyer with a big-shot attitude you will not be welcomed back. Use your knowledge to inform your customer, not to patronize him or show him that you are superior. Don't make your customer feel that you are looking down on him; such behavior will tempt him to buy from another salesman.
- The salesman who knows it all. If you claim to know everything you will only irritate your customers. Here's your reminder not to be "too smart": Your prospect or customer often knows as much as you do about your product.
- The salesman who knows nothing. If you fail to inform yourself about your product and your customer's needs you will remain an order-taker.
- The talkative salesman. Monopolize the interview and you will often talk yourself right out of a sale.
- The pressure salesman. If you try to high-pressure your customer into buying your product you will antagonize him .
- The salesman who misrepresents. If you oversell or give your customer false statements about your product you are inviting complaints and destroying your chances for a repeat sale.
- The salesman who bribes. Try to induce a buyer to purchase from you with a promise of reward and you will soon find yourself on his "unwanted" list.
- The "chummy" salesman. One way to damage customer relations is to abandon your professional status for a "let's be good friends" basis.
- The poorly groomed salesman. Buyers appreciate the respect you show them by appearing suitably dressed.

¶ 8062 Use enthusiasm as a sales aid

Make enthusiasm your most important sales aid and you'll boost your potential for added sales. A top buyer for a West Coast company told us that a salesman who generates enthusiasm has already taken the first big step in persuading him to buy. He added—

self-management to make a positive impression

"When a salesman shows me he's enthusiastic about his work, I feel he's confident about his product, and proud of the company he represents. His enthusiasm puts me in a buying mood."

How do you generate enthusiasm? First of all, you must have a winning attitude. You must believe that your product is the best—the only one your prospect should buy—and be prepared to back this belief with facts. In other words, know *everything* about your product.

Secondly, you must make your customer feel that he is important. Convince him that he will get all the attention he needs from you.

⇒WHAT TO DO→ Let him know right off the bat that you're enthusiastic about the meeting. Here are three things you should do:

(1) Concentrate on that first impression. Your smile, your facial expression, your manner of greeting a customer—your very words —help in establishing a good relationship, and encourage your prospect to respond favorably to you.

(2) Allow time for the prospect to express his views. While showing enthusiasm for your work—and your company's product is important, you should also be careful to give your prospect a chance to express his own views. Every buyer enjoys being heard. He also wants some manifestation from you that he is being heard.

⇒WHAT TO DO→ Recap when the prospect finishes. Then ask alert questions. This serves two purposes—(1) It shows him you were attentive and (2) in case something he said was fuzzy, the prospect will clear it up. If you're not sure of his objection or point, don't slide over it. You can say something like this:

I want to be sure I understand your objection. Are you saying . . . .?

Results: By showing that you're a good listener, you'll gain the prospect's respect. Then when you do offer your views, he'll be more receptive to whatever you have to offer.

(3) Offer encouragement and moral support. Make the person to whom you are speaking feel that you're interested in him and his problems and that you're willing to help him with those problems. If you can persuade the prospect to air his gripes and get his problems out in the open, you will build *his* confidence and enthusiasm. But more important, you've put the sale in motion.

⇒WHAT TO DO→ Talk to your prospect in a way that will mean something to *him*. Focus your attention on his needs, and treat him as a "unique" individual—not just another "prospect."

Result: He'll be eager to buy from you—not just once, but again and again.

¶ 8063 **Don't offend your customer by smoking**

The majority of the men you call on smoke or are entirely tolerant of others who do. Yet most of them definitely resent it if a salesman *enters* their office with a cigarette in hand or mouth.

No good salesman will "light up" once he is in the buyer's office, except under the following conditions: (1) when the buyer suggests it; (2) when the buyer himself is smoking; (3) when the salesman is on such a friendly basis with the buyer that he is *certain* his smoking will not be construed as an ill-mannered liberty.

¶ 8064 **Shake hands meaningfully**

A firm handshake is important in making a positive impression. Follow these directions to develop a meaningful handshake.

• Offer your full hand, not just the tips of your fingers.

• When your hand contacts your customer's, apply pressure. This will vary with the size and estimated strength of your customer.

• Make a clean break after you have shaken your customer's hand.

• Avoid "pumping" your customer's hand.

¶ 8065 **Walk with assurance**

The salesman who walks as if he had just closed a million dollar sale will impress others favorably; the man who saunters along in a half-spirited manner will make an unfavorable impression. Make your manner of walking give the best impression of yourself.

¶ 8066 **Practice poise**

There are times in the life of every salesman when pressures increase to the boiling point. When that happens to you, how do you meet the situation? If you allow yourself to get "steamed up" about each of the irritants, your enthusiasm evaporates as the pressure rises.

But if you manage to bear them with poise and assurance, you can still harness your enthusiasm and use it to help you over the rough periods.

The secret of maintaining poise in the face of mounting pressure—a run of bad breaks, a disappointing call, a new competitor who seems to be crowding you out—is to learn to control the little irritations.

¶ 8067 **Undue familiarity might damage customer relations**

Always let the customer lead the way when it comes to dispensing with normal, run-of-the-mill formalities.

If the *customer* begins to call you "Bill," you are perfectly safe, in the majority of cases, in calling him "Tom." The exceptions arise when the customer is much older than the salesman, or when his voice, manner, or some circumstance indicates that he doesn't *intend* the relationship to be one of full equality.

¶ 8068 **Enthusiasm doesn't condone brashiness**

Once you feel that you have "sold" your customer, don't run the risk of losing the sale by breaking the bounds of propriety. A customer chooses to buy from you because he feels that your product will benefit him most and that you will give him the best service. But even these reasons won't make him tolerate brashiness.

¶ 8069 **Keep your troubles to yourself**

A salesman must keep his troubles to himself. Customers may *sympathize* with the complaining salesman, but they rarely, if ever, react by *buying* from him as readily as they otherwise might.

The salesman must decide whether he can afford to follow the precept, "Misery loves company," or whether he is big and professional enough to live up to the maxim, "The show must go on." The answer will have a vital bearing on his sales results.

¶ 8070 **Why good speech is essential**

Your speech immediately identifies you as a salesman to listen to. A good definition of the importance of your speech is given by Johnnye Akin in her book, "And So We Speak"[1]: "Good speech is a badge of linguistic sophistication that gives security to those whose pursuits require exemplary speech."

Faulty speech can be eliminated and good speech habits substituted if you practice the following guides.

▶ *Awareness.* You do not become aware of the quality of your speech until you are in an environment where speech characteristics different from yours are dominant, or until someone points out your speech differences to you, or until you learn to look for them yourself. But not until you know what differences exist can you learn what to do about them. You must first learn to listen.

▶ *Listening.* Mere hearing will not enable you to correct your speech pattern. You must compare your speech characteristics with those of others who speak well before you will be in a position to correct yourself. Learn to listen intently to yourself and to others and the process of comparing and altering will become a habit. This will occur when you are properly motivated.

▶ *Motivation.* If you are properly motivated to change your speech you will have won half the battle. Consciousness that your speech characteristics are not as desirable as you would like them to be is perhaps the strongest motivation for correction.

An effective spoken word is the result of proper coordination of pronunciation, breathing, intonation, pitch, and rhythm. Fortunately for the busy salesman, it is not necessary to enter upon a formal course of voice culture in order to correct the majority of poor voice habits that affect salesmanship. What is required above all else is that the salesman become *voice conscious.* Few sales-killing voice mannerisms are caused by anything more serious than carelessness. Let the salesman become aware of his voice, and proper tone, speed, diction, pauses, and inflection usually result almost of their own accord.

¶ 8071 **How to use your voice effectively**

The following guides will direct you to proper management of your voice.

• Speak unhurriedly. Your customer should be able to hear every word that you have to tell him about your product.

• Speak clearly. You will inspire confidence in your customer when you give strength and importance to every word you say.

- Speak economically. Choose only those words that will state simply and effectively what you have to say.

- Speak with dignity. Give your product the importance it deserves by speaking of it with proper respect.

- Speak in a conversational tone. When you speak conversationally you reduce the possibility of tension developing between your customer and you. You will also become more persuasive.

- Smile when you speak. Smiling encourages your customer and indicates that you are willing to serve him.

- Use expressive words. Your speech can be improved if you find and use those words that best express the qualities of your product. See ¶ 5091 et seq.

IDEA IN ACTION Russell York is vice president of an average sized wholesale grocery concern. It is part of his job to talk with salesmen who call on his company to present various non-grocery products and services, such as stationery, office machines, insurance, trucks, warehouse equipment, and the like. He talks with eight or ten such salesmen each day.

The first man who called on him today was a "mumbler." "This chap must think he's talking to himself," mused York, as he cocked his right hand behind his ear to try to catch the salesmen's message.

Did the salesman catch the significance of this gesture? Not he! On he went, making it about as difficult for his words to "register" as possible.

But, more important, perhaps, is the fact that his method of speaking made it particularly easy for Mr. York to interrupt. He broke into the salesman's remarks, saying, "No, Mr. Hogan, we're really not interested in new lighting fixtures for our office. If you'll leave me your card . . ."

The caliber of the salesman's delivery *invited* interruption at will.

Mr. York's next visitor was of a different type. He told his story in a rasping voice that seemed to imply, "I just dare you to disagree with me!"

This chap was selling truck tires. Mr. York happened to have tire replacement on his mind, so he was an excellent prospect for the well known brand of tire this salesman was presenting. "Tell you what I'll do, Mr. Gregory," said Mr. York after about ten minutes of listening, "I'll check your prices against what we've been paying, and if there's no great difference, we'll try out your product. Is that fair enough?"

It was, of course, a crucial moment in the interview. Gregory knew the right answer, and he used the right words. "That's fair enough, Mr. York, but I just want to point out one thing more. I don't know what make of tire you've been buying, but if it's comparable to our own in quality and proven performance, price won't be an obstacle!"

It was an important point, well made, as far as *words* go. But there was that unfortunate *voice* quality—which made the whole remark seem almost a challenge.

As Mr. York asked his secretary to get him the necessary information, he thought to himself, "This chap doesn't sound as though he'd be too easy to get along with if something went wrong and needed adjustment. Seems a little on the belligerent side. Maybe we'd better stick to Joe, our regular tire man. *He's* so pleasant about everything!"

Mr. York's next two visitors used their voices to *good* advantage. But then along came a chap who was a "shouter." He bellowed his greeting, his message, his close. Furthermore, he committed one of the worst faults of salesmanship—he handed his prospect an important catalog sheet—but kept right on talking while Mr. York was supposed to be *reading* it!

This man, of course, talked himself out of any chance of getting an order. Few prospects fail to get annoyed when confronted with a "shouter." *No* prospect can *read* and *listen* at the same time. It was a bad performance indeed, voice-wise.

It may seem from the above that Mr. York had had a "bad day." Actually, Mr. York's day was *all too typical*.

¶ 8072 It's important to learn your sales talk perfectly

The difference between a presentation that has been learned perfectly and one that you only *think* you know well can mean the difference between making and losing a sale. Because it is extremely difficult to be objective in evaluating your own presentation, you should make a point to go through it before a person qualified to tell you how it sounds. He will be able to pick out the places where more effective words might be used, where rambling sentences might be cut down, and where important sales points might be clarified or emphasized.

IDEA IN ACTION Doug Curtis, an above average salesman, was called in by his sales manager to role-act the presentation the company had prepared a few months back. Doug sincerely thought he followed the presentation very well.

The sales manager, who listened critically, found these telling flaws in Doug's use of the presentation:

He had used the word "good" 17 times. (This colorless and almost meaningless word didn't appear once in the written presentation.)

He forgot completely to mention one rather important sales point.

He did not go into a close until he had finished his story, although the model presentation had three trial closes woven into it.

Finally, it took him four long minutes to deliver an inadequate version of a story that, in its suggested form, could be excellently covered in 90 seconds.

¶ 8073 How to train your memory

It is essential for you to remember the facts of your selling job: facts about your product, how to present it, names of prospects and customers [¶ 2065], your customer's needs and wants, a request, answers to objections, and the like. You can train yourself to remember the facts if you practice these memory-training techniques:

- Raise your interest in the things you want to remember. You will remember them more quickly and for a longer time.
- "Act out" the things you want to remember. Practice your presentation. This is particularly helpful if you must demonstrate your product and you can't afford to have anything go wrong.
- Learn details and characteristics. It's much easier to "peg" your memory to a specific detail than to a broad, ill-defined picture.
- Get a clear image of what you want to remember. Precise images will stay with you longer than blurred ones.
- Refer often to material you must remember. You refresh your memory with each review.
- Use your memory primarily for the most important aspects of your selling job. It is important that you "learn by heart" your presentation, your demonstration, and answers to possible objections. But make full use of prospect files, follow-up records, etc., in planning your work.

¶ 8074 Role-playing prepares you for the actual sale

Sales managers who use the personal coaching training method often play the part of a customer while the trainee goes through the selling process. This role-playing prepares the salesman for real selling situations in the field.

Whether or not you have had this type of coaching, you can use the technique to improve your skills. Take the time to rehearse imaginary sales. Practice what you will say and do when you are with your prospect or customer.

How to make the most of your personality

¶ 8091 Your personality is a composite of many factors

A salesman's personality is composite of *many* characteristics, all of which merge—in the prospect's mind—into one general impression. In dealing with management of his personality, the salesman must examine one facet at a time—just as a mechanic checks the carburetor, the spark plugs, and so forth, *individually*, to perform the only service that is of practical value—a *complete* tune-up. Only when the salesman understands this fundamental rule—that any one manifestation of personality may act as a sales handicap—is he prepared to think constructively of his own personality.

It is essential to understand the difference between the old-fashioned and modern concepts of "personality." Under the old way of thinking, a salesman whose appearance, voice, manner, and attire made an excellent first impression would automatically be rated as having an outstanding personality. Under the modern concept, if the same salesman indulges in minor misrepresentations or makes promises he isn't certain he can fully execute, he is rated as having a poor personality. The *modern* yardstick recognizes the reactions of others as the only true index.

In making the most of your personality, you

how to make the most of your personality

must consider your characteristics, your habits, and your conduct.

¶ 8092 Plug up 'personality leaks' to step up your sales

Plug up "personality leaks" and you'll plug in to big sales. Most salesmen—at one time or another—offend some of their customers by little actions that they may not even be conscious of doing at all.

Here are three personality leaks that can lose a sale:

(1) *Brusque telephone manners.* Many salesmen who are gracious face to face are as unreasonable and difficult when they use the telephone as they are when driving a car. And, you know how people act in traffic jams!

⇛WHAT TO DO→ Plan your phone calls like you plan your presentations. Know what you are going to say—but say it smoothly. Don't fly off the handle.

(2) *Curtness in letters.* This is another failing, a tendency to write curt, short, discourteous business letters. And many a salesman who is pleasant and ingratiating in person, sounds like an old bear when he dictates a letter to a good customer.

⇛WHAT TO DO→ Read your letters over when you finish them and ask yourself: "Would I say this if I were standing in front of my customer?"

(3) *Selfishness.* Customers resent the salesman who monopolizes all his time and doesn't allow him to voice his opinions. Selling is a 'give and take' situation.

⇛WHAT TO DO→ Make every customer you talk to feel like a bigger person. Ask him for his opinion. Then compliment him when he makes a good point. Avoid interrupting and acting bored.

If you treat your customers as if they are the most important people in the world—they will treat you likewise—and your sales record will show the results.

¶ 8093 Sincerity will pay off

If your customer feels that you are sincerely interested in helping him and his business you stand a better chance to make more sales.

You can show your sincerity in a number of ways. Take the time and interest to ask your customer about his changing needs and wants. You will convince him that you are genuinely interested in selling your product to him.

Answer his calls for service immediately. Your attention will convince him that you are truly interested in his continued business.

Make regular service calls. You will assure him that you are honestly interested to know that your product gives him all that he expects.

Treat your customer and his business with respect. He likes to have himself and his work taken seriously.

Take his questions seriously. Your frank attempts to give him an accurate picture will express your interest in satisfying him.

¶ 8094 Courtesy advances your customer relations

The salesman who has a reputation for courtesy is the one buyers will welcome back.

Show your courtesy by respecting your customer's time. Get through with your business as quickly as possible. Your customer will appreciate that you value *his* time as well as your own.

Have the courtesy to remember your customer's likes. If you do and say the things that you know will please him you will always find your customer courteous in return.

Your courtesy reflects itself in your attitude. Make a point of being pleasant with everyone you meet. Your reward will be their good opinion of you.

Remain silent and attentive to your customer when he speaks to you. (See ¶ 4082 for handling the talkative prospect.)

Be as mindful of courtesy on your latest call as you were on your first.

¶ 8095 Tact turns opposition into agreement

The tactful salesman is able to meet his customers on their own ground. Achieve the habit of tact and you will be able to turn opposition into sales.

A picture of tact is given by Emille Raux in his book, "The Salesman's Complete Ideas Handbook." He tells of the tugs that guide liners into the open sea; they do not meet the larger ships head-on, but ease alongside headed in the same direction. They soon have the ship moving in the direction they want it to go.[1]

¶ 8096 **Use your power of charm**

Charm is the power to influence your customer by pleasing him. You can have charm like that which sparks the personalities of top-ranking salesmen because it can be developed. Here are the essentials:

- Readiness to adapt. Adapt yourself to the personality of your customer and to the requirements of his business and you'll find him responding warmly.
- Eagerness to be interested. Interest in the customer can show itself in your courtesy and kindness. Your eagerness to be interested will generate charm power.
- Quickness to praise. Acknowledgment of your customer's accomplishments by a "pat on the back" will make you more charming to him.
- Desire to be yourself. "Being yourself" can be the most charming thing about you. However, acting naturally is not enough if you have not developed habits that please.

¶ 8097 **You can help keep at peak selling by acquiring patience**

Patience is the ability to endure circumstances that would otherwise hinder you from performing at selling peak. You can cultivate patience by learning to control yourself in situations that normally tend to be aggravating.

Help yourself to exercise patience while you wait for customers by taking along something to read—a trade journal, sales magazine, a card outlining the steps of your presentation, or even a good book.

Have the patience to learn and to like the many details that are part of your selling job. Patience with company reports, files, prospect cards, etc. will pay off in more sales.

Develop the forbearance to remain calm in trying situations, whether they occur with a prospect or in your personal life.

¶ 8098 **Overcome your prejudices**

Because an open mind is important to every salesman, it is harmful to harbor the "blind spots" of prejudice. Prejudice closes a person's mind to sources that might otherwise be used to advantage. To banish prejudice, these self-disciplining measures are recommended:

- Remain open-minded toward people. A salesman must have an open mind or he reduces the number of potential prospects.
- Be partial to new ideas.
- Do away with preconceived notions that are not based on facts or reason. Decisions based on unsubstantiated ideas or "feelings", rather than facts, cannot lead to resultful selling.
- Be fair. Injustice is the other half of prejudice.

¶ 8099 **Resolve that your prospect will find you friendly**

An immediate friendly impression will make your prospect willing to listen to you; the opposite impression will soon cause him to terminate the interview.

Control your gestures, your bearing, your facial expressions and the tone of your voice, for each is an advertisement of your eagerness to be friendly.

¶ 8100 **Learn to judge your prospect's mood**

Give your sales an additional plus. How? Be a judge—a judge of your prospect's mood, that is.

Reason: With so many products to be considered these days, and with strong pressure from the top to watch costs, there are times when buyers want a salesman to be quick. If a salesman ignores this "mood" of the buyer, chances are he'll lose the sale.

⟩⟩⟩WHAT TO DO #1→   Develop your ability to perceive other people's moods. Practice on everyone you meet. Try to quickly discover whether the person is impatient, irritable, or "jumpy."

When you're in the buyer's office, look for these clues to his mood:

1) Does his phone keep ringing? When he speaks does his voice seem to "snap" with impatience?

2) Do people continually enter his office with some important papers for him to act on?

3) Does he tell others, "Someone's here right now and I can't do anything until he leaves?"

WARNING: If these things occur, then watch out. He is in the mood for a quick presentation.

Of course, you may not have to look for clues. He may tell you as you enter his office that he is busy and can't afford to waste a minute.

⟩⟩⟩WHAT TO DO #2→   Decide which sections of your sales talk can safely be left out in an emergency. Practice the abbreviated presentations until you can, if necessary, meet a five- or a ten-minute deadline.

Now you can handle an irritable buyer with the promise, "I'll only take five minutes of your time, Mr. Prospect." And you will also be sure of including all the key facts.

¶ 8101 Capitalize a mark of individuality in your customer

If your customer has developed an unusual characteristic you can often please him by the way you show that you've observed it.

IDEA IN ACTION Tom Worth observed that one of his customers always smoked and enjoyed an extra-long cigar. Tom took this as a cue to do one of those little things, like remembering a hobby, that sincerely flatter the customer. He presented this customer with a large novelty cigar neatly embedded in a closed box. The customer was so tickled at this recognition of his pet enjoyment that he asked Tom out to dinner. Tom's observation of an unusual characteristic went a long way to cement his relationship with this buyer.

¶ 8102 You must be a self-starting salesman

It takes a determined, self-starting salesman to win out in today's highly competitive market. Self-starting power will put you far ahead of others who waste valuable selling time by postponing their work.

Here are guides to help you build your self-starting power.

• Begin immediately. Don't waste your time waiting for a vague impulse or someone else to get you started. Right now is the time for you to begin.

• Avoid putting-off. If you procrastinate you will disrupt your schedule and lose valuable selling hours.

• Finish the first job. Form the habit of finishing the first job you start. A completed job behind you will give you the necessary momentum to plunge into the day's work.

¶ 8103 You can strengthen your character through self-reliance

When you rely on yourself you learn to depend less on others. Your reward will be greater confidence in yourself and more conviction in your actions.

Self-reliance is a necessary virtue for the salesman who is largely his own boss and the maker or breaker of his own fortune.

¶ 8104 Check your habits

The sum total of all the habits you have acquired during your lifetime are reflected in your character. Good habits can be formed and strengthened. Undesirable habits can be stopped once you learn to recognize them. Remember that your habits are consciously acquired and can be consciously improved.

Check your habits by self-questioning. Here are some questions with which to get started:

• What habits do I have that give me a good start on the selling day?

• Do I make a habit of putting my customer's welfare before my own?

• Have I acquired the habit of positive thought and action?

• Do I practice habits that keep me physically strong?

• Do I practice habits that refresh me spiritually and keep me mentally alert?

• Do I make a habit of small courtesies?

• Have I acquired the habit of preparing myself thoroughly before I call on my customers?

Through self-management you can develop and strengthen good habits that will make the best impression on your customer.

¶ 8105 Personal mannerisms can affect a sale

A gesture that is used purposefully to emphasize a point or to add force to a demonstration can help make any sale. But a mannerism that diverts a prospect's attention from the business at hand or that irritates the prospect, is a fault to be corrected.

IDEA IN ACTION Herb Colby is a dynamic salesman who "burns up lots of nervous energy" in his work. His industry and enthusiasm, plus his mastery of selling technique in general, have made him a high score producer. Yet periodically he goes into a slump that he cannot account for.

The answer is simple. When he is having an uphill time of it, Herb uses several mannerisms that definitely distract attention from his presentation. As he makes an important point he frequently "pounds the desk" with the palm of his hand. Secondly, when it's the prospect's turn to talk, Herb is quite likely to shake his head in disagreement when an unfavorable point is made.

Herb is completely unaware of these mannerisms. Consequently, he does not realize that whenever the going gets really tough, he resorts to them even more than normally. It is this factor that accounts for his slumps.

Herb could easily school himself against these attention-diverters, and especially against his tendency to step them up when he is under a nervous strain. This would eliminate his periodic slumps as well as make his selling task easier.

⟶SUGGESTION→ A person who uses diverting mannerisms is almost always completely *unaware* of them. Watch your prospect's reactions to the way you act. Check yourself while actually giving a presentation, or ask a friend his opinion, if you want to be sure that your mannerisms are not distracting.

Most detrimental mannerisms can be detected by an honest checkup. To aid you, here is a list of the more common things to guard against:

- Strumming your fingers
- Chewing pencil or pen
- Toying with eyeglasses, pencil, etc.
- Constant crossing and uncrossing of legs
- Nodding or shaking head unnecessarily
- Exaggerated slapping or pounding table with hand or fist
- Toying with keys, coins, etc.
- Frequent interruption of prospect when he is talking
- Slumping in chair
- Looking bored while prospect is talking
- Exaggerated facial expressions
- Raising voice unreasonably when enthusiastic or excited

¶ 8106 **Punctuality shows that you are in control of your job**

If you fail to observe punctuality in your appointments you can never enjoy the full confidence of your customers. Meticulous care about commitments indicates that you are "on top of your job." Lack of this quality is interpreted as a mark of unreliability.

Most salesmen are put to the test of punctuality every day of their lives. When a customer specifies a certain shipping date, requests certain information or a quotation by a given time, or makes an appointment, he normally feels slighted if he is kept waiting. "I guess my business doesn't seem too important to him," is the usual conclusion. "This chap means well, but you can't rely on him," is a statement that every buyer makes from time to time.

A reputation for punctuality is easy to establish and maintain. Two things are required:
- Follow through to make certain that anything you undertake to do is actually performed on time.
- Explain immediately by note or phone call whenever this proves impossible.

¶ 8107 **Don't make yourself hard to buy from**

A customer will sometimes tip you off to what he wants to buy. When you get a "break" like this you must not try to sell him something else that you think he should buy. You must sell him what he has said he wants to buy.

IDEA IN ACTION Bill Morgan, selling electric signs, was offered an unusually large order. He had been told by his customer that there was no particular preference for color, design, and so forth. The only things he wanted were a type of sign that would suit his purpose, at a cost, on an order of 10,000 pieces, that would not exceed $15 per unit.

In spite of this guidance, Bill spent the first five minutes of the interview extolling the features of a sign which, he then blithely announced, could be bought for a mere $18. "Price isn't everything, you know," he countered as the buyer said that number wouldn't do. Bill then took three or four minutes to read a gratuitous lecture on the need to consider value in a deal of this sort. The buyer would remind Bill of the price, and Bill would go right on talking value and features—at prices that in each case were above $15.

Finally the buyer said, "Sorry, Mr. Morgan, but I guess you haven't got what we want."

"Wait a minute, I've just had an idea," said Bill. "We do have a sign that might fill your bill, but I still think you'd be better off with this other one."

As he wrote up his order for 2,000 fifteen dollar signs for a starter, Bill remarked, "When I got your message about a fifteen dollar sign, I thought you'd probably go a little higher for a better one, so I brought it along—just in case."

Bill's sale was smaller than it might otherwise have been. He ignored the obvious cues from the buyer and thus made himself hard to buy from.

¶ 8108 **Get the buyer in your corner: don't put him on the defensive**

You'll win more friends—and sales—by not creating a situation where the buyer feels it's necessary to challenge you on every point just to prove that he knows his business. *Reason:*

how to make the most of your personality

You may win the skirmish—but you'll never sell the buyer. And when you lose the sale, you've lost the war.

This type of situation may develop when a salesman backs the prospect against the ropes with any of the following:

1. "Of course, you know that our machine can do the job faster and better than the one you're using now."

Result: The buyer sees red. He's been put in a position where he has to defend his present machine. And there's a good chance that he probably made the *original* decision to buy it!

▶ **IDEA IN ACTION** "Mr. Buyer, would you mind going over these facts that I have prepared. I think you'll see that my machine can do the job for your company in a way that will save you money.

Result: The prospect doesn't feel that he has to defend himself; rather he can show himself as a fairminded man by agreeing to go over the figures. The basic reason for the different results is that the salesman has made his prospect feel like a hero instead of a heel.

2. "I think you should spread your business around." No matter what follows, the sale is lost. *Reason:* The buyer will resent, and rightly too, being told *how* to spend his company's money.

▶ **IDEA IN ACTION** "Mr. Buyer, I know that you give all your business to the Bay Company. What I want to do is offer you a plan that will *protect you* over the long run." (Note: *The salesman hasn't told the buyer how to spend his money. He's merely offering an idea. What's the difference? It could be a sale.*)

The new plan, of course, consists of the prospect switching some of his business so he won't be caught short if something happens to his present supplier. This time, the buyer is being approached from his viewpoint instead of the salesman's.

¶ 8109 Avoid putting a customer "on the spot"

It's never good strategy to put the buyer on a spot where he has no "out". His "out" is to turn down your proposition completely.

▶ **IDEA IN ACTION** Al Scott is introducing a new make of electric broiler. His company decides that the quickest way to launch their product is to run an initial advertising campaign direct to the consuming public, and to use the resulting leads and inquiries to convince local dealers that they should carry the line.

The home office accordingly sends to Al all the leads that come from various towns in his territory.

"Mr. Dealer," says Al on his first call, "we are introducing a new electric broiler that you can profitably sell. To prove its salability, we have advertised direct to the consumer. Here are some orders and leads that we want to turn over to you. You will, of course, get the full dealer's profit on these sales. We think this proves you can profitably stock and sell our line."

The dealer agreed and took on the line, ordering a dozen units in addition to those already sold.

Al then went to the next town in his territory, that was about three time as large as the first town. "This dealer should stock three dozen units," he said to himself. I think I'll tell him that we'll give him the orders from his town *provided* he orders three dozen extra."

"Young man," said the dealer when he had heard this proposition, "we aren't interested in carrying your line. You come in here with some orders and try to use these as a club to make us place an order that is much larger than we would otherwise place on a new item. Well, we don't like such tactics, and we aren't interested in your proposition."

¶ 8110 Use the right word to avert unpleasant situations

There are many times when the right word can turn a potentially unpleasant situation into an opporunity to cement customer relations.

▶ **IDEA IN ACTION** Salesman Smith finds himself provoked by a customer who tries to blame Smith and his product for his business slump. Smith says, "I understand that business is not as good as usual all over. Thank goodness we know that slumps are only preludes to peaks in business. I think this idea I have for you will help you be among the first to regain your usual high volume." His words of understanding make the customer's ill temper evaporate, and set up a healthy atmosphere for a successful sales talk.

At his next interview Smith is ushered into the office of a buyer who does not bother to acknowledge his presence, but continues to write at his desk. Smith could show his impatience in a number of ways or even leave. But he quietly stands there until the customer is forced to realize his breach of courtesy and offer him a seat. Smith makes a point to say "Thank you" warmly, indicating his willingness to overlook his customer's breach of courtesy.

Salesman Smith's next customer speaks sarcastically about the performance of Smith's product. Smith does not accept any blame or argue with his customer. He praises his customer for his good judgment and for not hesitating to express his opinions. Smith adds that he knows his product is a good one and that he is there to be of service to his customer. The customer's attitude soon softens, and by the time Smith invites him to repeat or write down his complaints most of them have disappeared.

Smith's last appointment for the day proves to be the most exasperating. The customer who had assured him that he would be free at 4:30 has not yet returned to his office. Bill does not let this affect him. He decides that the possibility to get an order is good, and that the dollar value of this customer warrants his waiting. He further reasons with himself that this customer has always been prompt before and rarely has kept him waiting. Smith's calmness in the face of exasperation pays off. The customer returns after 15 minutes, thanks Smith for waiting for him, then gives him a bigger order than he had expected.

¶ 8111 **A display of optimism can often make a sale**

Optimism, like enthusiasm, laughter, and other pleasant manifestations of your state of mind, tends to be contagious. Put your customer in an optimistic frame of mind, and you can often get him to buy.

▶ **IDEA IN ACTION** Stanley White, owner of a manufacturing business in Chicago, meets a neighbor on the morning train going to town. As they chat about the weather, politics, and business, the neighbor Owen Banks, mentions that his own business is "bad," and that he understands his competitors have felt a recession as well. "If you ask me, Stan," he continues, "we're in for some tough going. Things have been pretty good in our industry for quite a while, and I guess the old business cycle is catching up with us."

Mr. White arrives at his office feeling a shade depressed. "After all, business does have its ups and downs, and maybe Neighbor Banks is right in his conclusion that the cycle is on the downside.

"Maybe it would be wiser to hold off a bit on that advertising contract I was going to sign this morning," muses White as he digs into his morning mail.

At 11 o'clock a caller is announced. He is "Red" McNulty, a space salesman for an important national magazine.

"Red," says Mr. White, "I'm going to ask you to wait about a week on that contract. Business seems to be slipping off, and I don't want to sign up for a campaign of this size at the wrong time. Let me think it over, and call me in a week or so."

"Okay, Mr. White," says Red with an easy smile. "I know just how you feel. But if I thought we were in for a bit of a dip, I'd be the first one to say to all my accounts, 'Let's go easy.'"

"You mean you don't think things are tightening up?" asks White.

"Well, let's look at it this way," replies Red. "Yesterday, about 4 o'clock, I signed the *biggest contract* ever placed by the ABC Company. One of the country's biggest corporations—and they usually know what they're doing!"

"Yes," says White, "they're pretty smart operators!"

"But that's only part of the story," continues Red. "Earlier this week Hugh Simmons, our West Coast representative, wired in that he had just signed up the XYZ Corporation, who have never advertised with us before, but are now going to have a full page in each issue for 12 months."

"Say, you fellows are going to town!"

"Oh, I guess we're getting our share, all right! But what I get out of all this, Mr. White, is the fact that companies like those I've mentioned seem to figure that *they're* not going to just sit there and take it on the chin if sales do fall off a bit in their industries. No sir! Whether business goes up or down, they figure to *win* by keeping their names right in front of the buying public!"

Red's optimism was infectious. He had stated only two simple facts (about two companies), and one principle (the need for advertising in any event); two facts and one principle that many salesmen wouldn't even have bothered to mention. But "between the lines" Red's prospect could detect an attitude that *more* than offset what he had heard on the morning train.

Of course Red got his order. He got it by a display of *optimism*. Nothing else would have been likely to cause the prospect to buy at that time.

¶ 8112 **Six ways to change stress from enemy to friend**

Stress can be your worst enemy or your best friend. As an enemy it can wear you down in a number of subtle ways—hitting at body as well as mind—until you reach a point of no return. As a friend it may be essential to life, and it is indeed essential to personal progress and development. This is the conclusion of *Dr. Robert C. Page*, M.D., F.A.C.P., M.R.S.H., a leading authority on medical problems of the top executive.

▶ *Stress as an enemy.* The following types of stress situations, generally looked upon as dangerous, can be turned from vitality drainers to constructive exercises, according to Dr. Page.

(1) How to overcome fear of change. Aversion to "new ways" of doing things can become a nagging efficiency-sapper for even the most dynamic, most self-confident salesman. Every one of us, as we grow older, is faced more and more often with temptations to become set in our ways. Growing force of habit plus the natural tendency to follow the path of least resistance is just one of the "inevitable warts on the skin of humanity."

Case in Point: One salesman admits that he is immediately opposed to any really new idea that is presented to him. But the point is, he recognizes this tendency—and knows that everyone else shares it to some degree. So once he's got the "enemy" out in the open and unprotected, he annihilates it.

▶ **IDEA IN ACTION** The minute he feels that all-too-human opposition to a new idea welling up inside him, he remembers these words: *Will it work?* This is the only real criterion for any procedure in business. The fact that it also may involve a little effort to vault out of that "rut" should be immaterial.

Objective achieved—and more. This simple technique enables the salesman to judge a new suggestion *on its merits*. But what's perhaps more important, it also allows him to welcome the idea of change as an exciting stimulant to better performance, instead of dreading it as an irritation to be escaped.

▶ *Stress as a friend.* There's no need to waste words on the friendly aspects of stress. All you need to do is recognize the stress situations that are actually medicine for you.

(2) Keep a full schedule of activities every day. Beware, however, of letting your zest for work allow you to take on more than you can handle. As soon as you feel you are falling behind, take warning and adjust your pace accordingly.

(3) Set tough goals. Most competent men work best under pressure, provided it is not prolonged.

(4) Make opportunities to perform work at which you are good. You have certain talents or abilities at which you shine. The challenge that makes you put these particular talents into play is a first rate "battery-charge."

(5) Earn your moments of relaxation. The completion of a tough day's schedule will add savor to any form of evening relaxation.

(6) Get into nonvocational activities which you can do well. Any ego-boosting activity is good for you—as it is for anyone.

¶ 8113 **An effective last remark will often gain a second interview**

When you leave your customer on a high note you pave the way for a welcome return. You can make sure your customer will want to see you again if you spend a few moments planning what to say as you leave him. Suggestions:

• If you sell your customer, thank him for his business.

• If you do not sell your customer, thank him for his time.

• You can make your last remark a promise to bring something your customer may have requested.

• A friendly parting remark will leave a pleasant memory, particularly when it concerns something important to your customer such as his family or vacation.

⟶REMEMBER⟶ The salesman who has nothing gratifying to say when he departs will leave less incentive for his customer to grant him another interview.

¶ 8114 **Always keep the sales door open**

Every call a salesman makes doesn't result in a sale—but even "no-sale" calls can pay off in the long run. You must make sure you'll get another crack at the prospect by leaving like you've "just landed a big one."

It's sad but true that more than one salesman has killed a future sale by stalking out annoyed or making a snide remark after being turned down by a prospect.

The right way. A top salesman always thanks the prospect for listening to his proposal. He then says something to this effect: "When we meet across the sales table again, I hope to have better luck."

Payoff: He's already started to pitch for a future sale by saying he'll be back.

⟫WHAT TO DO→ Make sure you follow up your defeats. If you gain a prospect's respect the first time, chances are good you'll gain a sale the second time—if you come back with something new for him.

¶ 8115 Self-management can turn you into an expert closer

Through really good self-sales-management, a salesman can transform himself in a few weeks from a poor closer into a very good one.

▶ **IDEA IN ACTION** Ken Graye's trouble was that he was afraid to make a strong bid for an order. Time and again, when he had a man just about sold, he'd flunk out on some small objection like, "Well, maybe I'd better think it over for a day or two." He would take that as a signal to leave, instead of trying to show the customer why he had something to gain by acting immediately.

Then Ken's sales suddenly soared. He had looked at his record and seen that he had gotten nowhere during the past year, and that he still was weak at closing. He thought it was time for him to quit. This gave him an idea. He knew that if he were going to leave his territory in a week he could push his customers for all he was worth during the next few days.

Ken decided to make one final call on each of his customers. Whether they bought or not, it was going to be the last time he'd see them. He felt no need to hesitate, or accept the excuse "Next time." If a customer tried to brush him off Ken pulled no punches to get an order. He used the strong closing methods he should have used in the first place.

It is important to note that although Ken's new closing tactics seemed like "high pressure" to *him*, in actual fact they were nothing more than the tactics a strong closer uses all the time.

¶ 8116 Only you can follow through on self-management

It is not enough for you merely to recognize an area of self-management that needs improvement. To get results, you must follow through.

▶ **IDEA IN ACTION** Salesman Jones, in spite of his better-than-average ability, has been doing a below-average job. His sales manager calls Jones in to talk things over, and after a complete and frank discussion, Jones realizes that the trouble is due to his lack of proper planning. So he makes a firm resolve to lick that weak spot.

He succeeds, and after two months Jones finds himself leading the other salesmen in sales. Although he never would have found his error if he had been left to himself, neither his manager's analysis, nor his own resolve to correct the error would have been valuable if Jones hadn't followed through.

⟫OBSERVATION→ One or two efforts at self-management will not do the job. Regular and methodical self-management are necessary for any salesman who is aiming high.

¶ 8999 **Footnote references**

¶ 8002
  (1) "How I Raised Myself from Failure to Success in Selling," p. 8, published by Prentice-Hall, Inc., Englewood Cliffs, N. J.

¶ 8011
  (1) Published by Prentice-Hall, Inc., Englewood Cliffs, N. J.

¶ 8022
  (1) Pp. 4, 97-122, published by Prentice-Hall, Inc., Englewood Cliffs, N. J.

¶ 8024
  (1) Dockeray, Floyd C. and Lane, G. Gorham, "Psychology," p. 138, published by Prentice-Hall, Inc., Englewood Cliffs, N. J.

¶ 8051
  (1) Published by Prentice-Hall, Inc., Englewood Cliffs, N. J.

¶ 8070
  (1) Pp. 4-7, published by Prentice-Hall, Inc., Englewood Cliffs, N. J.

¶ 8095
  (1) P. 88, published by Prentice-Hall, Inc., Englewood Cliffs, N. J.

¶ 8102
  (1) "How I Raised Myself from Failure to Success in Selling," p. 17, published by Prentice-Hall, Inc., Englewood Cliffs, N.J.

PERSONAL RECORDS, INFORMATION SOURCES AND CASE PROBLEMS

Helpful Personal Records to Reach High-Bracket Goals
How to Find Information About People and Companies
Case Problems: How Would You Do It?

TABLE OF CONTENTS

Starts at Paragraph [¶]

HELPFUL PERSONAL RECORDS TO REACH HIGH-BRACKET GOALS

How to get maximum benefit from your personal records	9001
Combined prospect personal information card and record of calls (Forms 1-2)	9002
Prospect control records for call-backs (Form 3)	9003
Record of calls, inventory, and sales (Forms 4-5)	9004
Combined daily plan sheet and record of calls (Form 6)	9005
Route schedule (Form 7)	9006
Weekly work analysis form (Form 8)	9007
Personal Check Charts (Forms 9, 10, 11)	9008

HOW TO FIND INFORMATION ABOUT PEOPLE AND COMPANIES

Diversified publications give valuable information	9021
"Finder" for essential information	9022
Poor's Register of Directors and Executives	9023
Who's Who in Commerce and Industry	9024
Dun and Bradstreet Reference Book	9025
Moody's Industrial Manual	9026
Directories of banks and bankers (Polk's World Bank Directory; Rand McNally International Bankers Directory)	9027
Thomas' Register of American Manufacturers	9028
Directory of Directors in the City of New York (an example of a city directory of directors)	9029
Area directories (State and City)	9030
Marine News Directory (an example of a trade directory)	9031
Industrial Marketing (magazine) — Market Data and Directory (annual)	9032

Getting Information From Chambers of Commerce

Do Chambers of Commerce serve salesmen?	9033
What kind of information can you get from a Chamber of Commerce?	9034
Is information available in the form of a Directory?	9035
How do you go about getting information?	9036

CASE PROBLEMS: HOW WOULD YOU DO IT?

Is back scratching blackmail?	9051
Carpet laying, or is it lying?	9052
Let's look at the record	9053
What do we do for openers?	9054
Panning for gold	9055
Lighting Up or Striking Out	9056
Getting to see Mr. Big	9057
Are you really family?	9058
Sticking to the script	9059
Under-exposed benefits	9060
It's the sign of the times	9061
All the way in one play	9062

HELPFUL PERSONAL RECORDS TO REACH HIGH-BRACKET GOALS

¶ 9001 **How to get maximum benefit from your personal records**

Each record you keep should be tested against these three criteria:
- Will it serve an important purpose?
- Will it help you achieve top-level selling?
- Is it simple and easy to keep?

To get maximum value from your records, you must look upon them as an integral part of your objective to reach big selling, not as "paperwork to get done." Only by keeping and *using* records *with your earnings goal in mind* can they prove most profitable to you.

➤➤WHAT TO DO➤ 1. Select from the specimen forms given those that suit your needs. If your company supplies a particular form that serves the purpose of any offered here, use the company form, of course.

2. Make whatever changes are necessary in the form to suit your needs. Remember, each suggested form is merely a guide. Some of them may suit your needs perfectly just as they are; others might need slight changes.

3. Have a supply of the forms, changed to suit your needs, run off on a duplicating machine.

4. Record the information accurately and regularly.

5. *Use* the information you compile; *think* about it; *take action* to improve your selling record.

¶ 9002 **Combined prospect personal information card and record of calls (Forms 1 and 2)**

If your selling requires you to gather personal information about a prospect, some form of card or sheet, which classifies the information and contains the record of calls made, is usually necessary. Forms 1 and 2 are adaptable for this purpose. The survey information, of course, is determined by what you sell. Forms 1 and 2 contain sufficient detail to enable you to design a similar card to meet your needs.

▶ *How to use Form 1.* Numbers 1 to 31 at the top identify the days of the month, to be flagged for follow-up purposes. The abbreviations under "Other Investments" stand for savings banks (SB), savings and loan association accounts (BL), Government bonds (GB), securities (ST), real estate (RE). In the blank boxes opposite "Source" use your own code letters to identify the source of your prospect.

▶ *How to use Form 2.* This is the reverse side of Form 1. There is room at the top for insertion of additional personal information that you may want to include. In the "Interview Result" column, insert in the blank columns remarks similar to "out", "sold" that tell you what happened. In the "Further Action" column, if you need something more than "Call-back (C.B.) date," and "Literature (Lit.)," you can add other columns. The column "Radiation Names" is a reminder to you to get the names of possible prospects from your contact.

¶ 9003 **Prospect control record for call-backs (Form 3)**

It's important to know which product or product benefits you have already elaborated if you make call-backs on the same prospect. Your prospect is much more impressed, and more eager to listen to your proposition, if you always come up with new features that benefit him.

▶ *How to use Form 3 as a selling tool.* At the top of the chart, insert the items to be discussed with your prospect. The ideas are numbered. As each idea is discussed, insert the date in the proper block under the appropriate number. Under "Name," list the name of the company and the man that you called on. Then on each call, this chart will tell you what you have already discussed and what ideas you have left to discuss.

▶ *How to use Form 3 as a tickler followup.* This chart is also a tickler follow-up on your calls. On one chart, for instance, you can list all customers that should be called

personal records to reach high-bracket goals

1 2 3 4 5 6 7 8 9 10 11 12 13 14 15 16 17 18 19 20 21 22 23 24 25 26 27 28 29 30 31
(MR. MRS. MISS)

STREET	APARTMENT
CITY	☐ MARRIED ☐ WIDOW—ER
	☐ SINGLE ☐ DIVORCED
BUS. CONNECTION	OCCUPATION	MO. EARNINGS $ ACTUAL EST.

HOME ☐ OWN ☐ RENT	OTHER INVESTMENTS	BOY	GIRL	CHILDREN'S NAMES	AGE	AGE
☐ SINGLE	SB $				DATE	AP. AGE
☐ DUPLEX	BL $					
☐ FLAT ☐ APARTMENT	GB $				DATE OF BIRTH	
	ST $				DAY	MONTH	YEAR
MORTGAGE $	RE $	WIFE'S NAME			
INTEREST RATE %	TOTAL $				
SOURCE ☐A ☐C ☐B ☐V ☐R—FROM					

**Form 1. Prospect Personal Information Card
(Information Side)**

	ADDITIONAL PERSONAL INFORMATION	NOTES:
	OTHER DEPENDENTS:	
	FRIEND OF:	
	LODGE CHURCH	
	HOBBIES, RECREATIONS, ETC.	

DATE	INTERVIEW RESULT			FURTHER ACTION			REMARKS	TIME WITH PROSPECT	RADIATION NAMES
	OUT		SOLD	KILL	C.B. DATE	LIT.			

**Form 2. Additional Information and Record
of Calls (Reverse Side of Form 1.)**

personal records to reach high-bracket goals

```
                              PROSPECT CONTROL RECORD
              (Note: Insert opposite the numbers below the items to be talked about.)
    1.          6.                  11.             16.             21.
    2.          7.                  12.             17.             22.
    3.          8.                  13.             18.             23.
    4.          9.                  14.             19.             24.
    5.         10.                  15.             20.             25.
```

NAME	1	2	3	4	5	6	7	8	9	10	11	12	13	14	15	16	17	18	19	20	21	22	23	24	25	REMARKS

Form 3. Prospect Control Record

on twice a month. On another chart, those that should be called on monthly. You can have still another chart for those to be called on every 6 weeks, and still another for those to be called on every 2 months. File these charts in a tickler file according to the next date they are to be called on, by week. Then, when any given week comes up, pull out the charts for that week and this much of your week's work has been pre-planned.

¶ 9004 **Record of calls, inventory, and sales (Forms 4 and 5)**

A record like that shown in Forms 4 and 5 enables you to determine when to call back on a customer, and what items the customer will be interested in reordering *at the specified time*. The form is reproduced through the courtesy of The Shelby Salesbook Company, Shelby, Ohio.

▶ *How to use Form 4 as a prospect and customer card.* Before calling on a prospect, fill out the card with the name of the concern, zone, type of business, and financial rating. When you call on the prospect, get the name of the buyer as well as the names and titles of other executives whom it might be advisable to see. Enter this information on the card in the space under "Memoranda and Remarks," with the date of the call. In the "Follow-up" column, insert the date when you are to follow up.

▶ *How to use Form 5 as a customer sales and inventory record.* Use Form 5 to enter the items that the customer has bought, under "Record of Sales." Enter the customer's inventory of the various items in the upper half of the card.

⇒⇒OBSERVATION→ Shelby salesmen must, if possible, ascertain and note the quantity on hand of each different product used that the Shelby Salesbook Company can supply. If the prospect will not permit an actual count of the stock the salesman explains that by looking over the inventory he can offer suggestions on forms that had not been thought of previously. If this fails, the salesman notes on the card the prospect's or customer's estimate of how long his present stock will last. In any case, the salesman marks on the card the month and year in which he wants to follow up the account.

▶ *Arrangement of cards.* If you work your territory by zones, arrange the cards in each zone so that you can work up one side of the street and down the other. For follow-up purposes, tab the cards at the months indicated at the top. On the first of each month, go through the tabs, which are already arranged by zone, and pull those that are to be followed up.

¶9004

personal records to reach high-bracket goals

JAN.	FEB.	MAR.	APR.	MAY	JUNE	JULY	AUG.	SEP.	OCT.	NOV.	DEC.

FIRM NAME			SALESMAN		Zone	
STREET ADDRESS			BUYER(S)		Rating	
CITY	P.O. Zone	State			Bus. No.	
TYPE OF BUSINESS	Telephone No.		RECORD OF SPECIAL MAILINGS			
			Dept. Store Forum	Ind. Forum	Dist. Forum	Ret. Forum

RECORD OF CALLS

Date of Call			MEMORANDA AND REMARKS	Follow-Up	
Mon.	Day	Yr.		Mon.	Yr.

SALES CONTROL PLAN   SALESMAN'S WORK CARD   FORM No. 378

Form 4. Record of Calls

RECORD OF INVENTORY

Item No.	Form No. or Name	Type or Style of Stationery	Mfg. By	Average Monthly Usage	DATE AND QUANTITY ON HAND						
1											
2											
3											
4											
5											
6											
7											
8											
9											
10											

RECORD OF SALES

Item No.	Date	Quan.	Price	Item No.	Date	Quan.	Price	Item No.	Date	Quan.	Price

PROPERTY OF THE SHELBY SALESBOOK COMPANY, SHELBY, OHIO

Form 5. Record of Inventory—Record of Sales
(Reverse side of Form 4)

¶ 9005 **Combined daily plan sheet and record of calls (Form 6)**

Form 6 helps you plan your daily calls, the objectives of each call, and the means to achieve them. The information you record after completed calls becomes part of your permanent files; gives you a quick-glance history of what you have accomplished—what remains to be done to make the sale.

TODAY'S PLAN and CALL RECORD

DATE ....

TODAY'S PLAN
This is my plan for the day, to be made out in advance of calls.
List calls in the order I plan to make them, including more than I expect to make.

CALL RECORD
At the end of the day, record the results of my call. Cross off calls not made; add those made but not previously entered.
List classifications (N-R-U). Transfer pertinent data on each call to my permanent prospect and customer records.

CALLS		SUMMARY		ORDERS TAKEN					
				PRODUCT		PRODUCT		PRODUCT	
	NO.		NO.		NO.		NO.		NO.
New (N)		Demonstration							
Repeat (R)		Proposal							
Users (U)		Close							
TOTAL									

LOCATION	COMPANY	INDIVIDUAL	OBJECT-IVE	SALES TOOL	CLASS N. R. U.
RESULTS					
RESULTS					
RESULTS					
RESULTS					
RESULTS					
RESULTS					
RESULTS					
RESULTS					

OBJECTIVES				SALES TOOLS	
Inquiry (INQ)	Survey (SURV)	Complaint (CPLT)		Order Form (O. F.)	
Referral (REF)	Proposal (PROP)	Others--		Sales Manual (S. M.)	
Canvass (CANV)	Close (Cl)	(Specify)		Literature (LIT)	
Demo (D)	Maintenance (MAINT)			User List (U. L.)	
Competition (COMP)	Instruct (INST)			Movies (M)	
	Price Change (P. C.)			Testimonials (T)	

Form 6. Today's Plan and Call Record

▶ *How to use Form 6 as a plan of daily calls.* List in the appropriate columns the names of the companies, locations, and individuals you want to call on the following day. Beside each name, in the "Objective" column, add the specific objective of that particular call from the list of "Objectives" at the bottom of the form. Under the "Sales Tool" heading, list the selling aid you plan to use to achieve your objective.

⟫OBSERVATION→ Notice that the Objectives and Sales Tools are codified. If you add other objectives or sales tools, make an appropriate abbreviation. Entries on the record are by code letters.

▶ *How to use Form 6 as a record of your calls.* After each interview, indicate in the "Class" column whether the persons you called on were new prospects, call-backs, or users of your product. Also note the results of each call. Delete names of persons you were unable to see; add non-planned calls.

▶ *How to use Form 6 as a selling aid.* At the end of each day:

• Transfer the total of each class of calls to the "Calls" section at the top of the form. This section tells you whether you have made a sufficient number of calls on new prospects to assure a continued supply of fresh business. A large number of call-backs without closing might indicate a need for more careful consideration before a call-back is made.

• Use the summary of objectives, next to the "Calls" column, to record the number and kind of different objectives you actually reached. These figures tell you whether you are making your goals; whether your interviews are aimed at closes, demonstrations, etc. and not at less profitable objectives.

• If you are a multi-product salesman, refer to the "Orders Taken" section to see just which products you are selling; whether you are neglecting any in your line.

• Note the objective and result of each call to help you plan a new objective for your next call.

• Save your daily plan and call reports for a week or a month. Analyze the figures to see just how you spend your interview time, the percentage of goals you achieve, the parts of your planning that need strengthening, the products you need to sell harder, etc.

• Transfer important information from your daily record of calls to your permanent prospect and customer records (this is important).

¶ 9006 **Route schedule (Form 7)**

Use this form to plan your itinerary for the coming week if you are an "on the road" salesman.

▶ *How to use Form 7.* Enter the names of the towns you plan to stop at during your coming week's itinerary. Record the date you plan to arrive, and when you will leave. If you drive, add a "Mileage" column (filled in beforehand by referring to a map), to tell you just how far you have to go to get to your next destination.

List the hotels where you plan to stay. (Leave a copy with someone who can get in touch with you if necessary). If you go into a new territory, list and *rate* your hotels as you go along. The next time you go that way, a glance at your previous route schedule will tell you whether to stay there again or try somewhere else. Knowing where you stayed is useful if you leave something behind during your trip, or if you must send for a forwarded item that you missed.

Under the "Work Plan" heading, list the names of the people you plan to call on during your stay in town.

The "Advance Schedule Following Week" section at the bottom half of the form becomes, after changes, your new week's schedule.

⟫OBSERVATION→ Use the "Notes" section at the bottom of the form to record any unusual road conditions or information you will want to remember for your next trip.

¶ 9007 **Weekly work analysis form (Form 8)**

Analyze yourself by filling out Form 8. Your record of the week's accomplishments will show you how good you really are. The result, good as you may be, may open avenues of effort and new possibilities for increasing sales. The self-questioning at the bottom of the form is designed to make you find the new possibilities.

ROUTE SCHEDULE Week Beginning_____, 19__						
DATE	ARR.	TOWN (S)	STATE	HOTELS	LEAVE	WORK PLAN
ADVANCE SCHEDULE FOLLOWING WEEK						
NOTES:						

Form 7. Route Schedule

THINGS I ACCOMPLISHED DURING THE WEEK ENDING						
	Monday	Tuesday	Wednesday	Thursday	Friday	Saturday
No. of accounts called on						
On how many of the above calls did I get to the man or woman I wanted?						
No. of future appointments made						
No. of presentations made to NEW accounts						
No. of presentations made to REGULAR accounts						
No. of orders taken						
$ value of orders taken						
No. of contacts made in connection with merchandising activities						
No. of times sales portfolio was used						
During the past week have I worked out any new, unusual sales presentations which helped my business or created new INTEREST or ENTHUSIASM on the part of the buyer?						

As soon as you have recorded the week's activities, look this over and ask yourself these questions:

1. Am I planning my time AHEAD so that I can contact as many Buyers, Merchandise and Advertising men as possible EVERY DAY?

2. At the rate I am going, will I accomplish all I am CAPABLE of doing this year?

3. Am I applying TOO LITTLE effort to one or more important phases of my work?

4. Am I applying TOO MUCH effort on some relatively unimportant phase of my work, so that more important matters suffer as a result?

5. Does the above week's record show that I am USING MY TIME to the best possible advantage?

Form 8. Weekly Work Analysis Sheet

personal records to reach high-bracket goals

➤➤➤OBSERVATION➤ This form was used by salesmen of Jantzen Knitting Mills. Even a hard-boiled veteran found the self-analysis of accomplishments worthwhile.

▶ *How to use Form 8.* This form does not have to be filled in every week. Use it at regular intervals to assure a frequent complete checkup on performance. Save your record and compare the latest one with the preceding one—with the one several months back or a year back.

¶ 9008 **Personal Check Charts (Forms 9, 10, 11)**

A periodic check-up, say the first of every month, using a form that lets you rate yourself as *above average, good or average, fair or mediocre,* and *poor* on various personal questions, should be part of every salesman's self-improvement program.

The following three personal check charts (Forms 9, 10, 11) are recommended for your use. They are copyrighted by, and reproduced with the permission of, Salesmanship Institute of America, Sales Counselors and Trainers.

Each chart carries its own instructions for its use.

PERSONAL CHECK CHART (FORM 9)

Rate yourself honestly. You can only cheat yourself by a biased rating. It will seriously impair your chances for self-improvement. Rate yourself 4 on any question where you sincerely believe you are above average; 3 for good or average; 2 for fair or mediocre; and 1 for poor or weak. A total score of 70 to 80 means that you are above par and this is undoubtedly reflected in your present performance. If your score is 55 to 70, it shows that you are an average individual, and can easily and readily improve yourself by conscientiously trying. A score of 40 to 55 indicates that self-improvement should be started at once and diligently continued; and below 40 signifies that you are in real danger of failure and should adopt drastic, concentrated action to improve.

RATING

Do I really want to be successful? _____
Am I determined and have I the will to win? _____
Am I willing to put forth concentrated effort and work hard? _____
Am I willing to sacrifice some pleasures and comforts if need be? _____
When adverse conditions arise, do I steadfastly continue my efforts? _____
Do I have a clear picture of my ultimate major objective? _____
Am I setting small personal objectives as stepping-stones to more easily and surely attain my goal? _____
Am I constantly adding knowledge to make my efforts more effective? _____
Is my attitude right, so that I enjoy my work? _____
Have I the right feeling for the company for which I work? _____
Am I completely "sold" on the products I sell? _____
Do I have faith in and teamplay with my management? _____
Am I considerate of and do I give the right co-operation to my co-workers? _____
Am I aware of all the motives that should impel me toward success? _____
Do I have properly balanced motivation? _____
Do I really understand my customers, associates, and friends? _____
Do I consistently try to promote the customer's feelings of adequacy and gain his good will? _____
Do I command the confidence and respect of my customers? _____
Do I see the customer's point of view and settle any differences of opinion by reasoning and diplomacy? _____
Do I bend over backwards to give my customers service? _____

TOTAL _____

PERSONAL CHECK CHART (FORM 10)

Again check yourself conscientiously and rate yourself honestly. Award 4 for excellent; 3 for good; 2 for fair, and 1 for poor. A total score of 70 to 80 means you are in the top 10% bracket; 55 to 70 is good; 40 to 55 is the borderline and needs extensive improvement; and under 40 means "action now" before it is too late.

RATING

Do I prevent many complaints by explaining clearly and completely? _____
If complaints arise, do I always handle them cheerfully, quickly, and properly? _____

¶9008

Am I neat and clean, pleasant and friendly, smiling and cheerful? _____

Am I sociable, and generally well liked? _____

Do I create a pleasant first impression? _____

Do my speech, mood, and actions enhance this first impression? _____

Is my telephone personality outstanding? _____

Do I avoid such bad habits as poor personal taste and improper speech and actions? _____

Am I conscious of, and do I control, annoying nervous habits? _____

Have I eliminated all speech hesitancy, and do I avoid interrupting the customer's conversation? _____

Do I check myself periodically to determine if I have erased any old bad habits or have acquired any new ones? _____

Do I use my company's advertising and promotion to promote more sales? _____

Do I, where possible, use Suggestion Selling and "tie-in" wanted or needed related merchandise? _____

Do I, when advisable, "trade-up" or "trade-down" a sale—whichever will give the buyer the most satisfaction? _____

Are my initial greetings cordial and friendly? _____

Do my approaches get attention and arouse interest? _____

Do I occasionally ask "self-answering" questions to qualify my sales talk and check for customer-interest-maintenance? _____

Do I ask questions to find out my customer's wants and needs? _____

Do I understand and use the basic motives that create desire? _____

Is my explanation concise, clear, accurate, and informative? _____

TOTAL _____

PERSONAL CHECK CHART (FORM 11)

Rate yourself 4 on each question in which you are outstanding; 3 for good; 2 for fair; and 1 for poor. Again, 70 to 80 is tops; 55 to 70 is average; 40 to 55 is weak; and below 40 shows urgent need for self-improvement. It is well to note that anyone who cannot rate a total of at least 55 definitely lacks initiative. They are lazy and are not using the knowledge they have, are too indolent to try to acquire sufficient knowledge, or are too self-satisfied to realize their own inefficiency and shortcomings.

RATING

Do I increase the value of my explanation with demonstration and visuals, where possible? _____

Do I have a complete knowledge of my products? _____

Can I intelligently answer any and all questions about my product, to the customer's satisfaction? _____

Do I state the benefits and features (in that sequence) of each product as I sell it? _____

Do I know my stock, where it is and actually what I have on hand? _____

Do I have ample confirmation available and use it frequently to substantiate my sales talk? _____

Can I overcome sincere objections effectively without arguing or causing customer displeasure? _____

Can I eliminate sales resistance and unearth the real "non-buying" reason? _____

Do I, when in doubt, "test" before trying to close? _____

Do I use two or three different closes on each sale before giving it up as lost? _____

Do I voice and show real appreciation to every customer? _____

Do I have genuine self-confidence, because I have a thorough knowledge of myself, people, selling skills, and products? _____

Have I eliminated indecision, discouragement, and anxiety? _____

Am I aware of my limitations as well as my capacities? _____

Am I doing anything constructive to eliminate my shortcomings? _____

Am I consistently trying to enlarge my capacity to "think creatively"? _____

Am I honest, sincere, and dependable? _____

Do I work with a minimum of supervision necessary, and follow instructions cheerfully and implicitly? _____

Do I always plan my work and work my plan? _____

Is my plan always worked out in an organized, systematic fashion? _____

TOTAL _____

HOW TO FIND INFORMATION ABOUT PEOPLE AND COMPANIES

¶ 9021 Diversified publications give you valuable information

The reference sources explained in this section are published regularly by organizations whose business it is to gather and prepare important information about people, companies, and the products they make—information you can put to work in your day-to-day selling.

You can find most of these works in the libraries of medium-sized and large cities, and in libraries of universities having schools of commerce.

➤➤➤Note→ The size indicated for each publication is from the latest edition available when the MIRACLE SALES GUIDE went to press.

¶ 9022 "Finder" for essential information

The following 22 essential points of information you might look for about people, companies, and their products can be found in the publications explained at the paragraphs noted.

Addresses (company) . . ¶ 9073; 9075; 9076; 9077; 9078; 9079; 9080; 9081; 9084
Addresses (residence) . . ¶ 9073; 9074; 9079
Affiliated companies . . ¶ 9076; 9078; 9081
Biographies . . ¶ 9073; 9074
Branches . . ¶ 9077; 9078; 9080
Chamber of Commerce members . . ¶ 9084
Credit ratings (company) . . ¶ 9075; 9078
Directors of a company . . ¶ 9073; 9076; 9077; 9079; 9081
Executives of a company . . ¶ 9073; 9076; 9077; 9078; 9079; 9081; 9084
Financial strength (company) . . ¶ 9075; 9076; 9077
History (company) . . ¶ 9076; 9084
Industry data, trends, etc. . . ¶9082
Key personnel (company) . . ¶ 9073; 9077; 9080; 9081; 9084
Manufacturers of a product . . ¶ 9073; 9076; 9078; 9079; 9080; 9084
Maps (local) . . ¶ 9084
Number of employees . . ¶ 9073; 9076; 9080; 9084
Officers of a company . . ¶ 9073; 9076; 9077; 9078; 9079; 9080; 9081; 9084
Parent companies . . ¶ 9076; 9078; 9081
Plant locations of a company . . ¶ 9076
Products of a company . . ¶ 9073; 9076; 9078; 9080; 9081
Purchasing agents . . ¶ 9073; 9080; 9081; 9084
Subsidiaries . . ¶ 9076; 9078; 9081

¶ 9023 Poor's Register of Directors and Executives

Poor's Register of Directors and Executives gives you the answers to questions like these:
• What are the principal business affiliations of this prospect?
• What position does he hold in his company?
• What fraternal organizations does he belong to?

Publisher: Standard & Poor's Corporation, 345 Hudson St., New York, N. Y. 10014

When published: Annually (also quarterly supplements that include up-to-date changes)

Size: 3,207 pages

I. *What you can find out about people:*
   Name
   Home address
   Place of birth
   Name of college attended and year of graduation
   Fraternal memberships (other than college)
   Principal business affiliations
   Position held in business and professional organizations (officer, director, trustee, partner, etc.)

II. *What you can find out about companies:*
   1. Names of companies and the cities in which they are located, classified alphabetically by industry. For example, the category **Abrasive Wheels and Abrasives** includes companies engaged in manufacturing abrasive grinding wheels of emery, carborundum, corundum, etc.; abrasive stones, sticks, paper, bricks, and cloths; and buffing and polishing wheels. There are about 200 categories. Hundreds of names appear in the various categories.

¶9023

2. Name of corporation
   Address
   Officers' names, and title of office held (chairman, president and general manager, vice president, treasurer, secretary, general counsel, purchasing agent, etc.)
   Directors' names
   Number of employees
   Principal products

III. *What you can find out about products:*
   1. Names of companies that produce certain products
   2. Principal products manufactured by named corporations

IV. *How to Use Poor's Register:*

▶ *To find out about the person you contact.* Turn to the section "Register of Directors and Executives" (all section titles and page locations are listed in the "Table of Contents" at the beginning of the Register). The information you want to know is listed under the person's name. Names are listed in alphabetical order.

▶ *To find out about a prospect company or a present customer.* Turn to the section "Corporation Directory." The information you want to find is listed under the company's name. Companies are listed in alphabetical order.

▶ *To find prospects.* Turn to the section "Classified Index of Corporation Directory." You will find the kind of companies that are prospects for your product listed together under the same subject heading. For example, if your prospects are companies that manufacture electric products, turn to the headings "Electrical Appliances," "Electrical Equipment," and "Electrical Machinery." Select the prospect companies located in your territory.

⇒ OBSERVATION → Salesmen who work in specific areas can refer to the Geographical Index that rearranges all corporation listings by states and principal cities.

▶ *To find additional prospects in future years.* Turn to the section "New Companies in This Edition" and select the companies whose names indicate that they might be additional prospects for you. Find out about these prospects using the same steps outlined above.

⇒ OBSERVATION → A number of similar directories are compiled by other publishers on a regional and state basis. See ¶ 9079 for example.

¶ 9024   **Who's Who in Commerce and Industry**

> *Who's Who in Commerce and Industry* gives you the answers to questions like these:
> • How old is the man I am going to contact?
> • What organizations does he belong to?
> • Who is the ranking executive of my prospect's corporation?
> • Who are the ranking executives of any given corporation?

Publisher: Marquis — Who's Who, Chicago, Illinois 60611
When published: Biennially
Size: 1273 pages

I. *What you can find out about people:* The "Who's Who" gives "career sketches of leading businessmen and others noteworthy in the field of commerce and industry." The kind of information varies slightly. A typical sketch might give you this data:

Name
Address
Position (such as "utility official")
Place of birth
Date of birth
College and degree
Name of wife
When married
Name of children
Companies associated with
Dates of association
Positions held in various companies
Memberships in organizations
Memberships in clubs

II. *How to use Who's Who in Commerce and Industry:*

▶ *To find out about a prospect or customer.* Names of persons in the Who's Who are listed in alphabetical order in the "Roster of Ranking Executives." Turn to the listing that will give you the biography of the man you want to find out about.

▶ *To find the ranking executive of a company.* Use "The Indexed Catalog of Selected Principal Businesses" near the end of the reference. Names of selected companies are listed in alphabetical order. Find listed under it the names of the company's key executives, then refer to their biographical listings in the "Roster of Ranking Executives" arranged in the front of the book.

how to find information about people and companies

¶ 9025 Dun and Bradstreet Reference Book

> The *Dun and Bradstreet Reference Book* gives you the answers to questions like these:
> - What is the estimated financial strength of my prospect or customer company?
> - What is its composite credit appraisal?
> - What type of business is the XYZ Corp. engaged in?

Publisher: Dun and Bradstreet, Inc., 99 Church St., New York, N. Y. 10007
When published: Bimonthly (Jan., March, May, July, Sept., Nov.)
Size: Several thousand pages (4-vol.)

⟫⟫IMPORTANT→ The Dun & Bradstreet Reference Book is available only to subscribers and their representatives. Find out whether your company is a subscriber.

If you represent a company that subscribes to Dun & Bradstreet Service you can obtain on request a Service Card. With this card you can go to any Dun & Bradstreet office in the United States and Canada and consult the Reference Book or request credit information about any account in which you are interested. *Check with your employer about requesting credit information.*

For convenience of salesmen and others, Dun & Bradstreet also publishes the Reference Book in briefcase size State Editions, issued twice a year, in January and July.

I. *What you can find out about companies:*

▶ Rating for "estimated financial strength" of companies—merchants, manufacturers, and traders generally throughout the U.S. and Canada. The Reference Book contains a Key to Ratings which explains the letters used to show estimated financial strength.

▶ Rating for "composite credit appraisal." The Key to Ratings explains the symbols that designate the rating as "High," "Good," "Fair," or "Limited."

▶ The type of business, designated by Standard Industrial Classification numbers. A narrative description of line of business is also included.

⟫⟫CAUTION→ A rating, while representative when assigned, may not be representative a month later because of the dynamic nature of business. Reference Books are subject to constant revision in many particulars besides ratings. New names are added, old names deleted. Over 5,000 changes occur daily. Credit men supplement the Reference Book rating with more detailed information by ordering reports from Dun & Bradstreet.

II. *How to use Dun and Bradstreet Reference Book:*

▶ *To find financial information about a prospect company or a present customer.* The main section contains the names of companies, listed alphabetically by state and by city in the U.S. Turn to the state and city locations of the company you want to find out about. Then find the particular company listed in alphabetical order. For example, **Alabama**—Abbeville—Abbeville Equipment Co. In addition to the business name, each listing shows: line and function of business, year business was started, and rating indicating credit and financial strength. Newly added business names are preceded by the letter A, and a C precedes the name of a concern whose rating has changed.

⟫⟫SUGGESTION→ Use a State Edition:
- To find prospects among the business firms in the State, and to classify and qualify them.
- To locate new outlets.
- To concentrate your sales efforts on more profitable accounts.
- To follow the financial growth or decline of companies in your territory.

¶ 9026 Moody's Industrial Manual

> *Moody's Industrial Manual* gives you the answers to questions like these:
> - How big is the company I am going to sell?
> - Who are the top executives in the company?
> - What products does this company manufacture?
> - What do the balance sheet and income statement of the corporation show?

Publisher: Moody's Investors Service, 99 Church Street, New York, N. Y. 10007
When published: Annually, supplemented twice weekly.
Size: 2,944 pages

I. *What you can find out about people:*
Names of officers and directors of companies covered

City (directors only) (not always included)
Position held in business organization (officer, director, auditor, etc.)

II. *What you can find out about companies*:
Name of company
Address
History
Officers' names and title of office held (chairman, president, vice president, treasurer, secretary, etc.)
Directors' names and city
Number of employees
Number of stockholders
Business and products
Principal plants and properties: location by city, and kind of operation
Subsidiary's name, city, and business
Financial statement (income account, sales and earnings, balance sheet, and capital stock)

NOTE: This information is supplied for "American Industrial Companies" as well as "Canadian and Foreign Industrial Companies."

III. *What you can find out about products*:
The products of each company appear in a paragraph entitled "Business."

IV. *How to use Moody's Industrial Manual:*

▶ *To find out about a prospect company or a present customer.* Refer to the "Alphabetical Index" near the beginning of the Manual to find the page on which complete information about the company is given. The information is presented under clearly marked sub-headings.

▶ *To find special information.* The "Table of Contents" at the beginning of the Manual will direct you to the "Special Features" section. This section gives you special information about stocks, bonds, and other industrial securities.

▶ *To find prospects.* Turn to the first page of the "Special Features" section. It will guide you to the page location of the "Classification of Companies By Industries." There you will find listings of the more important corporations in each industry, from "Advertising" to "Wholesalers and Jobbers." Choose the kind of companies you sell to. Then refer to the page reference indicated for detailed information about each. Be sure to check the "Business" paragraph for the specific products manufactured by a company. This information will often give you a better idea of that company's need for your product.

⟫OBSERVATION→ Moody's Investors Service also publishes Moody's Bank and Finance Manual, Moody's Transportation Manual, Moody's Public Utility Manual.

¶ 9027 **Directories of Banks and Bankers (Polk's World Bank Directory, Rand McNally International Bankers Directory)**

Polk's and *Rand McNally* are the two outstanding directories in this area. They give you answers to questions like these:
• Which banks are the biggest potential customers for my product?
• Who are the officers of these banks?
• How can I get an idea of the sales potential of an unfamiliar territory?

Polk's World Bank Directory is published by R. L. Polk & Co., 130 Fourth Avenue, North, Nashville 3, Tennessee. It is published semi-annually, with cumulative supplements issued throughout the six-month period for each issue. Polk's World Bank Directory, March edition, reports December 31 and later information, while the September edition reports mid-year data. It has over 2350 pages for U. S. banks, plus separate sections for Canadian and Foreign banks and statistical information.

Rand McNally International Bankers Directory is published by Rand McNally & Company, P. O. Box 7600, Chicago 80, Illinois. It, too, is published semi-annually; the First Edition reports year-end financial statements, the Final Edition reports mid-year statements and changes. It has over 1900 pages for the U. S. section, plus separate sections for Canadian and Foreign banks and statistical information.

I. *What you can find out about banks from these Directories:*
Bank name
Address and phone
Town, county and population
Established date
Kind of bank: Commercial, Mutual Savings, Trust Co., Private, State
FDIC, Federal Reserve, and Association memberships
Officers and Directors (and Counsel, in Polk's)
Out-of-town branches
Transit number and check routing symbol
Assets and liabilities
Par value of stock (and dividend rate, in Polk's)

how to find information about people and companies

Principal correspondent banks

II. *How to use these Directories:*

▶ *To find out about a bank.* If banks are among your prospects, use these Directories for preapproach information. Each reference uses an alphabetical arrangement; for U.S. banks, listings are by state, then by town or city, and then by bank. Preceding each state and each foreign area or continent is an indexed map.

▶ *To find general banking information.* Both Directories have a Contents and a Detailed Index at the front to help you locate information. Here are examples of the data you can find:

- Accessible banking points for non-bank towns in the U.S.
- Bankers associations
- Government banking and financial agencies
- Explanation of transit numbers and routing symbols
- Discontinued banks for a five year period (Rand McNally lists them together; Polk's has them in their alphabetical places)
- Laws (the essentials of banking laws of the states)
- Maps
- Largest Commercial Banks in the U.S. (Polk's lists 300 largest, by deposits; Rand McNally lists 400 largest, by total resources)

▶ *Other uses.* Here are some other ways you might use these Directories:

• To help estimate a territory's sales potential. Look at the number of banks listed for the territory, their deposits and assets, and population figures.

• To determine a bank's potential as a prospect. Observe the size, number of branch offices, whether it lists a certain kind of department (Trust Department, for example) in which you are interested, and so on.

• To get credit information about a new account located in a distant town. Get the name of your customer's bank, then look it up. If your company's bank is listed as a correspondent of the customer's bank, you're in luck. Your company's bank, as a correspondent, can usually obtain credit information about the customer from his own bank. Have your credit department place the request.

¶ 9028 **Thomas' Register of American Manufacturers**

Thomas' Register of American Manufacturers gives you the answers to questions like these:
- Who are the manufacturers of marine goods that might be prospects for my product?
- Is Bethlehem Steel Co. a parent company or a subsidiary?
- Where are the branch offices of General American Transportation located?

Publisher: Thomas Publishing Co., N. Y., N. Y. 10001
When published: Annually
Size: Over 10,000 pages (four vol., index)

I. *What you can find out about people:*
   - Names of executives (only of Thomas' Register advertisers)
   - Position held in company (only of Thomas' Register advertisers)

II. *What you can find out about companies:*
   - Name of company
   - Address
   - Products made
   - Branches
   - Capital rating
   - Affiliation data where appropriate ("successor," "affiliate," and/or "subsidiary")
   - Cable address designation (where interested in overseas sales)

For advertisers in Thomas' Register (designated by bold face type), the following information is also given:
   - Trade mark display
   - Branches, sales offices, distributors (with local addresses)
   - Product Index of listings—showing ad locations
   - Other sales data (where available)

III. *What you can find out about products:*
   - Who manufactures a particular classification of product
   - Who manufactures specific products

IV. *How to use Thomas' Register:* Thomas' Register is divided into four volumes and an index. The first three volumes list, in alphabetical order, products manufactured in the U.S. The fourth volume lists, in alphabetical order, the manufacturers of those products.

Use Volumes I, II, and III:

▶ *To find the manufacturers of a class of product.* The first three volumes list, in alphabetical order, all the products of all U.S. manufacturers. Under each product classification the names of manufacturers are arranged alphabetically: first by states; second by cities and towns; third by name of manufacturer. Turn to the product, state and city to find the manufacturers you are interested in.

▶ *To find the manufacturers of a specific product.* Refer to the "Index to Contents" (Volume V), which lists products in alphabetical order. For example, to find manufacturers of marine doors, look in the Index under "M" for Marine. All marine items, including "doors," will be listed, and the page shown where each list of manufacturers appears.

Note: This Index to Contents (Volume V) also includes a list of advertisers in Thomas' Register.

Volumes I, II, and III give you answers to questions like these:

• Does anyone in Alabama make cast iron pipe?

• Who makes electric motors in Michigan?

• Is there a large manufacturer of rubber hose in Connecticut?

Use Volume IV (list of manufacturers, in alphabetical order):

• To find the address when you know only a company's name.

• To find products manufactured by a company.

• To find the capital rating of a company. "Estimate of approximate minimum capital" is given: AAAA for over $1 million, to H for over $500, and X to indicate "No Estimate".

• To find locations of branch offices of a company. The branches of companies are given, as, well as their state and city locations.

▶ *To find subsidiaries, affiliated, controlled or succeeding concerns.* An "S" or an "[A]" designation before or after a company name tips you off to its relationship with another company.

Company names *following* an "S" are subsidiaries, or affiliated with, or controlled by the concern that *precedes* the "S." For example, Calebaugh Self-Lubricating Carbon Co. (S Co-operative Utilities Co. Inc.) indicates that Calebaugh Self-Lubricating Carbon Co. has an affiliated or subsidiary company, the Co-operative Utilities Co. Inc.

A company name *preceding* the symbol "[A]" is affiliated with, subsidiary of, or controlled by the concern that *follows* the "[A]." For example, Co-operative Utilities Co. Inc. ([A] Calebaugh Self-Lubricating Carbon Co.) indicates that Co-operative Utilities Co. Inc. is affiliated with Calebaugh Self-Lubricating Carbon Co.

In many cases, subsidiaries, etc., are indicated by "(Sub. of ―――)".

Volume IV gives you answers to questions like these:

• Where are the plants of the Abbott Laboratories?

• Where is the home office of the Bristol Brass Corporation?

• Is Bethlehem Steel Co. a parent company or subsidiary?

• Where are the branch offices of the Stanley Tool Division?

• What companies does General American Transportation own or control?

▶ *To find the manufacturer who uses a special trade name.* To find the manufacturer of a special trademark or brand of any article, look for the trade name you want in the "Trademark Section" (in Volume IV). The trademark index is an alphabetically arranged list of names under which various products are stamped, labeled, advertised, etc. Following the trademark is the name and address of the manufacturer.

⋙OBSERVATION→ This trademark index is not limited to registered trademarks. Many of those listed are not registered.

¶ 9029   **Directory of Directors in the City of New York (an example of a city directory of directors)**

The *Directory of Directors in the City of New York* gives you the answers to questions like these:

• Who is the President of the corporation I am going to sell?

• Who are the Directors of the corporation?

• What is the residence address of the Vice President of the Company?

Publisher: Directory of Directors Co., Inc., 342 Madison Avenue, New York
When published: Annually
Size: 1000 pages

I. *What you can find out about people:*
   Names of officers, directors, trustees or partners of companies covered
   Addresses (business and residence)
   Name of company or companies with which associated
   Position held in company (president, vice president, secretary, etc.)

II. *What you can find out about companies:*
   Name
   Address
   Chairman of the Board

how to find information about people and companies

President
Vice presidents
Secretary
Treasurer
Controller
Directors
Type of business (for example, "rail equipment")

III. *How to use the New York City Directory of Directors:*

▶ *To find out about a director.* Turn to the alphabetical listing of directors in the first section. The information you want will be under the person's name.

▶ *To find out about a company.* Turn to the alphabetical listing of corporations and firms in the second section. The information you want will be under the company's name.

≫OBSERVATION→ To find out whether a particular city has a directory of directors, inquire at the main library in the particular city. Subscribers to the New York Directory of Directors can obtain this information from the New York office where a library of out-of-town directories is maintained.

¶ 9030 **Area Directories (State and City)**

(a) THE NEW JERSEY STATE INDUSTRIAL DIRECTORY (an example)

The New Jersey State Industrial Directory gives you the answers to questions like these:
• What companies are located in my territory?
• What industrial firms in New Jersey manufacture the products in which I'm interested?
• What out-of-state firms have plants or branch offices in New Jersey?
• Where is a particular corporation located in New Jersey?

Publisher: New Jersey State Industrial Directory, Port Authority Building, 111 Eighth Ave., N. Y., N. Y. 10011
When published: Annually

I. *What you can find out about people:*
Names and titles of officers, executives, and key management personnel of companies covered

II. *What you can find out about companies:*
Name
Names and titles of officers, executives and key management personnel
Number of male and female employees
Square footage
Description of product or service
Street address (postal address if different)
Telephone number
Main and branch offices
Geographical location

III. *What you can find out about products:*
Who manufactures a particular product

IV. *How to use the New Jersey Industrial Directory:*

▶ *To find the location of a firm.* Turn to the first section of the Directory, "Firm Names Alphabetical." This section lists more than 14,000 industrial firms in New Jersey with their locations by municipality and county. Turn to the company you want to find out about for its town and county location. Knowing a company's county location enables you to find additional information about that company.

▶ *To secure more details about a company.* Turn to the second section of the book, "Firm Names Geographical." The counties are arranged in alphabetical order, and the towns are in alphabetical order within their respective counties. The information about companies is under the town heading.

≫NOTE→ The advertising for the most recent edition of the New Jersey State Industrial Directory mentions a very effective use for this type of directory: direct-mail selling. The direct-mail seller has a complete list of potential customers — their addresses and their phone numbers — within the covers of one book. The advertising highlights the directory's advantages by listing the following:
Over 700 pages
Over 14,000 firms
Over 80,000 executives
Over 1,000 classified headings
Latest Zip codes

▶ *To find which firms offer a particular product or service.* Turn to the third section of the book, "New Jersey Industrial Market Place". This section is a guide to the entire state, arranged by product and service titles in alphabetical order. It lists all industrial firms, classified by their product or service and shows their location. For complete details about a firm, refer to the geographical section (section 2).

≫OBSERVATION 1→ Following this third section is a list of "Out of State Firms" that do business in New Jersey, but whose main offices are located in other states. New Jersey branch plants and offices are shown.

¶9030

⇒OBSERVATION 2→ Other states have industrial directories similar to the one described above. A complete list of these directories and where they may be obtained, giving price and indicating content, is sold at 35¢ per copy by the State Chamber of Commerce Service Department, Chamber of Commerce of the United States, Washington, D.C. See also ¶ 9085, describing directories published by various Chambers of Commerce.

(b) CITY DIRECTORIES

A City Directory gives you the answers to questions like these:
- Is the person I am calling on the head of the house and does he own his own home?
- What does he do for a living, and who are his neighbors?
- Who are the owners or officers of the business concern I am contacting?
- How many other firms are there in the community in the same kind of business?

Publishers: Members of the Association of North American Directory Publishers.

Coverage: An approximate 1,650 separate volumes are published, covering some 8,250 American and Canadian communities and listing an estimated 80 million adults.

When published: Most directories are published annually, and are completely re-compiled for every edition from information gathered in house-to-house enumeration.

I. *What a City Directory contains:*
   1. An alphabetical list of names and addresses of every adult resident, business concern, and institution.
   2. A Street and Avenue guide listing numerically every location on every street, and indicating where intersecting streets appear.
   3. A Classified Business Directory listing every business, classified as to type, and showing names and addresses.
   4. A Statistical and Historical Review of the city.

II. *What a City Directory tells you about an individual:*
   Name
   Address
   Job title
   Place of employment
   Marital status
   Wife's name
   Whether he owns or rents home
   Whether he has a telephone
   Whether he is the head of the household
   Whether he owns his own business
   Names of his neighbors

III. *What a City Directory tells you about a business concern:*
   Name and address
   Whether it is a partnership or corporation
   Names of partners, owners, or officers
   Names of other concerns in the same business

IV. *What a City Directory tells you about a locality:*
   Quickest way to get there
   Resident(s) at a given address
   Whether the home has a telephone
   Nearest street corner
   Nearest store, church, school, garage, etc.
   Occupants of an office building or apartment house

V. *What a City Directory tells you about an organization:*
   Name
   Headquarters
   Secretary

VI. *What a City Directory tells you about a community:*
   Latest population figures and other statistical information
   Names and locations of schools and churches
   Locations of hospitals, homes, and asylums

► A City Directory can be put to many uses by salesmen. It can be used to locate new markets, and to maintain up-to-date mailing lists. It is helpful in analyzing the buying power of a street or a community. A City Directory can be used to route salesmen efficiently. In many instances, it is the only means of locating residents of hotels or apartment buildings.

how to find information about people and companies

▶ As a public service, members of the Association of North American Directory Publishers cooperate in maintaining libraries of out-of-town city directories—usually at the local Chamber of Commerce—in over 740 cities.

¶ 9031 **Marine News Directory (an example of a trade directory)**

> The *Marine News Directory* gives you the answers to questions like these:
> - Who are the professionals (architects, engineers, surveyors, etc.) in the marine trade?
> - Who is the purchasing agent for the United States Navigation Company?
> - Who are the Tankship owners and operators in California? In Norway?

Publisher: Marine News Directory, 516 5th Ave., N. Y., N. Y. 10036
When published: Annually
Size: 588 pages

I. *What you can find out about people*:
Names of people in companies covered
Position held in company (president, vice president, treasurer, secretary, etc.)
Key personnel (by title: general manager, chief engineer, purchasing agent, etc.)
Professionals in the trade (naval architects, consulting engineers, surveyors, etc.)

II. *What you can find out about companies:*
Name
Address
Kind of business
Telephone number
Officers
Directors
Key personnel (under "Plant Directory," or "Operating Officials" designations)
Affiliations

III. *How to use the Marine News Directory:*

▶ *To find out about a company in the trade.* The Directory lists companies under four main headings: "American and Canadian Shipbuilding and Repair Yards," "American and Canadian Steamship and Waterway Lines," "Tankship Owners and Operators—American and Foreign," and "American and Canadian Dredging Companies." Turn to the section in which you think the company might be listed. Each section, except the last, is arranged by state, with an alphabetical listing of the companies in each state engaged in that particular business. Locate the company you are interested in for the information in category II above.

Because of the few names in the last section, "American and Canadian Dredging Companies," companies are listed in alphabetical order, followed by locations, without any state headings.

Foreign countries and companies, listed in alphabetical order, follow the state listings in the Tanker section.

▶ *To find the location of a company when you know only the name.* Turn to the appropriate Index in the back pages of the book. Companies are listed in alphabetical order, followed by the page where you will find detailed information about each.

▶ *To find professionals in the trade.* Turn to the section, "Naval Architects, Marine Engineers, Consulting Engineers, Surveyors and Chief Draftsmen." You will find persons in these professions listed in alphabetical order—one list under United States and one under Canada.

▶ *To find trade associations.* Turn to the section entitled "American Maritime Associations." Arranged in alphabetical order you will find listed all maritime associations, together with their addresses.

▶ *To find other trade information.* The table of contents at the beginning of the book guides you to sections that give other maritime trade data. Here are some examples of the additional trade information you can get: names of officials of government maritime organizations; names and addresses of companies that supply goods or services to ports throughout the United States; names of suppliers to the marine field; etc.

⟫OBSERVATION→ Many trades have their own directories. *The Marine News Directory* has been included here as a sample. A quick way to find out whether a particular trade has a directory, and what it's called, is to telephone one of the leading companies in the business. Any executive is quite certain to know its name.

¶ 9032 **Industrial Marketing (magazine) Market Data and Directory (annual)**

Publisher: Advertising Publications Inc., 200 E. Illinois St., Chicago 11, Ill.
When published: Monthly
Size: 184 pages

The Industrial Marketing magazine has a number of departments that cover, in article form, various aspects of business of interest to a salesman. Here are some samples, taken from a current issue:

¶9032

Departments:
  Sales Promotion Ideas
  Company Communications
  Industrial Shows
  Markets on the Move
Articles:
  "Let's take a new look at industrial sales psychology"
  "The mysteries of purchasing" (Why do industrial buyers buy?)
  "How to cut the cost of low-volume sales"

Market Data and Directory gives you the answers to questions like these:
• What are the current trends in the industries to which I sell?
• What sources of information can I go to for up-to-date information about the industries to which I sell?
• What products does a particular industry buy?
• What are the buying procedures and who are the specific "buying influences" I must contact to make a sale to plants in this industry?

Industrial Marketing's issue of *Market Data and Directory*, which appears annually, mid-year (642 pages), is of great value to salesmen, when used as indicated below.

I. *What you can find out about industries:*
  Industry composition (description of the various kinds of sub-industries that make up each "primary" industry—explained below)
  Current trends within the industry
  Basic statistics (plant population, services and materials consumed, sales, etc.)
  What the industry buys (typical products, services, etc.)
  How the industry buys (description of who does the buying, under what circumstances, etc.)
  Available market data (a guide to information sources pertaining to that industry: surveys, booklets, etc.)
  Associations that serve each industry
  Publications read by those in each industry

II. *How to use Market Data and Directory:*
▶ *To find above data about any field or industry.* For complete information about an industry, turn to the chapter outline at the beginning of the Directory. It shows you the page locations of the 73 "primary" industries and/or markets covered. The Directory is divided into 11 Industry Divisions; each covers a different group of primary industries. Within each main division are separate chapters devoted to the different primary industries that comprise the overall Division. Each chapter is divided into the headings listed under I, "What you can find out about industries." Turn to the page indicated for the industry that you are interested in.

⟫OBSERVATION⟶ There may be other information pertinent to an industry that is covered elsewhere in the Directory. To find additional information about a specific topic or market, turn to the "Subject Index" near the beginning of the Directory. This index contains almost 900 listings and covers subjects from "Abrasives" to "Zinc." Page locations are given where you will find all the data given in the issue about each subject.

▶ *To find the associations serving an industry.* Turn to the "Associations" heading near the end of each chapter for the associations covering that particular field or industry.

▶ *To find information about industry publications.* A "Publications Index," listing industry publications in alphabetical order, gives the page locations where you will find detailed information about the business publications listed. This information includes: address, editor, physical description (size, etc.), circulation, etc.
The list includes "U.S." as well as "Canadian" publications.

▶ *To find out about business reference publications.* The "Business Reference Publications Index" gives an alphabetical list of year books, catalog files, and other business reference publications. Detailed information about each publication will be found in the Industry Division and chapter relative to the field covered. The Index guides you to the correct page.

Getting information from Chambers of Commerce

¶ 9033 **Do Chambers of Commerce serve salesmen?**

Chambers of Commerce throughout the country are essentially interested in the economic growth of the areas they serve. Although they are concerned principally with providing information to firms that would be wealth-producing for the area, they recognize that the establishment of markets in the area also contributes to its economic development. They are therefore ready to be of service to salesmen from other geographical locations, within the limits of their facilities and policies.

how to find information about people and companies

¶ 9034 What kind of information can you get from a Chamber of Commerce?

The answer depends upon the particular Chamber of Commerce. Some can give you information on all of the points listed below which are of interest to salesmen; others on some of them.

- Company names
- Company addresses
- Name of the head of the company
- Names of chief management personnel
- Name of the purchasing agent
- Number of employees, usually within categories such as 25 to 100; 100 to 500; more than 500.
- Products and services available from members of the Chamber of Commerce.
- History of the company
- Men to see in particular departments
- Local maps

⇢ **OBSERVATION** → Chambers of Commerce do not as a rule supply financial information about their members. Because of their long association with business in the community, some may be able and willing to provide information about financial circumstances, or tell you of the reputation of a firm in the community. You may find that a Chamber of Commerce follows the policy of never giving derogatory information.

¶ 9035 Is information available in the form of a Directory?

Many Chambers of Commerce publish a "Blue Book" or Directory which includes information along the lines mentioned above. These directories are usually for sale to non-members of the Chamber of Commerce, at twice the charge to Chamber members.

EXAMPLE: The *Blue Book* published by the Indianapolis Chamber of Commerce is "a guide to reliable buying and selling in Indianapolis." Pages 1-45 is the classified section, arranged alphabetically according to commodities, products, services, etc., available from Chamber of Commerce members. The firm name, address and telephone number are listed, as is the classification symbol for the business operation.

Pages 46-83, the alphabetical section, gives the following information for each member of the Chamber:
   Name of the Chamber member
   Street address
   Telephone number
   Name of head of the company or manager

Wherever information has been supplied, this list also shows for each member:
   Name of sales official (s)
   Name of purchasing official (p)
   Classification of the business operation (designated by abbreviations)
   Number of employees (designated by symbol)

Some Chamber of Commerce directories are limited to lists of manufacturers; others are more extensive, including public, semi-public and private institutions, organizations, agencies, clubs and estates.

⇢ **SUGGESTION** → The Chamber of Commerce directories are excellent for finding prospects as well as information about them.

¶ 9036 How do you go about getting information?

Members of the American Chamber of Commerce Executives attempt to maintain a uniform policy throughout the nation with regard to answering inquiries. Under the uniform policy, inquiries originating out of the territory of a particular Chamber of Commerce are answered through a similar organization in the locality where they originate. (Exceptions to this policy include industrial and commercial projects, tourists, and school children requests.)

In other words, if you write to a Chamber of Commerce that follows the uniform policy, you are likely to receive a letter saying that if you are a member of your local Chamber of Commerce, and the request is made by them, they will furnish the information free of charge. If you are not a member of your local Chamber of Commerce, they will make a charge for the information. The letter you receive will probably list the charges for materials you request and inform you that the information will be mailed upon receipt of a letter from your local Chamber of Commerce. It may add that requests made by others than Chambers of Commerce must be accompanied by a check.

Many of the Chambers of Commerce will answer requests made in person, on the telephone, or by mail. Some prefer that requests be made in writing because of their limited facilities for handling personal and telephone inquiries.

⇢ **SUGGESTION** → Carry with you evidence of your membership, or your firm's membership, in your local Chamber of Commerce. It will help you get information quickly when you call at a Chamber of Commerce in your territory. Also, you might find it worthwhile to join the Chamber of Commerce in an area that you visit frequently.

Case problems: How would you do it?

¶ 9051 Is back scratching blackmail?

The Belson Chemical Company has a very broad industrial product mix. Packaging is of major importance to them because of the volatile and corrosive nature of the products, the variety of products, and the variety of sizes required. After much testing and trial and error procedures, Pulp Products Company emerged as one of Belson's major suppliers of containers.

Belson has been trying to develop a line of industrial cleaning products, which has never reached a satisfactory sales volume. They have put pressure on their salesmen to sell across the lines. Special incentive plans have been instituted for the industrial cleaners, and the sales volume for the line has been noted at the time of salesmen's personnel reviews.

One of Belson's salesmen, Dick Needham, called regularly on Pulp Products and sold them chemicals used in their industrial processes. He had never been able to get them to use the Belson industrial cleaners. The Pulp's purchasing agent insisted that the line they were using was of superior quality, was immediately available in small quantities, and was preferred by the maintenance foreman.

Dick felt that there was only one way to break through on the Pulp Products account. He succeeded in persuading his general manager to contact the Pulp Products sales manager and negotiate a reciprocal deal. The sales manager was reminded of the importance of the Belson account to Pulp Products and was requested to use his influence to get his company to switch to the Belson line of industrial cleaners, which was packaged in Pulp Product containers.

The maneuver worked and Dick was elated to pick up orders for industrial cleaners. The Pulp Products purchasing agent, however, was most unhappy. He voiced disapproval of Dick's methods and termed reciprocity as just another form of blackmail.

Questions:

1. Do you have any suggestions as to how Dick might have sold the industrial cleaning products without using the reciprocity approach?

2. Do you approve of Dick's actions? Why or why not?

3. How would you evaluate the future relations between Belson Chemical and Pulp Products? Between Dick and Pulp Products' purchasing agent?

¶ 9052 Carpet laying, or is it lying?

The Diamond Furniture Company had expanded into a small chain of six retail stores. They had done little in institutional or commercial furnishing and had maintained no outside salesmen. Rather than opening additional retail outlets, they decided to continue their growth efforts by opening a contract division. Their initial market target was small investors in duplexes and small apartments.

One of their new outside salesmen, Jack Small, was making a presentation to the Higbees, the owners of a four-unit apartment. He was trying to get them to install nylon shag carpeting in the apartments. Try as he might, he could not close them. Mrs. Higbee made a couple of references to Century Furnishers, the largest contract furnisher in the area. Jack had also noted some of Century's literature on a shelf behind the Higbees. He was pretty sure they had Century in mind when they said they wanted to look around, and he decided to meet the situation head on.

"You know we have always been home furnishers and have a tradition of quality. A lot of these new contract furnishers are too commercial, and they just don't offer quality.

I just happen to have some samples in the car of what Century is putting into the Woodacre condominiums. I'll bring it in."

Jack returned with a swatch of nylon carpeting. He compared the backing with that of the Diamond carpeting. He talked about the fastness of color, the number of tufts per inch, and how they are tied into the backing. He was able to convince the Higbees that the sample carpet was inferior to the Diamond carpeting. In this he was accurate, since it was of a cheaper grade. However, he inferred that the price was the same, although he knew that Century was selling it for an appropriate $2.00 a yard less. He also stated that this was the type of commercial carpeting which contract furnishers always installed, since they couldn't obtain the quality goods available to home furnishers. This, of course, was not the case, but Jack observed that they were impressed by the demonstration and he needed just a little more ammunition to convince them.

The Higbees signed the contract upon learning that the Diamond carpeting, in the shade they preferred, was limited in quantity and they might have a month's wait if they didn't order that day.

Questions:

1. How would you evaluate Jack's sales strategy?
2. Do you feel that there is anything unethical about Jack's sales presentation?
3. Evaluate Jack's closing technique.

¶ 9053 Let's look at the record

The Berryessa Carpet Mills has asked Mr. Nick Manarello, its National Sales Manager, to recommend one of his twelve salesmen for a special bonus award. The entire matter has been kept secret so the winning man can be surprised at the upcoming annual Sales Conference in New York City. Mr. Manarello has begun the task of trying to determine which of his men deserves the special award. So far, he has compiled the figures in Exhibit I. At this point, he wants to start narrowing his choice to make the final selection somewhat easier.

Questions:

1. Calculate as many of the performance measurements as you can (Exhibit II) for each salesman and the company average. Display your results in tabular form.
2. Which salesman do you think is doing the best job?
3. Which measurements are most reliable in determining whether a salesman is doing a good job?
4. For each man, write down your advice to help him improve his performance.

Exhibit II

Measurement of sales performance

1. Sales Volume. Might be more a reflection of the territory potential, than of the salesman's potential.
2. Market Penetration. Compares the sales of each man to the potential volume available to him or to the total market potential of his territory.
3. Gross Profit. Determines salesman's success in selling the firm's high profit items, found by subtracting the cost of manufacture or purchase from the selling price.
4. Calls per Day (Call Rate). Found by dividing the total number of calls made in a given period of time by the number of days worked.
5. Average Order Size. Found by dividing the total number of orders into the salesman's total sales volume.
6. Batting Average. Measures the ability to close sales. Found by dividing the number of orders by the number of calls made.
7. Expense Ratio. Found by dividing salesman's expenses by the number of calls he has
8. Cost per Call. Found by dividing salesman's expenses by the number of calls he has made.
9. Cost per Order. Found by dividing salesman's expenses by the number of orders obtained.

EXHIBIT I

	Al (CA) $	Norm (NYC) $	Dave (MT, ID, WY) $	George (MI, WI) $	Company Average $	Company Total $
Sales	2,200,000	900,000	320,000	1,100,000	760,000	9,120,000
Comm. (3)	66,000	27,000	9,600	33,000	22,800	
Calls	560	580	412	520	500	
Orders	410	285	370	406	360	
Days Worked	220	210	262	250	240	
New Accts.	68	48	20	42	38	
Lost Accts.	11	22	16	18	20	
Expenses	7,450	4,750	5,200	6,420	6,100	
Miles	14,800	7,730	16,250	14,820	14,200	
National Market Potential for carpet and room sized rugs in 1972 in billions	$3.5	$1.2	$ .32	$1.4		$12.0

Note: If total cost per call or order is desired, use field expenses plus salesman's compensation in the calculation.

10. Routing Efficiency. Found by dividing miles traveled by the number of calls made.

11. Non-Selling Activities. The number of each kind of special activity completed (e.g. co-op ads, window or interior displays, dealer training classes conducted, etc.)

¶ 9054 What do we do for openers?

Jim O'Brien is a pharmaceutical detail salesman for The Baxter-Warner Pharmaceutical Company. He has been on this job for eight months, having joined the company right after graduating from college. The firm markets a small line of ethical drugs. The salesman's primary mission involves telling (detailing) doctors about how and why his firm's products are better than those of competitors. In addition, Jim must make sure that the drug stores and drug wholesalers in his territory carry an adequate supply of all Baxter-Warner products.

Baxter-Warner is currently introducing a new liquid antacid. This preparation is primarily intended for the chronic ulcer patient who cannot get relief from the common proprietary remedies sold in rolls, tablets, and gel form. Nevertheless, the new product does face stiff competition from established prescription drugs.

The new antacid is named "Demulcimyn." One of its significant features, especially from the patient's viewpoint, is it palatability. Unlike competing products, it tastes very good. People most often describe it as "banana flavored."

To prepare himself for detailing DEMULCIMYN, salesman O'Brien is trying to decide what kind of information he should emphasize during his doctor calls. He knows from experience that he can count on only about three to five minutes of selling time with each doctor. During that time, he should remind the doctor of at least two other company products. He has literature and samples to leave, but he knows from industry studies that doctors learn more from the salesman himself than from reading literature or from patients' reports on the use of samples. The new drug has no particular price advantage, also no claim can be made that it is more effective than competing products.

Questions:

1. List the kinds of product knowledge Jim will need before detailing DEMULCIMYN.

2. What product features or benefits should be emphasized to the doctors?

3. What kind of an approach might Jim use to make a dramatic product introduction on each call? Include all words and actions required.

¶ 9055 Panning for gold

Bill Rodriggs is excited. Today he won out over seven other applicants for the sales representative job with Ad-Lite, Inc. Ad-Lite manufactures custom made outdoor neon and plexiglas signs. Now Bill will be starting his career as an outside salesman, something he's been anxious to do since beginning his A.A. degree program in marketing two years ago.

Although he is optimistic about his chances for success in this line of selling, Rodriggs is realistic enough to know it will take a lot of hard work. There's been a high turnover of salesmen in this company and in the industry as a whole. Bill believes that excessive turnover is mainly caused by salesmen who don't develop and live by a set of definite operating procedures.

One of the key strategies that Bill has already worked out for himself concerns his proposed prospecting system. Since he will be working on a draw against commission, Bill knows that a good prospecting system can make or break him in this job. His system is based on the observation that the little guy represents an almost completely untapped market. Competing sign salesmen fight each other for the big jobs (large restaurants, motels, banks, big stores, etc.) These sales typically fall into the $5,000 and up category, and although they make for big paydays when they hit, everybody and his brother is out to get them.

Bill reasons that just as a smart fisherman looks for a spot that isn't crowded with anglers, he will too. He thinks he's found it in all those small businesses that can't afford expensive signs, but need them badly. While the other fishermen are trying to bring in Moby

Dick, Bill figures he can grab plenty of smaller fish that will let him eat well enough and much more regularly. That's why he plans to steer clear of the big companies and concentrate (even become a specialist) on small businesses.

Questions:

1. Comment on Bill Rodrigg's prospecting plan. Is it sound? Why or why not?

2. Should Bill stay completely away from prospects who need expensive signs?

3. What other sources could Bill exploit?

¶ 9056 Lighting up or striking out

Fred Dobson was hired as a salesman by the Global Match Company. Book matches have always been a basic advertising specialty which fit well into the promotional programs of many industrial and service companies. Fred was advised to save time and travel by using the phone to make appointments.

He had met only limited success, but doggedly continued on through the yellow pages. One of his calls was to the Clark Correspondence Schools (C.C.S.) which had its branch office located in the city where he lived. After he dialed their number, it went like this:

C.C.S.: Good morning, Clark Correspondence Schools, Miss Kline speaking.
FRED: Hello, this is Fred Dobson. May I have the name of the owner please?
C.C.S.: Well, we are a corporation, but the president's name is Leland Clark.
FRED: Is he in?
C.C.S.: No, he is in New York.
FRED: When do you expect him back?
C.C.S.: We don't, his office is in New York.
FRED: Oh! Well, I guess I'd like to talk to the manager. What is his name?
C.C.S.: His name is Steve Jones. May I ask the nature of your call or the company you represent?
FRED: I am with the Global Match Company. Just tell him I am the Global man with a world of ideas.
C.C.S.: Go ahead, here is Mr. Jones now.
FRED: Hello Mr. Jones, this is Fred Dobson of the Global Match Company.
C.C.S.: What can I do for you?
FRED: It is not what you can do for me, it is what I can do for you. Do you know that you can increase the effectiveness of all the advertising you are doing by five times?
C.C.S.: I always knew that our advertising was only half as effective as it might be, but I didn't know which half.
FRED: Yes, well I am going to tell you how to do it. You see, people see your ads but turn the page and forget about them. With your ad on a book of matches a person sees your ad twenty times before he throws away the book.
C.C.S.: I think that match book advertising would cheapen our image.
FRED: No, you got it all wrong. You see it works on a synergistic basis. Kind of like two plus two equals five. When people see the matches, it reminds them of your other advertising and then when they see your other advertising, it reminds them of your match book message. See, your effectiveness is increased. And I know you are going to think it is too expensive. Well, that isn't the case, Steve. You know I can get the price down to one and six-tenths a book on 10,000 book lots.
C.C.S.: There would be a lot of problems in distributing the matches and a lot of waste. No, I don't think we are interested.
FRED: I have a special way of overcoming that problem. I have twenty-five high traffic locations such as restaurants, bars, bowling alleys that will distribute your matches. Now as I see it, you would probably want a snappy little slogan like— "You have to learn to earn"—and then give your name and address. We could really make the letters stand out like with yellow on black. This way you won't need any illustration, and it would save you money.
C.C.S.: No, we really are not interested.
FRED: Well look, Steve, I called to see if we could make an appointment. I want to go into all the details with you because then you will agree it's a winner.
C.C.S.: No, not now. If we ever decide to go that route we'll call you.

Questions:

1. Explain the advantages and drawbacks of making appointments over the telephone.

2. Evaluate Fred's telephone technique.

3. How should the telephone be used to get an interview appointment?

4. How would you have sought an interview by phone with the Clark Correspondence Schools?

¶ 9057 Getting to see Mr. Big

The Braun Industrial Linen Supply Company was struggling hard to compete against the larger Model Linen Service. Both companies extended similar service to their customers. They provided—in addition to linens—smocks, jackets, over-alls, and basic work clothes. Braun had developed a new fashion-lease program which offered suits, sport coats, and slacks for men, and suits, skirts, slacks, and pant suits for women on a contract lease basis. Many companies were seeking fringe benefits for their mid-management and supervisory personnel. The program also permitted enforcement of dress regulations for those employees who were in contact with the public.

Braun felt that this new line would enable them to open many new accounts as well as increasing the volume of their present accounts. They promoted Jim Haggarty, a route salesman, to sales representative for the fashion-lease service. Jim could also sell the linen service, and it was hoped that he could wedge out Model in many areas where they were firmly entrenched.

One of Jim's first efforts was with one of Model's accounts, the D'Amico grocery chain of 120 stores. They used women checkers exclusively, and their store managers were required to wear jackets. Jim wanted to sell them the idea of putting their checkers in distinctive pant suits and their managers in blazers and slacks.

Jim made calls on the purchasing agent in D'Amico's central office, but to no avail. His fashion-lease proposal was turned down primarily on the basis of additional cost. Although his basic linen and uniform prices were slightly lower than Model, the purchasing agent claimed they were very happy with the service and would make no changes.

Jim recognized that he was not getting to the right person and was considering what officials actually comprised the decision-making units in this case. The various functional divisions of D'Amico's were headed by the following top executves:

- Director of Personnel and Industrial Relations
- Director of Buying and Sales
- Director of Store Operations
- Director of Operating Services
- Director of General Office Services (Controller)
- Director of Real Estate

He knew that the purchasing agent reported to the Director of Operating Services but had a staff relationship with the Director of General Office Services (Controller). He was considering going over the purchasing agent's head and presenting his proposal directly to his immediate superior. Then he thought that since cost seemed to be the primary objection maybe he should go to the Controller and justify the cost of the proposed service.

Another idea came to Jim's mind. Maybe the key would be the Director of Personnel. If he could sell him on the beneficial employee relations aspect of the fashion-lease program, then maybe he would use his influence on the other directors to adopt the service. This would completely eliminate the hassle over cost.

Finally, he thought, "What have I got to lose? We aren't getting any business out of D'Amico's now, so why not play it bold and get right to Mr. Big? Why not go directly to Johnny D'Amico, the president of the company and son of the founder?" He felt that the fashion idea was one which might just fire up the aggressive and volatile president. If this were the case, he wouldn't have to worry about the various spheres of influence and strengths and weaknesess on down the line.

Questions:

1. Which division of D'Amico's do you think would be responsible for adopting and maintaining the fashion-lease program?

2. Which approach would you advise Jim Haggarty to take in this situation?

3. If Jim decides to go to someone else in the organization, should he ask permission of the purchasing agent? What if the purchasing agent refuses?

4. Do you feel that it would be wise to go to the president? Are there any cases when this would be appropriate?

¶ 9058 **Are you really family?**

Robert Bates was the sales representative for the college division of Wayne Publishing Company. He called regularly on Contra Mesa State College and had been successful in getting several texts adopted by professors for courses in a wide cross-section of departments. Bob majored in business administration in college, and he felt more comfortable selling business texts and talking with business professors.

Consequently he spent more time in the Business Department and made more sales in that department.

In Bob's job description was the duty of recruiting professors to author textbooks. Two of Contra Mesa's business professors had written books for Wayne Publishing, and a third was in the process of writing a manuscript. Although Bob's responsibility for authorships ended when he put the professor in touch with the editor, a closer relationship always resulted when a professor signed a contract with the publisher.

Bob had always been cordially received by all of the business faculty as he made his campus calls. He had been professional in his sales presentation. He had product knowledge of his offerings and of his competitors. He knew what each professor taught, what approach he used, and what texts were used. He was always neatly groomed, wearing either suit or sport coat with tie. He used his time, as well as the faculty's time, judiciously. He knew when to terminate an interview and leave.

As Bob became better acquainted with the faculty he became more relaxed. He joked and kidded with the receptionist and made small talk with the faculty in the halls of the office building. He felt that he was practically part of the academic family.

It was a particularly warm day in June just before the quarter's end when Bob "dropped by" the Contra Mesa Business Department. He wore a leather jacket with a Wallace Beery round neck sport shirt, flairs, boots, and dark sun glasses. He entered the workroom area of the department, where the faculty maintained a coffee pot and a refrigerator. He drew a cup of coffee, seated himself on the service counter, and prepared to enjoy a few quips with the faculty.

One of the older accounting professors entered the room. He looked at Bob for a momment and looked away. Bob felt that he had not been recognized so he took off his dark glasses. Knowing that the professor was writing an accounting book for another publisher he tried to open a conversation with: "Say Ralph, how is you bookkeeping book coming along?" The professor looked at him with a small light of recognition and said, "Well I have completed the debits, but what a time I am having with the credits." He left the room with a frown on his face and a couple of shakes of the head while Bob remained perched on the counter.

Questions:

1. *Should Bob have avoided informality and remained quite business-like in his contacts with the faculty?*
2. *Criticize or justify Bob's attire and conduct on that particularly warm day in June.*
3. *What suggestions do you have for Bob in regard to his future calls on the accounting professor?*
4. *Does familiarity breed contempt?*

¶ 9059 **Sticking to the script**

James Cowell has been selling recreational (pre-builder) land for Mountain Meadows Inc. for two months. Recently, the company opened up a new land development in Amador County in Northern California. Basically the company sells homesites ranging in price from $4990 to $7990 depending on their size and proximity to the Mokelumne River.

The company employs a team of telephone girls who find prospects for its salesmen to call on. Today, Cowell was given a telephone referral for a Tuesday evening appointment with Mr. Les Meyers. There was nothing listed under "Comments" on the prospect card given to Cowell except the notation, "sounds like a good one."

It is now Tuesday, and we find Mountain Meadows representative James Cowell ringing the doorbell of the Meyers' residence at exactly 7:00 p.m. As he stands waiting, Cowell feels a surge of optimism run through him. He likes all the early indications: upper class neighborhood, an expensive car in the garage, the neatly manicured and attractive landscaping. He doesn't think he'll have any money problems with this prospect.

MEYERS: *(opening door)* You must be the man from Mountain Meadows.
COWELL: Yes, that's me! How do you do, Mr. Meyers? My name is James Cowell.
MEYERS: You're right on time. Come in and have a chair.
COWELL: Thank you, sir. Is this one all right?
MEYERS: Fine. Now, tell me about your land development.

measurement of sales performance

COWELL: I'll be glad to Mr. Meyers, but before I start, may I ask you a few questions?
MEYERS: O.K., shoot.
COWELL: Have you lived in this area long?
MEYERS: About six years.
COWELL: Do you own other property besides your home here?
MEYER: I've got a 4-plex and I'm involved in a couple of real estate syndications.
COWELL: I see. Do you like camping, fishing or hiking?
MEYERS: No, not really, but my kids do.
COWELL: How many children do you have?
MEYERS: Two teenage girls and a boy, 12.
COWELL: Fine. Mr. Meyers, here are some statistics I'd like to show you. Unlike most statistics, these are anything but boring. They help explain why investing in California real estate has been so profitable for so many people.

COWELL FLIPS PAGES OF SALES BINDER AND COMMENTS ON MANY NEWSPAPER AND MAGAZINE ARTICLES AND STATISTICS SHOWING THE SCARCITY OF RECREATION LAND, POPULATION TRENDS, POLLUTION PROBLEMS, DRAMATIC INCREASES IN LAND VALUES, ETC.

MEYERS: What about Mountain Meadows itself? What's the dope on the property there?
COWELL: Mr. Meyers, I've got some beautiful color slides that will give you a clear picture of the area where our homesites are located.

COWELL SHOWS AND COMMENTS ON THE FOLLOWING SLIDES:

Slide 1	Map of the Mother Lode country
Slide 2	Sutter's Mill
Slide 3	French bakery and Community Church in Calaveras County
Slide 4	Fire house and old town in Auburn, Placer County
Slide 5	Longest covered bridge located in Bridgeport, Nevada County
Slide 6	Museum building, Downieville, Sierra County
Slide 7	Old Harrison Mine locomotive, Coulterville, Mariposa County
Slide 8	Fire house and Duchow building, Columbia State Historical Park, Tuolumne County
Slide 9	The Sierra Buttes
Slide 10	The American River
Slides 11-14	Angels Camp Jumping Frog contest, Calaveras County
Slide 15	Daffodil Hill at Eastertime
Slide 16	Inspiration Point
Slide 17	Bear River Dam
Slides 18-20	Mercer Caverns, town of Murphy's, Calaveras County
Slide 21	Murphy's Hotel
Slide 22	Calaveras Big Trees State Park
Slides 23-26	Town of Volcano, Old Ice Cream Parlor, Civil War cannon
Slide 27	Marshall Monument, Colma State Park
Slides 28-30	Carson Pass on the Scenic Emigrant Trail, Maiden's Grave, Tragedy Springs

AT THIS POINT, MRS. MEYERS COMES IN THE FRONT DOOR.

MEYERS: Hi, dear. How was the baby shower? Guess you didn't know we were going to have a picture show here tonight, huh?
MRS. M.: *(laughing)* No, I didn't.
MEYERS: This is Mr. Cowell. He's been showing me slides of the Mother Lode Country.
COWELL: Hello, Mrs. Meyers. Would you like to join us for some more pictures?
MEYERS: I'm afraid we won't be able to see any more slides tonight. I've promised to take my boy bowling. We've got a lane reserved for 8:15, and it's almost 8 o'clock now.
COWELL: I see. Well, I'd like to give you the details on our home sites, Mr. Meyers. Could I come back some other night this week? It wouldn't take long.
MEYERS: I'll call you when I see what my schedule is like. Can you leave me your card?
COWELL: Here you are. And here's a map of the Mother Lode. I've indicated our development in red felt tip pen.
MEYERS: Thank you. I'll be in touch.
COWELL: Fine. I'll look forward to seeing you both soon.
MEYERS: Goodbye, Mr. Cowell.
COWELL: Goodbye.

Questions:

1. What do you consider Cowell's most serious error in this sales call?
2. Is there anything intrinsically wrong with this standardized presentation?
3. Do you think Meyers really had a previous commitment to take his son bowling?
4. Do you think Cowell should have telephoned Mr. Meyers before going to see him?
5. Do you think that the Mountain Meadows telephone girls should do more preapproaching of prospects secured by phone?

¶ 9060 **Under-exposed benefits**

Ted Greener had always listed photography as his one and only hobby. After his first home-made cigar box camera, there came an accumulation of lenses, shutters, developers, printers, enlargers, projectors, the gamut of photographic equipment. While attending high school and then a community college, he worked part time in a camera store. Subsequently, he managed the laboratory for Ribera Color Processing before becoming a sales representative for the Bophors Company, a leading manufacturer of quality cameras.

Ted was making his first call on Mr. J. F. Deaton, the buyer of photography equipment for the Buffington Department Store group. Buffington's had carried some of Bophors accessory equipment and a few of their 35 millimeter cameras, but had never really pushed the line. Ted was most anxious to get them to buy the new Cinecamera 382, Bophor's entry into the super 8 movie camera field. We pick up Ted's presentation to Mr. Deaton as he takes the 382 out of its case.

TED: Our new Cinecamera 382 is fitted with the most advanced and dependable features. Electronics and miniaturization have been used, which insure better performance than any other mechanical means. Just look at this lens set-up. It has a 1" C mount — 32 threads per inch — standard extension f:1. 9 zoom lens with a focal length of 8 to 64 millimeters. It is fitted with our special Robomatic automatic diaphragm, a variable speed electric drive for the focal length adjustment ring and a macro cine-matographic control lever. Isn't that something?

DEATON: How does this compare with the Bolex C-4?

TED: No comparison at all. This is much better. And look at this super-luminous reflex view finder. It has a mirror set at 4 degrees on a guillotine-type shutter which alternately directs all light on to the viewfinder. The viewfinder eyepiece has a magnification of 25 times, which is really something when you couple it with a fine-grain ground-glass focussing screen.

DEATON: What national advertising will there be on this?

TED: I'm not sure, but they'll have some. Anyway a camera like this really doesn't need advertising. Let me tell you about its power supply. It has a nickel-cadmium accumulator battery which powers a high-sensitivity reflex cell which receives all the light rays coming through the lens. This cell triggers the micromotor, driving the electronically-controlled iris diaphragm of the lens itself. This control is performed by a shock-proof galvanometer fitted with a checking pointer visible in the viewfinder. A potentiometer adjusts the system according to the emulsion speed set. It is interconnected with the filming-speed mechanism. Now isn't that something?

DEATON: Sounds like quite a camera. Perhaps too much camera for our departments. This must list for over $750.

TED: Yes, it is $875, which is under $1,000. Anyone who knows anything about cameras would expect to pay over $1,000. Now you look at this transistorized electronic regulation system which allows a . . .

DEATON: Do you have any cooperative advertising, dealer aids, or demonstrator allowance in your promotional program?

TED: No, but I could tell your salesmen the same thing I am telling you. No trouble at all. This camera will knock your customer's eyes out. Now back to the transistorized electronic regulation system, which is really something . . .

DEATON: We are heavy on inventory now, and I would rather concentrate on the Kodak super 8's.

TED: You are making a big mistake, Mr. Deaton. Stores like yours need a little upgrading with some really quality merchandise. You could start attracting a really worthwhile camera trade.

DEATON: We can't be everything to everybody. I have an appointment now. Best of luck to you with the 382.

Questions:

1. Evaluate Ted's use of product knowledge in his sales presentation.

2. Explain how a retailer is motivated to buy for resale.

3. How would you improve Ted's presentation?

4. How would you alter the presentation if you were a retail salesman selling to a customer.

¶ 9061   **It's the sign of the times**

The St. George Hotel is a landmark in the city. This year it will celebrate its 40th year of operation. Old George is still in very good condition due to extensive renovations made by the management over the years. Almost all of the refurbishing has been done inside the hotel. Except for new paint, the outside looks the same as it always has. This is precisely what attracted the attention of John Newell, a

measurement of sales performance

salesman with Ad-Lites, Inc., makers of outdoor electrical signs.

Newell has preapproached Mr. Clarence G. Barron, vice-president and eldest son of the hotel's founder, to discover the best way to sell him on replacing the old neon sign that hangs over the main entrance. In the course of his investigation, John has found out some key information from hotel personnel. He has it listed on his prospect card like this:

1. Two firms have tried unsuccessfully to sell the St. George a new sign.

2. The reason for not buying boils down to putting all renovation money into rooms, kitchen, and other inside facilities.

3. It's been four months since anyone has approached Mr. Barron about sign work.

4. The General Manager seems to favor a new sign if it's the right design and right price.

5. Barron is an independent thinker. He won't be influenced by the General Manager or anyone else.

John Newell has succeeded in getting an appointment with Mr. Barron. He was lucky. The Sales Club he belongs to authorized him to check on hotel facilities for a state-wide convention to be held next Spring. John saw this as his one big door opening opportunity. He plans to discuss convention arrangements with Mr. Barron first, then switch over to the new sign idea. John has definitely decided not to use the convention as a wedge for three reasons:

1. He's pretty sure Barron would never stand for it.

2. He thinks the sign can be sold on its own merits, and—

3. He really doesn't have the final say on where the convention will be held, although his recommendation would carry much weight.

We pick up the conversation after Mr. Barron has explained why his hotel would be the ideal convention site.

NEWELL: You really do have a fine, comfortable place here, Mr. Barron.

BARRON: Thank you. I'm very proud of it, and the way we treat our guests.

NEWELL: Does it worry you when people get a mistaken impression of your hotel?

BARRON: A mistaken impression? What do you mean?

NEWELL: I was just thinking about people who would be surprised to see how modern and up-to-date your hotel is.

BARRON: Why would they be surprised? Our guests don't stay here because they want coal lamps and iron beds.

NEWELL: Of course not. But they see you from the INSIDE. What about people who aren't persuaded to come in the door? How do they know what the hotel is like on the inside?

BARRON: I get the feeling I'm being hustled for something. What are you trying to sell me?

NEWELL: Mr. Barron, you're a hotel expert. I wouldn't try to advise you on rooms, food, drink, laundry, maid service, or anything else that goes on inside your hotel. Besides, I like what I see here. However, I do think you are losing business you should be getting. Will you let me take a few minutes to show you some information, I've gathered that concerns your hotel?

BARRON: Well, all right. But I don't have much time.

NEWELL: Is there a table nearby?

BARRON: Let's go into this office. We won't be interrupted here. *(Smiling)* I'll let you sit down but don't figure on keeping your knees bent too long.

NEWELL: *(Smiling)* Mr. Barron, my knees are trained to unbend in a hurry. You know as well as I do that many people DO judge a book by its cover. You know too that people are judged every day by the clothes they wear or some other outward manifestation. Maybe you and I do the same thing once in a while ourselves. To use another cliché, appearances can be deceiving. I'm afraid this cliché applies to the St. George Hotel. Here are some photographs. What do you see here?

BARRON: Pictures of hotels.

NEWELL: Thirty-five people were shown these pictures and asked to describe each hotel. Here are the results. *(Hands sheet of paper to Barron)* As you can see, Mr. Barron, the word most often used to describe these hotels was "run-down."

BARRON: You're a pretty sneaky operator, Newell. Why didn't you tell me you were a sign salesman?

NEWELL: Would we be talking together now if I had? Not only that, I've been holding out on you, too. Notice there are seven hotels described in the survey and you've got only six pictures. Here's the picture that goes with description number seven.

BARRON: *(After studying the picture)* So you and thirty-five other people think my hotel looks run-down, and you think the place needs a new sign so we'll look modern. Then you and those thirty-five will rent rooms here. Is that it?

NEWELL: Mr. Barron, I want to convince you that a new sign will attract new people for dinner, for dancing, and for lodging too. It won't turn away any of your regular guests. There's one more picture I want you to see. *(pulls out artist's rendering of proposed new St. George sign)* Don't you think this represents what you have to offer better than your old sign does?

BARRON: You know that old sign has represented us for about twenty-six years. It's on all our letterheads and advertising material too.

NEWELL: I'm not recommending your old sign be replaced because it's twenty-six years old. I'm recommending a new sign because the old one no longer represents you in a positive way. It's like the clothes you yourself wore twenty-six years ago. Even if they were still in good condition and you still had them would you wear them today?

BARRON: I get your message.

NEWELL: Mr. Barron, when would you like us to install a new sign for you?

BARRON: Now wait a minute. You're going too fast. I don't even think much of this design you've got here.

NEWELL: That's fine. Our artists will be glad to show you some other possibilities. And we'd like all of your ideas on the kind of sign that will best represent the St. George. I know I've overstayed my time, so may I have your permission to discuss this further with you, say next Wednesday at lunch?

BARRON: I'm sorry, but I'm committed for lunch every day next week.

NEWELL: All right. If I come back next Thursday at 2:00 p.m., will you have some design ideas for me to take back to my artist?

BARRON: All right. At least I'll let you know then what kind of sign I *won't* buy.

NEWELL: Fine. I'll also bring some cost estimates and some lease-versus-buy information. *(as he gets up)* Thank you, Mr. Barron. I'll see you next Thursday at 2 o'clock.

BARRON: Very well. Goodbye.

Questions:

1. What did you think of the way Newell handled this interview? Be sure to comment on his use of the pictures and the survey.

2. Did Newell cut off the interview too soon? If so, how much farther should he have gone?

3. Was there anything in this interview that Newell did or said that you would have done or said differently?

4. From what has transpired so far, what are Newell's chances of making this sale?

5. Outline the steps Newell should cover on his next call.

6. Assume you are John Newell. Naturally you have to anticipate other objections that Mr. Barron might raise. Write out your answer to these:

a. "I want to get a quote from one or two other outfits before I decide."

b. "It's just too much money for that purpose. We still have some important capital expenditures to make on the inside." (Assume sign will cost $18,500)

c. "I think we better wait until the city council decides on its earthquake ordinance. That will probably affect the manufacturing specifications and the cost."

Presentation to distributors

¶ 9062   **All the way in one play**

HAND CALLING CARD TO PROSPECT

I'm with SPU. You've probably heard of us. We don't do the usual type of advertising—no TV, radio, or newspapers. We're sales boosters and are presently engaged in the greatest sales promotion ever devised, one that will absolutely guarantee you 200 new customers—or 500, or 1,000 as many as you want. It's the only sales promotion of its kind and has been 100% successful in every area. I don't mean 90% or 99%, but 100% successful for every merchant who's taken part in it. We're doing ———————County now, and I know you'll want to participate in the promotion. It'll take me just 2½ minutes to show it to you. May we set it on this counter?

TAKE UNIT FROM CONTAINER

Ever seen one of these? Before we started using them for our promotion, nearly half a million were sold in stationary stores for $6.95 plus batteries—$7.35 altogether.

REMOVE PERSONAL ADDRESS BOOK FROM POCKET

It's a telephone index like this but contains about twice as many listings and runs on batteries.

TURN ON LIGHT AND RUN TAPE TO ABOUT "G" AND BACK TO "C". OPEN WINDOW AND DEMONSTRATE SOLID WRITING SURFACE

Its owner can record his personal phone numbers—friends, relatives, doctor, baby sitter, and so forth.

CLOSE WINDOW AND MOVE TAPE A LITTLE WITH HAND KNOB

It also contains classified listings, which we sell, but that's not what I'm here to talk to you about. I've promised you hundreds of new customers, so let me show you how we're going to bring them to you. We're going to distribute _____ of these automatic telephone indexes in _____ County, and we're going to do it through local merchants such as you—pharmacies, cleaners, gas stations, florists, and so on —but (NAME PROSPECT'S BUSINESS) seem to do the best job for us and get the most benefit from distributing them. When I say distribute, I mean you're going to give them away free to your customers—free, that is, with a minimum purchase. And every time you give one away free, you'll make several dollars in immediate profit. I'll show you how in a moment, but first . . .

HOLD UP UNIT AND POINT TO PRINTING AS YOU DESCRIBE IT

. . . As a distributor, as opposed to an ordinary advertiser, your name, address, and phone number will appear here, or if you prefer we can move it up here and print it in larger letters, along with your slogan or emblem. That sits in front of the telephone in the customer's home all year long, giving you constant exposure every time a member of the family uses the phone. When they change batteries, they're again reminded that it was a gift from *you*. You also receive one classified listing on the tape. Note that these classified listings are just like those in the Yellow Pages, with one difference—no two companies are listed under the same classification. We never have our advertisers or distributors competing with each other in the same area. So you'll have an exclusive—you'll be the only (NAME TYPE OF BUSINESS) listed.

RUN TAPE TO FRONT END

Whenever they run the index tape to the end, they're again reminded that *you* gave it to them. It's also at the other end, after Z, constantly reminding them that *you* gave it to them. And never in the history of merchandising have customers ever been given a gift like this, a $7.35 value. The most they usually get is a ball point pen, and they get a dozen of those a year, or a key chain, or they get five calendars and throw four away. There's no appreciation to those things; it's something they've come to expect. But this is different, a $7.35 gift that has value, an item they can use daily, a nice piece of furniture to sit alongside their telephone, and it has novelty value, too. It's something they really *appreciate,* and every time they see it, they're reminded that *you* gave it to them. They see your name a dozen times a day; it gets burned into their minds, and soon they know your name better than that of any merchant in town. It has more advertising saturation power for that family than if you had 20 huge bill boards standing all over town.

PRODUCE INSTRUCTION SHEET, POINT TO LOWER RIGHT CORNER

And when occasionally they have to tighten the light bulb or change batteries, the instruction sheet again reminds them of you. On an average, these units will last from 3 to six years, depending upon how much abuse they get. And for all of those years, you've got a prominent ad sitting right in front of them in the most favorable position in the house—next to the phone, where they have nothing to do with their eyes while they're talking, so their eyes keep returning to the printing on the front of the case — they get to know not only your name, but your address and even your phone number *by heart* after staring at it a few hundred times. Now, here's how you give these $7.35 gifts away, and make money doing it . . .

PRODUCE BROCHURES

For each unit you agree to distribute free— and you can distribute as few as _____, or up to _____, depending upon how many new customers you want—but for each one you agree to distribute, we mail out five of these brochures to five families in your immediate area, or in whatever area you'd like to draw new customers from. These aren't handbills—we fold them, place them in envelopes and individually address them to the families. They invite the families to come here and get one free with a purchase. See here how a pharmacy, for instance, tied the gift with a 5 sale—a bank

¶ 9062

with every new account of $25. (CONTINUE SHOWING HOW EACH MERCHANT WORDED HIS BROCHURE. ASSUME IN THE BALANCE OF THIS PRESENTATION THAT YOU'RE SPEAKING TO A GAS STATION OWNER.) Here's the way a gas station sometimes does it, but more often they give a unit away with a lube, oil change, and *filter*. You make more money on a filter, and nearly all of the customers will have you put gas in at the same time anyhow.

SHOW BROCHURE THAT IS BLANK AFTER "FREE"

We print anything you want after the word "free." Let's assume, though, that you tie it in with lube, oil change, and filter, as most gas stations do. On a lube, oil change, and filter, plus some gas and whatever else you can sell the average customer when he has his car serviced—windshield wiper, plugs, antifreeze, brake adjustment, an occasional tire, and so forth—the average customer is going to spend $10 or more, usually more, on which you'll make a gross profit of from $4 to $6. I know you have an overhead, but that's taken care of already by the business you do *now*. This is *added* business, mostly *new* customers, that we're talking about—so your gross profit on this new business is virtually all *net* profit.

It takes an average of 3 1/4 brochures to bring a customer in when the merchant requires a minimum purchase of $10 or less. For gas stations it's only 2 4/5 brochures, because the guy has to have his car serviced anyhow and it doesn't cost him any more here then wherever else he might go. His wife gets this brochure, wants the $7.35 gift, so he comes here to get one the next time he's due for a lube. Most of those customers you'd never lay eyes on otherwise. So he comes in and you *immediately* make from $4 to $6 profit on him, what's equally important, you've got a chance to make a steady customer out of him. You won't make steady customers out of all of them, of course, not even half. But if you treat them right aside from giving them this gift, if you give them good service and friendliness, if they like you or one of your boys, you can make life-time customers out of some of them—maybe 10, 15, or 20% of them and each one you do make a steady customer of,

you'll not only make $4 to $6 on his first trip, but they'll each spend hundreds of dollars a year with you, year after year. On the other 80 or 90%, you'll only have made from $4 to $6 each, which isn't bad, considering it's profit added to what you already make, in most instances. Oh sure, a few of them who come in for their free gift will be your regular customers, but even with them, a $7.35 gift buys a lot of added loyalty. A man can't very well accept a valuable gift like this and go on using it every day, then go down the street to buy his gas.

So if you distribute 500 of these automatic indexes, or 200 or 2,000, whatever you say, but let's assume it's 500, you'll make from $4 to $6 immediate profit off each of them, which comes to somewhere between $2,000 and $3,000 added profit, and you'll pick up a few dozen permanent new customers on whom you'll make additional thousands of dollars in the next few years. The question is, what's it going to cost you to give these away. That's the ingenious part of this whole program. See these ads in here . . .

MOVE TAPE AROUND "A" AND "B" WITH HAND KNOB

We sell 120 ads on each tape. We also leave 120 blank lines where the owners can write their friends' numbers. We sell 120 of them. Our national and regional advertisers pay six cents for each listing, local advertisers more or less, depending on the area, but an overall average of six cents per listing. With 120 listings in each unit, MSA grosses $7.20 in advertising revenue for each unit you give away. I don't know what it costs my company to have these manufactured in the Orient, but I doubt it's more than a fourth, probably a fifth of that $7.20 they receive from the advertisers. The only trouble is, we can't sell a single ad until we can absolutely guarantee the advertisers that _____ will be distributed in this county. That's where you and other distributors come in. We *need* you to distribute these for us. We have to have signed agreements, backed by a cash deposit, to show our advertisers before we can sell a single ad. For instance, an advertiser wants to buy space in 10,000 units. At six cents each, that costs him $600. Before he lays out his $600, he wants to know who's going to distribute them, and he wants to know beyond any doubt that we have firm agreements from the merchants. So, as I said, we need you to distribute these for us, and to make sure you will, we offer you a distributorship under terms that no businessman, as you obviously are, can logically refuse. We offer you virtually nothing but pure profit! Here's what it costs you. . . .

REFER TO BROCHURE AGAIN

For each unit you agree to distribute free to your new customers, we send out up to five of these brochures. Actually it doesn't take five, so we'll spread the mailings over a ten, fifteen or twenty weeks period, depending upon how many you're going to distribute. Somewhere around midway through the mailings you'll find you're nearly out of the units and will ask us to stop mailing out the brochures. No sense mailing them all out at once anyhow, because you couldn't handle 500, 1,000, or even 200 extra lube jobs in one week. So we spread the mailings out, let's say over a twenty week period, and at the end of ten weeks, stop and take inventory. You won't want us to mail out so many that new customers show up with their brochures and you have no more units left to give them. You can't re-order, you know, and you're out to make friends, not enemies. So be sure to let us know when to stop mailing the brochures.

But at any rate, we contract to mail out up to five of the brochures for every unit you agree to distribute. If you were to take 500, for instance, we'd mail out up to 2,500 brochures to 2,500 different families in your area. The brochures, envelopes, addressing, and mailing at bulk rates costs us about seven cents each. That's thirty-five cents for the five brochures. It costs us another three cents to print your name and address and phone number on the units. That's a total of up to thirty-eight cents we spend promoting this give-away for you.

Well, sir, that's all it costs you! Just thirty-eight cents, and we spend it back on advertising your give-away, spend it to bring in the new customers for you. You pay nothing for the units. The advertisers pay for them — 120 advertisers at six cents each is $7.20 we collect from the advertisers for every unit you give away, and we're satisfied with that.

So every time you give away a unit—a $7.35 gift — to a new customer, you make from $4 to $6 on him, and all it costs you is the thirty-eight cents we spend to bring him in. Give it to him with *your* compliments. He has no way of knowing that it cost you nothing, that the advertisers paid for it. A $7.35 gift— he supposes that by buying them wholesale you got them for $3 or $4, and most of them appreciate it. I don't know of anyone who doesn't. You can buy a lot of loyalty for a $7.35 gift. They've never in their lives had a merchant give them anything anywhere near as valuable, and as they use it several times a day through the years, your name is right there in front of them, reminding them that you gave it to them.

PRODUCE AGREEMENT BUT DON'T SHOW IT TO HIM YET

And your expense is the thirty-eight cents we spend to bring the new customer in to you. Actually it doesn't cost us quite that much, because as I said, it takes an average of 3 1/4 brochures, in a gas station an average of 2 4/5 brochures, so you'll stop us before we mail out all of them, and we pick up a few cents for MSA out of your thirty-eight cents. But it still costs you the same, even if we only have to mail out two brochures for every unit you give away—we don't give one of our distributors an advantage over another; you all pay thirty-eight cents toward the promotion costs. Here let me show you the agreement. It's very simple, just what I've told you. There are no extras, unless you want more than one classified listing you're entitled to, in which event you'd pay half of what an ordinary advertiser pays. But one listing is probably all you'll need and I'm not here to sell you any extras. My job is just to line up the distribution so that the ad salesmen can go to work in this area.

SHOW HIM AGREEMENT, BUT HOLD IT SO HE CAN'T TAKE IT OUT OF YOUR HAND. USE YOUR PEN TO POINT TO EACH PARAGRAPH AS YOU REVIEW IT, BUT DON'T READ IT WORD FOR WORD —JUST TELL HIM WHAT'S IN EACH PARAGRAPH. FOR INSTANCE, WHEN YOU COME TO THE BOXED PORTION NEAR THE TOP OF THE PAGE, MERELY SAY:

¶ 9062

Ostensibly, you're just buying the advertising, so there's no sales tax. This box tells where your name goes on the unit, here, the one classified listing, the plug at both ends of the tape, and on the instruction sheet.

WHEN YOU COME TO THE LAST PARAGRAPH, IN SMALLER PRINT, MERELY SAY:

And in case war breaks out or something, this paragraph protects everyone. That's the entire agreement. There's nothing more to buy. There's nothing more to pay. It's just a question of how many new customers you want, bearing in mind that it costs you thirty-eight cents (even less if you take the cash discount) to bring in each new customer on whom you'll make an immediate $4 to $6, with a chance of making him a permanent customer on whom you'll eventually make hundreds of dollars.

NOW, GO TO BROCHURES AGAIN, PREPARED TO WRITE UNDER THE "FREE"

.... what would you like to tie this in with —a lube, oil change, and filter? Remember, he'll probably buy gas anyhow. Lube, oil change, and filter o.k.?

START WRITING THE AD. (Don't write on agreement until after the ad is completed.)
AFTER OBTAINING HIS SIGNATURE AND CHECK, AND CAUTIONING HIM TO SAVE SOME UNITS FOR LATE ARRIVALS, SAY GOODBYE QUICKLY AND MOVE ON TO NEXT PROSPECT.

Questions:

1. What buying motives does this presentation appeal to?

2. The answers to certain objections are incorporated in this presentation. Which objections does it try to forestall?

3. What objections might the prospect logically bring up to prevent the salesman from closing?

4. List the analogies contained in this presentation?

5. Should the presentation make more use of questions? If so, what should they be and where do they belong?

6. List the visual aids used in this presentation. Are there any others that might have helped dramatize the points made?

7. Comment on any aspects of this presentation that you feel should be changed. Are there any parts of it that you would feel uncomfortable saying?

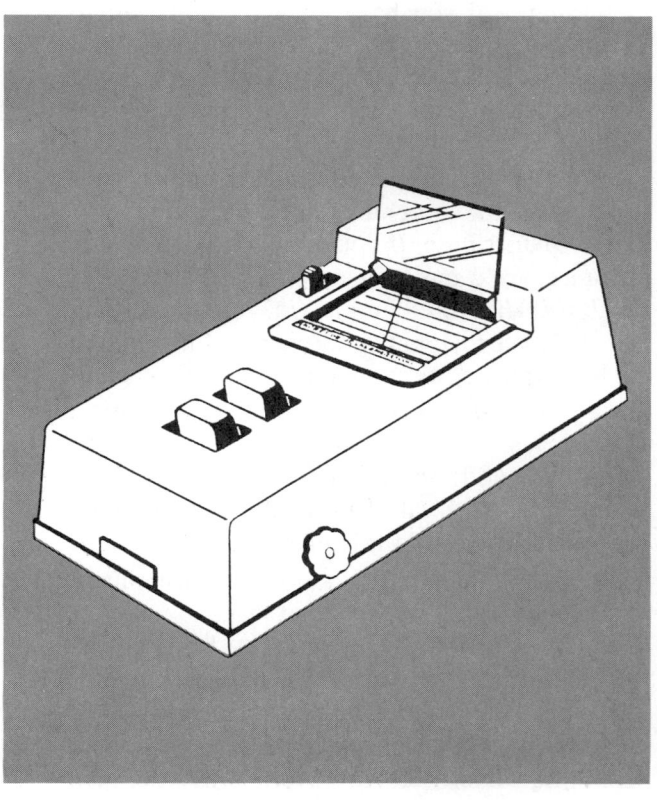

OPERATES ON ORDINARY FLASHLIGHT BATTERIES:

AUTOMATIC TELEPHONE INDEX

(Complete with batteries)

$7.35 Value

FREE

With lube, oil change & 10 gal. gas

at

Scotty's CHEVRON STATION

Corner 4th and Grant
Phone xxx-xxxx

TIRES, BATTERIES, TUNE-UPS, MINOR MECHANICAL REPAIRS

OPEN 7 A.M. to 11 P.M.

(Closed Sundays)

BRING THIS BROCHURE WITH YOU

LIMIT: One telephone index per car. Limited Supply.

presentation to distributors

Sales

Promotions   PARTICIPATION AGREEMENT

Unlimited

1968 - 1969 A D V E R T I S I N G   P R O M O T I O N

SPU agrees to supply _____ Model 12B automatic telephone indexes (complete with batteries) and five times as many brochures, to the distributor named below. The distributor agrees to distribute all of the indexes to the public within the _____ promotion period.

The distributor hereby purchases advertising to be imprinted by SPU on the units, as follows.

> The words "Compliments of," followed by the distributor's name and phone number on the bottom of the case; and,
>
> The same wording, plus his address, at both the beginning and end of the index tape and on the instruction sheet; and,
>
> His name, address, phone number and, if desired, his slogan, on the front of the case; and,
>
> One classified listing in the alphabetical index, consisting of only the classification and his name and phone number

PRICE: $38 per 100 units. Add $3 per 100 for each classified listing in excess of one.

SPU reserves the right to sell classified listings on the same alphabetical indexes to other advertisers, provided that no two advertisers shall be listed under the same classification.

Classified listings: _____
Slogan, if used: _____
Brochure wording after "FREE" _____

_____ Brochures to be mailed by SPU in distributor's immediate area over _____ week period.
No. of Display Boards (No charge): _____ 8 x 10 _____ 12 x 15 _____ 16 x 20

TOTAL PRICE: $_____

TERMS
5% Discount is paid in full with order
□
-OR-
Net: 50% with order, balance 30 days from this date □

SPU reserves the right to refund the merchant's money without penalty and cancel this contract at any time before delivery and during the promotion period if a national emergency, natural disaster, business conditions or other problem renders delivery impractical. Otherwise, this is a firm offer.

Make all checks payable to Sales Promotions Unlimited only.

Received herewith	Distributor_____
$_____ by check	Address_____
Balance due $_____	Town_____Phone_____
_____	X_____
SPU Representative	Authorized Signature Title
Date_____, 19___	

Distribution:
   WHITE: Home Office
   YELLOW: Western Division
   PINK: Distributor

Index

ABILITY — All References are to PARAGRAPH [¶] NUMBERS — **CLOSING**

Ability to pay, 2033, 2036
  sources for finding, 9025, 9026, 9027
Across-the-board selling, 1034
  creative idea for, 3056
Activities, review of your, 1014, 1015, 1067
Addresses, finding, 9022, 9034
Adjustments, handling, 8047
Advertising: in promotional mix, 808
Advertising, aid in selling, 3093, 4065, 5092
Affiliated companies, finding, 9022
Affiliations, prospect's, 9022
Agent middlemen: See Middleman
Aids, sales: See Sales tools, use of
American Marketing Association: definitions by, 802; 807
American Salesman, The, 3999, 6999, 7999
Analyzing your selling, 1014, 1015, 1067
Annual report, use of, 2054, 3058
Answer book, objections, 7048
Answering objections: See also Objections, 7001-7138
Appeals:
  buying motives, 4101-4110
  to senses, 5018, 5087
Appointments:
  advance cards, 4067
  by junior salesman, 2016
  interview without, 4071-4076
  need for, 4013
  punctuality, 8106
  telephoning for, 2041, 4021
Attitude, customer's, 4081-4090
Attitude, salesman's: See also Fear, overcoming
  after a no-sale, 8018
  as a professional salesman, 804
  courtesy, 8094
  customer complaint, 8047
  enthusiasm aided by, 8003, 8020
  for creative selling, 3031-3035, 3082
  glum, changing, 8020
  in:
    cold canvass, 3035
    dominating interview, 5176
    reselling prospect, 3080
  patience, 8097
  self-confidence, 8025
  sincerity in, 8093
  toward:
    answering objections, 7022, 7041-7048
    company policy, 1074
    competition, 1080

Attitude (continued):
  toward (continued):
    customer's misconceptions, 7042
    fear of big buyers, 1051
    losing a sale, 8114
    "No" in trial close, 6005
    paper work, 1087
    selling more to present customers, 1032
    suspicious prospect, 4089
    woman prospect, 4092
Authority to buy: See Buying, authority

Banks, bankers, facts about, 9027
Beard, Miriam, 809
Bell, Hugh, 9032
Benefits of product: See Product, your, benefits of
Bettger, Frank, 7096, 8002, 8011, 8102
Biographies of prospects, finding, 9022
Blue Book, Chamber of Commerce, 9035
Bluffing, 4072
"Born" salesman myth, 1072
Branches, finding location, 9022
Breaking into big selling, 1001-1088; See also Increasing sales
  mature salesmanship, 1071-1088
  selling bigger buyers, 1051-1054
  selling more to customers, 1031-1049
  setting sights, 1011-1016
  time planning, 1061-1068
  valuing your time, 1002-1008
  ways to increase sales, 1021-1022
Brush-off by receptionist, handling, 4072, 4074
Business: history of, 809
Business periodicals: See also News
  for economic news, 3094
  for industry trends, 9032
Business publications, 9021-9032
Buyers: See also Customers; Prospects
  attitude of, 1075, 4081-4090
  competition favored, 1080
  finding names of, 9022
  group, key man, 2051-2055
  interview policy, 1079
  one-item, increasing, 3056
  small, dropping, 1005, 1006
  welcome mat, leaving, 1043

Buyer's market, call-backs, 4121
Buying:
  ability, test, 2033, 2036
  authority:
    finding key man, 2054
    first contact, 2055
    test of, 2033, 2035
    when shifted, 3087
  motives, 925-940, 4101-4110
    appealing to, 5002, 5015
    disasters, creating, 2029
    emotional, 933
    family status, 932
    practical list, 934
    prospects reaction, 936
    rational, 933
    stimulated by ideas, 3040
  need, test of, 2033, 2034
  policy, guides to, 2035
  process, 932
  signal:
    closing on, 6009
    family status, 932
    objection as, 7010, 7011
    professional status, 932
    psychological age, 932
    psychological income, 932

Call-backs: See also Calls; Follow-up; User calls
  customer "too busy", 7096
  records for, 9003, 9004
  strategies, 4121-4127
  tickler file, 9003
  to group-buyers, 2051, 4121
Calling card:
  for repeat sales, 1013
  to gain prospects, 2014
Calls: See also Call-backs; Prospecting; User calls
  advance card, 4067
  analyzing results, 1067
  best time to make, 8051
  cold canvass: See Cold canvass
  customer "too busy", 7096
  deciding if worthwhile, 1005
  eliminating unprofitable, 1004
  fallacies to avoid, 1006
  follow-up, 1062, 2037
  increasing, need for, 1021
  making profitable, 2001-2029
  market knowledge before, 2020
  non-business, cutting, 8045
  persistence in, 3058
  prospect's habits and, 4091
  rainy days, 8050
  records, 2065
  route sheet, 1062
  routing: See Routing
  scheduling: See Schedule
  service, value of, 2007

Calls (continued):
  telephone: See Telephone
  timing, 1063, 8051
  user: See User calls
  weekly analysis, 9007
  weekly schedule, 9006
  work schedule for, 8049
Cancellations, reducing, 6045
"Canned" presentation, 5005
Canvassing, cold: See Cold canvass
Capacity to buy, 2033
Card, to get interview, 4067
Cards, customer and prospect, 1062
Catalog, use of, 5056
Chamber of Commerce, prospect source, 2079
Channel of distribution: See Marketing, Marketing mix
Chartered Life Underwriter, 823
Chartered Property and Casualty Underwriter, 823
Charts, use of, 5057, 5062
Choice, closing technique, 6015
City directories, 9029, 9030
Cliches, use of, 5096
Closing techniques, 6002-6045
  after presentation, 5176
  "ask for the order" close, 6025
  asking for hidden objection, 7031
  assumptive close, 6013
  choice close, 6015
  concession close, 6017
  creating your own, 6041
  creative idea for, 3043
  direct mail technique, 6010
  fear of loss technique, 6033
  "hat trick" close, 6024
  hooker, necessity for, 6031-6034
  inducement close, 6018
  last chance close, 6019
  Miracle Guide to, 6001
  misinformed prospect, 7027
  multiple-close, 6002
  narrative close, 6020
  objections leading to, 7001
  offering idea, 6044
  physical action close, 6014
  presentation leading into, 5151
  resistance, on prospect's, 5176
  self-management for, 8115
  summarizing before, 5146
  summary close, 6022
  testimonial close, 6021
  "tough" customer, 8026

CLOSING — CREATIVE

All References are to PARAGRAPH [¶] NUMBERS

Closing (continued):
  trade-ins, 7033
  trial:
    after buying signal, 6009
    after demonstration, 6008
    after objections, 6007, 7022
    after strong point, 6006
    attitude toward "No", 6005
    in presentation, 5031
    multiple-close technique, 6002
    when to make, 5002, 6003, 6004
    12 tested, 6011-6025
  using prospect's records, 6042
  using unique fact, 6043
  "why not" close, 6023
Clothes, salesman's, 8062
Cold canvass:
  creating prospects, 3036
  creative selling in, 3035
  getting by secretary, 3038
  method of prospecting, 2021
  observation during 2040
  qualifying prospects, 2039
Cold canvassing as direct salesman, 823
Commercial credit agencies, 2036
Commissions: See Earnings
Companies, facts about, 9071-9086
Company, your:
  accessibility, objection to, 7118
  advance cards from, 4067
  advertising, use of, 3093, 4064, 4065, 5092
  aid in answering objection, 7126
  bulletins for reproduction, 5065
  closing ideas from direct mail, 6010
  confidence, answering objection, 7112
  cooperation with, 1072-1074
  dealer aids, 7102
  facts from, 5143
  features, listing, 5014
  guarantee, objection to, 7106
  leads from, 2003, 2004
  loyalty to, 5174
  product features from, 5013
  relations with, for enthusiasm, 8016, 8017
  sales kit, 5055
  sales tools, 5053
  stating name, 5012
  statistical control by, 1085
  training programs, 918, 1086, 8016
    as product knowledge, 918
Comparison, in sales presentation, 5089

Compensation:
  plans, 826-828
    characteristics of good plans, 827
    examples, 827
    expense allowances, 828
    fringe benefits, 828
Competition:
  attitude toward, 1080
  belittling, 5174
  customer's loyalty to, answering objections, 7122-7125
  finding reason for loss to, 7032
  guarantee better, objection, 7106
  guarding customers against, 3084
  in modern selling, 1080
  in trade-in sales, 7033
  lower bid objection, 7080
  overcoming, 5133
    by creative selling, 3033
    by solving customer's problems, 1037
    on price, 7064, 7069
    through confidence, 7110, 7112
    through service, 1044, 3072
  price objection, 5071
  product benefits different from, emphasizing, 5017
  prospect misinformed by, 7027
  studying, 5016
Complaints:
  cheerfulness instead of, 8069
  inactive accounts, 2006
  saving time in handling, 8047
  user calls to check, 1041
Complete line, selling, 1034
Concert pitch, selling at: See Enthusiasm; Self-management
Concessions in closing, 1084, 6017
Confidence:
  customer's in you:
    comparison with competition, 1080
    delaying answer to objection, 7029
    ignoring "No", 8019
    integrity, source of, 8092
    testimonials, gaining by, 5064
    trade-in sale, 7033
    winning with facts, 1073
  in your company, overcoming rumors, 7117
  self:
    by increasing enthusiasm, 8011
    creative idea as aid, 3019, 3095
    emotions generating, 8022

Confidence (continued):
  self (continued):
    facts creating, 5142
    gaining by preparation, 5005, 5144
    in answering objections, 7022, 7041
    to your product, 7110, 7111
    in dominating interview, 5171, 5174
    in handling price, 5029, 5074
    in selling big buyers, 1051, 1054
    in "tough" jobs, 8020
    letter of introduction, aid, 4062
    news clippings, to build, 5066
    product knowledge, 5011, 8007
    prospect data, 4003
    punctuality creating, 8106
    reserve sales points, 5017
    responsibility for sale, 1040
    role-playing, giving, 8076
    self-reliance, aid to, 8103
    talking yourself into, 8025
    telephoning for appointment, 4023
    with "tough" customer, 8026
Consumption: See Economic system
Consumerism, 814
Continuity selling: See Salesmen, route
Conversation:
  after getting order, 5177
  cutting to gain time, 8045
  mentioning your product, 2064
  source of ideas, 3016
Convincing prospect, 5141, 5146
Cost control, effect of, 1085
Cost of goods: See Economic system
Courtesy, 8006, 8094
Creative salesman: See also Creative selling, ideas for
  applying ideas to yourself, 3091
  attitude of, 3031-3043
  buying motive and, 4106
  characteristics of, 3091-3095
  demand for, 3002
  increasing creativity, 3031-3043
  inventiveness of, 3077
  maintaining creativity, 3071-3087
  qualifying as, 3003
  training imagination, 3014
Creative selling, ideas for: See also Creative salesman; Increasing sales
  across-the-board selling, 3056

Creative (continued):
  adapting, 3015, 3018
  aided by publications, 3094
  associating need with knowledge, 1036
  attitude toward, 3031-3035
  bigger buyers, reaching, 3051, 3059
  borrowing, 3015, 3018
  bottlenecks leading to, 3033
  chance remark starts, 2026
  closing with, 3043
  curiosity stimulant, 3012
  demonstration and, 5043
  divulging, 3019
  enthusiasm created by, 8014
  exchanging, 4125
  favors won through, 3073, 3086
  for catalog, 5056
  for closing, 6041, 6044
  for dealers, 1007
  for each step of sale, 3035
  for proposals, 5062
  for prospecting, 2023-2026
  for repeat sale, 3084
  for retailer-customers, 3075
  for sales tools, 5060
  formula for, 3016, 3017
  fresh approach to old prospect, 3058
  hidden application, 3054
  imagination in, 3011, 3013
  importance of, 3002
  improving customer's product, 2024
  in answering objections, 7025
  in demonstration, 3041
  in getting by secretary, 3038
  in letters, 4046, 4066
  in making call-back, 4122
  in pre-approach, 3037
  increasing number of, 3018
  increasing sales to present customers, 1033
  increasing size of order, 3053
  lengthening season, 1065
  Miracle Guide to, 3001
  need for creativity, 3001-3003
  in reselling, 3080
  new product uses, 3055
  news as aid to, 2025, 3094
  originating, 3015, 3018
  persistence and, 3032
  planning sale around, 3078, 3095
  power of suggestion in, 3081
  preserving, 3018
  presuming need for product, 3085
  problems leading to, 3032, 3082
  product knowledge and, 3077
  prospects created by, 3036, 3057
  recording, 3018
  reorganization by customer, 3087

Creative (contniued):
  reviewing, 3018
  secondary sales points, 3083
  selling tools used in, 3093
  service as basis of, 3072
  showing more than savings, 3039
  to boost customer's business, 1031
  to get repeat orders, 3071
  to make bigger buyers, 3051
  to overcome objections, 3042
  to win dealers, 3074
  training dealers' salesmen, 3082
  training for, 3011-3019
  up-grading customers with, 3052
  user calls, 1042
  using existing equipment with product, 3076
  value analysis, use of, 3040
  when territory is cut, 2082
Credit agencies, 2036
Credit department, leads, 2066
Credit rating:
  finding, 9022
  importance of, 2036
Credit terms, objection to, 7078-7079
Cundiff, Edward, 814
Customers: See also Increasing sales; Prospects
  advance cards to, 4067
  as source of product knowledge, 921
  as source of prospects, 2008
  buying habits, 4091
  calling on most valuable, 2074
  calls on rainy days, 8050
  charm influencing, 8096
  complaints by, 1041, 2006, 8047
  courtesy toward, 8094
  dealers: See Dealers; Retailers
  dedication to, 1031
  demonstration in office, 5044
  dissatisfied, 1041, 2006, 8047
  'drop-outs', 2005
  eliminating unprofitable calls, 1004
  enthusiasm by pleasing, 8006
  familiarity with, 8067
  financial strength, 9072
  finding information about, 9071-9086
  getting value from product, 3084
  gossip to, 8112
  greeting, 5102, 8011
  ideas for, 1037
  ignoring cues from, 8017
  inactive, 2005, 2006, 2066
  increasing sales to, 1031-1049
  increasing use of product, 3084
  interview arranged by, 4061

Customers (continued):
  intimidating, 8109
  introductions from, 2014
  keeping suppliers competitive, 1080
  keeping your troubles from, 8069
  key, routing calls to, 2076
  knowing their progress, 1053
  knowledge of, aid to enthusiasm, 8007
  last remarks to, 8113
  making optimistic, 8111
  misinformed, 7027
  modern interview policy, 1079
  "No" from, 7041
  objections, answering: See also Objections, 7001-7138
  opinions about your product, 5012
  patience toward, 8097
  prejudice toward, 8098
  pride, appealing to, 7113
  propriety toward, 8068
  punctuality with, 8106
  putting yourself in place of, 8021, 8061
  records, 2065
  referrals, 2009
  selection of, 1008
  sincerity towards, 8093
  size, finding, 9022
  smoking in presence of, 8063
  social contacts with, 1075
  source of creative ideas, 3016, 3017, 3019
  source of prospect data, 4004
  tact towards, 8095
  telephoning: See Telephone
  testimonials from, 5064
  timing calls on, 8051
  "tough", overcoming fear, 8026
  types of, 4081-4090
  "unapproachable", understanding, 8100
  unique trait, capitalizing, 8101
  unsold, friendliness, 8018
  up-grading, 3052
  using name of, 2010
  using "right" word with, 8110
  waiting for, 8045, 8046
  when to drop, 1005
  winning favors from, 3086

Dartnell Corporation, 826, 827
Dealers: See also Customers; Retailers
  aids to, 3059, 3093
  answering objections of, 7113, 7114
    to price, 7062

Dealers (continued):
  answering (continued):
    when stocked-up, 7102-7105
  creative ideas for, 3059
  winning over, 3074
Dedication to customer, 1031
Demonstration:
  creative thinking, 3014
  definition, 5401
  guide to, 5041
  in user's office, 5044
  preparing for, 5027, 5041-5044
  presentation built around, 5182
  prospect participation, 5043
  trial close after, 6008
  word power in, 5094
Demonstrator, use of, 5052
  appealing to senses, 5087
Depression, stabilizing sales during, 1052
Detailing, 825
DeVoe, Merrill, 2072, 2078
Diagrams, use of, 5057, 5062
Dichter, Ernest, 932
Dictaphone Corporation, presentation, 5031, 5071, 5182
Direct mail, prospecting by, 2027
Directories, use of, 9022-9032
  Chamber of Commerce, 9035
Directors, finding names, 9022
Directory of Directors in the City of New York, 9029
Discussion, in sales presentation, 5176
Displays, getting dealers to use, 3059, 3093
Dissatisfied customers, 1041, 2006, 8047
Dolan, J. R., 812
Dramatizing the presentation, 3043, 5042, 5082
Drives, basic: See also Buying, motives, in explaining buying behavior, 930
Drop-in calls: See User calls
Drummer, 812
Dun and Bradstreet Reference Book, 2035

Earnings: See also Increasing sales
  increasing, 1011-1016
  through junior salesmen, 2016
  value per hours, 1003-1004
"Easy-to-sell" items, 1046
Economic system:
  consumption, 806
  cost of goods, 806
  marketing, 806
  production, 806

Economic (continued):
  purpose, 805
  utility, 805
    definition, 806
    form, 806
    place, 806
    possession, 806
    time, 806
Ego drive, 829
Empathy, 829
Employees, finding number, 9022
Encyclopedia of American Associations, 4005
Endicott, Frank S., 826
Enthusiasm:
  as a sales aid, 8062
  attitude affecting, 8020
  creating by:
    admiration, 8005
    association with successful people, 8009
    atmosphere, 8003
    belief in ability, 8011
    company relations, 8016, 8017
    creativeness, 8014
    evaluation and planning, 8028
    goals, 8010
    ignoring "No", 8019
    job done, 8013
    knowledge, 8007
    nerves, controlling your, 8016
    physical fitness, 8009
    planning, 8012
    pleasing customers, 8006
    self-confidence, 8025
    selling strength, 8003
    thinking, 8004
  emotions raising, 8022
  inclosing, 6022
  Miracle Guide to, 8001
  overcoming "defeatism", 8023, 8024
  overcoming dejection, 8021
  overcoming fear of "tough" customer, 8026
  power of, 8002
  propriety in showing, 8068
  renewing on no-sale, 8018
  under pressure, 8066
  voice quality, 8072
  when waiting for customer, 8046
  whole-heartedness, by-product of, 8015
Ethics:
  and society, 815
  as an individual, 816
  as a salesman, 817
Executives of companies:
  eliminating fear of, 1051
  finding names of, 9022, 9034
  getting through to, 3038, 4072, 4073
  getting to know top, 1045
Exhibits, use of, 5051, 5066

Index

All References are to PARAGRAPH [¶] NUMBERS

Expense account, tax deductions: See Entertainment expenses; Outside salesman; Reimbursed expenses; Travel expense

Facts, importance of knowing:
  about product: See Product, your, knowledge of
  in disputes, 8047
  no substitute for, 5042, 5043
Failures, analysis of, 1015
Family, selling to, 2051, 2052, 7130, 7131
Family status: See Buying, process
Fear, overcoming:
  enthusiasm as aid, 8002
  of answering objection, 7041
  of big buyers, 1051
  of "tough" customer, 8026
  of "tough" sale, 8020
  prospect's overcoming, 7028
Files: See Records, personal
Films, use of, 5053, 5063
Financial information:
  finding, 9022
  qualifying prospects, 2036
Flexibility of presentation, 5006
Follow-up: See also Call-backs; User calls
  after answering objections, 7024
  coinciding with reason to buy now, 2037
  industrial sale, 1041
  letters, for repeat sales, 1013
  of letters to gain interview, 4066
  records, 1062
Foreknowledge: See Pre-approach strategies
Form letters: See Letters
Form utility: See Economic system
Former buyers: See Inactive accounts
Forms: See also Records, personal
  customer card, 9004
  outline for presentation, 5024, 5025
  personal information card, 9002
  record of calls, 9002-9005
  route sheets, 1062
  weekly analysis, 1067
Formula:
  for selling a complete line, 1034
  for valuing your time, 1003
Friends:
  answering "personal Friend" objection, 7119
  leads from, 2018
Friendship, place in selling, 1073

Gayle, Willie, 9032
Gestures:
  friendly, to customers, 8099, 8100
  in presentation, 8105
  'no-sale', watch out for, 5042
"Getting in" without appointment, 4071
Goals:
  planning to achieve, 1013
  records to reach, 9001-9010
  setting daily, 1068
  setting long-range, 1013
  step up, 1011
  valuing time to reach, 1003, 1004
Goodwill, winning: 3019, 3075
  See also Service
Gore, Michael, 7061
Graphs, use of, 5057, 5062
Gras, N. S. B., 809
Greenberg, Herbert M., 829
Greeter, 812
Greeting customers, 5102, 8011
Greif, Edwin Charles, 3040
Grooming, 8062
Group buyers:
  call-backs to, 4121
  finding and rating key man, 2051, 2055
Guarantee:
  as product knowledge, 913
Guarantee, objections to, 7106

Habits:
  checking, 8104
  checklist of, 8104
  of role-playing, 8076
  of tact, 8095
  prospect's working, timing call, 8051
  speech, 8070
Health, of salesman, 8009, 8022
Hearing, appeal to, 5087
High pressure, what is, 1078
High-priced product, increasing sales of, 1035
History of company, finding, 9022
Hobbies:
  enthusiasm created by, 8021
  noting customers', 1031
Honesty:
  as a professional salesman, 804
  a success characteristic, 829
Honesty, pleasing customers with: See also Misrepresentation
"Hooker" to close:
  absence of, 6034
  necessity for, 6031
  supplied by prospect, 6032
  supplied by salesman, 6033
  to sell "hot" prospect, 2037
Hotels:
  keeping record of, 9006

House organ, customer's, ideas from, 3016
Husband and wife, selling to, 2051, 2052, 7031, 7032

Idea bank, 1031, 3018
Imagination:
  curiosity element, 3012
  development of, 3013
  in creative selling, 3003, 3011, 3039
  in getting by secretary, 3038
  training, 3014
Impression you make, 3081, 8061-8074
Inactive accounts:
  as leads, 2005, 2066
  handling grievance of, 2006
Increasing sales: See also Breaking into big selling
  after territory cut, 2082
  analysis of failures, 1015
  analysis of sales, 1067
  bigger buyers, moving up to, 1051-1054
  by answering objections, 7001-7038; See also Objections
  by creative selling, 3001-3095; See also Creative selling, ideas for
  by eliminating unprofitable calls, 1005
  by learning presentation, 8074
  by overcoming fears, 1051, 7041, 8020, 8026
  by reading publications, 3094
  creating closing techniques for, 6041
  credit department cooperation, 2066
  daily goals for, 1068
  dealer customers, 3093
  energize your personal goals, 1011
  5 ways, 1021, 1022
  ignoring customer's "No", 8019
  in unfamiliar field, 2063
  law of averages used in, 1012
  lengthening season, 1066
  long-range goals for, 1013
  mature salesmanship, 1071-1088; See also Modern selling
  Miracle Guide to, 1001
  new product sales, 3055
  of retailer-customers, 3075
  product knowledge checklist, 1022
  promptness in getting job done, 8106
  prospecting for, 2001
  put buyer in your corner, 8108
  questions for finding ways of, 1012

Increasing (continued):
  quoting quantity prices, 5076
  records for, 2065
  7 keys to, 1001
  through persistence, 3032
  through pre-approach, 4001-4067; See also Pre-approach strategies
  through service, 3053, 3072; See also Service
  through tact, 8095
  time-planning, 1061-1068; See also Time, planning for big selling
  to present customers:
    across the board selling, 1034
    answering biggest need, 1036
    assuming responsibility, 1040
    correct attitude, 1032
    creative selling, 1033
    dedication to customer, 1031
    "easy-to-sell" items as groundwork, 1046
    extra service, 1043, 1044
    giving advice on product use, 1038
    knowing top executives, 1045
    mail orders, 1048
    records for, 9004
    selling high-priced units, 1035
    showing cost of splitting business, 1039
    solving customer's problems, 1037
    telephoning for quick coverage, 1047
    up-grading, 1038, 3052
    user calls: See User calls
  utilizing rainy days, 8050
  valuing time for, 1002-1008
  "whopper sale" fallacy, 1007
  with catalog, 5056
Indianapolis Chamber of Commerce Directory, 9035
Inducement, to close, 1084, 6018
Industrial capitalism, 813
Industrial directory, example of, 9030
Industrial marketing, 9032
Industrial selling, 2054
  follow-up call, 1041
Industrial wholesale salesmen: See Salesmen
Industry, finding information about, 9022
Information, finding:
  about people and companies, 9021-9036
  industry data and trends, 9022
Insufficient funds objection, answering, 7081-7085

Index

INTANGIBLES — All References are to PARAGRAPH [¶] NUMBERS — **MODERN**

Intangibles selling, necessity of call-backs, 4121
International Minerals and Chemical Corporation, Presentation, 5132, 5146, 5184
Interruption of interview, 5073, 7029
Interviews: See also Call-back; Follow-up; Presentation
　advance card to arrange, 4067
　analysis of, 1015, 1067
　appointment for:
　　by letter, 4041-4057
　　by telephone, 4021-4031
　arranged by junior salesman, 2016
　banishing tension, 8027
　closing, 5151
　controlling, 5171
　　when delaying answer to objection, 7029
　　with prepared presentation, 5005
　dominating, 5172, 5174
　friendliness in, 8099
　gaining, 4011-4013, 4062
　granted under modern policy, 1079
　increasing time for, 8043
　initial:
　　techniques for gaining, 4013
　　written proposals for, 5061
　interruption of, 5073, 7029
　listening to prospect, 4095
　mailing material before, 4064
　misrepresentation to gain, 4028
　names, use of in, 5172
　need to sell, 4012
　objections to, handling, 7003
　personalizing, 5083
　planning around creative idea, 3095
　preparing for, 4002
　presentation manual in controlling, 5054
　price, quoting in, 5072
　prospect's friend arranging, 4061
　reception room, avoiding, 4076
　records for analyzing, 9007
　records for scheduling, 9005-9007
　rules for gaining, 4012
　selling before selling product, 4071
　specifics, getting down to, 4093
　subsequent:
　　literature in, 5058
　　paving way for, 8018, 8113
　time spent daily in, 5004
　T-V approach, 5177
　win over secretary, 4075

Interviews (continued):
　without appointment, 4071-4076
　without naming product, 4074
Introduction: See also Recommendations and referrals
　first step in presentation, 5012
　letters of, 4062
　use of cards for, 4062
Inventory, customer, record of, 9004
Itinerary, weekly, 9006

Junior salesman, 2016

Katz, Julius H., 9032
Key man in prospect group:
　family situation, 2051
　finding and rating, 2051-2055
　from non-competitive salesman, 2015, 2053
　husband-wife situation, 2052
　industrial situation, 2051, 2054
　partnership, 2051, 2053
Knowledge:
　as a professional salesman, 804
　need for, 1081
　of product: See Product, your, knowledge of

Laissez-faire, 813
Language, importance of, 5084: See also Word power
Larson, Henrietta M., 809
Law merchant, 809
Law of averages to raise sales, 1012
Leads: See Prospects
Letters:
　asking for interview, 4041-4057
　getting attention, 4045-4054
　how to write, 4044
　opener, 4054
　originality in, 4046, 4066
　product benefit stated in, 4049, 4055, 4056
　rules for writing, 4043
　weaknesses, 4042
　"you" approach in, 4047
　of introduction, examples, 4062
　pleasing customers with, 8006
　prospecting, 2027
　testimonial: See Testimonials
　transmittal of proposal, 5062

Libraries:
　as product knowledge, 920
List broker for direct mail prospecting, 2027
Listen, making prospects, 4081-4094
Listening to prospects, 4094
Lists:
　direct mail, 2027
　of markets, 2020
　of prospect sources, 2061
　　symbol system for, 2062
　use in telephoning, 2041
Literature:
　getting dealers to use, 3059, 3093
　to stimulate repeat sales, 1013
　use of, 5058
Lost customers and sales:
　analyzing failures, 1015
　bringing back, 2005, 2006, 2066
　reorganization of customer buying, 3087
Low pressure setting, 1078
　in telephoning for appointment, 4029
Loyalty:
　customer's, to other suppliers, overcoming, 7119, 7121, 7126
　your, to company and product, 7174

MacDonald, John A., 9032
Magazines, use of: See also News
　for economic news, 3094
　for industry trends, 9032
Management: See Executives of companies
Management, self: See Self-management
Management team, selling to, 2051-2055
Mannerisms, check-list of, 8104
Manuals, sales presentation, 5054
Manufacturer's agent: See Salesmen
Manufacturers of a product, finding, 9022
　from Chamber of Commerce, 9034
Manufacturer's representative: See Salesmen
Maps:
　for territory coverage, 2079
　local, as source of information, 7073
　routing on by zones, 2075
　used in routing, 2075
Marine News Directory, 9031
Market Data and Directory, 9032

Marketing:
　as a flow, 807
　concept, 814, 829
　definition, 807
　marketing mix, 808
　　channel of distribution, 808
　　personal selling, 808
　　price, 808
　　product, 808
　　promotion, 808
　　promotional mix, 808
　　sales promotion, 808
Marketing concept: See Marketing
Marketing mix: See Marketing
Markets:
　acquaintance with, 4005
　affected by population growth, 2081
　as source of prospects, 2020
　creating through imagination, 3014
　defined, 2020
　knowledge of, 3002
　mass, qualifying, 2031
　selective, qualifying, 2031
Martindale-Hubbell Law Directory, 2053
Mature salesmanship: See Modern selling
Mayer, David, 829
Medical detail salesman: See salesmen
Membership in organization, as lead source, 2018
Memory:
　names, 4093
　　in dominating interview, 5172
　prospect source list as aid to, 2061
　remembering empathic remarks, 7021
　remembering presentation, 5005, 5006, 8072
　training, 8073
Mercantile Capitalism, 809
Merchant middleman: See Middleman
Merchant princes, 810
Merger, saving account, 3087
Middleman:
　agent, 808
　definition, 808
　merchant, 808
Mill supply houses: See Salesmen
Misrepresentation:
　in answering objections, 7029
　in narrative close, 6020
　in quoting customers, 5064
　in stating "facts", 5142
　to gain interview, 4028
　to suspicious prospect, 4089
　to trusting prospect, 4088
Modern selling, 1071-1088
　attitude toward paperwork, 1087

| MODERN | All References are to PARAGRAPH [¶] NUMBERS | PLANNING |

Planning (continued):
  buyers granting interviews, 1079
  buyers more businesslike, 1075
  changes, keeping up with, 1088
  competition in, 1080
  cooperation with sales managers, 1071, 1074
  distribution cost control in, 1085
  informed salesmen required, 1081, 1082
  keeping up with, 1071
  low pressure required, 1078
  "natural-born salesman" myth, 1072
  need for trimming presentation, 1076
  no "psychological moment" for closing, 1083
  non-selling duties increased, 1086
  price dickering frowned on, 1084
  prima donna, no place for, 1074
  sales, not friendships, the goal, 1073
  selecting customers, 1008
  selling as continuous process, 1014
  value of persistence in, 1077
Moody's Industrial Manual, 9026
Motives, buying, 925-940, 4101-4110: See also Buying, motives
Moving pictures, use of, 5053

Names:
  Chambers of Commerce members, 9022
  importance of correct, 2065
  of executives, finding, 9022
  remembering, 4093
  using in interview, 5172
National Associations of the United States, 4005
Need for product:
  answering biggest, to up sale, 1036
  appointment letters to fit, 4043
  as qualifying test, 2034
  building, 5132
  creating, 3040
  determining in cold canvass, 2040
  discovering by walk through plant, 3073
  explaining in specialty selling, 4074
  keynote to demonstration, 5041
  presuming, 3085

Presentation (continued):
  product knowledge and, 3077
  prospect data to determine, 4003
  record showing customer's, 2065
  survey to establish, 5062
Needs, basic: See Drives, basic
Neighbors, prospect data from, 4004
New Jersey Industrial Directory, 9080
News:
  aid to creative selling, 3094
  clippings:
    as sales tools, 5066
    In letter to gain interview, 4052
    up-dating presentation with, 5066
  creative idea using, 2025, 3016
  opening talk with, 5118
  passing to customers, 8112
  prospecting from, 3094
  reproducing for evidence, 5065
"No", answering customer's: See Objections
Non-prospect, leads from, 2017
Non-selling duties, 1086
Norton Company, presentation, 5183

Objections:
  answering specific:
    adverse rumor, 7117
    already have it, 4029
    budget limitation, 7086-7087
    can't afford it, 3042
    consignment wanted, 7138
    credit terms unsatisfactory, 7078, 7079
    criticism of product, 7110-7114
    distance from supplier, 7118
    dividing business among suppliers, 1039
    guarantee unsatisfactory, 7106
    husband-wife situation, 7130, 7131
    insufficient funds, 7081-7085
    lower bid from competitor, 7080
    loyalty to present supplier, 7121-7125
    not in the market, 3059
    not interested, 7099-7101
    partner situation, 7127-7129
    personal ties, 7119-7120
    present equipment still good, 7132-7135
    price, 7062-7077

Presentation (continued):
preparing (continued):
  prior salesman criticized, 7116
  procrastination, 7088-7095
  product too new, 7109
  reciprocal buying, 7126
  second-hand machine will do, 7136, 7137
  stock up, 7102-7105
  too busy, 7096-7098
  trade association supplies information, 3057
  unknown company, 7107, 7108
making them work for you:
  after initial sale, 3080
  Answer Book tool, 7048
  basic rules for, 7002
  by capitalizing, 7007, 7008
  by introducing facts, 7027
  by raising nonexistent objections, 7026
  considering prospect's temperament, 7046
  converting into questions, 7022
  converting into reasons to buy, 7023
  creative ideas to overcome "No", 7034
  creativity in, 3042, 7025
  delaying answer, 7029
  eliminating fear of, 7041
  evading the objection, 7003, 7004, 7005
  finding hidden, 7009, 7031
  goal of presentation, 5002
  identifying buying signals, 7010, 7011
  identifying customer's stall, 7006
  in role-playing, 8076
  in trade-ins, 7003
  in trial closing, 6005
  lowering prospect's resistance, 7021
  meeting prospect's "excuse objections", 7030
  minimizing with facts, 7028
  Miracle Guide to, 7001
  misconceptions, basis of, 7042
  price, closing on answer, 6043
  prospect answering his own, 7024
  providing for in presentation, 5030
  tact in, 7044, 7045
  trial closing after answer, 6007
  when there is no answer, 7047
  without arguing, 7043
Observations:
  in cold canvassing, 2040
  walking through plant, 3073

Officers: See Executives of companies
One-price policy, 1084, 7075, 7077
Oral presentation, 5171-5177: See also Presentation
Organization chart, prospect's, use of, 2054
Outlining a presentation, 5021-5031
Overselling:
  the buyer, 1021
  yourself, 1073

Paper work:
  attitude toward, 1087
  when to do, 8044
Parent companies, finding out names of, 9022
Partnerships:
  answering objections, 7127
  selling to, 2051, 2053
Paying ability, 2033, 2036
  sources for finding, 9025, 9026, 9027
Peak and valley selling, avoiding, 1065
People, understanding, 8100
Performance:
  as a professional salesman, 804
Periodicals:
  creative use of, 3094
  pre-approach, use of, 4004
Persistence:
  creative idea justifies, 3095
  in creative selling, 3032
  in prospecting, 3058
  in reselling a prospect, 3080
  in telephoning for appointment, 4029
  low pressure, 1078
  modern viewpoint, 1077
  when to use, 1006
Personal information, prospect's, form for, 9002
Personal integrity, 829
Personal selling: See Marketing, marketing mix
Personality, your, 8061-8116: See also Self-management
Personnel of prospect, finding key names, 9022, 9034
Persuasion: See Selling
Petty capitalism, 809
Photographs, use of, 3079, 5053, 5062-5064
Photostat, use of, 5065
Pictures: See Sales tools, use of
Place utility: See Economic system
Planning: See also Routing; Time
  daily calls, form for, 9005
  daily review, 1067

Index

PLANNING — All References are to PARAGRAPH [¶] NUMBERS — **PRODUCT**

Modern (continued):
  "fixed route" or no route, 1062
  interview, around idea, 3078, 3095
  next day, 1068
  power-packed techniques, 1067
  presentation, 5021-5031
  records for, 9005-9007
  routes, 2072-2082
  sales to big buyers, 1051, 1052
  tickler file for call-backs, 9003, 9004
  to achieve goals, 1013
  weekly review, 1067
  weekly route form, 9006
Plants, customer's:
  finding location of, 9022
Poise, salesman's, 8066
Polk's World Bank Directory, 9027
Poor's Register of Directors and Executives, 9023
Popularity, overemphasizing, 1073
Positive attitude, 8005, 8011, 8021, 8022, 8024, 8025, 8111
Possession utility: See Economic system
Potential of prospects: See Qualifying prospects
Praise, use of, 4053, 8005
Pre-approach strategies:
  appointments, making, 4021-4067: See also Appointments
  creative ideas used in, 3037
  finding out about prospects, 4003-4005
  gaining interview: See Interviews
  market information, 4005
  sales material, 4064
  steps in, 4002
  to sell big buyer, 1054
Presentation:
  adding word power, 5091-5096: See also Word power
  buying motives affecting, 4110
  "canned", arguments against, 5005
  complete, examples, 5181-5184
    built around demonstration, 5182
    built around slides, 5184
    semi-technical, 5183
    two-call, 5181
  definition and objectives, 5002
  demonstration during, 5041-5044: See also Demonstration

Need (continued):
  developing, 5011-5018
    by listing product and company features, 5014
    by planning demonstration, 5018
    by studying competition, 5016
    from sales features, 5013
    knowing what you sell, 5011
    listing selling points, 5012
    selecting selling points, 5017
    turning facts into benefits, 5015
  dramatizing, 3043
  electric quality, 5081-5089
    appealing to senses, 5087
    asking questions, 5086
    dramatizing, 5082
    explaining with parallel situations, 5089
    language, 5084
    story-telling, 5085
    using examples, 5088
    "you" approach, 5083
  giving, 5171
    controlling, 5171, 5173
    controlling prospect, 5175
    dominating the interview, 5176
    making impression, 5172, 5174
  in reception room, avoiding, 4076
  interrupted by impulsive prospect, 4086
  interrupting to answer objection, 7029
  learning, 8074
  length, 1076, 5004
  "listening time" included in, 4094
  making dynamic, 8073
  manual, use of, 5054
  Miracle Guide to making, 5001
  outlining, 5021-5031
    example of, 5024, 5025
    including additional points, 5023
    including trial closings, 5031
    points to include in, 5022
    providing for answering questions, 5030
    providing for demonstration, 5027
    providing for price coverage, 5029
    providing for use of tools, 5028
    repeating important points, 5026
    value of, 5021
  preparing, 5001-5097
    achieving flexibility, 5006
    anticipating objections, 7001

Objections (continued):
  answering continued
    avoiding objections, 7030
    need for, 5005
    value of, 5001-5006
    prerequisites for success, 4001
    price, handling of, 5071-5077: See also Price of product
    sales tools, use of in, 5051-5066: See also Sales tools
    steps in, 5022
    stopping at buying signal, 7011
    time consumer in, 1076, 5004
    to key prospect in group, 2051
    to men and women, 4092
    to "proxy" for prospect, 4073
    to types of prospects, 4081-4094: See also Prospects, types
  up-dating, 5066
  using to gain prospects, 2011
  writing, 5101-5151
    bidding for order, 5151
    building interest, 5121
    building prospect's need, 5132
    conviction in, 5141-5146
    creating desire, 5131
    creating interest, 5121
    developing from outline, 5101
    dramatic openings, 5115
    exhibit of opening, 5117
    facts in, 5142, 5143
    gaining attention, 5111-5118
    glamorizing product, 5136
    introduction, 5102
    leading into close, 5151
    making benefits satisfy prospect, 5135
    need for specific information, 5142
    news item opening, 5118
    no name approach, 5116
    opening with offer to solve problem, 5113
    pointing out prospect's stake, 5134
    question opening, 5114
    showing product as best, 5133
    story opening, 5116
    summarizing, 5146
    thoroughness, 5144
    turning interest into desire, 5131-5136
    word power in, 5091-5096, 5145
Presumption, in closing, 6012-6015
Prevette, Earl, 5093, 8051
Price: See Marketing, marketing mix

Price of product:
  answering objection to, 7029, 7062-7077
  closing on answer, 6043
  change, telephoning to notify of, 1047
  covering in presentation, 5029
  delaying quotation, 5073
  dickering frowned on, 1084
  in preparing presentation, 5071-5077
  quoting in presentation, 5071
  quoting quantity prices, 5076
  soften up, 5074
  techniques for minimizing, 5075
  when to quote, 5072
Prima donna, faults of, 1074
Problems, looking for, in creative selling, 3082
Procrastination, overcoming, 7088
Product: See Marketing, marketing mix
Product, your:
  answering objections to, 7110-7114
  benefits of:
    answering objection by stating, 7121
    covering with presentation manual, 5054
    emphasizing to control prospect, 5175
    exclusive, overcoming price objection, 7065
    facts backing up, 5142
    facts converted into, 5015
    features converted into, 925-940
    goal of presentation, 5002
    illustrating, 5085
    in letter to gain interview, 4048, 4049, 4055, 4056
    in preparing presentation, 5121
    key to demonstration, 5041
    overcoming competition with, 5133
    primary, in closing, 6024
    record of, for developing presentation, 5012
    repeating in presentation, 5026
    samples to point up, 5051
    secondary, use of, 3083, 5176
    selecting for presentation, 5017
    stated from "you" approach, 5083
    stressed in proposal, 5061
    stressed on telephone, 4025, 4027
    summarizing in presentation, 5146
    summary of in proposal, 5062

PRODUCT — All References are to PARAGRAPH [¶] NUMBERS — **PROSPECTING**

Product (continued):
  summary (continued):
    tie-in with price, 5075
    use in trial closing, 6005
    word power in demonstrating, 5094
    word power in describing, 5092, 5093
  building need for, 5132
  buying motives for, 4102
  catalog, 5056
  creating desire for, 5131, 5134
  demonstration, 5041-5044: See also Demonstration
  dramatizing, 5042
  exclusive features, 5017
  explaining on telephone, 4027
  facts about in presentation, 5143
  finding uses for, 3055
  glamorizing, 5136
  hidden applications, uncovering, 3054
  Installing and servicing, saving time in, 8048
  interview sold before, 4012
  knowledge of:
    catalog source of, 5056
    checklist for, 1022
    company's history, 915
    competitive products, 916
    credit terms, 94
    customer needs and, 3077
    customers, 921
    enthusiasm gained by, 8007
    gaining in preparing presentation, 5005
    how to use, 909
    importance of, 902
    kinds of, 906
    manufacturing process, 912
    market, 2020
    modern selling need, 1081
    news item used with, 2025
    performance data, 910
    physical characteristics, 907
    presentation developed from, 5011
    prices, 914
    replacement parts, 908
    service policies, 913
    shipping terms, 914
    trade and industrial shows, 923
    trade journals, 922
    value, 5133
    values of, 905
    when selling to experts, 904
    when you don't know, 903
  loyalty to, 5174
  mentioning everywhere, 2064
  misconceptions about, 7027, 7042

Product (continued):
  need for: See Need for product
  newness of, answering objection, 7109
  personalizing, 5135
  price, 5071-5077: See also Price of product
  samples of, 5051
  selling after selling interview, 4071
  specialty, gaining interview without naming, 4074
  stages of development, camera used to show, 5063
  study of, 5012
  testimonial proof of, 5059
  unique fact to close sales, 6043
  used with existing equipment, 3076
  when selling to suspicious prospect, 4089
  withholding name, 4074
  working model to explain, 5052
Product analysis sheet:
  preparation, 398
  use of, 940
  value of, 939
Production: See Economic system
Products of prospects:
  creative idea for improving, 2024
  finding what companies produce, 9022
Profession:
  definition of, 804
Professional salesman: See Salesmen, professional
Professional status: See Buying process
Profit:
  definition, 805
Promises, care in making, 1043
Promotion: See Marketing, marketing mix
Promotional literature: See Literature
Promotional mix: See Marketing, marketing mix
Promotions, How execs choose salesmen for, 1015
Promptness, pleasing customers, 8006
Proposals, written:
  camera, use in, 5063
  finding product application for, 3054
  how to prepare, 5062
  use in first interview, 5061
Prospect record cards, 2039
Prospecting: See also Prospects; Calls
  aids to, 2061, 2066
  by telephone, 2041
  by word-of-mouth, 2064
  calling card used in, 2014

Prospecting (continued):
  chance remark as aid to, 2026
  cold canvass: See Cold canvass
  creative ideas in, 2023-2026: See also Creative selling, ideas for
  cutting time in, 2001
  guides to territory coverage, 2071-2082
  in cut territory, 2082
  letters, 4041-4057
  methods of, 2019
  Miracle Guide to, 2001
  news item used in, 2025
  partnerships, guide to, 2053
  persistence in, 3058
  referrals, 2009
  source list as aid to, 2061
  stressing service in, 2013
  telephone, 4021-4031
  territory change, 2081
  tests used in, 2032-2035
  using creative ideas for, 3019
  using customers' names in, 2010
  using presentation, 2011
  with help of others, 2003
Prospects: See also Customers; Prospecting
  advance cards to, 4067
  answering objections from, 7001-7138: See also Objections
  appointments with, 4013: See also Appointments
  arguing with, 7043
  building need for product, 5132
  buying habits, adjusting to, 4091
  buying signals from, 6009
  calls to on rainy days, 8050
  cold, telephoning, 4025
  controlling during interview, 5175
  controlling with presentation manual, 5054
  convincing, 5141, 5142
  creating desire for product, 5131
  creative ideas for, 3042
  creative ideas to find, 3036
  creative selling to open new group, 3057
  credit department leads, 2066
  customers' leads, 2008
  demonstration to: See Demonstration
  direct mail leads, 2027
  disasters as source of, 2029
  disinterested, how to handle, 7099-7101
  eliminating unprofitable, 1004
  enthusiasm from admiring, 8005
  evaluating, 1005

Prospects (continued)
  fallacies about, 1006
  financial strength, 2036
  finding and rating key man, 2051-2055
  finding bigger, 2001
  finding full-potential, 2001-2029
  finding information about, 3094, 4003-4005
  fresh approach with creative idea, 3058
  friendliness toward, 8099
  gaining attention of in presentation, 5111
  grouping, 2039
  "hot", a test to select, 2037
  husband-wife:
    answering objections, 7130
    test for qualifying, 2052
  impressing, 5005, 5172, 5174, 8061-8074
  inactive accounts, 2005
  industrial, selling to, 2054
  interview policy, 1079, 4012
  interview through friend of, 4061
  in unfamiliar field, 2063
  junior salesmen to discover, 2016
  keeping sources competitive, 1080
  list provided by company, 2004
  loyalty to present supplier, answering objections, 7122-7125
  mailing material to, 4064
  making them listen, 4081-4094
  mannerisms diverting, 8105
  markets as source of, 2020
  men and women, differences, 4092
  misconceptions of, 7042
  misrepresentation to: See Misrepresentation
  names, remembering, 4094, 5172
  new clients as source of, 2013
  news clippings for, 5066
  no decision by, 4052
  "No" from, 7041
  non-prospects as source, 2017
  participating in demonstration, 5043
  praising, in appointment letter, 4053
  presentation aimed at, 5134
  proposal prepared for, 5061, 5062
  protecting ego of, 7045
  proxy for, getting by, 4073
  purchasing policies of, 2036
  putting yourself in place of, 5017, 7021, 8061

PROSPECTING			SALESMEN

Prospects (continued):
qualifying, 2031-2041: See also Qualifying prospects
records, 2065
research before interview, 4003
salesmen, leads from, 2015
satisfying with benefits, 5135
saving face of, 7046
service department leads, 2007
size, finding out, 9022
smoking in presence of, 8063
social contacts as source, 2018
sources for:
  data about, 4005
  developed with others, 2003
  developed yourself, 2019
  importance of knowing, 2062
  list of, 2061
staying with, 3054, 4124
strengthening easy sales, 6045
testimonials to approach, 5059
trade exhibition leads, 2028
types, 4081
  bargainer, 7074
  deliberate, 4085
  fast-talking, 4084
  hesitant, 6026, 6034
  impatient, 7096-7098
  impulsive, 4086
  opinionated, 4090, 7046
  procrastinator, 7088
  silent, 4083, 6013
  stubborn, 7024
  suspicious, 4009
  talkative, 4082
  trusting, 4088
  vacillating, 4087
unanswerable objections from, 7047
unsold, leads from, 2012
work habits of, timing call, 8051
Prospectus: See Proposals, written
"Proxy" for prospect, handling, 4073
Psychological age: See Buying, process
Psychological income: See Buying, process
Psychological moment for closing, 1083
Publications: See also News
  creative use of, 3094
  information from, 9021
  source of prospect data, 4004
Punctuality, 8106
Purchasing agent:
  buying authority, 2035
  bypassing, 1078
  enlisting aid of, 7126

Purchasing (continued):
interview policy, 1079
keeping sources competitive, 1080
name of, finding, 9022, 9034
necessity for seeing, 2054, 2055

Qualifying prospects:
  at a glance, 2039
  before call-backs, 4121
  by telephone, 2041
  cold canvass, 2021, 2022
  credit department cooperation, 2066
  determined by product, 2031
  need test, 2034
  potential, importance of, 2032
  symbol system for, 2062
  tests for, 2032, 2033
    husband-wife, 2052
  what to find out, 4003
  who comes to you, 2038
Quantities, selling larger, 5076: See also Increasing sales
Questions:
  after a no-sale, 8018
  answering on telephone, 4027
  by prospect, minimizing, 5176
  checking your habits, 8104
  controlling interview with, 5175
  during demonstration, 5041
  during presentation, 5086
  in answering objections, 7024
  objections converted into, 7022
  opening presentation with, 5114
  power over procrastinator, 7090
  providing for in presentation, 5030
  sincerity in listening to, 8093
  to draw out hesitant prospect, 6026
  to draw out silent prospect, 4083
  to find buying motives, 4104
  to find hidden objections, 7009

Rack salesman: See Salesmen
Rand McNally International Bankers Directory, 9027
Rating yourself, 9008: See also Self-management
Raux, Emille, 8095
Reader's Guide to Periodical Literature, 920
Receptionist, treatment of:
  brush-off by, 4072

Receptionist (continued):
creative thinking to get by secretary, 3038, 4075
for partnership, 2053
"proxy" for prospect, 4073
withholding name of product, 4074
Reciprocal buying, objection to, 7126
Recommendations and referrals:
  customer, 2009
  from new clients, 2013
  getting customer to give, 2010
  interview gained by, 4061
  source of prospect data, 4004
  verbal, to gain interview, 4063
Records, personal:
  Answer Book for objections, 7048
  call-back control, 4123
  calls, 9002, 9005
  calls, inventory and sales, 9004
  customer or prospect, 1062
  daily plan and calls, 9005
  follow-up, 1062
  for creative ideas, 3018
  modern attitude toward, 1087
  personal, to reach goals, 9000-9010
    analyzing your selling, 9007
    criteria for, 9001
    planning your work, 9005-9007
    prospecting, 9002, 9003
    rating yourself, 9008
    sales to customers, 9004
  prospect personal information, 9005
  prospect's buying habits, 4091
  tickler for call-backs, 9003, 9004
  time spent in selling activities, 8043
  to increase sales, 2065
  watching growing buyers, 1053
  weekly analysis, 1067
  weekly route schedule, 9006
Referrals: See Recommendations and referrals
Related items, selling, 3075
Remington Rand, Inc., 3012, 5181
Reorders: See Repeat sales
Reorganization, keeping customers after, 3087
Repeat sales: See also Increasing sales to present customers
  creative idea leading to, 3071, 3084
  creative thinking to get, 3059

Repeat (continued):
increasing with displays, 3093
knowing top executives, 1045
planning to increase, 1013
records for anticipating, 9004
user calls to get, 1041
Reporting expenses: See Entertainment expenses; Travel expenses; Reimbursed expenses
Reports:
  to credit department, 2066
  to sales department, 1087, 8044
Reproductions, use of, 5065
Reselling a prospect, 3080
Responsibility, assuming, 1040
Résumé, personal, 830
Retailers: See also Customers; Dealers
  selling creatively, 3075
Review of selling activities, 1014, 1015
Right man: See also Buying, authority; key man in prospect group
  extra service to get to, 1043
  finding through creative idea, 3037, 3054
  "going for broke" to see, 4075
  meeting top executives, 1045
  purchasing agent: See Purchasing agent
  when selling specialty product, 4074
Roth, Charles B., 3043, 4110, 5093, 5094
Routing:
  around key customer, 2076
  by customer importance, 2074
  by zones, 2073
  door-to-door selling, 2078
  fixed and non-fixed routes, 1062
  for regular and frequent calls, 2075
  form for, 9006
  one town at a time, 2077
  plans, 2072

Sales engineers: See Salesmen
Sales kit, use of, 5055
Sales Manager:
  cooperation with, 1071
  enlisting aid of, 3041, 5030
  in role-playing, 8076
  source of testimonials, 5059
Salesmanship, definition of, 803
Sales manuals:
  as product knowledge, 919
Salesmen:
  advertising, 824
  become more valuable, 1083
  direct, 823

Index

Salesmen (continued):
 fellow, getting help from, 4125, 5012
 freight service, 824
 industrial wholesale, 824
 manufacturer's agent, 824
 manufacturer's representative, 824
 medical detail salesman, 825
 mill supply house, 824
 non-competitive:
  knowing key prospect, 2053
  leads from, 2015
 prospect data from, 4004
 professional, 804
 rack salesman, 825
 real estate, 823
 route, 823
 sales engineers, 824
 securities, 823
 service, 823
Sales points: See Product, your
Sales promotion: See Marketing, marketing mix
Sales resistance: See Objections
Sales tools, use of: See also Records
 appealing to senses with, 5087
 catalog, 5056
 charts and graphs, 5057
  proposal including, 5062
 company advertising, 4065
 creative thinking in, 3093
 exhibit, opener in presentation, 5117
 eyes, importance of, 5018
 illustrations, proposal including, 5062
 in preparing presentation, 5028, 5051-5066
 laboratory report, 5065
 literature, 5058
 news items, 5066, 5118
 photography, 3079, 5053, 5062-5064
 presentation manual, 5054
 promotional material, 4064
 proposals: See Proposals, written
 reproductions, 5065
 sales kit, 5055
 speaking habits, 5060
 samples, 5051
 testimonials, 5059, 5064: See also Testimonials
 visual aid, presentation built around, 5184
 working models, 5052
Samples, use of, 5051
Satisfaction: See Selling
Schedule: See also Planning; Routing
 daily calls, 9005
 daily work, 1067, 8049
 disrupting, 1007
 forms for making, 9005-9007

Schedule (continued):
 tickler file for call-backs, 9003
 weekly route, 9006
Seasonal selling, lengthening, 1066
Secretary: See Receptionist, treatment of
Self, ideal:
 definition, 931
Self, real:
 definition, 931
Self-improvement: See Self-management
Self-management:
 analysis for, 1014, 1015, 1021, 1067, 9005, 9007
 being a "good loser", 8114
 capitalizing customer's unique trait, 8101
 closing power from, 8115
 creativity in, 3092
 follow-through, 8116
 gaining selling time:
  by preparing work schedule, 8049
  collections, adjustments, complaints, 8047
  considering prospect's work habits, 8051
  cutting wasted time, 8045
  desk work last, 8044
  figuring earnings from, 8042
  installing and servicing product, 8048
  selling on rainy days, 8050
  timing selling activities, 8043
  waiting for customer, 8046
 making positive impression:
  appearance, 8062
  familiarity, 8067
  mastering presentation, 8073, 8074
  poise, 8066
  propriety, 8068
  shaking hands, 8064
  sizing up by buyer, 8061
  smoking, 8063
  voice, 8070, 8071
  walking, 8065
 memory training, 8073
 Miracle Guide to, 8041
 overselling yourself, 1073
 paving way for second interview, 8113
 personality:
  charm, 8096
  courtesy, 8094
  friendliness, 8099
  gossip, 8112
  habits, 8104
  initiative, 8108
  integrity, 8092
  mannerisms, 8105
  nature of, 8091
  optimism, 8111
  patience, 8097

Self-management (continued):
 performing services, 1031
 persistence, 1006
 prejudice, 8098
 punctuality, 8106
 self-reliance, 8103
 self-starting ability, 8102
 selling what customer wants, 8108
 sincerity, 8093
 tact, 8095
 understanding "unapproachable" customer, 8100
 using "right" word, 8110
 records to help in, 9001-9008
 role-playing, 8074
 typing yourself, 8061
Selling:
 as persuasion, 803
 definition, 802
 satisfaction as product, 803
Selling steps, 5022
 continuous process, 1014
Selling strategies: See Strategies
Selling yourself, 1073
Seltz, David, 2025
Service:
 by dedicated salesmen, 1031
 department, leads, 2007
 offering, 3019, 5174
 sincerity shown by, 8093
 solving customer's problems, 1037
 stressing, to gain referrals, 2013
 to increase sales, 3053, 3072
 to new customers, 2007
 when to refuse, 1043
 willingness to give, 5083
Sight, appeal to, 5018, 5087
Simmons, Harry, 3011
Slides, use of, 5053, 5184
Slumps, avoiding, 1065
Small buyers:
 dropping, 1005
 fallacies in keeping, 1006
Smith, Abbott P., 9032
Smith, Adam, 811
Smoking, 8063
Social contacts:
 leads from, 2018
 with customers, 1075
Sole supplier, whether to be, 1032
Specials, telephoning about, 1047
Specialty selling, nature of, 4074
Stalling, by customer, 7006, 7030, 7088-7095
Statistical control, 1085
"Staying with": See Persistence
Still, Richard R., 814
Story-telling:
 as opener, 5116
 in letter, 4050

Story-telling (continued):
 in closing, 6020
 in preparing presentation, 5085
 tension banished by, 8027
Strategies:
 bypassing purchasing agent, 1078-1079
 call-back, 4121-4127
 closing, 6002-6045
 discovering buying motives, 4101-4110
 gaining interview without appointment, 4071-4076
 importance to success, 4001
 in presentation, 5001-5096: See also Presentation
 making prospect listen, 4081-4094
 Miracle Guide to, 4001
 pre-approach, 4001-4067
 switching selling point, 3039
 word, 5096
Stress, how to change, 8112
Subsidiaries, finding information about, 9022
Success:
 characteristics, 829
Suggestion, power of, in creative selling, 3081
Suggestive selling, ideas for, 3075
Summarizing:
 avoiding objections by, 7030
 in closing, 6022
 in presentation, 5146, 5175
 trial close after, 6006
Survey:
 interviews for, 1086
 outline for selling, 5025
 proposal for selling, 5061, 5062

Tact, 7043, 7045, 8095
Talkative prospect, 4082
Telephone:
 appointment by, 4021-4031
 calls to please customers, 8006
 close by, 1048
 increasing sales by, 1031
 qualifying prospect by, 2041
 territory coverage by, 1047, 2080, 4027
 to maintain schedule, 1007
Television, 5117: See also Interviews
Territory: See also Routing
 adequate, 1011
 coverage, guides to, 2071-2082
 cold canvass, 2021
 telephone, 1047, 2080, 4027
 cut in:
  leading to more sales, 2082

Territory (continued):
  cut *(continued):*
    up-grading to overcome, 3052
    increasing sales in, 1021
    make-up, changes in, 2081
    maps, 2079
    names of companies in, finding, 9022
    new, opening, 2017
    stabilizing, 1052
    timing calls, 1063
    work schedule fitting, 8049
Testimonials:
  getting, 5044, 5064
  how to use, 5059
  in closing, 6021
  overcoming objections with, 7108, 7110, 7118
  overcoming rumors with, 7117
Thomas' Register of American Manufacturers, 9028
Tickler files, 9003, 9004
Time: See also Planning; Routing
  allotting to big buyers, 1052
  best use in cold canvass, 2021
  concise presentation, 1076, 5004
  customer's, respecting, 8094
  dividing among all products, 1034
  gaining through self-management, 8042-8051
  most profitable hours, 1004
  non-profitable, cutting, 8045
  non-selling, role-playing, 8076
  planning, for big selling, 1061-1068
    day-to-day, long-range, 1064
    doubling work day, 1064
    stabilizing peaks and valleys, 1065
  presentation and, 5004
  saving:
    by preparing presentation, 5005

Time (continued):
  by presentation manual, 5054
  correct routing, 2072, 2077
  junior salesmen for, 2016
  in adjustments, complaints, 8047
  in prospecting, 2001
  in travel, 2079
  through appointments, 4013
  through self-starting, 8102
  with photographs, 5063
  figuring value of, 8042
  hours in a year, 1004
  techniques for gaining, 8042-8051
  spent finding prospects, 2002
  spent with deliberate prospect, 4085
  telephone use and, 4026
  valuing your own, 1002-1008
    formula for, 1003
    objective, 1002
  waiting, using, 8046
  waste of, cutting, 8045
  working days in year, 1003
Time utility: See Economic system
Timing your calls, 8051
Tinker, 812
Trade associations:
  effect on competition, 1080
  source of prospect data, 4005
Trade channel: See Marketing, marketing mix
Trade directory, example of, 9031
Trade exhibitions, leads, 2028
Trade-ins, techniques, 7033, 7035
Trade magazines:
  creative ideas from, 3016
  prospect data from, 4005
Training dealers' salesmen, 3082
Transmittal letter, 5062
Travel time, reducing, 2071-2080: See also Routing
Trends, finding industry, 9022

Trial closing: See Closing techniques
Turnover, overcoming price objections, 7104
Types of prospects, 4081-4090

Upgrading customers, 1038, 1052
User calls:
  advantages, 1041
  creative ideas from, 3017
  giving advice on product use, 1038
  more sales from, 1037, 1042
  scheduling, 1041
  watching use of product, 3086
Utility: See Economic system

Value analysis: See Creativity
Valuing your time, 1002-1008: See also Time
Visual aids: See Sales tools, use of
"Vivid picture" language, 5091-5096
Voice, 8070, 8071

Warming up cold prospects, 1065
Warranty:
  as product knowledge, 913
Waste of time, reducing, 8045
Weaknesses, your own: See Self-management
Wealth of Nations, 811
Wheeler, Elmer, 7090
Who's Who in Commerce and Industry, 9024
"Why" technique: See also Questions
  in answering objections, 7024, 7090
  in lost sales, 7032
Wife and husband, selling to, 2051, 2052, 7031, 7032

Women, presentation to, 4092
Word power:
  by preparing presentation, 5005
  demonstrating product benefit, 5094
  describing product feature, 5093
  dramatic words, 5082
  importance of language, 5084
  in answering objections, 7021
  in appointment letter, 4048, 4054
  in preparing presentation, 5091-5096, 5145
  in stating facts, 5142
  in telephoning for appointment, 4025, 4027
  increasing word power, 5095
  minimizing price, 5075
  originality in letters, 4046
  presentation length and, 5004
  testing for, 5096
  trade terminology, 4005
  using parallel situations, 5089
  using "right" word, 8110
  voice control, 5175, 8071
  ways to increase, 5092
  with examples, 5088
  with questions, 5086
  with stories, 5085
Work planning: See Planning
Working days in a year, 1003
Working hours in a year, 1003

Yankee peddlers, 812
"You" emphasis:
  in letters for appointment, 4047
  in presentation, 5083

Zoning, routing by, 2073